GOVT¹⁰

PRINCIPLES OF AMERICAN GOVERNMENT

EDWARD SIDLOW
Eastern Michigan University

BETH HENSCHEN
Eastern Michigan University

CENGAGE

Australia • Brazil • Mexico • Singapore • United Kingdom • United States

GOVT10

Edward Sidlow, Beth Henschen

Senior Vice President, Higher Ed Product, Content, and Market Development: Erin Joyner

Sr. Product Manager: Bradley Potthoff

Content/Media Developer: Colin Grover

Product Assistant: Danielle Gidley

Marketing Manager: Valerie Hartman

Sr. Content Project Manager: Martha Conway

Sr. Art Director: Bethany Bourgeois

Text Designer: Chris Miller, Cmiller Design

Cover Designer: Lisa Kuhn, Curio Press, LLC / Chris Miller, Cmiller Design

Cover Image: MerveKarahan/E+/Getty Images

Intellectual Property Analyst: Alexandra Ricciardi

Intellectual Property Project Manager: Nick Barrows

Indexer: Terry Casey

Production Service/Compositor: Alison Kuzmickas, SPi Global

Design elements: world flags as keyboard, Scanrail1/Shutterstock.com; video camera viewfinder, IxMaster/Shutterstock.com; microphone and U.S. flag, DenisFilm/Shutterstock.com

Library of Congress Control Number: 2017950884

Student Edition ISBN: 978-1-337-40529-4

Student Edition with MindTap ISBN: 978-1-337-40528-7

Cengage
20 Channel Center Street
Boston, MA 02210
USA

Cengage is a leading provider of customized learning solutions with employees residing in nearly 40 different countries and sales in more than 125 countries around the world. Find your local representative at **www.cengage.com.**

Cengage products are represented in Canada by Nelson Education, Ltd.

To learn more about Cengage platforms and services, visit **www.cengage.com.**

To register or access your online learning solution or purchase materials for your course, visit **www.cengagebrain.com.**

Printed in the United States of America
Print Number: 04   Print Year: 2019

SIDLOW / HENSCHEN

GOVT¹⁰

BRIEF CONTENTS

MerveKarahan/E+/Getty Images

CONTENTS

1 AMERICA IN THE TWENTY-FIRST CENTURY 2

2 THE CONSTITUTION 24

Part II
OUR LIBERTIES AND RIGHTS 72

Part III
THE POLITICS OF DEMOCRACY 122

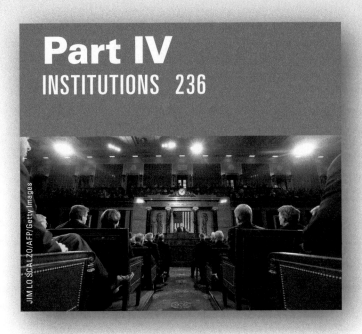

Part IV
INSTITUTIONS 236

JIM LO SCALZO/AFP/Getty Images

Part V
PUBLIC POLICY 334

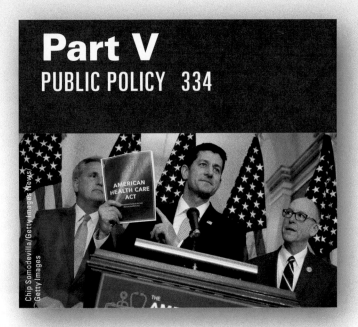

Chip Somodevilla/Getty Images News/
Getty Images

Rawpixel.com/Shutterstock.com

SKILL PREP

A Study Skills Module

Welcome!

With this course and this textbook, you've begun what we hope will be a fun, stimulating, and thought-provoking journey into the world of American government and politics.

In this course, you will learn about the foundation of the American system, culture and diversity, interest groups, political parties, campaigns, elections, the media, our governing institutions, public policy, and foreign policy. Knowledge of these basics will help you think critically about political issues and become an active citizen.

We have developed this study skills module to help you gain the most from this course and this textbook. Whether you are a recent high school graduate or an adult returning to the classroom after a few years, you want

results when you study. You want to be able to understand the issues and ideas presented in the textbook, talk about them intelligently during class discussions, and remember them as you prepare for exams and papers.

This module is designed to help you develop the skills and habits you'll need to succeed in this course. With tips on how to be more engaged when you study, how to get the most out of your textbook, how to prepare for exams, and how to write papers, this guide will help you become the best learner you can be!

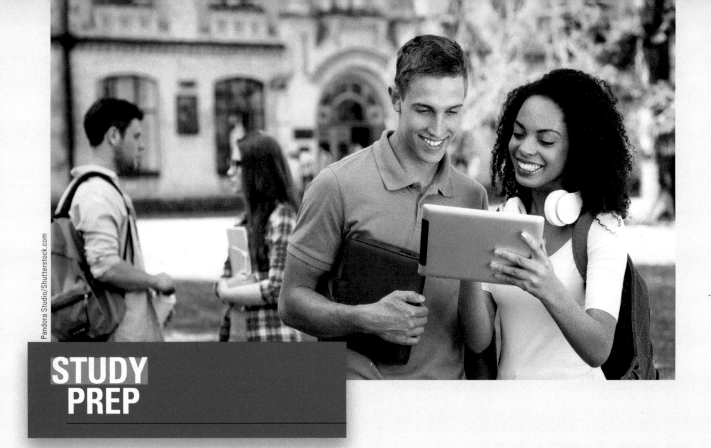

STUDY PREP

What does it take to be a successful student? You may think success depends on how naturally smart you are. However, the truth is that successful students aren't born, they're made. Even if you don't consider yourself "book smart," you can do well in this course by developing study skills that will help you understand, remember, and apply key concepts.

Reading for Learning

Your textbook is the foundation for information in a course. It contains key concepts and terms that are important to your understanding of the subject. For this reason, it is essential that you develop good reading skills. As you read your textbook with the goal of learning as much of the information as possible, work on establishing the following habits:

FOCUS

Make an effort to focus on the book and tune out other distractions so that you can understand and remember the information it presents.

TAKE TIME

To learn the key concepts presented in each chapter, you need to read slowly, carefully, and with great attention.

REPEAT

To read for learning, you have to read your textbook a number of times. Follow a preview-read-review process:

1. **PREVIEW: Look over the chapter title, section headings, and highlighted or bold words. This will give you a good preview of important ideas in the chapter.** Notice that each major section heading in this textbook has one or more corresponding **Learning Objectives.** You can increase your understanding of the material by rephrasing the headings and subheadings in your textbook into questions, and then try to answer them. Note graphs, pictures, and other visual illustrations of important concepts.

   QUICK TIP! Log in to GOVT10 MindTap with your access code to find interactive figures and tables from the chapters and to quiz yourself on the important material in the book.

2. **READ: It is important to read with a few questions in mind:** What is the main point of this paragraph or section? What does the author want me to learn from this? How does this relate to what I read before? Keeping these questions in mind will help you be an attentive reader who is actively focusing on the main ideas of the passage.

Also during this phase, it is helpful to take notes while reading in detail. You can mark your text or write an outline, as explained later in this module. Taking notes will help you read actively, identify important concepts, and remember them. When it comes time to review for the exam, the notes you've made should make your studying more efficient.

3. REVIEW: When reviewing each section of the text and the notes you've made, ask yourself this question: What was this section about? You'll want to answer the question in some detail, readily identifying the important points. Use the Learning Objectives in the text to help focus your review.

QUICK TIP! Tear out the Chapter Review cards in the back of the textbook for on-the-go review!

A reading group is a great way to review the chapter. After completing the reading individually, group members should meet and take turns sharing what they learned. Explaining the material to others will reinforce and clarify what you already know. Getting a different perspective on a passage will increase your knowledge, because different people will find different things important during a reading.

Take Notes

Being *engaged* means listening to discover (and remember) something. One way to make sure that you are listening attentively is to take notes. Doing so will help you focus on the professor's words and will help you identify the most important parts of the lecture.

The physical act of writing makes you a more efficient learner. In addition, your notes provide a guide to what your instructor thinks is important. That means you will have a better idea of what to study before the next exam if you have a set of notes that you took during class.

Make an Outline

As you read through each chapter of your textbook, you might want to make an outline—a simple method for organizing information. You can create an outline as part of your reading or at the end of your reading. Or you can make an outline when you reread a section before moving on to the next one. The act of physically writing an outline for a chapter will help you retain the material in this text and master it.

To make an effective outline, you have to be selective. Your objectives in outlining are, first, to identify the main concepts and, second, to add the details that support those main concepts.

Your outline should consist of several levels written in a standard format. The most important concepts are assigned Roman numerals; the second-most important, capital letters; and the third-most important, numbers. Here is a quick example.

ESB Professional/Shutterstock.com

I. What Are Politics and Government?
  A. Defining Politics and Government
        1. Politics and Conflict
        2. Government and Authority
  B. Resolving Conflicts
  C. Providing Public Services
        1. Services for All and Services for Some
        2. Managing the Economy
  D. Defending the Nation and Its Culture
II. Different Systems of Government
  A. Undemocratic Systems
        1. Monarchy
        2. Dictatorship
  B. Democratic Systems
        1. The Athenian Model of Direct Democracy
        2. Direct Democracy Today
        3. Representative Democracy
        4. Types of Representative Democracy
  C. Other Forms of Government

Mark Your Text

If you own your own textbook for this course and plan to keep it, you can improve your learning by marking your text. By doing so, you will identify the most important concepts of each chapter, and at the same time, you'll be making a handy study guide for reviewing material at a later time. Marking allows you to become an active participant in the mastery of the material. Researchers have shown that the physical act of marking, just like the physical acts of note-taking during class and outlining, increases concentration and helps you better retain the material.

WAYS OF MARKING

The most common form of marking is to underline important points. The second-most commonly used method is to use a felt-tipped highlighter or marker, in yellow or some other transparent color. You can put a check mark next to material that you do not understand. Work on better comprehension of the checkmarked material after you've finished the chapter. Marking also includes circling, numbering, using arrows, jotting brief notes, or any other method that allows you to remember things when you go back to skim the pages in your textbook prior to an exam.

TWO POINTS TO REMEMBER WHEN MARKING

▶ **Read one section at a time before you do any extensive marking.** You can't mark a section until you know what is important, and you can't know what is important until you read the whole section.

▶ **Don't overmark.** Don't fool yourself into thinking that you have done a good job just because each page is filled with arrows, circles, and underlines. Be selective in your marking, so that each page allows you to see the most important points at a glance. You can follow up your marking by writing out more in your subject outline.

> Researchers have shown that the physical act of marking, just like the physical act of note-taking during class increases concentration and helps you better retain the material.

Try These Tips

Here are a few more hints that will help you develop effective study skills.

▶ **Do schoolwork as soon as possible after class.** The longer you wait, the more likely you will be distracted by television, the Internet, video games, or friends.

▶ **Set aside time and a quiet, comfortable space where you can focus on reading.** Your school library is often the best place to work. Set aside several hours a week of "library time" to study in peace and quiet. A neat, organized study space is also important. The only work items that should be on your desk are those that you are working on that day.

▶ **Reward yourself for studying!** Rest your eyes and your mind by taking a short break every twenty to thirty minutes. From time to time, allow yourself a break to do something else that you enjoy. These interludes will refresh your mind, give you more energy required for concentration, and enable you to study longer and more efficiently.

▶ **To memorize terms or facts, create flash (or note) cards.** On one side of the card, write the question or term. On the other side, write the answer or definition. Then use the cards to test yourself or have a friend quiz you on the material.

QUICK TIP! In GOVT10 MindTap, flash cards are available for all key terms (with definitions).

▶ **Mnemonic (pronounced ne-mon-ik) devices are tricks that increase our ability to memorize.** A well-known mnemonic device is the phrase ROY G BIV, which helps people remember the colors of the rainbow—red, orange, yellow, green, blue, indigo, violet. You can create your own mnemonic devices for whatever you need to memorize. The more fun you have coming up with them, the more useful they will be.

▶ **Take notes twice.** First, take notes in class. Writing down your instructor's key points will help you be a more active, engaged listener. Taking notes will also give you a record of what your instructor thinks is important. Later, when you have a chance, rewrite your notes. The rewrite will act as a study session for you to think about the material again.

sirtravelalot/Shutterstock.com

TEST PREP

You have worked hard throughout the term, reading the book, paying close attention in class, and taking good notes. Now it's test time, and you want to show mastery of the material you have studied. To be well prepared, you should know which reading materials and lectures will be covered. You should also know whether the exam will contain essays, objective questions, or both. Finally, you should know how much time you will have to take the exam. The following steps can help to reduce any anxiety you may feel, allowing you to approach the test with confidence.

Follow Directions

Students are often in a hurry to start an exam, so they take little time to read the instructions. The instructions can be critical, however. In a multiple-choice exam, for example, if there is no indication that there is a penalty for guessing, then you should never leave a question unanswered. Even if only a few minutes are left at the end of an exam, you should guess on the questions that you remain uncertain about.

Additionally, you need to know the weight given to each section of an exam. In a typical multiple-choice exam, all questions have equal weight. In other types of exams, particularly those with essay questions, different parts of the exam carry different weights. You should use these weights to apportion your time. If the essay portion of an exam accounts for 20 percent of the total points on the exam, you should not spend 60 percent of your time on the essays.

Finally, you need to make sure you are marking the answers correctly. Some exams require a No. 2 pencil to fill in the dots on a machine-graded answer sheet. Other exams require underlining or circling. In short, you have to read and follow the instructions carefully.

Objective Exams

An objective exam consists of multiple-choice, true/false, fill-in-the-blank, or matching questions that have only one correct answer. Students usually commit one of two errors when they read objective exam questions: (1) they read things into the questions that do not exist, or (2) they skip over words or phrases. Most test questions include key words such as:

>ALL   >NEVER
>ALWAYS   >ONLY

If you miss any of these key words, you may answer the question incorrectly even if you know the information being tested.

Whenever the answer to an objective question is not obvious, start with the process of elimination. Throw out the answers that are clearly incorrect. Typically, the easiest way to eliminate incorrect answers is to look for those that are meaningless, illogical, or inconsistent. Often, test authors put in some answers that make perfect sense and are indeed true, but do not answer the question under study. Here are a few more tips that will help you become an efficient, results-oriented student.

▸ **Review your notes thoroughly** as part of your exam preparation. Instructors usually lecture on subjects they think are important, so those same subjects are also likely to be on the exam.

- **Create a study schedule** to reduce stress and give yourself the best chance for success. At times, you will find yourself studying for several exams at once. When this happens, make a list of each study topic and the amount of time needed to review that topic.

- **Form a small group for a study session.** Discussing a topic out loud can improve your understanding of that topic and will help you remember the key points that often come up on exams.

- **Study from old exams.** Some professors make old exams available, either by posting them online or by putting them on file in the library. Old tests can give you an idea of the kinds of questions the professor likes to ask.

- **Avoid cramming just before an exam.** Cramming tires the brain unnecessarily and adds to stress, which can severely hamper your testing performance. If you've studied wisely, have confidence that you will be able to recall the information when you need it.

- **Be sure to eat** before taking a test so you will have the energy you need to concentrate.

- **Be prepared.** Make sure you have everything you will need for the exam, such as a pen or pencil. Arrive at the exam early to avoid having to rush, which will only add to your stress. Good preparation helps you focus on the task at hand.

- **When you first receive your exam, make sure that you have all the pages.** If you are uncertain, ask your professor or exam proctor. This initial scan may uncover other problems as well, such as illegible print or unclear instructions.

- **With essay questions, look for key words** such as "compare," "contrast," and "explain." These will guide your answer. Most important, get to the point without wasting your time (or your professor's) with statements such as "There are many possible reasons for . . . ."

- **Review your answers** when you finish a test early. You may find a mistake or an area where some extra writing will improve your grade.

- **Keep exams in perspective.** Worrying too much about a single exam can have a negative effect on your performance. If you do poorly on one test, it's not the end of the world. Rather, it should motivate you to do better on the next one.

GaudiLab/Shutterstock.com

WRITE PREP

A key part of succeeding as a student is learning how to write well. Whether writing papers, presentations, essays, or even e-mails to your instructor, you have to be able to put your thoughts into words and do so with force, clarity, and precision. In this section, we outline a three-phase process that you can use to write almost anything.

Phase 1: Getting Ready to Write

First, make a list. Divide the ultimate goal—a finished paper—into smaller steps that you can tackle right away. Estimate how long it will take to complete each step. Start with the date your paper is due and work backward to the present: For example, if the due date is December 1, and you have about three months to write the paper, give yourself a cushion and schedule November 20 as your targeted completion date. Then list what you need to get done by October 1 and November 1.

PICK A TOPIC

To generate ideas for a topic, any of the following approaches work well:

- **Brainstorm with a group.** There is no need to create in isolation. You can harness the energy and the natural creative power of a group to assist you.

- **Speak it.** To get ideas flowing, start talking. Admit your confusion or lack of clear ideas. Then just speak. By putting your thoughts into words, you'll start thinking more clearly.

- **Use free writing.** Free writing, a technique championed by writing teacher Peter Elbow, is also very effective when trying to come up with a topic. There's only one rule in free writing: Write without stopping. Set a time limit—say, ten minutes—and keep your fingers dancing across the keyboard the whole time. Ignore the urge to stop and rewrite. There is no need to worry about spelling, punctuation, or grammar during this process.

> There is no need to create in isolation. Brainstorm ideas for a topic with a group. Ask for feedback from your instructor or a friend as you prepare an outline and revise your first draft.

REFINE YOUR IDEA

After you've come up with some initial ideas, it's time to refine them:

- **Select a topic and working title.** Using your instructor's guidelines for the paper, write down a list of topics that interest you. Write down all of the ideas you think of in two minutes. Then choose one topic. The most common pitfall is selecting a topic that is too broad. "Political Campaigns" is probably not a useful topic for your paper. Instead, consider "The Financing of Modern Political Campaigns."

- **Write a thesis statement.** Clarify what you want to say by summarizing it in one concise sentence. This sentence, called a *thesis statement*, refines your working title. A thesis is the main point of the paper—it is a declaration of some sort. You might write a thesis statement such as "Recent decisions by the Supreme Court have dramatically changed the way that political campaigns are funded."

SET GOALS

Effective writing flows from a purpose. Think about how you'd like your reader or listener to respond after considering your ideas.

- If you want to persuade someone, make your writing clear and logical. Support your assertions with evidence.

- If your purpose is to move the reader into action, explain exactly what steps to take, and offer solid benefits for doing so.

To clarify your purpose, state it in one sentence—for example, "The purpose of this paper is to discuss and analyze the role of women and minorities in law enforcement."

BEGIN RESEARCH

At the initial stage, the objective of your research is not to uncover specific facts about your topic. That comes later. First, you want to gain an overview of the subject. Say you want to advocate for indeterminate sentencing. You must first learn enough about determinate and indeterminate sentencing to describe the pros and cons of each one.

MAKE AN OUTLINE

An outline is a kind of map. When you follow a map, you avoid getting lost. Likewise, an outline keeps you from wandering off topic. To create your outline, follow these steps:

1. **Review your thesis statement** and identify the three to five main points you need to address in your paper to support or prove your thesis.

2. **Next, focus on the three to five major points** that support your argument and think about what minor points or subtopics you want to cover in your paper. Your major points are your big ideas. Your minor points are the details you need to fill in under each of those ideas.

3. **Ask for feedback.** Have your instructor or a classmate review your outline and offer suggestions for improvement. Did you choose the right points to support your thesis? Do you need more detail anywhere? Does the flow from idea to idea make sense?

DO IN-DEPTH RESEARCH

Dig in and start reading. Keep a notebook, tablet, or laptop handy and make notes as you read. It can help to organize your research into three main categories:

1. **Sources** (bibliographical information for a source),

2. **Information** (nuggets of information from a correctly quoted source)

3. **Ideas** (thoughts and observations that occur to you as you research, written in your own words)

You might want to use these categories to create three separate documents as you work. This will make it easy to find what you need when you write your first draft.

When taking research notes, be sure to:

▸ Copy all of the information correctly.

▸ Include the source and page number while gathering information. With Internet searches, you must also record the date a site was accessed.

▸ Stay organized; refer to your outline as you work.

GaudiLab/Shutterstock.com

Phase 2: Writing a First Draft

To create your draft, gather your notes and your outline (which often undergoes revision during the research process). Then write about the ideas in your notes. It's that simple. Just start writing. Write in paragraphs, with one idea per paragraph. As you complete this task, keep the following suggestions in mind:

▸ **Remember that the first draft is not for keeps.** You can worry about quality later. Your goal at this point is simply to generate words and ideas.

▸ **Write freely.** Many writers prefer to get their first draft down quickly and would advise you to keep writing, much as in free writing. You may pause to glance at your notes and outline, but avoid stopping to edit your work.

▸ **Be yourself.** Let go of the urge to sound "scholarly" and avoid using unnecessary big words or phrases. Instead, write in a natural voice.

▸ **Avoid procrastination.** If you are having trouble getting started, skip over your introduction and just begin writing about some of your findings. You can go back later and organize your paragraphs.

  ▸ **Get physical.** While working on the first draft, take breaks. Go for a walk. From time to time, practice relaxation techniques and breathe deeply.

  ▸ **Put the draft away for a day.** Schedule time for rewrites, and schedule at least one day between revisions so that you can let the material sit. After a break, problems with the paper or ideas for improvement will become more evident.

Phase 3: Revising Your Draft

During this phase, keep in mind the saying, "Write in haste; revise at leisure." When you are working on your first draft, the goal is to produce ideas and write them down. During the revision phase, however, you need to slow down and take a close look at your work. One guideline is to allow 50 percent of writing time for planning, researching, and writing the first draft. Then use the remaining 50 percent for revising.

Here are some good ways to revise your paper:

1. **READ IT OUT LOUD.** The combination of speaking and hearing forces us to pay attention to the details. Is the thesis statement clear and supported by enough evidence? Does the introduction tell your reader what's coming? Do you end with a strong conclusion that expands on your introduction rather than just restating it?

2. **HAVE A FRIEND LOOK OVER YOUR PAPER.** This is never a substitute for your own review, but a friend can often see mistakes you miss. With a little practice, you will learn to welcome feedback, because it provides one of the fastest ways to approach the revision process.

3. **CUT.** Look for excess baggage. Also, look for places where two (or more) sentences could be rewritten as one. By cutting text you are actually gaining a clearer, more polished product. For efficiency, make the larger cuts first—sections, chapters, pages. Then go for the smaller cuts—paragraphs, sentences, phrases, words.

4. **PASTE.** The next task is to rearrange what's left of your paper so that it flows logically. Look for consistency within paragraphs and for transitions from paragraph to paragraph and section to section.

5. **FIX.** Now it's time to look at individual words and phrases. Define any terms that the reader might not know. In general, focus on nouns and verbs. Too many words add unnecessary bulk to your writing. Write about the details, and be specific. Also, check your writing to ensure that you:

   ▸ **Prefer the active voice.** Write *"The research team began the project"* rather than *"A project was initiated,"* which is a passive statement.

   ▸ **Write concisely.** Instead of *"After making a timely arrival and observing the unfolding events, I emerged totally and gloriously victorious,"* be concise with *"I came, I saw, I conquered."*

   ▸ **Communicate clearly.** Instead of *"The speaker made effective use of the television medium, asking in no uncertain terms that we change our belief systems,"* you can write specifically, *"The senatorial candidate stared straight into the television camera and said, 'Take a good look at what my opponent is doing! Do you really want six more years of this?'"*

wavebreakmedia/Shutterstock.com

6. **PREPARE.** Format your paper following accepted standards for margin widths, endnotes, title pages, and other details. Ask your instructor for specific instructions on how to cite the sources used in writing your paper. You can find useful guidelines in the *MLA Handbook for Writers of Research Papers.* If you are submitting a hard copy (rather than turning it in online), use quality paper for the final version. For an even more professional appearance, bind your paper with a plastic or paper cover.

7. **PROOFREAD.** As you ease down the home stretch, read your revised paper one more time, and look for the following:

   ▸ A clear thesis statement.

   ▸ Sentences that introduce your topic, guide the reader through the major sections of your paper, and summarize your conclusions.

   ▸ Details—such as quotations, examples, and statistics—that support your conclusions.

   ▸ Lean sentences that have been purged of needless words.

   ▸ Plenty of action verbs and concrete, specific nouns.

   ▸ Spelling and grammar mistakes. Use contractions sparingly, if at all. Use spell-check by all means, but do not rely on it completely, as it will not catch everything.

Academic Integrity: Avoiding Plagiarism

Using another person's words, images, or other original creations without giving proper credit is called *plagiarism.* Plagiarism amounts to taking someone else's work and presenting it as your own—the equivalent of cheating on a test. The consequences of plagiarism can range from a failing grade to expulsion from school.

To avoid plagiarism, ask an instructor where you can find your school's written policy on this issue. Don't assume that you can resubmit a paper you wrote for another class for a current class. Almost all schools will regard this as plagiarism even though you wrote the paper. The basic guidelines for preventing plagiarism are to cite a source for each phrase, sequence of ideas, or visual image created by another person. While ideas cannot be copyrighted, the specific way that an idea is *expressed* can be. You also need to list a source for any idea that is closely identified with a particular person. The goal is to clearly distinguish your own work from the work of others. There are several ways to ensure that you do this consistently:

▶ **Identify direct quotes.** If you use a direct quote from another source, put those words in quotation marks. If you do research online, you might copy text from a website and paste it directly into your notes. This is a direct quote. You must use quotation marks or if the quote is long, an indented paragraph.

▶ **Paraphrase carefully.** Paraphrasing means restating the original passage in your own words, usually making it shorter and simpler. Students who copy a passage word for word and then just rearrange or delete a few phrases are running a serious risk of plagiarism. Remember to cite a source for paraphrases, just as you do for direct quotes. When you use the same sequence of ideas as one of your sources—even if you have not paraphrased or directly quoted—cite that source.

▶ **Note details about each source.** For books, include the author, title, publisher, publication date, location of publisher, and page number. For articles from print sources, record the author, date, article title, and the name of the magazine or journal as well. If you found the article in an academic or technical journal, also include the volume and number of the publication. A librarian can help identify these details.

▶ **Cite online sources correctly.** If your source is a website, record as many identifying details as you can find—author, title, sponsoring organization, URL, publication date, and revision date. In addition, list the date that you accessed the page. Be careful when using Internet resources, as not all sites are considered legitimate sources. For example, many professors don't regard Wikipedia as an acceptable source.

▶ **Include your sources as endnotes or footnotes to your paper.** Ask your instructor for examples of the format to use. You do not need to credit wording that is wholly your own. Nor do you need to credit general ideas, such as the suggestion that people use a to-do list to plan their time. But if you borrow someone else's words or images to explain the idea, do give credit.

▶ **When in doubt, don't.** Sometimes you will find yourself working against a deadline for a paper, and in a panic, you might be tempted to take shortcuts. You'll find a source that expressed your idea perfectly, but you must cite it or completely rephrase the idea in your own words. Professors are experts at noticing a change in tone or vocabulary that signals plagiarism. Often, they can simply Google a phrase to find its source online. Do not let a moment's temptation cause you to fail the course or face an academic integrity hearing.

LOFTFLOW/Shutterstock.com

Rawpixel.com/Shutterstock.com

TAKE ACTION

A Guide to Political Participation

It's easy to think of politics as a spectator sport—something that politicians do, pundits analyze, and citizens watch. But there are many ways to get engaged with politics, to interact with the political world and participate in it, and even to effect change.

GET INFORMED

Find Out Where You Fit and What You Know

- You already have some opinions about a variety of political issues. Do you have a sense of where your views place you on the political map? Get a feel for your ideological leanings by taking *The World's Smallest Political Quiz*: **theadvocates.org/quiz**.

- Which Founder Are You? The National Constitutional Center can help you with that. Go to **constitutioncenter. org/foundersquiz** to discover which Founding Father's personality most resembles your own.

- The U.S. Constitution is an important part of the context in which American politics takes place. Do you know what the Constitution says? *Take the Constitution I.Q. Quiz:* **constitutionfacts.com**. Was your score higher than the national average?

- At the National Constitution Center, you can explore the interactive Constitution and learn more about the provisions in that document: **constitutioncenter. org/interactive-constitution**.

Rich Koele/Shutterstock.com

- Find out what those who want to become U.S. citizens have to do—and what they have to know. Go to the U.S. Citizenship and Immigration Services website at **uscis. gov/**. What is involved in applying for citizenship? Take the *Naturalization Self-Test* at **https://my.uscis. gov/prep/test/civics**. How did you do?

Think about How Your Political Views Have Been Shaped

- Consider how agents of political socialization—your family, your schools, and your peers, for example— have contributed to your political beliefs and attitudes. Then have conversations with people in your classes or where you live about the people, institutions, and experiences that influenced the way they view the political world. Try to understand how and why your views might differ.

- Explore how your views on political issues compare with those of a majority of Americans. There are a number of good polling sites that report public opinion on a range of topics.

  o The Pew Research Center for the People & the Press conducts monthly polls on politics and policy issues: **people-press.org**.

  o Public Agenda reports poll data and material on major issues: **publicagenda.org**.

  o The results of recent polls and an archive of past polls can be found at Gallup: **gallup.com**.

  o The Roper Center for Public Opinion Research is a leading archive of data from surveys of public opinion: **ropercenter.cornell.edu**.

GET CONNECTED

News

Keep up with news—print, broadcast, and online. Don't avoid certain news sources because you think you might not agree with the way they report the news. It's just as important to know how people are talking about issues as it is to know about the issues themselves.

- One way to follow the news is to get your information from the same place that journalists do. Often they take their cues or are alerted to news events by news agencies such as the nonprofit cooperative Associated Press: **ap.org**.

- Installing a few key apps on your phone or tablet can help you stay informed. Try downloading the Associated Press (AP) app for timely updates about news around the world. There are tons of other great political apps—some are fairly polarizing, some are neutral, and still others are just plain silly.

Blogs

The blogosphere affords views of politics that tend to be slanted according to the political orientation of the blog sponsor. In the last several decades, blogs have surged in popularity as a source for political news and opinion.

Social Media

Staying connected can be as simple as following local, national, or international politics on social media. Former President Barack Obama, Senator Elizabeth Warren, House Speaker Paul Ryan, and even the White House have Instagram accounts worth following. Most politicians and political outlets are also on Twitter and Facebook.

Check the Data

- It's not always easy to figure out whether a news report or public statement is accurate. PolitiFact, a project of the *Tampa Bay Times*, is a good place to go to get the facts: **politifact.com**. Check out the Truth-O-Meter, and get it on your smartphone or tablet.

- A project of the Annenberg Public Policy Center, **factcheck.org** is a nonpartisan, nonprofit "consumer advocate" for voters that monitors the factual accuracy of what political players are saying in TV ads, speeches, and interviews.

Rawpixel.com/Shutterstock.com

Keep Up during Election Season

- Project Vote Smart offers information on elections and candidates: **votesmart.org**.

- Nate Silver's FiveThirtyEight features election analysis, in addition to covering sports and economics: **fivethirtyeight.com**.

- Stay connected to the horse-race aspect of electoral politics by tracking election polls. There are many good sources:

    o For a comprehensive collection of election polls, go to the RealClearPolitics website: **realclearpolitics. com/polls**. RealClearPolitics is a good source for other political news and opinions as well.

    o Polls for U.S. federal elections, including state-by-state polls, can be found at **electoral-vote.com**.

    o HuffPost Pollster publishes pre-election poll results combined into interactive charts: **elections. huffingtonpost.com/pollster**. During presidential elections, additional maps and electoral vote counts can be found at HuffPost Politics Election dashboard.

- If you have the opportunity, attend a speech by a candidate you're interested in.

Monitor Money and Influence in Politics

The Center for Responsive Politics website is an excellent source for information about who's contributing what amounts to which candidates: **opensecrets.org**. You can also use the lobbying database to identify the top lobbying firms, the agencies most frequently lobbied, and the industries that spend the most on lobbying activities.

Connect with Congress

You can, of course, learn a lot about what's going on in Congress from the websites of the House of Representatives and the Senate: **house.gov** and **senate.gov**. Look up the names and contact information for the senators and the representative from your area. If you want your voice to be heard, simply phone or e-mail your senators or your representative. Members of Congress listen to their constituents and often act in response to their constituents' wishes. Indeed, next to voting, contacting those who represent you in Congress is probably the most effective way to influence government decision making.

Check GovTrack to find out where your representative and senators fall on the leadership and ideology charts, and learn about their most recently sponsored bills and votes on legislation: **govtrack.us**.

Dragon Images/Shutterstock.com

financial health, account-ability and transparency, and reporting of results.

Design Your Own Ways to Take Action

- Start a network to match those who need assistance and those who want to help. For example, there may be people on your campus who, because of a disability or recent injury, need someone to help carry belongings, open doors, or push wheel-chairs.

- Do you want to raise awareness about an issue? Is there a cause that you think needs attention? Talk with friends. Find out if they share your concerns. Turn your discussions into a blog. Create videos of events you think are newsworthy and share them online. Sign or start a petition.

Join a Group on Campus

You probably see flyers promoting groups and recruiting members posted all over campus. Chances are, there's a group organized around something you're interested in or care about.

Maybe it's an organization that works to bring clean water to remote parts of the world. The American Red Cross may be looking for help with campus blood drives. You'll find groups organized around race, culture, or political parties; groups that go on spring break trips to serve communities in need; service organizations of all kinds; and groups that focus on the environment. The list goes on and on.

If you have an interest that isn't represented by the groups on your campus, start your own. Your college or university should have an office of campus life (or something similar) that can help you establish a student organization.

Vote (but Don't Forget to Register First)

- You can learn about the laws governing voting in your state by going to the website of the National Conference

GET INVOLVED

Take an Interest in Your Community—Offer to Help

Every community—large and small—can use energetic people willing to help where there is a need. Local non-profit agencies serving the homeless, battered women, or troubled teens often welcome volunteers who are willing to pitch in.

The Internet also has abundant resources about nonprofits and charities and how you can get involved:

- **Idealist.org** is a great place to find organizations and events that are looking for employees, interns, and volunteers. Filter by type and area of focus (women, disaster relief, animals, etc.) to find a cause that fits you.

- **Tinyspark.org** is a watchdog for nonprofits and charity organizations. It highlights individuals and groups that are doing good things around the globe and investigates those who may not be doing as much good as you'd think. Tiny Spark also has a podcast.

- **Charitynavigator.org** is another tool for check-ing on charities. It evaluates and rates charities on

of State Legislatures and its link to Voter Identification Requirements: **ncsl.org/research/elections-and-campaigns/voter-id**.

- Register: Enter "register to vote in [your state]" in a search engine. The office in your state that administers voting and elections will have a website that outlines the steps you will need to follow. You can also find out how to obtain an absentee ballot.

- If you want to view a sample ballot to familiarize yourself with what you'll see at the polls, you will probably be able to view one online. Just enter "sample ballot" in a search engine. Your local election board, the League of Women Voters, or your district library often post a sample ballot online.

- Vote: Familiarize yourself with the candidates and issues before you go to the polls. If you'd like to influence the way things are done in your community, state, or Washington, D.C., you can do so by helping to elect local, state, and federal officials whose views you endorse and who you think would do a good job of running the government. Make sure you know the location and hours for your polling place.

Support a Political Party

Getting involved in political parties is as simple as going to the polls and casting your vote for the candidate of one of the major parties—or of a third party. You can also consider becoming a delegate to a party convention. Depending on the state, parties may hold conventions by U.S. House district, by county, or by state legislative district. In many states, the

LHF Graphics/Shutterstock.com

lowest-level conventions (or, in some states, caucuses) are open to anyone who shows up. Voting rights at a convention, however, may be restricted to those who are elected as precinct delegates in a party primary.

In much of the country, precinct delegate slots go unfilled. If this is true in your area, you can become a precinct delegate with a simple write-in campaign, writing in your own name and persuading a handful of friends or neighbors to write you in as well. Whether you attend a convention as a voting delegate or as a guest, you'll have a firsthand look at how politics operates. You'll hear debates on resolutions. You might participate in electing delegates to higher-level conventions—perhaps even the national convention if it is a presidential election year.

Work for a Campaign

Candidates welcome energetic volunteers. So do groups that are supporting (or opposing) ballot measures. While sometimes tiring and frustrating, working in campaign politics can also be exhilarating and very rewarding.

Find the contact information for a campaign you're interested in on its website, and inquire about volunteer opportunities. Volunteers assemble mailings, answer the telephone, and make calls to encourage voters to support their candidate or cause. Even if you have little free time or are not comfortable talking to strangers, most campaigns can find a way for you to participate.

Be Part of Campus Media

Do you have a nose for news and do you write well? Try reporting for the university newspaper. Work your way up to an editor's position. If broadcast media are your thing, get involved with your college radio station or go on air on campus TV.

Joseph Sohm/Shutterstock.com

baur/Shutterstock.com

Engage with Political Institutions, Government Agencies, and Public Policymakers— at Home and Abroad

- **Visit the government websites for your state and community and learn about your representatives.** Contact them with your thoughts on matters that are important to you. Attend a city council meeting. You can find the date, location, and agenda on your city's website. And if you're passionate about a local issue, you can even sign up to speak.

- **Check to see if internships or volunteer opportunities are available close to home.** Your U.S. representative has a district office, and your U.S. senators also have offices in various locations around the state. If you plan to be in Washington, D.C., and want to visit Capitol Hill, book a tour in advance through your senators' or representative's offices. That's also where you can obtain gallery passes to the House and Senate chambers.

- **Spend some time in Washington, D.C.** Many colleges and universities have internship programs with government agencies and institutions. Some have semester-long programs that will bring you into contact with policymakers, journalists, and a variety of other prominent newsmakers. Politics and government will come alive, and the contacts you make while participating in such programs can often lead to jobs after graduation.

- **If you're interested in the Supreme Court** and you're planning a trip to Washington D.C., try to watch oral arguments. Go to the Court's website to access the link for oral arguments: **supreme court.gov**. You'll find the argument calendar and a visitor's guide. (The secret is to get in line early.)

- **Become a virtual tourist.** If you can't make it to Washington, D.C., for a semester-long program or even a few days, take the U.S. Capitol Virtual Tour: **https://www.capitol.gov**.

- **You can take a virtual tour of the Supreme Court** at the website of the Oyez Project at IIT Chicago-Kent College of Law: **www.oyez.org/tour**. You can also listen to Supreme Court oral arguments wherever you are. Go to the Oyez site and check out ISCOTUSnow (blogs.kentlaw.iit.edu/iscotus/).

- **Check with the study-abroad office** at your college or university. Studying abroad is a great way to expand your horizons and get a feel for different cultures and the global nature of politics and the economy. There are programs that will take you almost anywhere in the world.

- **Participate in the Model UN Club** on your campus (or start a Model UN Club if there isn't one). By participating in Model UN, you will become aware of international issues and conflicts and gain hands-on experience in diplomacy.

**GET INFORMED.
GET CONNECTED.
GET INVOLVED.**

Rommel Canlas/Shutterstock.com

Every day in America, almost 12,000 people turn age 18 and become eligible to vote. Each vote makes a difference!

Rock the Vote! is the largest nonprofit and nonpartisan organization providing the tools college students need to get registered to vote. It also provides resources about becoming a more active citizen.

Go to the website below and get involved. Let your voice be heard!

Go to the Rock the Vote website below and ...

1 AMERICA IN THE TWENTY-FIRST CENTURY

bbernard/Shutterstock.com

LEARNING OUTCOMES

After reading this chapter, you should be able to:

1-1 Explain what is meant by the terms *politics* and *government*.

1-2 Identify the various types of government systems.

1-3 Summarize some of the basic principles of American democracy and basic American political values.

1-4 Define common American ideological positions, such as "conservatism" and "liberalism."

After finishing this chapter, go to **PAGE 22** for **STUDY TOOLS**

AMERICA AT ODDS | Do We Still Need the "Mainstream Media"?

razihusin/Shutterstock.com

During the first week of the Trump administration, press secretary Sean Spicer announced that the new administration was not going to let the "mainstream media get away with anything." During the years leading up to his presidential victory, Trump relied heavily on communications methods that bypassed the mainstream media. He was, and still is, famous for his constant barrage of tweets.

But even before Trump and his blizzard of tweets, the great news institutions of the twentieth century were fading. These include print newspapers, weekly news magazines, and the televised evening news, presented by trusted anchorpersons. With the advent of the Internet, social media, and unlimited access to videos and blogs, we now live in a world of hyper information, most of it unfiltered. Does that mean that we can forget about the mainstream media and just let them ride off into the sunset?

Forget the Mainstream Media—They Are Biased Anyway

Trump's people certainly seem to believe that the mainstream media are doomed. They see these sources as a collection of has-beens with liberal biases who can't accept that the world has changed. As chief White House strategist Steve Bannon told the *New York Times*: "The media should be embarrassed and humiliated and keep its mouth shut and just listen for awhile."

Leaving aside the contention that the mainstream media are pro-liberal and anti-Trump, more and more news consumers today use mobile devices to find out what is happening. Young people simply have no interest in reading the print edition of any newspaper or magazine. They get their news from Twitter, Facebook, online bloggers, and just about any place except the mainstream media.

In the past, most Americans had to put up with the opinions of their local newspaper and network anchorpersons, whether they agreed with those opinions or not. That is no longer necessary. You can find the news presented in whatever way you wish on hundreds of Internet news sites and thousands of blogs.

Don't Kid Yourself—We Need Real Reporters and Real Facts

Defenders of the mainstream media have a very different view of what is happening. The real world is not just made up of tweets, retweets, and Facebook's news feed. If all we rely on are tweets from politicians and their supporters, we are in for real trouble. When a president tweets a falsehood, it takes the mainstream media to fight back so that the public knows the truth. Politifact, a Pulitzer Prize–winning fact-checker, has found that more than two out of every three statements made by Trump are mostly false, false, or "pants on fire."

The mainstream media have and will continue to serve a civic role, one in which they function as useful filters of information. They sort facts from lies. Rather than simply criticizing the mainstream media as irrelevant, we should be looking for ways to strengthen them. And that does cost money. After all, journalists have families to feed and thus must be paid. Companies that are part of the mainstream media must make profits to stay in business. New types of media are all very fine, but we also need to support and encourage the media that have served us well since this nation was founded.

Where do you stand?

1. What is the danger, if any, in obtaining news only from your friends, tweets, and Facebook's trending topics?
2. What methods could you use to find out whether your favorite news sources are biased?

Explore this issue online

- Search for "state of the news media" to see a comprehensive report by the Pew Research Center.
- Ann Arbor is now the largest city in the nation without a for-profit daily newspaper. (The University of Michigan still supports a daily.) See what replaced the *Ann Arbor News* at www.mlive.com/ann-arbor.

INTRODUCTION

Regardless of how Americans feel about government, one thing is certain: they can't live without it. James Madison (1751–1836) once said, "If men were angels, no government would be necessary." Today, his statement still holds true. People are not perfect. People need an organized form of government and a set of rules by which to live.

Government performs a wide range of extremely important functions. From the time we are born until the day we die, we constantly interact with various levels of government. Most (although not all) students attend government-run schools. All of us travel on government-owned streets and highways. Many of us serve in the military—a completely government-controlled environment. A few of us get into trouble and meet up with the government's law enforcement system. Every citizen reaching the age of sixty-five can expect the government to help with medical and living expenses. To fund all these functions, the government collects taxes.

In a representative democracy such as ours, it is politics that controls what the government decides to do. What combination of taxes and government services is best? When should our leaders use military force against foreign nations or rebellions in foreign countries? As discussed in this chapter's opening *America at Odds* feature, how do citizens gain the information they need to make these decisions? How the nation answers these and many other questions will have a major impact on your life—and participation in politics is the only way you can influence what happens.

1-1 WHAT ARE POLITICS AND GOVERNMENT?

LO Explain what is meant by the terms *politics* and *government*.

institution An ongoing organization that performs certain functions for society.

social conflict Disagreements among people in a society over what the society's priorities should be.

Even if—contrary to Madison's observation—people were perfect, they would still need to establish rules to guide their behavior. They would somehow have to agree on how to divide up a society's resources,

> "The ultimate rulers
> of our democracy
> are ... *the voters*
> of this country."
>
> FRANKLIN D. ROOSEVELT
> THIRTY-SECOND PRESIDENT
> OF THE UNITED STATES 1933–1945

such as its land, among themselves and how to balance individual needs and wants against those of society generally.

These perfect people would also have to decide *how* to make these decisions. They would need to create a process for making rules and a form of government to enforce those rules. It is thus not difficult to understand why government is one of humanity's oldest and most universal **institutions.**

As you will read in this chapter, a number of different systems of government exist in the world today. In the United States, we have a democracy in which decisions about pressing issues ultimately are made politically by the people's representatives in government.

Because people rarely have identical thoughts and feelings about issues, it is not surprising that in any democracy citizens are often at odds over many political and social problems. Throughout this book, you will read about contemporary controversies that have brought various groups of Americans into conflict with one another.

Differences in political opinion are essential parts of a democratic government. Ultimately, these differences are resolved, one way or another, through the American political process and our government institutions.

1-1a Defining Politics and Government

Politics means many things to many people. There are also many different notions about the meaning of government. How should we define these two central concepts?

Politics and Conflict   To some, politics is an expensive and extravagant game played in Washington, D.C., in state capitols, and in city halls, particularly during election time. To others, politics involves all of the tactics and maneuvers carried out by the president and Congress. Most formal definitions of politics, however, begin with the assumption that **social conflict**—disagreements among people in a society over what the society's priorities should be—is inevitable. Conflicts will naturally arise over how the society should use its scarce resources and who should receive various benefits, such as health care and higher education. Resolving such conflicts is the essence of **politics**. Political scientist Harold Lasswell perhaps said it best in his classic definition of politics as the process of determining "who gets what, when, and how" in a society.[1]

Government and Authority

Disputes over how to distribute a society's resources inevitably arise because valued resources, such as property, are limited, while people's wants are unlimited. To resolve such disputes, people need ways to determine who wins and who loses, and how to get the losers to accept those decisions. Who has the legitimate power—the *authority*—to make such decisions? This is where governments step in.

From the perspective of political science, **government** can best be defined as the individuals and institutions that make society's rules and also possess the power and authority to enforce those rules. Generally, in any country, government uses its authority to serve at least three essential purposes:

▸ **Resolving conflicts,**

▸ **providing public services, and**

▸ **defending the nation and its culture against attacks by other nations.**

1-1b Resolving Conflicts

Governments decide how conflicts will be resolved so that public order can be maintained. Governments have **power**—the ability to influence the behavior of others. Power is getting someone to do something that he or she would not otherwise do. Power may involve the use of force (often called coercion), persuasion, or rewards. Governments typically also have **authority,** which they can exercise only if their power is legitimate. As used here, the term *authority* means the ability to use power that is collectively recognized and accepted by society as legally and morally correct. Power and authority are central to a government's ability to resolve conflicts by making and enforcing laws, placing limits on what people can do, and developing court systems to make final decisions.

For example, the judicial branch of government—specifically, the United States Supreme Court—resolved

Transportation Security Administration (TSA) and Secret Service agents set up security equipment outside an upcoming rally by senator and presidential candidate Bernie Sanders (D., Vt.) in Santa Cruz, California. *Why is passenger screening at airports carried out by federal government employees such as TSA staff?*

Matthew Corley/Shutterstock.com

the highly controversial question of whether the Second Amendment to the Constitution grants individuals the right to bear arms. In 2008 and 2010, the Court affirmed that such a right does exist. Because of the Court's stature and authority as a government body, there was little resistance to its decision, even from gun control advocates.

1-1c Providing Public Services

Another important purpose of government is to provide **public services**—essential services that many individuals cannot provide for themselves. Governments undertake projects that individuals usually would not or could not carry out on their own.

politics The process of resolving conflicts over how society should use its scarce resources and who should receive various benefits, such as public health care and public higher education.

government The individuals and institutions that make society's rules and possess the power and authority to enforce those rules.

power The ability to influence the behavior of others, usually through the use of force, persuasion, or rewards.

authority The ability to legitimately exercise power, such as the power to make and enforce laws.

public services Essential services that individuals cannot provide for themselves, such as building and maintaining roads, establishing welfare programs, operating public schools, and preserving national parks.

These projects include building and maintaining roads, establishing welfare programs, operating public schools, and preserving national parks. Governments also provide such services as law enforcement, fire protection, and public health and safety programs. As Abraham Lincoln once stated:

> The legitimate object of government is to do for a community of people, whatever they need to have done, but cannot do, *at all*, or cannot, *so well* do, for themselves— in their separate, individual capacities. In all that the people can individually do as well for themselves, government ought not to interfere.[2]

Services for All and Services for Some Some public services are provided equally to all citizens of the United States. For example, government services such as national defense and domestic law enforcement allow all citizens, at least in theory, to feel that their lives and property are safe. Laws governing clean air and safe drinking water benefit all Americans.

Other services are provided only to citizens who are in need at a particular time, even though they are paid for by all citizens through taxes. Such services include health and welfare benefits. For example, a program such as Social Security Disability Insurance provides a source of income to people whose ability to work is limited by a notable disability. Americans contribute to the program through the Social Security payroll tax, regardless of whether they ever become disabled.

Managing the Economy One of the most crucial public services that the government is expected to provide is protection from hardship caused by economic recessions or depressions. From 2008 on, this governmental objective became more important than almost any other, due to the severity of the Great Recession that began in December 2007.

One of the most damaging consequences of the recession has been low rates of employment, which have continued into the present, even though the recession officially ended in June 2009 when economic growth resumed. True, the official *unemployment* rate was 4.7 percent at the beginning of 2017, down from a high of 10 percent. Yet the unemployment rate counts only people who are actively looking for work. The share of Americans of prime working age without a job in 2017 was almost 2 percentage points higher than in 2007. That translates into more than 2 million people who have not gone back to work. As you will learn later in this chapter, when many Americans continue to face economic hardships, they often have negative views about how well our government is "running the ship."

1–1d Defending the Nation and Its Culture

Historically, matters of national security and defense have been given high priority by governments and have demanded considerable time, effort, and expense. The U.S. government provides for the common defense and national security with its Army, Navy, Marines, Air Force, and Coast Guard. The departments of State, Defense, and Homeland Security, plus the Central Intelligence Agency, National Security Agency, and other agencies, also contribute to this defense network.

As part of an ongoing policy of national security, many departments and agencies in the federal government are constantly dealing with other nations. The Constitution gives our national government exclusive power over relations with foreign nations. No individual state can negotiate a treaty with a foreign nation.

A U.S. Navy SEAL with diving gear and weapons. As of early 2017, participation by U.S. troops in Syria was limited to special operations forces such as the SEALs. *Why would the federal government be reluctant to introduce regular infantry soldiers into that conflict?*

Of course, in defending the nation against attacks by other nations, a government helps to preserve the nation's culture, as well as its integrity as an independent unit. Failure to defend successfully against foreign attacks may have significant consequences for a nation's culture. For example, consider what happened in Tibet in the 1950s. When that country was taken over by the People's Republic of China, the conquering Chinese set out on a systematic program, the effective result of which was large-scale cultural destruction.

Attacks by foreign governments are not the only threat that nations must address. Since the terrorist attacks on the World Trade Center and the Pentagon in 2001, defending the homeland against future terrorist attacks has become a priority of our government. Terrorists often operate independently of any foreign authority, even if they are inspired from abroad. Examples include the killings in San Bernardino, California, in December 2015 and the massacre at a gay nightclub in Orlando, Florida, in 2016.

CRITICAL THINKING

▶ *Would it be a good idea to send U.S. ground forces to attack ISIS in Iraq or Syria, or would doing so lead to even greater problems than we already face? Explain your answer.*

1–2 DIFFERENT SYSTEMS OF GOVERNMENT

LO Identify the various types of government systems.

Through the centuries, the functions of government just discussed have been performed by many different types of structures. A government's structure is influenced by a number of factors, such as a country's history, customs, values, geography, resources, and human experiences and needs. No two nations have exactly the same form of government. Over time, however, political analysts have developed ways to classify different systems of government. One of the most meaningful ways is according to *who* governs. Who has the power to make the rules and laws that all must obey?

1–2a Undemocratic Systems

Before the development of modern democratic systems, the power of the government was typically in the hands of an authoritarian individual or group. When such power is exercised by an individual, the system is called an **autocracy.** Autocrats can gain power by traditional or nontraditional means.

Monarchy One form of autocracy, known as a **monarchy,** is government by a king or queen, an emperor or empress—or a person with some other aristocratic title, such as emir, grand duke, or prince. In a monarchy, the monarch, who usually acquires power through inheritance, is the highest authority in the government.

Historically, many monarchies were *absolute monarchies*, in which the ruler held complete and unlimited power. Until the eighteenth century, the theory of "divine right" was widely accepted in Europe. This **divine right theory,** variations of which had existed since ancient times, held that God gave those of royal birth the unlimited right to govern other men and women. In other words, those of royal birth had a "divine right" to rule, and only God could judge them. Thus, all citizens were bound to obey their monarchs, no matter how unfair or unjust they seemed to be. Challenging this power was regarded not only as treason against the government but also as a sin against God.

Most modern monarchies, however, are *constitutional monarchies*, in which the monarch shares governmental power with elected lawmakers. Over time, the monarch's power has come to be limited, or checked, by other government leaders and perhaps by a constitution or a bill of rights. Most constitutional monarchs today serve merely as ceremonial leaders of their nations, as in Spain, Sweden, and the United Kingdom (Britain).

Dictatorship Undemocratic systems that are not supported by tradition are called **dictatorships.** Often, a dictator is a single individual, although dictatorial power can be exercised by a group, such as the Communist Party of China. Dictators are not accountable to anyone else.

A dictatorship can be *totalitarian*, which means that a leader or group of leaders seeks to control almost all aspects of social and economic life. The leadership establishes the goals of society. Citizens must conform to the government's dictates in all fields of endeavor—in the economy, in literature and entertainment, and even in private conversation. Typically, these collective goals

> **autocracy** A form of government in which the power and authority of the government are in the hands of a single person.
>
> **monarchy** A form of autocracy in which a king, queen, or other aristocrat is the highest authority in the government. Monarchs usually obtain their power through inheritance.
>
> **divine right theory** The theory that a monarch's right to rule was derived directly from God rather than from the consent of the people.
>
> **dictatorship** A form of government in which absolute power is exercised by an individual or group whose power is not supported by tradition.

benefit only the leaders and are damaging to the nation as a whole.

Examples of the totalitarian form of government include Adolf Hitler's Nazi regime in Germany from 1933 to 1945 and Joseph Stalin's dictatorship in the Soviet Union (Russia) from 1929 to 1953. A more contemporary example of a totalitarian dictator is the latest leader of North Korea, Kim Jong-un.

1–2b Democratic Systems

The most familiar form of government to Americans is **democracy,** in which the supreme political authority rests with the people. The word *democracy* comes from the Greek *demos*, meaning "the people," and *kratia*, meaning "rule." The main idea of democracy is that government exists only by the consent of the people and reflects the will of the majority. Figure 1–1 shows the extent of democracy in the world today—with "democratic" defined as "free."

> **democracy** A system of government in which the people have ultimate political authority. The word is derived from the Greek demos ("the people") and kratia ("rule").
>
> **direct democracy** A system of government in which political decisions are made by the people themselves rather than by elected representatives. This form of government was practiced in some parts of ancient Greece.

The Athenian Model of Direct Democracy

Democracy as a form of government began long ago. In its earliest form, democracy was simpler than the system we know today. What we now call **direct democracy** exists when the people participate directly in government decision making. In its purest form, direct democracy was practiced in Athens and several other ancient Greek city-states about 2,500 years ago. Every Athenian citizen participated in the governing assembly and voted on all major issues. Some consider the Athenian form of direct democracy ideal because it demanded a high degree of citizen participation. Others point out that most residents in the Athenian city-state (women, foreigners, and slaves) were not considered citizens. Thus, they were not allowed to participate in government.[3]

Direct Democracy Today Clearly, direct democracy is possible only in small communities in which citizens can meet in a chosen place and decide key issues and policies. Nowhere in the world does pure direct democracy exist today. Some New England towns, though, and a few of the smaller political subunits, or cantons, of Switzerland still use a modified form of direct democracy.

Another modern institution with some of the characteristics of direct democracy is the ballot proposal,

FIGURE 1–1 FREE AND UNFREE NATIONS OF THE WORLD, JANUARY 2017

In this classification of nations by Freedom House, green means free, yellow means partly free, and blue means unfree. Bear in mind that these are the assessments of a single organization. *Why might another organization come up with a different system of classification?*

Sources: Arch Puddington and Tyler Roylance, *Populists and Autocrats: The Dual Threat to Global Democracy* (Washington, D.C.: Freedom House, 2017). Outline map adapted from Wikimedia.

In this rather idealized painting by Norman Rockwell, a working man rises to speak at a New England town meeting. The 1943 work, titled "Freedom of Speech," was one of four. The others illustrated freedom of worship, freedom from want, and freedom from fear. *Why would Rockwell paint such images in the middle of World War II (1939–1945)?*

In a **representative democracy,** the will of the majority is expressed through smaller groups of individuals elected by the people to act as their representatives. These representatives are responsible to the people for their conduct and can be voted out of office.

Our founders preferred to use the term **republic,** which means essentially a representative system with one qualification. A democratic republic, by definition, has no king or queen. Rather, the people are sovereign. In contrast, a representative democracy may be headed by a monarch. For example, as Britain evolved into a representative democracy, it retained its monarch as the head of state (but with no real power).

Types of Representative Democracy In the modern world, there are basically two forms of representative democracy: presidential and parliamentary. In a *presidential democracy*, the lawmaking and law-enforcing branches of government are separate but equal. For example, in the United States, Congress is charged with the power to make laws, and the president is charged with the power to carry them out.

In a *parliamentary democracy*, the lawmaking and law-enforcing branches of government are united. In Britain, for example, the prime minister and the cabinet are members of the legislature, called Parliament, and are responsible to that body. A **parliament** thus both enacts the laws and carries them out.

CRITICAL THINKING

▶ *Chinese Communist leader Mao Zedong (1893–1976) once said, "Political power grows out of the barrel of a gun." Was Mao right? Why or why not?*

in which the voters themselves decide a specific question rather than letting their elected officials resolve the issue. Ballot proposals are used in many American states. In one type, the *referendum*, the legislature sends a ballot proposal to the voters. The *initiative* differs in that a question is placed on the ballot by gathering signatures, not by action of the legislature. A related process is *recall*, an initiative to remove an elected official immediately, before his or her term of office comes to an end.

Representative Democracy Although the founders of the United States were aware of the Athenian model and agreed that government should be based on the consent of the governed, they believed that direct democracy would deteriorate into mob rule. They thought that large groups of people meeting together would ignore the rights and opinions of people in the minority and would make decisions without careful thought. They believed that representative assemblies were superior because they would enable public decisions to be made in a calmer and more deliberate manner.

 1-3 ## AMERICAN DEMOCRACY

LO Summarize some of the basic principles of American democracy and basic American political values.

"This country, with all its institutions, belongs to the people who inhabit it. Whenever they shall grow weary of the existing government, they can exercise their constitutional right to

representative democracy A form of democracy in which the will of the majority is expressed through groups of individuals elected by the people to act as their representatives.

republic Essentially, a representative system in which there is no king or queen and the people are sovereign.

parliament The national legislative body in countries governed by a parliamentary system, such as Britain and Canada.

amend it, or their revolutionary right to dismember or overthrow it."[4]

With these words, Abraham Lincoln underscored the most fundamental concept of American government: the people, not the government, are ultimately in control.

1–3a The British Legacy

In writing the U.S. Constitution, the framers incorporated two basic principles of government that had evolved in England: *limited government* and *representative government*. In a sense, then, the beginnings of our form of government are linked to events that occurred centuries earlier in England. They are also linked to the writings of European philosophers, particularly the English political philosopher John Locke (1632–1704). From these writings, the founders of our nation derived ideas to justify their rebellion against Britain and their establishment of a "government by the people."

Limited Government   At one time, the English monarch claimed to have almost unrestricted powers. This changed in 1215, when King John was forced by his nobles to accept the Magna Carta, or the Great Charter. This monumental document provided for a trial by a jury of one's peers (equals). It prohibited the taking of a free man's life, liberty, or property except through due process of law. The Magna Carta also forced the king to obtain the nobles' approval of any taxes he imposed on them. Government thus became a contract between the king and his subjects.

The importance of the Magna Carta to England cannot be overemphasized, because it clearly established the principle of **limited government**—a government on which strict limits are placed, usually by a constitution. This form of government is characterized by institutional checks to ensure that it serves public rather than private interests. Hence, the Magna Carta signaled the end of the monarch's absolute power. Although many of the rights provided under the original Magna Carta applied only to the nobility, the document formed the basis of the future constitutional government for England and eventually the United States.

Representative Government   In a representative government, the people, by whatever means, elect individuals to make governmental decisions for all of the citizens. Usually, these representatives of the people are elected to their offices for specific periods of time. In England, as mentioned earlier, this group of representatives is called a *parliament*. The English form of government provided a model for Americans to follow. Each of the American colonies established its own legislature.

In 1689, the English Parliament passed the English Bill of Rights, which further extended the concepts of limited and representative government. This document included several important ideas:

▶ **The king or queen could not interfere with parliamentary elections.**

▶ **The king or queen had to have Parliament's approval to levy (collect) taxes or to maintain an army.**

▶ **The king or queen had to rule with the consent of the people's representatives in Parliament.**

The English colonists in North America were also English citizens, and nearly all of the major concepts in the English Bill of Rights became part of the American system of government.

Political Philosophy: Social Contracts and Natural Rights   Our democracy resulted from what can be viewed as a type of **social contract** among early Americans to create and abide by a set of governing rules. Social-contract theory was developed in the seventeenth and eighteenth centuries by philosophers such as John Locke. According to this theory, individuals voluntarily agree with one another, in a "social contract," to give up some of their freedoms to obtain the benefits of orderly government. The government is given adequate power to secure the mutual protection and welfare of all individuals.

limited government
A form of government based on the principle that the powers of government should be clearly limited either through a written document or through wide public understanding.

social contract
A voluntary agreement among individuals to create a government and to give that government adequate power to secure the mutual protection and welfare of all individuals.

Locke also argued that people are born with **natural rights** to life, liberty, and property. He theorized that the purpose of government was to protect those rights. If it did not, it would lose its legitimacy and need not be obeyed. When the American colonists rebelled against British rule, such concepts as natural rights and a government based on a social contract became important theoretical tools in justifying the rebellion.

Corbis Yellow/RF/Corbis

1–3b Principles of American Democracy

We can say that American democracy is based on at least five fundamental principles:

▶ *Equality in voting.* Citizens must have equal opportunities to express their preferences about policies and leaders.

▶ *Individual freedom.* All individuals must have the greatest amount of freedom possible without interfering with the rights of others.

▶ *Equal protection of the law.* The law must entitle all persons to equal protection.

▶ *Majority rule and minority rights.* The majority should rule, while guaranteeing the rights of minorities.

▶ *Voluntary consent to be governed.* The people who make up a democracy must collectively (not individually) agree to be governed by the rules laid down by their representatives.

These principles frame many of the political issues that you will read about in this book. They also frequently lie at the heart of America's political conflicts. Does the principle of minority rights mean that minorities should receive preferential treatment in hiring and firing decisions to make up for past mistreatment? Does the principle of individual freedom mean that individuals can express whatever they want on the Internet, including hateful, racist comments? Above all, how much should the government *do?* We address that last question in this chapter's *Join the Debate* feature.

Such conflicts over individual rights and freedoms and over society's priorities are natural and inevitable. Resolving these conflicts is what politics is all about. The key point is that Americans are frequently able to reach acceptable compromises because of their common political heritage.

1–3c American Political Values

Historically, as the nations of the world emerged, the boundaries of each nation normally coincided with the boundaries of a population that shared a common ethnic heritage, language, and culture. From its beginnings as a nation, however, America has been defined less by the culture shared by its diverse population than by the ideas that make up its political culture.

A **political culture** can be defined as a patterned set of ideas, values, and ways of thinking about government and politics. Our political culture is passed from one generation to another through families, schools, and the media. This culture is powerful enough to win over most new immigrants. Indeed, some immigrants come to America precisely because they are attracted by American values.

The ideals and standards that constitute American political culture are embodied in the Declaration of Independence, one of the founding documents of this nation, presented in its entirety in Appendix A. The political values outlined in the Declaration of Independence include natural rights (to life, liberty, and the pursuit of happiness), equality under the law, government by the consent of the governed, and limited government powers. In some ways, the Declaration of Independence defines Americans' sense of right and wrong. It presents a challenge to anyone who might wish to overthrow our democratic processes or deny our citizens their natural rights.

The rights to liberty, equality, and property are fundamental political values shared by most Americans. These values provide a basic framework for American political discourse and debate because they are shared, yet Americans often interpret their meanings quite differently. The result of these differences can be sharp conflict in the political arena.

natural rights Rights that are not bestowed by governments but are inherent within every man, woman, and child by virtue of the fact that he or she is a human being.

political culture The set of ideas, values, and attitudes about government and the political process held by a community or a nation.

For much of America's history, there was little discussion about whether our government had grown too large. The government, after all, wasn't that big. Since the Great Depression of the 1930s, however, the government has grown by leaps and bounds.

Americans are at odds over the proper size of government. Indeed, the size of government lies at the very heart of the traditional differences between Republicans and Democrats. Republicans in Congress have called for large cuts to the federal budget. Democrats, however, believe that large cuts may endanger important programs such as Medicare and Medicaid. (Medicare provides health-care funding to the elderly, and Medicaid provides it to low-income persons.) As a candidate, Donald Trump was more open to large government than most Republican leaders. As president, however, Trump's proposals have been more traditionally Republican, and it is not clear what will happen to the size of government.

Big Government Must Shrink

Many of those who believe that big government must shrink admit that government programs can help many people who need, for example, medical care or education. The problem is that once government programs are in place, they expand. Opponents of big government believe that too many people seek government assistance rather than taking care of their problems by themselves or with the help of family and friends.

Conservatives argue that government spending must be held back to avoid higher taxes. Even if the government supports its spending by borrowing, it will have to make up the difference by imposing new taxes at some time in the future. The federal budget deficit cannot rise forever, and most of us know that. Further, the government is inefficient. Private citizens can almost always make better use of funds than the government can. Finally, taxing some people to support other people is fundamentally unfair.

We Need What the Government Does

Liberals reject the argument that taxation must injure the economy. In the 1990s, Democrats under President Bill Clinton raised taxes to reduce the federal budget deficit. Conservatives predicted disaster. In fact, America then experienced some of the strongest economic growth in its history.

More generally, liberals argue that we need the programs that a big government can provide. Medicare, Medicaid, and Social Security together make up half of all federal spending. These programs assist people who cannot get by with just the help of family or friends.

Liberals agree that government should do whatever it can to limit wasteful spending. But when we must choose between higher taxes and eliminating crucial services, we will simply have to pay for the benefits we need. America can do this if we need to. Back in the 1970s, the top marginal income tax rate was 75 percent higher than what it is today. In the 1950s it was higher still.

Critical Analysis

Are tax increases a legitimate policy option—or should they be out of the question?

Liberty The term *liberty* can be defined as a state of being free from external controls or restrictions. In the United States, the Constitution sets forth our *civil liberties*, including the freedom to practice whatever religion we choose and to be free from any state-imposed religion. Our liberties also include the freedom to speak freely on any topic and issue. Because people cannot govern themselves unless they are free to voice their opinions, freedom of speech is a basic requirement in a true democracy.

Clearly, though, if we are to live together with others, there have to be some restrictions on individual liberties. If people were allowed to do whatever they wished, without regard for the rights or liberties of others, chaos would result. Hence, a more accurate definition of

A young girl celebrates the Fourth of July. *What function does "flag waving" have?*

liberty would be *the freedom of individuals to believe, act, and express themselves as they choose so long as doing so does not infringe on the rights of other individuals in the society.*

While almost all Americans believe strongly in liberty, differing ideas of what liberty should mean have led to some of our most heated political disputes. Should women be free to obtain abortions? Should employers be free to set the wages and working conditions of their employees? Should individuals be free to smoke marijuana? Over the years, Americans have been at odds over these and many other issues that concern liberty.

Equality The goal of **equality** has always been a central part of American political culture. The Declaration of Independence confirmed the importance of equality to early Americans by stating, "We hold these Truths to be self-evident, that all Men are created equal." Because of the goal of equality, the Constitution prohibited the government from granting titles of nobility. (The Constitution did not prohibit slavery, however.)

But what, exactly, does *equality* mean? Does it mean simply political equality—the right to vote and run for political office? Does it mean that individuals should have equal opportunities to develop their talents and skills? What about those who are poor, suffer from disabilities, or are otherwise at a competitive disadvantage? Should it be the government's responsibility to ensure that such individuals also have equal opportunities?

Although most Americans believe that all persons should have the opportunity to fulfill their potential, few contend that it is the government's responsibility to totally eliminate the economic and social differences that lead to unequal opportunities. Indeed, some contend that efforts to achieve equality, in the sense of equal treatment for all, are fundamentally incompatible with the value of liberty.

Property As noted earlier, the English philosopher John Locke asserted that people are born with natural rights and that among these rights are life, liberty, and *property*. The Declaration of Independence makes a similar assertion: people are born with certain "unalienable" rights, including the right to life, liberty, and the *pursuit of happiness*. For Americans, property and the pursuit of happiness are closely related. Americans place a great value on home ownership, on material possessions, and on their businesses. Property gives its owners political power and the liberty to do what they want—within limits.

Property and Capitalism. Private property in America is not limited to personal possessions such as automobiles and houses. Property also consists of assets that can be used to create and sell goods and services, such as factories, farms, and shops. Private ownership of wealth-producing property is at the heart of our capitalist economic system. **Capitalism** enjoys such widespread support in the United States that we can reasonably call it one of the nation's fundamental political values. In addition to the private ownership of productive property, capitalism is based on *free markets*—markets in which people can freely buy and sell goods, services, and financial investments without undue constraint by the government. Freedom to make binding contracts is another element of the capitalist system. The preeminent capitalist institution is the privately owned corporation.

liberty The freedom of individuals to believe, act, and express themselves as they choose so long as doing so does not infringe on the rights of other individuals in the society.

equality A concept that holds, at a minimum, that all people are entitled to equal protection under the law.

capitalism An economic system based on the private ownership of wealth-producing property, free markets, and freedom of contract. The privately owned corporation is the preeminent capitalist institution.

Capitalism and Government. Although capitalism is supported by almost all Americans, there is no equivalent agreement on the relationship between capitalism and the government. Is it best for the government to leave businesses alone in almost all circumstances—or would this lead to excessive inequality and unethical business practices that injure consumers? As with the values of liberty and equality, Americans are divided over what the right to property should mean.

1-3d Political Values and a Divided Electorate

Differences among Americans in interpreting our collectively held values underlie the division between the Republican and Democratic parties. Election results in the twenty-first century suggest that the voters are split right down the middle. Elections have often been close. In 2000, for example, Republican George W. Bush won the presidency in one of the closest presidential elections in U.S. history. In election years since 2000, support for the two major parties has swung back and forth, sometimes dramatically. The years 2006 and 2008 were very good for the Democrats, at first because of public dissatisfaction with the war in Iraq and later because of the economic crisis that struck while Bush was still president. The Republicans, in turn, enjoyed a banner year in 2010, based in part on the widespread belief that President Barack Obama and the Democrats were going too far in an attempt to carry out their liberal party platform. Despite the earlier swing to the Democrats and the later Republican victories, the underlying reality remained— the nation was closely divided in its political preferences.

The 2012 and 2014 Elections By 2012, many moderate voters were apparently concerned that Republican threats to popular social programs outweighed Democratic fondness for "big government." Also, in a presidential election year such as 2012, more Democratic-leaning young people and minority group members could be expected to vote. (Often, such voters stay home in *midterm election* years such as 2010 and 2014, when presidential candidates are not on the ballot.) In the end, President Obama won reelection in 2012 by a comfortable margin. In 2014, however, voter turnout was lower than it had been in any year since 1942, when the vote took place in the middle of World War II. One result was the largest number of Republicans in Congress since the 1920s.

The 2016 Elections The political battles of the twenty-first century have been intense. Public opinion polls report that increasing numbers of Republicans and Democrats consider the other party to be not merely misguided, but a danger to the country. The 2016 elections, therefore, were certain to be hard-fought. Voter turnout was higher than in the 2012 presidential election year, not to mention the midterm years 2010 and 2014. The Democrats did, in fact, post a net gain of two senators and eight members of the House, although this result did not come close to threatening Republican control of either chamber. In addition, Democratic presidential candidate Hillary Rodham Clinton won the national popular vote by a margin of 2.1 percent.

In the United States, however, presidential elections are not decided by the popular vote but by votes in the *electoral college*. The members of the college— *electors*—are chosen by the individual states, plus the District of Columbia. Republican presidential candidate Donald J. Trump carried the electoral college easily. Trump's victory was decided in the so-called heartland, the industrial Midwest plus Pennsylvania. His margins in states such as Michigan, Pennsylvania, and Wisconsin were narrow, however. Clinton ran up unprecedented margins in states such as California, but that state was going to vote Democratic anyway. In effect, Clinton's extra votes in states such as California were wasted.

Republicans in Power For the first time since December 2010, one party was in full control of the national government. In January 2017, President Trump nominated a conservative candidate to fill a vacancy on the United States Supreme Court, in an attempt to ensure that the Republicans would enjoy a sympathetic hearing from the judiciary. The practical consequences of the Republican sweep were not clear. That party was expected to pass much conservative legislation, but new laws would need Trump's approval. On many points, Trump's nationalist politics differed from traditional Republican small-government conservatism. Trump's influence on Congress, however, turned out to be surprisingly modest.

Trump's Policies In an almost endless number of ways, Trump was an unprecedented presidential candidate. His background, campaign style, and positions on the issues were quite different from those of past Republican candidates. For years, a core Republican objective had been cuts in tax rates, especially for upper-income Americans. Republican leaders were willing to fund such reductions by cutting programs such as Social Security and Medicare. Many ordinary Republicans, however, saw these programs as a right earned by years of paying taxes. For many of these people, opposition to immigration was the number one issue. In contrast, business-oriented establishment Republicans often supported immigration and steps to improve the status of illegal immigrants.

Trump, in contrast, promised to defend Social Security and Medicare. His hostility to immigration and to foreign imports was legendary. In Trump's view, foreign trade was responsible for a dramatic fall in the number of manufacturing jobs. He expressed his opinions on trade and immigration with some of the most inflammatory language ever employed by a major-party presidential candidate. He began his campaign in 2015 by denouncing Mexican immigrants: "They're bringing drugs. They're bringing crime. They're rapists."

Trump's Followers Those Trump supporters who attended his rallies may have applauded such language, but for most of his voters economic issues were at least as important as concerns about the changing nature of American society. Trump did best in areas with two characteristics. One was an unusually large number of white voters with no more than a high school diploma. Such people are commonly identified as members of the white working class (although earlier in history that term was based on employment, not education). A second characteristic of districts that voted strongly for Trump was that people in these areas were more likely to suffer from poor health. Death rates in Trump counties were also well above the national average.

Trump clearly struck a nerve among voters in areas suffering from serious economic and social stress. Voter turnout was up substantially in districts with such problems. Trump's new voters were generally not the hardest-pressed members of the white working class, however. Rather, they were somewhat more prosperous individuals who believed that their communities were unraveling around them. When combined with regular Republican voters, who mostly rallied to Trump, this new group of voters was enough to elect Trump president.

1–3e Political Values in a Changing Society

From the time of the earliest European settlers, America's population has always had widely differing origins. Early commentators, such as Alexis de Tocqueville, wrote of the three races of North America—Europeans, Africans, and Indians. Many years were to pass, however, before African Americans and American Indians—and later, Hispanic Americans—were widely accepted as members of the national community. Immigrants from Europe found acceptance to be easier. Still, most Americans expected that white immigrants would abandon their

> "People often say that, in a democracy, decisions are made by a majority of the people. Of course, that is not true. Decisions are made by a majority of . . . the people who vote—a very different thing."
>
> ~ WALTER H. JUDD,
> U.S. REPRESENTATIVE FROM MINNESOTA, 1943–1963

cultural distinctions and assimilate the language and customs of earlier Americans.

One of the outgrowths of the civil rights movement of the 1960s was an emphasis on *multiculturalism*, the belief that the many cultures that make up American society should remain distinct and be protected—and even encouraged—by our laws. Trump's 2016 presidential campaign, however, revealed that some Americans continue to see multiculturalism as an unacceptable value.

Despite their differing views about multiculturalism, Americans of all backgrounds remain committed to the values described in the last few sections of this text. The variety of ways that different groups interpret these values, however, add to our political divisions. African Americans, for example, given their collective history, often have a different sense of what equality should mean than do Americans whose ancestors came from Europe.

Race and Ethnicity The racial and ethnic makeup of the United States has changed dramatically in the last two decades and will continue to change, as shown in Figure 1–2. Already, non-Hispanic whites are a minority in California. For the nation as a whole, non-Hispanic whites will be in the minority before 2050. Some Americans fear that rising numbers of immigrants will threaten traditional American political values and culture. Others are confident that newcomers will adopt American values.

Even as new Hispanic and Asian citizens assimilate into American culture, they remain more likely to vote for Democrats than

> **working class** Today, persons with no more than a high school diploma. Formerly, families in which the head of household was employed in manual or unskilled labor.

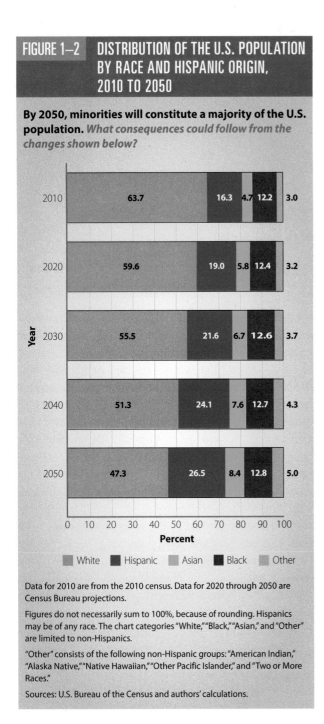

FIGURE 1–2 DISTRIBUTION OF THE U.S. POPULATION BY RACE AND HISPANIC ORIGIN, 2010 TO 2050

By 2050, minorities will constitute a majority of the U.S. population. *What consequences could follow from the changes shown below?*

Year	White	Hispanic	Asian	Black	Other
2010	63.7	16.3	4.7	12.2	3.0
2020	59.6	19.0	5.8	12.4	3.2
2030	55.5	21.6	6.7	12.6	3.7
2040	51.3	24.1	7.6	12.7	4.3
2050	47.3	26.5	8.4	12.8	5.0

Percent

■ White ■ Hispanic ■ Asian ■ Black ■ Other

Data for 2010 are from the 2010 census. Data for 2020 through 2050 are Census Bureau projections.

Figures do not necessarily sum to 100%, because of rounding. Hispanics may be of any race. The chart categories "White," "Black," "Asian," and "Other" are limited to non-Hispanics.

"Other" consists of the following non-Hispanic groups: "American Indian," "Alaska Native," "Native Hawaiian," "Other Pacific Islander," and "Two or More Races."

Sources: U.S. Bureau of the Census and authors' calculations.

An Older Society In 2010, Americans aged 65 or above made up 13 percent of the total population. By 2040, however, that figure is expected to exceed 21 percent. The aging of America means that in future years there will be more retired people collecting Social Security, Medicare, and private pensions, compared with the number of working adults. Inevitably, the question of how to share the national income among the generations will become an ever-greater problem. In many foreign countries, however, the aging population poses a much greater threat than in the United States. Our population is expected to grow throughout the coming century. Nations such as Germany, Japan, Russia, and even China can expect to see their populations shrink, which will make it much harder for them to support their older citizens.

Socialization and Crime The people of the United States are not only older and more diverse, but they are also, on the whole, better behaved. Few people realize it, but crime rates have fallen dramatically in recent decades. For example, the murder rate per 100,000 persons peaked at 10.2 in 1980. By 2014, it was 4.5, almost an all-time low. Measurements of sexual violence, divorce, births to teenage mothers, and many others are headed in a positive direction.

Since 2014, the murder rate appears to have gone up slightly, but it remains far below what it was in the 1980s and 1990s. The uptick is partly due to a rate increase in a limited number of neighborhoods in cities such as Baltimore and Chicago, and it appears to be associated with a breakdown in trust between law enforcement and community members.

Digging into crime statistics reveals an unexpected fact: crime rates overall are down among minority youth—and up among middle-age whites. California has the most complete statistics. According to a recent report, in that state about as many minority youth were arrested for felonies in 2008 as middle-age whites. By 2014, more than twice as many middle-age whites were arrested as minority youth.[5] Death rates for rural whites are up—by 48 percent among white women ages 35 to 39. This is happening at a time when death rates for every other group are falling. These results may be due to an epidemic of drug and alcohol abuse among rural whites, another sign of a cultural and economic crisis that helped elect Donald Trump.

▶ *It's an old saying: "Your freedom to swing your arm ends where my nose begins." Can you think of other examples where one person's liberty interests conflict with those of another person?*

Republicans. In other words, demographic change may provide a substantial future benefit to the Democratic Party. In recent elections, however, this benefit has been counteracted by another effect. A growing number of non-Hispanic whites—especially older ones—have been drawn to conservatism by their concern over the changing nature of American society. As we have observed, such concerns played a role in electing Donald Trump as president in 2016. We take a closer look at the immigration issue in this chapter's *Perception vs. Reality* feature.

PERCEPTION VS. REALITY

Do Immigrants Take American Jobs?

America was founded by immigrants, and few restrictions on immigration existed until the twentieth century. Today, however, immigration is a major issue. A special concern is the large number of unauthorized immigrants, also called illegal immigrants. There are probably about 11 million of these people currently in the country. The number of unauthorized immigrants has been stable since 2008 due to a collapse in rates of immigration from Mexico. (In fact, the annual number of Mexican immigrants—legal and illegal—returning home now exceeds the number of new arrivals.) Still, many people fear that immigrants, whether legal or illegal, take jobs away from American citizens.

The Perception

Many believe that increased immigration leads to more competition for jobs. Low-skilled immigrants drive down the wages of low-skilled citizens. Even highly skilled immigrants can take jobs away from engineers and other educated individuals born in the United States.

The Reality

Immigrants fill jobs, but they also create them. Economic growth can increase the amount of employment that is available. And economic studies show that highly skilled immigrants promote economic growth, increasing employment even among high-tech workers.

The number of well-educated immigrants from China, India, and other Asian countries is growing rapidly. The annual number of immigrants from Asia now exceeds the number from Latin America. A quarter of the engineering and technology companies started in the United States from 1995 to 2005 had at least one founder who was foreign-born. Some of the world's brightest brains and most cutting-edge innovators come to the United States to study—and often to stay. Foreign students earn more than half of U.S. science and engineering doctorates. Yet many of these students are forced to leave the country after graduation because there are not enough visas available for professionals.

Even low-skilled immigrants benefit the overall economy. The United States has jobs available at the bottom as well as the top. With unemployment at 10 percent in 2009 and 2010,

farmers on the West Coast still could not find U.S. citizens willing to pick fruits and vegetables.

Studies suggest that while low-skilled—and especially illegal—immigrants may have an impact on low-end wages, those most likely to not be hired are *other low-skilled immigrants*. These immigrants often speak English poorly, if at all. That gives native-born citizens an employment advantage in most parts of the country. They can compete successfully for jobs that require English competency, such as store-clerk positions. More immigration means more economic growth, and more of all kinds of jobs, including jobs that require English-speaking applicants.

Blog On

Enter "immigration and american jobs" into an Internet search engine such as Google. Several informative articles will appear, including ones from the **New York Times** *and* **The Atlantic.**

1-4 ## AMERICAN POLITICAL IDEOLOGY

LO Define common American ideological positions, such as "conservatism" and "liberalism."

In a general sense, **ideology** refers to a system of political ideas. These ideas typically are rooted in religious or philosophical beliefs about human nature, society, and government.

When it comes to ideology, Americans are often placed in two broad political camps: conservatives and liberals. The term *conservative* originally referred to persons who wished to conserve—keep—traditional social and political habits and institutions. The term *liberal* referred to those

> **ideology** Generally, a system of political ideas that are rooted in religious or philosophical beliefs concerning human nature, society, and government.

Donald Trump introduces Indiana governor Mike Pence as his vice-presidential running mate. *How is Trump different from past Republican candidates?*

who wanted to be free from tradition and to establish new policies and practices. In today's American political arena, however, these simple definitions of *liberalism* and *conservatism* are incomplete. Both terms mean much more.

1-4a Conservatism

Modern American **conservatism** does indeed value traditions—specifically, American ones. For much of U.S. history, business enterprise was largely free from government control or regulation. That freedom began to break down during the administration of Franklin D. Roosevelt (1933–1945). Roosevelt's New Deal programs, launched in an attempt to counter the effects of the Great Depression, involved the government in the American economy to an extent previously unknown. Roosevelt gave conservatives a common cause: opposition to the New Deal and to big government. One tradition that conservatives sought to maintain, therefore, was a version of capitalism that was free of government regulation or control. Another tradition has been that groups that held a preeminent position in American society in the past—such as business and religious leaders—should continue to receive respect.

conservatism A set of political beliefs that include a limited role for the national government in helping individuals and in the economic affairs of the nation, as well as support for traditional values and lifestyles.

conservative movement An ideological movement that arose in the 1950s and 1960s and continues to shape conservative beliefs.

liberalism A set of political beliefs that include the advocacy of active government, including government intervention to improve the common welfare and to protect civil rights.

The Conservative Movement The emergence of the **conservative movement** in the 1950s and 1960s was essential to the development of modern conservatism. Previously, economic conservatives were often seen as individuals who feared that government activity might personally cost them wealth or power. The conservative movement, in contrast, was clearly ideological. It provided a complete way of viewing the world, and it attracted millions of followers who were not necessarily motivated by narrow economic self-interest. The conservative movement emerged as a major force in 1964, when Arizona senator Barry Goldwater won the Republican presidential nomination on a relatively radical platform. Goldwater was soundly defeated by Democrat Lyndon B. Johnson (1963–1969). In 1980, however, Republican Ronald Reagan became the first "movement conservative" to win the White House. While the beliefs of President Trump and his most ardent supporters differ from those of movement conservatism, they are clearly within the broader conservative tradition.

Conservatism Today A key element in conservative thinking is the belief that the distribution of social and economic benefits that would exist if the government took little or no action is usually optimum. Conservatives believe that individuals and families should take responsibility for their own economic circumstances, and if that means that some people have less, so be it. Conservatives also place a high value on the principle of order, on family values, and on patriotism. Conservatism has always included those who want society and the government to reflect traditional religious values, and Christian conservatives remain an important part of the conservative coalition today.

1-4b Liberalism

While modern American **liberalism** can trace its roots to the New Deal programs of Franklin D. Roosevelt, the ideology did not take its fully modern form until the 1960s, during the Johnson administration. Johnson went well beyond the programs of Roosevelt with new

Alex Wong/Getty Images News/Getty Images

U.S. senator Elizabeth Warren (D., Mass.) at a 2017 hearing of the Senate Armed Services Committee. The topic was the situation in Afghanistan. An ally of Senator Bernie Sanders (D., Vt.), Warren has been mentioned as a possible presidential candidate in 2020. *What is her ideology?*

economic initiatives, such as Medicare and Medicaid. These programs—and more recent health-care reforms—reflect the strong liberal belief that the social and economic outcomes that exist in the absence of government action are frequently unfair. Conservatives commonly accuse liberals of valuing "big government" for its own sake. Liberals reject that characterization and argue that big government is simply a necessary tool for promoting the common welfare.

The Civil Rights Revolution In the 1960s, liberals in the Democratic Party were able to commit their party firmly to the cause of African American equality, permanently overriding those Democratic conservatives who still supported legal segregation of the races. In a matching development, conservatives in the Republican Party began to appeal to traditionalist whites who were upset by the African American civil rights movement. As the party of Lincoln, the Republicans had once been the natural political home of African Americans. This was no longer true.

Support for minority rights of all kinds became an integral part of liberal ideology, while conservatism came to include skepticism toward minority claims. As one example, consider the Black Lives Matter movement that arose in 2015 following claims that many police officers were too willing to use deadly force against African Americans. Democratic presidential candidates expressed sympathy for the movement, but most Republican candidates accused it of being antipolice.

Other Liberal Values The Vietnam War (1965–1975) also influenced liberal thinking. Although American participation in the conflict was initiated by President Johnson, liberals swung against the war more strongly than other Americans. Liberalism therefore came to include a relatively negative view of American military initiatives abroad. (That distrust has declined in recent years, however.)

Liberals strongly favor the separation of church and state. They generally think that the government should avoid laws that endorse or impose traditional religious values. Examples include laws that limit the rights of gays and lesbians. These beliefs sharply contrast with those of religious conservatives. In this area, at least, liberals do not stand for big government, but rather the reverse.

Liberals and Progressives Not all political labels are equally popular, and the term *liberal* has taken a particular beating in the political wars of the last several decades. One result is that most politicians who might have called themselves liberals in the past have labeled their philosophy progressivism instead. The term *progressive* dates back to the first years of the twentieth century, when it referred to a reform movement that was active in both major political parties. Later, the progressive label fell into disuse, until it was resurrected in recent years.

1–4c The Traditional Political Spectrum

Traditionally, liberalism and conservatism have been regarded as falling within a political spectrum that ranges from the left to the right. As illustrated in Figure 1–3, modern conservatives typically identify themselves politically as Republicans. Similarly, liberals—or progressives—identify with the Democratic Party. The identification of the parties with specific ideologies is clear today but was not always so noticeable in the past. Conservative Democrats and liberal Republicans were once common, but they are now rare.

People whose views fall in the middle of the traditional political spectrum are generally called **moderates.** By definition, moderates do not classify themselves as either liberal or conservative. Moderates may vote for either

> **progressivism** Today, an alternative, more popular term for the set of political beliefs also known as liberalism.
>
> **moderates** Persons whose views fall in the middle of the political spectrum.

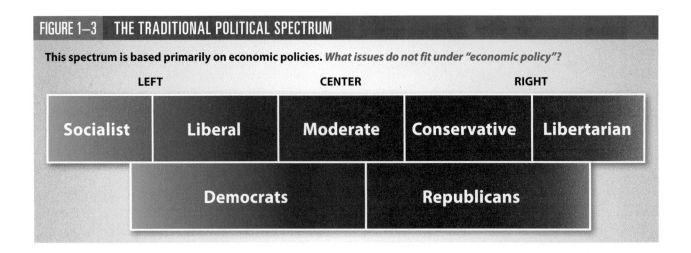

FIGURE 1–3 THE TRADITIONAL POLITICAL SPECTRUM

This spectrum is based primarily on economic policies. *What issues do not fit under "economic policy"?*

LEFT		CENTER		RIGHT
Socialist	Liberal	Moderate	Conservative	Libertarian

Democrats	Republicans

Republicans or Democrats, although in public opinion polls Democrats are about twice as likely as Republicans to identify themselves as moderates. Still, a large number of moderates do not support either major political party and often describe themselves as *independent*.

1–4d Beyond Conservatism and Liberalism

Many Americans do not adhere firmly to a particular political ideology. Some are not interested in political issues. Others may have opinions that do not neatly fit under the liberal or conservative label. For example, conservatives typically support restrictions on the availability of abortion. They also may favor banning the procedure altogether.

Liberals usually favor the right to have an abortion. Many liberals believe that the government ought to guarantee that everyone can find a job. Conservatives generally reject this idea. Millions of Americans, however, support restrictions on abortion while supporting government jobs programs. Many other citizens would oppose both of these positions. Conservatism and liberalism, in other words, are not the only ideological possibilities.

socialism A political ideology, often critical of capitalism, that lies to the left of liberalism on the traditional political spectrum. Socialists are scarce in the United States but common in many other countries.

libertarianism The belief that government should do as little as possible, not only in the economic sphere, but also in regulating morality and personal behavior.

Socialism To the left of liberalism on the traditional ideological spectrum lies **socialism.** This ideology has relatively few adherents in the United States, although a handful of Democrats and independents accept the label, including senator and 2016 presidential candidate Bernie Sanders (D., Vt.). In much of the world, however, the main left-of-center party descends from the socialist tradition. These *social democrats* have a stronger commitment to egalitarianism than do U.S. liberals and a greater tolerance for strong government. Indeed, in the first half of the twentieth century, most socialists advocated government ownership of major businesses. Few social democrats endorse such proposals today, however.

Social democrats strongly support democracy, but early in the twentieth century an ultra-left breakaway from the socialist movement—the Communists—established a series of brutal dictatorships, initially in Russia (the Soviet Union). Communists remain in power in China and a few other nations. Despite Communist rule, in recent years capitalist businesses have thrived in China.

Libertarianism Even as socialism is weak in America compared with the rest of the world, the right-of-center ideology of **libertarianism** is unusually strong. Libertarians oppose almost all government regulation of the economy and government redistribution of income.

Many ardent conservatives share these beliefs. What distinguishes true libertarians, however, is that libertarians also oppose government involvement in issues of private morality. In this belief, they often have more in common with liberals than they do with conservatives. For most people, however, economic issues remain the more important ones, and a majority of libertarians ally with conservatives politically and support the Republicans.

Economic Progressives, Social Conservatives Many other voters are liberal on economic issues even as they favor conservative positions on social matters. These people support government intervention to promote both economic "fairness" *and* moral values. Low-income people frequently are economic progressives and social conservatives. A large number of African Americans and Hispanics fall into this camp. While it is widespread within the electorate, this "anti-libertarian" point of view has no agreed-upon name.

In sum, millions of Americans do not fit neatly into the traditional liberal–conservative spectrum. We illustrate an alternative, two-dimensional political classification in Figure 1–4.

CRITICAL THINKING

▸ *Suppose you are a representative in Congress who ran for office on a platform that clearly articulated your strong beliefs. Should you be willing to compromise with others in the hopes of obtaining at least some of what you favor—or is it better to stand on principle, even if you lose?*

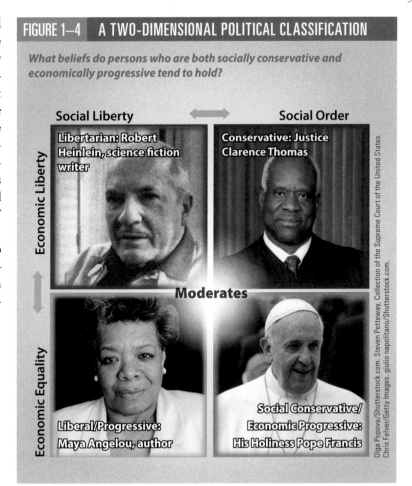

FIGURE 1–4 A TWO-DIMENSIONAL POLITICAL CLASSIFICATION

What beliefs do persons who are both socially conservative and economically progressive tend to hold?

Social Liberty ⟷ Social Order

Economic Liberty

Libertarian: Robert Heinlein, science fiction writer

Conservative: Justice Clarence Thomas

Moderates

Economic Equality

Liberal/Progressive: Maya Angelou, author

Social Conservative/ Economic Progressive: His Holiness Pope Francis

Olga Popova/Shutterstock.com. Steven Petteway, Collection of the Supreme Court of the United States. Chris Felver/Getty Images. giulio napolitano/Shutterstock.com.

AMERICA AT ODDS | America in the Twenty-First Century

As you learned in this chapter, Americans are united by a common political culture. At the same time, however, Americans are at odds over how much weight should be given to various fundamental principles. We can summarize these most basic disputes as follows:

- *How much of a problem does immigration pose for the United States? Does it create economic difficulties? If so, what are they? To what extent does it challenge the established character of our nation? Does it matter which countries immigrants come from? Why or why not? What changes to policy would be desirable, if any?*

- *How large should our government be? Should it offer a wide range of services, along with the resulting taxes—or should it provide relatively few services and collect less in taxes?*

- *Should businesses be strictly regulated to ensure the common good—or should regulation be minimized to promote economic freedom and growth?*

- *More generally, should we place a greater value on economic liberty and property rights—or on economic egalitarianism and improving the condition of those who are less well off?*

- *How active should the government be in promoting moral behavior? Should the government support traditional values—or place a high value on social liberty?*

READY TO STUDY? IN THE BOOK, YOU CAN:

☐ Review what you've read with the following chapter quiz.

☐ Check your answers in Appendix D at the back of the book.

☐ Rip out the Chapter Review Card, which includes key terms and chapter summaries.

ONLINE AT WWW.CENGAGEBRAIN.COM, YOU CAN:

☐ Watch videos to get a quick overview.

☐ Expedite your studying with Major Player readings and Focus Activities.

☐ Check your understanding with Chapter Quizzes.

FILL-IN

Learning Outcome 1–1

1. _____ can best be defined as the individuals and institutions that make society's rules and also possess the power and authority to enforce those rules.

2. In any country, government generally serves at least three essential purposes: _____, _____, _____

Learning Outcome 1–2

3. In a/an _____, the power and authority of the government are in the hands of a single person.

4. In a/an _____, the will of the majority is expressed through groups of individuals elected by the people to act as their representatives.

Learning Outcome 1–3

5. The philosopher John Locke argued that people are born with natural rights to _____, _____, _____

6. American democracy is based on five fundamental principles: _____, _____, _____, _____, _____

Learning Outcome 1–4

7. When it comes to ideology, Americans are often placed in two broad political camps: _____, _____.

8. Arizona senator Barry Goldwater and President Ronald Reagan were well-known political _____.

9. People whose views fall in the middle of the traditional political spectrum are generally called _____.

10. _____ oppose almost all government regulation of the economy and government redistribution of income, while also opposing government involvement in issues of private morality.

MULTIPLE CHOICE

Learning Outcome 1–1

11. Political scientist Harold Lasswell defined _____ as the process of determining "who gets what, when, and how" in a society.
    a. government   **b.** power   **c.** politics

12. When the government's ability to exercise power is widely viewed as legitimate, we say that the government
    a. has authority.
    b. is representative.
    c. is limited.

Learning Outcome 1–2

13. The system of government in the United States is best described as a _____ democracy.
    a. parliamentary
    b. presidential
    c. direct

14. The principal difference between an absolute monarchy and a dictatorship is that
    a. Unlike a dictatorship, an absolute monarchy allows freedom of speech and religion.
    b. Dictators may be women, but monarchs never are.
    c. An absolute monarchy is based on tradition, but a dictatorship is not.

Learning Outcome 1–3

15. Which of the following best describes a social contract?
    a. The set of ideas, values, and attitudes about govern-ment and politics held by a community or a nation.
    b. A voluntary agreement among individuals to create a government and to give that government adequate power to secure the mutual protection and welfare of all individuals.
    c. An economic system based on the private ownership of wealth-producing property, free markets, and freedom of contract.

16. Because of the political value of _____, Article I, Section 9, of the U.S. Constitution prohibits the government from granting titles of nobility.
    a. equality
    b. liberty
    c. multiculturalism

Learning Outcome 1–4

17. Today's Republican Party differs from the party that existed a century ago in that it
    a. no longer has strong support from business interests.
    b. is less reliant on the support of religious conservatives.
    c. no longer enjoys the support of most African Americans.

18. American liberalism took its fully modern form in the _____.
    a. 1960s, during the administration of Lyndon Johnson.
    b. 1990s, during the administration of Bill Clinton.
    c. 2000s, during the administration of Barack Obama.

2 | THE CONSTITUTION

Hulton Archive/Getty Images

LEARNING OUTCOMES

After reading this chapter, you should be able to:

2-1 Point out some of the influences on the American political tradition in the colonial years.

2-2 Explain why the American colonies rebelled against Britain.

2-3 Describe the structure of government established by the Articles of Confederation and some of the strengths and weaknesses of the Articles.

2-4 List the major compromises made by the delegates at the Constitutional Convention, and discuss the Federalist and Anti-Federalist positions on ratifying the Constitution.

2-5 Summarize the Constitution's major principles of government, and describe how the Constitution can be amended.

After finishing this chapter, go to **PAGE 47** for **STUDY TOOLS**

AMERICA AT ODDS | Should We Elect the President by Popular Vote?

Krista Kennell/Shutterstock.com

When Americans cast their ballots for president, they do not vote directly for the candidates. Rather, they vote for electors—persons chosen in each state by the political parties to cast the state's electoral votes for the candidate who wins that state's popular vote. This system is known as the electoral college. Each state has as many electoral votes as it has members in the U.S. Senate and House of Representatives. (In addition, the District of Columbia has three.) There are currently 538 electoral votes. To win, a presidential candidate must get 270 of these votes.

Most states have a "winner-take-all" system, in which the candidate who receives more of the popular votes than any other candidate receives all of the electoral votes, even if the margin of victory is slight. A candidate who wins the popular vote nationally may yet lose in the electoral college. In 2016, Democratic candidate Hillary Clinton won the popular vote by a margin of about 2,870,000 votes, roughly 2.1 percent. Yet she lost to Republican Donald Trump in the electoral college. This situation has happened before—in 2000, Democrat Al Gore won the popular vote but narrowly lost the electoral college to Republican George W. Bush. Many Americans believe that we should let the popular vote decide who becomes president. Others are not so sure.

The Electoral College Ensures Stability

Supporters of the electoral college argue that it helps to protect the small states from being overwhelmed by the large states. It also helps to maintain a relatively stable party system. If the president were elected by popular vote, we might have multiple parties vying for the nation's highest office. The current system helps to discourage single-issue or regional candidates—candidates who are not focused on the interests of the nation as a whole. To prevail in the electoral college, a candidate must build a national coalition.

Even in 2016, the college worked as intended. Trump's vote was more broadly distributed geographically than Clinton's. Her popular vote majority was based on a 4,270,000-vote margin in California. But why should that state get to pick the president?

Finally, with the electoral college, a disputed presidential election could force a recount in one or more close states. A close election in a popular vote system, however, might require recounts in every corner of the country.

Let the People Elect Our President

Opponents of the electoral college believe that it is simply unfair. Consider that one electoral vote in California corresponds to roughly 725,000 people, while an electoral vote in Wyoming represents only about 197,000. Clearly, the votes of Americans are not weighted equally, and this inequality is contrary to the "one person, one vote" principle of our democracy. As to the California argument just advanced, you can change the outcome of any election if you disregard some of the votes. When California chose Clinton over Trump by a two-to-one margin, that should have meant something. It didn't.

It's true that getting rid of the electoral college would require a constitutional amendment, and the small states would never agree to that. There is an alternative. The National Popular Vote Interstate Compact would give the electoral votes of every participating state to the national popular vote winner. The compact would go into effect if the participating states had 270 votes—enough to control the electoral college. Currently, the compact states (ten states and the District of Columbia) have 165 votes.

Where do you stand?

1. Do you believe that a candidate elected by popular vote would be more representative of the nation than a candidate elected by the electoral college? Why or why not?

2. Why might the electoral college issue threaten to become a partisan one?

Explore this issue online

- You can find the website of National Popular Vote Inc., a sponsor of the proposal, at www.nationalpopularvote.com.

- The conservative website The New American opposes the National Popular Vote Interstate Compact. Find its arguments by searching for "popular vote threatens republic."

INTRODUCTION

The Constitution, which was written more than two hundred years ago, continues to be the supreme law of the land. Time and again, its provisions have been adapted to the changing needs and conditions of society. The challenge before today's citizens and political leaders is to find a way to apply those provisions to a society and an economy that could not possibly have been anticipated by the founders. Will the Constitution survive this challenge? Most Americans assume that it will—and with good reason: no other written constitution in the world today is as old as the U.S. Constitution. Americans tend to revere their Constitution despite its quirks, such as the one discussed in the chapter-opening *America at Odds* feature.

To understand the principles of government set forth in the Constitution, you have to go back to the beginnings of our nation's history.

2–1 THE BEGINNINGS OF AMERICAN GOVERNMENT

LO Point out some of the influences on the American political tradition in the colonial years.

When the framers of the Constitution met in Philadelphia in 1787, they brought with them some valuable political assets. One asset was their English political heritage. Another was the hands-on political experience they had acquired during the colonial era. Their political knowledge and experience enabled them to establish a constitution that could meet not only the needs of their own time but also the needs of generations to come.

The American colonies had been settled by individuals from many nations, including France, Germany, Ireland, the Netherlands, Spain, and Sweden. The majority of the colonists, though, came from England and Scotland. The British colonies in North America were established by private individuals and private trading companies, and were under the rule of the British Crown. The colonies, which were located along the Atlantic seaboard of today's United States, eventually numbered thirteen.

Although American politics owes much to the English political tradition, the colonists derived most of their understanding of social compacts, the rights of the people, limited government, and representative government from their own experiences. Years before Parliament adopted the English Bill of Rights or John Locke wrote his *Two Treatises of Government*, the American colonists were already putting the ideas expressed in those documents into practice.

2–1a The First English Settlements

The first permanent English settlement in North America was Jamestown, in what is now Virginia.[1] Jamestown was established in 1607 as a trading post of the Virginia Company of London.[2]

Plymouth Colony   The first New England colony was founded by the Plymouth Company in 1620 at Plymouth in what is today Massachusetts. Most of the settlers at Plymouth were Pilgrims, a group of English Protestants who came to the New World on the ship *Mayflower*. Even before the Pilgrims went ashore, they drew up the **Mayflower Compact,** in which they set up a government and promised to obey its laws.

The reason for the compact was that the group was outside the territory assigned to the Virginia Company, which had arranged for them to settle in what is now New York, not Massachusetts. Fearing that some of the passengers might decide that they were no longer subject to any rules of civil order, the leaders on board the *Mayflower* agreed that some form of governmental authority was necessary.

The Mayflower Compact was essentially a social contract. It has historical significance because it was the first of a series of similar contracts among the colonists to establish fundamental rules of government.[3] The Compact reflected the fact that Plymouth was essentially a religious colony, and early colonial attitudes toward religion were different from those of the revolutionary era. We address that point in this chapter's *Join the Debate* feature.

More Colonies, More Constitutions   The Massachusetts Bay Colony was established as another trading outpost in New England in 1628. In 1636, following disputes in the Massachusetts Bay Colony, settlers from Massachusetts organized the Connecticut Colony at Hartford. In 1639, they adopted America's first written constitution, which was called the Fundamental Orders of Connecticut. This document called for the laws to be made by an assembly of elected representatives from

Mayflower Compact
A document drawn up by Pilgrim leaders in 1620 on the ship *Mayflower*. The document set up a provisional government.

JOIN THE DEBATE

Was the United States Meant to Be a Christian Nation?

The Pilgrims established a religious colony when they landed in New England. In early Virginia, failure to attend Church of England services was a serious crime. By the time the Constitution was written, several states still had established (state-supported) churches. Christian beliefs were strong among the population in that era. Most Americans considered themselves to be part of a Christian—indeed, a Protestant—people. (Anti-Catholicism was widespread.)

Yet the Declaration of Independence never refers to Christ. The Constitution does not contain the word *God*. It refers to religion twice. Article VI states, ". . . no religious Test shall ever be required as a Qualification to any Office or public Trust under the United States." The world-famous First Amendment begins, "Congress shall make no law respecting an establishment of religion, or prohibiting the free exercise thereof . . . ."

Considering these facts, was the United States meant to be a Christian nation—or not? The answer to that question depends in part on what we mean by "Christian nation."

Yes, America Is a Christian Nation

By *nation*, do we mean a country's government or its people? If we say "people," it is hard to deny that the United States has been a Christian nation. According to the Pew Research Center, 70.6 percent of Americans today consider themselves to be Christian. Some conservatives, however, have argued that "Christian nation" should mean more than that. Most of the founders, even those whose private commitment to Christianity was questionable, agreed that religion was essential to a just and harmonious society. The founders would have been astonished to learn that public school teachers today may not lead their students in prayer.

According to Christian conservatives, constitutional principles are inseparable from Christianity, and the First Amendment means only that the government must not pick and choose among Christian churches. Limits on "anti-Western" religions, such as bans on Islamic mosques, are appropriate.

The "Christian Nation" Idea Would Violate Our Rights

It is hard to imagine how the founders could have sought to establish a Christian nation when many of them were not Christians at all, in the modern sense. George Washington never took communion or referred to Christ. John Adams was a Unitarian—that is, he did not believe that Jesus was divine. Thomas Jefferson thought likewise. It is impossible to say what James Madison and James Monroe believed, because they avoided issues of doctrine even in their private correspondence. Not until Andrew Jackson (1829–1837) did we have a president who openly endorsed Christianity in the way we now expect of political candidates.

Opponents of the "Christian nation" concept argue that the First Amendment should be interpreted strictly. It is essential to tolerate the adherents of all religions—including Muslims and, for that matter, atheists. This is an issue about which the founders were quite explicit.

Critical Analysis

Christian conservatives argue that discrimination against Christians is widespread in modern America. Is anti-Christian discrimination a problem? Why or why not?

each town. The document also provided for the popular election of a governor and judges.

Other colonies, in turn, established fundamental governing rules. The Massachusetts Body of Liberties of 1641 protected individual rights. The Pennsylvania Frame of Government, passed in 1682, and the Pennsylvania Charter of Privileges of 1701 established principles that were later expressed in the U.S. Constitution and the **Bill of Rights** (the first ten amendments to the Constitution). By 1732, all thirteen colonies had been established, each with its own political documents and constitution (see Figure 2–1).

2–1b Colonial Legislatures

Bill of Rights The first ten amendments to the U.S. Constitution. They list the freedoms—such as the freedoms of speech, press, and religion—that a citizen enjoys and that cannot be infringed on by the government.

As mentioned, the British colonies in America were under the rule of the British monarchy. Britain, however, was thousands of miles away—it took two months to sail across the Atlantic. Thus, to a significant extent, colonial legislatures carried on the "nuts and bolts" of colonial government. These legislatures, or *representative assemblies*, consisted of representatives elected by the colonists. The earliest colonial legislature was the Virginia House of Burgesses, established in 1619. By the time of the American Revolution, all of the colonies had representative assemblies. Many had been in existence for more than a hundred years.

Through their participation in colonial governments, the colonists gained crucial political experience. Colonial leaders became familiar with the practical problems of governing. They learned how to build coalitions among groups with diverse interests and how to make compromises. Indeed, by the time of the American Revolution in 1776, Americans had formed a complex, sophisticated political system.

The colonists benefited from their political experiences. They were quickly able to establish their own constitutions and state governments after they declared their independence from Britain in 1776. Eventually, they were able to set up a national government as well.

CRITICAL THINKING

▶ *When first founded, each of the colonies had very few people. How might that have made it easier to draw up founding documents?*

2–2 THE REBELLION OF THE COLONISTS

LO Explain why the American colonies rebelled against Britain.

FIGURE 2–1   THE THIRTEEN COLONIES BEFORE THE AMERICAN REVOLUTION

The western boundary of the colonies was set by the Proclamation Line of 1763, which banned European settlement in western territories that were reserved for Native Americans. Note that Vermont, which is striped, was claimed by both New York and New Hampshire. *What would have happened if the founders had tried to limit the number or powers of new states?*

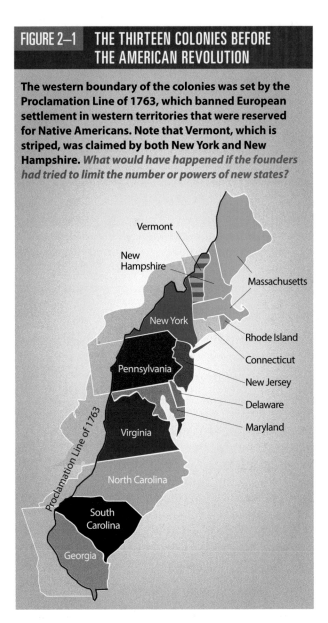

Scholars of the American Revolution point out that by and large, the American colonists did not want to become independent of Britain. For the majority of the colonists, Britain was the homeland, and ties of loyalty were strong. Why, then, did the colonists revolt against Britain and declare their independence? What happened to sever the political, economic, and emotional bonds that tied the colonists to Britain? The answers to these questions lie in a series of events in the mid-1700s that culminated in a change in British policy toward the colonies. Table 2–1 shows some major political events in early U.S. history.

One of these events was the French and Indian War (1754–1763) between Britain and France. (In Europe, the fighting began in 1756, and Europeans call that conflict the *Seven Years' War*.) (In North America, the fighting began in 1754, and Americans call that conflict the *French and Indian War*.) The British victory in the

TABLE 2–1	SIGNIFICANT EVENTS IN EARLY U.S. POLITICAL HISTORY
1607	Jamestown established—Virginia Company lands settlers.
1620	Mayflower Compact signed.
1628	Massachusetts Bay Colony set up.
1639	Fundamental Orders of Connecticut adopted.
1641	Massachusetts Body of Liberties adopted.
1682	Pennsylvania Frame of Government passed.
1701	Pennsylvania Charter of Privileges adopted.
1732	Last of thirteen colonies established (Georgia).
1754	French and Indian War breaks out.
1765	Stamp Act—Stamp Act Congress meets.
1773	Boston Tea Party.
1774	First Continental Congress meets.
1775	Second Continental Congress. Revolutionary War begins.
1776	Declaration of Independence signed.
1777	Articles of Confederation drafted.
1781	Last state signs Articles of Confederation.
1783	"Critical period" in U.S. history begins. Weak national government until 1789.
1786	Shays' Rebellion.
1787	Constitutional Convention held.
1788	Constitution ratified.
1791	Bill of Rights ratified.

Seven Years' War permanently altered the relationship between Britain and its American colonies. After successfully ousting the French from North America, the British expanded their authority over the colonies. To pay its war debts and to finance the defense of its expanded North American empire, Britain needed revenues. The British government decided to obtain some of these revenues by imposing taxes on the American colonists and exercising more direct control over colonial trade.

At the same time, Americans were beginning to distrust the expanding British presence in the colonies. Having fought alongside British forces, Americans thought they deserved more credit for the victory. The British, however, attributed the victory solely to their own efforts.

Furthermore, the colonists began to develop a sense of identity separate from the British. Americans were shocked at the behavior of some of the British soldiers and the cruel punishments meted out to enforce discipline among the British troops. The British, in turn, had little good to say about the colonists alongside whom they had fought. They considered them brutish, uncivilized, and undisciplined. It was during this time that the colonists began to use the word *American* to describe themselves.

2–2a "Taxation without Representation"

In 1764, the British Parliament passed the Sugar Act, which imposed a tax on all sugar imported into the American colonies. Some colonists, particularly in Massachusetts, vigorously opposed this tax and proposed a boycott of certain British imports. This boycott developed into a "nonimportation" movement that soon spread to other colonies.

The Stamp Act of 1765   The following year, in 1765, Parliament passed the Stamp Act, which imposed the first direct tax on the colonists. Under the act, all legal documents and newspapers had to use specially embossed (stamped) paper that was purchased from the government. Items such as playing cards and dice were also subject to this requirement.

The Stamp Act generated even stronger resentment among the colonists than the Sugar Act. James Otis, Jr., a Massachusetts attorney, declared that there could be "no taxation without representation." The American colonists were not represented in the British Parliament. They viewed Parliament's attempts to tax them as contrary to the principle of representative government. The British saw the matter differently. From the British perspective, it was only fair that the colonists pay taxes to help support the costs incurred by the British government in defending its American territories. Troops were permanently stationed in the colonies following the Seven Years' War.

In October 1765, nine of the thirteen colonies sent delegates to the Stamp Act Congress in New York City. The delegates prepared a declaration of rights and grievances, which they sent to King George III. This action marked the first time that a majority of the colonies had joined together to oppose British rule. The British Parliament repealed the Stamp Act.

Further Taxes and the Coercive Acts   Soon, however, Parliament passed new laws designed to bind the colonies more tightly to the central government in London. Laws that imposed taxes on glass, paint, lead, and many other items were passed in 1767. The colonists protested by boycotting all British goods. In 1773, anger over taxation reached a powerful climax at the Boston Tea Party, in which colonists dressed as Mohawk Indians dumped almost 350 chests of British tea into Boston Harbor as a gesture of tax protest.[4]

The British Parliament was quick to respond to the Tea Party. In 1774, Parliament passed the Coercive Acts (sometimes called the "Intolerable Acts"), which closed Boston Harbor and placed the government of Massachusetts under direct British control.

2-2b The Continental Congresses

In response to the "Intolerable Acts," New York, Pennsylvania, and Rhode Island proposed a colonial congress. The Massachusetts House of Representatives requested that all colonies select delegates to send to Philadelphia for the congress.

The First Continental Congress The First Continental Congress met on September 5, 1774, at Carpenters' Hall in Philadelphia. Of the thirteen colonies, only Georgia did not participate. The congress decided that the colonies should send a petition to King George III to explain their grievances, which they did. The congress also called for a continued boycott of British goods and required each colony to establish an army.

To enforce the boycott and other acts of resistance against Britain, the delegates to the First Continental Congress urged that "a committee be chosen in every county, city and town . . . whose business it shall be attentively to observe the conduct of all persons." The committees of "safety" or "observation," as they were called, organized militias, held special courts, and suppressed the opinions of those who remained loyal to the British Crown. Committee members spied on neighbors' activities and reported to the press the names of those who violated the boycott against Britain. The names were then printed in the local papers, and the transgressors were harassed and ridiculed in their communities.

The Second Continental Congress Almost immediately after receiving the petition from the First Continental Congress, the British government condemned the actions of the congress as open acts of rebellion. Britain responded with even stricter and more repressive measures. On April 19, 1775, British soldiers (Redcoats) fought against colonial citizen soldiers (Minutemen) in the towns of Lexington and Concord in Massachusetts—the first battles of the American Revolution.

> "We have it in our power
> *to begin*
> *the world over again.*"
>
> ~ PATRICK HENRY
> AMERICAN PLANTATION OWNER
> AND POLITICIAN 1736–1799

First Continental Congress A gathering of delegates from twelve of the thirteen colonies, held in 1774 to protest the Coercive Acts.

Second Continental Congress The congress of the colonies that met in 1775 to assume the powers of a central government and to establish an army.

Less than a month later, delegates from all thirteen colonies gathered in Pennsylvania for the Second Continental Congress, which immediately assumed the powers of a central government. The Second Continental Congress declared that the militiamen who had gathered around Boston were now a full army. It also named George Washington, a delegate to the congress who had some military experience, as its commander in chief.

The delegates to the Second Continental Congress still intended to reach a peaceful settlement with the British Parliament. One declaration stated specifically that "we [the congress] have not raised Armies with ambitious Designs of separating from Great Britain, and establishing independent States." The continued attempts to effect a reconciliation with Britain, even after the outbreak of fighting, underscore the colonists' reluctance to sever their relationship with the home country.

2-2c Breaking the Ties: Independence

Public debate about the problems with Britain continued to rage, but the stage had been set for declaring independence. One of the most rousing arguments in favor of independence was presented by Thomas Paine, a former English schoolmaster and corset maker, who wrote a pamphlet called *Common Sense*.

Paine's *Common Sense* Paine's pamphlet was published in Philadelphia in January 1776. In it, Paine addressed the crisis using "simple fact, plain argument, and common sense." He mocked King George III and attacked every argument that favored loyalty to the king. He called the king a "royal brute" and a "hardened, sullen-tempered Pharaoh [Egyptian king in ancient times]."[5]

Paine's writing went beyond a personal attack on the king. He contended that America could survive economically on its own and no longer needed its British connection. He wanted the developing colonies to become a model republic in a world in which other nations were oppressed by strong central governments.

None of Paine's arguments was new. In fact, most of them were commonly heard in tavern debates throughout the land. Instead, it was the wit and eloquence of Paine's words that made *Common Sense* so effective:

A government of our own is our natural right: and when a man seriously reflects on the precariousness of human affairs, he will become convinced, that it is infinitely wiser and safer, to form a constitution of our own in a cool and deliberate manner, while we have it in our power, than to trust such an interesting event to time and chance.[6]

Revolution and Popular Opinion

Many historians regard Paine's *Common Sense* as the single most important publication of the American Revolution. The pamphlet became a best seller. More than one hundred thousand copies were sold within a few months after its publication. (The equivalent in today's publishing world would be a book that sells between 9 million and 11 million copies in its first year of publication.) It put independence squarely on the agenda. Above all, *Common Sense* helped sever the remaining ties of loyalty to the British monarch, thus removing the final psychological barrier to independence. Indeed, later John Adams would ask,

> What do we mean by the Revolution? The War? That was no part of the Revolution. It was only an effect and consequence of it. The Revolution was in the minds of the people, and this was effected, from 1760 to 1775, in the course of fifteen years before a drop of blood was drawn at Lexington.[7]

Independence from Britain—The First Step

By June 1776, the Second Continental Congress had voted for free trade at all American ports with all countries except Britain. The congress had also suggested that all colonies establish state governments separate from Britain. The colonists realized that a formal separation from Britain was necessary if the new nation was to obtain supplies for its armies and commitments of military aid from foreign governments. On June 7, 1776, the first formal step toward independence was taken when Richard Henry Lee of Virginia placed the following resolution before the congress:

> RESOLVED, That these United Colonies are, and of right ought to be, free and independent States, that they are absolved from allegiance to the British Crown, and that all political connection between them and the state of Great Britain is, and ought to be, totally dissolved.

The congress postponed consideration of Lee's resolution until a formal statement of independence could be drafted. On June 11, a "Committee of Five" was appointed to draft a declaration that would present to the world the colonies' case for independence.

Thomas Paine, the author of *Common Sense*. Paine argued that the United States could stand on its own economically. *How important do you think that argument was?*

The Significance of the Declaration of Independence

Adopted on July 4, 1776, the Declaration of Independence is one of the world's most famous documents. Like Paine, Thomas Jefferson, who wrote most of the document, elevated the dispute between Britain and the American colonies to a universal level. Jefferson opened the second paragraph of the declaration with the following words, which have since been memorized by countless American schoolchildren and admired the world over:

> We hold these Truths to be self-evident, that all Men are created equal, that they are endowed by their Creator with certain unalienable Rights, that among these are Life, Liberty, and the Pursuit of Happiness—That to secure these Rights, Governments are instituted among Men, deriving their just Powers from the Consent of the Governed, that whenever any Form of Government becomes destructive of these Ends, it is the Right of the People to alter or to abolish it, and to institute new Government.

Library of Congress Prints and Photographs Division [LC-USZ62-96219]

Three members of the committee chosen to draft a declaration of independence are shown here: Benjamin Franklin, John Adams, and Thomas Jefferson. *What would the British have done if they had managed to arrest these people?*

The concepts expressed in the Declaration of Independence clearly reflect Jefferson's familiarity with European political philosophy, particularly the works of John Locke.[8] Jefferson's "life, liberty, and the pursuit of happiness" is clearly modeled on Locke's "life, liberty, and property."

From Colonies to States

Even before the Declaration of Independence, some of the colonies had transformed themselves into sovereign states with their own permanent governments. In May 1776, the Second Continental Congress had directed each of the colonies to form "such government as shall . . . best be conducive to the happiness and safety of their constituents [those represented by the government]."

Before long, all thirteen colonies had created constitutions. Eleven of the colonies had completely new constitutions. The other two,

unicameral legislature
A legislature with only one chamber.

Rhode Island and Connecticut, made minor modifications to old royal charters. Seven of the new constitutions contained bills of rights that defined the personal liberties of all state citizens. All constitutions called for limited governments.

Republicanism

Many citizens were fearful of a strong central government because of their recent experiences under the British Crown. They opposed any form of government that resembled monarchy in any way. This antiroyalist—or *republican*—sentiment pervaded the colonies.

The Impact of Republicanism. Wherever antiroyalist sentiment was strong, the legislature—composed of elected representatives—became all-powerful. In Pennsylvania and Georgia, for example, **unicameral** (one-chamber) **legislatures** were unchecked by any executive authority. Indeed, the executive branch was extremely weak in all thirteen states.

The republican spirit was strong enough to seriously interfere with the ability of the new nation to win the Revolutionary War. (For example, republican sentiments made it difficult for the national government to raise the funds needed to adequately supply General Washington's army.) Republicans of the Revolutionary Era (not to be confused with supporters of the later Republican Party) were suspicious not only of executive authority in their own states but also of national authority as represented by the Continental Congress.

This antiauthoritarian, localist impulse contrasted with the *nationalist* sentiments of many of the nation's founders, especially such leaders as George Washington and Alexander Hamilton. Nationalists favored an effective central authority. Of course, many founders, such as Thomas Jefferson, harbored both republican and nationalist impulses.

Who Were the Republicans? Like all political movements of the time, the republicans were led by men of "property and standing." Leaders who were strongly republican, however, tended to be less prominent than their nationalist or moderate counterparts. Small farmers may have been the one group that was disproportionately republican. Significantly, small farmers made up a majority of the voters in every state.

CRITICAL THINKING

▶ *The American colonists did not have the right to elect members of the British Parliament. How might American history have been different if the British had permitted such representation?*

2-3 THE CONFEDERATION OF STATES

LO Describe the structure of government established by the Articles of Confederation and some of the strengths and weaknesses of the Articles.

Republican sentiments influenced the thinking of the delegates to the Second Continental Congress, who formed a committee to draft a plan of confederation. A **confederation** is a voluntary association of *independent* states. The member states agree to let the central government undertake a limited number of activities, such as forming an army, but do not allow the central government to place many restrictions on the states' own actions. The member states typically can still govern most state affairs as they see fit.

On November 15, 1777, the Second Continental Congress agreed on a draft of the plan, which was finally signed by all thirteen colonies on March 1, 1781. The **Articles of Confederation,** the result of this plan, served as our first national constitution and represented an important step in the creation of our system of government.[9]

2-3a The Articles of Confederation

The Articles of Confederation established the Congress of the Confederation as the central governing body. This congress was a unicameral (one-chamber) assembly of representatives—or ambassadors, as they were called—from the various states. Although each state could send from two to seven representatives to the congress, each state, no matter what its size, had only one vote. The issue of sovereignty was an important part of the Articles of Confederation:

> Each State retains its sovereignty, freedom, and independence, and every power, jurisdiction, and right, which is not by this Confederation expressly delegated to the United States in Congress assembled.

The structure of government under the Articles of Confederation is shown in Figure 2–2.

> **confederation** A league of independent states that are united only for the purpose of achieving common goals.
>
> **Articles of Confederation** The nation's first constitution, which established a national form of government following the American Revolution. The Articles provided for a confederal form of government in which the central government had few powers.

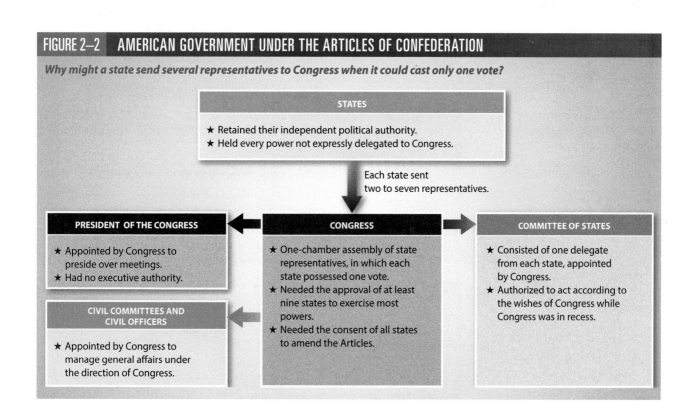

FIGURE 2–2   AMERICAN GOVERNMENT UNDER THE ARTICLES OF CONFEDERATION

Why might a state send several representatives to Congress when it could cast only one vote?

STATES
★ Retained their independent political authority.
★ Held every power not expressly delegated to Congress.

Each state sent two to seven representatives.

PRESIDENT OF THE CONGRESS
★ Appointed by Congress to preside over meetings.
★ Had no executive authority.

CIVIL COMMITTEES AND CIVIL OFFICERS
★ Appointed by Congress to manage general affairs under the direction of Congress.

CONGRESS
★ One-chamber assembly of state representatives, in which each state possessed one vote.
★ Needed the approval of at least nine states to exercise most powers.
★ Needed the consent of all states to amend the Articles.

COMMITTEE OF STATES
★ Consisted of one delegate from each state, appointed by Congress.
★ Authorized to act according to the wishes of Congress while Congress was in recess.

Powers under the Articles Congress had several powers under the Articles of Confederation, and these enabled the new nation to achieve a number of objectives (see Figure 2–3). The Northwest Ordinance settled states' claims to many of the western lands and established a basic pattern for the government of new territories. Also, the 1783 peace treaty negotiated with Britain granted to the United States all of the territory from the Atlantic Ocean to the Mississippi River and from the Great Lakes and Canada to what is now northern Florida.

Lack of Powers under the Articles In spite of these accomplishments, the central government created by the Articles of Confederation was quite weak. The Congress of the Confederation had no power to raise revenues for the militia or to force the states to meet military quotas. Essentially, this meant that the new government did not have the power to enforce its laws. Even passing laws was difficult because the Articles of Confederation provided that nine states had to approve any law before it was enacted. Figure 2–4 lists powers that the central government lacked under the Articles of Confederation.

The Articles and the Constitution Nonetheless, the Articles of Confederation proved to be a good "first draft" for the Constitution, and at least half of the text of the Articles would later appear in the Constitution. The Articles were an unplanned experiment that tested some of the principles of government that had been set forth earlier in the Declaration of Independence. Some argue that without the experience of government under the Articles of Confederation, it would have been difficult, if not impossible, to arrive at the compromises that were necessary to create the Constitution several years later.

2–3b A Time of Crisis—The 1780s

The Revolutionary War ended on October 18, 1781. The Treaty of Paris, which confirmed the colonies' independence from Britain, was signed in 1783. Peace with the British may have been won, but peace within the new nation was hard to find. The states bickered among themselves and refused to support the new central government in almost any way. As George Washington stated, "We are one nation today and thirteen tomorrow. Who will treat [with] us on such terms?"

FIGURE 2–3 POWERS OF THE CENTRAL GOVERNMENT UNDER THE ARTICLES OF CONFEDERATION

Although the Articles of Confederation were later scrapped, they did allow the early government of the United States to achieve several important goals, including winning the Revolutionary War. *Why might the Post Office have been such a successful early institution?*

WHAT THE CONGRESS COULD DO	ACCOMPLISHMENT
Congress could establish and control the armed forces, declare war, and make peace.	The United States won the Revolutionary War.
Congress could enter into treaties and alliances.	Congress negotiated a peace treaty with Britain.
Congress could settle disputes among the states under certain circumstances.	Congress passed the Northwest Ordinance, which settled certain states' land claims.
Congress could regulate coinage (but not paper money) and set standards for weights and measures.	Congress carried out these functions (but the inability to regulate paper money proved a major weakness).
Congress could borrow money from the people.	Congress did borrow money (but without the power to tax, it had trouble repaying the loans or obtaining new ones).
Congress could create a postal system, courts to address issues related to ships at sea, and government departments.	Congress created a postal system and departments of foreign affairs, finance, and war.

FIGURE 2–4 LACK OF CENTRAL GOVERNMENT POWERS UNDER THE ARTICLES OF CONFEDERATION

The government's lack of certain powers under the Articles of Confederation taught the framers of the Constitution several important lessons, which helped them create a more effective government under that new document. *Why would the inability of the national government to regulate interstate commerce have been so important?*

WHAT THE CONGRESS COULD NOT DO	RESULT
Congress could not force the states to meet military quotas.	The central government could not draft soldiers to form a standing army.
Congress could not regulate commerce between the states or with other nations.	Each state was free to tax goods imported from other states. Economic quarrels broke out among the states and with other nations.
Congress could enter into treaties but could not enforce them.	The states were not forced to respect treaties. Many states entered into treaties independent of Congress.
Congress could not directly tax the people.	The central government had to rely on the states to collect taxes, which the states were reluctant to do.
Congress had no power to enforce its laws.	The central government depended on the states to enforce its laws, which they rarely did.
Any amendment to the Articles required all thirteen states to consent.	In practice, the powers of the central government could not be changed.
There was no national judicial system.	Most disputes among the states could not be settled by the central government.
There was no executive branch.	Coordinating the work of the central government was almost impossible.

Indeed, the national government, such as it was, did not have the ability to prevent the various states from entering into agreements with foreign powers, despite the danger that such agreements could completely disrupt the confederation, pitting state against state. When Congress proved reluctant to admit Vermont into the Union, Britain began negotiations with influential Vermonters with the aim of annexing the district to Canada. Britain also held a variety of forts on territory that was undeniably American by treaty. Likewise, Spain occupied forts as far north as Memphis.

The states increasingly taxed each other's imports and at times even prevented trade altogether. By 1784, the new nation was suffering from a serious economic depression. States started printing their own money at dizzying rates, which led to inflation. Banks were calling in old loans and refusing to issue new ones. Individuals who could not pay their debts were often thrown into prison.

Shays' Rebellion The tempers of indebted farmers in western Massachusetts reached the boiling point in August 1786. Former Revolutionary War captain Daniel Shays, along with approximately two thousand armed farmers, seized county courthouses and disrupted the debtors' trials. Shays and his men then launched an attack on the national government's arsenal in Springfield. **Shays' Rebellion** continued to grow in intensity and lasted into the winter, when it was finally stopped by the Massachusetts volunteer army, which was paid by Boston merchants.[10]

Similar disruptions occurred throughout most of the New England states and in some other areas as well. The upheavals were an important catalyst for change. The revolts frightened American political and business leaders and caused more and more Americans to realize that a *true* national government had to be created.

Shays' Rebellion A rebellion of angry farmers in western Massachusetts in 1786, led by former Revolutionary War captain Daniel Shays.

The Annapolis Meeting The Virginia legislature called for a meeting of representatives from all of the states in Annapolis, Maryland, on September 11, 1786, to consider extending national authority to issues of commerce. Five of the thirteen states sent delegates, two of whom were Alexander Hamilton of New York and James Madison of Virginia. Both of these men favored a strong central government.[11] They persuaded the other delegates to issue a report calling on the states to hold a convention in Philadelphia in May of the following year.

The Congress of the Confederation at first was reluctant to give its approval to the Philadelphia convention. By mid-February 1787, however, seven of the states had named delegates to the Philadelphia meeting. Finally, on February 21, the Congress called on the states to send delegates to Philadelphia "for the sole and express purpose of revising the Articles of Confederation." That Philadelphia meeting became the **Constitutional Convention.**

Alexander Hamilton was among the key delegates to the Constitutional Convention that convened on May 25, 1787. *What kind of government did he want America to have?*

CRITICAL THINKING

▶ *Given that all Americans would have benefited from an army capable of keeping the peace and defending the country, why would the states have been so reluctant to fund the national government?*

2-4 DRAFTING AND RATIFYING THE CONSTITUTION

LO List the major compromises made by the delegates at the Constitutional Convention, and discuss the Federalist and Anti-Federalist positions on ratifying the Constitution.

Constitutional Convention The convention of delegates from the states that was held in Philadelphia in 1787 for the purpose of amending the Articles of Confederation. In fact, the delegates wrote a new constitution (the U.S. Constitution) that established a federal form of government.

Although the convention was supposed to start on May 14, 1787, few of the delegates had actually arrived in Philadelphia on that date. The convention formally opened in the East Room of the Pennsylvania State House on May 25, after fifty-five of the seventy-four delegates had arrived.[12] Only Rhode Island, where feelings were strong against creating a more powerful central government, did not send any delegates.

2-4a Who Were the Delegates?

Among the delegates to the Constitutional Convention were some of the nation's best-known leaders. George Washington was present, as were Alexander Hamilton, James Madison, George Mason, Robert Morris, and Benjamin Franklin (who, at eighty-one years old, had to be carried to the convention on a portable chair).

Some notable leaders were absent, including Thomas Jefferson and John Adams, who were serving as ambassadors in Europe, and Patrick Henry, who did not attend because he "smelt a rat." (Henry was one of Virginia's most strongly republican leaders.)

For the most part, the delegates were from the best-educated and wealthiest classes. Thirty-three delegates were lawyers, nearly half of the delegates were college graduates, three were physicians, and seven were former chief executives of their respective states. Six owned large plantations, at least nineteen owned slaves, eight were important business owners, and twenty-one had fought in the Revolutionary War.

In other words, the delegates to the convention constituted an elite assembly. No ordinary farmers or merchants were present. Indeed, in his classic work on the Constitution, Charles Beard maintained that the Constitution was produced primarily by wealthy bondholders who had made loans to the government under the Articles and wanted a strong central government that could prevent state governments from repudiating debts.[13] Later historians, however, rejected Beard's thesis, concluding that bondholders played no special role in writing the Constitution.

2-4b The Virginia Plan

James Madison had spent months reviewing European political theory before he went to the Philadelphia convention. His Virginia delegation arrived before anybody else, and he immediately put its members to work. On the first day of the convention, Governor Edmund Randolph of Virginia was able to present fifteen resolutions outlining what was to become known as the *Virginia Plan*. This was a masterful political stroke on the part of the Virginia delegation. Its proposals immediately set the agenda for the remainder of the convention.

The fifteen resolutions contained in the Virginia Plan proposed an entirely new national government under a constitution. The plan, which favored large states such as Virginia, called for the following:

▶ **A bicameral (two-chamber) legislature. The lower chamber was to be chosen by the people. The smaller, upper chamber was to be chosen by the elected members of the lower chamber. The number of representatives would be in proportion to each state's population (the larger states would have more representatives). The legislature could void any state laws.**

▶ **A national executive branch, elected by the legislature.**

▶ **A national court system, created by the legislature.**

The smaller states immediately complained because they would have fewer representatives in the legislature. After two weeks of debate, they offered their own plan— the *New Jersey Plan*.

2-4c The New Jersey Plan

William Paterson of New Jersey presented an alternative plan favorable to the smaller states. He argued that because each state had an equal vote under the Articles of Confederation, the convention had no power to change this arrangement. The New Jersey Plan proposed the following:

▶ **Congress would be able to regulate trade and impose taxes.**

▶ **Each state would have only one vote.**

> ## "The Constitution only gives people the right to pursue happiness. You have to catch it yourself."
>
> ~ ANONYMOUS—ATTRIBUTED TO BENJAMIN FRANKLIN, AMERICAN STATESMAN, 1706–1790

▶ **Acts of Congress would be the supreme law of the land.**

▶ **An executive office of more than one person would be elected by Congress.**

▶ **The executive office would appoint a national supreme court.**

2-4d The Compromises

Most delegates were unwilling to consider the New Jersey Plan. When the Virginia Plan was brought up again, however, delegates from the smaller states threatened to leave, and the convention was in danger of dissolving. On July 16, Roger Sherman of Connecticut broke the deadlock by proposing a compromise plan. Compromises on other disputed issues followed.

The Great Compromise   Roger Sherman's plan, which has become known as the **Great Compromise** (or the Connecticut Compromise), called for a legislature with two chambers:

▶ **A lower chamber (the House of Representatives), in which the number of representatives from each state would be determined by the number of people in that state.**

▶ **An upper chamber (the Senate), which would have two members from each state. The members would be elected by the state legislatures.**

The Great Compromise gave something to both sides: the large states would have more representatives in the House of Representatives than the small states, yet each state would be granted equality in the Senate— because each state, regardless of size, would have

bicameral legislature
A legislature made up of two chambers, or parts.

Great Compromise
A plan for a bicameral legislature in which one chamber would be based on population and the other chamber would represent each state equally. Also known as the Connecticut Compromise.

Delegates to the Constitutional Convention sign the final document under the view of George Washington, the convention chair. *What advantages may have followed from naming Washington to preside over the convention?*

two senators. The Great Compromise thus resolved the small-state/large-state controversy.

The Three-Fifths Compromise   A second compromise had to do with how many representatives each state would have in the House of Representatives. Although slavery was legal in parts of the North, most slaves and slave owners lived in the South. Indeed, in the southern states, slaves constituted about 40 percent of the population. Counting the slaves as part of the population would thus greatly increase the number of southern representatives in the House. The delegates from the southern states wanted the slaves to be counted as persons, but the delegates from the northern states disagreed.

Eventually, the **three-fifths compromise** settled this deadlock: each slave would count as three-fifths of a person in determining representation in Congress.

three-fifths compromise A compromise reached during the Constitutional Convention by which three-fifths of all slaves were to be counted for purposes of representation in the House of Representatives.

interstate commerce Trade that involves more than one state.

(The three-fifths compromise was eventually overturned in 1868 by the Fourteenth Amendment.)

Slave Importation   The three-fifths compromise did not satisfy everyone at the Constitutional Convention. Many delegates wanted slavery to be banned completely in the United States. The delegates compromised on this question by agreeing that Congress could prohibit the importation of slaves into the country beginning in 1808. The issue of slavery itself, however, was never really addressed by the delegates to the Constitutional Convention. As a result, the South won twenty years of unrestricted slave trade and a requirement that escaped slaves who had fled to the northern states be returned to their owners. Domestic slave trading was untouched.

Banning Export Taxes   The South's economic health depended in large part on its exports of agricultural products. The South feared that the northern majority in Congress might pass taxes on these exports. This fear led to yet another compromise: the South agreed to let Congress have the power to regulate **interstate commerce** as well as commerce with other nations. In exchange, the Constitution guaranteed that no export taxes would be imposed on products exported by the states. Today, the United States is one of the few countries that does not tax its exports.

2-4e Defining the Executive and the Judiciary

The Great Compromise was reached by mid-July. Still to be determined was the makeup of the executive branch and the judiciary.

The Executive One of the weaknesses of the Confederation had been the lack of an independent executive authority. The Constitution remedied this problem by creating an independent executive—the president—and by making the president the commander in chief of the army and navy and of the state militias when called into national service. The president was also given extensive appointment powers, although Senate approval was required for major appointments.

To insulate the presidency from the masses, the position was to be filled by members of an *electoral college*, not directly by the people, as explained in the chapter-opening *America at Odds* feature. Each state was to have a number of electors (members of the electoral college) equal in number to the total number of senators and representatives from that state.[14] In the long run, the electoral college failed to prevent ordinary voters from choosing the president. As of 1796, electors were typically pledged to specific presidential candidates. Voting for an elector was therefore equivalent to voting for a presidential candidate.

For a number of decades, electors in several states were selected by the state legislature, not the people. By 1796, however, the creation of political parties meant that voters could effectively choose the presidential candidate of a particular party by voting for that party's state legislative candidates. The creation of the electoral college did accomplish one goal—it kept the national Congress from choosing the president.

The Judiciary and the Impeachment Process Another problem under the Confederation was the lack of a judiciary that was independent of the state courts. The Constitution established the United States Supreme Court and authorized Congress to establish other "inferior" federal courts.

To protect against possible wrongdoing, the Constitution also provided a way to remove federal officials from office—through the impeachment process. The Constitution provides that a federal official who commits "Treason, Bribery, or other high Crimes and Misdemeanors" may be *impeached* (accused of, or charged with, wrongdoing) by the House of Representatives and tried by the Senate. If found guilty of the charges by a two-thirds vote in the Senate, the official can be removed from office and prevented from ever assuming another federal government post.

2-4f The Final Draft Is Approved

A five-man Committee of Detail handled the executive and judicial issues, plus other remaining work. In August, it presented a rough draft to the convention. In September, a committee was named to "revise the stile [style] of, and arrange the Articles which had been agreed to" by the convention. The Committee of Style was headed by Gouverneur Morris of Pennsylvania.[15] On September 17, 1787, the final draft of the Constitution was approved by thirty-nine of the remaining forty-two delegates (some delegates had left early).

As we look back on the drafting of the Constitution, an obvious question emerges: Why didn't the founders ban slavery outright? Certainly, many of the delegates thought that slavery was morally wrong and that the Constitution should ban it entirely. Many Americans have since regarded the framers' failure to deal with the slavery issue as a betrayal of the Declaration of Independence, which proclaimed that "all Men are created equal."

A common argument supporting the framers' action (or lack of it) with respect to slavery is that they had no alternative but to ignore the issue. If they had taken a stand on slavery, the Constitution certainly would not have been ratified. Indeed, if the antislavery delegates had insisted on banning slavery, the delegates from the southern states might have walked out of the convention—and there would have been no Constitution to ratify. For another look at this issue, however, see this chapter's *Perception vs. Reality* feature.

2-4g The Debate over Ratification

The ratification of the Constitution set off a national debate of unprecedented proportions. The battle was fought chiefly by two opposing groups—the **Federalists** (those who favored a strong central government and the new Constitution) and the **Anti-Federalists** (those who opposed a strong central government and the new Constitution).

In the debate over ratification, the Federalists had several advantages. They assumed a positive name, leaving their opposition with a negative label.

> **Federalists** A political group, led by Alexander Hamilton and John Adams, that supported the adoption of the Constitution and the creation of a federal form of government.
>
> **Anti-Federalists** A political group that opposed the adoption of the Constitution.

In the Declaration of Independence, Thomas Jefferson, a Virginia slave owner, pronounced that "all Men are created equal." Jefferson considered slavery a "hideous blot" on America. George Washington, also a slave owner, regarded the institution of slavery as "repugnant." Patrick Henry, another southerner, also publicly deplored slavery. Given such views among the leading figures of the era, why didn't the founders stay true to the Declaration of Independence and free the slaves?

The Perception

Most Americans assume that southern economic interests and racism alone led the founders to abandon the principles of equality expressed in the Declaration of Independence. African slaves were the backbone of American agriculture, particularly for tobacco, the most profitable export. Without their slaves, southern plantation owners would not have been able to earn such high profits. Presumably, southerners would not have ratified the Constitution unless it protected the institution of slavery.

The Reality

The third chief justice of the United States Supreme Court, Oliver Ellsworth, declared that "as population increases, poor laborers will be so plenty as to render slaves useless. Slavery in time will not be a speck in our country."[16] He was wrong, of course. But according to historian Gordon S. Wood, Ellsworth's sentiments mirrored those of most prominent leaders in the United States in the years leading up to the creation of our Constitution. Indeed, great thinkers of the time firmly believed that the liberal principles of the Revolution would destroy the institution of slavery.

At the time of the Constitutional Convention, slavery was disappearing in the northern states (it would be eliminated there by 1804). Many founders thought the same thing would happen in the southern states. After all, there were more antislavery societies in the South than in the North. The founders also thought that the ending of the international slave trade in 1808 would eventually end slavery in the United States. Consequently, the issue of slavery was taken off the table when the Constitution was created simply because the founders had a mistaken belief about the longevity of the institution. They could not have predicted that, within a relatively short time, rapid growth of cotton production in the southern states would give slavery a new lease on life.[17]

Blog On

"Slavery and the Constitution" is just one of many subjects that you can read about in the Legal History Blog, which you can find at legalhistoryblog.blogspot.com. If you scroll down far enough, you'll find a list of topics on the right-hand side of the screen. Click on "slavery" to see postings on this topic.

(Instead, the Anti-Federalists could well have called themselves republicans and their opponents nationalists.) The Federalists also had attended the Constitutional Convention and thus were familiar with the arguments both in favor of and against various constitutional provisions. The Anti-Federalists, in contrast, had no actual knowledge of those discussions because almost none of them had attended the convention.

The Federalists also had time, funding, and prestige on their side. Their impressive list of political thinkers and writers included Alexander Hamilton, John Jay, and James Madison. The Federalists could communicate with one another more readily because many of them were bankers, lawyers, and merchants who lived in urban areas, where communication was easier. Accordingly, the Federalists organized a quick and effective ratification campaign to elect themselves as delegates to each state's ratifying convention.

The Federalists Argue for Ratification Alexander Hamilton, a leading Federalist, enlisted John Jay and James Madison to help him write newspaper columns in support of the new Constitution. In a period of less than a year, these three men wrote a series of eighty-five essays in defense of the Constitution. These essays, which were printed in newspapers throughout the states, are known collectively as the *Federalist Papers*.

Generally, the papers attempted to allay the fears expressed by the Constitution's critics. One fear was that the rights of those in the minority would not be protected. Many critics also feared that a republican form of government would not work in a nation the size of the United States. Various groups, or **factions,** would struggle for power, and chaos would result.

Madison responded to the latter argument in *Federalist Paper* No. 10 (see Appendix C), which is considered a classic in political theory. Among other things, Madison argued that the nation's size was actually an advantage in controlling factions: in a large nation, there would be so many diverse interests and factions that no one faction would be able to gain control of the government.[18]

The Anti-Federalists' Response Perhaps the greatest advantage of the Anti-Federalists was that they stood for the status quo. Usually, it is more difficult to institute changes than it is to keep what is already known and understood. Among the Anti-Federalists were such patriots as Patrick Henry and Samuel Adams. Patrick Henry said of the proposed Constitution, "I look upon that paper as the most fatal plan that could possibly be conceived to enslave a free people."

In response to the *Federalist Papers*, the Anti-Federalists published their own essays. They also wrote brilliantly, attacking nearly every clause of the new document. Many Anti-Federalists contended that the Constitution had been written by aristocrats and would lead the nation to aristocratic **tyranny** (the exercise of absolute, unlimited power). Other Anti-Federalists feared that the Constitution would lead to an overly powerful central government that would limit personal freedom.[19]

The Anti-Federalists argued vigorously that the Constitution needed a bill of rights. They warned that without a bill of rights, a strong national government might take away the political rights won during the American Revolution.

The Federalists generally did not think that a bill of rights was necessary. Some worried that listing specific rights might imply that other rights could be denied. (The Ninth Amendment addressed that issue.) Nevertheless, to gain the necessary political support, the Federalists finally promised to add a bill of rights to the Constitution as the first order of business under the new government. This promise turned the tide in favor of the Constitution.

2-4h Ratification

The contest for ratification was close in several states, but the Federalists finally won in all of the state conventions. In 1787, Delaware, Pennsylvania, and New Jersey voted to ratify the Constitution, followed by Georgia and Connecticut early in the following year. Even though the Anti-Federalists were perhaps the majority in Massachusetts, a successful political campaign by the Federalists led to ratification by that state on February 6, 1788.

Following Maryland and South Carolina, New Hampshire became the ninth state to ratify the Constitution on June 21, 1788, thus formally putting the Constitution into effect. New York and Virginia had not yet ratified, however, and without them the Constitution would have no true power. That worry was dispelled in the summer of 1788, when both Virginia and New York ratified the new Constitution. North Carolina waited until November 21 of the following year to ratify the Constitution, and Rhode Island did not ratify until May 29, 1790.

2-4i Did a Majority of Americans Support the Constitution?

Some historians have called the Constitution an aristocratic document that lacked majority support. We cannot conclusively say what most Americans thought of the Constitution, however, because the great majority of adults did not have the right to vote.

Slaves, women, and American Indians, of course, could not vote. Furthermore, free men could not vote unless they held sufficient property. A typical voting requirement, used by several states, was possession of land or other property worth forty British pounds. At the time, this sum would buy about a hundred acres of average U.S. farmland. Many of the men who could not vote, it has been argued, were strong republicans.

Still, support for the Constitution seems to have been widespread in all social classes. Both rich and poor Americans were troubled by the weakness of the national government under the Articles of Confederation.

CRITICAL THINKING

▶ *Suppose that Rhode Island had refused to ratify the Constitution and join the Union. Would American history have been seriously altered by such an event?*

 2-5 ## THE CONSTITUTION'S MAJOR PRINCIPLES OF GOVERNMENT

LO Summarize the Constitution's major principles of government, and describe how the Constitution can be amended.

The framers of the Constitution were fearful that the national government might become like the powerful British monarchy, against which they had so recently rebelled. At the same time,

faction A group of individuals forming a cohesive minority.

tyranny The arbitrary or unrestrained exercise of power by an oppressive individual or government.

they wanted a central government strong enough to prevent the kinds of crises that had occurred under the weak central authority of the Articles of Confederation. The principles of government expressed in the Constitution reflect both of these concerns.

2–5a Limited Government, Popular Sovereignty, and the Rule of Law

The Constitution incorporated the principle of limited government, which means that government can do only what the people allow it to do through the exercise of a duly developed system of laws. This principle can be found in many parts of the Constitution. For example, while Articles I, II, and III indicate exactly what the national government *can* do, the first nine amendments to the Constitution list the ways in which the government *cannot* limit certain individual freedoms.

Popular Sovereignty   Implicitly, the principle of limited government rests on the concept of popular sovereignty. Remember the phrases that frame the Preamble to the Constitution: "We the People of the United States . . . do ordain and establish this Constitution for the United States of America." In other words, it is the people who form the government and decide on the powers that the government can exercise. If the government exercises powers beyond those granted to it by the Constitution, it is acting illegally.

The Rule of Law   The idea that no one, including government officers, is above the law is often called the **rule of law.** Ultimately, the viability of a democracy rests on the willingness of the people and their leaders to adhere to the rule of law. A nation's written constitution may guarantee numerous rights and liberties for its citizens. Yet, unless the government of that nation enforces those rights and liberties, the law does not rule the nation. Rather, government leaders decide what the rules will be.

rule of law A basic principle of government that requires those who govern to act in accordance with established law.

federal system A form of government that provides for a division of powers between a central government and several regional governments.

commerce clause The clause in Article I, Section 8, of the Constitution that gives Congress the power to regulate interstate commerce (commerce involving more than one state).

2–5b The Principle of Federalism

The Constitution also incorporated the principle of *federalism*, or a **federal system** of government, in which the central (national) government shares sovereign powers with the various state governments. Federalism was the solution to the debate over whether the national government or the states should have ultimate sovereignty.

National Powers   The Constitution gave the national government significant powers—powers that it had not had under the Articles of Confederation. For example, the Constitution expressly states that the president is the nation's chief executive as well as the commander in chief of the armed forces. The Constitution also declares that the Constitution and the laws created by the national government are supreme—that is, they take precedence over conflicting state laws. Other powers given to the national government included the power to coin money, to levy and collect taxes, and to regulate interstate commerce, a power granted by the **commerce clause.** Finally, the national government was authorized to undertake all laws that are "necessary and proper" for carrying out its expressly delegated powers.

James Madison (1751–1836). Madison's contributions at the Constitutional Convention in 1787 earned him the title "Master Builder of the Constitution." *Why might he have been the one chosen to draft the Bill of Rights?*

State Powers Because the states feared too much centralized control, the Constitution also allowed for many states' rights. These rights include the power to regulate commerce within state borders and generally the authority to exercise any powers that are not delegated by the Constitution to the central government.

2-5c Separation of Powers

As James Madison once said, after you have given the government the ability to control its citizens, you have to "oblige it to control itself." To force the government to "control itself" and to prevent the rise of tyranny, Madison devised a scheme, the Madisonian Model, in which the powers of the national government were separated into different branches: legislative, executive, and judicial.[20] The legislative branch (Congress) passes laws, the executive branch (the president) administers and enforces the laws, and the judicial branch (the courts) interprets the laws. By separating the powers of government, the framers ensured that no one branch would have enough power to dominate the others. This principle of **separation of powers** is laid out in Articles I, II, and III of the Constitution.

2-5d Checks and Balances

A system of **checks and balances** was also devised to ensure that no one group or branch of government can exercise exclusive control. Even though each branch of government is independent of the others, it can also check the actions of the others.

Look at Figure 2–5 and you can see how this is done. As the figure shows, the president checks Congress by

Madisonian Model The model of government devised by James Madison, in which the powers of the government are separated into three branches: legislative, executive, and judicial.

separation of powers The principle of dividing governmental powers among the legislative, executive, and judicial branches of government.

checks and balances A major principle of American government in which each of the three branches is given the means to check (to restrain or balance) the actions of the others.

FIGURE 2–5 CHECKS AND BALANCES AMONG THE BRANCHES OF GOVERNMENT

What negative consequences could result from the American system of limited government?

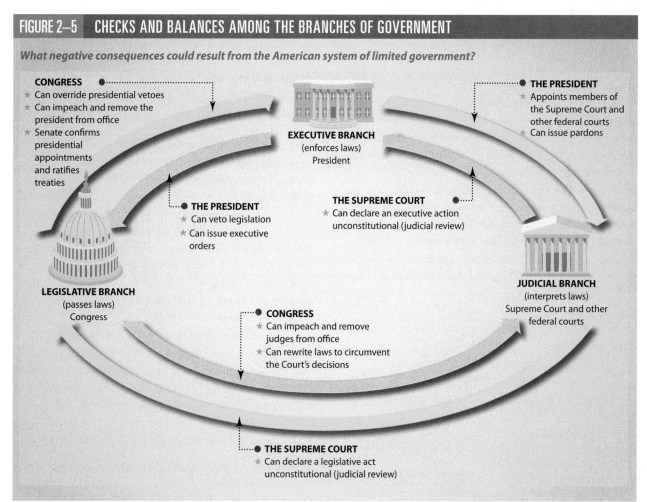

CONGRESS
★ Can override presidential vetoes
★ Can impeach and remove the president from office
★ Senate confirms presidential appointments and ratifies treaties

EXECUTIVE BRANCH
(enforces laws)
President

THE PRESIDENT
★ Appoints members of the Supreme Court and other federal courts
★ Can issue pardons

THE PRESIDENT
★ Can veto legislation
★ Can issue executive orders

THE SUPREME COURT
★ Can declare an executive action unconstitutional (judicial review)

LEGISLATIVE BRANCH
(passes laws)
Congress

JUDICIAL BRANCH
(interprets laws)
Supreme Court and other federal courts

CONGRESS
★ Can impeach and remove judges from office
★ Can rewrite laws to circumvent the Court's decisions

THE SUPREME COURT
★ Can declare a legislative act unconstitutional (judicial review)

Theresa May, a member of the Conservative Party, is prime minister of the United Kingdom (Britain). She took office in 2016 after Britain voted in a referendum to leave the European Union. That vote led to the resignation of the previous prime minister. *Why are American politicians reluctant to resign from office?*

holding a **veto power,** which is the ability to return bills to Congress for reconsideration. Congress, in turn, controls taxes and spending, and the Senate must approve presidential appointments. The judicial branch can check the other branches of government through *judicial review*—the power to rule congressional or presidential actions unconstitutional.[21] In turn, the president and the Senate exercise some control over the judiciary through the president's power to appoint federal judges and the Senate's role in confirming presidential appointments.

Among the other checks and balances built into the American system are staggered terms of office. Members of the House of Representatives serve for two years, members of the Senate for six, and the president for four. Federal court judges are appointed for life but may be impeached and removed from office by Congress for misconduct. Staggered terms and changing government personnel were supposed to make it difficult for individuals within the government to form controlling factions.

2-5e Limited versus Effective Government

Such American constitutional principles as the separation of powers and a system of checks and

> **veto power** A constitutional power that enables the chief executive (president or governor) to reject legislation and return it to the legislature with reasons for the rejection. This either prevents or delays the bill from becoming law.

balances are not universal among representative democracies. Compared with the United States, many countries place less emphasis on limited government and a higher value on "effective government." (The alternative term "efficient government" is also used.) The *parliamentary system* is a constitutional form that reflects such values. We describe it in this chapter's *The Rest of the World* feature.

2-5f The Bill of Rights

To secure the ratification of the Constitution in several important states, the Federalists had to promise a bill of rights. At the state ratifying conventions, delegates set forth specific rights that should be protected. James Madison considered these recommendations as he labored to draft the Bill of Rights.

After sorting through more than two hundred state recommendations, Madison came up with sixteen amendments. Congress tightened the language somewhat and eliminated four of the amendments. Of the remaining twelve, two—one dealing with the apportionment of representatives and the other with the compensation of the members of Congress—were not ratified by the states during the ratification process.[22] By 1791, all of the states had ratified the ten amendments that now constitute our Bill of Rights.

2-5g Amending the Constitution

Since the Constitution was written, more than eleven thousand amendments have been introduced in Congress. Nonetheless, in the years since the ratification of the Bill of Rights, only seventeen proposed amendments have actually survived the amendment process and become a part of our Constitution. Some contend that members of Congress use the amendment process simply as a political ploy. By introducing an amendment, a member of Congress often can show her or his position on an issue, knowing that the odds against the amendment's being adopted are high.

One of the reasons there are so few amendments is that the framers, in Article V, made the formal amendment process difficult (although it was easier than it had been under the Articles of Confederation). There are two ways to propose an amendment and two ways to ratify one. As a result, there are four possible ways for an amendment to be added to the Constitution.

Methods of Proposing an Amendment The two methods of proposing an amendment are as follows:

1. Following the introduction of an amendment, a two-thirds vote in the Senate and in the House

THE REST OF THE WORLD

The Parliamentary Alternative

An alternative to our form of government is the parliamentary system. Britain—the United Kingdom—has a typical *parliamentary system*. In contrast to the American system, the British one is based on the *fusion* of powers rather than the *separation* of powers.

First, a Few Basics

Members of Parliament (MPs) are elected just as we elect members of Congress. Here the similarity ends. British voters do not directly choose a chief executive, as we do when we vote for president. Rather, the chief executive is chosen by the lower house of Parliament—the House of Commons, analogous to our House of Representatives. (There is an upper house, the House of Lords, but it has little power.)

Each political party selects a leader well before the general elections. If one party wins a majority of the seats in the House of Commons, it can name its leader as the prime minister—the chief executive of the nation.

The Fusion of Powers

MPs who join the *government* (what we would call the administration) keep their seats in Parliament. The prime minister is both the chief executive of the nation and the leader of his or her party in the legislature. The legislature and the executive are fused, not separated. In contrast, the U.S. Constitution explicitly requires members of Congress who join the president's administration to resign from Congress.

Americans often view the parliamentary system as undemocratic because voters cannot choose the chief executive. Citizens of parliamentary countries do not see the system in quite that way, however. Voters know who the party leaders are in advance of the elections. When they vote, they are choosing a party and its leader. The identity of their own local MP usually has little impact on how they cast their ballots.

What the parliamentary system really does is prevent voters from choosing a chief executive from one party and a legislative representative from another. In America, during the six years after the 2010 elections, for example, Democratic president Barack Obama faced a House of Representatives controlled by the Republicans. (In 2014, Republicans gained control of the Senate as well.) That kind of divided government is impossible under the parliamentary system.

Coalition Governments

The parliamentary system does encourage the formation of multiple major parties, thus providing voters with more options than is common in America. But what if no party wins a majority in the lower house of Parliament? Two options are possible. The largest party can form a *minority government* with the acquiescence of other parties. Alternatively, two, three, or more parties can agree to form a *coalition government*. Many countries that use the parliamentary system are normally governed by coalitions.

Critical Analysis

Why is it so hard to form effective third parties in the United States?

---

of Representatives is required. All of the twenty-seven existing amendments have been proposed in this way.

2. If two-thirds of the state legislatures request that Congress call a national amendment convention, then Congress must call one. The convention may propose amendments to the states for ratification. No such convention has ever been convened.

The notion of a national amendment convention is exciting to many people. Many leaders, however, are uneasy about the prospect of convening a body that conceivably could do what the Constitutional Convention did—create a new form of government.

Methods of Ratifying an Amendment There are two methods of ratifying a proposed amendment:

1. Three-fourths of the state legislatures can vote in favor of the proposed amendment. This method is considered the "traditional" ratification method and has been used twenty-six times.

2. The states can call special conventions to ratify the proposed amendment. If three-fourths of the states approve, the amendment is ratified. This

method has been used only once—to ratify the Twenty-first Amendment.[23]

You can see the four methods for proposing and ratifying amendments in Figure 2–6. As you can imagine, to meet the requirements for proposal and ratification, any amendment must have wide popular support throughout the country.

▶ **Is amending the Constitution too difficult? Why or why not?**

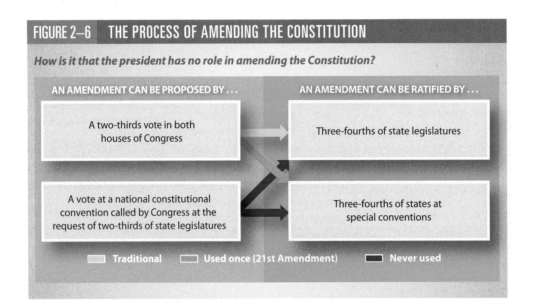

FIGURE 2–6   THE PROCESS OF AMENDING THE CONSTITUTION

How is it that the president has no role in amending the Constitution?

AN AMENDMENT CAN BE PROPOSED BY ...	AN AMENDMENT CAN BE RATIFIED BY ...
A two-thirds vote in both houses of Congress	Three-fourths of state legislatures
A vote at a national constitutional convention called by Congress at the request of two-thirds of state legislatures	Three-fourths of states at special conventions

▢ **Traditional**   ▢ **Used once (21st Amendment)**   ▢ **Never used**

AMERICA AT ODDS | The Constitution

Americans engaged in intense disputes about the ratification of the Constitution, as you have learned in this chapter. The most important of these disputes was over the relative power of the states and the national government. This dispute is central to the topic of federalism. Proposed constitutional amendments have also been the source of many controversies throughout U.S. history. These controversies include the following:

- *The Equal Rights Amendment of 1972 stated, "Equality of rights under the law shall not be denied or abridged by the United States or by any state on account of sex." The amendment failed to win approval from enough states. Should it be revived—or are equal rights for women unacceptable because women could not then be exempted from a military draft?*

- *Progressive groups have called for a constitutional amendment to overturn the Supreme Court's decision in* Citizens United v. Federal Election Commission. *In that case, the Court removed many existing limits on contributions to political campaigns. Should we reimpose such limits to curb corruption—or would that violate freedom of speech?*

- *Conservatives have campaigned for a constitutional amendment to require the federal government to balance its budget. Would such a measure be desirable—or would it introduce a disastrous lack of flexibility into national finances?*

- *What about an amendment to ban the destruction of the American flag as an act of protest? Is such a ban important to the dignity of our fallen soldiers—or would it be an unacceptable limit on free speech?*

READY TO STUDY? IN THE BOOK, YOU CAN:

☐ Review what you've read with the following chapter quiz.

☐ Check your answers in Appendix D at the back of the book.

☐ Rip out the Chapter Review Card, which includes key terms and chapter summaries.

ONLINE AT WWW.CENGAGEBRAIN.COM, YOU CAN:

☐ Watch videos to get a quick overview.

☐ Expedite your studying with Major Player readings and Focus Activities.

☐ Check your understanding with Chapter Quizzes.

FILL-IN

Learning Outcome 2–1

1. Even before the Pilgrims went ashore, they drew up the _____, in which they set up a government and promised to obey its laws.

Learning Outcome 2–2

2. After the Seven Years' War, the British government decided to obtain revenues to pay its war debts and to finance the defense of its North American empire by _____.

3. The British Parliament imposed several taxes on the colonists, including the _____.

Learning Outcome 2–3

4. The Articles of Confederation established the _____ as the central governing body.

5. _____, a rebellion of angry farmers in western Massachusetts in 1786, along with similar uprisings throughout most of the New England states, emphasized the need for a true national government.

Learning Outcome 2–4

6. At the Constitutional Convention in 1787, the delegates forged the Great Compromise, which established a bicameral legislature composed of the _____.

7. The Constitution provides that a federal official who commits "_____" may be impeached by the House of Representatives and tried by the Senate.

8. During the debate over ratification, the Anti-Federalists argued that the Constitution needed a _____ because a strong national government might take away the political rights won during the American Revolution.

Learning Outcome 2–5

9. The principle of dividing governmental powers among the legislative, the executive, and the judicial branches of government is known as the _____.

10. Among the checks and balances built into the American system of government is the court's power of _____.

MULTIPLE CHOICE

Learning Outcome 2–1

11. The majority of American colonists came from
    a. Germany and Spain.
    b. France and Ireland.
    c. England and Scotland.

Learning Outcome 2–2

12. Before the mid-1700s, the majority of American colonists were
    a. secretly planning to declare their independence from Britain.
    b. loyal to the British monarch and viewed Britain as their homeland.
    c. politically indifferent.

Learning Outcome 2–3

13. Under the Articles of Confederation, the new nation
    a. could not declare war.
    b. could enter into treaties and alliances.
    c. could regulate interstate commerce.

Learning Outcome 2–4

14. The three-fifths compromise reached at the Constitutional Convention had to do with
    a. how slaves would be counted in determining representation in Congress.
    b. the imposition of export taxes.
    c. the regulation of commerce.

Learning Outcome 2–5

15. All of the existing amendments to the Constitution have been proposed
    a. by a two-thirds vote in the Senate and in the House of Representatives.
    b. by a vote in three-fourths of the state legislatures.
    c. at national constitutional conventions.

3 | FEDERALISM

GEOFF ROBINS/AFP/Getty Images

LEARNING OUTCOMES

After reading this chapter, you should be able to:

3-1 Explain what federalism means, how federalism differs from other systems of government, and why it exists in the United States.

3-2 Indicate how the Constitution divides governing powers in our federal system.

3-3 Summarize the evolution of federal-state relationships in the United States over time.

3-4 Describe developments in federalism in recent years.

3-5 Explain what is meant by the term *fiscal federalism*.

After finishing this chapter, go to **PAGE 70** for **STUDY TOOLS**

AMERICA AT ODDS

Should Recreational Marijuana Be Legal?

Teri Virbickis/Shutterstock.com

The history of marijuana in America is long and varied. Before the 1920s, marijuana was either not regulated or lightly regulated throughout the United States. By the mid-1930s, however, pot was illegal almost everywhere. Current national law is based on the Controlled Substances Act of 1970, which lists marijuana as a "Schedule I" substance with no medical use and a high potential for abuse.

Times have changed, and so have state laws. According to a Gallup poll, a majority of Americans now favor legalizing marijuana. As of 2017, marijuana remained fully illegal in only five states. One state—Nebraska—has simply decriminalized it. That means Nebraska does not treat simple possession as a criminal offense. Twelve states have legalized varieties of medical marijuana that won't easily get someone stoned. Another twelve states have legalized "psychoactive" medical marijuana. Yet another twelve have both medical marijuana and decriminalization laws. Finally, eight states and the District of Colombia have legalized recreational marijuana. The states are Alaska, California, Colorado, Maine, Massachusetts, Nevada, Oregon, and Washington. With our federal system, though, the national government can still arrest individuals for possession and use of marijuana everywhere.

Legalize Marijuana at Our Peril

Opponents of marijuana legalization say that if you like the huge expense of alcohol and tobacco abuse, then you will love the costs of legal marijuana. Use of alcohol and tobacco is common—65 percent of Americans use alcohol, and 30 percent use tobacco. If we were to add legalized marijuana to that list, how many people would abuse the drug? More than do so now, surely.

Just as long-term use of alcohol and tobacco affects the body and the brain, so, too, does long-term marijuana use. The results are memory loss, reduced ability to concentrate, and poor coordination. Long-term abuse from an early age yields diminished attention spans and reduced ability for abstract reasoning. Adolescents face the greatest risk if we legalize marijuana.

A final point: Legalization advocates claim that legal pot will cut crime rates. Yet most drug-related violence and gang activity are not due to marijuana. Violence most commonly follows the production and sale of cocaine, heroin, and methamphetamines. Do we want to legalize these?

The Benefits Outweigh the Costs

Those in favor of marijuana legalization point out the obvious: In a typical year, 40 to 50 million Americans use marijuana recreationally at least once. If we were to repeal current federal legislation and let the states do as they wish, we would relieve our overworked police, courts, and prisons. Arresting hundreds of thousands of people each year for marijuana use is simply a waste of resources. Those who are arrested, even if they do not serve time in prison, will have a police record for life, reducing their chances for employment.

Tobacco smokers die an average of seven years before nonsmokers. Thousands of people die from alcohol poisoning each year, but it is essentially impossible to die of a pot overdose. Marijuana users are not as aggressive as those who are intoxicated with alcohol. In fact, a third of those arrested for crimes were drunk when they broke the law. What sense does it make to ban marijuana when these legal drugs are so much more dangerous?

Where do you stand?

1. Instead of legalizing marijuana, would it make sense to ban alcoholic beverages? Why or why not?
2. What benefits might states gain if they legalize the recreational use of marijuana?

Explore this issue online:

- John Hawkins argues against marijuana legalization on the conservative Townhall blog. Find the article by searching for "hawkins marijuana."

- Renee Jacques makes the case for legalization on the Huffington Post site. Search for "marijuana should be legal everywhere."

INTRODUCTION

Clearly, those who work for the national government would like the states to cooperate fully in the implementation of national policies. At the same time, those who work in state government don't like to be told what to do by the national government, especially when the implementation of a national policy is costly for the states. (Sometimes, this attitude can lead to conflicts, such as the one described in the chapter-opening *America at Odds* feature.) Finally, those who work in local governments would like to run their affairs with the least amount of interference from both their state governments and the national government.

Such conflicts arise because our government is based on the principle of **federalism,** which means that government powers are shared by the national government and the states. When the founders of this nation opted for federalism, they created a practical and flexible form of government capable of enduring for centuries. At the same time, however, they planted the seeds for future conflict between the states and the national government over how government powers should be shared. As you will read in this chapter—and throughout this book—many of today's most pressing issues have to do with which level of government should exercise certain powers.

3–1 FEDERALISM AND ITS ALTERNATIVES

> **LO** Explain what federalism means, how federalism differs from other systems of government, and why it exists in the United States.

There are various ways of ordering relations between central governments and local units. Federalism is one of these ways. Learning about federalism and how it differs from other forms of government is important to understanding the American political system.

3–1a What Is Federalism?

federalism A system of shared sovereignty between two levels of government—one national and one subnational—occupying the same geographic region.

Nowhere in the Constitution does the word *federalism* appear. This is understandable, given that the modern concept of federalism was an invention of the founders.

Ever since the Federalists and the Anti-Federalists argued more than two hundred years ago about what form of government we should have, hundreds of definitions of federalism have been offered. Basically, government powers in a *federal system* are divided between a central government and regional, or subnational, governments.

Defining Federalism   Although the definition given here seems straightforward, its application certainly is not. After all, almost all nations—even the most repressive totalitarian regimes—have some kind of subnational governmental units. Thus, the existence of national and subnational governmental units by itself does not make a system federal. *For a system to be truly federal, the powers of both the national units and the subnational units must be specified and limited.*

Under true federalism, individuals are governed by two separate governmental authorities (national and state authorities) whose expressly designated powers cannot be altered without changing the fundamental nature of the system—for example, by amending a written constitution. Table 3–1 lists some of the countries that have a federal system of government.[1]

TABLE 3–1	COUNTRIES THAT HAVE A FEDERAL SYSTEM TODAY

What influence might the example of the United States have had on the adoption of federal systems in other countries?

Country	Population (in Millions)
Argentina	43.9
Australia	24.4
Austria	8.8
Brazil	207.1
Canada	36.4
Ethiopia	101.9
Germany	82.8
India	1,311.5
Malaysia	31.9
Mexico	130.2
Nigeria	191.8
Pakistan	196.3
Switzerland	8.4
United States	324.5

Source: Official estimates by governments of the listed nations or by the United Nations.

U.S. Federalism in Practice Federalism in theory is one thing—federalism in practice is another. As you will read shortly, the Constitution sets forth specific powers that can be exercised by the national government and provides that the national government has the implied power to undertake actions necessary to carry out its expressly designated powers. All other powers are "reserved" to the states. The broad language of the Constitution, though, has left much room for debate over the specific nature and scope of state and national powers. Thus, the actual workings of our federal form of government have depended, to a great extent, on the historical application of the broad principles outlined in the Constitution.

To further complicate matters, the term *federal government*, as it is used today, refers to the national, or central, government. When individuals talk of the federal government, they mean the national government based in Washington, D.C. They are not referring to the federal *system* of government, which is made up of both the national government and the state governments.

3–1b Alternatives to Federalism

Perhaps an easier way to define federalism is to discuss what it is *not*. A majority of the nations in the world today have a **unitary system** of government. In such a system, the constitution vests all powers in the national government. If the national government so chooses, it can delegate some activities to subnational units. In a unitary system, any subnational government is a "creature of the national government." The governments of Britain, France, Israel, Japan, and the Philippines are examples of unitary systems.

In the United States, because the Constitution does not mention local governments (cities and counties), we say that city and county governmental units are "creatures of state government." That means that state governments can—and do—both give powers to and take powers from local governments. The individual American states, in other words, are also unitary systems.

The Articles of Confederation created a confederal system, a second alternative to federalism. In a **confederal system,** the national government exists and operates only at the direction of the subnational governments. Few true confederal systems are in existence today, although some people contend that the European Union (EU)—a group of twenty-eight European nations that has established many common institutions—qualifies as such a system. (In 2016, Britain voted to leave the EU, effective 2019.)

3–1c Federalism—An Optimal Choice for the United States?

The Articles of Confederation failed because they did not allow for a sufficiently strong central government. The framers of the Constitution, however, were also fearful of tyranny and a too-powerful central government. The outcome had to be a compromise—a federal system.

Advantages of Federalism The appeal of federalism was that it retained state powers and local traditions while establishing a strong national government capable of handling common problems, such as national defense. A federal form of government also furthered the goal of creating a division of powers (to be discussed shortly). There are other reasons why the founders opted for a federal system, and a federal structure of government continues to offer many advantages for U.S. citizens.

Advantage: Size. One of the reasons a federal form of government is well suited to the United States is our country's large size. Even when the United States consisted of only thirteen states, its geographic area was larger than that of England or France. In those days, travel was slow and communication was difficult, so people in outlying areas were isolated. The news of any particular political decision could take several weeks to reach everyone. Therefore, even if the framers of the Constitution had wanted a more centralized system (which most of them did not), such a system would have been unworkable.

Look at Figure 3–1. As you can see, to a great extent the practical business of governing this country takes place in state and local governmental units. Indeed, the most common type of governmental unit in the United States is the *special district*—an independent unit of government that is separate from general-purpose local governments such as counties, cities, and townships. Special districts enjoy substantial administrative and financial independence.

A special district is generally concerned with a specific issue such as solid waste disposal, mass transportation, or fire protection. Often, the jurisdiction of special districts crosses the boundaries of other governmental units, such as cities or counties. Compared to other local governments, special

unitary system A centralized governmental system in which local or subdivisional governments exercise only those powers given to them by the central government.

confederal system A league of independent sovereign states, joined together by a central government that has only limited powers over them.

FIGURE 3–1 GOVERNMENTAL UNITS IN THE UNITED STATES TODAY

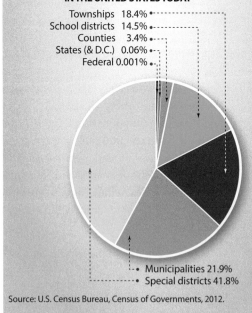

How could the number of governments in the United States create problems for voters?

THE NUMBER OF GOVERNMENTS IN THE UNITED STATES TODAY

Government	Number
Federal government	1
State governments and District of Columbia	51
Local governments	
Counties	3,031
Municipalities (mainly cities or towns)	19,522
Townships (less extensive powers)	16,364
Special districts (water, sewer, and so on)	37,203
School districts	12,884
Subtotal local governments	89,004
Total	**89,056**

PERCENTAGE OF ALL GOVERNMENTS IN THE UNITED STATES TODAY

Townships 18.4%
School districts 14.5%
Counties 3.4%
States (& D.C.) 0.06%
Federal 0.001%

Municipalities 21.9%
Special districts 41.8%

Source: U.S. Census Bureau, Census of Governments, 2012.

districts tend to have fewer restrictions as to how much debt they can incur and so are created to finance large building projects.

Advantage: Experimentation. The existence of numerous government subunits in the United States also makes it possible to experiment with innovative policies and programs at the state or local level. Many observers, including Supreme Court justice Louis Brandeis (1856–1941), have emphasized that in a federal system, state governments can act as "laboratories" for public-policy experimentation. For example, many states have adopted minimum-wage laws that establish a higher minimum wage than the one set by national legislation. State governments also have a wide variety of policies on how or whether state employees can form labor unions.

Depending on the outcome of a specific experiment, other states may (or may not) implement similar programs. State innovations can also serve as models for federal programs. For instance, California was a pioneer in air-pollution control. Many of that state's regulations were later adapted by other states and eventually by the federal government.

Advantage: Subcultures. We have always been a nation of different political subcultures. The Pilgrims who founded New England were different from the settlers who established the agricultural society of the South. Both of these groups were different from those who populated the Middle Atlantic states. The groups that founded New England had a religious focus, while those who populated the Middle Atlantic states were more business oriented. Those who settled in the South were more individualistic than the other groups. That is, they were less inclined to act as a collective and more inclined to act independently of each other. A federal system of government allows the political and cultural interests of regional groups to be reflected in the laws governing those groups. By far the most important of these regional interests was slavery. Federalism allowed northern states to ban the institution, while southern states maintained it.

As we noted earlier, nations other than the United States have benefited from the principle of federalism. One of them is Canada. Because federalism permits the expression of varying regional cultures, Canadian federalism naturally differs from the American version, as you will discover in this chapter's *The Rest of the World* feature.

Some Drawbacks to Federalism Federalism offers many advantages, but it also has some drawbacks. Consider that although federalism in many ways promotes greater self-rule, or democracy, some scholars point out that local self-rule may not always be in society's best interests. These observers argue that the smaller the political unit, the higher the probability that it will be dominated by a single political group, which may or may not be concerned with the welfare of many of the local unit's citizens. For example, entrenched segregationist politicians in southern states denied African Americans their civil rights and voting rights for decades.

Canadian versus American Federalism

By land area, Canada is the second-largest country in the world. Physically, the country seems designed for a federal system of government. And indeed, Canada has a federal system similar in some ways to that of the United States—but it also has some big differences. When the 1867 Constitution Act created modern Canada, the United States had just concluded the Civil War. Canada's founders blamed that war on the weakness of the U.S. central government. Therefore, the Canadian Constitution gave far more power to the central government than did the U.S. Constitution.

The Powers of Lower-Level Governments

Our lower levels of government are called states, whereas in Canada they are called provinces. Right there, the powers of the central government are emphasized. The word state implies sovereignty. A *province*, however, is never sovereign and is typically set up for the convenience of the central government.

In the United States, the powers of the national government are limited to those listed in the Constitution. In the Canadian Constitution, it is the powers of the provinces that are limited by a list. The Tenth Amendment to the U.S. Constitution reserves residual powers to the states or to the people. In Canada, residual powers rest with the national government. Under the 1867 Canadian Constitution, the central government could veto any provincial legislation. No such clause appears in the U.S. Constitution.

The Provinces Gain Strength

Over time, the powers of the U.S. federal government grew at the expense of the states. The opposite happened in Canada. By the end of the nineteenth century, the Canadian government in practice had abandoned the power to veto provincial legislation. The Great Depression of the 1930s strengthened the national government in the United States. In Canada, it strengthened the provinces.

Two Languages

Another striking difference between Canada and the United States is that Canada has two national languages. A majority of Canadians speak English, but most of the population of Québec speak French. The Parti Québécois (PQ), which wants Québec to be a separate country, gained power in that province in 1976 and 1994. Both times, it held referendums on whether Québec should demand "sovereignty-association," a euphemism for independence. In 1995, the PQ almost obtained a majority vote for its position. The PQ returned to power in 2012 but without enough votes to hold another referendum. In 2014, it was defeated by the Liberal Party. Nevertheless, the possibility exists that Canada could actually break apart someday.

Critical Analysis

The Canadian Constitution is based on the principles of "peace, order, and good government." Contrast that phrase with the words in the Declaration of Independence—"life, liberty, and the pursuit of happiness." How do the statements differ?

Powerful state and local interests can impede national plans. State and local interests often diverge from those of the national government. For example, the health-care reforms adopted by the national government in 2010 sought to expand the number of poor persons eligible for Medicaid. As of 2017, however, nineteen states had refused to participate in the expansion program, even though the national government was to pick up the entire cost until 2020. (In 2017, as part of its attempt to repeal Obamacare, both the House and Senate considered legislation that would have drastically cut Medicaid benefits. None of the bills passed, however.)

Finding acceptable solutions to such conflicts has not always been easy. Indeed, as will be discussed shortly, in the 1860s, war—not politics—decided the outcome of a struggle over states' rights.

Federalism has other drawbacks as well. One of them is the lack of uniformity of state laws, which can complicate business transactions that cross state borders. Another problem is the difficulty of coordinating government policies at the national, state, and local levels. Additionally, the simultaneous regulation of business by all levels of government creates red tape that imposes substantial costs on the business community.

In a federal system, there is always the danger that national power will be expanded at the expense of the states. President Ronald Reagan (1981–1989) once said, "The Founding Fathers saw the federalist system as constructed something like a masonry wall. The States are the bricks, the national government is the mortar. . . . Unfortunately, over the years, many people have increasingly come to believe that Washington is the whole wall."[2]

CRITICAL THINKING

▶ *The national government imposed a uniform highway speed limit on the entire country from 1974 until its repeal in 1995. Why should we leave speed limits to the states—or why should they be a federal responsibility?*

3–2 THE CONSTITUTIONAL DIVISION OF POWERS

LO Indicate how the Constitution divides governing powers in our federal system.

division of powers
A basic principle of federalism established by the U.S. Constitution, by which powers are divided between the national and state governments.

expressed powers
Constitutional or statutory powers that are expressly provided for by the U.S. Constitution; also called *enumerated powers.*

implied powers
The powers of the federal government that are implied by the expressed powers in the Constitution, particularly in Article I, Section 8.

necessary and proper clause Article I, Section 8, Clause 18, of the Constitution, which gives Congress the power to make all laws "necessary and proper" for the federal government to carry out its responsibilities; also called the *elastic clause.*

The founders created a federal form of government by dividing sovereign powers into powers that could be exercised by the national government and powers that were reserved to the states. Although there is no systematic explanation of this **division of powers,** the original Constitution, along with its amendments, provides statements on what the national and state governments can (and cannot) do.

3–2a The Powers of the National Government

The Constitution delegates certain powers to the national government. It also prohibits the national government from exercising certain powers.

Powers Delegated to the National Government The national government possesses three types of powers: expressed powers, implied powers, and inherent powers.

Expressed Powers. Article I, Section 8, of the Constitution expressly enumerates twenty-seven powers that Congress may exercise. Two of these **expressed powers,** or *enumerated powers*, are the power to coin money and the power to regulate interstate commerce. Constitutional amendments have provided for other expressed powers. For example, the Sixteenth Amendment, added in 1913, gives Congress the power to impose a federal income tax.

One power expressly granted to the national government is the right to regulate commerce not only among the states, but also "with the Indian Tribes." As a result, relations between Native American tribal governments and the rest of the country have always been a national responsibility. A further consequence is that state governments face significant limits on their authority over American Indian reservations within their borders.

Implied Powers. The constitutional basis for the **implied powers** of the national government is found in Article I, Section 8, Clause 18, often called the **necessary and proper clause.** This clause states that Congress has the power to make "all Laws which shall be necessary and proper for carrying into Execution the foregoing [expressed] Powers, and all other Powers vested by this Constitution in the Government of the United States, or in any Department or Officer thereof." The necessary and proper clause is often referred to as the *elastic clause*, because it gives elasticity to our constitutional system.

The U.S. Flag flies above the Texas state flag in Austin, Texas. *Which level of government has responsibility for Indian affairs?*

An example of an implied power is the power to print paper currency such as dollar bills. The Constitution says only that Congress has the power to "coin money," presumably in the form of gold or silver coins. Congress also has the expressed power to borrow, however, and on that basis it eventually issued paper currency that represented sums owed by the government.[3]

Inherent Powers. The national government also enjoys certain inherent powers—powers that governments must have simply to ensure the nation's integrity and survival as a political unit. For example, any national government must have the inherent ability to make treaties, regulate immigration, acquire territory, wage war, and make peace. While some inherent powers are also enumerated in the Constitution, such as the powers to wage war and make treaties, others are not. For example, the Constitution does not speak of regulating immigration or acquiring new territory. Although the national government's inherent powers are few, they are important.

Federal Lands. One inherent power is older than the Constitution itself—the power to own land. The United States collectively owned various western lands under the Articles of Confederation. The Northwest Territory, which included the modern states of Illinois, Indiana, Michigan, Ohio, Wisconsin, and part of Minnesota, joined United States' lands together with lands given up by New York and Virginia. The Northwest Territory was organized during the ratification of the Constitution. Indeed, establishing the territory as the collective property of the entire Union was necessary to secure support for ratification in several states, including Maryland.

The United States then sold land to new settlers—land sales were a major source of national government income throughout much of the 1800s. To this day, the national government owns most of the acres in most far western states, a fact that annoys many Westerners.

Powers Prohibited to the National Government The Constitution expressly prohibits the national government from undertaking certain actions, such as imposing taxes on exports, and from passing laws restraining certain liberties, such as the freedom of speech or religion. Most of these prohibited powers are listed in Article I, Section 9, and in the first eight amendments to the Constitution. Additionally, the national government is implicitly prohibited from exercising certain powers. For example, most authorities believe that the federal government does not have the power to create a national public school system, because such power is not included among those that are expressed and implied.

3–2b The Powers of the States

The Tenth Amendment to the Constitution asserts that powers that are not delegated to the national government by the Constitution nor prohibited to the states "are reserved to the States respectively, or to the people." The Tenth Amendment thus gives numerous powers to the states, including the power to regulate commerce within their borders and the power to maintain a state militia.

Police Powers In principle, each state has the ability to regulate its internal affairs and to enact whatever laws are necessary to protect the health, safety, welfare, and morals of its people. These powers of the states are called police powers. The establishment of public schools and the regulation of marriage and divorce have traditionally been considered to be entirely within the purview of state and local governments.

Because the Tenth Amendment does not specify what powers are reserved to the states, these powers have been defined differently at different times in our history. In periods of widespread support for increased regulation by the national government, the Tenth Amendment tends to recede into the background. When the tide of support turns, the Tenth Amendment is resurrected to justify arguments supporting increased states' rights (see, for example, the discussion of the new federalism later in this chapter). Because the United States Supreme Court is the ultimate arbiter of the Constitution, the outcome of disputes over the extent of state powers often rests with the Court.

> "This country's planted thick with laws from coast to coast . . . and if you cut them down . . . d'you really think you could stand upright in the winds that would blow then?"
>
> ~ ROBERT BOLT
> *A MAN FOR ALL SEASONS*

inherent powers The powers of the national government that, although not always expressly granted by the Constitution, are necessary to ensure the nation's integrity and survival as a political unit.

police powers The powers of a government body that enable it to create laws for the protection of the health, safety, welfare, and morals of the people. In the United States, most police powers are reserved to the states.

Powers Prohibited to the States Article I, Section 10, denies certain powers to state governments, such as the power to tax goods that are transported across state lines. States are also prohibited from entering into treaties with other countries. In addition, the Thirteenth, Fourteenth, Fifteenth, Nineteenth, Twenty-fourth, and Twenty-sixth Amendments prohibit certain state actions. (The complete text of these amendments is included in Appendix B.)

The fact remains that, under the Constitution, the states have considerable scope for action under their police powers. Some have even argued that state-level laws and regulations can be more burdensome than national legislation. This chapter's *Perception vs. Reality* feature reports on that concern.

3–2c Interstate Relations

The Constitution also contains provisions relating to interstate relations. The states have constant commercial and social interactions among themselves, and these interactions often do not directly involve the national

---

PERCEPTION VS. REALITY
The Best Government Is Local Government

Our government has certainly grown in size since World War II. Many Americans complain about "big government." Taxes are too high. Regulations take away our freedom. The "government" in question is the one in Washington, D.C.

The Perception

Big government is the problem, and big government means the federal government. Government closest to the people governs best. Therefore, state and local governments should have more power, and the federal government should have less.

The Reality

In recent years, more and more commentators have begun arguing that regulations imposed by state and local governments are even more costly than the ones imposed by the feds. Consider housing policies. The zoning regulations that control housing construction are almost entirely local. Typically, zoning restricts development to ensure low population densities in our major urban areas. City dwellers want to keep out new high-rises. Suburbanites want to stop the construction of town houses and apartment buildings. As a result, cities with highly productive industries, such as Boston, New York, Los Angeles, San Francisco, and Seattle, don't have enough housing for all the people who would like to live there.

The law of supply and demand takes its course: the cost of the housing that does exist rises astronomically. Americans willing to move in search of economic opportunity are priced out. Instead, they go to places where the cost of housing is tolerable—places such as Houston, which has no zoning code. *But jobs don't pay as well in Houston as they do in San Francisco.* The national cost of excessive residential zoning, therefore, may run into hundreds of billions of dollars.

As another example, look at state (and sometimes local) occupational licensing requirements. Of course, it's generally agreed that not everyone who wants to should be a surgeon or a lawyer. We need to be sure that people who handle matters of life and death know what they are doing.

But do we really need to license interior designers, as is done in Florida? Do barbers really have to be licensed? Should dental hygienists be required to work for dentists, who then get a cut of their income? Some 29 percent of American workers need a state-issued license to do their jobs legally.

Excessive licensing not only makes the services we buy more expensive, but also restricts job opportunities. These restrictions simply serve the interests of those already in particular trades by reducing the number of competitors.

Blog On

New York Magazine columnist Jonathan Chait is best known for his aggressive criticism of conservatives. In "The Worst Governments in America Are Local," however, he takes on both political parties. Find this article by searching on "chait worst governments."

Rena Schild/Shutterstock.com

Supporters of same-sex marriage celebrate at the United States Supreme Court after it legalized same-sex marriage in all fifty states in June 2015.
Why has same-sex marriage been an issue for our federal system?

government. The relationships among the states in our federal system of government are sometimes referred to as *horizontal federalism*.

The Full Faith and Credit Clause   The Constitution's full faith and credit clause requires each state to honor every other state's public acts, records, and judicial proceedings. This constitutional mandate posed a problem in the years from 2004 to 2015, when same-sex marriage was legal in some—but not all—of the states. Already in 1996, members of Congress feared that one or more states might recognize such marriages. If a gay couple was legally married in one state, would all the others be forced to recognize the marriage? To prevent this result, Congress passed the Defense of Marriage Act (DOMA), which provided that no state was required to treat a relationship between persons of the same sex as a marriage, even if the relationship was considered a marriage in another state. A second part of the law barred the national government from recognizing same-sex marriages in states that legalized them. The constitutionality of both parts of the law was subject to debate.

United States v. Windsor   The United States Supreme Court never took up the question of whether DOMA violated the full faith and credit clause. In 2013, however, in *United States v. Windsor*, the Court did find that the second part of the law, which banned national

recognition of such marriages, was unconstitutional.[4] The *Windsor* case was, in a way, a vindication of states' rights—the national government could not interfere with state decisions on whether to recognize same-sex marriage.

Obergefell v. Hodges   By 2015, thirty-seven states and the District of Columbia permitted same-sex marriage. In June of that year, in *Obergefell v. Hodges*, the Supreme Court found laws against same-sex marriage to be unconstitutional throughout the entire United States.[5] With that ruling, the question of whether DOMA violated the full faith and credit clause became irrelevant.

Interstate Compacts   Horizontal federalism also includes agreements, known as *interstate compacts*, among two or more states to regulate the use or protection of certain resources, such as water or oil and gas. California and Nevada, for example, have formed an interstate compact to regulate the use and protection of Lake Tahoe, which lies on the border between those states.

3–2d Concurrent Powers

Concurrent powers can be exercised by both the state governments and the federal government. Generally, a state's concurrent powers apply only within the geographic area of the state and do not include functions that the Constitution delegates exclusively to the national government, such as the coinage of money and the negotiation of treaties.

An example of a concurrent power is the power to tax. Both the states and the national government have the power to impose income taxes—and a variety of other taxes. States, however, are prohibited from imposing tariffs (taxes on imported goods), and, as noted, the federal government may not tax articles exported by any state.

Figures 3–2 and 3–3 summarize the powers granted and denied by the Constitution, respectively, and list other concurrent powers.

3–2e The Supremacy Clause

The Constitution makes it clear that the federal government holds ultimate

> **Concurrent powers**
> Powers held by both the federal and the state governments in a federal system.

FIGURE 3–2   POWERS GRANTED BY THE CONSTITUTION

The Constitution grants certain powers to the national government and certain powers to the state governments. Some powers, called *concurrent powers*, can be exercised at either the national or the state level, but generally the states can exercise these powers only within their own borders. *There are limits on what states can do using their police powers. Give some examples of actions that would not be allowed.*

NATIONAL

- To coin money
- To conduct foreign relations
- To regulate interstate commerce
- To declare war
- To raise and support the military
- To establish post offices
- To admit new states
- To exercise powers implied by the necessary and proper clause

CONCURRENT

- To levy and collect taxes
- To borrow money
- To make and enforce laws
- To establish courts
- To provide for the general welfare
- To charter banks and corporations

STATE

- To regulate intrastate commerce
- To conduct elections
- To provide for public health, safety, welfare, and morals
- To establish local governments
- To ratify amendments to the federal Constitution
- To establish a state militia

power. Article VI, Clause 2, known as the **supremacy clause,** states that the U.S. Constitution and the laws of the federal government "shall be the supreme Law of the Land." In other words, states cannot use their reserved or concurrent powers to counter national policies. Whenever state or local officers, such as judges or sheriffs, take office, they become bound by an oath to support the U.S. Constitution. National government power always takes precedence over any conflicting state action.[6]

CRITICAL THINKING

▸ *Under current court rulings, it is very difficult for states to collect taxes on goods that their citizens buy through the Internet. National legislation, however, could make such tax collection more feasible. Should Congress pass such legislation? Why or why not?*

 3–3

THE STRUGGLE FOR SUPREMACY

LO Summarize the evolution of federal-state relationships in the United States over time.

supremacy clause
Article VI, Clause 2, of the Constitution, which makes the Constitution and federal laws superior to all conflicting state and local laws.

Much of the political and legal history of the United States has involved conflicts between the supremacy of the national government and the desire of the states to preserve their sovereignty. The most extreme example of this conflict was the Civil War in the 1860s. Through the years, because of the Civil War and several important Supreme Court decisions, the national government has increased its power.

3–3a Early United States Supreme Court Decisions

Two Supreme Court cases, both of which were decided in the early 1800s, played a key role in establishing the constitutional foundations for the supremacy of the national government. Both decisions were issued while John Marshall was chief justice of the Supreme Court. In his thirty-four years as chief justice (1801–1835), Marshall did much to establish the prestige and the independence of the Court.

In *Marbury v. Madison*, Marshall clearly enunciated the principle of *judicial review*, under which the courts can determine that laws or executive actions are unconstitutional.[7] Judicial review has since become an important part of the checks and balances in the American system of government. William Marbury was appointed a judge by President John Adams, a member of the Federalist Party, when Adams was about to leave office. The incoming president, Thomas Jefferson, was leader of the rival Republican Party. Adams sought to pack the judiciary, thus preventing Jefferson from filling judicial posts. James Madison, now secretary of state under Jefferson, refused to issue Marbury's appointment. Marbury sued. Marshall's court found Marbury's suit to be unconstitutional on a technicality, thus resolving a troublesome issue. Under Marshall's leadership, the Supreme Court

FIGURE 3–3 POWERS DENIED BY THE CONSTITUTION

The Constitution denies certain powers to the national government and denies certain powers to the state governments.
What would happen if the states had the right to coin their own money?

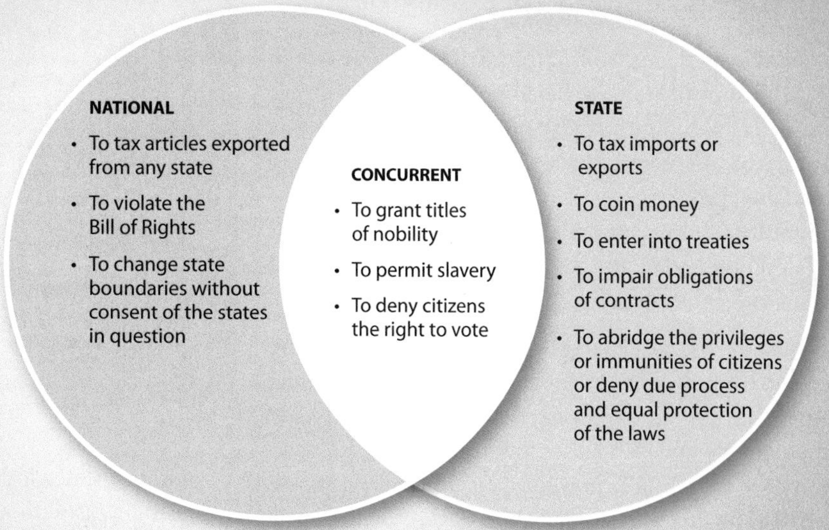

NATIONAL

- To tax articles exported from any state
- To violate the Bill of Rights
- To change state boundaries without consent of the states in question

CONCURRENT

- To grant titles of nobility
- To permit slavery
- To deny citizens the right to vote

STATE

- To tax imports or exports
- To coin money
- To enter into treaties
- To impair obligations of contracts
- To abridge the privileges or immunities of citizens or deny due process and equal protection of the laws

also established, through the following cases, the superiority of federal authority under the Constitution.

McCulloch v. Maryland (1819)

The issue in *McCulloch v. Maryland*, a case decided in 1819, involved both the necessary and proper clause and the supremacy clause.[8] When the state of Maryland imposed a tax on the Baltimore branch of the Second Bank of the United States, the branch's chief cashier, James McCulloch, declined to pay the tax. The state court ruled that McCulloch had to pay it, and the national government appealed to the United States Supreme Court.

The Necessary and Proper Clause. The case involved much more than a question of taxes. At issue was whether Congress had the authority under the Constitution's necessary and proper clause to charter and contribute capital to the Second Bank of the United States. A second constitutional issue was also involved: If the bank was constitutional, could a state tax it? In other words, was a state action that conflicted with a national government action invalid under the supremacy clause?

Chief Justice Marshall pointed out that no provision in the Constitution grants the national government the *expressed* power to form a national bank. Nevertheless, if establishing such a bank helps the national government exercise its expressed powers, then the authority to do so could be implied. Marshall also said that the necessary and proper clause included "all means that are appropriate" to carry out "the legitimate ends" of the Constitution.

The Doctrine of National Supremacy. Having established this doctrine of implied powers, Marshall then answered the other important constitutional question before the

Court and established the doctrine of *national supremacy*. Marshall declared that no state could use its taxing power to tax an arm of the national government. If it could, the Constitution's declaration that the Constitution "shall be the supreme Law of the Land" would be empty rhetoric without meaning. From that day on, Marshall's decision became the basis for strengthening the national government's power.

Gibbons v. Ogden (1824)

Article I, Section 8, of the Constitution gives Congress the power to regulate commerce "among the several States." But the framers of the Constitution did not define the word *commerce*. At issue in *Gibbons v. Ogden* was how the *commerce clause* should be defined and whether the national government had the exclusive power to regulate commerce involving more than one state.[9]

The New York legislature had given Robert Livingston and Robert Fulton the exclusive right to operate steamboats in New York waters, and Livingston and Fulton licensed Aaron Ogden to operate a ferry between New York and New Jersey. Thomas Gibbons, who had a license from the U.S. government to operate boats in interstate waters, decided to compete with Ogden, but he did so without New York's permission. Ogden sued Gibbons in the New York state courts and won. Gibbons appealed.

In ruling on the case, Chief Justice Marshall defined *commerce* as including all business dealings, including steamboat travel. Marshall also stated that the power to regulate interstate commerce was an *exclusive* national power and had no limitations other than those specifically found in the Constitution. Since this 1824 decision, the national government has used the commerce clause repeatedly to justify its regulation of almost all areas of economic activity.

3–3b The Civil War— The Ultimate Supremacy Battle

The great issue that provoked the Civil War (1861–1865) was the future of slavery. Because people in different sections of the country had radically different beliefs about slavery, the slavery issue took the form of a dispute over states' rights versus national supremacy. The war brought to a bloody climax the ideological debate that had been outlined by the Federalist and Anti-Federalist factions even before the Constitution was ratified.

A Shift to States' Rights As just discussed, the Supreme Court headed by John Marshall interpreted the commerce clause in such a way as to increase the power of the national government at the expense of state powers. By the late 1820s, however, a shift back to states' rights had begun, and the question of the regulation of commerce became one of the major issues in federal-state relations. When the national government, in 1828 and 1832, passed laws imposing tariffs (taxes) on goods imported into the United States, southern states objected, believing that such taxes were against their interests.

One southern state, South Carolina, attempted to *nullify* the tariffs, or to make them void. South Carolina claimed that in conflicts between state governments and the national government, the states should have the ultimate authority to determine the welfare of their citizens. President Andrew Jackson was prepared to use force to uphold national law, but Congress reduced the tariffs. The crisis passed temporarily.

States' Rights, Slavery, and Secession The defense of slavery and the promotion of states' rights were both important in the South's decision in favor of secession—withdrawal from the Union—in 1860 and 1861. Indeed, the two concepts were commingled in the minds of Southerners of that era. Which of these two was the more important remains a matter of controversy even today. Modern defenders of states' rights and those who distrust governmental authority often present southern secession as entirely a matter of states' rights. Liberals and those who champion the rights of African Americans see slavery as the sole cause of the crisis.

To understand this dispute more fully, it is worth recognizing that "states' rights," by itself, is a relatively abstract concept. It gains meaning only when you answer the question: "The rights of the states to do *what*?" The declarations of secession issued by the

secession The act of formally withdrawing from membership in an alliance; the withdrawal of a state from the federal Union.

> "We here highly resolve that . . . This Nation . . . shall have a new birth of freedom; and that government of the people, by the people, for the people, shall not perish from the earth."
>
> ~ ABRAHAM LINCOLN, GETTYSBURG ADDRESS, 1863

southern states left no doubt that the defense of slavery was the reason they were leaving the Union.

When the South was defeated in the war, the idea that a state has a right to secede from the Union was defeated also. Although the Civil War occurred because of the South's desire for increased states' rights, the result was just the opposite—an increase in the political power of the national government. The "Civil War amendments" to the Constitution—the Thirteenth, Fourteenth, and Fifteenth Amendments—gave the national government the power to enforce significant new rights. These included the power to:

▸ **abolish laws that allowed slavery,**

▸ **ensure that states would guarantee all persons "due process of law" and "the equal protection of the laws," and**

▸ **require states to recognize the right of African Americans to vote.**

Courtesy of the Supreme Court of the United States Washington, DC

John Marshall, chief justice of the United States Supreme Court (1801–1835). *How did Marshall strengthen the national government?*

3-3c Dual Federalism—From the Civil War to the 1930s

Scholars have devised various models to describe the relationship between the states and the national government at different times in our history. These models are useful in describing the evolution of federalism after the Civil War.

The model of **dual federalism** assumes that the states and the national government are more or less equals, with each level of government having separate and distinct functions and responsibilities. The states exercise sovereign powers over certain matters, and the national government exercises sovereign powers over others.

For much of our nation's history, this model of federalism prevailed. After the expansion of national authority during the Civil War, the courts again tended to support the states' rights to exercise police powers and tended to strictly limit the powers of the federal government under the commerce clause. In 1918, for example, the Supreme Court ruled unconstitutional a 1916 federal law excluding from interstate commerce the products created through the use of child labor. The law was held unconstitutional because it attempted to regulate a local problem.[10] The era of dual federalism came to an end in the 1930s, when the United States was in the depths of the greatest economic depression it had ever experienced.

3-3d Cooperative Federalism and the Growth of the National Government

The model of **cooperative federalism,** as the term implies, involves cooperation by all branches of government. This model views the national and state governments as complementary parts of a single governmental mechanism, the purpose of which is to solve the problems facing the entire United States. For example, federal law enforcement agencies, such as the Federal Bureau of Investigation, lend technical expertise to solve local crimes, and local officials cooperate with federal agencies.

Roosevelt's New Deal Cooperative federalism grew out of the desire to solve the pressing national problems caused by the Great Depression, which began in 1929. In an attempt to bring the United States out of the Depression, President Franklin D. Roosevelt (1933–1945) launched his **New Deal,** which involved many government regulation, spending, and public-assistance programs. Roosevelt's New Deal legislation not only ushered in an era of cooperative federalism, which has more or less continued until the present day, but also marked the real beginning of an era of national supremacy.

President Franklin D. Roosevelt proposed many new federal programs during the Great Depression. *How did our conception of federalism change during his presidency?*

Catwalker/Shutterstock.com

Before the period of cooperative federalism could be truly established, it was necessary to obtain the concurrence of the United States Supreme Court. As mentioned, in the early part of the twentieth century, the Court held a very restrictive view of what the federal government could do under the commerce clause. In the 1930s, the Court ruled again and again that various economic measures were unconstitutional.

In 1937, Roosevelt threatened to "pack" the Court with up to six new members who presumably would be more favorable to federal action. This move was widely considered to be an assault on the Constitution, and Congress refused to support it. Later that year, however, Roosevelt had the opportunity—for the first time since taking office—to appoint a new member of the Supreme Court. Hugo Black, the new justice, tipped the balance on the Court. After 1937, the Court ceased its attempts to limit the scope of the commerce clause.

Cooperative Federalism and the "Great Society" The 1960s and 1970s saw an even greater expansion of the national government's role

dual federalism A system of government in which the federal and the state governments maintain diverse but sovereign powers.

cooperative federalism A model of federalism in which the states and the federal government cooperate in solving problems.

New Deal The policies ushered in by the Roosevelt administration in 1933 in an attempt to bring the United States out of the Great Depression.

in domestic policy. The Great Society legislation of President Lyndon B. Johnson (1963–1969) created Medicaid, Medicare, the Job Corps, Operation Head Start, and other programs. The Civil Rights Act of 1964 prohibited discrimination in public accommodations, employment, and other areas on the basis of race, color, national origin, religion, or gender. In the 1970s, national laws protecting consumers, employees, and the environment imposed further regulations on the economy. Today, few activities are beyond the reach of the regulatory arm of the national government.

Nonetheless, the massive social programs undertaken in the 1960s and 1970s also resulted in greater involvement by state and local governments. The national government simply could not implement those programs alone. For example, Head Start, a program that provides preschool services to children of low-income families, is administered by local nonprofit organizations and school systems, although it is funded by federal grants.

The model in which every level of government is involved in implementing a policy is sometimes referred to as **picket-fence federalism.** In this model, the policy area is the vertical picket on the fence, while the levels of government are the horizontal support boards.

Cornerstones of Cooperative Federalism

The regulatory powers that the national government enjoys today rest on constitutional cornerstones laid by the Supreme Court decisions discussed at the beginning of this section. The commerce clause and the doctrine of federal preemption have been crucial.

> **picket-fence federalism** A model of federalism in which specific policies and programs are administered by all levels of government—national, state, and local.
>
> **preemption** A doctrine rooted in the supremacy clause of the Constitution that provides that national laws or regulations governing a certain area take precedence over conflicting state laws or regulations governing that same area.
>
> **new federalism** A plan to limit the federal government's role in regulating state governments and to give the states increased power in deciding how they should spend government revenues.

The Commerce Clause.

From 1937 on, the Supreme Court consistently upheld Congress's power to regulate domestic policy under the commerce clause. Even activities that occur entirely within a state were rarely considered to be outside the regulatory power of the national government. For example, in 1942 the Supreme Court held that wheat production by an individual farmer intended wholly for consumption on his own farm was subject to federal regulation. The Court reasoned that the home consumption of wheat reduced the demand for wheat and thus could have an effect on interstate commerce.[11]

In 1980, the Supreme Court acknowledged that the commerce clause had "long been interpreted to extend beyond activities actually in interstate commerce to reach other activities that, while wholly local in nature, nevertheless substantially affect interstate commerce."[12] Today, Congress can regulate almost any kind of economic activity, no matter where it occurs. In recent years, though, the Supreme Court has, for the first time since the 1930s, occasionally curbed Congress's regulatory powers under the commerce clause. You will read more about this development shortly.

Federal Preemption. John Marshall's validation of the supremacy clause of the Constitution has also had significant consequences for federalism. One important effect of the supremacy clause today is that the clause allows for federal preemption of certain areas in which the national government and the states have concurrent powers. When Congress chooses to act exclusively in an area in which the states and the national government have concurrent powers, Congress is said to have *preempted* the area. In such cases, the courts have held that a valid federal law or regulation takes precedence over a conflicting state or local law or regulation covering the same general activity.

CRITICAL THINKING

▸ *Although marijuana is illegal under national law, as of 2017 eight states had moved to legalize and tax it. Should the federal government take a hands-off approach or crack down on these states? In either case, why?*

 3-4

FEDERALISM TODAY

LO Describe developments in federalism in recent years.

By the 1970s, some Americans had begun to question whether the national government had acquired too many powers. Had the national government gotten too big? Had it become, in fact, a threat to the power of the states and the liberties of the people? Should steps be taken to reduce the regulatory power and scope of the national government? Since that time, the model of federalism has evolved in ways that reflect these and other concerns.

3-4a The New Federalism— More Power to the States

Starting in the 1970s, several administrations attempted to revitalize the doctrine of dual federalism, which they renamed the "new federalism." The **new federalism** involved a shift from *nation-centered* federalism to *state-centered* federalism. One of the major goals of the new federalism was to return to the states certain powers that had been exercised by the national government since the 1930s. The term **devolution**—the transfer of powers to political subunits— is often used to describe this process.

Although a product of conservative thought and initiated by Republicans, the devolutionary goals of the new federalism were also espoused by Democrats during the Clinton administration (1993–2001). An example of the new federalism is the welfare reform legislation passed by Congress in 1996, which gave the states more authority over public-assistance programs.

A marijuana grower in Colorado sprays the plants with neem oil, an organic method of combating spider mates and mildew. Colorado is one of eight states to legalize recreational marijuana. *How might the national government respond to legalization?*

Cyrus McCrimmon/The Denver Post/Getty Images

3–4b The Supreme Court and the New Federalism

During the late 1900s and the early 2000s, the Supreme Court played a significant role in furthering the cause of states' rights. A variety of decisions either limited the power of the federal government or enhanced the power of the states.

Limiting the Power of the National Government   In a landmark 1995 decision, *United States v. Lopez*, the Supreme Court held, for the first time in sixty years, that Congress had exceeded its constitutional authority under the commerce clause.[13] The Court concluded that the Gun-Free School Zones Act of 1990, which banned the possession of guns within one thousand feet of any school, was unconstitutional because it attempted to regulate an area that had "nothing to do with commerce."

In a 1997 decision, the Court struck down portions of the Brady Handgun Violence Prevention Act of 1993, which obligated state and local law enforcement officers to do background checks on prospective handgun buyers until a national instant-check system could be implemented. The Court stated that Congress lacked the power to "dragoon" state employees into federal service through an unfunded **federal mandate** of this kind.[14]

In 2000, the Court invalidated a key provision of the federal Violence Against Women Act of 1994, which allowed women to sue in federal court when they were victims of gender-motivated violence, such as rape. The Court upheld a federal appellate court's ruling that the commerce clause did not justify national regulation of noneconomic, criminal conduct.[15]

Forcing the National Government to Act   In *Massachusetts v. Environmental Protection Agency*, Massachusetts and several other states sued the Environmental Protection Agency (EPA) for failing to regulate greenhouse-gas emissions.[16] The states asserted that the agency was required to do so by the Clean Air Act of 1990. The EPA argued that it lacked the authority under the Clean Air Act to regulate greenhouse-gas emissions alleged to promote climate change. In a 2007 decision, the Court ruled for the states, holding that the EPA was required under the Clean Air Act to regulate such emissions and should take steps to do so.

3–4c The Shifting Boundary between Federal and State Authority

Clearly, the boundary between federal and state authority has been shifting. Notably, issues relating to the federal structure of our government, which at one time were not at the forefront of the political arena, have in recent years been the subject of heated debate among Americans and their leaders. The federal government and the states seem to be in a constant tug-of-war over federal regulations, federal programs, and federal demands on the states.

devolution The surrender or transfer of powers to local authorities by a central government.

federal mandate A requirement in federal legislation that pressures states and municipalities to comply with certain rules.

A Syrian refugee, center, arrives at O'Hare Airport in Chicago in February 2017. Earlier, she and her family had been banned from entry into the United States due to an executive order by President Donald Trump. *Do we have an obligation to take in migrants whose lives are threatened in their home countries?*

The Politics of Federalism The Republican Party is often viewed as the champion of states' rights. Certainly, the party has claimed such a role. For example, when the Republicans took control of both chambers of Congress in 1995, they promised devolution—which, as already noted, refers to a shifting of power from the national level to the individual states. Smaller central government and state-centered federalism have long been regarded as the twin pillars of Republican ideology. In contrast, Democrats usually have sought greater centralization of power in Washington, D.C.

Since the Clinton administration, however, there have been times when the party tables seem to have turned. As mentioned earlier, it was under Clinton that welfare reform legislation giving more responsibility to the states—a goal that had been endorsed by the Republicans for some time—became a reality. Conversely, the No Child Left Behind Act of 2001, passed at the request of Republican president George W. Bush, gave the federal government a much greater role in education and educational funding than ever before. Finally, the Bush administration made repeated attempts to block California's medical-marijuana initiative and Oregon's physician-assisted suicide law.

The Supreme Court Weighs In Again In the last several years, the Supreme Court has again issued rulings that have affected the shape of our federal system. Sometimes, that has meant upholding the authority of the national government, as in an immigration case

involving Arizona. More often, the Court has extended the rights of the states, as it did in opinions on health-care reform and voting rights.

Immigration. In 2012, in *Arizona v. United States*, the Supreme Court confirmed national authority over immigration by striking down three provisions of a tough Arizona immigration law.

The rejected provisions would have (1) subjected illegal immigrants to criminal penalties for activities such as seeking work, (2) made it a state crime for immigrants to fail to register with the federal government, and (3) allowed police to arrest people without warrants if they had reason to believe that the individuals were deportable.

The Court did allow Arizona to check the immigration status of individuals arrested for reasons other than immigration status. But it reserved the right to rule against Arizona on that issue, too, if the state was shown to practice racial discrimination in its arrests.[17]

Health-Care Reform. Another 2012 ruling concerned the constitutionality of the Affordable Care Act, popularly known as Obamacare. In this case, *National Federation of Independent Business v. Sebelius*, the Court upheld most of the law. Two of Chief Justice John Roberts's arguments, however, set limits on the powers of the national government.

Writing the majority opinion, Roberts contended that the federal government cannot, under the commerce clause of the Constitution, *require* individuals to purchase something—in this case, health-care insurance. The government can encourage such behavior through the tax code, however, which is what the Affordable Care Act did. Roberts also stated that the national government cannot force the states to expand Medicaid by threatening to take away all of their Medicaid funds if they do not. Roberts argued that cutting the states off completely would do too much damage to their budgets.[18] This portion of the ruling was widely and incorrectly seen as setting a new precedent, as we explain in this chapter's *Join the Debate* feature.

Although Obamacare survived the decision, the case did appear to demonstrate that the Court was more willing to challenge the national government on its use of the commerce clause than at any time since 1937. Indeed, four of the nine justices advocated positions

About 11 million people currently live in the United States without legal authorization to be here. These people, termed *unauthorized immigrants* by the national government, are also called "illegal immigrants." About half are from Mexico. How to respond to this population has been a major political issue for years. Should they all be deported—or given a path to citizenship?

Some jurisdictions have taken steps to make deportation more difficult. A *sanctuary city* is one in which local law enforcement does not cooperate with federal deportation efforts. Often, this simply means not asking persons about their immigration status when they come in contact with police. Some local governments also refuse to cooperate with federal immigration agencies altogether. As of 2017, about forty cities had some kind of sanctuary policy, as did more than 350 counties and four states. The existence of such policies raises three questions: (1) Are sanctuary cities a good idea, (2) are they even legal, and (3) should the national government penalize local governments that have sanctuary policies? Americans disagree over these questions.

The National Government Should Crack Down on Sanctuary Cities

Those who would penalize sanctuary cities claim that such policies serve only to protect lawbreakers. The very fact that people are in this country illegally means that they have violated our immigration laws. Also, many illegal immigrants have committed terrible crimes. True, immigration law is the responsibility of the national government. The United States Supreme Court has ruled, in an Arizona case, that states can't impose immigration laws that are tougher than federal laws. Why should they be allowed to have laws that are looser? Setting immigration law is a federal matter, and therefore local authorities should cooperate with the national government in carrying it out. If localities will not cooperate, they should lose federal funds.

President Trump had it right when he said, "We will end the sanctuary cities that have resulted in so many needless deaths." If sanctuary policies are banned, we will be able to expel more dangerous criminals from this country.

Our Constitution Protects Sanctuary Cities

Defenders of sanctuary policies argue that they make cities safer because they encourage unauthorized immigrants to cooperate with the police—without having to worry that doing so could lead to deportation. Serious criminals can still be deported.

Further, the national government cannot make local officials enforce national laws. It is up to the feds to enforce their own laws. Washington does have the power to persuade state and local governments by offering or withholding grants, but its power to *coerce* is limited. In 1987, the Supreme Court held that the federal government could pressure states to raise the age for buying alcohol by threatening to withhold 5 to 10 percent of their highway funds. Anything much beyond that would be unconstitutional.[19] It should not, therefore, have been a surprise when, in its ruling on Obamacare, the Court found that withholding *all* of a state's Medicaid funding would be unacceptable. A move to defund sanctuary cities would surely be thrown out by the courts.

Critical Analysis

In **McCulloch v. Maryland,** *the Court ruled that a state cannot tax an arm of the national government. If the federal government requires local police to devote time and effort to enforcing a national law, is that the same as taxing a state government? Why or why not?*

---

on the commerce clause that, in terms of recent legal understanding, were almost revolutionary.

Voting Rights. The Voting Rights Act of 1965 was one of the most important pieces of civil rights legislation in American history. It included a variety of provisions to guarantee African Americans and others the right to vote. (This right was widely violated in many Southern states at the time.) One provision was known as *preclearance*. State and local governments with a history of voting rights violations could not change voting procedures or district boundaries without approval by either the U.S. Attorney General or the U.S. District Court for the District of Columbia.

In June 2013, in *Shelby County v. Holder*, the Court held that the methods used to determine whether a state or local government should be subject to preclearance were obsolete.[20] The preclearance system was therefore unconstitutional until Congress could agree on new methods for determining eligibility. The chances that Congress would pass such legislation anytime soon were negligible.

The ruling was seen as a great victory for the rights of the affected states. The ruling does not prevent the national government from suing state and local governments *after* new procedures or district boundaries are put in place. Such lawsuits, however, are less effective than the preclearance system. It is also unlikely that the Trump administration will take much interest in suits of this nature.

CRITICAL THINKING

▶ *With Republicans in control of Congress and the presidency after the 2016 elections, Democrats are expected to become champions of certain states' rights. What kinds of state actions are they likely to defend against federal authority?*

3-5 **THE FISCAL SIDE OF FEDERALISM**

LO Explain what is meant by the term *fiscal federalism.*

Since the advent of cooperative federalism in the 1930s, the national government and the states have worked hand in hand to implement programs mandated by the national government. Whenever Congress passes a law that preempts a certain area, the states are, of course, obligated to comply with the requirements of that law.

As already noted, a requirement that a state provide a service or undertake some activity to meet standards specified by a federal law is called a *federal mandate.* Many federal

fiscal federalism The allocation of taxes collected by one level of government (typically the national government) to another level (typically state or local governments).

categorical grant A federal grant targeted for a specific purpose as defined by federal law.

"**Taxes,** *after all, are the dues that we pay for the privilege of membership in an organized society.*"

~ FRANKLIN D. ROOSEVELT
THIRTY-SECOND PRESIDENT
OF THE UNITED STATES
1933–1945

mandates concern civil rights or environmental protection. Recent federal mandates require the states to provide persons with disabilities access to public buildings, sidewalks, and other areas; to establish minimum water-purity and air-purity standards; and to extend Medicaid coverage to all poor children.

To help the states pay for some of the costs associated with implementing national policies, the national government gives back some of the tax dollars it collects to the states in the form of grants. As you will see, the states have come to depend on grants as an important source of revenue. When taxes are collected by one level of government (typically the national government) and spent by another level (typically state or local governments), we call the process **fiscal federalism.**

3-5a Federal Grants

Even before the Constitution was adopted, the national government granted lands to the states to finance education. Using the proceeds from the sale of these lands, the states were able to establish elementary schools and, later, *land-grant colleges.* Cash grants started in 1808, when Congress gave funds to the states to pay for the state militias. Federal grants were also made available for other purposes, such as building roads and railroads.

Only in the twentieth century, though, did federal grants become an important source of funds to the states. The major growth began in the 1960s, when the dollar amount of grants quadrupled to help pay for the Great Society programs of the Johnson administration. Grants became available for education, pollution control, conservation, recreation, highway construction and maintenance, and other purposes. There are two basic types of federal grants: categorical grants and block grants.

Categorical Grants A **categorical grant** is targeted for a specific purpose as defined by federal law. The federal government defines hundreds of categories of state and local spending. Categorical grants give the national government control over how states use the funds by imposing certain conditions. For example, a categorical grant may require that the funds be used for the purpose of repairing interstate highways and that the projects cannot pay below the local prevailing wage. Depending on the project, the government might require that an environmental impact statement be prepared.

Block Grants A block grant is given for a broad area, such as criminal justice or mental-health programs. The term *block grant* was coined in 1966 to describe a series of programs initiated by President Johnson, although a number of federal grants issued earlier in our history shared some of the characteristics of modern block grants.

A block grant gives the states more discretion over how the funds will be spent. Nonetheless, the federal government can exercise control over state decision-making through these grants by using **cross-cutting requirements,** or requirements that apply to all federal grants. Title VI of the 1964 Civil Rights Act, for example, bars racial discrimination in the use of all federal funds, regardless of their source.

3-5b Federal Grants and State Budgets

Currently, about one-fifth of state and local revenue comes from the national government. In fiscal year 2017, the federal government transferred about $694 billion to state and local governments— more than half a trillion dollars. By far, the largest transfer was for Medicaid, the health-care program for the poor. It totaled $386 billion. The federal government provided the states with about $59 billion for education. Highway grants ran about $44 billion.

When the media discuss state and local budgets, they typically refer just to the general fund budgets, which are largely supported by state and local taxes. But, in fact, state and local taxes support only slightly more than half of state and local spending. Federal funds aren't listed in general fund budgets. Further, about one-quarter of state and local spending goes to fee-for-service operations, in which governments charge for the services they provide. This spending applies to:

▶ functions such as water supplies, sewers, and other public utilities,

▶ fees charged by government-owned hospitals,

▶ airport fees, and

▶ college tuition.

Typically, these operations are also excluded from general fund budgets. Figure 3–4 summarizes state and local revenue sources.

3-5c Federalism and Economic Cycles

Unlike the federal government, state governments are supposed to balance their budgets. A practical result is that when a major recession occurs, the states are faced with severe budget problems. Because state citizens are earning and spending less, state income and sales taxes fall. During a recession, state governments may be forced either to reduce spending and lay off staff—or to raise taxes. Either choice may make the recession worse. State spending patterns tend to make economic booms more energetic and busts more painful—in a word, they are *procyclical*.

The federal government has no difficulty in spending more on welfare, unemployment compensation, and Medicaid during

> **block grant** A federal grant given to a state for a broad area, such as criminal justice or mental-health programs.
>
> **cross-cutting requirements** Requirements that apply to all federal grants.

FIGURE 3–4   STATE AND LOCAL GOVERNMENT REVENUE SOURCES

Do the sizes of any of these pie slices surprise you? If so, which ones?

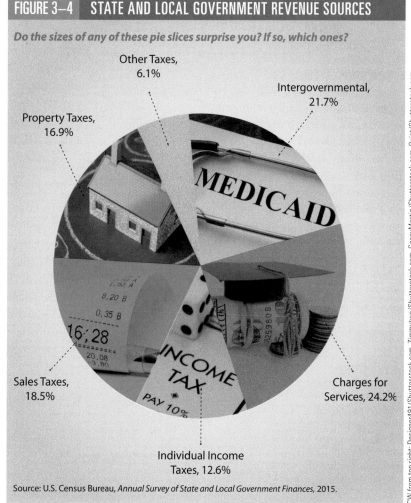

- Other Taxes, 6.1%
- Intergovernmental, 21.7%
- Property Taxes, 16.9%
- Sales Taxes, 18.5%
- Individual Income Taxes, 12.6%
- Charges for Services, 24.2%

Source: U.S. Census Bureau, *Annual Survey of State and Local Government Finances*, 2015.

CW from top right: Designer491/Shutterstock.com, Zimmytws/Shutterstock.com, CaseyMartin/Shutterstock.com, Qvist/Shutterstock.com, ChameleonsEye/Shutterstock.com

a recession. Also, the federal government often cuts tax rates in a recession to spur the economy. It makes up the difference by going further into debt. In a recession, the actions of the federal government are normally *anticyclical*.

One method of dealing with the procyclical nature of state spending is to increase federal grants to the states during a recession. Such grants were included in the February 2009 stimulus legislation championed by President Obama following the onset of the Great Recession. By the middle of 2010, however, the grants had largely dried up. From 2010 through 2012, the states laid off a substantial number of employees.

3–5d Using Federal Grants to Control the States

Grants of funds to the states from the national government are one way that the Tenth Amendment to the U.S. Constitution can be bridged. Remember that the Tenth Amendment reserves all powers not delegated to the national government to the states and to the people. You might well wonder, then, how the federal government has been able to exercise control over matters that traditionally have been under the authority of state governments. The answer involves the giving or withholding of federal grant dollars.

For example, in 1984 the national government forced the states to raise the minimum drinking age to twenty-one by threatening to withhold federal highway funds from states that did not comply. Still, Supreme Court rulings on the minimum drinking age and the Affordable Care Act, described earlier in this chapter, place some limits on the ability of the federal government to coerce the states.

The education reforms embodied in the No Child Left Behind Act relied on federal funding for their implementation as well. The states received block grants for educational purposes and, in return, had to meet federally imposed standards for testing and accountability. In time, No Child Left Behind proved to be unpopular. Conservatives disliked the degree of national control imposed by the act. Teachers complained that too much class time was devoted to "teaching to the test." Also, some of the national standards were impossibly strict. As a result, the Obama administration was able

> **competitive federalism** A model of federalism in which state and local governments compete for businesses and citizens, who in effect "vote with their feet" by moving to jurisdictions that offer a competitive advantage.

to gain substantial leverage over the states by waiving the harshest requirements in exchange for state concessions. In December 2015, No Child Left Behind was replaced by the Every Student Succeeds Act. The new legislation lets states create their own evaluation systems and standards.

3–5e The Cost of Federal Mandates

In some areas, the federal government can order states to comply with federal authority outright. An example is that states must grant persons "the equal protection of the laws," as provided by the Fourteenth Amendment to the Constitution. In addition, when federal laws require the states to implement certain programs, the states usually find that they must comply—but compliance with federal mandates can be costly. The cost of compliance has been estimated at $29 billion annually, but some believe the true figure to be much higher. Although Congress passed legislation in 1995 to curb the use of unfunded federal mandates, that legislation was more rhetoric than reality.

Even when funding is provided, it may be insufficient, resulting in an *underfunded* federal mandate. As mentioned earlier, for example, states receive block grants for educational purposes in return for meeting standards imposed by the national government. Critics argue that the national government does not supply the states with enough funds to implement these programs properly.

3–5f Competitive Federalism

The debate over federalism is sometimes reduced to a debate over taxes. Which level of government will raise taxes to pay for government programs, and which will cut services to avoid raising taxes?

The Right to Move How states answer that question gives citizens an option: they can move to a state with fewer services and lower taxes, or to a state with more services but higher taxes. Political scientist Thomas R. Dye calls this model of federalism **competitive federalism**.[21] State and local governments compete for businesses and citizens. If the state of Ohio offers tax advantages for locating a factory there, for example, a business may be more likely to build its factory in Ohio, thereby providing more jobs for Ohio residents.

If Ohio has very strict environmental regulations, however, that same business may choose not to build there, no matter how beneficial the tax advantages, because complying with the regulations would be costly. Although Ohio citizens lose the opportunity for more jobs, they may enjoy better air and water quality than citizens of the state where the new factory is ultimately built.

Advantages and Disadvantages of Competition Some observers consider such competition an advantage: Americans have several variables to consider when they choose a state in which to live. Others consider it a disadvantage: a state that offers more social services or lower taxes may experience an increase in population as people "vote with their feet" to take advantage of that state's laws. The resulting population increases can overwhelm the state's resources and force it to cut social services or raise taxes. Regulations that make it easier to build new housing may also draw in new residents. Recent studies suggest that much of the difference in population growth rates among states in recent decades may be due to differences in the cost of housing.

It appears likely, then, that the debate over how our federal system functions, as well as the battle for control between the states and the federal government, will continue. The Supreme Court, which has played umpire in this battle, is also likely to continue issuing rulings that influence the balance of power.

An elementary school teacher helps his students. Under the federal 2015 Every Student Succeeds Act, states are designing tests to determine whether schools are doing an adequate job of teaching their students. *Are such tests desirable? Why or why not?*

CRITICAL THINKING

▶ *What kinds of factors might cause you to consider moving to a different state? Are any of these factors under the control of state governments? Local governments?*

AMERICA AT ODDS | Federalism

The topic of federalism raises one of the most enduring disputes in American history—the relative power of the national government versus that of state governments. Americans have been at odds over the strength of the central government since well before the American Revolution. The issue of centralization versus decentralization has taken a number of specific forms:

- *Is it right for the national government to use its financial strength to pressure states into taking actions such as raising the drinking age by threatening to withhold subsidies—or are such pressures an abuse of the federal system?*

- *Should the national government let some states get away with legalizing recreational marijuana—or should it crack down on these states?*

- *Should the commerce clause be interpreted broadly, granting the federal government much power to regulate*

the economy—or should it be interpreted as narrowly as possible to keep the government from interfering with the rights of business owners?

- *Should the federal government have a role in setting national policies for public education—or should that be left entirely to the states?*

- *Should the federal government establish a national system for funding health care—or should that, too, be left to the states or to the private sector?*

READY TO STUDY? IN THE BOOK, YOU CAN:

☐ Review what you've read with the following chapter quiz.

☐ Check your answers in Appendix D at the back of the book.

☐ Rip out the Chapter Review Card, which includes key terms and chapter summaries.

ONLINE AT WWW.CENGAGEBRAIN.COM, YOU CAN:

☐ Watch videos to get a quick overview.

☐ Expedite your studying with Major Player readings and Focus Activities.

☐ Check your understanding with Chapter Quizzes.

FILL-IN

Learning Outcome 3–1

1. The advantages of a federal system of government in the United States include _____.

Learning Outcome 3–2

2. The constitutional basis for the implied powers of the national government is the _____ clause.

3. The Constitution's _____ clause requires each state to honor every other state's public acts, records, and judicial proceedings.

Learning Outcome 3–3

4. In *McCulloch v. Maryland*, a case decided in 1819, the United States Supreme Court established the doctrines of _____.

5. Cooperative federalism grew out of the need to solve the pressing problems caused by _____.

Learning Outcome 3–4

6. The relationship of national, state, and local levels of government in implementing massive social programs in the 1960s and 1970s is often referred to as _____ federalism.

7. A _____ is a requirement in federal legislation that pressures states and municipalities to comply with certain rules.

8. When tax revenue collected by one level of government is passed on to another level, we call this _____.

Learning Outcome 3–5

9. The national government effectively pressured the states to raise the minimum drinking age to twenty-one by _____.

10. In 2015, the Every Student Succeeds Act replaced the earlier _____ Act, which according to many people had given the national government too much control over education.

MULTIPLE CHOICE

Learning Outcome 3–1

11. In a unitary system,
    a. subdivisional governments exercise only those powers given to them by the central government.
    b. sovereign states are joined together by a central government that has only limited powers over them.
    c. there are no local or subdivisional governments.

12. There are _____ governmental units in the United States today.
    a. 51
    b. nearly 3,000
    c. almost 90,000

Learning Outcome 3–2

13. Article I, Section 8, of the U.S. Constitution enumerates twenty-seven powers that Congress may exercise. Two of these _____ powers are the power to coin money and the power to regulate interstate commerce.
    a. concurrent
    b. expressed
    c. inherent

14. The relationships among the states in our federal system of government are sometimes referred to as _____ federalism.
    a. picket-fence
    b. cooperative
    c. horizontal

Learning Outcome 3–3

15. The era of _____ federalism came to an end in the 1930s.
    a. dual
    b. new
    c. competitive

Learning Outcome 3–4

16. The welfare reform legislation passed by Congress in 1996 is an example of _____ federalism.
    a. dual
    b. cooperative
    c. new

Learning Outcome 3–5

17. Block grants
    a. are targeted for specific purposes by law.
    b. are federal grants given to a state for broad areas, such as criminal justice or mental-health programs.
    c. give the states less discretion than categorical grants over how funds will be spent.

4 | CIVIL LIBERTIES

Frantic Studio/Shutterstock.com

LEARNING OUTCOMES

After reading this chapter, you should be able to:

4-1 Define the term *civil liberties*, explain how civil liberties differ from civil rights, and state the constitutional basis for our civil liberties.

4-2 List the religious freedoms guaranteed by the First Amendment, and explain how the courts have interpreted and applied these freedoms.

4-3 Describe how freedom of speech is protected by the First Amendment, and show how the courts have implemented this freedom.

4-4 Discuss why Americans are increasingly concerned about privacy rights.

4-5 Summarize how the Constitution and the Bill of Rights protect the rights of accused persons.

After finishing this chapter, go to **PAGE 96** for **STUDY TOOLS**

AMERICA AT ODDS | Do U.S. Citizens Really Need Military-Style Rifles?

Guy J. Sagi/Shutterstock.com

The Second Amendment to the U.S. Constitution states that the people have the right "to keep and bear arms." The Supreme Court has ruled that this right is enjoyed by individuals, not just state militias. In these rulings, however, the Court has also said that the national and state governments may limit the types of weapons that individuals may possess. Should ordinary citizens have a right to own rifles based on military weapons?

This issue came to the fore after a shooter killed twenty-six children and teachers in December 2012 at the Sandy Hook Elementary School in Connecticut. The shooter used a semiautomatic rifle based on the military's M4 carbine. In June 2016, a shooter inspired by ISIS terrorists killed forty-nine people and wounded fifty-three others in an attack on a gay nightclub in Orlando, Florida. Most victims were Hispanic. The killer used a rifle based on an advanced design developed for U.S. special operations forces. Still, Americans remain at odds about whether military-style rifles and high-round magazines should be legal.

The Second Amendment Means What It Says

Those who do not believe that Congress should ban military-style rifles maintain that such weapons are fully covered by the constitutional right to bear arms. The most popular military-style rifle is the AR-15, based on the military's M16. Other rifles are based on the similar but lighter M4 of the Sig Sauer MCX used by special operations forces. These civilian rifles are semiautomatic, which means that the trigger must be pulled once for each shot. That makes these weapons different from fully automatic military weapons that can spray bullets like water from a hose. Plenty of civilian weapons other than the AR-15 are semiautomatic, including many handguns and deer rifles. Yet they were exempt from the recent proposed legislation to limit military-style arms.

From 1994 to 2004, the Federal Assault Weapons Ban outlawed such weapons. This law did not reduce the national murder rate. Although the murder rate fell throughout this period, the decline would have occurred even if these weapons had not been banned. After all, only 2.6 percent of all murders are committed using any type of rifle.

Citizens Don't Need Military-Style Rifles

Although the National Rifle Association claims that semiautomatic military-style rifles are useful for hunting, target practice, and home defense, they are not. The AR-15's .223 caliber ammunition is too light for deer hunting and useless for waterfowl. The low-power .22 rimfire cartridge—not the high-power .223—is the international standard for target competition. An ordinary 12-gauge shotgun is vastly superior for home protection, and a handgun is best for self-defense in other circumstances.

The AR-15/M16 was designed in 1957 for the U.S. Army. This rifle, like the M4 and the MCX, is optimized for one purpose only—killing the largest number of enemy possible on the battlefield. How can such a weapon be legitimate in a civilian context? Let's face it: military-style rifles are popular because they appeal to owners' dangerous fantasies of domestic chaos or insurrection. Fantasies of a zombie apocalypse are not an acceptable basis for national policy.

Where do you stand?

1. Under the Second Amendment, what limits, if any, should be placed on the kinds of weapons that ordinary civilians can own?

2. Could a citizens' militia possibly be effective against an attempt to install a dictator?

Explore this issue online:

- For a defense of the right to bear the AR-15, search on "lott wsj assault weapons" for an article by John Lott.

- Justin Peters criticizes the usefulness of the AR-15— enter "slate peters AR-15."

- Finally, Matt Steinglass attacks the fantasies of AR-15 owners at "economist gun treason Steinglass."

INTRODUCTION

The debate over military-style rifles, discussed in the chapter-opening *America at Odds* feature, is but one of many controversies concerning our civil liberties. **Civil liberties** are legal and constitutional rights that protect citizens from government actions.

Perhaps the best way to understand what civil liberties are and why they are important to Americans is to look at what might happen if we did not have them. If you were a student in China, for example, you would have to exercise some care in what you said and did. That country prohibits various kinds of speech, notably any criticism of the leading role of the Communist Party. If you criticized the government in e-mail messages to your friends or on your website, you could end up in court on charges that you had violated the law—and perhaps even go to prison.

Note that some Americans confuse *civil liberties* with *civil rights* and use the terms interchangeably. Scholars, however, make a distinction between the two. They point out that civil liberties limit government action, setting forth what the government *cannot* do. Civil rights, in contrast, specify what the government *must* do—for example, ensure equal protection under the law for all Americans.

4-1 THE CONSTITUTIONAL BASIS FOR OUR CIVIL LIBERTIES

civil liberties Individual rights protected by the Constitution against the powers of the government.

writ of *habeas corpus* An order that requires an official to bring a specified prisoner into court and explain to the judge why the person is being held in jail.

bill of attainder A legislative act that inflicts punishment on particular persons or groups without granting them the right to a trial.

***ex post facto* law** A criminal law that punishes individuals for committing an act that was legal when the act was committed.

LO Define the term *civil liberties*, explain how civil liberties differ from civil rights, and state the constitutional basis for our civil liberties.

The founders believed that the constitutions of the individual states contained ample provisions to protect citizens from government actions. Therefore, the founders did not include many references to individual civil liberties in the original version of the Constitution. Many of our liberties were added by the Bill of Rights, ratified in 1791.

Nonetheless, the original Constitution did include some safeguards to protect citizens against an overly powerful government.

4-1a Safeguards in the Original Constitution

Article I, Section 9, of the Constitution provides that the writ of *habeas corpus* (a Latin phrase that roughly means "produce the body") will be available to all citizens except in times of rebellion or national invasion. A **writ of *habeas corpus*** is an order requiring that an official bring a specified prisoner into court and explain to the judge why the prisoner is being held in jail. If the court finds that the imprisonment is unlawful, it can order the prisoner to be released. If our country did not have such a constitutional provision, political leaders could jail their opponents without giving them the opportunity to plead their cases before a judge. Without this opportunity, many opponents might conveniently be left to rot away in prison.

The Constitution also prohibits Congress and the state legislatures from passing bills of attainder. A **bill of attainder** is a legislative act that directly punishes a specifically named individual (or a group or class of individuals) without a trial. For example, no legislature can pass a law that punishes a named Hollywood celebrity for unpatriotic statements.

Finally, the Constitution prohibits Congress from passing *ex post facto* laws. The Latin term *ex post facto* roughly means "after the fact." An ***ex post facto* law** punishes individuals for committing an act that was legal when it was committed.

4-1b The Bill of Rights

As you have read, one of the contentious issues in the debate over ratification of the Constitution was the lack of protections for citizens from government actions. Although many state constitutions provided such protections, the Anti-Federalists wanted more. The promise of the addition of a bill of rights to the Constitution ensured its ratification.

The Bill of Rights was ratified by the states and became part of the Constitution on December 15, 1791. Look at the text of the Bill of Rights in Table 4–1. As you can see, the first eight amendments grant the people specific rights and liberties. The remaining two amendments reserve certain rights and powers to the people and to the states.

Basically, in a democracy, government policy tends to reflect the view of the majority. A key function of the Bill of Rights, therefore, is to protect the rights of those in the minority against the will of the majority. When

TABLE 4–1 THE BILL OF RIGHTS AND WHAT IT MEANS

Half of these amendments deal with criminal justice issues. *Why might the founders have focused on that topic?*

Amendment I.
Religion, Speech, Press, Assembly, and Petition

Congress shall make no law respecting an establishment of religion, or prohibiting the free exercise thereof; or abridging the freedom of speech, or of the press; or the right of the people peaceably to assemble, and to petition the Government for a redress of grievances.

Congress may not create an official church or enact laws limiting the freedom of religion, speech, the press, assembly, and petition. These guarantees, like the others in the Bill of Rights, are not absolute—each right may be exercised only with regard to the rights of other persons.

Amendment II.
Militia and the Right to Bear Arms

A well regulated Militia, being necessary to the security of a free State, the right of the people to keep and bear Arms, shall not be infringed.

Each state has the right to maintain a volunteer armed force. Although individuals have the right to bear arms, states and the federal government may regulate the possession and use of firearms by individuals.

Amendment III.
The Quartering of Soldiers

No Soldier shall, in time of peace be quartered in any house, without the consent of the Owner, nor in time of war, but in a manner to be prescribed by law.

Before the Revolutionary War, it had been common British practice to quarter soldiers in colonists' homes. Military troops do not have the power to take over private houses during peacetime.

Amendment IV.
Searches and Seizures

The right of the people to be secure in their persons, houses, papers, and effects, against unreasonable searches and seizures, shall not be violated, and no Warrants shall issue, but upon probable cause, supported by Oath or affirmation, and particularly describing the place to be searched, and the persons or things to be seized.

Here, the word warrant refers to a document issued by a magistrate or judge indicating the name, address, and possible offense committed. Anyone asking for a warrant, such as a police officer, must be able to convince the magistrate or judge that an offense probably has been committed.

Amendment V.
Grand Juries, Self-Incrimination, Double Jeopardy,
Due Process, and Eminent Domain

No person shall be held to answer for a capital, or otherwise infamous crime, unless on a presentment or indictment of a Grand Jury, except in cases arising in the land or naval forces, or in the Militia, when in actual service in time of War or public danger; nor shall any person be subject for the same offense to be twice put in jeopardy of life or limb; nor shall be compelled in any criminal case to be a witness against himself, nor be deprived of life, liberty, or property, without due process of law; nor shall private property be taken for public use, without just compensation.

There are two types of juries. A grand jury considers physical evidence and the testimony of witnesses and decides whether there is sufficient reason to bring a case to trial. A petit jury hears the case at trial and decides it. "For the same offense to be twice put in jeopardy of life or limb" means to be tried twice for the same crime. A person may not be tried for the

same crime twice or forced to give evidence against herself or himself. No person's right to life, liberty, or property may be taken away except by lawful means, called the due process of law. Private property taken for public purposes must be paid for by the government.

Amendment VI.
Criminal Court Procedures

In all criminal prosecutions, the accused shall enjoy the right to a speedy and public trial, by an impartial jury of the State and district wherein the crime shall have been committed, which district shall have been previously ascertained by law, and to be informed of the nature and cause of the accusation; to be confronted with the witnesses against him; to have compulsory process for obtaining witnesses in his favor, and to have the Assistance of Counsel for his defence.

Any person accused of a crime has the right to a fair and public trial by a jury in the state in which the crime took place. The charges against that person must be made clear. Any accused person has the right to a lawyer to defend him or her and to question those who testify against him or her, as well as the right to call people to speak in his or her favor at trial.

Amendment VII.
Trial by Jury in Civil Cases

In Suits at common law, where the value in controversy shall exceed twenty dollars, the right of trial by jury shall be preserved, and no fact tried by a jury, shall be otherwise re-examined in any Court of the United States, than according to the rules of the common law.

A jury trial may be requested by either party in a dispute in any case involving more than $20. If both parties agree to a trial by a judge without a jury, the right to a jury trial may be put aside.

Amendment VIII.
Bail, Cruel and Unusual Punishment

Excessive bail shall not be required, nor excessive fines imposed, nor cruel and unusual punishments inflicted.

Bail is that amount of money that a person accused of a crime may be required to deposit with the court as a guarantee that she or he will appear in court when requested. The amount of bail required or the fine imposed as punishment for a crime must be reasonable compared with the seriousness of the crime involved. Any punishment judged to be too harsh or too severe for a crime shall be prohibited.

Amendment IX.
The Rights Retained by the People

The enumeration in the Constitution, of certain rights, shall not be construed to deny or disparage others retained by the people.

Many civil rights that are not explicitly enumerated in the Constitution are still held by the people.

Amendment X.
Reserved Powers of the States

The powers not delegated to the United States by the Constitution, nor prohibited by it to the States, are reserved to the States respectively, or to the people.

Those powers not delegated by the Constitution to the federal government or expressly denied to the states belong to the states and to the people. This clause in essence allows the states to pass laws under their "police powers."

---

there is disagreement over how to interpret the Bill of Rights, the courts step in.

The United States Supreme Court, as our nation's highest court, has the final say as to how the Constitution, including the Bill of Rights, should be interpreted. The

civil liberties that you will read about in this chapter have all been shaped over time by Supreme Court decisions. For example, it is the Supreme Court that determines where freedom of speech ends and the right of society to be protected from certain forms of speech begins.

4–1c The Incorporation Principle

For many years, the courts assumed that the Bill of Rights limited only the actions of the national government, not the actions of state or local governments. In other words, if a state or local law was contrary to a basic freedom, such as the freedom of speech or the right to due process of law, the federal Bill of Rights did not come into play. The founders believed that the states, being closer to the people, would be less likely to violate their own citizens' liberties. Moreover, state constitutions, most of which contain bills of rights, protect citizens against state government actions. The United States Supreme Court upheld this view when it decided, in *Barron v. Baltimore* (1833), that the Bill of Rights did not apply to state laws.[1]

Eventually, however, the Supreme Court began to take a different view. Because the Fourteenth Amendment played a key role in this development, we look next at the provisions of that amendment.

The Right to Due Process   In 1868, three years after the end of the Civil War, the Fourteenth Amendment was added to the Constitution. The **due process clause** of this amendment requires that state governments protect their citizens' rights. (A similar requirement, binding on the federal government, was provided by the Fifth Amendment.) The due process clause reads, in part, as follows:

> No State shall . . . deprive any person of life, liberty, or property, without due process of law.

The right to **due process of law** is simply the right to be treated fairly under the legal system. That system and its officers must follow "rules of fair play" in making decisions, in determining guilt or innocence, and in punishing those who have been found guilty. Due process has two aspects—procedural and substantive.

due process clause
The constitutional guarantee, set out in the Fifth and Fourteenth Amendments, that the government will not illegally or arbitrarily deprive a person of life, liberty, or property.

due process of law
The requirement that the government use fair, reasonable, and standard procedures whenever it takes any legal action against an individual.

Procedural Due Process. *Procedural* due process requires that any governmental decision to take life, liberty, or property be made equitably. For example, the government must use "fair procedures" in determining whether a person will be subjected to punishment or have some burden imposed on him or her. Fair procedure has been interpreted as requiring that the person have at least an opportunity to object to a proposed action before an impartial, neutral decision maker (who need not be a judge).

Substantive Due Process. *Substantive* due process focuses on the content, or substance, of legislation. If a law or other governmental action limits a *fundamental right*, it will be held to violate substantive due process, unless it promotes a *compelling* or *overriding state interest*. All First Amendment rights plus the rights to interstate travel, privacy, and voting are considered fundamental. Compelling state interests could include, for example, the public's safety.

Other Liberties Incorporated   The Fourteenth Amendment also states that no state "shall make or enforce any law which shall abridge the privileges or immunities of citizens of the United States." For some time, the Supreme Court considered the "privileges and immunities" referred to in the amendment to be those conferred by state laws or constitutions, not the federal Bill of Rights.

Starting in 1925, however, the Supreme Court gradually began using the due process clause to say that states could not abridge a civil liberty that the national government could not abridge. In other words, the Court *incorporated* the protections guaranteed by the national Bill of Rights into the liberties protected under the Fourteenth Amendment. As you can see in Table 4–2, the Supreme Court was particularly active during the 1960s in broadening its interpretation of the due process clause to ensure that states and localities could not infringe on civil liberties protected by the Bill of Rights.

Today, the liberties still not incorporated include the right to a grand jury hearing. The right to refuse to quarter soldiers has been affirmed by a U.S. appeals court, but not by the Supreme Court, and so that liberty is fully guaranteed in only a few states. The right to bear arms described in the Second Amendment was incorporated only in 2010.

Who Is Covered under the Fourteenth Amendment?   The language of the due process clause refers to "persons," not citizens. The choice of words was deliberate. The authors of the amendment sought in this way to avoid questions about who was covered by the guarantee. One group of persons has only limited protection, however—noncitizens seeking to enter or remain in the United States. The government can bar noncitizens from entry into the country without raising any constitutional questions.

Noncitizens living in the United States can be deported even if their presence here is lawful. In 1903,

TABLE 4–2 INCORPORATING THE BILL OF RIGHTS INTO THE FOURTEENTH AMENDMENT

Year	Issue	Amendment Involved	Court Case
1925	Freedom of speech	I	*Gitlow v. New York*, 268 U.S. 652
1931	Freedom of the press	I	*Near v. Minnesota*, 283 U.S. 697
1932	Right to a lawyer in capital punishment cases	VI	*Powell v. Alabama*, 287 U.S. 45
1937	Freedom of assembly and right to petition	I	*De Jonge v. Oregon*, 299 U.S. 353
1940	Freedom of religion	I	*Cantwell v. Connecticut*, 310 U.S. 296
1947	Separation of church and state	I	*Everson v. Board of Education*, 330 U.S. 1
1948	Right to a public trial	VI	*In re Oliver*, 333 U.S. 257
1949	No unreasonable searches and seizures	IV	*Wolf v. Colorado*, 338 U.S. 25
1961	Exclusionary rule (See "The Rights of the Accused" section later in this chapter.)	IV	*Mapp v. Ohio*, 367 U.S. 643
1962	No cruel and unusual punishments	VIII	*Robinson v. California*, 370 U.S. 660
1963	Right to a lawyer in all criminal felony cases	VI	*Gideon v. Wainwright*, 372 U.S. 335
1964	No compulsory self-incrimination	V	*Malloy v. Hogan*, 378 U.S. 1
1965	Right to privacy	Various	*Griswold v. Connecticut*, 381 U.S. 479
1966	Right to an impartial jury	VI	*Parker v. Gladden*, 385 U.S. 363
1967	Right to a speedy trial	VI	*Klopfer v. North Carolina*, 386 U.S. 213
1969	No double jeopardy	V	*Benton v. Maryland*, 395 U.S. 784
1982	Right to refuse to quarter soldiers	III	*Engblom v. Carey*, 677 F.2d 957 (2d Cir.)
2010	Right to bear arms	II	*McDonald v. Chicago*, 561 U.S. 3025

however, the Supreme Court ruled that the government could not deport someone without a hearing that meets constitutional due process standards.[2] Still, the courts have often accepted government arguments that noncitizens cannot make constitutional claims. We discuss that issue further in this chapter's *The Rest of the World* feature.

▶ *Congress often passes laws that are so narrow in scope that only one individual or corporation is covered by the legislation. Should such laws be considered bills of attainder and thus unconstitutional? Why or why not?*

 4–2 **FREEDOM OF RELIGION**

LO List the religious freedoms guaranteed by the First Amendment, and explain how the courts have interpreted and applied these freedoms.

The First Amendment sets forth some of our most important civil liberties. Specifically, the First Amendment guarantees the freedoms of religion, speech, the press, and assembly, as well as the right to petition the government. In the pages that follow, we look closely at the first three of these freedoms and discuss how, over time, Supreme Court decisions have defined their meaning and determined their limits.

The First Amendment prohibits Congress from passing laws "respecting an establishment of religion, or prohibiting the free exercise thereof." The first part of this amendment is known as the **establishment clause.** The second part is called the **free exercise clause.**

4–2a Laws on Religion in the Colonies

That freedom of religion was the first freedom mentioned in the Bill of Rights is not surprising. After all, many colonists came to America to escape religious persecution. Nonetheless, these same colonists showed little tolerance for religious freedom within the communities they established. For example, in 1610 the Jamestown colony enacted a law requiring attendance at religious services on Sunday "both in the

establishment clause
The section of the First Amendment that prohibits Congress from passing laws "respecting an establishment of religion."

free exercise clause
The provision of the First Amendment stating that the government cannot pass laws "prohibiting the free exercise" of religion.

THE REST OF THE WORLD

Do Foreigners Have Constitutional Rights in the United States?

As we have explained, the national government has almost complete freedom to ban foreign citizens from entering this country. For example, British singer Yusuf Islam (formerly known as Cat Stevens) was banned more than a decade ago for obscure reasons. About the same time, the government banned Narendra Modi, currently the prime minister of India. In those years, Modi was chief minister (governor) of the Indian state of Gujarat. Anti-Muslim riots there had led to thousands of deaths, and the government blamed Modi for turning a blind eye to the killings.

What If You Are Already Here?

Under ordinary circumstances, persons already in the United States—legally or illegally—who are facing deportation are entitled to a hearing before an immigration judge and to representation by a lawyer, if they can afford one. Still, the courts have waived these protections under some conditions. Under the Antiterrorism and Effective Death Penalty Act of 1996, the government has the power to deport noncitizens for alleged terrorism without any court review of the deportation order, based on secret evidence that the deportee is not allowed to see. Expedited deportation is also available in cases where a migrant is arrested shortly after crossing the border.

Also, First Amendment rights to freedom of association may not apply to noncitizens. In 1999, the Court approved the deportation of a group of noncitizens associated with the Popular Front for the Liberation of Palestine (PFLP). Members of the PFLP in Israel had carried out terrorist acts, but there was no evidence of criminal acts by those arrested in the United States.[3]

President Trump's Executive Order on Immigration

President Donald Trump appears to have tested the limits of the government's power to ban entry into the United States. As one of his first acts as president, Trump issued a hastily drafted executive order banning people from seven majority-Muslim countries—and most refugees—from entering the United States. Initially, the order applied even to permanent legal residents who were out of the country temporarily, though that part of the ban was quickly lifted. On the face of it, the president would seem to have clear powers to issue such an order, given the sweeping grants of authority that Congress has given the president on immigration. Congress has also prohibited religious discrimination in immigration cases, however. In February 2017, a federal judge suspended the executive order. A replacement order was blocked as well. In June 2017, the Supreme Court temporarily reinstated the order for those with no "credible claim of a bona fide relationship with a person or entity in the United States."

CRITICAL ANALYSIS

Trump's executive order was issued without input from cabinet members or legal counsel. Would it have been more successful if he had solicited the advice of these individuals? Why or why not?

---

morning and the afternoon." Repeat offenders were subjected to particularly harsh punishments. For those who twice violated the law, for example, the punishment was a public whipping. For third-time offenders, the punishment was death.

These examples of religious laws provide a context that is helpful in understanding why, in 1802, President Thomas Jefferson—a great proponent of religious freedom and tolerance—wanted the establishment clause to be "a wall of separation between church and state." The context also helps to explain why even state leaders who supported state religions might have favored the establishment clause—to keep the national government from interfering in such state matters. After all, the First Amendment says only that *Congress* can make no law respecting an establishment of religion. It says nothing about whether the *states* can make such laws.

4-2b The Establishment Clause

The establishment clause forbids the government from establishing an official religion or church. This makes the United States different from countries that are ruled by religious governments, such as the Islamic government of Iran. It also makes us different from nations that have in the past strongly discouraged the practice of any religion at all, such as the People's Republic of China.

The Establishment Clause in Practice What does this separation of church and state mean in practice? For one thing, religion and government, though constitutionally separated in the United States, have never been enemies or strangers. The establishment clause does not prohibit government from supporting religion *in general*. Religion remains a part of public life.

Most government officials take an oath of office in the name of God, and our coins and paper currency carry the motto "In God We Trust." Clergy of different religions serve in each branch of the armed forces. Public meetings and even sessions of Congress open with prayers. (The Supreme Court endorsed such practices as recently as 2014 in *Town of Greece v. Galloway*.)[4] Indeed, the establishment clause often masks the fact that Americans are, by and large, religious and prefer that their political leaders be people of faith.

The Wall of Separation The "wall of separation" that Thomas Jefferson referred to, however, does exist and has been upheld by the Supreme Court on many occasions. An important ruling by the Supreme Court on the establishment clause came in 1947. The case involved a New Jersey law that allowed the state to pay for bus transportation of students who attended parochial schools (schools run by churches or other religious groups).

The Court stated, "No tax in any amount, large or small, can be levied to support any religious activities or institutions." Nevertheless, the Court upheld the New Jersey law because it did not aid the church *directly* but provided for the safety and benefit of the students.[5] The ruling both affirmed the importance of separating church and state and set the precedent that not *all* forms of state and federal aid to church-related schools are forbidden under the Constitution.

A full discussion of the various church-state issues that have arisen in American politics would fill volumes. Here, we examine three of these issues: prayer in the schools, the teaching of evolution versus creationism or intelligent design, and government aid to parochial schools.

The First Amendment to the Constitution mandates separation of church and state. Nonetheless, references to God are common in public life, as the phrase "In God We Trust" on this coin demonstrates.

4-2c Prayer in the Schools

Public opinion polls reveal that a substantial majority of Americans believe that public school teachers ought to be able to lead students in prayer. The Supreme Court disagrees, however.

The Regents' Prayer Case On occasion, some public schools have promoted a general sense of religion without proclaiming allegiance to any particular church or sect. Whether the states have a right to allow this was the main question presented in 1962 in *Engel v. Vitale*, also known as the "Regents' Prayer case."[6] The State Board of Regents in New York had composed a nondenominational prayer (a prayer not associated with any particular church) and urged school districts to use it in classrooms at the start of each day. The prayer read as follows:

> Almighty God, we acknowledge our dependence upon Thee, and we beg Thy blessings upon us, our parents, our teachers, and our Country.

Some parents objected to the prayer, contending that it violated the establishment clause. The Supreme Court agreed and ruled that the Regents' Prayer was unconstitutional. Speaking for the majority, Justice Hugo Black wrote that the First Amendment must at least mean "that in this country it is no part of the business of government to compose official prayers for any group of the American people to recite as a part of a religious program carried on by government."

Since the *Engel v. Vitale* ruling, the Supreme Court has continued to shore up the wall of separation between church and state in a number of decisions. For example, in a 1980 case, the Supreme Court ruled that a Kentucky law requiring that the Ten Commandments be posted in all public schools violated the establishment clause.[7] Many groups around the country opposed this ruling.

Moments of Silence and Other Issues
Another controversial issue is whether "moments of silence" in the schools are constitutional. In 1985, the Supreme Court ruled that an Alabama law authorizing a daily one-minute period of silence for meditation and voluntary prayer was unconstitutional. Because the law specifically endorsed prayer, it appeared to support religion.[8] Since then, the lower courts have generally held that a school may require a moment of silence, but only if it serves a clearly secular purpose (such as to meditate on the day's activities).[9]

Yet another issue concerns prayers said before public school sporting events, such as football games. In 2000, the Supreme Court held that student-led pregame prayer using the school's public-address system was unconstitutional.[10]

In sum, the Supreme Court has ruled that public schools, which are agencies of government, cannot sponsor religious activities. It has *not*, however, held that individuals cannot pray, when and as they choose, in schools or in any other place. Nor has it held that the schools are barred from teaching *about* religion, as opposed to engaging in religious practices.

4–2d Evolution versus Creationism

Certain religious groups have long opposed the teaching of evolution in public schools. These groups contend that evolutionary theory, a theory with overwhelming scientific support, directly counters their religious belief that human beings did not evolve but were created fully formed, as described in the biblical story of the creation. In fact, surveys have shown that up to one-third of Americans believe that humans were directly created by God rather than having evolved from other species. The Supreme Court, however, has held that state laws forbidding the teaching of evolution in the schools are unconstitutional.

For example, in a case decided in 1968, the Supreme Court held that an Arkansas law prohibiting the teaching of evolution violated the establishment clause because it imposed religious beliefs on students.[11] In 1987, the Supreme Court also held unconstitutional a Louisiana law requiring that the biblical story of the creation be taught along with evolution. The Court deemed the law unconstitutional in part because it had as its primary purpose the promotion of a particular religious belief.[12]

Evolution Versus Intelligent Design Some activists have advocated the concept of "intelligent design" as an alternative to the teaching of evolution. This concept posits that an intelligent cause, rather than an undirected process such as natural selection, lies behind the creation and development of the universe and living things. Proponents of intelligent design claim that it is a scientific theory and thus that its teaching does not violate the establishment clause in any way. Opponents contend that the "intelligent cause" is simply another term for God.

These arguments were tested in 2004 in Dover, Pennsylvania, when the local school board required ninth-grade biology classes to use a textbook that endorsed intelligent design. In November 2005, the board members who supported the requirement were voted out of office. In December, a federal district court judge ruled that intelligent design was not science, that it was inherently religious, and that the school board's actions were unconstitutional.[13]

Members of a campus Bible study group pray together. If public schools and colleges allow student clubs to use school facilities after hours, they must allow religious groups the same rights as any other organizations. *Why would that be so?*

Monkey Business Images/Shutterstock.com

"Teach the Controversy" Various groups continue their efforts to restrict the teaching of evolution. One strategy is a campaign known as "Teach the Controversy," promoted by the Discovery Institute, an antievolution group. Proponents of this campaign argue that it is only fair to present both sides of the question—that is, both evolution and other views, such as intelligent design.

Biologists, however, point out that there is no controversy within the scientific community. Evolution is a "theory" only in the sense that scientists speak of a "theory of gravity." Debate over evolution exists solely in the domains of religion and politics. If the controversy is taught at all, it should be taught in classes that deal with those topics. Indeed, the Dover ruling just mentioned dismissed the "teaching the controversy" tactic as insincere at best.

4–2e Aid to Parochial Schools

Americans have long been at odds over whether public tax dollars should be used to fund activities in parochial schools. Over the years, the courts have often had to decide whether specific types of aid do or do not violate the establishment clause. Aid to church-related schools in the form of transportation, equipment, or special educational services for disadvantaged students has been held permissible. Other forms of aid, such as funding teachers' salaries and paying for field trips, have been held unconstitutional.

The *Lemon* Test Since 1971, the Supreme Court has held that, to be constitutional, a state's school aid must meet three requirements: (1) the purpose of the financial aid must be clearly secular (not religious), (2) its primary effect must neither advance nor inhibit religion, and (3) it must avoid an "excessive government entanglement with religion." The Court first used this three-part test in *Lemon v. Kurtzman*, and hence it is often referred to as the *Lemon* **test.**[14]

In the 1971 *Lemon case*, the Court denied public aid to private and parochial schools even for the salaries of teachers of secular courses and for textbooks and instructional materials in certain secular subjects. The Court held that the establishment clause is designed to prevent three main evils: "sponsorship, financial support, and active involvement of the sovereign [the government] in religious activity."

School Voucher Programs Another contentious issue has to do with the use of school vouchers—educational certificates, provided by state governments, that students can use at any school, public or private. In

> "The purpose of separation of church and state is to keep forever from these shores the ceaseless strife that has soaked the soil of Europe in blood for centuries."
>
> ~ JAMES MADISON, DRAFTER OF THE BILL OF RIGHTS AND U.S. PRESIDENT, 1809–1817

an effort to improve their educational systems, a number of school districts have been experimenting with voucher systems. Twelve states and the District of Columbia now have limited voucher programs, under which some schoolchildren may attend private elementary or high schools using vouchers paid for by taxpayers' dollars. In six of these states, vouchers are limited to children with special needs.[15] In addition, seventeen states have scholarship tax credit programs. These provide a tax credit for contributions to scholarships for students who attend private schools.

In 2002, the United States Supreme Court ruled that a voucher program in Cleveland, Ohio, was constitutional. Under the program, the state provided up to $2,250 to low-income families, who could use the funds to send their children to either public or private schools. The Court concluded that the taxpayer-paid voucher program did not unconstitutionally entangle church and state because the funds went to parents, not to schools. The parents theoretically could use the vouchers to send their children to nonreligious private academies or charter schools, even though 95 percent used the vouchers at religious schools.[16]

Despite the 2002 Supreme Court ruling, several constitutional questions surrounding school vouchers remain unresolved. For example, some state constitutions are more explicit than the federal Constitution in denying the use of public funds for religious education. Even after the Supreme Court ruling in the Ohio case, a Florida

***Lemon* test** A three-part test enunciated by the Supreme Court in the 1971 case of *Lemon v. Kurtzman* to determine whether government aid to parochial schools is constitutional.

school voucher An educational certificate, provided by a government, that allows a student to use public funds to pay for a private or a public school chosen by the student or his or her parents.

In New York City, a Hunter College graduate stands with her parents following graduation ceremonies. She is a first-generation Syrian American. *What civil liberties protect her right to wear a head scarf at a public college?*

court ruled in 2002 that a voucher program in that state violated Florida's constitution.[17]

4-2f The Free Exercise Clause

As mentioned, the second part of the First Amendment's statement on religion consists of the free exercise clause, which forbids the passage of laws "prohibiting the free exercise of religion." This clause protects a person's right to worship or to believe as he or she wishes without government interference. No law or act of government may violate this constitutional right.

Belief and Practice Are Distinct The free exercise clause does not necessarily mean that individuals can act in any way they want on the basis of their religious beliefs. There is an important distinction between belief and practice. The Supreme Court has ruled consistently that the right to hold any *belief* is absolute. The right to *practice* one's beliefs, however, may have some limits. As the Court itself once asked, "Suppose one believed that human sacrifice were a necessary part of religious worship?"

The Supreme Court first dealt with the issue of belief versus practice in 1878 in *Reynolds v. United States*.[18] Reynolds was a member of the Latter-Day Saints (Mormons) who had two wives. Polygamy, or the practice of having more than one spouse simultaneously, was encouraged by the customs and teachings of his church at that time. Polygamy was prohibited by federal law, however. Reynolds was convicted and appealed the case, arguing that the law violated his constitutional right to freely exercise his religious beliefs. The Court did not agree. It said that to allow Reynolds to practice polygamy would make religious doctrines superior to the law. In 1890, the Latter-Day Saints issued a manifesto prohibiting new polygamist marriages.

Medical Treatment for Children Another issue under the free exercise clause is the right to refuse medical treatment. In most cases, adults have such a right. The right of parents to refuse treatment for their children, however, is much more limited. The courts have long held that a refusal by a parent to allow lifesaving treatments for a child can be considered a serious crime.

This principle also extends to vaccination. As a public health measure, states may require all children attending public schools to be vaccinated against common diseases. Typically, state law allows parents to opt out for religious reasons. Some states allow opt-outs based on philosophical beliefs as well. Such opt-outs are not required by the Constitution, however. California, Mississippi, and West Virginia allow no opt-outs except when a physician advises that a vaccination might endanger a child's health.

Vaccination has been in the news lately because of a movement against vaccination among some Americans. Although medical science is united in its support for vaccination, some parents have chosen not to have their children vaccinated. In turn, the increase in the number of unvaccinated children has left some communities open to outbreaks of diseases such as measles. As a result, several states have sought to toughen their vaccination laws.

Religious Practices and the Workplace The free exercise of religion in the workplace was bolstered by Title VII of the Civil Rights Act of 1964, which requires employers to accommodate their employees' religious practices unless such accommodation causes an employer to suffer an "undue hardship." Thus, if an employee claims that religious beliefs prevent him or her from working on a particular day of the week, such as Saturday or Sunday, the employer must try to accommodate the employee's needs if possible.

Several cases have come before lower federal courts concerning employer dress codes that contradict the religious customs of employees. In 1999, the Third Circuit Court of Appeals ruled in favor of two Muslim police officers in Newark, New Jersey, who claimed that they were required by their faith to wear beards and would not shave them to comply with the police department's grooming policy.[19] Since then, Muslims, Rastafarians, and others have refused to change their dress or grooming habits and have been successful in court. For example, in 2015, the Supreme Court ruled against Abercrombie & Fitch, a chain of clothing stores. The company had refused to hire a young Muslim woman who wore a headscarf for religious reasons.[20] "This is really easy," Justice Antonin Scalia said in announcing the decision.

Insurance for Birth Control A recent free exercise controversy involved the question of whether businesses could be required to supply health-insurance coverage for birth control measures. Such coverage was required in health-insurance plans that met the standards of the 2010 Affordable Care Act. Churches and other religious organizations that objected to contraception on principle were exempt from the requirement. In 2012, however, the government ruled that universities, hospitals, and similar organizations had to provide coverage for contraception even if they were affiliated with churches that opposed birth control.

The result was a storm of opposition from organizations such as the Roman Catholic Church, which rejects contraception. These groups argued that they were being forced to support activities to which they were morally opposed. Such a requirement was, in their opinion, a violation of their free exercise rights. An alternative view was that the churches were attempting to impose their religious values on employees not directly involved in religious activities.

President Barack Obama proposed a compromise under which church-affiliated hospitals and schools would not have to pay for the insurance coverage, but employees would still receive the benefit. This plan satisfied many schools and hospitals. It was not acceptable to the Catholic bishops, however, who filed a lawsuit aimed at overturning the requirement.

In 2014, in *Burwell v. Hobby Lobby*, the Supreme Court held that a closely held for-profit corporation could be exempted from the requirement to provide certain forms of birth control coverage if its owners objected on religious grounds.[21] The ruling was based on congressional legislation rather than the free exercise clause. It therefore left many questions unanswered.

CRITICAL THINKING

▸ *The establishment of religious chaplains in the armed forces has been justified on the basis that, without them, service members on active duty would have no access to religious services and counseling. Do you agree with this argument? Why or why not?*

 4-3 ## FREEDOM OF EXPRESSION

LO Describe how freedom of speech is protected by the First Amendment, and show how the courts have implemented this freedom.

No one in this country seems to have a problem protecting the free speech of those with whom they agree. The real challenge is protecting unpopular ideas. The protection needed is, in Justice Oliver Wendell Holmes's words, "not free thought for those who agree with us but freedom for the thought that we hate." The First Amendment is designed to protect the freedom to express *all* ideas, including those that may be unpopular. Many foreign nations do not protect unpopular ideas in the way that the United States does. Note, however, that in the United States, private organizations—such as Facebook—are not bound by the First Amendment.

> "Free speech is the whole thing, the whole ball game. Free speech is life itself."
>
> ~ SALMAN RUSHDIE,
> INDIAN-BORN BRITISH WRITER, BORN 1947

The First Amendment has been interpreted to protect more than merely spoken words. It also protects **symbolic speech**— speech involving actions

symbolic speech The expression of beliefs, opinions, or ideas through forms other than verbal speech or print. Also speech involving actions and other nonverbal expressions.

and other nonverbal expressions. Some common examples include picketing in a labor dispute or wearing a black armband in protest of a government policy. Even burning the American flag as a gesture of protest has been held to be protected by the First Amendment.

4–3a The Right to Free Speech Is Not Absolute

Although Americans have the right to free speech, not *all* speech is protected under the First Amendment. Our constitutional rights and liberties are not absolute. Rather, they are what the Supreme Court—the ultimate interpreter of the Constitution—says they are.

Although the Court has zealously safeguarded the right to free speech, at times it has imposed limits on speech in the interests of protecting other rights of Americans. These rights include security against harm to one's person or reputation, the need for public order, and the need to preserve the government. As Justice Holmes once said, even "the most stringent protection of free speech would not protect a man in falsely shouting fire in a theatre and causing a panic."[22] We look next at some of the ways that the Court has limited the right to free speech.

4–3b Subversive Speech

At times in our nation's history, various individuals have opposed our form of government. The government, in responding to these individuals, has drawn a line between legitimate criticism and the expression of ideas that may seriously harm society. Clearly, the government may pass laws against violent acts. But what about subversive or **seditious speech,** which urges resistance to lawful authority or advocates overthrowing the government?

As early as 1798, Congress took steps to curb seditious speech when it passed the Sedition Act, which made it a crime to utter "any false, scandalous, and malicious" criticism of the government. The act was considered unconstitutional by many but was never tested in the courts. Several dozen individuals were prosecuted under the Sedition Act, and some were actually convicted. In 1801, President Thomas Jefferson pardoned those sentenced under the act, and it was not renewed after it expired in 1801.

The Bad Tendency and Clear and Present Danger Tests During World War 1, Congress passed the Espionage Act of 1917, which prohibited attempts to interfere with operations of the military forces, the war effort, or the process of recruitment. A 1918 amendment to the act (also known as the Sedition Act) made it a crime to "willfully utter, print, write, or publish any disloyal . . . or abusive language about the government."

In judging whether this restriction on free speech was constitutional, the Supreme Court used several tests. The predominant test at the time was the *bad tendency test*, which held that speech could be restricted if it was likely to have harmful consequences. Using this broad test, the Court upheld the Espionage Act's restrictions on speech in several cases.[23]

The Court used a somewhat different rule in the 1919 case of *Schenck v. United States*, although the outcome was still to uphold the Espionage Act. Under the *clear and present danger test*, expression could be restricted if it would cause a dangerous condition, actual or imminent, that Congress had the power to prevent.[24]

The Imminent Lawless Action Test The current standard for evaluating the legality of speech opposing the government was established by the Supreme Court in 1969. Under the **imminent lawless action test,** speech can be forbidden only when it is "directed to inciting . . . imminent [immediate] lawless action."[25] This is a hard standard for prosecutors to meet. As a result, subversive speech receives far more protection today than it did in the past. In the wake of massive demonstrations following the inauguration of President Trump, Republican legislators in at least ten states introduced laws to curb the actions of demonstrators. All of these proposals went nowhere.

4–3c Limited Protection for Commercial Speech

Advertising, or **commercial speech,** is also protected by the First Amendment, but not as fully as regular speech. Generally, the Supreme Court has considered a restriction on commercial speech to be valid as long as the restriction

1. Seeks to implement a substantial government interest.

2. Directly advances that interest.

3. Goes no further than necessary to accomplish its objective.

seditious speech
Speech that urges resistance to lawful authority or that advocates the overthrow of a government.

imminent lawless action test The current Supreme Court doctrine for assessing the constitutionality of subversive speech. To be illegal, speech must be "directed to inciting . . . imminent lawless action."

commercial speech
Advertising statements that describe products. Commercial speech receives less protection under the First Amendment than ordinary speech.

Problems arise, though, when restrictions on commercial advertising achieve one substantial government interest yet are contrary to the interest in protecting free speech and the right of consumers to be informed. In such cases, the courts have to decide which interest takes priority.

Liquor advertising is a good illustration of this kind of conflict. In one case, Rhode Island argued that its law banning the advertising of liquor prices served the state's goal of discouraging liquor consumption (because the ban discouraged bargain hunting and thus kept liquor prices high). The Supreme Court, however, held that the ban was an unconstitutional restraint on commercial speech. The Court stated that the First Amendment "directs us to be especially skeptical of regulations that seek to keep people in the dark for what the government perceives to be their own good."[26]

4–3d Unprotected Speech

Certain types of speech receive no protection under the First Amendment. Speech has never been protected when the speech itself is part of a crime. An act of fraud, for example, often may be carried out entirely through spoken words. Accused fraudsters who attempted to defend their actions by standing on their First Amendment rights would get nowhere. Other types of unprotected speech include defamation (libel and slander) and obscenity.

Libel and Slander   No person has the right to libel or slander another. **Libel** is a published report of a falsehood that tends to injure a person's reputation or character. **Slander** is the public utterance (speaking) of a statement that holds a person up for contempt, ridicule, or hatred. To prove libel or slander, certain criteria must be met. The statements made must be untrue, must stem from an intent to do harm, and must result in actual harm.

The Supreme Court has ruled that public figures (public officials and others in the public limelight) cannot collect damages for remarks made against them unless they can prove the remarks were made with "reckless" disregard for accuracy. Generally, it is believed that because public figures have greater access to the media than ordinary persons do, they are in a better position to defend themselves against libelous or slanderous statements.

The End of Obscenity   Traditionally, obscenity was a form of expression not protected under the First Amendment. The courts, however, have found the term **obscenity** hard to define. In 1973, the Supreme Court finally came up with a three-part test in *California v. Miller*.[27] To be ruled obscene, a work must

Comedian and actor Russell Brand won a substantial libel settlement from the *Sun on Sunday*, a London newspaper. The *Sun* falsely accused Brand of cheating on his girlfriend. *Why would a celebrity such as Brand have a harder time winning such a case in the United States?*

1. excite unwholesome sexual desire under present-day community standards,

2. offensively depict prohibited sexual conduct, and

3. lack serious literary, artistic, political, or scientific value.

Under "community standards," the definition of obscenity could vary from one part of the country to another.

The *Miller* test was handed down at a time when American attitudes toward sexual expression were undergoing a revolution. A few years earlier, major literary works such as *Ulysses* by James Joyce and *Lady Chatterley's Lover* by D. H. Lawrence were illegal. By the early 1980s, however, it was possible in almost all parts of

> **libel** A published report of a falsehood that tends to injure a person's reputation or character.
>
> **slander** The public utterance (speaking) of a statement that holds a person up for contempt, ridicule, or hatred.
>
> **obscenity** Indecency or offensiveness in speech, expression, behavior, or appearance.

the country to rent pornographic videotapes that left nothing to the imagination.

The Internet was the final blow to the concept of obscenity. By the end of the twentieth century, U.S. officials no longer tried to impose obscenity restrictions on printed or visual material. Attempts by Congress in 1996 and 1998 to ban Internet obscenity that might be seen by minors were ruled unconstitutional by the Supreme Court.[28]

Remaining Restrictions on Pornography

Several types of restrictions survive. The First Amendment applies only to governments, so private, voluntary restrictions are possible. Most mainstream movie theaters, for example, will not show a film that has received a "no [child] 17 and under admitted" (NC-17) rating from the Motion Picture Association of America. In addition, the government retains the right to impose restrictions on activities that it subsidizes or media that it controls, such as the broadcast spectrum. Thus, restrictions on radio and broadcast television remain in effect.

Finally, the courts have upheld laws aimed at protecting children. Making or possessing pornographic videos or photographs of underage persons remains a serious crime, based on the argument that such depictions are acts of child abuse. Ironically, this argument demonstrates the collapse of obscenity as a legal concept—child pornography is *not* banned because it is obscene. Writings or drawings, including animation, that depict underage sexuality are tolerated because no actual children are involved.

4-3e Free Speech for Students?

America's schools and college campuses experience an ongoing tension between the guarantee of free speech and the desire to restrain speech that is offensive to others. Typically, cases involving free speech in the schools raise the following question: Where should the line between unacceptable speech and merely offensive speech be drawn? Schools at all levels—elementary schools, high schools, and colleges and universities—have grappled with this issue.

Elementary and High Schools

Generally, the courts allow elementary and middle schools wide latitude to define what students may and may not say to other students. At the high school level, the Supreme Court has allowed some restraints to be placed on the freedom of expression. For example, as you will read shortly in the discussion of freedom of the press, the Court allows school officials to exercise some censorship over high school publications. And, in a controversial 2007 case, the Court upheld a school principal's decision to suspend a high school student who unfurled a banner reading "Bong Hits 4 Jesus" at an event off the school premises. School officials maintained that the banner appeared to advocate illegal drug use in violation of school policy. Many legal commentators and scholars strongly criticized this decision.[29]

Colleges and Universities

A difficult question that many colleges and universities face today is whether the right to free speech includes the right to make hateful remarks about others based on their race, gender, or sexual orientation. Some claim that allowing people with extremist views to voice their opinions can lead to violence. In response to this question, several universities have gone so far as to institute speech codes to minimize the disturbances that hate speech might cause. Speech codes at public colleges have been ruled unconstitutional on the ground that they restrict freedom of speech.[30] Such codes continue to exist on many college campuses, however.

Actions by University Administrations. Race-based incidents on university campuses gave rise to free speech questions in 2015. At the University of Oklahoma (UO), a YouTube video showed fraternity brothers chanting a racist song. The lyrics, which proclaimed that blacks would never join the fraternity, were highly insulting to African Americans and possibly threatening as well. UO promptly closed the fraternity and expelled two students. Some observers thought that this reaction violated the students' First Amendment rights. The students in question did not contest their punishment, however—perhaps because doing so might have exposed them to further public humiliation.

Actions by Students. The First Amendment applies only to the national government and to state governments, including state university administrations. But what if the persons accused of limiting free speech are private individuals, such as students? This question is raised by

> "The only security of all is in a *free press*. . . . it is necessary, to keep the waters pure."
>
> ~ THOMAS JEFFERSON
> THIRD PRESIDENT
> OF THE UNITED STATES
> 1801–1809

the issue of **political correctness.** Typically, political correctness means criticizing others for speech that is offensive to minority group members, women, or LGBT persons. (*LGBT* stands for lesbian, gay male, bisexual, or transgender.) Conservatives—and some liberals—have claimed that freedom of speech is threatened on many campuses by political correctness. Others contend that so-called political correctness is itself a form of speech. Denunciations of political correctness were a major theme of Donald Trump's presidential campaign.

Alleged political correctness becomes much more controversial when it goes beyond words. An example is the attempt by students on some campuses to prevent speeches by persons they consider offensive. In 2014, former secretary of state Condoleezza Rice cancelled a scheduled commencement address at Rutgers University because of student protests. The students, who objected to Rice's role in the Iraq War under President George W. Bush, were subject to near-universal criticism.

A less clear-cut case was the decision by the police department of the University of California, Berkeley, to cancel an appearance by Milo Yiannopoulos, an ultra-right Internet provocateur. Yiannopoulos was famous for using the most extreme possible language to denounce liberals, minority group members, and feminists. He had also, in previous campus appearances, identified specific students by name and photograph, thus exposing them to harassment. Police cancelled the speech due to a riot by about 150 masked "anarchists," few of whom were University of California students. Those condemning these actions included many of the several thousand peaceful demonstrators who had also assembled.

4-3f Freedom of the Press

The framers of the Constitution believed that the press should be free to publish a wide range of opinions and information, and generally the free speech rights just discussed also apply to the press. The courts have placed certain restrictions on freedom of the press, however. Over the years, the Supreme Court has developed various guidelines and doctrines to use in deciding whether freedom of speech and the press can be restrained.

The Preferred-Position Doctrine   One major guideline, called the *preferred-position doctrine*, states that certain freedoms—including freedom of speech and of the press—are so essential to a democracy that they hold a preferred position. According to this doctrine, any law that limits these freedoms should be presumed unconstitutional unless the government can show that the law is absolutely necessary. The idea behind this doctrine

is that freedom of speech and the press should rarely, if ever, be diminished, because spoken and printed words are the prime tools of the democratic process.

Prior Restraint   Stopping an activity before it actually happens is known as *prior restraint*. With respect to freedom of the press, prior restraint means *censorship*, which occurs when an official removes objectionable materials from an item before it is published or broadcast. An example of censorship and prior restraint would be a court's ruling that two paragraphs in an upcoming article in the local newspaper had to be removed before the article could be published. The Supreme Court has generally ruled against prior restraint, arguing that the government cannot curb ideas before they are expressed.

In certain circumstances, however, the Court has allowed prior restraint. For example, in a 1988 case, a high school principal deleted two pages from the school newspaper just before it was printed. The pages contained stories on students' experiences with pregnancy and discussed the impact of divorce on students at the school. The Supreme Court, noting that students in school do not have exactly the same rights as adults in other settings, ruled that high school administrators can censor school publications. The Court said that school newspapers are part of the school curriculum, not a public forum. Therefore, administrators have the right to censor speech that promotes conduct inconsistent with the "shared values of a civilized social order."[31]

CRITICAL THINKING

▸ *Libel and slander are hard to prove in the United States. Should it be easier to win libel and slander suits than it is now? Why or why not?*

 4-4   THE RIGHT TO PRIVACY

LO Discuss why Americans are increasingly concerned about privacy rights.

In a dissenting opinion written in 1928, Supreme Court justice Louis Brandeis stated that the right to privacy is "the most comprehensive of rights and the right most valued by civilized men."[32] The majority of the justices on the Supreme Court at that

political correctness
Criticism or other actions taken against others for speech that is offensive to minority group members, women, or LGBT persons. (*LGBT* stands for lesbian, gay male, bisexual, or transgender.)

time did not agree. In the 1960s, however, Court opinion began to change.

In 1965, in the landmark case of *Griswold v. Connecticut*, the Supreme Court held that a right to privacy is implied by other constitutional rights guaranteed in the First, Third, Fourth, Fifth, and Ninth Amendments.[33] For example, consider the words of the Ninth Amendment: "The enumeration in the Constitution, of certain rights, shall not be construed to deny or disparage others retained by the people." In other words, just because the Constitution, including its amendments, does not specifically mention the right to privacy does not mean that this right is denied to the people.

Although Congress and the courts have acknowledged a constitutional right to privacy, the nature and scope of this right are not always clear. For example, Americans continue to debate whether the right to privacy includes the right to have an abortion or the right of terminally ill persons to commit physician-assisted suicide. Since the terrorist attacks of September 11, 2001, another pressing privacy issue has been how to monitor potential terrorists to prevent another attack without violating the privacy rights of all Americans.

Pro-life activists at the annual March for Life in Washington, D.C. The activists gather every year to mark the anniversary of *Roe v. Wade*, the Supreme Court decision that legalized abortion. *Why does abortion continue to be an explosive topic?*

4-4a The Abortion Controversy

One of the most divisive and emotionally charged issues debated today is whether the right to privacy means that women can choose to have abortions.

Abortion and Privacy In 1973, in the landmark case of *Roe v. Wade*, the Supreme Court, using the *Griswold* case as a precedent, held that the "right of privacy . . . is broad enough to encompass a woman's decision whether or not to terminate her pregnancy."[34] The right is not absolute throughout pregnancy, however. The Court also said that any state could impose certain regulations to safeguard the health of the mother after the first three months of pregnancy and, in the final stages of pregnancy, could act to protect potential life.

Since the *Roe v. Wade* decision, the Supreme Court has adopted a more conservative approach and has upheld restrictive state laws requiring counseling, waiting periods, notification of parents, and other actions prior to abortions.[35] Yet the Court has never overturned the *Roe* decision. In fact, in 1997 and again in 2000, the Supreme Court upheld laws requiring "buffer zones"

around abortion clinics to protect those entering the clinics from unwanted counseling or harassment by antiabortion groups.[36] In 2014, however, the Court ruled that a thirty-five-foot buffer zone established by Massachusetts was excessive.[37]

Partial-Birth Abortions In 2000, the Supreme Court invalidated a Nebraska statute banning "partial-birth" abortions, a procedure used during the second trimester of pregnancy.[38] Abortion rights groups contend that the procedure, known to physicians as "intact dilation and extraction," is sometimes the best way to protect the health of the mother. In any event, the government should not outlaw particular medical procedures. Antiabortion activists disagree and claim that the procedure destroys the life of a fetus that might be able to live outside the womb.

Undeterred by the fate of the Nebraska law, President George W. Bush signed the Partial-Birth Abortion Ban Act in 2003. In a close (five-to-four) and controversial 2007 decision, the Supreme Court upheld the constitutionality of the 2003 act.[39]

Many were surprised at the Court's decision on partial-birth abortion, given that the federal act banning this practice was quite similar to the Nebraska law that had been struck down by the Court in 2000, just seven years earlier. The Court became more conservative in 2006, however, when President George W. Bush

Xavier Ascanio/Shutterstock.com

appointed Justice Samuel Alito to replace Justice Sandra Day O'Connor. Dissenting from the majority opinion in the case, Justice Ruth Bader Ginsburg said that the ruling was an "alarming" departure from three decades of Supreme Court decisions on abortion.

In reality, how easy is it for women to access abortion services today? We examine that question in this chapter's *Perception vs. Reality* feature.

4-4b Do We Have the "Right to Die"?

Whether it is called euthanasia (mercy killing) or assisted suicide, it all comes down to one basic question: Do terminally ill persons have, as part of their civil liberties, a right to die and to be assisted in the process by physicians or others? Phrased another way, are state laws banning physician-assisted suicide in such circumstances unconstitutional?

In 1997, the issue came before the Supreme Court, which characterized the question as follows: Does the liberty protected by the Constitution include a right to commit suicide, which itself includes a right to assistance in doing so? The Court's clear and categorical answer to this question was no. To hold otherwise, said the Court, would be "to reverse centuries of legal doctrine and practice, and strike down the considered policy choice of almost every state."[40]

Although the Court upheld the states' rights to ban such a practice, the Court did not hold that state laws *permitting* assisted suicide were unconstitutional. In 1997, Oregon became the first state to implement such a law. Five additional states now allow the practice—California, Colorado, Montana, Vermont, and Washington. Oregon's law was upheld by the Supreme Court in 2006.[41]

4-4c Privacy and Personal Information

A major concern among Americans in recent years is that their personal information could be collected by individuals or organizations that use the data improperly. Some kinds of data have been collected and disseminated for many years. Any economically active person has a credit rating, and a poor credit rating can make it impossible to borrow money for a car or house. Recently, information technology has made it easier for businesses and other institutions to collect vast quantities of personal data. Grocery stores, for example, may collect data on every purchase you make in an effort to sell you more goods. Another looming privacy issue is the use of drones to collect information. Both governments and private parties may be tempted to use such devices as they become more widespread.

Privacy Legislation The 1960s marked the beginning of Congress's attempts to pass laws protecting the privacy rights of individuals. The 1966 Freedom of Information Act allows any person to request copies of information about her or him contained in government files. In 1974, Congress passed the Privacy Act, which restricts government disclosure of data to third parties.

The Driver's Privacy Protection Act, passed in 1994, prevents states from disclosing or selling a driver's personal information without the driver's consent.[42] In late 2000, the federal Department of Health and Human Services issued a regulation protecting the privacy of medical information. Health-care providers and insurance companies are restricted from sharing confidential information about their patients. In 2011, however, the Supreme Court struck down a Vermont law that prevented pharmacies from selling the prescription records of physicians to drug companies. The Court concluded that such limits violated free speech rights.[43]

The vast amount of information available about individuals on the Internet has led to additional attempts to safeguard privacy. In Europe, for example, courts have come up with a new doctrine aimed at protecting privacy—the "right to be forgotten." In some cases, individuals can obtain a court order requiring Google and other search engines to remove personal information from their search results. (The information is not deleted, but it becomes difficult to locate.) Most experts doubt that such a right could be extended to the United States because of our First Amendment guarantees of free speech. California, however, has adopted a new law that requires websites to let persons under the age of eighteen erase material that they have posted on the sites.

Online Harassment The Internet gives individuals a potent platform for communicating information about each other, including highly damaging information and even outright lies. The resulting online harassment has been called *cyberbullying*. Recently, several cyberbullies have been charged with crimes.

Cases of Cyberbullying. One example is the case of a Rutgers University student who committed suicide after his roommate secretly taped a sexual encounter he had with another man and then posted it online. The roommate was convicted of multiple computer-related crimes. All but one of the convictions, however, were overturned on appeal. Another example is a woman who pretended online to be a boy so as to harass one of her daughter's classmates. The young victim committed suicide. The woman's conviction was overturned on appeal, because the statute under which she was charged was inapplicable.

The Availability of Abortion

Before 1973, abortion was illegal in much of the United States. In that year, the United States Supreme Court issued its decision in *Roe v. Wade*. The outcome of this landmark case seemed to settle the abortion issue once and for all. Women had the right to terminate their pregnancies.

The Perception

The highest court in the land made it clear—women can have an abortion if they so decide, and no state laws may prevent this, at least during the first trimester of pregnancy. During the second trimester, only state laws that limit the procedure to protect the health of pregnant women are constitutional. It follows that abortion should be freely available throughout the land.

The Reality

The pro-life and pro-choice sides of the abortion debate seem to agree on one thing. In practice, *Roe v. Wade* is no longer the law of the land. From 2010 through the end of 2017, state legislatures adopted a total of 338 new laws aimed at limiting access to abortion, according to the Guttmacher Institute.

Twenty-seven states have a waiting period between required counseling and the time an abortion can be performed. Nineteen states require that counseling include statements that the medical profession considers false or unproven. Twenty-three place limits on how late in the pregnancy an abortion can be performed that are stricter than those specified in *Roe v. Wade*. Fourteen require an ultrasound before an abortion can be performed.

Other legislation is aimed at closing down abortion clinics. Twenty-one states require that abortion facilities must meet structural standards equivalent to those for surgical facilities. In some states, this requirement is easy to meet. In Texas, however, many clinics would have to move into new and expensive custom-built facilities. Four states require that clinic physicians have admitting privileges at a local hospital. The states can then rely on hospitals to refuse such privileges.

Most of these new laws violate *Roe v. Wade* and subsequent Supreme Court rulings. Supporters of abortion rights, however, have been reluctant to challenge the laws because they are afraid that the Supreme Court might narrow abortion rights further. Still, recent laws have forced abortion clinics to defend themselves in court. As a result, dozens of state laws have been overturned by the federal courts. In June 2016, the Supreme Court struck down the Texas law that set clinic structural standards and required hospital admitting privileges. Still, for all practical purposes, women today cannot get an abortion in several small-population Great Plains and Rocky Mountain states.

Blog On

For up-to-date information on state laws concerning abortion, visit the Guttmacher Institute website at www.guttmacher.org/geography/united-states.

Both of these cases raise troubling questions about whether verbal harassment may be protected by the First Amendment. While all states have laws against harassment, not all of the laws are equally effective.

Trolling and Doxxing. Some instances of Internet harassment are perpetrated by individuals whose motives go beyond personal grievances. The practice of online *trolling*, for example, is as old as the Internet itself, and it has been employed for political ends. A typical form of trolling is to post online messages designed to provoke or upset other members of the community. Such trolling can be handled by ignoring the offensive post, as in the slogan "Please don't feed the trolls." Sometimes, however, trolling becomes outright harassment. A well-known example is the "Gamergate" controversy that erupted in 2014. Persons using the Twitter hashtag Gamergate targeted women in the video game industry who had called for the development of more women-friendly games and for less misogyny in male-oriented ones. The campaign—which involved real-world as well as Internet harassment—included death, rape, and even bomb threats, and it led some of the women involved to go into hiding.

Another incident involved Milo Yiannopoulos, mentioned earlier in this chapter as the focus of a Berkeley riot. Yiannopoulos managed to get himself banned from Twitter (a rare event) because he helped organize a campaign of harassment against African American actress Leslie Jones. Yiannopoulos and others were upset that the 2016 film *Ghostbusters: Answer the Call* featured a female cast that included Jones.[44]

Another form of online harassment has become known as *doxxing*. This practice involves locating facts about a targeted individual, such as their name, address, telephone number, and even employer. This information is then disseminated widely in an attempt to encourage harassment. Doxxing has been used to attack feminists and LGBT persons, but also conservatives.

Revenge Porn. Another form of harassment is the practice of posting online sexually explicit photographs or videos of a former partner. Such postings may include the name, address, and employer of the victim. This practice, aptly dubbed *revenge porn*, can have devastating effects on the targeted person. If the photos go into wide circulation, it may be impossible to track them down and delete them.

Still, a revenge porn victim may have more legal options than a victim of cyberbullying. Thirty-four states and the District of Columbia now outlaw the act explicitly. Victims can also pursue civil lawsuits on a variety of grounds. If, as is often the case, a posted photo was taken by the victim—if it was a "selfie"—the victim may even be able to allege copyright violation. Perpetrators who took the photos themselves, however, have claimed First Amendment rights to do what they wish with the images.

4-4d Personal Privacy and National Security

Since the terrorist attacks of September 11, 2001, the news media and Congress have debated how the United States can strengthen national security while still protecting civil liberties, particularly the right to privacy.

The USA Patriot Act Several laws and programs that infringe on Americans' privacy rights were created in the wake of 9/11 in an attempt to protect the nation's security. For example, the USA Patriot Act of 2001 gave the government broad latitude to investigate people who are only vaguely associated with terrorists. Under this law, the government can access personal information on American citizens to an extent never before allowed.

The Federal Bureau of Investigation was also authorized to use "National Security Letters" to demand personal information about individuals from private companies (such as banks and phone companies). The companies supplying the information are not allowed to inform their customers about the requests. In one of the most controversial programs, the National Security Agency (NSA) was authorized to monitor certain domestic phone calls without first obtaining a warrant. When Americans learned of the NSA's actions in 2005, the ensuing public furor forced the Bush administration to obtain warrants for such activities.

National Security under President Obama
During his 2008 campaign, Obama promised to make a clean break with the policies of the Bush administration on national security. It did not take long, however, for observers to realize that the differences between the Obama and Bush administrations were more a matter of presentation than of substance. For example, Obama restated the Bush policy that suspected terrorists could be held indefinitely without trial.

Another issue was the treatment of individuals who passed national security information to the press. By 2013, the administration had brought felony charges against seven such persons under the Espionage Act of 1917. It had been almost thirty years since the government last charged anyone under the act based on leaks to the press. One of the most serious cases involved

Cyberbullying is a major problem, especially among younger people.
Why is it so hard for the law to address this issue?

Edward Snowden, who leaked secret materials from the National Security Agency.
Should Snowden be pardoned or prosecuted to the full extent of the law?

place to be searched, and the persons or things to be seized."

Cloud Computing. Another program, known as PRISM, was designed to accumulate vast quantities of data from the servers of corporations such as AOL, Apple, Facebook, Google, Skype, and others. The information included e-mails, chats, photos, and more, and was collected worldwide. In particular, the NSA considered itself free to access any data stored on a U.S. server by a foreign citizen. As a former NSA chief put it, "The Fourth Amendment is not an international treaty." This policy threatened to create major problems for American companies that offer "cloud computing" services worldwide. (In *cloud computing*, users store their information on a remote server so that they can access it from any system, anywhere.)

Private First Class Bradley Manning, who was convicted in 2013 of giving huge amounts of classified material to WikiLeaks, a website. Before conviction, Manning was held in solitary confinement under conditions some considered abusive. Manning has since chosen to become a woman and has adopted the first name of Chelsea. In January 2017, President Obama commuted Manning's sentence, and she was released in May.

The NSA Revelations   In June 2013, materials released to the press by Edward Snowden, a national security contractor, revealed that surveillance by the NSA had been more universal than most people had previously assumed. Snowden, aware of the treatment of leakers such as Manning, was in Hong Kong by the time his identity was released. Learning that the Chinese government might turn him over to the United States, he fled to Russia, where he was granted asylum.

Collecting Metadata. Under one NSA program publicized by Snowden's revelations, the agency had been collecting information about every landline phone call made in the entire United States—not the content of the call, but the time, number called, and number making the call. (Such information *about* phone calls—as opposed to actual contents of communications—has been called *metadata*.) Although this program was undertaken pursuant to a secret court-ordered search warrant, its scope seems hard to square with the text of the Fourth Amendment, which states that "no Warrants shall issue, but upon probable cause . . . and particularly describing the

Bugging Foreign Leaders. It was also revealed that the NSA had collected massive quantities of data on foreign phone calls. The agency tapped the telephones of dozens of foreign leaders, including German chancellor Angela Merkel, Brazil's president Dilma Rousseff, and dozens of others. It bugged the offices of European Union negotiators in advance of trade talks with the United States. Other surveillance also seemed to be aimed more at gaining U.S. economic advantage than at combating terrorism. These revelations created serious diplomatic problems for the U.S. government.

The USA Freedom Act   In June 2015, several key provisions of the USA Patriot Act expired. Debate in Congress on whether to renew the provisions was fierce. In an unusual coalition, Republican libertarians united with left-leaning Democrats in an attempt to place limits on the NSA's activities. The result was the USA Freedom Act.

The new act reauthorized most of the provisions of the USA Patriot Act. Still, it also sought to control the NSA's collection of metadata on domestic phone calls. Further, it attempted to shine some light on the Foreign Intelligence Surveillance Court (FISC). This secret court is responsible for authorizing searches by the NSA and other intelligence agencies. The FISC must now release justifications for key rulings. A new panel is to review search requests and challenge them if necessary. Civil liberties advocates argued that the new legislation would have little practical effect—massive data sweeps would continue under the authority of other laws.

▶ *Could the government's current policies on screening airline passengers be considered a violation of privacy rights? Why or why not?*

4–5 THE RIGHTS OF THE ACCUSED

LO Summarize how the Constitution and the Bill of Rights protect the rights of accused persons.

The United States has one of the highest murder rates in the industrialized world. It is therefore not surprising that many Americans have extremely strong opinions about the rights of persons accused of criminal offenses. Indeed, some Americans complain that criminal defendants have too many rights.

Why do criminal suspects have rights? The answer is that all persons are entitled to the protections afforded by the Bill of Rights. If criminal suspects were deprived of their basic constitutional liberties, all people would suffer the consequences, because there is nothing to stop the government from accusing anyone of being a criminal. In a criminal case, a state official (such as the district attorney, or D.A.) prosecutes the defendant, and the state has immense resources that it can bring to bear against the accused person. By protecting the rights of accused persons, the Constitution helps to prevent the arbitrary use of power by the government.

4–5a The Rights of Criminal Defendants

The basic rights, or constitutional safeguards, provided for criminal defendants are set forth in the Bill of Rights. These safeguards include the following:

▶ The Fourth Amendment protection from unreasonable searches and seizures.

▶ The Fourth Amendment requirement that no warrant for a search or an arrest be issued without **probable cause**—cause for believing that there is a substantial likelihood that a person has committed or is about to commit a crime.

▶ The Fifth Amendment requirement that no one be deprived of "life, liberty, or property, without due process of law." As discussed earlier in this chapter, this requirement is also included in the Fourteenth Amendment, which protects persons against actions by state governments.

▶ The Fifth Amendment prohibition against **double jeopardy**—being tried twice for the same criminal offense.

▶ The Fifth Amendment provision that no person can be required to be a witness against (incriminate) himself or herself. This is often referred to as the constitutional protection against **self-incrimination.** It is the basis for a criminal suspect's "right to remain silent" in criminal proceedings.

▶ The Sixth Amendment guarantees of a speedy trial, a trial by jury, a public trial, and the right to confront witnesses.

▶ The Sixth Amendment guarantee of the right to counsel at various stages in some criminal proceedings. The right to counsel was strengthened in 1963 in *Gideon v. Wainwright.*[45] The Supreme Court held that if a person is accused of a felony and cannot afford an attorney, an attorney must be made available to the accused person at the government's expense.

▶ The Eighth Amendment prohibitions against excessive bail and fines and against cruel and unusual punishments. Should the death penalty be considered a cruel and unusual punishment? We discuss that question in this chapter's *Join the Debate* feature.

4–5b The Exclusionary Rule

Any evidence obtained in violation of the constitutional rights spelled out in the Fourth Amendment normally is not admissible at trial. This rule, which has been applied in the federal courts since at least 1914, is known as the **exclusionary rule.** The rule was extended to state court proceedings in 1961.[46]

The reasoning behind the exclusionary rule is that it forces law enforcement personnel to gather evidence properly. If they do not, they will be unable to introduce the evidence at trial to convince the jury that the defendant is guilty.

probable cause Cause for believing that there is a substantial likelihood that a person has committed or is about to commit a crime.

double jeopardy The prosecution of a person twice for the same criminal offense. Prohibited by the Fifth Amendment in all but a few circumstances.

self-incrimination Providing damaging information or testimony against oneself in court.

exclusionary rule A criminal procedural rule stating that illegally obtained evidence is not admissible in court.

Is the Death Penalty a Cruel and Unusual Punishment?

The Eighth Amendment to the U.S. Constitution explicitly states that the government cannot inflict "cruel and unusual punishments." But what exactly is considered "cruel and unusual"? What about the death penalty, also called capital punishment?

Criminals have been executed in America since the earliest days of the republic. In addition to murder, a variety of crimes have been punished by death. In the 1700s, for example, citizens were executed for robbery, forgery, and illegally cutting down trees.

No state executes people for such crimes today. Furthermore, although a majority of Americans continue to support the death penalty for crimes such as murder, fewer states are executing people at all. Nineteen states—most recently, Delaware—and the District of Columbia have abolished the death penalty. The death penalty has also been suspended officially in eight states and unofficially in eight more. Pharmaceutical companies have refused to sell to the states the drugs that are necessary for executions by lethal injection. Only twenty persons

were executed in the United States in 2016, the lowest number in twenty five years. Do these developments suggest that in our modern world the death penalty itself is seen as cruel and unusual, and therefore a violation of the Eighth Amendment?

An Eye for an Eye Makes the Whole World Blind

Some argue that the death penalty is inappropriate even for someone who has committed murder. Violence and death may always be with us, but the law should not encourage violent sentiments. Already in 1764, the Italian jurist Cesare Beccaria asserted that "the death penalty cannot be useful, because of the example of barbarity it gives men."

Face it—capital punishment is barbaric whether it is carried out by a firing squad, an electric chair, a gas chamber, lethal injection, or hanging. Nations other than the United States that frequently employ capital punishment are not ones that we would seek to emulate: they include China, Iran, North Korea, and Saudi Arabia. Almost all of our allies have abolished the practice.

There Is Nothing Cruel and Unusual about Executing a Murderer

Strangely enough, some who are against capital punishment have argued that life in prison without parole is crueler than death. Prisoners are confined in an environment of violence where they are treated like animals, and the suffering goes on for decades. If you think about it, this is an argument that the death sentence can be merciful.

In any event, capital punishment is not cruel and unusual as meant by the Eighth Amendment. Indeed, the current method of execution used in most states—lethal injection—appears quite civilized compared with methods of execution used in England back in the 1700s, which included drawing and quartering and burning at the stake. Practices such as these are what the founders sought to ban.

Critical Analysis

Can there be a humane method of extinguishing someone's life? Why or why not?

In a 2014 landmark case, the Supreme Court brought the exclusionary rule into the modern age. The Court held unanimously that searching the digital contents of a cell phone during an arrest is unconstitutional unless law enforcement personnel have a search warrant. Chief Justice John Roberts wrote: "Modern cell phones are not just another technological convenience. With all they contain and all they may reveal, they hold for many Americans 'the privacies of life.' The fact that technology now allows an individual to carry such information in his

hand does not make the information any less worthy of the protection for which the Founders fought."[47]

4–5c The *Miranda* Warnings

In the 1950s and 1960s, one of the questions facing the courts was not whether suspects had constitutional rights—that was not in doubt—but how and when those rights could be exercised. For example, could the right to remain silent (under the Fifth Amendment's prohibition against self-incrimination) be exercised during pretrial interrogation proceedings or only during the trial? Were confessions obtained from suspects admissible in court if the suspects had not been advised of their right to remain silent and other constitutional rights?

To clarify these issues, in 1966 the Supreme Court issued a landmark decision in *Miranda v. Arizona*.[48] In that case, the Court enunciated the *Miranda* **warnings** that are now familiar to almost all Americans:

> Prior to any questioning, the person must be warned that he has a right to remain silent, that any statement he does make may be used against him, and that he has a right to the presence of an attorney, either retained or appointed.

A protester is arrested in New York City for blocking Seventh Avenue. He was part of a 2016 demonstration against police shootings of black men. *Is it appropriate for cities to ban protesters from marching in the streets without a parade permit?*

a katz/Shutterstock.com

The Erosion of *Miranda* As part of a continuing attempt to balance the rights of accused persons against the rights of society, the Supreme Court has made a number of exceptions to the *Miranda* ruling. In an important 1991 decision, the Court stated that a suspect's conviction will not be automatically overturned if the suspect was coerced into making a confession. If the other evidence admitted at trial is strong enough to justify the conviction without the confession, then the fact that the confession was obtained illegally can be, in effect, ignored.[49] In 2011, however, the Court ruled that because children are more susceptible to pressure than adults, police officers must take extra care in ensuring the *Miranda* rights of child suspects.[50]

Recording Confessions *Miranda* may eventually become obsolete regardless of any decisions made in the courts. A relatively new trend in law enforcement has been for agencies to digitally record interrogations and confessions. Thomas P. Sullivan, a former U.S. attorney in Chicago, and his staff interviewed personnel in more than 230 law enforcement agencies in thirty-eight states that record interviews of suspects who are in custody. Sullivan found that nearly all police officers said the procedure saved time and money, created valuable evidence to use in court, and made it more difficult for defense attorneys to claim that their clients had been illegally coerced.[51] Some scholars have suggested that recording all custodial interrogations would satisfy the Fifth Amendment's prohibition against coercion and in the process render the *Miranda* warnings unnecessary.

> **Miranda warnings**
> A series of statements informing criminal suspects, on their arrest, of their constitutional rights, such as the right to remain silent and the right to counsel. Required by the Supreme Court's 1966 decision in *Miranda v. Arizona*.

CRITICAL THINKING

▶ *In many states, public defenders—court-appointed attorneys—suffer from low pay and excessive workloads. Why might this be so?*

AMERICA AT ODDS | Civil Liberties

Civil liberties represent a contentious topic, and Americans are at odds over many civil liberties issues. Almost all Americans claim to believe in individual rights, but how should this freedom be defined? Often, one right appears to interfere with another. Some of the resulting disputes include the following:

- *Should the First Amendment's establishment clause be interpreted strictly, so that no one's rights are infringed on by government sponsorship of religion—or should it be interpreted loosely, to recognize that the United States is a very religious country?*

- *What kinds of religious practices should be allowed under the free exercise clause? For example, should religious groups that limit or ban participation by gay men and lesbians receive the same government benefits as any other group—or should they be penalized for discrimination?*

- *Should advertising receive the same free speech rights as any other kind of speech—or should advertisers be held accountable for making false claims?*

- *Has the government gone too far in restricting liberties in an attempt to combat terrorism—or are the restrictions trivial compared with the benefits?*

- *Consider the most intense controversy of all: Should women have a privacy right to terminate a pregnancy for any reason—or should abortion be a crime?*

STUDY TOOLS 4

READY TO STUDY? IN THE BOOK, YOU CAN:

- ☐ Review what you've read with the following chapter quiz.
- ☐ Check your answers in Appendix D at the back of the book.
- ☐ Rip out the Chapter Review Card, which includes key terms and chapter summaries.

ONLINE AT WWW.CENGAGEBRAIN.COM, YOU CAN:

- ☐ Watch videos to get a quick overview.
- ☐ Expedite your studying with Major Player readings and Focus Activities.
- ☐ Check your understanding with Chapter Quizzes.

1. The _____ clause of the Fourteenth Amendment to the U.S. Constitution guarantees that state governments will not arbitrarily deprive any person of life, liberty, or property.

Learning Outcome 4–2

2. The *Lemon* test, enunciated by the Supreme Court in 1971 to determine whether government aid to parochial schools is constitutional, states that the aid must _____.

Learning Outcome 4–3

3. The current Supreme Court standard for assessing the constitutionality of _____ is the imminent lawless action test.

4. _____ is a published report of a falsehood that tends to injure a person's reputation or character.

Learning Outcome 4–4

5. Under the USA Patriot Act of 2001, the FBI is authorized to use _____ to demand personal information about individuals from private companies, such as banks and phone companies.

6. In _____, the Supreme Court held that the "right of privacy . . . is broad enough to encompass a woman's decision whether or not to terminate her pregnancy."

Learning Outcome 4–5

7. The _____ Amendment includes protection from unreasonable searches and seizures.

8. Upon arrest, suspects must be advised of their constitutional rights through _____.

MULTIPLE CHOICE

Learning Outcome 4–1

9. A/An _____ is an order requiring that an official bring a specified prisoner into court and explain to the judge why the prisoner is being held.
   a. *ex post facto* law
   b. writ of *habeas corpus*
   c. bill of attainder

10. The Supreme Court has used the incorporation principle to
    a. extend First Amendment protections to corporations.
    b. require state governments to observe protections listed in the national Bill of Rights.
    c. guarantee all citizens the right to vote.

Learning Outcome 4–2

11. The Supreme Court has ruled that public schools
    a. cannot sponsor religious activities.
    b. are allowed to determine for themselves the number of religious exercises they will sponsor.
    c. are barred from teaching about religion.

Learning Outcome 4–3

12. The Supreme Court's _____ doctrine states that certain freedoms are so essential that any law limiting these freedoms should be presumed to be unconstitutional unless the government can show that it is absolutely necessary.
    a. prior-restraint
    b. due-process
    c. preferred position

Learning Outcome 4–4

13. The Supreme Court, in *Griswold v. Connecticut* (1965), held that a right to privacy is implied by other constitutional rights guaranteed in the
    a. Magna Carta.
    b. First, Third, Fourth, Fifth, and Ninth Amendments.
    c. Declaration of Independence.

Learning Outcome 4–5

14. The Fifth Amendment
    a. includes a protection against self-incrimination.
    b. guarantees a speedy trial and a trial by jury.
    c. guarantees the right to counsel at various stages in some criminal proceedings.

5 | CIVIL RIGHTS

Erik McGregor/Pacific Press/LightRocket/Getty Images

LEARNING OUTCOMES

After reading this chapter, you should be able to:

5–1 Explain the constitutional basis for our civil rights and for laws prohibiting discrimination.

5–2 Discuss the reasons for the civil rights movement and the changes it caused in American politics and government.

5–3 Describe the political and economic achievements of women in this country over time, and identify some obstacles to equality that women continue to face.

5–4 Summarize the struggles for equality that other groups in America have experienced.

5–5 Explain what affirmative action is and why it has been so controversial.

After finishing this chapter, go to **PAGE 120** for **STUDY TOOLS**

AMERICA AT ODDS

Do the Police Use Excessive Force against African Americans?

Scott Olson/Getty Images News/Getty Images

In the years since 2015, Americans have been confronted with a major issue—police relations with minority communities. Above all, the question has been whether law enforcement officers have employed excessive force against African Americans—especially young men. Incidents in which unarmed black men were killed during interactions with police have led to riots in cities as varied as Ferguson, Missouri; Baltimore, Maryland; and Charlotte, North Carolina. In addition, protests and expressions of concern have taken place across the nation.

Another issue: police regularly subject black drivers and pedestrians, especially young men, to investigatory stops—stops made without evidence of a crime. African Americans refer to these stops as the "crime of driving while black." Whites, including white males, almost never experience investigatory stops. Of course, the more often African Americans are stopped, the more likely it is that an incident will turn out badly. Is police racism, then, a serious problem in this country?

The Police Are Just Trying to Do Their Job

Those who defend the police say racism, while it may exist in some forces, is not the whole story. After all, many of the officers involved in recent incidents—such as those implicated in the death of Freddie Gray while in custody in Baltimore—are themselves African American.

There are other reasons why men of color—black and Latino—are arrested more frequently than whites. Through no fault of their own, many young men in black and Latino neighborhoods grow up in an environment that seems designed to push them toward a life of crime. Finding a job seems impossible. Criminals, in contrast, receive respect and money. And it is a fact that African Americans are far more likely to commit many kinds of crime than white Americans.

Furthermore, police advocates contend that demonstrations and activism make it harder for police officers to do their jobs. Police may pull back and make fewer arrests if they fear that the community will resist rather than support them. In Baltimore, murder rates are 150 percent of what they were before the Freddie Gray incident.

The Police Have Created the Problem, Not the Protesters

African Americans say they have good reasons to be afraid of the police. Consider the statistics. The Propublica website calculates that black teens are twenty-one times more likely than white teens to be shot and killed by police. Consider, too, that most complaints about police brutality are never investigated. Even when a complaint is investigated, only rarely is the officer convicted, particularly when a minority male is the alleged victim. And when there is a conviction, the disciplinary action is often trivial.

It is a long-standing truism that the police cannot combat crime all by themselves. They need the cooperation of the local community if they are to be effective. Victims must be prepared to report crimes to the authorities. Witnesses must be willing to come forward and talk. If members of an impoverished African American or Latino community are afraid that any interaction with the police can have disastrous consequences, they will avoid the police at all costs. And in fact, the police are seen as an army of occupation in many neighborhoods. Such a force can only breed resentment, not solve crimes.

Where do you stand?

1. Do you think that having officers wear cameras to record interactions with the public would be a good solution? Why or why not?

2. There is a disparity in drug arrests among racial groups. Will that gap be reduced in states that have legalized recreational marijuana? Why or why not?

Explore this issue online:

- Former FBI director James Comey discusses police-community relations at "comey georgetown university."

- For a description of investigatory stops, see an article by Charles Epp and Steven Maynard-Moody at "how to rebuild trust epp moody."

INTRODUCTION

As noted earlier, people sometimes confuse civil rights with civil liberties. Generally, though, the term **civil rights** refers to the rights of all Americans to equal treatment under the law, as provided by the Fourteenth Amendment.

As you will read in this chapter, the struggle of various groups in American society to obtain equal treatment has been a long one, and it continues. African Americans make up one such group, and we discussed an issue that concerns them in this chapter's opening *America at Odds* feature.

In a sense, the history of civil rights in the United States is a history of discrimination against various groups. Discrimination against women, African Americans, and Native Americans dates back to the early years of this nation. More recently, other groups, including persons with disabilities and the LGBT community, have struggled for equal treatment under the law. This chapter discusses each of these groups. Inevitably, though, a single short chapter must omit discussion of some groups that have experienced discrimination. Two such groups are American Muslims and older Americans.

Central to any discussion of civil rights is the interpretation of the equal protection clause of the Fourteenth Amendment to the Constitution. For that reason, we look first at that clause.

5-1 THE EQUAL PROTECTION CLAUSE

LO Explain the constitutional basis for our civil rights and for laws prohibiting discrimination.

You read about the due process clause of the Fourteenth Amendment earlier in this text. Equal in importance to the due process clause is the **equal protection clause** in Section 1 of that amendment, which reads as follows: "No State shall . . . deny to any person within its jurisdiction the equal protection of the laws." Section 5 of the amendment provides a legal basis for federal civil rights legislation: "The Congress shall have power to enforce, by appropriate legislation, the provisions of this article."

The equal protection clause has been interpreted by the courts, and especially the United States Supreme Court, to mean that states must treat all persons equally and may not discriminate *unreasonably* against a particular group or class of individuals. The task of distinguishing between reasonable and unreasonable discrimination is difficult. Generally, in deciding this question, the Supreme Court balances the constitutional rights of individuals to equal protection against government interests in protecting the safety and welfare of citizens.

Over time, the Court has developed various tests, or standards, for determining whether the equal protection clause has been violated. These standards are strict scrutiny, intermediate scrutiny, and ordinary scrutiny (the rational basis test).

5-1a Strict Scrutiny

If a law or action prevents some group of persons from exercising a **fundamental right** (such as one of our First Amendment rights), the law or action will be subject to the **strict scrutiny standard.** Under this standard, the law or action must be necessary to promote a *compelling state interest* and must be narrowly tailored to meet that interest. A law based on a **suspect classification,** such as race, is also subject to strict scrutiny by the courts, meaning that the law must be justified by a compelling state interest.

---

civil rights The rights of all Americans to equal treatment under the law, as provided by the Fourteenth Amendment to the Constitution.

equal protection clause Section 1 of the Fourteenth Amendment, which says that no state shall "deny to any person within its jurisdiction the equal protection of the laws."

fundamental right A basic right of all Americans, such as First Amendment rights. Any law or action that prevents some group of persons from exercising a fundamental right is subject to the *strict scrutiny standard.*

strict scrutiny standard A standard under which a law or action must be necessary to promote a compelling state interest and must be narrowly tailored to meet that interest.

suspect classification A classification, such as race, that provides the basis for a discriminatory law. Any law based on a suspect classification is subject to strict scrutiny by the courts, meaning that the law must be justified by a compelling state interest.

All Americans are entitled to *equal treatment under the law*, as provided by the Fourteenth Amendment.

5-1b Intermediate Scrutiny

Because the Supreme Court had difficulty deciding how to judge cases in which men and women were treated differently, another test was developed—the *intermediate scrutiny standard*. Under this standard, also known as *exacting scrutiny*, laws based on gender classifications are permissible if they are "substantially related to the achievement of an important governmental objective."

For example, a law punishing males but not females for statutory rape (sex with an underage person) has been ruled valid by the courts. The reasoning is that there is an important governmental interest in preventing teenage pregnancy in those circumstances, and almost all of the harmful consequences of teenage pregnancies fall on young females.[1] A law prohibiting the sale of beer to males under twenty-one years of age and to females under eighteen years would not be valid, however.[2]

Generally, since the 1970s, the Supreme Court has scrutinized gender classifications closely and has declared many gender-based laws unconstitutional. In 1979, the Court held that a state law allowing wives to obtain alimony judgments against husbands but preventing husbands from receiving alimony from wives violated the equal protection clause.[3] In 1982, the Court declared that Mississippi's policy of excluding males from the School of Nursing at Mississippi University for Women was unconstitutional.[4]

5-1c The Rational Basis Test (Ordinary Scrutiny)

A third test used to decide whether a discriminatory law violates the equal protection clause is the **rational basis test.** This test is employed only when there is no classification—such as race or gender—that would require a higher level of scrutiny. When applying this test to a law that classifies or treats people or groups differently, the courts ask whether the discrimination is rational. In other words, is it a reasonable way to achieve a legitimate government objective? Few laws tested under the rational basis test—or the *ordinary scrutiny standard*, as it is also called—are found invalid, because few laws are truly unreasonable.

A municipal ordinance that prohibits certain vendors from selling their wares in a particular area of the

Increasingly, women are filling traditionally male jobs, such as police officer. *What benefits can a police force obtain by hiring more women officers?*

John Roman Images/Shutterstock.com

city, for example, will be upheld if the city can meet this rational basis test. The rational basis for the ordinance might be the city's legitimate interest in reducing traffic congestion in that particular area.

CRITICAL THINKING

▸ *When evaluating cases of discrimination against gay men or lesbians, some judges have employed the rational basis test, while others have applied intermediate scrutiny. Which standard do you consider appropriate, and why?*

5-2 AFRICAN AMERICANS

> **LO** Discuss the reasons for the civil rights movement and the changes it caused in American politics and government.

The equal protection clause was originally intended to protect the newly freed slaves after the Civil War (1861–1865). In the early years after the war, the U.S. government made an effort to protect the rights of African Americans living in the states of the former Confederacy. The Thirteenth Amendment (which granted freedom to the slaves), the Fourteenth Amendment (which

> **rational basis test** A test (also known as the *ordinary scrutiny standard*) used by the Supreme Court to decide whether a discriminatory law violates the equal protection clause of the Constitution. It is used only when there is no classification—such as race or gender—that would require a higher level of scrutiny.

guaranteed equal protection under the law), and the Fifteenth Amendment (which stated that voting rights could not be abridged on account of race) were part of that effort.

By the late 1880s, however, southern legislatures had begun to pass a series of *segregation* laws—laws that separated the white community from the black community. Such laws were commonly called "Jim Crow" laws (from a song that was popular in minstrel shows that caricatured African Americans). Some of the most common Jim Crow laws called for racial segregation in the use of public facilities, such as schools, railroads, and, later, buses. These laws were also applied to housing, restaurants, hotels, and many other facilities.

5–2a Separate But Equal

In 1892, a group of Louisiana citizens decided to challenge a state law that required railroads to provide separate railway cars for African Americans. A man named Homer Plessy, who was seven-eighths European and one-eighth African, boarded a train in New Orleans and sat in the railway car reserved for whites. When Plessy refused to move at the request of the conductor, he was arrested for breaking the law.

Four years later, in 1896, the Supreme Court provided a constitutional basis for segregation laws. In *Plessy v. Ferguson*,[5] the Court held that the law did not violate the equal protection clause if *separate* facilities for blacks were *equal* to those for whites.

The lone dissenter, Justice John Marshall Harlan, disagreed: "Our Constitution is colorblind, and neither knows nor tolerates classes among citizens." The majority opinion, however, established the **separate-but-equal doctrine,** which was used to justify segregation in many areas of American life for nearly sixty years. Separate facilities for African Americans, when they were provided at all, were in practice almost never truly equal.

5–2b Violence and Vote Suppression

Segregation was far from the only problem faced by African Americans in the years following the abolition of slavery. Perhaps the most important was denial of the right to vote.

separate-but-equal doctrine A Supreme Court doctrine holding that the equal protection clause of the Fourteenth Amendment did not forbid racial segregation as long as the facilities for blacks were equal to those for whites.

Loss of the Franchise The Fifteenth Amendment explicitly extended the *franchise* (the right to vote) to African Americans.

For several decades following the Civil War, black men (but not yet women) were in fact able to vote throughout much of the former Confederacy. In the 1880s and 1890s, however, Southern leaders launched major efforts to disenfranchise black voters. They used a number of techniques to accomplish this goal, including the following:

▶ *Literacy tests*, which African Americans were guaranteed to fail.

▶ The *poll tax*, a tax on voting, which disenfranchised poor whites as well as blacks.

▶ The *grandfather clause*, which effectively limited voting to those whose ancestors could vote before the Civil War.

▶ The *white primary*, which prevented African Americans from voting in Democratic primary elections.

Social Control through Violence These restrictive laws were backed up by the threat of violence directed at African Americans who were brave enough to try to vote. The *Ku Klux Klan* was famous for its use of force to keep black citizens "in their place," but white violence was not limited to Klan members. The threat of *lynching*—execution and even torture at the hands of a mob—was employed to keep African Americans from voting. Violence and economic coercion were also used to impose an elaborate code of conduct on African Americans. They were expected to behave humbly toward whites.

5–2c The *Brown* Decisions and School Integration

In the late 1930s and the 1940s, the Supreme Court gradually moved away from the separate-but-equal doctrine discussed earlier. The major breakthrough, however, did not come until 1954, in a case involving an African American girl who lived in Topeka, Kansas.

In the 1950s, Topeka's schools, like those in many cities, were segregated. Mr. and Mrs. Oliver Brown wanted their daughter, Linda Carol Brown, to attend a white school a few blocks from their home instead of an all-black school that was twenty-one blocks away. With the help of lawyers from the National Association for the Advancement of Colored People (NAACP), Linda's parents sued the board of education to allow their daughter to attend the nearby school. (NAACP is always pronounced as "N-double-A-C-P.")

In 1954, in *Brown v. Board of Education of Topeka*,[6] the Supreme Court reversed *Plessy v. Ferguson*. The Court unanimously held that segregation by race in public education is unconstitutional. Chief Justice Earl Warren wrote as follows:

> Does segregation of children in public schools solely on the basis of race, even though the physical facilities and other "tangible" factors may be equal, deprive the children of the minority group of equal educational opportunities? We believe that it does. . . . [Segregation generates in children] a feeling of inferiority as to their status in the community that may affect their hearts and minds in a way unlikely ever to be undone. . . . We conclude that in the field of public education the doctrine of "separate but equal" has no place. Separate educational facilities are inherently unequal.

In 1955, in *Brown v. Board of Education*[7] (sometimes called *Brown II*), the Supreme Court ordered desegregation to begin "with all deliberate speed," an ambiguous phrase that could be (and was) interpreted in a variety of ways.

Reactions to School Integration   The Supreme Court ruling did not go unchallenged. Bureaucratic loopholes were used to delay desegregation. Another reaction was "white flight." As white parents sent their children to newly established private schools, some formerly white-only public schools became 100 percent black. In Arkansas, Governor Orval Faubus used the state's National Guard to block the integration of Central High School in Little Rock in 1957. A federal court demanded that the troops be withdrawn. Only after President Dwight D. Eisenhower federalized the Arkansas National Guard and sent in additional troops did Central High finally become integrated.

By 1970, *de jure* **segregation**—segregation that is established by law—had been abolished by school systems. But that meant only that no public school could legally identify itself as being reserved for all whites or all blacks. It did not mean the end of *de facto* **segregation**—segregation that is not imposed by law but is produced by circumstances, such as neighborhoods populated mostly by African Americans. Attempts to overcome *de facto* segregation have included redrawing school district lines, reassigning pupils, and busing.

Busing   As it applies to civil rights, busing is the transporting of students by bus to schools physically outside their neighborhoods in an effort to achieve racially desegregated schools. The Supreme Court first endorsed busing in 1971 in a case involving the school system in Charlotte, North Carolina.[8] Nevertheless, busing was unpopular with many groups from its inception. By the mid-1970s, the courts had begun to retreat

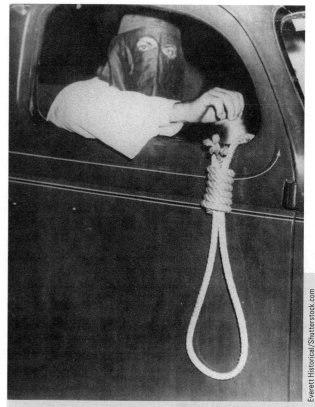

A member of the Ku Klux Klan in Miami, Florida, in 1939. He was part of a campaign to intimidate potential black voters. *How successful were campaigns such as this in the South?*

from their former support for busing. Today, courts no longer issue busing orders to end *de facto* segregation. Indeed, *de facto* segregation in America's schools is still widespread.

5–2d The Civil Rights Movement

In 1955, one year after the first *Brown* decision, an African American woman named Rosa Parks, a long-time activist in the NAACP, boarded a public bus in Montgomery, Alabama. When it became crowded, she refused to move to the "colored section" at the rear of the bus. She was arrested and fined for violating local segregation laws. Her arrest spurred the local African American community to organize a year-long boycott of the entire Montgomery bus system.

The protest was led by a twenty-seven-year-old Baptist minister, the

de jure segregation
Racial segregation that occurs because of laws or decisions by government agencies.

de facto segregation
Racial segregation that occurs not as a result of government actions but because of social and economic conditions and residential patterns.

Reverend Dr. Martin Luther King, Jr. During the protest period, he was jailed and his house was bombed. Yet, despite white hostility and what appeared to be overwhelming odds against them, the protesters were triumphant in the end.

In 1956, a federal court prohibited the segregation of buses in Montgomery, and the era of the civil rights movement—the movement by minorities and concerned whites to end racial discrimination—had begun. The movement was led by a number of groups and individuals, including Martin Luther King, Jr., and his Southern Christian Leadership Conference (SCLC). Other groups, such as the Congress of Racial Equality (CORE), the NAACP, the Student Nonviolent Coordinating Committee (SNCC), and the Urban League, also sought to secure equal rights for African Americans.

> "Injustice anywhere is a threat to justice everywhere."
>
> ~ MARTIN LUTHER KING, JR.
> U.S. CIVIL RIGHTS LEADER
> 1929–1968

Nonviolence as a Tactic

Civil rights protesters in the 1960s began to apply the tactic of nonviolent civil disobedience—the deliberate and public refusal to obey laws considered unjust—in civil rights actions throughout the South. Activists were trained in the tools of nonviolence—how to use nonthreatening body language, how to go limp when dragged or assaulted, and how to protect themselves from clubs and police dogs.

Greensboro: An Example.

In 1960, for example, four African American students in Greensboro, North Carolina, sat at the "whites only" lunch counter at Woolworth's and ordered food. The waitress refused to serve them, and the store closed early, but more students returned the next day to sit at the counter, with supporters picketing outside. Sit-ins spread to other lunch counters across the South.

In some instances, students participating in sit-ins were heckled or even dragged from Woolworth's by angry whites. But the protesters never reacted with violence. They simply returned to their seats at the counter, day after day. Within months of the first sit-in, lunch counter managers began to reverse their policies of segregation.

civil rights movement The movement in the 1950s and 1960s, by minorities and concerned whites, to end racial discrimination.

civil disobedience The deliberate and public act of refusing to obey laws thought to be unjust.

sit-ins A tactic of nonviolent civil disobedience. Demonstrators enter a business, college building, or other public place and remain seated until they are forcibly removed or until their demands are met.

The National Reaction.

As the civil rights movement gained momentum, media images increasingly showed nonviolent protesters being assaulted by police, sprayed with fire hoses, and attacked by dogs. These pictures shocked and angered Americans across the country. The resulting public backlash led to nationwide demands for reform. The March on Washington for Jobs and Freedom, led by Martin Luther King, Jr., in 1963, aimed in part to demonstrate widespread public support for legislation to ban discrimination in all aspects of public life.

Civil Rights Legislation

As the civil rights movement demonstrated its strength, Congress began to pass civil rights laws. While the Fourteenth Amendment prevented the *government* from discriminating against individuals or groups, the private sector—businesses, restaurants, and the like—could still freely refuse to employ and serve nonwhites. Therefore, Congress sought to address this issue.

The Civil Rights Act of 1964.

The Civil Rights Act of 1964 was the first and most comprehensive civil rights law. It forbade discrimination on the basis of race, color, religion, gender, and national origin. The major provisions of the act were as follows:

▶ It outlawed discrimination in public places of accommodation, such as hotels, restaurants, movie theaters, and public transportation.

▶ It provided that federal funds could be withheld from any federal or state government project or facility that practiced any form of discrimination.

▶ It banned discrimination in employment.

▶ It outlawed arbitrary discrimination in voter registration.

▶ It authorized the federal government to sue to desegregate public schools and facilities.

Voting and Housing Rights.

Other significant laws were passed by Congress during the 1960s as well. The Voting Rights Act of 1965 made it illegal to interfere with anyone's right to vote in any election held in this country. The Civil Rights Act of 1968 prohibited discrimination in housing.

The Black Power Movement

Not all African Americans embraced nonviolence. Several outspoken leaders in the mid-1960s were outraged at the slow pace of change in the social and economic status of blacks.

Malcolm X, a speaker and organizer for the Nation of Islam (also called the Black Muslims), rejected the goals of integration and racial equality espoused by the civil rights movement. He called instead for black separatism and "black pride." Although he later moderated some of his views when he converted to a more orthodox version of Islam, his rhetorical style and powerful message influenced many African American young people.

Both Malcolm X and Martin Luther King, Jr., were assassinated—Malcolm X in 1965 and King in 1968. In the late 1960s, a series of "race riots" (actually, insurrections against perceived police abuses) shook African American neighborhoods across the nation. The riots helped destroy much of the goodwill generated by nonviolent civil disobedience. By the end of the decade, the high tide of the civil rights movement was clearly over.

Civil rights leader the Reverend Dr. Martin Luther King, Jr. (1929–1968), at the March on Washington in 1963. King gave his most celebrated speech ("I Have a Dream") at this event. *What were the goals of the demonstration?*

5-2e African Americans in Politics Today

As mentioned earlier, in many jurisdictions African Americans were prevented from voting for years after the Civil War, despite the Fifteenth Amendment (1870). These discriminatory practices persisted in the twentieth century. In the early 1960s, only 22 percent of African Americans of voting age in the South were registered to vote, compared with 63 percent of voting-age whites. In Mississippi, the most extreme example, only 6 percent of voting-age African Americans were registered to vote. Such disparities led to the enactment of the Voting Rights Act of 1965, which ended discriminatory voter-registration tests and gave federal voter registrars the power to prevent racial discrimination in voting.

Today, the percentages of eligible blacks and whites registered to vote are nearly equal. As a result of this dramatic change, political participation by African Americans has increased, as has the number of African American elected officials.

Representation in Office More than nine thousand African Americans now serve in elective office in the United States. Following the 2016 elections, forty-seven African Americans were members of Congress.

A number of African Americans have achieved high office in the executive branch, including Colin Powell, who served as President George W. Bush's first secretary of state, and Condoleezza Rice, his second secretary of state. Of course, in 2008 Barack Obama, a U.S. senator from Illinois, became the first African American president of the United States. Obama's election reflects a significant change in public opinion. Fifty years ago, only 38 percent of Americans said that they would be willing to vote for an African American as president. Today, this number has risen to more than 90 percent. Nonetheless, only two African Americans have been elected to a state governorship since the Reconstruction period that followed the Civil War.

The Supreme Court Weakens the Voting Rights Act In June 2013, the Voting Rights Act received a significant setback at the hands of the Supreme Court. In *Shelby County v. Holder*, the Court ruled that Section 4 of the Voting Rights Act was unconstitutional.[9] This section defined which state and local governments were subject to special federal oversight.

These governments could not change voting procedures or district boundaries without *preclearance*, or approval, from the federal government. The governments identified by Section 4 had a history of voting rights violations in the 1960s, but the Court argued that basing current law on events that far in the past was unacceptable. In principle, Congress could adopt a new Section 4. The chances of such a measure passing today's Congress are remote, however. Meanwhile, the Department of Justice can still challenge election procedures after they have been implemented, but such lawsuits are less effective than the preclearance system. It is an open question whether President Trump's attorney general, Jeff Sessions, will be interested in pursuing any voting rights lawsuits.

The Impact of Voting Restrictions Progressives feared that the Court's decision would result in new state laws that would make it difficult for many low-income persons to vote. Indeed, in recent years, a substantial number of new laws have threatened to reduce turnout among poor—and minority—voters. These laws have included limits on early voting and requirements that voters produce photographic IDs. In several states, federal judges blocked the new laws in time for the 2016 elections. In North Carolina, a judge stated that the legislature had targeted black voters with "surgical precision." Failure to open enough voting sites in black areas was also a major problem.

5-2f Continuing Challenges

Although African Americans no longer face *de jure* segregation, they continue to struggle for income and educational parity with whites. Recent census data show that average incomes in black households are only 59 percent of those in non-Hispanic white households. The poverty rate for blacks is roughly three times that for whites. The loss of jobs caused by the recent Great Recession tended to make matters worse for African Americans and other minority group members.

Problems with Law Enforcement Criminal activity is commonplace in the impoverished neighborhoods where many African Americans live. As a result, African Americans are disproportionately victimized by crime. They are also arrested for crimes in numbers that substantially exceed their share of the population.

Some statistics suggest that African Americans probably do commit a disproportionate share of violent crime. Other statistics paint an alternative picture, however. Blacks are nearly four times as likely to be arrested for possession of marijuana as are whites, even though studies show that the two groups use and sell "weed" at

similar rates. African Americans make up 12 percent of the total population of drug users, but almost 40 percent of those arrested for drug offenses and 60 percent of those in state prisons for drug offenses.

Indeed, African Americans constitute nearly 1 million of the 2.3 million persons in prison. Add Hispanics, and these two groups make up 60 percent of all prisoners, even though they represent about 30 percent of the U.S. population. Such data raise the suspicion that U.S. law enforcement is biased against minority group members. We examined that question in further detail in the chapter-opening *America at Odds* feature.

Problems with Education The education gap between blacks and whites also persists despite continuing efforts by educators and by government to reduce it. Federal legislation aimed at this goal has included the No Child Left Behind Act, now replaced by the Every Student Succeeds Act. Recent studies show that, on average, African American students in high school read and do math at the level of whites in junior high school. Also, while black students have narrowed the gap with whites in earning high school diplomas, the disparity has widened for college degrees.

These problems tend to feed on one another. Schools in poorer neighborhoods generally have fewer educational resources available, resulting in lower achievement levels for their students. A persistent problem is that as talented teachers gain experience, they often transfer from struggling schools to schools in prosperous neighborhoods where students are better prepared. Thus, some educational experts suggest that it all comes down to money. In fact, many parents of minority students in struggling school districts are less concerned about integration than they are about funds for their children's schools.

Class versus Race in Educational Outcomes Researchers have known for decades that when students enrolled at a particular school come almost entirely from impoverished families, regardless of race, the performance of the students at that school is seriously depressed. When low-income students attend schools where the majority of the students are middle class, again regardless of race, their performance improves dramatically—without dragging down the performance of the middle-class students. These studies appear to provide evidence for the Supreme Court's earlier ruling in *Brown v. Board of Education*. Because of this research and recent Supreme Court rulings that have struck down some racial integration plans, several school systems have adopted policies that integrate students on the basis of socioeconomic class, not race.

CRITICAL THINKING

▶ *Why might low-income students do better in their studies, on average, when most of their classmates are middle class instead of poor?*

5–3 WOMEN

LO Describe the political and economic achievements of women in this country over time, and identify some obstacles to equality that women continue to face.

In 1848, Lucretia Mott and Elizabeth Cady Stanton organized the first "woman's rights" convention in Seneca Falls, New York. The three hundred people who attended approved a Declaration of Sentiments: "We hold these truths to be self-evident: that all men *and women* are created equal." In the following years, other women's groups held conventions in various cities in the Midwest and the East. With the outbreak of the Civil War, though, women's rights advocates devoted their energies to the war effort.

5–3a The Struggle for Voting Rights

The movement for political rights gained momentum again in 1869, with the founding of two organizations devoted to gaining **suffrage**—the right to vote—for women. The National Woman Suffrage Association, formed by Susan B. Anthony and Elizabeth Cady Stanton, saw suffrage as only one step on the road toward greater social and political rights for women. In contrast, the American Woman Suffrage Association, founded by Lucy Stone and others, believed that the right to vote should be the only goal.

The Suffrage Campaign By 1890, the two organizations had joined forces, and the resulting National American Woman Suffrage Association had indeed only one goal—enfranchisement (being given the right to vote). When little progress was made, small, radical splinter groups took to the streets. Parades, hunger strikes, arrests, and jailings soon followed.

World War I (1914–1918) marked a turning point in the battle for women's rights. The war offered many opportunities for women. Several thousand women served in the U.S. Navy, and about a million women joined the workforce, holding jobs vacated by men who had entered military service.

> ## "The right of citizens of the United States to vote shall not be denied or abridged . . . on account of sex."
>
> ~ THE NINETEENTH AMENDMENT TO THE UNITED STATES CONSTITUTION, 1920

The Nineteenth Amendment After the war, President Woodrow Wilson wrote to Carrie Chapman Catt, one of the leaders of the women's movement: "It is high time that [that] part of our debt should be acknowledged." Two years later, in 1920, seventy-two years after the Seneca Falls convention, the Nineteenth Amendment to the Constitution was ratified: "The right of citizens of the United States to vote shall not be denied or abridged by the United States or by any State on account of sex."

5–3b The Feminist Movement

For many years after winning the right to vote, women engaged in little independent political activity. In the 1960s, however, a new women's movement arose—the feminist movement. Women who faced discrimination in employment and other circumstances were inspired in part by the civil rights movement and the campaign against the war in Vietnam.

The National Organization for Women (NOW), founded in 1966, was the most important new women's organization. But the feminist movement also consisted of thousands of small, independent "women's liberation" and "consciousness-raising" groups established on campuses and in neighborhoods throughout the nation. **Feminism,** the goal of the movement, meant full political, economic, and social equality for women.

Combating Gender Discrimination During the 1970s, NOW and other organizations sought to win passage of the Equal Rights Amendment (ERA) to the Constitution, which would have written equality into the heart of the nation's laws. The amendment did not win support from enough state legislatures, however, and it failed. Campaigns to change state and

suffrage The right to vote; the franchise.

feminism A doctrine advocating full political, economic, and social equality for women.

A female U.S. Army soldier on patrol. Servicewomen in Afghanistan are encouraged—but not required—to wear headscarves when interacting with the local population. *Is this an appropriate gesture of respect to local sensibilities or a violation of American cultural norms? In either case, why?*

5-3c Women in American Politics Today

More than ten thousand members have served in the U.S. House of Representatives. Only 1 percent of them have been women, and women continue to face a "men's club" atmosphere in Congress. In 2002, however, a woman, Nancy Pelosi (D., Calif.), was elected minority leader of the House of Representatives. She was the first woman to hold this post. Pelosi again made history when, after the Democratic victories in the 2006 elections, she was elected Speaker of the House of Representatives, the first woman ever to lead the House. After the Republicans took control of the House in 2011, Pelosi again became minority leader.

In the 2016 elections, women continued to win a substantial number of seats in Congress. Twenty-one women now serve in the Senate, and eighty-three were elected to the House.

Women have also been underrepresented in the executive branch. Franklin D. Roosevelt (1933–1945) appointed the first woman to a cabinet post—Frances Perkins, who was secretary of labor from 1933 to 1945. A variety of women have held cabinet posts in more recent administrations. All of the last three presidents prior to Donald Trump have appointed women to the most senior cabinet post—secretary of state. Bill Clinton (1993–2001) appointed Madeleine Albright to this position, George W. Bush (2001–2009) picked Condoleezza Rice for the post in his second term, and Barack Obama chose New York senator Hillary Clinton to be secretary of state during his first term.

In addition, Ronald Reagan (1981–1989) appointed the first woman to sit on the Supreme Court, Sandra Day O'Connor. Bill Clinton appointed Ruth Bader Ginsburg to the Supreme Court. Barack Obama selected Sonia Sotomayor for the Court in 2009 and Elena Kagan in 2010.

5-3d Women in the Workplace

An ongoing challenge for American women is to obtain equal pay and equal opportunity in the workplace. In spite of federal legislation and programs to promote equal treatment of women in the workplace, women continue to face various forms of discrimination.

Wage Discrimination In 1963, Congress passed the Equal Pay Act. The act requires employers to pay an equal wage for substantially equal work—males cannot be paid more than females who perform essentially the same job. The following year, Congress passed the Civil Rights Act of 1964, Title VII of which prohibits employment discrimination on the basis of race, color, national

national laws affecting women were much more successful. Congress and the various state legislatures enacted a range of measures to provide equal rights for women. The women's movement also enjoyed considerable success in legal action. Courts at all levels accepted the argument that *gender discrimination* violated the Fourteenth Amendment's equal protection clause.

Abortion and Other Issues In addition to fighting against gender discrimination, the feminist movement took up a number of other issues important to women. Some campaigns, such as the one to curb domestic violence, have been widely supported. Others have resulted in heated debate. Perhaps the most controversial issue of all has been the right to have an abortion.

origin, gender, and religion. Still, women continue to face wage discrimination.

The Lilly Ledbetter Fair Pay Act of 2009. In 2007, however, the Supreme Court ruled that employers could not be sued under Title VII if the decision to discriminate in pay was made more than 180 days before the claim was made.[10] The plaintiff in this case was Lilly Ledbetter. In 2009, President Obama signed a law that negated the Court's decision. Under the new law, the 180-day statute of limitations resets with each new discriminatory paycheck.

Pay Equity Today. It is estimated that for every dollar earned by men, women earn about 83 cents. Although the wage gap has narrowed significantly since 1963, it still remains. This is particularly true for women in management positions and older women. Notably, when the workers in a particular occupation include a disproportionately high number of women, the wages that are paid in that occupation tend to be relatively low.

Recent research suggests that wage inequality is concentrated in fields in which staff members are expected to put in very long hours. Finance, where long hours are expected, may have the most unequal pay structure of any industry. In contrast, pay differentials are zero among dental hygienists and advertising salespeople. In effect, women may be penalized because child-care responsibilities make it hard for them to work far more than forty hours a week.[11]

The Glass Ceiling   Even though an increasing number of women now hold business and professional jobs once held only by men, relatively few of these women are able to rise to the top of the career ladder in their firms. They are held back by the so-called **glass ceiling**—an invisible but real discriminatory barrier that prevents women and minorities from rising to top positions of power or responsibility. Today, less than one-sixth of the top executive positions in the largest American corporations are held by women.

Sexual Harassment   Title VII's prohibition of gender discrimination has also been extended to prohibit sexual harassment. **Sexual harassment** occurs when job opportunities, promotions, salary increases, or even the ability to retain a job depends on whether an employee complies with demands for sexual favors. A special form of sexual harassment, called *hostile environment harassment*, occurs when an employee is subjected to sexual conduct or comments in the workplace that interfere with the employee's job performance or that create an intimidating, hostile, or offensive environment.

On a number of occasions, the Supreme Court has upheld the right of persons to be free from sexual harassment on the job. In 1998, the Court made it clear that sexual harassment includes harassment by members of the same sex.[12] In the same year, the Court held that employers are liable for the harassment of employees by supervisors unless the employers can show that (1) they exercised reasonable care in preventing such problems (by implementing antiharassment policies and procedures, for example), and (2) the employees failed to take advantage of any corrective opportunities provided by the employers.[13]

The Civil Rights Act of 1991 greatly expanded the remedies available for victims of sexual harassment. Under the act, victims can seek damages as well as back pay, job reinstatement, and other compensation.

Sexual Assault on Campus   Title IX of the Education Amendments of 1972 prohibits gender-based discrimination in schools that receive federal money. Title IX is best known for requiring equal opportunities in sports for men and women. Sexual assault is also considered discrimination under Title IX, however.

Sexual assault on campus, ranging from unwanted touching to acts of violence, is a long-standing problem. Use of alcohol is a major contributing factor. Under the broadest definition, about one in five college women has experienced sexual assault. Yet few women report assault to school authorities, and those who do often receive little help. In some cases, victims have actually been penalized for making complaints.

Beginning in 2011, the Obama administration began cracking down on the problem. By 2016, more than three hundred colleges and universities had been investigated for mishandling complaints. Many were also under investigation for retaliating against persons reporting an assault. Schools that failed to improve their procedures were at risk of losing federal funds.

Today, many students are unwilling to accept policies or language that they consider discriminatory, whether the target is women or minority group members. Criticisms of *language* that is alleged to be discriminatory or hostile, however, have led to a reaction. Many observers, especially conservatives, reject attempts to "police" such language, calling them *political correctness*. We look at this issue in this chapter's *Join the Debate* feature.

> **glass ceiling** An invisible but real discriminatory barrier that prevents women and minorities from rising to top positions of power or responsibility.
>
> **sexual harassment** Unwanted physical contact, verbal conduct, or abuse of a sexual nature that interferes with a recipient's job performance, creates a hostile environment, or carries with it an implicit or explicit threat of adverse employment consequences.

▶ *In recent years, the percentage of young women who have received college diplomas has exceeded the percentage for young men. In the future, how might this development change the social and economic roles of women and men?*

5–4 SECURING RIGHTS FOR OTHER GROUPS

LO Summarize the struggles for equality that other groups in America have experienced.

In addition to African Americans and women, a number of other groups in U.S. society have faced discriminatory treatment. One lingering result of past discrimination can be that a group suffers from below-average incomes and relatively high rates of poverty. Figure 5–1 shows the percentage of persons with incomes below the poverty line for five major racial or ethnic groups. The chart provides statistics for children as well as the overall population. Note that in all groups, children are more likely than adults to live in poverty. This reality makes poverty that much more damaging.

FIGURE 5–1 PERSONS IN POVERTY IN THE UNITED STATES BY RACE AND HISPANIC ORIGIN

Blacks, Hispanics, and American Indians are more likely than whites or Asians to have incomes below the poverty line. *Why are children more likely than adults to live in families with incomes below the poverty line?*

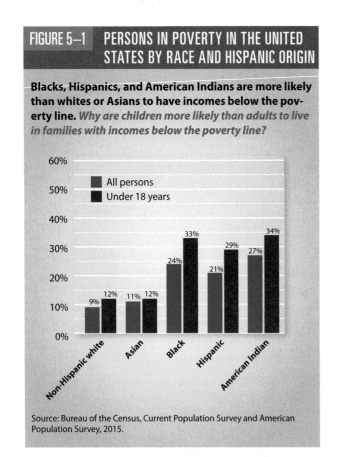

Source: Bureau of the Census, Current Population Survey and American Population Survey, 2015.

Next, we look at three groups that have had to struggle for equal treatment—Latinos, Asian Americans, and American Indians (or Native Americans). Then we examine the struggles of several other groups of Americans—persons with disabilities, gay men and lesbians, and transgender persons.

5–4a Latinos

Latinos, or Hispanics, constitute the largest ethnic minority in the United States. Whereas African Americans represent 12.6 percent of the U.S. population, Latinos now constitute 17.1 percent. Each year, the Hispanic population grows by more than 1 million people, one-third of whom are newly arrived legal immigrants. By 2050, Latinos are expected to constitute almost 30 percent of the U.S. population. Still, Hispanic immigration has declined in recent years. For example, the number of persons returning to Mexico every year now exceeds the number of new arrivals.

Who Are the Hispanics? According to the U.S. Census Bureau definition, Hispanics can be of any race. Note that while *Hispanic* is official U.S. government terminology, some members of this group prefer the term *Latino*—or *Latina* in the feminine case. Opinion polls report that among Hispanics, the two terms are roughly equal in popularity. Actually, though, most Latinos prefer to identify with their country of origin rather than be categorized as either Hispanics or Latinos.

Countries of Origin. As you can see in Figure 5–2, the largest Hispanic group consists of Mexican Americans, who constitute 63.9 percent of the Latino population

FIGURE 5–2 HISPANICS LIVING IN THE UNITED STATES BY PLACE OF ORIGIN

Why do Mexicans make up such a large share of Latino immigrants?

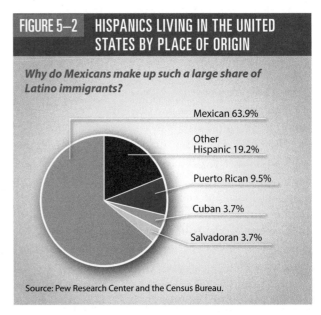

Mexican 63.9%

Other Hispanic 19.2%

Puerto Rican 9.5%

Cuban 3.7%

Salvadoran 3.7%

Source: Pew Research Center and the Census Bureau.

Is "Political Correctness" a Real Problem?

Political correctness has been much in the news of late. For example, as a Republican presidential candidate, Donald Trump, after insulting Fox News reporter Megyn Kelly, dismissed criticism of his language, saying that such criticism was "politically correct." Many commentators, including some liberals as well as conservatives, argue that political correctness (or PC) has created a "reign of terror" on college and university campuses. Are these people right? Is political correctness a real problem?

The Language Police Are Perverting Liberalism

New York Magazine columnist Jonathan Chait certainly believes that PC is a major problem. Chait contends that PC leftists threaten the very foundations of liberalism by rejecting free speech as a universal value. "Political correctness is a style of politics in which the more radical members of the left attempt to regulate political discourse by defining opposing views as bigoted and illegitimate," he writes.

Chait's examples of PC behavior go beyond verbal criticism of alleged racism or sexism. Examples include student campaigns to disinvite commencement speakers such as Bill Maher and Ayaan Hirsi Ali. These proposed speakers had called Islam an illegitimate religion. Chait concludes that the new political correctness "has bludgeoned even many of its own supporters into despondent silence." Yet politics is "based on getting people to agree with you, not making them afraid to disagree."

Political Correctness Doesn't Hinder Free Speech—It Expands It

Others do not think that political correctness is a real problem. After all, schools invite commencement speakers in part to honor them, but no one has the *right* to be honored. Typically, however, PC means calling people out on their offensiveness. When Trump calls a reporter a "bimbo," in what universe is that anything other than colossal rudeness?

As to "defining opposing views as bigoted and illegitimate," journalist Lindsay Beyerstein notes that "some views are bigoted and illegitimate." The so-called N-word, once constantly applied to African Americans, is today largely unprintable. That is PC in action. It is also not a problem.

PC's defenders say that you may have the right to make offensive comments, but others have the right to respond. Lindy West writes that "a bunch of college students, on the cusp of finding their voices, [are] being publicly berated by high-profile writers . . . because they don't like what [the students] have to say. Are you sure you know who's silencing whom?"

Critical Analysis

President Obama refused to use the term "radical Islamic terrorism" (he was fine with "Islamist"). Was this an example of PC run amok—or a legitimate attempt to avoid blaming all Muslims for the crimes of a few?

living in the United States. Some 9.5 percent of Latinos are Puerto Ricans. Persons from El Salvador make up 3.7 percent, and 3.7 percent are Cuban Americans. Most of the remaining Hispanics are from Central and South American countries.

Low Incomes. Economically, Hispanic households are often members of this country's working poor. As Figure 5–1 shows, many have incomes below the government's official poverty line. Latino leaders tend to attribute the low income levels to language problems, lack of job training, and continuing immigration. Immigration disguises statistical progress because language problems and lack of job training are usually more notable among new immigrants than among those who have lived in the United States for many years.

Party Identification In their party identification, Latinos tend to follow some fairly well-established patterns. Traditionally, Mexican Americans and Puerto Ricans identify with the Democratic Party, which has favored more government assistance and support programs for disadvantaged groups.

PERCEPTION VS. REALITY

We Are Too Lax in Vetting Refugees

Protect our borders. Keep extremists out of our country. Make America safe for Americans. These slogans represent one response to the current concern over how well we "vet" refugees who wish to come to America, especially from the Middle East.

The Perception

The federal government has done little to ensure that Americans are kept safe from potential terrorists who ask for asylum in the United States. Therefore, the government needs to institute more extreme measures to keep out would-be terrorists.

The Reality

A common political tactic in recent times has been to denounce the government for failing to do something that, in fact, it is already doing. The call for intensified vetting of refugees, especially those from war-torn Syria, is one example of this practice. Vetting was already extreme before President Trump took office.

For the past fifteen years, a typical refugee from the Middle East has had to wait up to two years before being admitted to this country. A twenty-one-step screening process starts with registration and interviews with the United Nation's High Commissioner for Refugees. Only after the UN has granted a person or family refugee status can it refer them to the United States for possible resettlement.

Then, the U.S. State Department takes over. It conducts an initial interview and background check. Many refugees receive two additional background checks. These steps are followed by three fingerprint screenings. Each case is then reviewed by U.S. immigration authorities from the Department of Homeland Security. Additional steps apply to anyone from Syria, including extensive in-person interviews with a Homeland Security officer, usually in Jordan or Turkey. Finally, each refugee undergoes multiagency security checks before leaving for the United States. A final security check takes place at a U.S. airport.

The result: no refugee who has undergone the federal government's screening procedures since the 9/11 attack has committed an act of terrorism in the United States. Indeed, none of the participants in 9/11 were from any of the seven majority-Muslim nations listed in President Trump's January 2017 executive order that barred entry into the United States. (Most of the 9/11 terrorists were from Egypt or Saudi Arabia, nations not covered by the order.) A majority of the criminals responsible for subsequent terror attacks were born in the United States.

Blog On

Haeyoun Park and Larry Buchanan provide a detailed list of asylum security steps in the New York Times. To find it, search for "Park Buchanan vetting." The government has also been criticized for not taking measures at the Mexican border that are already in effect. Check out an article by NBC's Leigh Ann Caldwell at "Caldwell border security."

The Cuban Exception. Cubans, in contrast, tend to identify with the Republican Party. This is largely because of a different history. Cuban émigrés fled from Cuba during and after the Communist revolution led by Fidel Castro. The strong anti-Communist sentiments of the Cubans propelled them toward the more conservative party—the Republicans. Today, relations with Communist Cuba continue to be a key political issue for Cuban Americans. Cubans of the younger generation, however, are much more open to voting for Democrats than their parents were.

The Immigration Issue. A problem for the Hispanic community is that many of its members arrived in this country illegally. (It is almost impossible for a poorly educated Mexican or Central American to gain legal admission.) Demand for the labor of such persons has been high, however, and in fact most unauthorized immigrants came to the United States to work. Others are small children. Many families have members who are U.S. citizens, often children born in this country, while other family members are unauthorized. As a result, deporting illegal immigrants can split up families—or force U.S. citizens into exile.

It follows that immigration reform has been an important issue for many Latinos. In recent years, the Republican Party has taken a stand against any reform that would let unauthorized immigrants regularize their status. This stand has pushed many Latinos toward the Democrats. Of course, Republican president Donald Trump's hostility toward immigration has been one of his strongest characteristics. Hispanics are not the only immigrants threatened by the policies of the new administration, as you saw in this chapter's *Perception vs. Reality* feature.

Latinos in American Politics Today

Generally, Latinos in the United States have had a comparatively low level of political participation. This is understandable, given that more than one-third of Hispanics are below voting age and also that more than one-fourth are not citizens and thus cannot vote. Although voter turnout among Latinos is generally low compared with the population at large, the Latino voting rate is rising as more immigrants become citizens and as more Hispanics reach voting age. Indeed, when comparing citizens of equal incomes and educational backgrounds, Latino citizens' participation rate is higher than average. In the 2016 elections, Latinos made up 11 percent of the electorate, up from 10 percent in 2012 and 9 percent in 2008. In the midterm elections of 2014, however, when voter turnout was depressed, Latino participation fell back to 8 percent.

Latinos increasingly hold political office, particularly in states with large Hispanic populations. Today, more than 5 percent of the state legislators in Arizona, California, Colorado, Florida, New Mexico, and Texas are of Hispanic ancestry. Cuban Americans have been notably successful in gaining local political power, particularly in Dade County, Florida. Latinos are also increasing their presence in Congress, albeit slowly. After the 2016 elections, Latino representation in Congress reached thirty-eight members. Two senators of Cuban heritage—Ted Cruz (R., Tex.) and Marco Rubio (R., Fla.)—were candidates for president in 2016.

5-4b Asian Americans

Asian Americans have also suffered, at times severely, from discriminatory treatment. The Chinese Exclusion Act of 1882 prevented people from China and Japan from coming to the United States to prospect for gold or to work on the railroads or in factories in the West. After 1900, immigration continued to be restricted—only limited numbers of Chinese or Japanese individuals were allowed to enter the United States. Those who were allowed into the country faced severe racial prejudice. In 1906, after the San Francisco earthquake, Japanese American students were segregated into special schools so that white children could use their buildings.

Internment of Japanese Americans

The Japanese bombing of Pearl Harbor in 1941, which launched the entry of the United States into World War II (1939–1945), intensified Americans' fear of the Japanese. Actions taken under an executive order issued by President Franklin D. Roosevelt in 1942 subjected many Japanese Americans to curfews, excluded them from certain "military areas," and evacuated most of the West Coast Japanese American population to internment camps (also called "relocation centers").[14] In 1988, Congress provided funds to compensate former camp inhabitants—$1.25 billion for approximately sixty thousand people.

A "Model Minority"?

Today, Asian Americans lead other minority groups in median income and median education. Indeed, Asians who have immigrated to the United States since 1965 (including immigrants from India) represent the most highly skilled immigrant groups in American history. Nearly 40 percent of Asian Americans over the age of twenty-five have college degrees. Recently, Asians have replaced Hispanics as the group with the greatest number of immigrants entering the United States each year.

An Asian American student works on a paper at the library. Some Asian Americans argue that they face discrimination in Ivy League admissions. *How important is it to get into a top college?*

The image of Asian Americans as a "model minority" has created certain problems for its members, however. Some argue that top private colleges and universities have discriminated against Asian Americans in admissions because so many of them apply. By one estimate, Asian Americans make up as many as 30 percent of the top college candidates as determined by SAT scores. In the Ivy League, however, Asian admissions have consistently run below 20 percent. Still, many good schools below the Ivy level admit Asian Americans freely.

More than a million Indochinese war refugees, most from Vietnam, have immigrated to the United States since the 1970s. Many came with relatives and were sponsored by American families or organizations. Thus, they had support systems to help them get started. Some immigrants from other parts of Indochina, however, have experienced difficulties because they come from cultures that have had very little contact with the practices of developed industrial societies.

5–4c American Indians

When we consider population figures since 1492, we see that American Indians experienced one catastrophe after another. We cannot know exactly how many people lived in the New World when Columbus arrived. Current research estimates the population of what is now the continental United States to have been anywhere from 3 million to 8 million. The Europeans brought with them diseases to which these Native Americans had no immunity. As a result, after a series of terrifying epidemics, the population of the continental United States was reduced to perhaps eight hundred thousand people by 1600. Death rates elsewhere in the New World were comparable. When the Pilgrims arrived at Plymouth, the Massachusetts coast was lined with abandoned village sites due to a recent epidemic.[15]

In subsequent centuries, the American Indian population continued to decline, bottoming out at about half a million in 1925. These were centuries in which the European American and African American populations experienced explosive growth. By 2016, the Native American population had recovered to almost 3 million, or more than 5 million if we count individuals who are only part Indian.

In 1789, Congress designated the native tribes as foreign nations so that the government could sign land and boundary treaties with them. As members of foreign nations, Native Americans had no civil rights under U.S. laws. This situation continued until 1924, when the citizenship rights spelled out in the Fourteenth Amendment to the Constitution were finally extended to American Indians.

Early Policies toward Native Americans

The Northwest Ordinance, passed by Congress under the Articles of Confederation in 1787, stated that "the utmost good faith shall always be observed towards the Indians; their lands and property shall never be taken from them without their consent." Over the next hundred years, these principles were violated more often than they were observed.

In 1830, Congress instructed the Bureau of Indian Affairs (BIA), which Congress had established in 1824 as part of the War Department, to remove all tribes to reservations west of the Mississippi River in order to free land east of the Mississippi for white settlement.

This member of the Navajo Code Talkers is proud of his heritage. His native language was an unbreakable code for transmitting information on the battlefields during World War II. *Why might many Americans be sympathetic to the Indian rights movement?*

The resettlement was a catastrophe for Indians in the eastern states.

In the late 1880s, the U.S. government changed its policy. The goal became the "assimilation" of American Indians into American society. Each family was given a parcel of land within the reservation to farm. The remaining acreage was sold to whites, thus reducing the number of acres in reservation status from 140 million to about 47 million. Tribes that would not cooperate with this plan lost their reservations altogether.

American Indian Activism Native Americans have always found it difficult to obtain political power. In part, this is because the tribes are small and scattered, making organized political movements difficult. Today, American Indians remain fragmented politically because large numbers of their population live off the reservations. Nonetheless, beginning in the 1960s, some Indians formed organizations to strike back at the U.S. government and to reclaim their heritage, including their lands. Most recently, Native Americans in North Dakota have organized against an oil pipeline that they believe threatens the water supply of their reservation. Many non-Indians joined the protest. As a result, President Obama suspended work on the pipeline, but President Trump has called for its resumption.

Compensation for Injustices of the Past As more Americans became aware of the sufferings of Native Americans, Congress began to compensate them for past injustices. In 1990, Congress passed the Native American Languages Act, which declared that American Indian languages are unique and serve an important role in maintaining Indian culture and continuity. Courts, too, have shown a greater willingness to recognize Native American treaty rights. For example, in 1985, the Supreme Court ruled that three tribes of Oneida Indians could claim damages for the use of tribal land that had been unlawfully transferred in 1795.[16]

The Indian Gaming Regulatory Act of 1988 allows American Indians to have gambling operations on their reservations. Although the profits from casinos have helped to improve the economic and social status of many Native Americans, poverty and unemployment remain widespread on the reservations.

5-4d Persons with Disabilities

Discrimination based on disability crosses the boundaries of race, ethnicity, gender, and religion. Persons with disabilities, especially those with facial deformities or severe mental impairments, face social bias. Although attitudes toward persons with disabilities have changed considerably in the last several decades, such persons continue to suffer from discrimination.

Persons with disabilities first became a political force in the 1970s, and in 1973 Congress passed the initial legislation protecting this group—the Rehabilitation Act. This act prohibited discrimination against persons with disabilities in programs receiving federal aid. The Individuals with Disabilities Education Act (formerly called the Education for All Handicapped Children Act of 1975) requires public schools to provide children with disabilities with free, appropriate, and individualized education in the least restrictive environment appropriate to their needs. The Americans with Disabilities Act (ADA) of 1990, however, is by far the most significant legislation protecting the rights of this group of Americans.

Gregory Reed/Shutterstock.com

U.S. Representative Tammy Duckworth (D., Ill.) walks to the podium at the 2016 Democratic National Convention. Duckworth lost both legs when her helicopter was shot down in Iraq. In 2016, she was elected to the U.S. Senate. *What accommodations are appropriate for persons with disabilities?*

The Americans with Disabilities Act The ADA requires that all public buildings and public services be accessible to persons with disabilities. The act also mandates that employers "reasonably accommodate" the needs of workers or job applicants with disabilities who are otherwise qualified for particular jobs unless to do so would cause the employer to suffer an "undue hardship."

The ADA defines persons with disabilities as persons who have physical or mental impairments that "substantially limit" their everyday activities. Health conditions that have been considered disabilities under federal law include blindness, a history of alcoholism, heart disease, cancer, muscular dystrophy, cerebral palsy, paraplegia, diabetes, and acquired immune deficiency syndrome (AIDS). The ADA, however, does not require employers to hire or retain workers who, because of their disabilities, pose a "direct threat to the health or safety" of their co-workers.

Limiting the Scope of the ADA From 1999 to 2002, the Supreme Court handed down a series of rulings that substantially limited the scope of the ADA. The Court found that any limitation that could be remedied by medication or by corrective devices such as eyeglasses did not qualify as a protected disability. According to the Court, even carpal tunnel syndrome was not a disability.[17] In 2008, however, the ADA Amendments Act overturned most of these limits. Carpal tunnel syndrome and other ailments may again qualify as disabilities. (The need for eyeglasses was not, however, covered by the new law.)

In 2001, the Supreme Court reviewed a case raising the question of whether suits under the ADA could be brought against state government employers. The Court concluded that states are immune from lawsuits brought to enforce rights under this federal law.[18]

5–4e Gay Men and Lesbians

Today, many Americans—including seven members of Congress—are openly gay, lesbian, or bisexual. Until the late 1960s and early 1970s, though, gay men and lesbians tended to keep quiet about their

LGBT persons Individuals who are lesbian, gay men, bisexual, or transgender.

A participant in the Women's March held in multiple cities on January 21, 2017, to express concern over the policies of President Donald Trump. The demonstrations were among the largest in U.S. history. *How much power does a president actually have over transgender rights?*

Justin Starr Photography/Shutterstock.com

sexual orientation because exposure usually meant facing harsh consequences. This attitude began to change after a 1969 incident in the Greenwich Village neighborhood of New York City. When the police raided the Stonewall Inn—a bar popular with gay men and lesbians—on June 27 of that year, the bar's patrons responded by throwing beer cans and bottles at the police. The riot continued for two days. The Stonewall Inn uprising launched the "gay power" movement. By the end of the year, gay men and lesbians had formed about fifty organizations, including the Gay Activist Alliance and the Gay Liberation Front.

Today, the broad movement in favor of sexual identity rights typically defends **LGBT persons,** that is, lesbians, gay men, bisexuals, and transgender individuals. The term *LGBTQ* is also in use—with "Q" standing for "queer" or "questioning." It represents persons with an alternative sexuality that is not easily categorized.

A Changing Legal Landscape The number of gay and lesbian organizations has grown from fifty in 1969 to several thousand today. These groups have exerted significant political pressure on legislatures, the media, schools, and churches. In the decades following Stonewall, more than half of the forty-nine states that had sodomy laws repealed them. (*Sodomy laws* prohibit intimate homosexual conduct and certain other forms of sexual activity.) In seven other states, the courts invalidated such laws. Then, in 2003, the United States

Supreme Court issued a ruling that effectively invalidated all remaining sodomy laws in the country.

Gaining Legal Status. In *Lawrence v. Texas*,[19] the Court ruled that sodomy laws violated the Fourteenth Amendment's due process clause. According to the Court, "The liberty protected by the Constitution allows homosexual persons the right to choose to enter upon relationships in the confines of their homes and their own private lives and still retain their dignity as free persons."

Changing Attitudes. Social attitudes toward LGBT individuals have changed greatly since the 1960s. Liberal political leaders started supporting gay rights at least two decades ago. Conservative politicians also have increasingly softened their stance on the issue. By 2011, polling organizations reported that, for the first time ever, an absolute majority of those questioned supported same-sex marriage.

Today, twenty-two states have laws prohibiting discrimination in employment and housing based on sexual orientation. Eleven ban employment discrimination only for state employment. About 250 cities and counties also have anti-discrimination laws.

Same-sex Marriage On June 26, 2015, in *Obergefell v. Hodges*, the Supreme Court ruled by a five-to-four margin that the Constitution guarantees a right to same-sex marriage in every state.[20] At the time of the ruling, gay marriage was still illegal in thirteen Midwestern and Southern states. The speed with which same-sex marriage became established was striking. As of January 2003, the number of states recognizing the right was zero. Massachusetts became the first state to recognize same-sex marriage in 2003.[21]

In many states, legalization of same-sex marriage was preceded by laws establishing same-sex domestic partnerships. Vermont pioneered this institution in 2000. These partnerships provided many, if not all, of the benefits of marriage under state law but denied couples the dignity of the marriage title. *Obergefell v. Hodges* did not automatically eliminate this status or convert domestic partnerships into marriages. The ruling did, however, make the institution of domestic partnership a minor part of the legal landscape in the United States, though the status is common elsewhere in the world.

Gays and Lesbians in the Military Gay men and lesbians who wish to join the military have faced a number of obstacles. Until recently, one was the "don't ask, don't tell" policy. This policy, which banned openly gay men and lesbians from the military, was implemented in 1993 by President Bill Clinton when it became clear that more liberal alternatives would not be accepted. In December 2010, Congress finally repealed the policy, effective in 2011. As a result, gay men and lesbians may now serve openly in the nation's armed forces. In 2016, the right to serve openly was extended to transgender individuals.

Issues Facing Transgender Persons What would it be like to grow up in the body of a boy—even as you sense that you are truly a girl? Or *vice versa*? People facing this issue are **transgender persons.** Their existence has been recorded throughout human history. More than two hundred women donned male clothing and fought in the U.S. Civil War, and some then lived the rest of their lives as men. In the mid-twentieth century, physicians in Germany and Scandinavia developed procedures for sex reassignment surgery. Today, such procedures are well established. Not all transgender persons wish to undergo such invasive surgery, however. In forty-six states, birth certificates can be altered to change a person's recorded sex, but in twenty-eight states such a change is possible only after surgery.

Discrimination against transgender persons—not to mention outright acts of violence—has been common. In the wake of the gay rights movement, transgender individuals also have come forward and demanded equal rights. Some cultural conservatives have pushed back. A key tactic, as exemplified by the state of North Carolina, has been to ban transgender persons from using public restrooms that do not accord with the sex listed on their birth certificates. Some have claimed that trans women (formerly men) would use their access to women's facilities to sexually harass women. North Carolina came under heavy criticism for its bathroom law, and the Obama administration announced that such bans in public schools would threaten their federal funding. The Trump administration reversed this Obama policy, however. North Carolina later repealed the bathroom ban, but it also retained other rules that many people saw as discriminatory.

CRITICAL THINKING

▶ *The number of Latinos in the United States continues to grow. What impact do you think this will have on American culture and politics?*

transgender person
Someone born with the physical characteristics of one sex, but whose sense of gender and identity corresponds with that of the other sex.

5-5 BEYOND EQUAL PROTECTION— AFFIRMATIVE ACTION

LO Explain what affirmative action is and why it has been so controversial.

One provision of the Civil Rights Act of 1964 called for prohibiting discrimination in employment. Soon after the act was passed, the federal government began to legislate programs promoting *equal employment opportunity*.

Such programs require that employers' hiring and promotion practices guarantee the same opportunities to all individuals. Experience soon showed that minorities often had fewer opportunities to obtain education and relevant work experience than did whites. Because of this, minorities were still excluded from many jobs. Even though discriminatory practices were made illegal, the change in the law did not make up for the results of years of discrimination. Consequently, under President Lyndon B. Johnson (1963–1969), a new policy was developed.

Called **affirmative action,** this policy required employers to take positive steps to remedy *past* discrimination. Affirmative action programs involved giving special consideration, in jobs and college admissions, to members of groups that were discriminated against in the past.

5-5a Affirmative Action Tested

The Supreme Court first addressed the issue of affirmative action in 1978 in *Regents of the University of California v. Bakke.*[22] Allan Bakke, a white male, had been denied admission to the University of California's medical school at Davis. The school had set aside sixteen of the one hundred seats in each year's entering class for applicants who wished to be considered as members of designated minority groups. Many of the students admitted through this special program had lower test scores than Bakke.

affirmative action
A policy that gives special consideration, in jobs and college admissions, to members of groups that have been discriminated against in the past.

reverse discrimination
Discrimination against those who have no minority status.

quota system A policy under which a specific number of jobs, promotions, or other types of placements, such as university admissions, are given to members of selected groups.

Bakke sued the university, claiming that he was a victim of **reverse discrimination**—discrimination against whites. Bakke argued that the use of a **quota system,** in which a specific number of seats were reserved for minority applicants only, violated the equal protection clause. A majority on the Supreme Court concluded that although both the Constitution and the Civil Rights Act of 1964 allow race to be used as a factor in making admissions decisions, race cannot be the *sole* factor. Because the university's quota system was based solely on race, it was unconstitutional.

5-5b Strict Scrutiny Applied

In 1995, the Supreme Court issued a landmark decision in *Adarand Constructors, Inc. v. Peña.*[23] The Court held that any federal, state, or local affirmative action program that uses racial classifications as the basis for making decisions is subject to "strict scrutiny" by the courts. As discussed earlier in this chapter, this means that, to be constitutional, a discriminatory law or action must be narrowly tailored to meet a *compelling* government interest.

In effect, the *Adarand* decision narrowed the application of affirmative action programs. An affirmative action program can no longer make use of quotas or preferences and cannot be maintained simply to remedy past discrimination by society in general. It must be narrowly tailored to remedy actual discrimination that has occurred, and once the program has succeeded, it must be changed or dropped.

5-5c The Diversity Issue

Following the *Adarand* decision, several lower courts faced cases raising the question of whether affirmative action programs designed to achieve diversity on college campuses were constitutional.

The University of Michigan Cases In 2003, the Supreme Court reviewed two cases based on such issues. Both cases involved admissions programs at the University of Michigan.

In *Gratz v. Bollinger,* two white applicants who were denied undergraduate admission to the university alleged reverse discrimination.[24] The university's system automatically awarded every minority applicant one-fifth of the points needed to guarantee admission. The Court held that this policy violated the equal protection clause.

In contrast, in *Grutter v. Bollinger,* the Court held that the University of Michigan Law School's admissions policy was constitutional.[25] The difference between the two admissions policies was that the law school's approach did not apply a mechanical formula giving "diversity bonuses." The Court concluded that diversity on college campuses was a legitimate goal and that limited affirmative action programs could be used to attain this goal.

The Supreme Court Revisits the Issue In 2007, another case involving affirmative action in education came before the Court. The case concerned the policies of two school districts—one in Louisville, Kentucky, and one in Seattle, Washington. Both districts were trying to achieve a more diversified student body by giving preference to minority students if space in the schools was limited and a choice among applicants had to be made. Parents of white children who were turned away from schools because of these policies sued the school districts, claiming that the policies violated the equal protection clause. Ultimately, the Supreme Court held in favor of the parents.[26] The Court's decision did not overrule the 2003 case involving the University of Michigan Law School, however.

The Court's most recent rulings on affirmative action came in two cases, both named *Fisher v. University of Texas*. The Court sent the first case back to the lower courts for further argument in 2013. In the second case, in 2016, the Court found that diversity was a legitimate goal, and that the university's policies were "narrowly tailored" to reach that goal, as the law requires.[27]

5-5d State Actions

Beginning in the mid-1990s, some states have taken actions to ban affirmative action programs or replace them with alternative policies.

Bans on Affirmative Action In 1996, by a ballot initiative, California amended its state constitution to prohibit any "preferential treatment to any individual or group on the basis of race, sex, color, ethnicity, or national origin in the operation of public employment,

This student is a Republican who attends Pepperdine University, a school with a conservative reputation. He received a $1,000 scholarship open only to minority group members. Anti-affirmative-action groups have complained about the scholarship to the Department of Education. *Do the groups have a point? Why or why not?*

Lawrence K. Ho/Los Angeles Times/Getty Images

public education, or public contracting." Seven other states have also ended affirmative action.

In 2006, a ballot initiative in Michigan banned affirmative action in that state just three years after the Supreme Court decisions discussed above. In 2012, a federal appeals court overturned the voter-approved ban. In April 2014, however, the Supreme Court reversed the appeals court ruling, arguing that state voters had the right to eliminate affirmative action programs.[28] This decision gave support to bans on affirmative action in other states.

"Race-Blind" Admissions In the meantime, many public universities are trying to find "race-blind" ways to attract more minority students to their campuses. For example, Texas has established a program under which the top students at every high school in the state are guaranteed admission to the University of Texas at Austin. Originally, the guarantee applied to students who were in the top 10 percent of their graduating class. Today, the percentage varies from year to year. Beginning in 2005, the university reinstated an affirmative action plan, but it was limited to students who were not admitted as part of the top-student guarantee.

The guarantee ensures that the top students at minority-dominated inner-city schools can attend the state's leading public university. It also assures admission to the best white students from rural, often poor, communities. Previously, many of these students could not have hoped to attend the University of Texas. The losers are students from upscale metropolitan neighborhoods or suburbs who have high test scores but are not the top students at their schools. One result is that more students with high test scores enroll in less famous schools, such as Texas Tech University and the University of Texas at Dallas—to the benefit of these schools' reputations.

CRITICAL THINKING

▶ *Is the Texas plan to admit the top students from each high school to the University of Texas fair? Why or why not?*

AMERICA AT ODDS | Civil Rights

During the first part of the twentieth century, discrimination against African Americans and members of other minority groups was a social norm in the United States. Indeed, much of the nation's white population believed that the ability to discriminate was a constitutionally protected right. Today, the "right to discriminate" has very few defenders. America's laws—and its culture—now hold that discrimination on the basis of race, gender, religion, national origin, and many other characteristics is flatly unacceptable.

Even if civil rights are now broadly supported and protected by law, however, questions remain as to how far these protections should extend. Americans are at odds over a number of civil rights issues, including the following:

- *Is police misconduct directed against minorities—especially black men—a burning issue, or is its importance overrated?*

- *When the Department of Defense decided to allow women soldiers to serve in combat roles, was that a positive development— or a mistake?*

- *Was the Supreme Court correct to legalize same-sex marriages nationwide—or was that a step too far?*

- *Is affirmative action still a necessary policy—or should it be abandoned?*

- *When colleges and universities consider admissions, is it legitimate to promote racial, ethnic, gender, and socioeconomic diversity—or are such considerations just new forms of discrimination?*

STUDY TOOLS 5

READY TO STUDY? IN THE BOOK, YOU CAN:

☐ Review what you've read with the following chapter quiz.

☐ Check your answers in Appendix D at the back of the book.

☐ Rip out the Chapter Review Card, which includes key terms and chapter summaries.

ONLINE AT WWW.CENGAGEBRAIN.COM, YOU CAN:

☐ Watch videos to get a quick overview.

☐ Expedite your studying with Major Player readings and Focus Activities.

☐ Check your understanding with Chapter Quizzes.

FILL-IN

Learning Outcome 5–1

1. A law based on a _____, such as race, is subject to strict scrutiny by the courts.

Learning Outcome 5–2

2. In *Plessy v. Ferguson* (1896), the Supreme Court established the _____ doctrine, which was used to justify racial segregation in many areas of life for nearly sixty years.

3. The Civil Rights Act of 1964 forbade discrimination on the basis of _____.

Learning Outcome 5–3

4. The feminist movement that began in the 1960s sought _____ for women.

5. It is estimated that for every dollar earned by men, women earn about _____.

Learning Outcome 5–4

6. _____ constitute the largest ethnic minority in the United States.

7. Actions taken under an executive order issued by President Franklin D. Roosevelt in 1942 subjected many _____ Americans to curfews and evacuated those on the West Coast to "relocation centers."

8. The major legislative act protecting the rights of disabled persons is the _____.

Learning Outcome 5–5

9. Affirmative action is best defined as a policy _____.

10. In *Adarand Constructors, Inc. v. Peña* (1995), the Supreme Court held that any federal, state, or local affirmative action program that uses racial classifications as the basis for making decisions is subject to _____ scrutiny by the courts.

MULTIPLE CHOICE

Learning Outcome 5–1

11. The equal protection clause of the _____ Amendment reads: "No State shall . . . deny to any person within its jurisdiction the equal protection of the laws."
    a. Fifth
    b. Fourteenth
    c. Nineteenth

Learning Outcome 5–2

12. "Jim Crow" laws
    a. separated the white community from the black community.
    b. were justified by the Supreme Court's decision in *Brown v. Board of Education of Topeka* (1954).
    c. required an end to segregation.

Learning Outcome 5–3

13. _____ appointed the first woman to serve as a justice of the Supreme Court.
    a. Ronald Reagan
    b. George W. Bush
    c. Barack Obama

Learning Outcome 5–4

14. In 1789, Congress designated the Native American tribes as _____ so that the government could sign land and boundary treaties with them.
    a. enemies
    b. sovereign states composed of American citizens
    c. foreign nations

15. The Supreme Court ruling that guaranteed same-sex couples the right to marry was
    a. *Lawrence v. Texas* (2003).
    b. *Obergefell v. Hodges* (2015).
    c. *University of California v. Bakke* (1978).

Learning Outcome 5–5

16. The Supreme Court has ruled that states
    a. may ban affirmative action by state universities.
    b. cannot ban affirmative action programs that are used to meet diversity goals.
    c. can ban affirmative action for university admissions but not state government employment.

6 | INTEREST GROUPS

a katz/Shutterstock.com

LEARNING OUTCOMES

After reading this chapter, you should be able to:

6–1 Explain what an interest group is, why interest groups form, and how interest groups function in American politics.

6–2 Identify the various types of interest groups.

6–3 Discuss how the activities of interest groups help to shape government policymaking.

6–4 Describe how interest groups are regulated by government.

After finishing this chapter, go to **PAGE 142** for **STUDY TOOLS.**

AMERICA AT ODDS | Are Farmers Getting a Deal That's Too Good?

Ljupco Smokovski/Shutterstock.com

Many people, including those who live in large cities, have a romantic view of farming and farmers. This view is one of many reasons why interest groups representing farmers are so successful in winning support from the federal government. Over the last five years, about 2 million farmers received subsidies. The federal government's farm program is authorized by five-year farm bills. Farm bills have traditionally passed with bipartisan support because farm programs were in the same bill as the Supplemental Nutrition Assistance Program (SNAP, or food stamps). That ensured that liberals would join with rural legislators to support the bill.

When the last farm bill expired in 2012, however, Congress had become highly polarized, and no new farm bill passed until 2014. The 2014 bill provided $4.4 billion per year for commodity programs, $5.6 billion per year for conservation, and $9.0 billion per year for crop insurance. *Direct payments* were abolished. These payments used to go to growers of corn, cotton, rice, soybeans, and wheat regardless of whether they actually planted the crops. Almost all of the funds saved were added back as crop insurance subsidies, however. Are farmers getting too good a deal? Should farm subsidies be cut?

Agriculture Works— Don't Mess with Success

Farming is one of the riskiest businesses around. Farmers are ten times as likely to be killed on the job as the average worker. The weather is a constant worry. Every year, thousands of farmers lose their crops to floods or drought. Further, unlike many businesses, farmers can't set their own prices for what they sell. If you manufacture dishwashers, you expect that you can set a price for them that will cover your costs. Not so in agriculture. Prices are set by world commodity markets, where prices can swing wildly from month to month.

Despite the dangers, agriculture is a success story. Farm exports are booming as poor countries become richer and their people demand better diets—and the United Nations predicts that farmers will need to produce 70 percent more food by 2050 to keep up with population increases. Farm programs are an important safety net that helps keep our farmers in business. At less than half a percent of the federal budget, these programs are also a bargain.

Wealthy Farmers Don't Need These Subsidies

Everybody loves small farmers, but most of the subsidies don't go to these farmers. Only 20 percent of all farmers receive federal payments. Farms with a gross cash farm income in excess of $350,000 receive 70 percent of all payments. These farmers typically have net incomes in the hundreds of thousands of dollars and wealth in the millions. Why are we giving so much federal aid to people who are that well off?

There's no doubt that farming is risky. That's why the great majority of farmers carry crop insurance, which—as noted above—is subsidized. Typically, two-thirds of the cost of the insurance is covered by the government. Further, the 2014 bill contains an extra provision to cover policy deductibles. How can you lose? Some may claim that we need disaster assistance and conservation programs. But commodity programs and excessive insurance subsidies need to be cut back dramatically. American food consumers and taxpayers have paid too much for too long.

Where do you stand?

1. What effect might farm programs have on rural residents who are not farmers?
2. Soybeans are the nation's second-largest crop, after corn. Half of all U.S. soybeans are exported, many of them to feed Chinese pigs. If China made large cuts in U.S. soybean imports due to a trade dispute, how would this affect U.S. farmers?

Explore this issue online:

- You can find the site of the Environmental Working Group (EWG), a critic of farm subsidies, at www.ewg.org. The EWG has a database that contains a complete record of farm program recipients and what they were paid.
- To find arguments in support of the farm programs, visit the website of the Farm Bureau at www.fb.org.

INTRODUCTION

The groups supporting and opposing farm programs provide but one example of how Americans form groups to pursue or protect their interests. All of us have interests that we would like to have represented in government. Labor unionists would like it to be easier to organize unions, for example. Young people want good educational opportunities. Environmentalists want cleaner air and water.

The old saying that there is strength in numbers is certainly true in American politics. Special interests significantly influence American government and politics. Indeed, some Americans think that this influence is so great that it jeopardizes representative democracy. Others maintain that interest groups are a natural consequence of democracy. After all, throughout our nation's history, people have organized into groups to protect special interests. Because of the important role played by interest groups in the American system of government, we examine such groups in this chapter. We look at what they are, why they are formed, and how they influence policymaking.

 6–1 ## INTEREST GROUPS AND AMERICAN GOVERNMENT

> **LO** Explain what an interest group is, why interest groups form, and how interest groups function in American politics.

An **interest group** is an organized group of people sharing common objectives who actively attempt to influence government policymakers through direct and indirect methods. Whatever their goals—more or fewer social services, higher or lower prices—interest groups pursue these goals on every level and in every branch of government.

On any given day in Washington, D.C., you can see national interest groups in action. If you eat breakfast in the Senate dining room, you might see congressional committee staffers reviewing testimony with representatives from a small business group. Later that morning, you might visit the United States Supreme Court and watch a civil rights lawyer arguing on behalf of a client in a discrimination suit. Lunch in a popular Washington restaurant might find you listening in on a conversation between an agricultural lobbyist and a congressional representative.

> **interest group**
> An organized group of individuals sharing common objectives who actively attempt to influence policymakers.

That afternoon, you might visit an executive department, such as the Department of Labor, and watch bureaucrats working out rules and regulations with representatives from a business interest group. Then you might stroll past the headquarters of the National Rifle Association (NRA), AARP (formerly the American Association of Retired Persons), or the National Wildlife Federation.

6–1a The Constitutional Right to Petition the Government

The right to form interest groups and to lobby the government is protected by the Bill of Rights. The First Amendment guarantees the right of the people "to petition the Government for a redress of grievances." This important right sometimes gets lost among the other, more well-known First Amendment guarantees, such as the freedoms of religion, speech, and the press. Nonetheless, the right to petition the government is as important and fundamental to our democracy as the other First Amendment rights.

The right to petition the government allows citizens and groups of citizens to lobby members of Congress and other government officials, to sue the government, and to submit requests to the government. Whenever someone e-mails her or his congressional representative for help with a problem, such as not receiving a Social Security payment, that person is petitioning the government.

6–1b Why Interest Groups Form

The United States is a vast country of many regions, scores of ethnic groups, and a huge variety of businesses and occupations. The number of potential interests that can be represented is therefore very large. Beyond the sheer size of the country, however, there are a number of specific reasons why the United States has as many interest groups as it does.

Becoming an Interest Group It is worth remembering that not all groups are interest groups. A group becomes an interest group when it seeks to affect the policies or practices of the government. Many groups do not meet this standard. A social group, for example, may be formed to entertain or educate its members, with no broader purpose. Churches, organized to facilitate worship and community, frequently have no political aims. (Indeed, certain political activities, such as campaigning for or against candidates for office, could cost a church its tax-exempt status.)

A group founded with little or no desire to influence the government can become an interest group, however, if its members decide that the government's policies are important to them. Alternatively, lobbying the government may initially be only one of several activities pursued by a group and may then grow to become the group's primary purpose.

The National Rifle Association (NRA) provides an example of this process. From its establishment in 1871 until the 1930s, the group took little part in politics. As late as the 1970s, a large share of the NRA's members joined for reasons that had nothing to do with politics. Many joined solely to participate in firearms training programs or to win marksman certifications. The NRA continues to provide such services today, but it is now so heavily politicized that anyone likely to take out a membership is certain to broadly agree with the NRA's political positions.

More Government, More Interest Groups

Interest groups may form—and existing groups may become more politically active—when the government expands its scope of activities. More government, in other words, means more interest groups. Prior to the 1970s, for example, the various levels of government were not nearly as active in attempting to regulate the use of firearms as they were thereafter. This change provides one explanation of why the NRA is much more politically active today than it was years ago.

Consider another example—AARP, formerly the American Association of Retired Persons. AARP is a major lobbying force that seeks to preserve or enhance Social Security and Medicare benefits for citizens sixty-five years of age and older. Before the creation of Social Security in the 1930s, however, the federal government did not provide income support to the elderly, and there would have been little reason for an organization such as AARP to exist.

Defending the Group's Interests Interest groups also may come into existence in response to a perceived threat to a group's interests. In the example of the NRA, the threat was an increase in the frequency of attempts to regulate or even ban firearms. This increase threatened the interests of gun owners. As another example, the National Right to Life Committee formed in response to *Roe v. Wade*, the Supreme Court's

decision that legalized abortion. Interest groups can also form in reaction to the creation of other interest groups, thus pitting two groups against each other. Political scientist David B. Truman coined the term *disturbance theory* to describe this kind of defensive formation of interest groups.[1]

The Importance of Leaders Political scientist Robert H. Salisbury provided another analysis of the organization of interest groups that he dubbed *entrepreneurial theory*. This line of thought focuses on the importance of the leaders who establish the organization. The desire of such individuals to guarantee a viable organization is important to the group's survival.[2] AARP is an example of a group with a committed founder—Dr. Ethel Percy Andrus, a retired high school principal. Andrus organized the group in 1958 to let older Americans purchase health-care insurance collectively. Like the NRA, AARP did not develop into a lobbying powerhouse until years after it was founded.

Incentives to Join a Group The French political observer and traveler Alexis de Tocqueville wrote in 1835 that Americans have a tendency to form "associations" and have perfected "the art of pursuing in common the object of their common desires. . . . In no other country of the world, has the principle of association been more successfully used or applied to a greater multitude of objectives than in America."[3] Of course, Tocqueville could not have foreseen the thousands of associations that now exist in this country. Surveys show that more than 85 percent of Americans belong to at least one group. Table 6–1 shows the percentage of Americans who belong to various types of groups today.

> "Politics is about *people*, not politicians."
> ~ SCOTT SIMMS
> CANADIAN POLITICIAN
> BORN 1969

TABLE 6–1 PERCENTAGE OF AMERICANS BELONGING TO VARIOUS GROUPS	
Social clubs	17%
Neighborhood groups	18
Hobby, garden, and technology clubs	19
PTA and school groups	21
Professional and trade associations	27
Health, sport, and country clubs	30
Religious groups	61

Source: AARP.

Political scientists have identified various reasons why people join interest groups. Often, people have one or more incentives to join such organizations.

▶ If a group stands for something that you believe is very important, you can gain considerable satisfaction in taking action from within that group. Such satisfaction is referred to as a **purposive incentive.**

▶ Some people enjoy the camaraderie and sense of belonging that come from associating with other people who share their interests and goals. That enjoyment can be called a **solidary incentive.**

▶ Some groups offer their members material incentives for joining, such as discounts on products, subscriptions, or group insurance. Each of these could be characterized as a **material incentive.**

Sometimes, though, none of these incentives is enough to persuade people to join a group.

The Free Rider Problem　The world in which we live is one of scarce resources that can be used to create *private goods* and *public goods*. Most of the goods and services that you use are private goods. If you consume them, no one else can consume them at the same time. If you eat a sandwich, no one else can have it.

With public goods, however, your use of a good does not diminish its use by someone else. National defense is a good example. If this country is protected through its national defense system, your protection from enemy invasion does not reduce any other person's protection.

People cannot be excluded from enjoying a public good, such as national defense, just because they did not pay for it. As a result, public goods are often provided by the government, which can force people to pay for the public good through taxation.

The existence of persons who benefit but do not contribute is called the **free rider problem.** Much of what we know about the free rider problem comes from Mancur Olson's classic work of political science, *The Logic of Collective Action.*[4]

Alexis de Tocqueville (1805–1859), a French writer, took a keen interest in America. He toured the United States and collected his observations in *Democracy in America*, published in 1835. *What U.S. institution would he have seen that was undemocratic?*

Interest Groups and Public Goods.　Lobbying, collective bargaining by labor unions, and other forms of representation can also be public goods. If an interest group is successful in lobbying for laws that will improve air quality, for example, everyone who breathes that air will benefit, whether they paid for the lobbying effort or not.

Addressing the Problem.　In some instances, the free rider problem can be overcome. For example, social pressure may persuade some people to join or donate to a group for fear of being ostracized. This motivation is more likely to be effective for small, localized groups than for large, widely dispersed groups like AARP, however.

The government can also step in to ensure that the burden of lobbying for the public good is shared by all. When the government classifies interest groups as nonprofit organizations, it confers on them tax-exempt status. The groups' operating costs are reduced because they do not have to pay taxes, and the impact of the government's lost revenue is absorbed by all taxpayers.

purposive incentive
A reason to join an interest group—satisfaction resulting from working for a cause in which one believes.

solidary incentive
A reason to join an interest group—pleasure in associating with like-minded individuals.

material incentive
A reason to join an interest group—practical benefits such as discounts, subscriptions, or group insurance.

free rider problem
The existence of persons who benefit from the actions of a group but do not contribute to the group.

Everett Historical//Shutterstock.com

6-1c How Interest Groups Function in American Politics

Despite the bad press that interest groups tend to get in the United States, they do serve several purposes in American politics:

▸ Interest groups help bridge the gap between citizens and government—and enable citizens to explain their views on policies to public officials.

▸ Interest groups help raise public awareness and inspire action on various issues.

▸ Interest groups often provide public officials with specialized and detailed information that might be difficult to obtain otherwise. This information may be useful in making policy choices.

▸ Interest groups serve as another check on public officials to make sure that they are carrying out their duties responsibly.

Access to Government   In a sense, the American system of government invites the participation of interest groups by offering many points of access for groups wishing to influence policy. Consider the possibilities at just the federal level.

An interest group can lobby members of Congress to act in the interests of the group. If the House of Representatives passes a bill opposed by the group, the group's lobbying efforts can shift to the Senate. If the Senate passes the bill and the president signs it, the group can try to influence the new law's application by lobbying the executive agency that is responsible for implementing the law. The group might even challenge the law in court. This can happen directly—by filing a lawsuit—or indirectly—by filing a brief as an *amicus curiae*, or "friend of the court." (The phrase is pronounced ah-*mee*-kus kure-ee-eye.)

Interest groups can seek a variety of different benefits when lobbying the government. A frequent goal is favorable treatment under federal or state regulations. Groups may also seek outright subsidies that benefit their members. An increasingly popular objective is special treatment in the tax code. Tax breaks for a special interest can be easier to obtain than subsidies because the breaks don't look like government spending.

Pluralist Theory   The pluralist theory of American democracy focuses on the participation of groups in a decentralized government structure that offers many points of access to policymakers. According to the pluralist theory, politics is a contest among various interest groups. These groups vie with one another—at all levels of government—to gain benefits for their members.

Pluralists maintain that the influence of interest groups on government is not undemocratic because individual interests are indirectly represented in the policymaking process through these groups. Although not every American belongs to an interest group, inevitably some group will represent at least some of the interests of each individual. Thus, each interest is satisfied to some extent through the compromises made in settling conflicts among competing interest groups.

Pluralists also contend that because of the extensive number of interest groups vying for political benefits, no one group can dominate the political process. Additionally, because most people have more than one interest, conflicts among groups do not divide the nation into hostile camps. Not all scholars agree that this is how American democracy functions, however.

Majoritarianism and Elite Theory   Political scientists have two other theories to describe American democracy: majoritarianism and elite theory. Majoritarianism is the belief that public policy should be set in accordance with the opinions of a majority of the people. Majoritarianism is highly popular, but political scientists find it to be a startlingly poor description of how politics actually works. Elite theory contends that, as a practical matter, the government is controlled by one or more elite groups, typically drawn from the wealthiest members of society. One version of elite theory posits that multiple elites compete for power. It is worth noting that many interest groups are largely funded—or even controlled—by wealthy individuals, so pluralism (described previously) and elite theory may overlap.

Evaluating the Theories   How valid are these three theories as explanations of how policy is made? Many political scientists have long believed that both pluralism and elite theory contain elements of truth and that majoritarianism is only an ideal. Political scientists Martin Gilens and Benjamin Page recently tried to find evidence for this belief through a major study. They found that the preferences of interest groups and of economic elites did indeed have a strong influence on policy. The

pluralist theory A theory that views politics as a contest among various interest groups—at all levels of government—to gain benefits for their members.

majoritarianism The belief that public policy is or should be set in accordance with the opinions of a majority of the people.

elite theory The belief that the government is controlled by one or more elite groups.

influence of average citizens, however, when separated from the preferences of interest groups or elites, was effectively zero.[5] It follows that ordinary citizens have a good reason to join interest groups. Only by doing so will they be heard.

6-1d How Do Interest Groups Differ from Political Parties?

Although both interest groups and political parties are groups of people joined together for political purposes, they differ in several important ways. A political party is a group of individuals who organize to win elections, operate the government, and determine policy. Interest groups, in contrast, do not seek to win elections or operate the government, although they do seek to influence policy. Interest groups differ from political parties in the following ways:

▶ Interest groups are often policy *specialists*, whereas political parties are policy *generalists*. Political parties are broad-based organizations that must attract the support of many opposing groups and consider a large number of issues. Interest groups, in contrast, may have only a handful of key policies to promote. An environmental group, obviously, will not be as concerned about the economic status of Hispanics as it is about polluters. A manufacturing group is more involved with pushing for fewer regulations than it is with inner-city poverty.

▶ Interest groups are usually more tightly organized than political parties. They are often financed through contributions or dues-paying memberships. Organizers of interest groups communicate with members and potential members through conferences, mailings, newsletters, and electronic formats such as e-mail, Facebook, and Twitter.

▶ A political party's main sphere of influence is the electoral system. Parties run candidates for political office. Interest groups may try to influence the outcome of elections, but unlike parties, they do not compete for public office. Although a candidate for office may be sympathetic to—or even be a member of—a certain group, he or she does not run for election as a candidate of that group.

CRITICAL THINKING

▶ *Identify some public goods other than national defense. Are any of these public goods associated with a significant free rider problem? Why or why not?*

LO Identify the various types of interest groups.

American democracy embraces almost every conceivable type of interest group, and the number is increasing rapidly. No one has ever compiled a *Who's Who* of interest groups, but you can get an idea of the number and variety by looking through the annually published *Encyclopedia of Associations*.

Some interest groups have large memberships. AARP, for example, has more than 38 million members. Others, such as the Colorado Auctioneers Association, have fewer than one hundred members. Some, such as the U.S. Chamber of Commerce, are household names and have been in existence for many years, while others crop up overnight. Some are highly structured and are run by full-time professionals, while others are loosely structured and informal.

The most common interest groups are those that promote private interests. These groups seek public policies that benefit the economic interests of their members and work against policies that threaten those interests.

6-2a Business Interest Groups

Business has long been well organized for effective action. Hundreds of business groups are now operating in Washington, D.C., in the fifty state capitals, and at the local level across the country. Table 6–2 lists some top business interests and their campaign contributions through the 2016 elections.

Two umbrella organizations that include small and large corporations and businesses are the U.S. Chamber

TABLE 6–2 TOP BUSINESS CAMPAIGN DONORS, 1990–2016 ELECTION CYCLES

Firm or Group	Total, 1990–2016
1. The Fahr Group (executive recruitment)	$165,918,297
2. Las Vegas Sands (casinos)	$113,473,114
3. Renaissance Technologies (hedge fund)	$92,053,788
4. National Association of Realtors	$83,852,698
5. Adelson Drug Clinic (casinos)	$81,211,318
6. Newsweb Corp. (media)	$78,024,311
7. AT&T	$71,030,263
8. Soros Fund Management	$69,432,648
9. Goldman Sachs (bank)	$56,959,986
10. Elliot Management (hedge fund)	$56,679,369

Source: Center for Responsive Politics.

of Commerce and the National Association of Manufacturers (NAM). In addition to representing more than 3 million individual businesses, the Chamber has more than three thousand local, state, and regional affiliates. It has become a major voice for millions of small businesses.

Trade Organizations The hundreds of trade organizations are far less visible than the Chamber of Commerce and the NAM, but they are also important in seeking policies that assist their members. Trade organizations usually support policies that benefit specific industries. For example, people in the oil industry work for policies that favor the development of oil as an energy resource. Other business groups work for policies that favor the development of coal, solar power, or nuclear power. Trucking companies work for policies that would lower their taxes. Railroad companies would, of course, not want other forms of transportation to receive special tax breaks, because that would hurt their business.

How Business Interest Groups Support Both Parties Traditionally, business interest groups have been viewed as staunch supporters of the Republican Party. This is because Republicans are more likely to promote government policies friendly toward business. Since 2000, however, donations from corporations to the Democratic National Committee have more than doubled.

Why would business groups make contributions to the Democratic National Committee? One reason is that in some fields, business leaders are more likely to be Democrats than in the past. Financial industry leaders were once almost entirely Republican, but today some of them support the Democrats. Information technology, a relatively new industry, contains both Republicans and Democrats. An additional reason why many business interests support both parties is to ensure that they will benefit regardless of who wins elections. There is another possible motivation: campaign contributions may be made not to gain political favors but rather to avoid political disfavor that could damage the interests of a business.

Agricultural Interest Groups In our capitalist society, farms clearly are businesses. They are a particular kind of business, however, and deserve special attention.

A Walmart store manager reviews the previous day's sales at a meeting with staff members. Much of Walmart's inventory consists of low-cost goods imported from China and elsewhere. Its managers and staff therefore worry about possible restrictions on imports under the Trump administration. *How important are low-cost goods to low-income Americans?*

Producers of various specific farm commodities, such as dairy products, soybeans, grain, fruit, corn, cotton, beef, and sugar beets, have formed their own organizations to promote their interests. In addition, many groups work for general agricultural interests. Three broad-based agricultural groups represent millions of American farmers, from peanut farmers to dairy producers to tobacco growers. They are the American Farm Bureau Federation (Farm Bureau), the National Grange, and the National Farmers Union. The Farm Bureau, representing more than 5.5 million families (a majority of whom are not actually farm families), is the largest and generally the most effective of the three.

Interest groups representing farmers have been spectacularly successful in winning subsidies from the federal government, as we explained in the chapter-opening *America at Odds* feature. Subsidies are not the only way in which the federal government can assist growers of a particular crop. The government can also restrict imports of a specific commodity, such as sugar. The restrictions raise the price of sugar, which benefits sugar beet growers at the expense of consumers.

trade organization
An association formed by members of a particular industry, such as the oil or trucking industries, to develop common standards and goals for the industry. Trade organizations, as interest groups, lobby government for legislation or regulations that specifically benefit their members.

6–2b Labor and Professional Interest Groups

Interest groups representing labor have been some of the most influential groups in our country's history. They date back to at least 1886, when the American Federation of Labor (AFL) was formed. The largest and most powerful labor interest group today is the AFL-CIO (the American Federation of Labor–Congress of Industrial Organizations), a confederation of fifty-five unions representing 12.5 million organized workers and 3.2 million members of community affiliates (affiliates are community groups that are not unions).

Unions not affiliated with the AFL-CIO also represent millions of members. The Change to Win federation consists of four unions and 4.2 million workers. Dozens of other unions are independent. Examples include the National Education Association, the United Electrical Workers (UE), and the Major League Baseball Players Association. We list some top labor campaign donors in Table 6–3.

Union Goals   Like labor unions everywhere, American unions press for policies to improve working conditions and ensure better pay for their members. Unions may compete for new members. In many states, for example, the National Education Association and the AFL-CIO's American Federation of Teachers compete fiercely for members.

TABLE 6–3	TOP LABOR CAMPAIGN DONORS, 1990–2016 ELECTION CYCLES	
Union or Group		**Total, 1990–2016**
1. Service Employees International Union		$272,230,427
2. National Education Association		$119,863,839
3. Amer. Fed. of State, County, and Municipal Employees		$107,918,931
4. Carpenters & Joiners Union		$96,893,960
5. American Federation of Teachers		$92,014,596
6. Laborers Union (construction)		$84,801,586
7. Int'l. Brotherhood of Electrical Workers		$74,069,571
8. United Food & Commercial Workers Union		$69,518,700
9. AFL-CIO		$62,384,819
10. United Auto Workers		$53,713,997

Source: Center for Responsive Politics.

The goals of unions, however, are not necessarily limited to measures that directly benefit their own members. An example is the national campaign for a $15 minimum wage, which has received heavy union support. Very few of those who would benefit from a higher minimum wage are union members or likely to join in the future. Still, some argue that a higher minimum wage would tend to push up wages generally, which would benefit all workers, including union members.

Another major issue for the labor movement has been foreign trade. Unions have traditionally been hostile to trade agreements such as the North American Free Trade Agreement (NAFTA), believing that they cost American jobs. President Donald Trump has also taken this view, but most unions disagree with the Republican Party on so many other issues that supporting Trump was out of the question. We look more closely at the trade issue in this chapter's *Perception vs. Reality* feature.

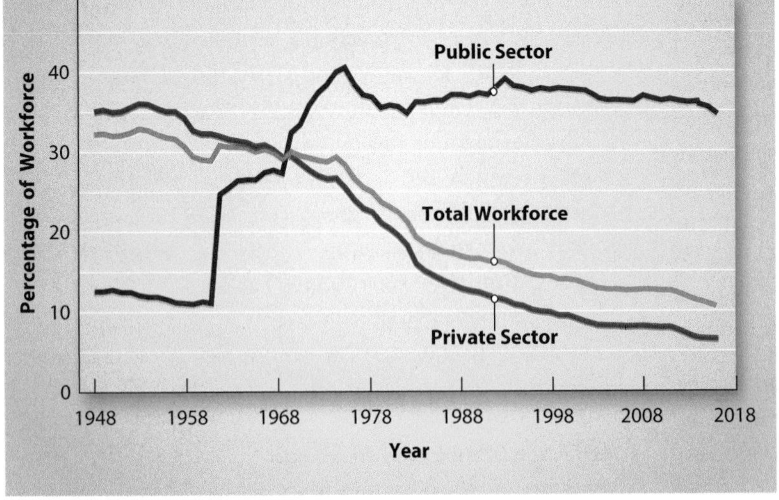

The Decline of Unions   Although unions were highly influential in the 1930s, 1940s, and 1950s, their strength and political power have waned in the last several decades, as you can see in Figure 6–1. Today, members of organized labor make up only 10.7 percent of all wage and salary workers. Unions also represent many workers who are not members. Therefore, the percentage of workers represented by a union is larger than the percentage who are members.

FIGURE 6–1   UNION MEMBERSHIP, 1952 TO PRESENT

This figure shows the percentage of wage and salary workers who have been union members from 1952 to the present. *Why has the share of union members in the labor force fallen?*

The United States Can Bring Back Factory Jobs

President Trump's slogan "Make America Great Again" was, in part, a promise to bring lost factory jobs back to this country. Indeed, after Trump's election, a number of U.S. firms announced that they would cancel plans to move jobs from the United States to Mexico.

The Perception

U.S. companies have moved millions of jobs to countries such as China and Mexico because these countries don't pay their workers as well as we do. Too many of our factory workers have lost their jobs because of this unfair competition. If we stand up to these foreign countries, we can get our jobs back.

The Reality

It is certainly true that the United States has fewer manufacturing jobs than in the past. In 1980, the number of such jobs was almost 19 million, whereas today there are barely 12 million. But that doesn't mean that America no longer makes things. In fact, the inflation-adjusted output of the U.S. manufacturing sector today is more than two-and-a-half times what it was in 1980.

How can that be? The answer is increased productivity. Year after year, U.S. manufacturers have become more efficient. We can produce more output with fewer and fewer workers. Consider that it costs $8 an hour to use a robot for spot welding as opposed to $25 for a U.S. worker. If we did manage to bring back work from China or Mexico, the jobs wouldn't go to people. They would go to machines. Economists have calculated that 80 to 90 percent of the manufacturing jobs that have disappeared since 1980 vanished because of productivity gains.

Yet if foreign competition is at least a small part of the problem, then shouldn't we blame—as Trump does—international trade deals, such as the North American Free Trade Agreement (NAFTA)? Not really. In fact, the impact of special trade deals such as NAFTA on employment is so small as to be almost invisible. The real source of disturbance has been China, with which we have no special trade deals. The economy of China is now more than *two hundred times larger* than it was in 1970. There is no way that U.S. economic policies could have

prevented the emergence of such a mighty competitor.

And here is something else. If we restrict international trade, say by a tariff (tax) on imports, there will ultimately be fewer jobs in the United States. Why? Because the books must balance. Taken together, our imports of goods, services, and investments must match our exports. If we stop the world from sending us imports, the world won't be able to buy our exports. That would be lethal for soybean farmers in Iowa and aircraft builders in Seattle. Also, if we do in fact tax imports, one inevitable result will be higher prices for the American consumer.

Blog On

University of California economics professor Brad DeLong provides much additional insight in an article that, among other things, compares the United States with Germany. Find it by searching for "vox delong trade."

Reasons for Labor's Decline. There are several reasons why the power of organized labor has declined in the United States. One is the continuing fall in the proportion of the nation's workforce employed in such blue-collar activities as manufacturing and transportation. These sectors have always been among the most heavily unionized.

Another important factor in labor's decline, however, is the general political environment. Forming and maintaining unions is more difficult in the United States than in most other industrial nations. Among the world's

wealthy democracies, the United States is one of the most politically conservative, at least on economic issues. Economic conservatives are traditionally hostile to labor unions. Further, many business owners in the United States do not accept unions as legitimate institutions and will make strong efforts to ensure that their own businesses remain nonunionized.

Differing State Laws. The impact of the political environment on labor's organizing ability can be easily seen by comparing rates of unionization in various states. These rates are especially low in conservative southern states. Georgia and South Carolina are both major manufacturing states, but unions represent only 3.9 percent of those employed in Georgia and only 1.6 percent in South Carolina.

Compare these figures with rates in more liberal states, such as California and New York: unions represent 15.9 percent of the workforce in California and 23.6 percent in New York. One factor that depresses unionization rates is that many states in the South and West have so-called **right-to-work laws.** These laws ban unions from collecting dues or other fees from workers whom they represent but who have not actually joined the union. Such laws create a significant free rider problem for unions. Twenty-eight states have right-to-work laws. The most recent states to adopt such laws are West Virginia (in 2016), and Kentucky and Missouri (in 2017).

Public-Sector Unions

While organized labor has suffered from declining numbers and a resulting loss in lobbying power, labor has held the line in one industry—government. In the 1960s and 1970s, public-sector unions enjoyed rapid growth. The percentage of government workers who are union members then leveled off, but it remains high. More than one-third of all public-sector workers are union members today.

In contrast to unions in the private sector, public-sector unions do not have the right to strike over wages and working conditions. Still, they are influential. Unlike workers in private industry, public-sector employees—in their role as citizens—have the right to vote for their own bosses. As a result, elected officials are often reluctant to antagonize public-sector unions. One consequence of the influence of these unions is that government workers typically enjoy pension benefits that are substantially more generous than those received by comparable employees in the private sector.

Since the 2010 elections, several Republican governors in the Midwest have attempted to curtail the bargaining rights of state and local government employee unions. These governors argue that pension benefits and other perks won by the unions threaten the financial stability of state and local governments. The role and status of public-sector unions, therefore, have become important political issues.

right-to-work laws
Laws that ban unions from collecting dues or other fees from workers whom they represent but who have not actually joined the union.

public-interest group
An interest group formed for the purpose of working for the "public good." Examples are the American Civil Liberties Union and Common Cause.

Professional Interest Groups

Employees are not the only members of the labor force who find a need to organize interest groups. Most professions that require advanced education or specialized training have organizations to protect and promote their interests. These groups are concerned mainly with the standards of their professions, but they also work to influence government policy.

Major professional groups include the American Medical Association (AMA), representing physicians; the American Bar Association, representing lawyers; and the American Association for Justice, representing trial lawyers. In addition, there are dozens of less well-known and less politically active professional groups, such as the National Association of Social Workers and the American Political Science Association.

Competing interests sometimes divide professional interest groups from one another. For example, medical groups contend that it is too easy for lawyers to sue physicians, insurance companies, and other businesses, and that generous settlements drive up the cost of health care and other goods. The AMA generally favors restrictions on such lawsuits. The American Association for Justice, naturally, opposes such changes.

6-2c Public-Interest and Other Types of Groups

Some interest groups have aims other than benefiting narrow economic interests. These include so-called **public-interest groups,** which are formed with the broader goal of working for the "public good." The American Civil Liberties Union and Common Cause are examples.

Let there be no mistake, though, about the name *public interest.* There is no such thing as a clear public interest in a nation of 325 million diverse people. The two public-interest groups just mentioned represent only a relatively small part of the American population. In reality, all lobbying groups, organizations, and other political entities represent special interests.

Consumer Interest Groups

Groups organized for the protection of consumer rights were very active in the 1960s and 1970s. Some are still active today. One well-known group is Consumers Union, a nonprofit organization started in 1936. In addition to publishing *Consumer Reports* magazine, Consumers Union has been influential in pushing for the removal of phosphates from detergents, lead from gasoline, and pesticides from food. Consumers Union strongly criticizes government agencies when they appear to act against consumer interests. Other major groups include Consumer Action, the Consumer Federation of America, and Public Citizen.

Consumer groups are active in many cities. They deal with such problems as substandard housing, discrimination against minorities and women, discrimination in the granting of credit, and business inaction on consumer complaints.

Identity Interest Groups

Americans who share the same race, ethnicity, gender, or other characteristics often have important common interests. African Americans, for example, have a powerful interest in combating the racism and racial discrimination that have marked American history from the beginning. Slaves, of course, were not able to form interest groups. For many years after the abolition of slavery, organizing African American interest groups remained impossibly dangerous. Such groups did not come into existence until the twentieth century.

Young Los Angeles protesters participate in a rally to condemn the killing of unarmed black men by police officers. *Are such demonstrations likely to be effective?*

African American Interest Groups. The National Association for the Advancement of Colored People (NAACP) was founded in 1909, and the National Urban League was created in 1910. During the civil rights movement of the 1950s and 1960s, African Americans organized a number of new groups, some of which lasted (the Southern Christian Leadership Conference, founded in 1957) and some of which did not (the Student Nonviolent Coordinating Committee, organized in 1960). Among the most recent interest groups formed to defend African Americans is the loosely organized Black Lives Matter movement. This movement seeks to end alleged police violence toward African Americans and other minority group members.

Other Identity Interest Groups. The campaigns for dignity and equality of Native Americans, Latinos, women, LGBT persons, Americans with disabilities, and many others have all resulted in important interest groups. Older American citizens are numerous, are politically active, and have a great deal at stake in debates over certain programs, such as Social Security and Medicare. As a result, groups representing them, such as AARP, can be a potent political force.

Ideological Interest Groups Some interest groups are organized to promote not an economic interest or a collective identity but a shared political perspective or ideology. Examples include MoveOn, an Internet-oriented liberal group, and the Club for Growth, a conservative antitax organization.

The Tea Party Movement. The highly decentralized Tea Party movement, which sprang into life in 2009, has been described as an ideological interest group. Still, some Tea Party groups have attempted to gain control of local Republican Party organizations. It may be only a matter of terminology, but political scientists refer to groups that compete for control of a political party as *factions*, not interest groups.

Environmental Groups. Environmental groups have supported water pollution controls, wilderness protection, and clean-air legislation. They have opposed strip mining, nuclear power plants, logging activities, chemical waste dumps, and many other potential environmental hazards. Environmental interest groups range from traditional organizations, such as the National Wildlife Federation with more than 4 million members, to more radical groups, such as Greenpeace USA with a membership of 250,000.

In the past, environmental groups have been characterized as single-interest groups, not ideological organizations. Issues such as climate change, however, have led many modern environmental groups to advocate sweeping changes to the entire economy. Groups with such broad agendas could be considered a type of ideological interest group.

Religious Groups. Religious organizations are another type of group that could be included in the ideological category. Many religious groups work on behalf of conservative social causes. Others take a strong interest in the well-being of those suffering from poverty. Indeed, for decades, many mainstream religious groups have lobbied on behalf of those suffering from poverty. These include Catholic organizations, Lutherans, the National Council of Churches, the Friends (Quakers), and many others. Liberal groups have also played a major role in such lobbying. We list some top ideological and miscellaneous interest groups that have made campaign contributions in Table 6–4.

Single-Issue Interest Groups Numerous interest groups focus on a single issue. For example, Mothers Against Drunk Driving (MADD) lobbies for stiffer penalties for drunk driving. Formed in 1980, MADD now boasts more than 3 million members and supporters. The abortion debate has created various single-issue groups, such as the National Right to Life organization (which opposes abortion) and NARAL Pro-Choice America (founded as the National Association for the Repeal of Abortion Laws in 1969, when abortion was widely illegal). Other examples of single-issue groups are the NRA and the American Israel Public Affairs Committee (a pro-Israel group).

Government Interest Groups Efforts by state and local governments to lobby the federal government have escalated in recent years. When states experience budget shortfalls, these governments often lobby in Washington, D.C., for additional federal funds. The federal government has sometimes lobbied in individual states, too. Until 2009, for example, the U.S. Attorney General's office lobbied against medical marijuana use in states that were considering ballot measures on the issue.

The Unrepresented Poor As we have noted, liberal and religious interests have done for the poor what the poor cannot do for themselves. As a result, low-income taxpayers are largely exempt from income taxes. They pay only payroll taxes, and in many cases, they can get rebates on these. On the

> **direct technique** Any method used by an interest group to interact with government officials directly to further the group's goals.

TABLE 6–4	TOP IDEOLOGICAL AND MISCELLANEOUS CAMPAIGN DONORS, 1990–2016 ELECTION CYCLES
Group	**Total, 1990–2016**
1. NextGen Climate Action	$58,400,407
2. EMILY's List (Democratic)	$45,063,529
3. Republican Governors Association	$37,839,719
4. Priorities USA (Democratic)	$33,753,682
5. Victory Campaign 2004 (Democratic)	$33,038,925

Source: Center for Responsive Politics.

spending side, the Brookings Institution has estimated that all federal low-income programs together cost more than $800 billion a year. These programs include food stamps (now called the Supplemental Nutrition Assistance Program, or SNAP), Medicaid, and the Earned-Income Tax Credit.

If there were no federal tax and spending programs aimed at low-income persons, as many as 25 percent of U.S. families would have incomes below the official poverty line. If you take into account all benefits that low-income families obtain, that number drops to about 10 percent.

CRITICAL THINKING

▸ *Are you a member of any interest groups? If so, why? If not, which existing groups might best serve your interests? Again, why?*

 HOW INTEREST GROUPS SHAPE POLICY

LO Discuss how the activities of interest groups help to shape government policymaking.

Interest groups operate at all levels of government and use a variety of strategies to steer policies in ways beneficial to their interests. Sometimes, they attempt to influence policymakers directly, but at other times they try to exert indirect influence on policymakers by shaping public opinion. The extent and nature of the groups' activities depend on their goals and their resources.

6–3a Direct Techniques

Lobbying and providing election support are two important **direct techniques** used by interest groups to influence government policy.

Lobbying   Today, lobbying refers to all of the attempts by organizations or by individuals to influence the passage, defeat, or contents of legislation or to influence the administrative decisions of government. (The term *lobbying* arose because, traditionally, individuals and groups interested in influencing government policy would gather in the foyer, or lobby, of the legislature to corner legislators and express their concerns.) A lobbyist is an individual who handles a particular interest group's lobbying efforts. Most of the larger interest groups have lobbyists in Washington, D.C. These lobbyists often include former members of Congress or former employees of executive bureaucracies who are experienced in the methods of political influence and who "know people." Table 6–5 summarizes some of the basic methods by which lobbyists directly influence legislators and government officials.

Mega-lobbyist Heather Podesta (center) greets a government official at a Washington, D.C., reception. *Why do former members of Congress often become lobbyists?*

Lobbying can be directed at the legislative branch of government or at administrative agencies. As mentioned earlier, lobbying can also be directed at the courts, by filing a lawsuit or an *amicus curiae* brief. Many lobbyists also work at state and local levels. In fact, lobbying at the state level has increased in recent years as states have begun to play a more significant role in policymaking.

Providing Election Support
Interest groups often become directly involved in the election process. Many group members join and work with political parties to influence party platforms and the nomination of candidates. Interest groups provide campaign support for legislators who favor their policies and sometimes encourage their own members to try to win posts in party organizations.

Most important, interest groups urge their members to vote for candidates who support the views of the group. They can also threaten legislators with the withdrawal of votes. No candidate can expect to have support from all interest groups, but if the candidate is to win, she or he must have support from many of the strongest ones.

Political Action Committees (PACs).   Since the 1970s, federal laws governing campaign financing have allowed corporations, labor unions, and special interest groups to raise funds and make campaign contributions through political action committees (PACs). Both the number of PACs and the amount of money PACs spend on elections have grown astronomically in recent years. There were about 1,000 PACs in 1976. Today, there are more than 4,500 PACs. In 1973, total spending by PACs amounted to $19 million. In the 2015–2016 election cycle, contributions to federal candidates by PACs totaled about $450 million.

Even with their impressive growth, PACs provided a smaller share of campaign spending in the years after 1988, principally because of the development of other funding sources, such as "soft money" and issue ads. (We discuss these sources shortly.)

Note that although campaign contributions do not guarantee that officials will vote the way the groups wish, contributions usually do ensure that the groups will have the ear of the public officials they have helped to elect.

Super PACs.   In 2010, the Supreme Court upended the world of campaign finance in *Citizens United v. Federal Election Commission*.[6] The Court ruled that PACs could accept unlimited contributions from individuals, unions, and corporations for the purpose of making independent expenditures. These are expenditures that

lobbying All of the attempts by organizations or by individuals to influence the passage, defeat, or contents of legislation or to influence the administrative decisions of government.

lobbyist An individual who handles a particular interest group's lobbying efforts.

political action committees (PACs) A committee that is established by a corporation, labor union, or special interest group to raise funds and make campaign contributions on the establishing organization's behalf.

independent expenditure An expenditure for activities that are independent from (not coordinated with) those of a political candidate or a political party.

TABLE 6–5 DIRECT LOBBYING TECHNIQUES

Technique	Description
Making Personal Contacts with Key Legislators	A lobbyist's personal contacts with key legislators or other government officials—in their offices, in the halls of Congress, or on social occasions such as dinners, boating expeditions, and the like—are one of the most effective direct lobbying techniques.
Providing Expertise and Research Results for Legislators	Lobbyists often have knowledge and expertise that are useful in drafting legislation, and these can be major strengths for an interest group. Harried members of Congress cannot possibly be experts on everything they vote on and therefore eagerly seek information to help them make up their minds.
Offering "Expert" Testimony before Congressional Committees	Lobbyists often provide "expert" testimony before congressional committees for or against proposed legislation. Each expert offers as much evidence as possible to support her or his position.
Providing Legal Advice to Legislators	Many lobbyists assist legislators in drafting legislation or prospective regulations. Lobbyists are a source of ideas and sometimes offer legal advice on specific details.
Following Up on Legislation	Because executive agencies responsible for carrying out legislation can often change the scope of the new law, lobbyists may also try to influence the bureaucrats who implement the policy.

© 2018 Cengage Learning

are not coordinated with a candidate's campaign or a political party. This ruling led, in short order, to the creation of super PACs, which channeled almost $1.8 billion into election spending in the 2016 election cycle. Many super PACs were funded by wealthy individuals, and many of them concentrated on running negative ads.

6–3b Indirect Techniques

Interest groups also try to influence public policy indirectly through the general public. The effects of such **indirect techniques** may appear to be spontaneous, but indirect techniques are generally as well planned as the direct lobbying techniques just discussed. Indirect techniques can be particularly effective because public officials are often more impressed by contacts from voters than from lobbyists.

Shaping Public Opinion Public opinion weighs significantly in the policymaking process, so interest groups cultivate their public images carefully. If public opinion favors a certain group's interests, then public officials will be more ready to listen and more willing to pass legislation favoring that group. An interest group's efforts to cultivate public opinion may include online campaigns through social media and e-mail, television publicity, advertisements, and mass mailings. In general, groups use public relations techniques to improve the group's image.

indirect technique
Any method used by interest groups to influence government officials through third parties, such as voters.

rating system A system by which a particular interest group evaluates (rates) the performance of legislators based on how often the legislators have voted with the group's position on particular issues.

For example, environmental groups often run television ads to dramatize threats to the environment. Oil companies may respond to criticism about gasoline prices with advertising that shows how hard they are working to develop new sources of energy. The goal of all these activities is to influence public opinion.

Rating Systems Some interest groups also try to influence legislators through **rating systems.** A group selects legislative issues that it believes are important to its goals and rates legislators according to the percentage of times they voted favorably on those issues. For example, a score of 90 percent on the Americans for Democratic Action (ADA) rating scale means that the legislator supported that liberal group's position to a high degree.

Other groups use telling labels to tag members of Congress who support (or fail to support) their interests to a significant extent. For instance, the Communications Workers of America refers to policymakers who take a position consistent with its views as "Heroes" and those who take the opposite position as "Zeroes." Needless to say, such tactics can be an effective form of indirect lobbying, particularly with legislators who do not want to earn a low ADA score or be placed on the "Zeroes" list.

Issue Ads One of the most powerful indirect techniques used by interest groups is the "issue ad"—a television or radio ad taking a position on a particular issue. The Supreme Court has made it clear that the First Amendment's guarantee of free speech protects interest groups' rights to set forth their positions on issues when they fund such activities through independent expenditures that are not coordinated with a candidate's campaign or a political party. Nevertheless, issue advocacy is controversial because the funds spent to air issue ads have had a clear effect on the outcome of elections.

Both political parties have benefited from such interest group spending.

527 and 501(c)4 Organizations The Bipartisan Campaign Reform Act of 2002 banned unlimited donations to campaigns and political parties, called *soft money*. In subsequent years, interest groups that had previously given soft money to parties set up new groups called "527s" (after the provision of the tax code that covers them). The 527s engaged in such practices as voter registration, but they also began making large expenditures on issue ads—which were legal so long as the 527s did not coordinate their activities with candidates' campaigns.

In the run-up to the 2008 presidential elections, clever campaign finance lawyers hit upon a new type of group, the 501(c)4 organization, also named after a section of the tax code. Groups such as the Sierra Club and Citizens Against Government Waste have set up special 501(c)4 organizations.

Lawyers argued that a 501(c)4 group could spend some of its funds on direct campaign contributions as long as most of the group's spending was on issue advocacy. Further, a 501(c)4 group could conceal the identity of its contributors. Federal agencies and the courts have not yet determined the legality of these claims.

Mobilizing Constituents Interest groups sometimes urge members and other constituents to contact government officials—by e-mail, Facebook, Twitter, text message, or telephone—to show their support for or opposition to a certain policy. Such efforts are known as *grassroots organizing*.

Large interest groups can generate hundreds of thousands of letters, e-mail messages, texts, tweets, and phone calls. Interest groups often provide pre-written form messages for constituents to use. The NRA has successfully used this tactic to fight strict federal gun control legislation by delivering half a million letters to Congress within a few weeks. Policymakers recognize that such communications are initiated by interest groups, however, and are impressed only when the volume of communications is very large.

In some cases, interest groups are not membership organizations. Instead, they are established by political fundraisers or wealthy individuals. Sometimes, such groups try to disguise their efforts as grassroots campaigns. Campaigns that masquerade as grassroots mobilizations, but are not, have been given the apt label *Astroturf lobbying*. An Astroturf lobbyist might, for example, make anonymous postings online that appear to be from concerned citizens but that actually come from the sponsoring organization.

Going to Court The legal system offers another avenue for interest groups to influence the political

> "Never doubt that a small group of thoughtful, committed citizens can change the world; indeed, it's the only thing that ever has."
>
> ~ MARGARET MEAD, AMERICAN ANTHROPOLOGIST, 1901–1978

process. In the 1950s and 1960s, civil rights groups paved the way for interest group litigation with major victories in cases concerning equal housing, school desegregation, and employment discrimination. Environmental groups, such as the Sierra Club, have also successfully used litigation to press their concerns.

For example, an environmental group might challenge in court an activity that threatens to pollute the environment or that will destroy the natural habitat of an endangered species. The legal challenge forces those engaging in the activity to defend their actions and may delay the project. In fact, much of the success of environmental groups has been linked to their use of lawsuits.

***Amicus Curiae* Briefs** An interest group can also influence the outcome of litigation without being a party to a lawsuit. Frequently, an interest group files an *amicus curiae* brief. The brief states the group's legal argument in support of its desired outcome in a case.

For example, the case *Arizona v. United States*, heard by the Supreme Court in 2012, turned on whether a state government could enact immigration laws tougher than those adopted by the federal government. The Court ruled that part, but not all, of the Arizona legislation was unconstitutional.[7] Dozens of organizations filed *amicus* briefs on one side or the other of the issue. Conservative and anti-immigration groups supported the state. Naturally, so did Arizona elected officials, including the state legislature. Those backing the federal government, which had challenged the Arizona law, included the Catholic bishops, labor unions, and the American Bar Association. A variety of civil rights and civil liberties groups, plus the government of Mexico, also opposed the Arizona law.

Often, in such briefs, interest groups cite statistics and research that support their position on a certain issue. This research can have considerable influence on the judges deciding the case.

Demonstrations Some interest groups stage protests to make a statement in a dramatic way. The Boston Tea Party of 1773, in which American colonists dressed as Native Americans and threw tea into Boston Harbor to protest British taxes, is testimony to how long this tactic has been around. Over the years, many groups have organized protest marches and rallies to support or oppose legalized abortion, LGBT rights, and the treatment of Native Americans. Other issues raised by demonstrators have included restrictions on the use of federally owned lands in the West and the killing of black men by police officers.

In 2016, demonstrators protested an oil pipeline in North Dakota that allegedly threatened the water supply of an Indian reservation. In January 2017, about 4.2 million people across the country joined women's marches against President Trump's policies. The women's marches—also attended by many men—may have been the largest demonstrations in U.S. history. Many members of Congress regularly set up "town hall" meetings to hear from their constituents. In February 2017, Republican meetings were packed with angry citizens defending the health care insurance they receive under the Affordable Care Act (Obamacare). Taking a protest directly to a member of Congress in this way is an unusually effective technique.

Not all demonstration techniques are peaceful. Some environmental groups, for example, have used such dangerous tactics as spiking trees and setting traps on logging roads to puncture truck tires. "Pro-life" groups have bombed abortion clinics, and members of the Animal Liberation Front have broken into laboratories and freed animals being used for experimentation. Some evidence suggests that violent demonstrations can be counterproductive—that is, that they can hurt the demonstrators' cause by angering the public. Historians continue to debate whether violent demonstrations against the Vietnam War (1965–1975) helped or hurt the antiwar cause.

CRITICAL THINKING

▶ Why might some lawmakers pay more attention to contacts by ordinary people than contacts by lobbyists?

6–4 TODAY'S LOBBYING ESTABLISHMENT

LO Describe how interest groups are regulated by government.

Without a doubt, interest groups and their lobbyists have become a permanent feature in the landscape of American government. All the major interest groups have headquarters in Washington, D.C., close to the center of government. Professional lobbyists and staff members of various interest groups move freely between their groups' headquarters and congressional offices and committee rooms. Interest group representatives are routinely consulted when Congress drafts new legislation. As already mentioned, interest group representatives are frequently asked to testify before congressional committees or subcommittees on the effect or potential effect of particular legislation or regulations. In sum, interest groups are an integral part of the American government system.

AP Images/Rick Bowmer

Citizens shout at Representative Jason Chaffetz (R., Utah). Most of the two thousand people at the "town hall" meeting opposed attempts to repeal the Affordable Care Act (Obamacare) and Chaffetz's refusal, as chair of the House Oversight Committee, to investigate the Trump administration. *Why would a Republican member of Congress refuse to investigate a Republican president?*

As interest groups have become a permanent feature of American government, lobbying has developed into a profession. A professional lobbyist—one who has mastered the techniques of lobbying discussed earlier in this chapter—is a valuable ally to any interest group seeking to influence government. Professional lobbyists can and often do represent a number of different interest groups over the course of their careers.

In recent years, it has become increasingly common for those who leave positions with the federal government to become lobbyists or consultants for the private-interest groups they helped to regulate. In spite of legislation and regulations designed to reduce this "revolving door" syndrome, it is still functioning quite well.

6–4a Why Do Interest Groups Get Bad Press?

Despite their importance to democratic government, interest groups, like political parties, are often criticized by both the public and the press. Our image of interest groups and their special interests is not very favorable. You may have run across political cartoons depicting lobbyists standing in the hallways of Congress with briefcases stuffed with money. These cartoons are not entirely factual, but they are not entirely fictitious either.

Examples of Questionable Activities Consider a few examples. In 2004, the chief executive officer of a coal company donated $3 million to the election campaign of a candidate for the West Virginia Supreme Court. That sum amounted to most of what was spent in the race. At that time, the coal company had a $50 million case pending before the court, which eventually found in the coal company's favor. (In 2009, the United States Supreme Court ruled that the recipient of the largesse should not have participated in the court proceedings.)[8]

In 2015 and 2016, Republicans alleged that foreign interests had benefited from donations to the Clinton Foundation. The foundation is a charity organized by former secretary of state Hillary Clinton and her husband, former president Bill Clinton. Critics were unable to show, however, that the secretary of state had participated in approving the trade benefits supposedly enjoyed by the foreign interests.

> **"An honest politician is one who, when he is bought, *will* *stay bought.*"**
>
> ~SIMON CAMERON
> U.S. FINANCIER AND POLITICIAN
> 1799–1889

Concentrated Benefits, Dispersed Costs

A major complaint by critics of interest groups is that the benefits these groups obtain are not in the general public interest. One reason for this situation is the "enthusiasm gap" between supporters and opponents of any given subsidy. Sugar producers, for example, benefit greatly from restrictions on sugar imports. They work hard to ensure that these restrictions continue. Yet for sugar consumers—all the rest of us—the price of sugar is a trivial matter. Candy-makers aside, end users of sugar have little incentive to organize. This enthusiasm gap is referred to as "concentrated benefits, dispersed costs."

We tend to think of restrictions on economic activity that provide concentrated benefits as resulting from federal regulation. Many of the restrictions that can hobble economic activity, however, are imposed at the state and local level. For example, Florida requires an individual to obtain an expensive license to work as an interior decorator. This law resulted from lobbying by those already working as interior decorators. We describe a recent dispute over economic restrictions in this chapter's *Join the Debate* feature.

6–4b The Regulation of Lobbyists

In an attempt to control lobbying, Congress passed the Federal Regulation of Lobbying Act in 1946. The major provisions of the act are as follows:

▶ Any person or organization that receives money to influence legislation must register with the clerk of the House and the secretary of the Senate.

▶ Any groups or persons registering must identify their employer, salary, amount and purpose of expenses, and duration of employment.

▶ Every registered lobbyist must make quarterly reports on his or her activities.

▶ Anyone violating this act can be fined up to $10,000 and be imprisoned for up to five years.

The act did not succeed in regulating lobbying to any great degree for several reasons. First, the Supreme Court restricted the application of the law to only those lobbyists who sought to influence federal legislation directly.[9] Any lobbyist seeking to influence legislation indirectly through public opinion did not fall within the scope of the law.

Until recently, taxis and, to an extent, limousines were the only services that would pick you up and take you from one point to another in a car. Today, depending on where you live, you may have other choices—specifically, Uber or Lyft. These "transportation network" companies directly compete with taxis. These services are built around the Internet. All you need to summon a car is a smartphone app. You use the app to locate the nearest Lyft or Uber driver. You communicate directly with that driver. You must already have a credit card number on file with the company—no cash changes hands. The driver picks you up, and your credit card is automatically charged at the end of your ride. Transportation network companies use both full-time and part-time drivers, all of whom own their own cars.

These competitors to taxis are a new type of service and are therefore unregulated. This fact has provoked controversy. Some city councils have banned the services outright. Others are trying to regulate them. (In 2015, for example, California determined that Uber and Lyft drivers are employees, not independent contractors.) Should they just be left alone instead?

Public Safety Is at Issue, and It's Also Unfair Competition

Opponents of Uber, Lyft, and other such services point out that taxi services are heavily regulated in most cities. The goal of the regulations is twofold: to ensure public safety and to allow taxi drivers to make a living wage.

In many cities, you must pay for a license to own a cab. Drivers for Uber and similar companies do not pay anything. Taxis must also carry expensive vehicle-for-hire insurance. They are regularly inspected to protect public safety. Another point— because you must have a credit card to use Uber or Lyft, these companies discriminate against poor people who don't have credit cards or smartphones. In sum, these new services do not compete fairly with licensed, regulated taxi drivers.

It's All about the Taxi Lobby

Supporters of the new "ride-share" systems say that talk of unfair competition and public safety is a smokescreen. Taxi lobbies simply want to eliminate competition. Uber, Lyft, and similar app-based services perform background checks on their drivers. Passengers have the names and mobile phone numbers of their drivers. They rate the drivers, and those who receive low ratings get fewer and fewer calls. Localities that regulate the new services, such as the state of California, require extra insurance.

The ride-share market works just as well as any other market. Banning these services simply guarantees that current taxi owners—not necessarily drivers—make high profits and passengers have fewer choices.

Critical Analysis

What might motivate a city council to ban Uber or Lyft services?

Second, only persons or organizations whose principal purpose was to influence legislation were required to register. Many groups avoided registration by claiming that their principal function was something else. Third, the act did not cover those whose lobbying was directed at agencies in the executive branch or lobbyists who testified before congressional committees. Fourth, the public was almost totally unaware of the information in the quarterly reports filed by lobbyists. Not until 1995 did Congress finally address those loopholes by enacting new legislation.

6–4c The Lobbying Disclosure Act of 1995

In 1995, Congress passed new, expanded lobbying legislation—the Lobbying Disclosure Act—that reformed the 1946 act in the following ways:

▶ Strict definitions now apply to determine who must register with the clerk of the House and the secretary of the Senate as a lobbyist. A lobbyist is anyone who either spends at least 20 percent of his or her time lobbying members of Congress, their staffs, or executive-branch officials, or is paid more than $5,000 in a six-month period for such work. Any organization that spends more than $20,000 in a six-month period conducting such lobbying activity must also register. These amounts have since been altered to $2,500 and $10,000 per quarter, respectively.

▸ Lobbyists must report their clients, the issues on which they lobbied, and the agency or chamber of Congress they contacted, although they do not need to disclose the names of those they contacted.

Tax-exempt organizations, such as religious groups, were exempted from these provisions, as were organizations that engage in grassroots lobbying, such as a media campaign that asks people to write or call their congressional representative. Nonetheless, the number of registered lobbyists nearly doubled in the first few years after the new legislation took effect.

Uber is now worldwide—this is what its app looks like in Malaysia. The San Francisco Cab Drivers Association reports that nearly one-third of the city's licensed taxi drivers have stopped driving taxis and have begun driving for ride-sharing services. *Why would they switch?*

6-4d Later Reform Efforts

In 2005, a number of lobbying scandals in Washington, D.C., came to light. As a result, following the midterm elections of 2006, the new Democratic majority in the Senate and House of Representatives undertook a lobbying reform effort. This involved changes to the rules that the two chambers impose on their own members.

Bundled campaign contributions, in which a lobbyist arranges for contributions from a variety of sources, would have to be reported. Expenditures on the sometimes lavish parties to benefit candidates would have to be reported as well. (Of course, partygoers were expected to pay for their food and drink with a check written out to the candidate.) The new rules covered PACs as well as registered lobbyists, which led one lobbyist to observe sourly that this wasn't lobbying reform but campaign-finance reform.

President George W. Bush signed the Honest Leadership and Open Government Act in 2007. The new law increased lobbying disclosure requirements and placed further restrictions on the receipt of gifts and travel by members of Congress paid for by lobbyists and the organizations they represent. The act also included provisions requiring the disclosure of lawmakers' requests for earmarks in legislation. Earmarks—that is, special provisions benefiting a lawmaker's constituents—are also known as "pork barrel legislation," or simply *pork*.

In March 2010, the Republican-led House Appropriations Committee banned earmarks that benefit profit-making corporations. About a thousand such earmarks had been authorized in the previous year, to the value of $1.7 billion. The ban was renewed in 2012. As it turned out, legislators proved remarkably creative in finding ways around the ban on pork, though the ban did at least limit its prevalence.

CRITICAL THINKING

▸ *As noted at the beginning of this chapter, the right to lobby is protected by the Constitution. If that weren't so, would it be a good idea to ban lobbying? Why or why not?*

Interest groups are one of the most controversial features of our democratic system. The right to lobby may be protected by the First Amendment, but many people consider lobbying by interest groups to be a source of corruption within the political system. Of course, people can readily see the problems with lobbying when it is done for a cause that they oppose. In contrast, it is easy to support political action for something you believe in, regardless of what others might think of it. Some of the controversies surrounding interest group lobbying include the following:

- *Should labor unions be allowed to organize workplaces by obtaining signed cards—or are secret-ballot elections an essential safeguard?*

- *Are farm subsidies a valid protection for an important industry—or just another giveaway to the politically powerful?*

- *Does lobbying always harm legislation—or can lobbying improve it?*

- *Free riders benefit from a particular activity without paying their share of its costs. Is free riding inherently unfair—or is it only a problem when it is so pervasive that it makes the activity in question (for example, lobbying by consumer groups) unaffordable?*

- *Are there too many lobbyists—or is the real problem that there aren't enough lobbyists for ordinary people?*

STUDY TOOLS 6

READY TO STUDY? IN THE BOOK, YOU CAN:

☐ Review what you've read with the following chapter quiz.

☐ Check your answers in Appendix D at the back of the book.

☐ Rip out the Chapter Review Card, which includes key terms and chapter summaries.

ONLINE AT WWW.CENGAGEBRAIN.COM, YOU CAN:

☐ Watch videos to get a quick overview.

☐ Expedite your studying with Major Player readings and Focus Activities.

☐ Check your understanding with Chapter Quizzes.

FILL-IN

Learning Outcome 6–1

1. The right to form interest groups and to lobby the government is protected by the _____ Amendment to the U.S. Constitution.

2. _____ theory describes the defensive formation of interest groups.

Learning Outcome 6–2

3. Today, members of organized labor make up only _____ percent of the labor force.

4. _____ laws ban unions from collecting dues or other fees from workers whom they represent but who have not actually joined the union.

5. An interest group that unites persons who share the same race, ethnicity, gender, or age can be called a/an

   _____.

Learning Outcome 6–3

6. Lobbying refers to _____.

7. Interest groups can influence the outcome of litigation without being a party to a lawsuit by filing _____.

Learning Outcome 6–4

8. The Supreme Court has guaranteed the rights of interest groups to set forth their position on issues when they fund such activities through independent expenditures that _____.

9. It has become increasingly common for those who leave positions with the federal government to become lobbyists or consultants for the private-interest groups they helped to regulate. This is called the _____ syndrome.

MULTIPLE CHOICE

Learning Outcome 6–1

10. There are various reasons why people join interest groups. Some people find that they gain considerable satisfaction from supporting causes that they agree with. Such satisfaction is referred to as a _____ incentive.
    a. free rider   **b.** purposive   **c.** material

11. Interest groups
    a. are often policy generalists.
    b. compete for public office.
    c. help bridge the gap between citizens and government.

Learning Outcome 6–2

12. The American Association for Justice represents the interests of
    a. trial lawyers.
    b. children.
    c. senior citizens.

13. MoveOn and the Club for Growth are _____ interest groups.
    a. business
    b. consumer
    c. ideological

Learning Outcome 6–3

14. _____ is a direct technique used by interest groups to influence public policy.
    a. The use of rating systems
    b. Providing election support
    c. Staging demonstrations

15. Lobbying campaigns that masquerade as grassroots mobilizations have been labeled _____ lobbying.
    a. Bluegrass
    b. Turfgrass
    c. Astroturf

Learning Outcome 6–4

16. When a benefit is provided to a limited number of people, the enthusiasm gap between recipients of the benefit and everyone else is called
    a. concentrated costs and dispersed benefits.
    b. the free rider problem.
    c. concentrated benefits and dispersed costs.

7 | POLITICAL PARTIES

Kobby Dagan/Shutterstock.com

LEARNING OUTCOMES

After reading this chapter, you should be able to:

7-1 Summarize the origins and development of the two-party system in the United States.

7-2 Describe the current status of the two major parties.

7-3 Explain how political parties function in our democratic system.

7-4 Discuss the structure of American political parties.

7-5 Describe the different types of third parties and how they function in the American political system.

After finishing this chapter, go to **PAGE 166** for **STUDY TOOLS**

AMERICA AT ODDS | Is Trump the Future of the Republican Party?

Christopher Halloran/Shutterstock.com

To all appearances, by 2017 the Republican Party was in a stronger position than it had been in decades. Republican Donald Trump held the presidency. Republicans controlled the U.S. Senate and the House of Representatives. Thirty-three out of fifty state governors were Republican, and the party controlled more state legislatures than at any time in over a century. Still, there were signs that this imposing structure rested on shaky foundations. From 1992 through 2016, the Republicans lost the popular vote for president in six out of seven elections. In 2012, the Republicans won a 33-vote majority in the U.S. House—yet Democratic House candidates secured about 1.4 million more votes than the Republicans.

After the 2012 elections, the Republican National Committee released a report arguing that the party needed to increase its levels of support among Latino and Asian voters by supporting immigration reform. It did not take long to learn that a majority of Republican voters had other ideas. Despite his flaws as a candidate, Donald Trump won popularity and votes running on a platform hostile to immigration and foreign trade. Does Trump's win open up a new path to victory for the Republican Party—or will it lead to an eventual dead end?

Trump's New Coalition Is the Republican Future

Trump's most enthusiastic supporters believe that his victories reveal a Republican electorate in open revolt against the party's establishment—the small-government, anti-tax politicians and the wealthy donors who support them. For establishment Republicans, nothing is more important than reducing tax rates on upper-income individuals. Funding these cuts requires reducing Social Security and Medicare benefits, which together make up more than 40 percent of the federal budget. Immigration and imports from China are not problems for these politicians.

Trump was the only Republican candidate in 2016 who vowed to protect Social Security and Medicare. His radical policy proposals and insults were music to the ears of desperate low-income conservatives. If the Republican Party is to have a future, it must find a way to address the problems of these people. To do so, it must break free from the libertarian values that block such steps. Together, loyal Republicans and Trump's new voters were enough to win in 2016, and they can form a winning coalition for years to come.

Trump's Successes Will Be Short-Lived

Those who believe that "Trumpism" is a dead end for the Republicans agree that Trump voters have reason to be angry. Low-income conservatives were hit hard by the 2008 economic catastrophe. Millions are still out of the workforce. An epidemic of drug abuse among less-educated whites has driven up their mortality rates. Yet the question remains whether Trump can really help the white working class. Certainly, he has the ability to pour scorn on the people his followers dislike—foreigners, immigrants, and latte-sipping liberals. Yet small-government, anti-tax Republicans continue to dominate the party at all levels. They hold the whip hand in Congress, and it is their priorities that the party will represent, not Trump's.

What happens to the Trump coalition if Republican legislation harms its members directly? Repeal of Obamacare would be a financial disaster for millions of Trump voters. Further, the number of Hispanic and young college-educated voters rises year after year. If these people conclude that Republicans see them as "the enemy," the party will be in big, long-term trouble.

Where do you stand?

1. Can a president who is a political "outsider" help us deal with our problems? Why or why not?
2. For a politician to succeed, how important is it to take stands that are mainly symbolic? To what extent can symbolism replace legislation that has practical consequences?

Explore this issue online

- Columnist Ross Douthat argues for pro-working-class reform while supporting the Republican Party. Follow him at twitter.com/douthatnyt.
- For full-throttle conservatism, visit Rush Limbaugh's site at www.rushlimbaugh.com.

INTRODUCTION

Political ideology can spark heated debates among Americans, as you read in the chapter-opening *America at Odds* feature. Today, political ideologies are typically embodied in political parties. A **political party** can be defined as a group of individuals who organize to win elections, operate the government, and determine policy.

Political parties were an unforeseen development in American political history. The founders defined many other important institutions, such as the presidency and Congress, and described their functions in the Constitution. Political parties, however, are not even mentioned in the Constitution. In fact, the founders decried factions and parties. Thomas Jefferson probably best expressed the founders' antiparty sentiments when he declared, "If I could not go to heaven but with a party, I would not go there at all."[1]

If the founders did not want political parties, though, who was supposed to organize political campaigns and mobilize supporters of political candidates? Clearly, there was a practical need for some kind of organizing group to form a link between citizens and their government. Even our early national leaders, for all their antiparty feelings, soon realized this. Several of them were active in establishing or organizing the first political parties.

> "Both of our political parties ... agree conscientiously in the same object: the *public good*; but they differ essentially in what they deem the means of promoting that good."
>
> ~THOMAS JEFFERSON
> IN A LETTER TO ABIGAIL ADAMS, 1804

7-1 A SHORT HISTORY OF AMERICAN POLITICAL PARTIES

LO Summarize the origins and development of the two-party system in the United States.

Throughout the course of our history, several major parties have formed, and some have disappeared. Even today, although we have only two major political parties, a few others always exist at any one time, as will be discussed later in this chapter.

political party A group of individuals who organize to win elections, operate the government, and determine policy.

7-1a The First Political Parties

The founders rejected the idea of political parties because they believed, as George Washington said in his Farewell Address, that the "spirit of party ... agitates the community with ill-founded jealousies and false alarms, kindles the animosity of one part against another, foments occasionally riot and insurrection."[2] At some point in the future, the founders feared, a party leader might even seize power as a dictator.

Federalists and Anti-Federalists In spite of the founders' fears, two major political factions—the Federalists and the Anti-Federalists—were formed even before the Constitution was ratified. The Federalists pushed for the ratification of the Constitution because they wanted a stronger national government than the one that had existed

John Adams (1735–1826) was the Federalists' candidate to succeed George Washington. Adams defeated Thomas Jefferson in 1796 but lost to him in 1800. *What did the Federalists stand for?*

Thomas Jefferson (1743–1826) became our third president and served two terms. Jefferson's Republicans (not to be confused with the later Republican Party of Abraham Lincoln) dominated American politics for more than two decades. *What kinds of people supported this party?*

Andrew Jackson (1767–1845) led the newly formed Democratic Party. Jackson won the presidential election in 1828, defeating the candidate of the National Republicans (soon to be known as the Whigs). *Were the Democrats or the Whigs more like the Federalists? Why?*

under the Articles of Confederation. The Anti-Federalists argued against ratification. They supported states' rights and feared a too-powerful central government.

Federalists and Republicans The Federalist and Anti-Federalist factions continued, in somewhat altered form, after the Constitution was ratified. Alexander Hamilton, the first secretary of the Treasury, became the leader of the Federalist Party, which Vice President John Adams also joined. The Federalists supported a strong central government that would encourage the development of commerce and manufacturing. The Federalists generally thought that a republic should be ruled by its wealthiest and best-educated citizens.

Opponents of the Federalists and Hamilton's policies referred to themselves as Republicans. Today, they are often referred to as Jeffersonian Republicans or Democratic Republicans (names never used at the time), to distinguish this group from the later-established Republican Party. Jefferson's Republicans favored a more limited role for government. They believed that the nation's welfare would be best served if the states had more power than the central government. In their view, Congress should dominate the government, and government policies should serve farming interests rather than promote commerce and manufacturing.

7–1b From 1796 to 1860

The nation's first two parties clashed openly in the elections of 1796, in which John Adams, the Federalists' candidate to succeed George Washington as president, defeated Thomas Jefferson. Over the next four years, Jefferson and James Madison worked to extend the influence of their Republican Party. In the presidential elections of 1800 and 1804, Jefferson won the presidency, and his party also won control of Congress.

Triumph of the Jeffersonians The transition of political power from the Federalists to Jefferson's party is the first example in American history of what political scientists have called a **realignment.** In a realignment, a substantial number of voters change their political allegiance, which usually also changes the balance of power between the two major parties. In fact, the Federalists never returned to power and thus became the first (but not the last) American party to go out of existence. (See the time line of American political parties in Figure 7–1.)

> **realignment** A process in which the popular support for and relative strength of the parties shift, and the parties are reestablished with different coalitions of supporters.

FIGURE 7–1 A TIME LINE OF U.S. POLITICAL PARTIES

Many of these parties—including the Constitutional Union Party, Henry Wallace's Progressive Party, and the States' Rights Democrats—were important during only one presidential election. *Do you find any of these party platforms attractive? Why?*

ANTI-FEDERALISTS
Nonparty faction formed to prevent ratification of the Constitution.

JEFFERSON'S REPUBLICAN PARTY
Formed to oppose Federalist policies. Initially led by Thomas Jefferson.

DEMOCRATIC PARTY
Emerged when Andrew Jackson ran against John Quincy Adams, presidential nominee of the National Republican Party.

PEOPLE'S PARTY
Appealed to farmers. Wanted to create inflation to help debtors pay off their obligations.

SOCIALIST PARTY
Labor oriented. Sought to replace capitalism with a system based on government or worker control of corporations.

BULL MOOSE PROGRESSIVE PARTY
Formed by Theodore Roosevelt. Prevented President Taft's reelection for president by splitting the Republican Party.

HENRY WALLACE'S PROGRESSIVE PARTY
Formed to elect Wallace to the presidency and end segregation. Was seen as too sympathetic to Communists.

GREEN PARTY
Supports environmentalism and opposes corporate influence.

Timeline years: 1787, 1790, 1792, 1800, 1810, 1820, 1828, 1830, 1836, 1840, 1850, 1854, 1860, 1870, 1880, 1887, 1890, 1900, 1901, 1910, 1912, 1920, 1930, 1940, 1948, 1950, 1960, 1968, 1971, 1980, 1990, 1996, 2000, 2010

FEDERALISTS AND LATER THE FEDERALIST PARTY
Formed to promote ratification of the Constitution.

NATIONAL REPUBLICAN PARTY
Split off from Jefferson's Republican Party. Formed by John Quincy Adams and Henry Clay to promote a strong national government. The National Republicans later became the Whig Party.

WHIG PARTY
Stood for national unity, public works, and limited presidential power. Essentially a reorganized version of the National Republican Party.

REPUBLICAN PARTY
Formed to oppose slavery. Took the name of Jefferson's old party.

CONSTITUTIONAL UNION PARTY
Formed to save the Union from the Civil War. Mostly former southern Whigs.

STATES' RIGHTS DEMOCRATS
Organized by dissident southern Democrats to promote segregation and states' rights.

AMERICAN INDEPENDENT PARTY
Formed by Alabama governor George Wallace. Opposed the civil rights movement.

LIBERTARIAN PARTY
Advocates the least possible intervention by the government in economic and social matters.

REFORM PARTY
Formed by H. Ross Perot to seek the presidency. Opposed federal budget deficits.

Jefferson's Republicans dominated American politics for the next twenty years. Jefferson was succeeded in the White House by two other members of the party—James Madison and James Monroe. In the mid-1820s, however, Jefferson's Republicans split into two groups. This was the second realignment in American history. Supporters of Andrew Jackson, who was elected president in 1828, called themselves Democrats. The Democrats appealed to small farmers and the growing class of urbanized workers. The other group, the National Republicans (later the Whig Party), was led by John Quincy Adams, Henry Clay, and the great orator

Daniel Webster. It had the support of bankers, business owners, and many southern planters.

The Impending Crisis As the Whigs and Democrats competed for the White House from 1835 to 1854, the two-party system as we know it today emerged. Both parties were large, with well-known leaders and supporters across the nation. Both had grassroots organizations of party workers committed to winning as many political offices (at all levels of government) for the party as possible. Both the Whigs and the Democrats tried to avoid the issue of slavery.

By 1856, the Whig coalition had fallen apart. Most northern Whigs were absorbed into the new Republican Party, which opposed the extension of slavery into new territories. Campaigning on this platform in 1860, the Republicans succeeded in electing Abraham Lincoln—the first president elected under the banner of the new Republican Party.

7-1c From the Civil War to the Great Depression

When the former Confederate states rejoined the Union after the Civil War, the Republicans and Democrats were roughly even in strength. The Republicans, though, were more successful in presidential contests. It was in this period that the Republicans picked up the nickname GOP, for "grand old party."

In the 1890s, however, the Republicans gained a decisive advantage. In that decade, the Democrats allied themselves with the Populist movement, which consisted largely of indebted farmers in the West and South. The Populists—the People's Party—advocated inflation as a way of lessening their debts. Urban workers in the Midwest and East strongly opposed this program, which would erode the value of their paychecks. After the realigning elections of 1896, the Republicans established themselves in the minds of many Americans as the party that knew how to manage the nation's economy. We illustrate the results of the 1896 presidential elections in Figure 7–2.

In 1912, however, the Republicans

temporarily split between the "Republican regulars" and Theodore Roosevelt's "Bull Moose Progressives." As a result of this Republican split, the Democrats under Woodrow Wilson won power from 1912 to 1920. Otherwise, the Republicans remained dominant in national politics until the onset of the Great Depression.

7-1d After the Great Depression

The Great Depression of the 1930s destroyed the belief that the GOP could better manage the economy and contributed to another realignment in the two-party system. In a realignment, the minority (opposition) party may emerge as the majority party, and this is certainly what happened in 1932. The election of 1932 brought Franklin D. Roosevelt to the presidency and the Democrats back to power at the national level.

A Civil Rights Plank Roosevelt's programs to fight the Depression were called the *New Deal*. Those who joined the Democrats during Roosevelt's New Deal included a substantial share of African Americans—many of Roosevelt's relief programs were open to people of all races. (Until the 1930s, African Americans had been overwhelmingly Republican.) In 1948, for the first time ever, the Democrats adopted a civil rights plank as part of the party platform at their national convention. A number of southern Democrats revolted and ran a separate States' Rights ticket for president.

> **GOP** A nickname for the Republican Party—"grand old party."

From the election of Abraham Lincoln in 1860 until 1932, the Republican Party was the more successful party in presidential politics. *In what geographical areas were the Republicans strong?*

Library of Congress, Prints & Photographs Division

The realigning election of 1932 brought Franklin Delano Roosevelt to the presidency and the Democrats back to power at the national level. *Why did the Democrats win in 1932?*

Library of Congress, Prints & Photographs Division

FIGURE 7–2 THE 1896 PRESIDENTIAL ELECTION RESULTS

This map shows the 1896 presidential election results by state. This pattern held in subsequent elections. Note that it is almost a complete reverse of the modern political pattern, reflecting the change in the Democrats from a party of segregation and small government to a party of civil rights and government activism. *How did this transformation occur?*

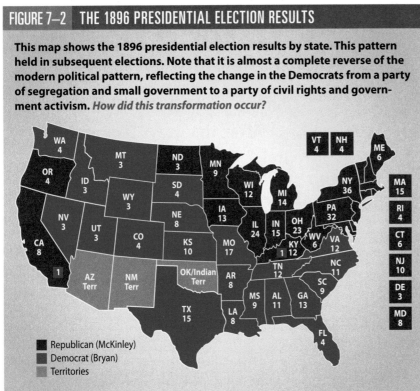

- ■ Republican (McKinley)
- ■ Democrat (Bryan)
- ■ Territories

A Closely Divided Nation. The result of this "rolling realignment" was that the two major parties were fairly evenly matched. The elections of 2000 were a striking demonstration of how closely the electorate was now divided. Republican George W. Bush won the presidency in that year by carrying Florida with a margin of 537 votes. Democrat Al Gore actually received about half a million more popular votes than Bush. Following the elections, the Senate was made up of fifty Republicans and fifty Democrats. The GOP controlled the House by a razor-thin margin of seven seats. We show the changing levels of support for the major parties in Figure 7–3.

CRITICAL THINKING

▸ *If you could create a new party, what would be its most important principles?*

In 1964, the Democrats, under incumbent president Lyndon Johnson, won a landslide victory, and liberals held a majority in Congress. In the political environment that produced this election result, a coalition of northern Democrats and Republicans crafted the major civil rights legislation described earlier in this text. The subsequent years were turbulent, with riots and marches in major cities and student protests against the Vietnam War (1965–1975).

A "Rolling Realignment" Conservative Democrats did not like the direction in which their party seemed to be taking them. Under President Richard Nixon, the Republican Party was receptive to these conservative Democrats, and over a period of years, most of them became GOP voters. This was a major alteration in the political landscape, although it was not exclusively associated with a single election. Republican president Ronald Reagan helped cement the new Republican coalition.

Turnover in Congress. The Democrats continued to hold majorities in the House and Senate until 1994, but partisan labels were somewhat misleading. During the 1970s and 1980s, a large bloc of Democrats in Congress, mostly from the South, sided with the Republicans on almost all issues. In time, these conservative Democrats were replaced by conservative Republicans.

 AMERICA'S POLITICAL PARTIES TODAY

LO Describe the current status of the two major parties.

Historically, political parties drew together like-minded individuals. Today, too, individuals with similar characteristics tend to align themselves more often with one or the other major party. Such factors as race, age, income, education, marital status, and geography all influence party identification.

7–2a Red States versus Blue States

Geography is one of the many factors that can determine party identification. Examine the map of the 2016 presidential elections shown in Figure 7–4. Like past Republicans, Donald Trump did well in the South, the Great Plains, and parts of the Mountain West. He also carried most of the Midwest, a new development. Democrat Hillary Clinton did well in the Northeast, the West Coast, and in certain other states such as Illinois. Beginning with the presidential elections of 2000, the press has made much of the supposed cultural differences between the "blue" states that vote for the Democratic

FIGURE 7–3   PARTY IDENTIFICATION OVER THE YEARS

This chart shows the levels of popular identification with the two major parties and with the *independent* label. In practice, most independents almost always support one of the major parties. The number of true independents may be as low as 10 percent. *Why would people who normally support one party call themselves independents?*

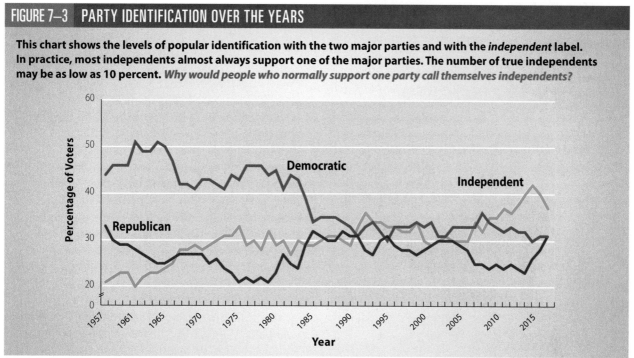

Sources: 1957–1989 and 2015–2016, the Gallup Organization; 1990–2014, the Pew Research Center.

candidate and the "red" states that vote for the Republican.[3] In reality, though, many states could better be described as "purple"—that is, a mixture of red and blue. These states could give their electoral votes to either party.

For another way to consider the influence of geography, see the map of Minnesota in Figure 7–5.

Most of Minnesota is red, and a quick glance might lead you to think that Trump carried the state. In fact, Clinton carried Minnesota by 1.5 percentage points. Minnesota looks red because Trump carried almost all of the rural parts of the state. The Clinton counties had larger populations.

This pattern was seen all over the country: the more urban the county, the more likely it was to vote Democratic.

7-2b Shifting Political Fortunes

As noted earlier, by 2000 the two major parties were very closely matched in terms of support. But that situation soon began to shift.

Troubles for Both Parties   During 2005, the seemingly endless war in Iraq began to cut into support for the Republicans. In 2006, the Democrats regained control of

FIGURE 7–4   THE 2016 PRESIDENTIAL ELECTION RESULTS

Donald Trump made major gains in the Midwest. (Maine awards two of its electoral votes by congressional district, and the pink square reflects Trump's victory in one of them.) *Is it fair for a candidate to win in the electoral college while losing the popular vote?*

■ Won by Hillary Clinton in 2016
■ Won by Donald Trump in 2016
■ Won by Obama in 2012 and Trump in 2016

FIGURE 7–5 THE 2016 PRESIDENTIAL ELECTION RESULTS IN MINNESOTA

This map displays the Minnesota counties carried by Hillary Clinton (blue) and Donald Trump (red) in the 2016 presidential elections. Clinton took the state by winning the three largest metro areas—the Twin Cities, Rochester, and Duluth. (She also carried two small mining counties in the far northeast.) *Why might the Republicans do better in the countryside?*

the House and Senate. In 2008, in the shadow of a global financial crisis, Americans elected Democrat Barack Obama as president.

Within one year of Obama's inauguration, the Democratic advantage had vanished. Continued high rates of unemployment were one major reason. Also, a sharp increase in government activity during Obama's first two years in office appeared to bother many voters. In November 2010, the voters handed the U.S. House to the Republicans. (The Democrats still controlled the Senate.) Republican successes in 2010 were backed up by the growth in new conservative movements such as the Tea Party. Founded after Barack Obama became president, the grassroots **Tea Party movement** opposed current levels of government and taxation, and also resisted political compromise.

Tea Party movement
A grassroots conservative movement that arose in 2009 after Barack Obama became president. The movement opposes big government and current levels of taxation, and also rejects political compromise.

Recent Elections By 2012, some were beginning to wonder whether the strong conservatism of the newly elected Republicans might be alienating independent voters. In fact, in the 2012 elections, Democratic presidential candidate Barack Obama prevailed by almost 4 percentage points.

In 2014, however, Republicans won control of the U.S. Senate and did well in state-level races. At least one cause of that party's success is that America has recently had two very different electorates, one for the midterms and one when presidential candidates are on the ballot. The midterm electorate now is significantly more Republican than the presidential one. In recent years, younger voters have become more Democratic, even as older ones have moved toward the Republicans. Voter turnout declines across the board in the midterms, but the falloff among younger voters (and minority group members) is especially large. This helps to explain why, since at least 2010, Republicans have done much better in midterm elections than in presidential ones.

Trump's Triumph The 2016 elections revealed a continuing shift in sources of support for the two major political parties. You can see signs of these changes in Figure 7–4. By narrow margins, Trump picked up a swath of states in the industrial heartland—Iowa, Wisconsin, Michigan, Ohio, and Pennsylvania—that had not gone Republican in twelve years and, in some cases, much longer than that. (He also carried Florida.) These are states with above-average numbers of less-well-educated, white, working-class voters, precisely the demographic group most drawn to Trump. College-educated voters narrowly broke for Clinton—in 2012, a majority of this group voted for Republican Mitt Romney.

These developments tended to move the country away from the red-blue map of earlier years. The Democrats were becoming a coalition of minority groups, plus Northern white progressives of all socioeconomic classes. The Republicans were continuing to shed minority voters as they became more and more the party of self-conscious whites. Behind everything lay the growing recognition that the United States would be a majority-minority nation by 2050. In one sense, it already was—as of 2016, minorities were in the majority among Americans aged three years and under.

Radical Partisanship A key characteristic of recent politics has been the extreme partisanship of party activists and members of Congress. In the 1960s, party coalitions included a variety of factions with differing politics. The rolling realignment after the elections of 1968 resulted in parties that were much more homogeneous. Political scientists have concluded that already by 2009, the most conservative Democrat in the House was to the left of the most moderate Republican.

Making the Other Party Look Weak. Ideological uniformity has made it easier for the parties to maintain discipline in Congress. Personal friendships across party lines, once common in Congress, have become rare. The belief has grown that compromise with the other party is a form of betrayal. According to this view, the minority party should not attempt to improve legislation proposed by the majority. Instead, it should oppose majority-party measures in an effort to make the majority appear ineffective. The Republican Party employed such tactics almost immediately after President Obama's inauguration, and the Democrats likewise adopted them as soon as President Trump took office.

The Tea Party. Political polarization grew even more severe after the 2010 elections. Many of the new Republican members of Congress were pledged to the Tea Party philosophy of no-compromise conservatism. (In later years, the Freedom Caucus in the House largely displaced the Tea Party as a home for that chamber's most conservative members.) Tea Party—and later, Freedom Caucus—members of Congress espoused conventional small-government conservatism, which gave many a misleading sense of what Tea Party voters actually believed. Political scientists Theda Skocpol and Vanessa Williamson interviewed a large number of Tea Party supporters and came away with a more nuanced understanding.[4]

Often, Tea Party advocates were not opposed to government benefits as such. Rather, they opposed benefits that, in their opinion, went to undeserving recipients. Immigrants were the number-one "undeserving" group. Other undeserving groups could include members of racial and ethnic minorities—and even young people. In contrast, most Social Security and Medicare recipients were seen as deserving. The belief by Tea Party activists that the government supports the undeserving was combined with the sense that they were losing control of their country to new groups that were culturally, morally, and politically alien.

These beliefs correspond closely with Donald Trump's campaign rhetoric and the beliefs of many of his supporters. The Tea Party movement, in other words, can be seen as a precursor to "Trumpism." This point of view has some obvious similarities to the ideas of nationalist movements and parties in Europe, as we explain in this chapter's *The Rest of the World* feature.

7-2c Realignment, Dealignment, and Tipping

Despite the narrowness of the Republican margin after 2000, Republican strategists dreamed of a new realignment that would force the Democrats into the minority. These hopes were not fulfilled. After 2006, many Democrats anticipated a realignment that would benefit the Democrats. These dreams were shattered as well. For a major realignment to take place, a large number of voters must conclude that their party is no longer capable of representing their interests and ideals, and that another party can do better. While some relatively small groups of voters appear to be in play, it is hard to identify large groups of voters who could be swayed to support a different party today.

Dealignment One political development that may rule out realignment is the growth in the number of independent voters. By the 2016 elections, fully 42 percent of the electorate claimed to be independent. True, many of

A supporter of U.S. Senate candidate Catherine Cortez Masto takes a selfie with her. In November 2016, Masto, a Democrat, was elected to represent Nevada in the Senate. *Why might Nevada be trending Democratic in presidential election years?*

Ethan Miller/Getty Images News/Getty Images

Even as the slogan "America First" is still in the air in the United States, similar slogans have become common throughout Europe. Far-right nationalist parties have gained popularity in Austria, Finland, France, Germany, Greece, the Netherlands, and Sweden. Nationalist parties currently govern Hungary and Poland. All of these parties are commonly described as *right-wing populist*, though this label can be misleading. All share a nostalgia for the "good old days," an idealized past that was never as great as people remember it. Some examples follow.

France for the French

Ever since France suffered through multiple terrorist attacks in Paris, Nice, and elsewhere, the popularity of Marine Le Pen and her right-wing National Front party has grown. Her message is simple: "Keep immigrants out." The underlying message, which is not heavily masked, is hostility toward Muslims. Another of Le Pen's messages, one that is shared by her counterparts in the countries just mentioned, is anti-globalization. Le Pen would pull France out of the euro currency zone and perhaps even the European Union. The consequences of such a divorce are incalculable.

Unlike American small-government conservatives, Le Pen endorses what is called *welfare chauvinism*. That is the belief that generous social programs are appropriate—as long as the benefits are limited to the ethnically homogeneous native population. Le Pen, in other words, tells the white French majority that a strong "safety net" is desirable—as long as those who benefit are just like you. These ideas are common among the new nationalist parties of Europe.

Ms. Le Pen was the top vote-getter in the first stage of the 2017 French presidential elections, held in April 2017. She was therefore one of the two candidates to advance to the runoff elections. Still, she lost the runoffs badly to Emmanuel Macron, a moderate candidate.

Agree with Dutch Values, or Get Out of the Netherlands

For years, Geert Wilders and his Dutch Party for Freedom were barely respectable. His appeal increased, though, after a flood of Muslim refugees entered Europe, beginning in 2015. (Many of the migrants were from war-torn Syria.) In the Netherlands elections of March 2017, Wilders's party gained seats in the House of Representatives. Still, with only 20 members out of a total of 150, his party's influence was limited. Some Dutch politicians, however, felt that they needed to embrace a few of the far right's positions in order to win. Prime Minister Mark Rutte, a moderate conservative and leader of the largest Dutch political party, wrote an open letter to his people suggesting that anyone who disliked Dutch values should leave the country.

Critical Thinking

In what ways do President Trump's ideas resemble those of the nationalist parties of Europe? In what ways are they different?

these voters admitted to leaning toward the Republicans or the Democrats. Still, anyone claiming to be an independent has a weakened attachment to the parties.

Some political scientists argue that with so many independent voters, the concept of realignment becomes irrelevant. Realignment has been replaced by **dealignment.** In such an environment, politics would be unusually volatile, because independents could swing from one party to another. The dramatic changes in fortune experienced by the two major parties in recent years provide some evidence to support the dealignment theory.

Tipping Realignment and dealignment are not the only processes that can alter the political landscape. What if the various types of voters maintain their political identifications—but one type of voter becomes substantially more numerous? This can happen due to migration

dealignment Among voters, a growing detachment from both major political parties.

between states or between nations, or even due to changes in education levels and occupations. The result could tip a state from one party to another.

In 2002, John Judis and Ruy Teixeira published *The Emerging Democratic Majority*.[5] Judis and Teixeira argued that in the future, a growing number of Latinos and young urban professionals would give the Democratic Party an edge. For some years thereafter, the authors' thesis was met with a certain amount of scorn. Beginning in 2008, however, a growing number of Mexican American voters turned several western states to the Democrats in presidential races. Also, new citizens and urban professionals from the North turned Republican Virginia into a swing state. Could it be that Judis and Teixeira were onto something?

To a degree, they were. The problem for their thesis is that, in recent elections, growing white working-class support for the Republicans has effectively counteracted the growth in the Democratic immigrant and urban professional votes. Still, the Republicans face a potential problem. Many new Latino citizens are already here as children, and they will begin voting when they grow up. The Republicans face a long-term danger of running out of newly conservative whites before the Democrats run out of new minority and progressive white voters.

CRITICAL THINKING

▶ *Demographers expect that minority group members will form a majority of the U.S. population by 2050. How might this affect the two major parties?*

7–3 WHAT DO POLITICAL PARTIES DO?

LO Explain how political parties function in our democratic system.

As noted earlier, the Constitution does not mention political parties. Historically, though, political parties have played a vital role in our democratic system. Their main function has been to link the people's policy preferences to actual government policies. Political parties also perform many other functions.

7–3a Selecting Candidates and Running Campaigns

One of the most important functions of the two political parties is to recruit and nominate candidates for political office. This function simplifies voting choices for the electorate. Political parties take the large number of people who want to run for office and narrow the field. They accomplish this by the use of the **primary,** which is a preliminary election to choose a party's final candidate. This candidate then runs against the opposing party's candidate in the general election.

Primary Elections   Voter turnout for primaries is lower than it is for general elections. The voters who do go to the polls are often strong supporters of their party. Indeed, in many states, independents cannot participate in primary elections, even if they lean toward one or the other of the two major parties. As a result, the Republican primary electorate is very conservative, and Democratic primary voters are quite liberal. Candidates often find that they must run to the political right or left during the primaries. Traditionally, candidates then often moved to the center during the general election campaign, though such a "pivot to the center" has been much less common in recent years.

Running Campaigns   Through their national, state, and local organizations, parties coordinate campaigns. Political parties take care of a large number of small and routine tasks that are essential to the smooth functioning of the electoral process. For example, they work at getting party members registered and at conducting drives to recruit new voters. Sometimes, party volunteers staff the polling places.

7–3b Informing the Public

Political parties help educate the public about important political issues. In recent years, these issues have included environmental policies, health-care reform, the tax system, immigration, and ways to stimulate the economy. Each party presents its views on these issues through television announcements, newspaper articles and ads, website materials, campaign speeches, and debates. These activities help citizens learn about the issues, form opinions, and consider proposed solutions.

7–3c Coordinating Policymaking

In our complex government, parties are essential for coordinating policy among the various branches of the government. The political party is usually the major institution through which the executive and legislative branches cooperate with each other. Each president, cabinet head, and member of Congress is normally a member of the

> **primary** A preliminary election held for the purpose of choosing a party's final candidate.

Democratic Party or the Republican Party. The president works through party leaders in Congress to promote the administration's legislative program.

Ideally, the parties work together to fashion compromises—legislation that is acceptable to both parties and that serves the national interest. Yet in recent years, as we noted earlier, there has been little bipartisanship in Congress. Parties also act as the glue of our federal structure by connecting the various levels of government—state and national—with a common bond.

7-3d Checking the Power of the Governing Party

The party with fewer members in the legislature is the **minority party.** The party with more members is the **majority party.** Whether we're considering control of the legislature or of the executive branch, the party that is not in control plays a vital function in American politics. The "out" party does what it can to influence the "in" party and its policies, and to check the actions of the party in power.

For example, depending on how evenly Congress is divided, the out party, or minority party, may be able to attract to its side some of the members of the majority party to pass or defeat certain legislation. The minority party will also work to inform voters of the shortcomings of the majority party's agenda and to plan strategies for winning the next election.

7-3e Balancing Competing Interests

Political parties are often described as vast umbrellas under which Americans with diverse interests can gather. Political parties are essentially **coalitions**—alliances of individuals and groups with a variety of interests and opinions who join together to support the party's platform, or parts of it.

The Democratic Party, for example, includes a number of groups with different views on such issues as health care, immigration, and climate change. The role of party leaders in this situation is to adopt a view broad enough on these issues that no group will be alienated. In this way, different groups can hold their individual views and still come together under the umbrella of the Democratic Party.

Like the Democrats, the Republicans are a coalition. The Republican coalition, however, rests on different principles than the Democratic one. Much more than the Democrats, the Republicans are held together by a shared set of ideas. In a recent study, political scientists Matt Grossmann and David Hopkins found evidence that "the Republican Party is primarily the agent of an ideological movement whose supporters prize doctrinal purity, while the Democratic Party is better understood as a coalition of social groups seeking concrete government action."[6] The rise of Donald Trump might seem to suggest that Republican ideological unity is overestimated. Yet even after Trump's election as president, the overwhelming majority of Republican officeholders remain committed to an ideology of small-government conservatism.

This asymmetry reflects an essential truth about the American electorate. Time and again, observers have noted that Americans express ideological support for a smaller, less active government. At the same time, they also support almost every program undertaken by the federal government. It makes sense, then, that a conservative party would benefit from an ideological appeal to voters. The Democrats, in turn, would benefit when they highlight actual programs, such as Social Security or minimum wage laws. Regardless of whether a party is oriented toward small-government ideology or positive government action, however, it still needs to promote unity among diverse party factions.

CRITICAL THINKING

▶ *Presidents often have political goals that are different from those of senators and representatives from the president's own party. What might these presidential goals be?*

7-4 HOW AMERICAN POLITICAL PARTIES ARE STRUCTURED

LO Discuss the structure of American political parties.

Each of the two major American political parties consists of three components: the party in the electorate, the party organization, and the party in government.

1. The party in the **electorate** is the largest component, consisting of all of those people who describe themselves as Democrats or

---

minority party The political party that has fewer members in the legislature than the opposing party.

majority party The political party that has more members in the legislature than the opposing party.

coalition An alliance of individuals or groups with a variety of interests and opinions who join together to support all or part of a political party's platform.

electorate All of the citizens eligible to vote in a given election.

Republicans. In most states, a voter can register as a Democrat or a Republican, but registration can be changed at will.

2. Each major party has a nationwide organization with national, state, and local offices. As will be discussed later in this section, the party organizations include several levels of people who maintain the party's strength between elections, make its rules, raise money, organize conventions, help with elections, and recruit candidates.

3. The party in government consists of all of the party's candidates who have won elections and now hold public office.

Like sports teams, the parties have mascots. The Republican elephant and the Democratic donkey date to the nineteenth century. Both were first drawn by a Republican cartoonist. The elephant was supposed to illustrate the large size of the GOP in the northern states. *Given that the donkey was drawn by a Republican, what do you think it was meant to represent?*

7–4a The Party in the Electorate

Let's look more closely at the largest component of each party—the party in the electorate. What does it mean to belong to a political party? In many European countries, being a party member means that you actually join a political party. You get a membership card to carry in your wallet, you pay dues, and you vote to select your local and national party leaders. In the United States, becoming a member of a political party is far less involved.

In most states, voters may declare a party preference when they register to vote. This declaration allows them to participate in party primaries. Some states do not register party preferences, however. In short, to be a member of a political party, an American citizen has only to think of herself or himself as a Democrat or a Republican (or a member of a third party, such as the Green Party or the Libertarian Party). Members of parties do not have to work for the party or attend party meetings. Nor must they support the party platform.

Identifiers and Activists   Generally, the party in the electorate consists of **party identifiers** (those who identify themselves as being members of the party) and **party activists** (party members who choose to work for the party and may even become candidates for office). Political parties need year-round support from the latter group to survive. During election campaigns in particular, candidates depend on active party members and volunteers to answer phones, conduct door-to-door canvasses,

participate in Web campaigns, organize speeches and appearances, and, of course, donate money.

Between elections, parties also need active members to plan the upcoming elections, organize fund-raisers, and stay in touch with party leaders in other communities to keep the party strong. The major functions of American political parties are carried out by the party activists.

Elite Groups   Most members of the party in the electorate are ordinary citizens. Even party activists are generally not known outside their own circles. Yet the party in the electorate is not limited to those who lack fortune or fame. It is also made up of elites of various kinds—opinion leaders, media personalities, and prominent persons in all walks of life. It includes fund-raisers, former politicians, and nationally famous political operatives.

Consider talk radio personality Rush Limbaugh and deep-pocket campaign contributors Charles and David Koch. These people have no official position in government or in the Republican Party. They may be members of the party in the electorate, but their influence on the GOP is considerable. Likewise, comedian Jon Stewart and Rachel Maddow of MSNBC are influential among Democrats. A large number of

party identifiers A person who identifies himself or herself as being a supporter of a particular political party.

party activists A party member who helps to organize and oversee party functions and planning during and between campaigns, and may even become a candidate for office.

John Kennedy, a Republican candidate for the U.S. Senate in Louisiana, greets fans before a football game between Louisiana State University and the University of Alabama. Kennedy was elected to the Senate in a runoff election in December 2016. *Why might Republicans be popular in Louisiana?*

entertainment celebrities are ardent Democrats, though some are Republicans.

Various interest groups are also considered to be part of the party coalitions. Labor unions are almost always seen as a base of support for the Democrats. Business groups such as the U.S. Chamber of Commerce are likewise viewed as key Republican players.

Why People Join Political Parties

In a few countries, such as the People's Republic of China, people belong to a political party because doing so will help them to get ahead in life, regardless of whether they agree with the party's ideas and candidates. In the United States, though, people generally belong to a political party because they agree with many of its main ideas and support some of its candidates. Just as with interest groups, people's reasons for choosing one party over another may include solidarity, material, and purposive incentives.

Solidarity Incentives. Some people join a particular party to express their **solidarity,** or mutual agreement, with the views of friends, loved ones, and other likeminded people. People also join parties because they enjoy the excitement of engaging in politics with likeminded others.

solidarity Mutual agreement among the members of a particular group.

patronage A system of rewarding the party faithful with government jobs or contracts.

Material Incentives. Many believe that by joining a party, they will benefit materially through better employment or personal career advancement. The traditional institution of **patronage**—rewarding the party faithful with government jobs or contracts— lives on, even though it has been limited to prevent abuses.[7] Back in the nineteenth century, when almost all government employees got their jobs through patronage, people spoke of it as the "spoils system," as in "the spoils of war."

Purposive Incentives. Finally, some join political parties because they wish to actively promote a set of ideals and principles that they feel are important to American politics and society. As a rule, people join political parties because of their overall agreement with what a particular party stands for.

Thus, when asked why they support the Democratic Party, people may make such remarks as the following: "The economy is better when the Democrats are in control." "The Democrats stand for civil rights." People might say about the Republican Party: "The Republicans favor a smaller government." "The Republicans want to put America first."

7-4b The Party Organization

In theory, each of the major American political parties has a standard, pyramid-shaped organization. This theoretical structure is much like that of a large company, in which the bosses are at the top and the employees are at various lower levels.

Actually, neither major party is a closely knit or highly organized structure. Both parties are fragmented and *decentralized*, which means there is no central power with a direct chain of command. If there were, the national chairperson of the party, along with the national committee, could simply dictate how the organization would be run, just as if it were Apple or Google. In reality, state party organizations are all very different and are only loosely tied to the party's national structure. Local party organizations are often quite independent from the state organization.

In short, no single individual or group directs all party members. Instead, a number of personalities, frequently at odds with one another, form loosely identifiable leadership groups.

State Organizations

In general, the state party organization is built around a central committee and a chairperson. The committee works to raise funds, recruit new party members, maintain a strong party organization, and help members running for state offices.

The state chairperson is usually a powerful party member chosen by the committee. In some instances, however, the chairperson is selected by the governor or a senator from that state.

Local Organizations

Local party organizations differ greatly, but generally there is a party unit for each district in which elective offices are to be filled. These districts include congressional and legislative districts, counties, cities and towns, wards, and precincts.

A **ward** is a political division or district within a city. A **precinct** can be either a political district within a city, such as a block or a neighborhood, or a rural portion of a county. Polling places are located within the precincts. The local, grassroots foundations of politics are formed within voting precincts.

The National Party Organization

On the national level, the party's presidential candidate is considered to be the leader of the party. Well-known members of Congress may also be viewed as national party leaders. In addition to the party leaders, the structure of each party includes four major elements: the national convention, the national committee, the national chairperson, and the congressional campaign committees.

> "Under democracy one party always devotes its chief energies to trying to prove that the other party is *unfit to rule*—and both commonly succeed."
>
> ~ H. L. MENCKEN
> AMERICAN JOURNALIST
> 1880–1956

The National Convention. Much of the public attention that the party receives comes at the national convention, which is held every four years during the summer before the presidential elections. The news media always cover the conventions, and as a result, these gatherings have become quite extravagant. Lobbyists, big business, and interest groups provide millions of dollars to put on these events. Such organizations have an interest in government subsidies, tax breaks, and regulatory favors.

The conventions inspire and mobilize party members throughout the nation. They provide the voters with an opportunity to see and hear the candidates directly, rather than through a media filter or characterizations provided by supporters and opponents. Candidates' speeches at conventions draw huge audiences.

For example, in 2016 more than 30 million people watched the acceptance speeches of Donald Trump and Hillary Clinton. President Obama's speech at the 2016 convention was even more widely viewed.

The national conventions are attended by delegates chosen by the states. The delegates' most important job is to nominate the party's presidential and vice-presidential

Ronna Romney McDaniel became chair of the Republican National Committee in January 2017. *How much control does she have over state party organizations?*

ward A local unit of a political party's organization, consisting of a division or district within a city.

precinct A political district within a city, such as a block or a neighborhood, or a rural portion of a county. The smallest voting district at the local level.

national convention The meeting held by each major party every four years to nominate presidential and vice-presidential candidates, write a party platform, and conduct other party business.

candidates, who together make up the **party ticket.** A select group of key delegates also writes the **party platform,** which sets forth the party's positions on national issues. Essentially, through its platform, the party promises to initiate certain policies if it wins the presidency. Despite the widespread perception that candidates can and do ignore these promises once they are in office, in fact, many of the promises become law.

The National Committee. Each state elects a number of delegates to the **national party committee.** The Republican National Committee and the Democratic National Committee direct the business of their respective parties during the four years between national conventions. The committees' most important duties, however, are to organize the next national convention and to plan how to support the party's candidate in the next presidential election.

The National Chairperson. Each party's national committee elects a **national party chairperson** to serve as administrative head of the national party. The main duty of the national chairperson is to direct the work of the national committee from party headquarters in Washington, D.C. The chairperson is involved in raising funds, providing for publicity, promoting party unity, encouraging the development of state and local organizations, recruiting new voters, and other activities. In presidential election years, the chairperson's attention is focused on the national convention and the presidential campaign.

The Congressional Campaign Committees. Each party has a campaign committee in each chamber of Congress. In each chamber, members are chosen by their colleagues and serve for two-year terms. The committees work to help elect party members to Congress.

> "I am not a member of any organized political party. *I am a Democrat.*"
>
> ~WILL ROGERS
> AMERICAN HUMORIST
> 1879–1935

party ticket A list of a political party's candidates for various offices. In national elections, the party ticket consists of the presidential and vice-presidential candidates.

party platform The document drawn up by each party at its national convention that outlines the policies and positions of the party.

national party committee The political party leaders who direct party business during the four years between the national party conventions, organize the next national convention, and plan how to support the party's candidate in the next presidential election.

national party chairperson An individual who serves as a political party's administrative head at the national level and directs the work of the party's national committee.

7–4c The Party in Government

Even though candidates above the local level almost always run for office as either Democrats or Republicans, members of a given party do not always agree with one another on government policy. The party in government helps to organize the government's agenda by coaxing and convincing its own party members in office to vote for its policies. If the party is to translate its promises into public policies, the job must be done by the party in government.

A political party succeeds at the national level when it wins the presidency or control of one or more chambers of Congress. It then has the opportunity to carry out the party platform it developed at its national convention. The platform represents the official party position on various issues. As noted, though, neither all party members nor all candidates running on the party's ticket are likely to share these positions exactly.

For an example of how such divisions can create trouble for a party, consider the Republican approach to health-care insurance after they gained full control of the national government in the 2016 elections. Ever since the Affordable Care Act (Obamacare) was adopted in 2010, Republicans were united in calling for its repeal. In time, Republicans came to realize that straightforward repeal would be a disaster for health-care insurance markets, and so their slogan became "repeal and replace." Still, at the time they assumed power, the Republicans had not yet come to an agreement on what "replace" ought to look like.

House Speaker Paul Ryan sought to rally the party around a replacement bill titled the "American Health Care Act." The bill maintained much of the structure of Obamacare but substantially reduced subsidies to low-income persons. It also made large cuts to Medicaid benefits. Freedom Caucus Republicans opposed the legislation because it was too similar to Obamacare. More moderate Republicans opposed the cuts. Ryan eventually modified the bill enough to satisfy conservatives. He also put enough pressure on moderates that the bill narrowly passed the House. In the Senate, versions of the legislation faced the same opposition from both left and right. This time, however, Senate Majority Leader Mitch McConnell was unable to find the necessary votes, and the Senate voted down all repeal proposals.

▶ *The parties often hope they can win additional votes in a state by holding their national convention in that state. Do you think this strategy is likely to be effective? Why or why not?*

7-5 THE DOMINANCE OF OUR TWO-PARTY SYSTEM

LO Describe the different types of third parties and how they function in the American political system.

Thomas Perez was elected chair of the Democratic National Committee in February 2017. *How much influence does Perez have over Democratic Party policy?*

In the United States, as noted, we have a **two-party system.** This means that the two major parties—the Democrats and the Republicans—dominate national politics. Why has the two-party system become so firmly entrenched in the United States? According to some scholars, the first major political division between the Federalists and the Anti-Federalists established a precedent that continued over time and ultimately resulted in the domination of the two-party system.

7-5a The Self-Perpetuation of the Two-Party System

One of the major reasons for the perpetuation of the two-party system is simply that there is no alternative. Minor parties, called **third parties,**[8] have found it extremely difficult to compete with the major parties for votes. There are many reasons for this, some of which are described in the following subsections.

Political Socialization   When young people or new immigrants learn about U.S. politics, they tend to absorb the political views of those who are providing them with information. Parents find it easy to pass their political beliefs on to their children, often without even trying. Those beliefs frequently involve support for one of the two major parties.

To be sure, about two-fifths of voters today regard themselves as independents (although they may lean toward one party or another). These voters apparently believe that neither major party fully represents their views. Such attitudes, however, do not mean that independents are looking for a third party. Typically, true independents are content to swing between the Democrats and the Republicans.

Election Laws Favoring Two Parties   American election laws tend to favor the major parties. In many states, for example, the established major parties need relatively few signatures to place their candidates on the ballot, whereas a third party must get many more signatures. The number of signatures required is often based on the total party vote in the last election, which penalizes a new party that is competing for the first time. The rules governing campaign financing also favor the major parties.

Institutional Barriers to a Multiparty System   The structure of many of our institutions prevents third parties from enjoying electoral success. The nature of the election process works against third-party candidates, as does the nature of single-member districts.

> "Let us not seek the Republican answer or the Democratic answer, but the right answer."
>
> ~ JOHN FITZGERALD KENNEDY,
> THIRTY-FIFTH PRESIDENT OF THE UNITED STATES,
> 1961–1963

two-party system A political system in which two strong and established parties compete for political offices.

third party In the United States, any party other than the two major parties (Republican and Democratic).

The Election Process. One of the major institutional barriers to third parties is the election, by the people, of governors and (through the electoral college) the president. Voting for governors and members of the electoral college takes place on a statewide, winner-take-all basis. (Maine and Nebraska are exceptions—they can, under certain circumstances, split their electoral votes.) Third-party candidates find it hard to win when they must campaign statewide instead of appealing to voters in a smaller district that might be more receptive to their political positions.

The popular election of executive officers contrasts with the parliamentary system described earlier in this text. In that system, parliament—not the voters—chooses the nation's executive officers. Third-party voters therefore have a greater chance of affecting the outcome by electing a few members of parliament. Even if the party's delegation is small, it may be able to participate in a coalition government with other parties.

Single-Member Districts versus Proportional Systems. Another institutional barrier to a multiparty system is the single-member district. Today, all federal and most state legislative districts are single-member districts—that is, voters elect one member from their district to the House of Representatives and to their state legislature.[9] In some countries, by contrast, districts are drawn as multimember districts and are represented by multiple elected officials from different parties, according to the proportion of the vote each party received.

In many democracies that use single-member districts to choose members of parliament, additional members are chosen from statewide or nationwide party lists. The number of additional members elected from the party lists is calculated to guarantee that the election results are *proportional*. Under a proportional election system, one party might receive 40 percent of the national vote, another party 35 percent, and a third party 25 percent. Each party can expect to obtain a share of seats in the national parliament that closely reflects its percentage of the vote.

Nonpartisan Elections. While third parties are rarely successful in the United States, the two major parties do not compete in all elections. Some state offices and many local offices are filled by *nonpartisan elections*, in which party identification never appears on the ballot. Are there benefits to the nonpartisan system? We examine that question in this chapter's *Join the Debate* feature.

7–5b Third Parties in American Politics

Despite difficulties, throughout American history third parties have competed for influence in the nation's two-party system. Indeed, as mentioned earlier, third parties have been represented in most of our national elections. These parties are as varied as the causes they represent, but all have one thing in common: their members and leaders want to challenge the major parties because they believe that certain needs and values are not being properly addressed. Table 7–1 lists the most successful American third parties since the Civil War (1861–1865).

TABLE 7–1   THE MOST SUCCESSFUL THIRD-PARTY PRESIDENTIAL CAMPAIGNS SINCE 1865

This table includes all third-party candidates winning more than 5 percent of the popular vote or any electoral votes since 1865. It does not count "unfaithful electors" in the electoral college who did not vote for the candidate to whom they were pledged. *What kinds of issue positions might make a third party especially popular?*

Year	Third Party	Third-Party Presidential Candidate	Percent of the Popular Vote	Electoral Votes	Winning Presidential Candidate and Party
1892	Populist	James Weaver	8.5%	22	Grover Cleveland (D)
1912	Progressive	Theodore Roosevelt	27.4	88	Woodrow Wilson (D)
	Socialist	Eugene Debs	6.0	—	
1924	Progressive	Robert LaFollette	16.6	13	Calvin Coolidge (R)
1948	States' Rights	Strom Thurmond	2.4	39	Harry Truman (D)
1960	Independent Democrat	Harry Byrd	0.4	15*	John F. Kennedy (D)
1968	American Independent	George Wallace	13.5	46	Richard Nixon (R)
1980	National Union	John Anderson	6.6	—	Ronald Reagan (R)
1992	Independent	Ross Perot	18.9	—	Bill Clinton (D)
1996	Reform	Ross Perot	8.4	—	Bill Clinton (D)

*Byrd received fifteen electoral votes from unpledged electors in Alabama and Mississippi.
Source: Dave Leip's Atlas of U.S. Presidential Elections at www.uselectionatlas.org.

It's hard to miss the partisan battles in Washington, D.C. To a lesser extent, nasty fights also occur in state legislatures and even city councils. As you've learned, the framers of the U.S. Constitution never mentioned political parties. They thought that the nation would be better off without them. Dream on. We will never eliminate partisan elections at the federal level. But what about the state and, particularly, the local levels? Would the states be better off with nonpartisan elections?

Take the Nastiness Out of Elections—Go Nonpartisan

Advocates of nonpartisan elections believe that the two major political parties are the reason that many states are "ungovernable." Political deadlock would be eliminated if state senators and representatives were voted into office without a party label.

Currently, ideological activists—Republicans and Democrats—largely determine the identity of state legislative candidates. Where does that leave independents and moderates? The answer is: underrepresented.

More than two-thirds of American cities have embraced nonpartisan voting. After all, local issues are very different from national ones, and knowing that a candidate is a Republican or a Democrat tells you little about that candidate's policy positions on local issues. It's time to extend nonpartisan elections to state legislatures as well. Nebraska, for one, has such a legislature already.

Nonpartisan Elections Lead to Less-Informed Voters

While enticing in theory, nonpartisan elections do not result in better government, according to their opponents. In some nonpartisan systems, candidates are still affiliated with political parties. Even so, without party labels on the ballot, citizens find it more difficult to cast an informed vote. Ordinary citizens cannot take the time to analyze in any detail the political positions of legislative candidates. Take the example of nonpartisan state elections in Minnesota before 1973.

There, prominent local figures were able to win elections even when their politics were unrepresentative of their districts. After partisan labels were introduced in 1973, the state legislature was transformed politically.

According to law professor David Schleicher, nonpartisan balloting at the city level also leaves voters poorly informed and reduces turnout in elections. True, party labels provide less information in municipal contests than in national elections. They provide at least some information, however, and without them, citizens often know nothing at all. As a result, Schleicher says, voters tend to rely on racial or ethnic clues in candidates' names.

Critical Analysis

If you were independently wealthy and could finance an expensive campaign, would you prefer partisan or nonpartisan elections? Why?

Some third parties have tried to appeal to the entire nation. Others have focused on particular regions, states, or local areas. Most third parties have been short-lived. A few, however, such as the Socialist Party (founded in 1901 and disbanded in 1972), lasted for a long time. The number and variety of third parties make them difficult to classify, but most fall into one of the general categories discussed in the following subsections.

Issue-Oriented Parties An issue-oriented third party is formed to promote a particular cause or timely issue. For example, the Free Soil Party was organized in 1848 to oppose the expansion of slavery into the western territories. The Prohibition Party was formed in 1869 to advocate banning the manufacture and use of alcoholic beverages.

Most issue-oriented parties fade into history as the issue that brought them into existence fades from public attention, is taken up by a major party, or is resolved. Some issue-oriented parties endure, however, when they expand their focus beyond a single area of concern. For example, the Green Party was founded in 1972 to raise awareness of environmental issues, but it is no longer a single-issue party. Today, the Green Party campaigns against alleged corporate greed and the major parties' ostensible indifference to a number of issues, including poverty, the excesses of globalism, and the failure of the war on drugs.

Ideological Parties A *political ideology* is a system of political ideas rooted in beliefs about human nature, society, and government. An ideological party supports a particular political doctrine or a set of beliefs.

For example, the Party for Socialism and Liberation, a communist party centered in California, advocates a "socialist transformation of society." Capitalism is to be abolished, and the existing political system replaced with a "new government of working people." In contrast, the Libertarian Party opposes almost all forms of government interference with personal liberties and private enterprise.

Splinter or Personality Parties A splinter party develops out of a split within a major party. This split may be part of an attempt to elect a specific person. For example, when Theodore Roosevelt did not receive the GOP nomination for president in 1912, he created the Bull Moose Party (also called the Progressive Party) to promote his candidacy. From the Democrats have come Henry Wallace's Progressive Party and the States' Rights (Dixiecrat) Party, both formed in 1948. In 1968, the American Independent Party was formed to support George Wallace's campaign for president.

Most splinter parties have been formed around a leader with a strong personality, which is why they are sometimes called *personality parties*. When that person steps aside, the party usually collapses. An example of a personality party is the Reform Party, which was formed in 1995 mainly to provide a campaign vehicle for H. Ross Perot. (The party was later taken over by others and adopted a platform of conservative nationalism.)

7–5c The Effects of Third Parties

Although most Americans do not support third parties or vote for their candidates, third parties have influenced American politics in several ways.

Third Parties Bring Issues to the Public's Attention Third parties have brought many political issues to the public's attention. They have exposed and focused on unpopular or highly debated issues that major parties have preferred to ignore. Third parties are in a position to take bold stands on issues that major parties avoid because third parties are not trying to be all things to all people.

Some people have argued that third parties are often the unsung heroes of American politics, bringing new issues to the forefront of public debate. Progressive social reforms such as the minimum wage, women's right to vote, railroad and banking legislation, and old-age pensions were first proposed by third parties. The Free Soil Party (1848–1854) was the first true antislavery party, and the Populists and Progressives put many social reforms on the political agenda. Although some of the ideas proposed by third parties were never accepted, others were taken up by the major parties as those ideas became increasingly popular.

Third Parties Can Affect the Vote Third parties can also influence election outcomes. On occasion, they have taken victory from one major party and given it to another, thus playing the "spoiler" role.

For example, in 1912, when the Progressive Party split from the Republican Party, the result was three major contenders for the presidency: Woodrow Wilson, the Democratic candidate; William Howard Taft, the regular Republican candidate; and Theodore Roosevelt, the Progressive candidate. The presence of the Progressive

Everett Historical/Shutterstock.com

Eugene V. Debs was the Socialist Party candidate for president in five elections. *Why would a self-identified socialist—such as Vermont senator Bernie Sanders—be more successful running as a Democrat?*

Party "spoiled" the Republicans' chances for victory and gave the election to Wilson, the Democrat. Without Roosevelt's third party, Taft might have won. Similarly, some commentators contended that third parties may have helped determine the results of the 2016 presidential elections. The third-party vote was unusually large that year, with the Libertarians winning more than 3 percent of the vote and the Green Party winning more than 1 percent. Given how close the results were in the key states of Wisconsin, Michigan, and Pennsylvania, Clinton might have won if the Green Party had not "spoiled" her chances. The assumption is that Green voters would be much more likely to vote for Clinton than for Trump.

Third Parties Provide a Voice for Dissatisfied Americans Third parties also provide a voice for voters who are frustrated with and alienated from the Republican and Democratic parties. Americans who are unhappy with the two major political parties can still participate in American politics through third parties that reflect their opinions on political issues. For example, many new Minnesota voters turned out during the 1998 elections to vote for Jesse Ventura, a Reform Party candidate for governor in that state. Ventura won.

Ultimately, third parties in national elections find it difficult to break through in an electoral system that perpetuates their failure. Because third parties normally do not win elections, Americans tend not to vote for them or to contribute to their campaigns, so they continue not to win. As long as Americans hold on to the perception that third parties can never win an election, the current two-party system is likely to persist.

CRITICAL THINKING

▶ *Some have argued that, given the polarization of the two major parties, Americans should organize a new party based on moderate politics. Why might such an initiative fail—or succeed?*

AMERICA AT ODDS | Political Parties

By their very nature, arguments about the parties are some of the most divisive conflicts in politics. We list only a sampling of the disputes:

- *Can an alliance between Trump enthusiasts and small-government conservatives continue to propel the Republicans to victory—or will such an alliance drive off voters that the Republicans will eventually need? For that matter, must the Democrats change their policies to obtain victories in the future?*

- *Is it better when the two chambers of Congress and the presidency are held by the same party, thus promoting effective government—or is it better when Congress and the presidency are held by different parties, so that the two parties can check each other?*

- *Is the increasing importance of political independents a positive development—or is it a sign that citizens are becoming dangerously detached from our political system?*

- *Are political parties desirable and inevitable—or should elections be nonpartisan whenever possible?*

- *Is it better to support a third party when you are in greater agreement with its positions than with those of either major party—or should you avoid wasting your vote and always support the major party that is closer to your politics?*

- *Finally, looking forward, do the Republicans or the Democrats offer the best solutions for our problems?*

STUDY TOOLS 7

READY TO STUDY? IN THE BOOK, YOU CAN:

☐ Review what you've read with the following chapter quiz.

☐ Check your answers in Appendix D at the back of the book.

☐ Rip out the Chapter Review Card, which includes key terms, chapter summaries, and answers to the following quiz.

ONLINE AT WWW.CENGAGEBRAIN.COM, YOU CAN:

☐ Watch videos to get a quick overview.

☐ Expedite your studying with Major Player readings and Focus Activities.

☐ Check your understanding with Chapter Quizzes.

FILL-IN

Learning Outcome 7–1

1. The nation's first two political parties, the _____ and the _____ clashed openly in the elections of 1796.

2. From 1835 until 1854, the _____ Party was the major opponent of the Democratic Party.

3. After the election of 1896, the _____ Party established itself in the minds of many Americans as the party that knew how to manage the economy.

Learning Outcome 7–2

4. Since 1957, the number of independents has gone up and the number of _____ has gone down.

5. Dealignment among voters refers to _____.

Learning Outcome 7–3

6. A _____ is a preliminary election held for the purpose of choosing a party's final candidate.

Learning Outcome 7–4

7. The Republican and Democratic candidates for president and vice president are nominated at each party's _____.

Learning Outcome 7–5

8. The third-party presidential campaign of _____ resulted in the election of Democrat Woodrow Wilson as president in 1912.

MULTIPLE CHOICE

Learning Outcome 7–1

9. A process in which a substantial number of voters change their political allegiance is called
   a. realignment.
   b. dealignment.
   c. tipping.

Learning Outcome 7–2

10. After the 2010 elections, many of the new Republican members of Congress were pledged to the Tea Party philosophy of
   a. moving the Republican Party toward the center.
   b. breaking political deadlock in Washington.
   c. no-compromise conservatism.

Learning Outcome 7–3

11. Functions of the political parties include
   a. conducting elections, articulating an ideology, and coordinating policymaking among those elected to various offices.
   b. selecting candidates, coordinating policymaking, and balancing competing interests within the party.
   c. managing membership, selecting candidates, and balancing competing interests.

Learning Outcome 7–4

12. To be a member of a political party in the United States
    a. you must join the party and pay membership dues.
    b. you must support the party platform.
    c. you need only think of yourself as a member of the party—as a Democrat or a Republican (or a member of a third party).

Learning Outcome 7–5

13. An issue-oriented third party
    a. supports a particular political doctrine or set of beliefs.
    b. is formed to promote a particular cause.
    c. is also referred to as a splinter party.

8 | PUBLIC OPINION AND VOTING

Rob Crandall/Shutterstock.com

LEARNING OUTCOMES

After reading this chapter, you should be able to:

8-1 Describe the political socialization process.

8-2 Discuss the different factors that affect voter choices.

8-3 Explain how public opinion polls are conducted, problems with polls, and how they are used in the political process.

8-4 Indicate some of the factors that affect voter turnout, and discuss what has been done to improve voter turnout and voting procedures.

After finishing this chapter, go to **PAGE 190** for **STUDY TOOLS**

AMERICA AT ODDS

How Important Is It to Target Independents?

The share of the electorate that claims to be independent—not supporting any political party—now hovers around 40 percent. That simple fact would suggest that independent voters are important in elections, especially presidential ones. It may be true that many "independents" are really Democrats or Republicans in disguise, but other independents—about 10 percent of the total electorate—are true swing voters. It seems to make sense, therefore, that any candidate, particularly one running for president, should try to win independents to her or his side.

But not everyone agrees that this is an effective strategy. Some claim that presidential candidates are better off catering to the "base" of their party. The goal is to get the largest number of faithful party supporters to the ballot box. After all, in the presidential election year of 2016, voter turnout was 60 percent. In 2014, an off year with just senators and representatives on the national ballot, turnout was only 36 percent. That's a difference of 24 percent. In any swing state, the turnout gap will be substantially larger than the percentage of true swing voters. In 2000 and 2004, Republican presidential candidate George W. Bush attempted to mobilize Republican turnout at the expense of appealing to moderate voters—and he won.

If You Don't Win Swing Votes, You Won't Be Elected

Those who argue that independents are crucial say the numbers tell it all. Winning over independents is the key to winning a presidential election. Look at Gallup's figures for the eve of the 2016 elections. Of those polled, 27 percent were Republicans and 16 percent were independents leaning Republican, for a total of 43 percent. Democrats were at 31 percent and Democratic leaners, 15 percent, for a total of 46 percent. With those numbers, how on earth can you win without swing voters?

According to many political scientists, swing voters are capable of responding to either liberal or conservative arguments. That is because they carry both liberal and conservative value systems in their heads. As long as there are independents who can be attracted to both conservative and progressive beliefs, they will swing between the parties. Therefore, politicians should moderate their positions to appeal to the center.

But You Will Also Lose If You Abandon Your Values

Other political scientists argue that the moderate swing voter is largely a myth. Many "moderate" voters seem moderate because they hold some conservative positions and some liberal ones. Many of these opinions are actually quite radical. A voter might, for example, endorse large increases in Social Security benefits, a liberal position. That same voter might favor the deportation of all 11 million unauthorized immigrants, a decidedly conservative stand. Typically, these voters are uninterested in politics and may have little political information.

Because such voters swing from party to party, politicians still want to appeal to them. Attempting to take moderate positions will not necessarily help, however, because many of these voters are not really moderate. Instead, a conservative candidate is better off presenting himself or herself as the most attractive possible conservative. Progressives should follow this strategy as well. It's not just ideas that win elections, but qualities such as optimism, empathy, and a consistent set of values.

Where do you stand?

1. If you were a candidate for the presidency, what "moderate" positions would you take?
2. Is there any way for any candidate to appeal to all voters? Why or why not?

Explore this issue online

- Linda Killian contends that the moderate middle is real enough. Search for "swing voters real killian."
- Ezra Klein argues that moderates are mostly a statistical artifact. Find his article at "klein moderate myth."

INTRODUCTION

For a democracy to be effective, members of the public must form opinions and openly express them to their elected officials. Only when the opinions of Americans are communicated effectively to elected representatives can those opinions form the basis of government action.

Citizens use many methods to communicate with elected officials, including tweets, e-mail, texting, telephone calls, and attendance at rallies or "town hall" meetings with representatives. The most accurate way of gauging overall public opinion between elections, however, is through public opinion polls, which we describe in this chapter.

The ultimate way that citizens communicate their views, of course, is by casting ballots for their preferred candidates. Many factors affect the political beliefs that motivate voters, and we discuss these factors in this chapter. We also look at the mechanics of voting, which can have a definite impact on election results.

> "A government can be no better than the *public opinion* that sustains it."
>
> ~ FRANKLIN DELANO ROOSEVELT
> THIRTY-SECOND PRESIDENT OF THE
> UNITED STATES
> 1933–1945

8-1 HOW DO PEOPLE FORM POLITICAL OPINIONS?

LO Describe the political socialization process.

What exactly is **public opinion**? We define it as the sum total of a complex collection of opinions held by many people on issues in the public arena, such as taxes, health care, Social Security, clean-air legislation, and unemployment. When asked, most Americans are willing to express an opinion on such issues. Not one of us, however, was born with these opinions. Most people acquire their political attitudes, opinions, beliefs, and knowledge through a complex learning process called **political socialization.** This process begins early and continues throughout life.

public opinion The views of the citizenry about politics, public issues, and public policies. A complex collection of opinions held by many people on issues in the public arena.

political socialization The learning process through which most people acquire their political attitudes, opinions, beliefs, and knowledge.

agents of political socialization People and institutions that influence the political views of others.

Most political socialization is informal, and it usually begins during early childhood, when the dominant influence on a child is the family. Although parents normally do not sit down and say to their children, "Let us explain to you the virtues of becoming a Republican," their children nevertheless come to know the parents' feelings, beliefs, and attitudes. The strong early influence of the family later gives way to the multiple influences of school, church, peers, television, co-workers, and other groups. People and institutions that influence the political views of others are called **agents of political socialization.**

8-1a The Importance of Family

As just suggested, most parents or caregivers do not deliberately set out to form their children's political ideas and beliefs. They are usually more concerned with the moral, religious, and ethical values of their offspring. Yet a child first sees the political world through the eyes of his or her family, which is perhaps the most important force in political socialization. Children do not "learn" political attitudes the same way they learn to master inline skating. Rather, they learn by hearing their parents' everyday conversations about politicians and issues, and by observing their parents' actions and reactions.

The family's influence is strongest when children can clearly perceive their parents' attitudes, and most can. In one study, more high school students could identify their parents' political party affiliation than their parents' other attitudes or beliefs. The political party of the parents often becomes the political party of the children, particularly if both parents support the same party.

8-1b Schools and Churches

Education also strongly influences an individual's political attitudes. From their earliest days in school, children learn about the American political system. They say the Pledge of Allegiance and sing patriotic songs. They celebrate national holidays, such as Presidents' Day and Veterans Day, and learn about the history and symbols associated with them. In the upper grades, young people acquire more knowledge about government and democratic procedures through civics classes and participation in student government and various clubs. They also learn citizenship skills through school rules and regulations. Generally, those

Monkey Business Images/Shutterstock.com

Family support for going to college often matters. *Why might it be important to encourage youth from minority families to attend college?*

with more education have more knowledge about politics and policy than do those with less education. The level of education also influences a person's political values, as will be discussed later in this chapter.

A majority of Americans hold strong religious beliefs, and these attitudes can also contribute significantly to political socialization. For example, if a family's church emphasizes that society has a collective obligation to care for the poor, the children in that family may be influenced in a liberal direction. If the church instead depicts the government as irreligious and morally threatening, children will receive a conservative message.

8-1c The Media

The **media**—newspapers, magazines, television, radio, and the Internet—also have an impact on political socialization. The most influential of these media is television, which continues to be a leading source of political information for older voters. As explained later in this chapter, older citizens turn out to vote significantly more often than younger ones.

Still, the Internet—and social media in particular—is an extremely important source of information for younger citizens. Social media are also important for politicians. Even after President Obama left office, @BarackObama had just under 86 million followers on Twitter, for third place worldwide. Despite President Trump's well-known fondness for Twitter, @realDonaldTrump was only

forty-fourth, with almost 27 million followers. Obama and Trump, however, were the only U.S. politicians to make the Twitter Top 100.

Some contend that the media's role in shaping public opinion has increased to the point that the media are as influential as the family, particularly among high school students. For example, in her analysis of the media's role in American politics, media scholar Doris A. Graber points out that high school students, when asked where they obtain the information on which they base their attitudes, mention the Internet and social media far more than they mention their families, friends, and teachers.[1]

Other studies have shown that the media's influence on people's opinions may not be as great as some have thought. Typically, people go online, watch television, or read articles with preconceived ideas about the issues. These preconceived ideas act as a kind of perceptual screen that blocks out information that is not consistent with the ideas. Generally, the media tend to wield the most influence over the views of persons who have not yet formed opinions about various issues or candidates.

8-1d Opinion Leaders

Every city or community has well-known citizens who are able to influence the opinions of their fellow citizens. These people may be public officials, religious leaders, teachers, or celebrities. They are the people to whom others listen and from whom others draw ideas and convictions about various issues of public concern. These *opinion leaders* play a significant role in the formation of public opinion.

Opinion leaders often include politicians and former politicians. Opinion leaders are not limited to political figures, however. In different ways, both Lady Gaga and Kate Middleton, Duchess of Cambridge, are opinion leaders (though British royals are required to stay out of politics). Media figures such as actress Angelina Jolie and pastor Rick Warren are opinion leaders as well.

> **media** Newspapers, magazines, television, radio, the Internet, and any other printed or electronic means of communication.

8-1e Major Life Events

Often, the political attitudes of an entire generation of Americans are influenced by a major event. For example, consider the Great Depression (1929–1939), the most severe economic depression in modern U.S. history. This event persuaded many Americans who lived through it that the federal government should step in when the economy is in decline. A substantial number of voters came to believe that the New Deal programs and policies of President Franklin Roosevelt showed that the Democratic Party was concerned about the fate of ordinary people. As a result, they became supporters of that party.

The generation that lived through World War II (1939–1945) tends to believe that American intervention in foreign affairs is good. In contrast, the generation that came of age during the Vietnam War (1965–1975) is more skeptical of American interventionism. A national tragedy, such as the terrorist attacks of September 11, 2001, is also likely to influence the political attitudes of a generation. The recent Great Recession and the financial crisis that struck in September 2008 will surely affect popular attitudes in years to come.

8-1f Peer Groups

Once children enter school, the views of friends begin to influence their attitudes and beliefs. From junior high school on, the **peer group**—friends, classmates, co-workers, club members, or religious group members—becomes a significant factor in the political socialization process.

Most of this socialization occurs when the peer group is involved with political activities or other causes. For example, your political beliefs might be influenced by a peer group with which you are working on a common cause, such as cleaning up a local riverbank or campaigning for a favorite candidate. Your political beliefs probably are not as strongly influenced by peers with whom you, say, snowboard regularly or attend concerts.

8-1g Economic Status and Occupation

A person's economic status may influence her or his political views. For example, poorer people are more likely to favor government assistance programs. On an issue such as abortion, lower-income people are more likely to be conservative—that is, to be against abortion—than are higher-income groups (of course, there are many exceptions).

peer group Associates, often close in age to one another. May include friends, classmates, co-workers, club members, or religious group members.

Where a person works also affects her or his opinions. Co-workers who spend a great deal of time working together tend to influence one another. For example, labor union members working together for a company may have similar political opinions, at least on issues of government involvement in the economy. Individuals working for a nonprofit agency that depends on government funds will tend to support government spending in that area. Business managers are more likely to favor tax laws helpful to businesses than are factory workers.

CRITICAL THINKING

▶ *Thinking about your own life, what sources of political socialization were most important to you? How did they influence your beliefs?*

8-2 WHY PEOPLE VOTE AS THEY DO

LO Discuss the different factors that affect voter choices.

What prompts some citizens to vote Republican and others to vote Democratic? What persuades voters to choose certain kinds of candidates? Researchers have collected more information on voting than on any other form of political participation in the United States. These data shed some light on why people decide to vote for particular candidates.

8-2a Party Identification and Ideology

Many voters have a standing allegiance to a political party, or a *party identification*, although the proportion of the population that does so has fallen in recent decades. For established voters, party identification is one of the most important and lasting predictors of how a person will vote. Party identification is an emotional attachment to a party that is influenced by family, age, peer groups, and other factors that play a role in the political socialization process discussed earlier.

A large number of voters call themselves independents. As mentioned before, despite this label, many independents actually support one or the other of the two major parties quite regularly.

Ideology is another indicator of voting behavior, one that is closely linked with party identification. Recent polls indicate that 37 percent of Americans consider themselves to be conservatives, 24 percent consider themselves liberals, and 35 percent identify themselves as moderates.

Trump supporters wait for him to arrive for a speech in Costa Mesa, California. *How did Republican Party leaders initially react to Trump's candidacy?*

Typically, liberals and some moderates vote for Democrats, and conservatives vote for Republicans. The large numbers of Americans who fall in the political center do not adhere strictly to a liberal or conservative ideology. (We looked at the political beliefs of so-called moderates in the chapter-opening *America at Odds* feature.)

8–2b Perception of the Candidates

Voters often base their decisions on the perceived character of the candidates rather than on their qualifications or policy positions. Such perceptions were important in 2010 and 2012. Following each of these elections, many political analysts concluded that the Republican Party had forfeited two to three U.S. Senate races by nominating Tea Party–supported candidates who were regarded by many voters as "too extreme." This perception was, to a large extent, based not on the political positions taken by the candidates, but on personal attitudes.

In 2014, Republican leaders made a major effort to ensure that the party's candidates were not the kinds of people who would be seen as unacceptable. By and large, the party succeeded.

Of course, the kind of candidate-vetting that Republicans engaged in during 2014 only works if voters are willing to listen to the "party elders." What if major sections of a party are in open rebellion against the leadership? If that is so, the primary candidates who win may be ones perceived as sharing that rebellious spirit. In 2016, Donald

Trump benefited from just such circumstances. When members of the Republican establishment attacked Trump, his supporters actually saw the attacks as a validation of his candidacy.

8–2c Policy Choices

When people vote for candidates who share their positions on particular issues, they are engaging in policy voting. If a candidate for senator in your state opposes gun control laws, for example, and you decide to vote for him or her for that reason, you have engaged in policy voting.

Historically, economic issues have had the strongest influence on voters' choices. When the economy is doing well, it is very difficult for a challenger, particularly at the presidential level, to defeat the incumbent. In contrast, when the country is experiencing inflation, rising unemployment, or high interest rates, the incumbent may be at a disadvantage.

One factor that limits the impact of the issues on voting decisions is that party identification can define policy choices for voters. For example, a Republican who believes that global warming is a serious problem is likely to be uncomfortable in a party that rejects that opinion. Rather than adjust their partisan identification, many people find themselves adjusting their position on the issues instead.

8–2d Socioeconomic Factors

Some factors that influence how people vote can be described as socioeconomic. These factors include educational attainment, occupation and income, age, gender, religion, geographic location, and race. Some of these factors have to do with the circumstances into which individuals are born. Others have to do with personal choices. Figure 8–1 shows how various groups voted in the 2016 presidential elections.

Educational Attainment   Traditionally, people with more education were more likely to vote Republican. In part, this tendency was due to the fact that educational attainment is linked to income level. (Higher incomes have always indicated Republican preferences.) One study has shown that among students from families with incomes in the bottom fifth of the population, only 12 percent earn a bachelor's degree by the age of

FIGURE 8–1   VOTING BY GROUPS IN THE 2016 PRESIDENTIAL ELECTIONS

Do any of these results surprise you? If so, which ones and why?

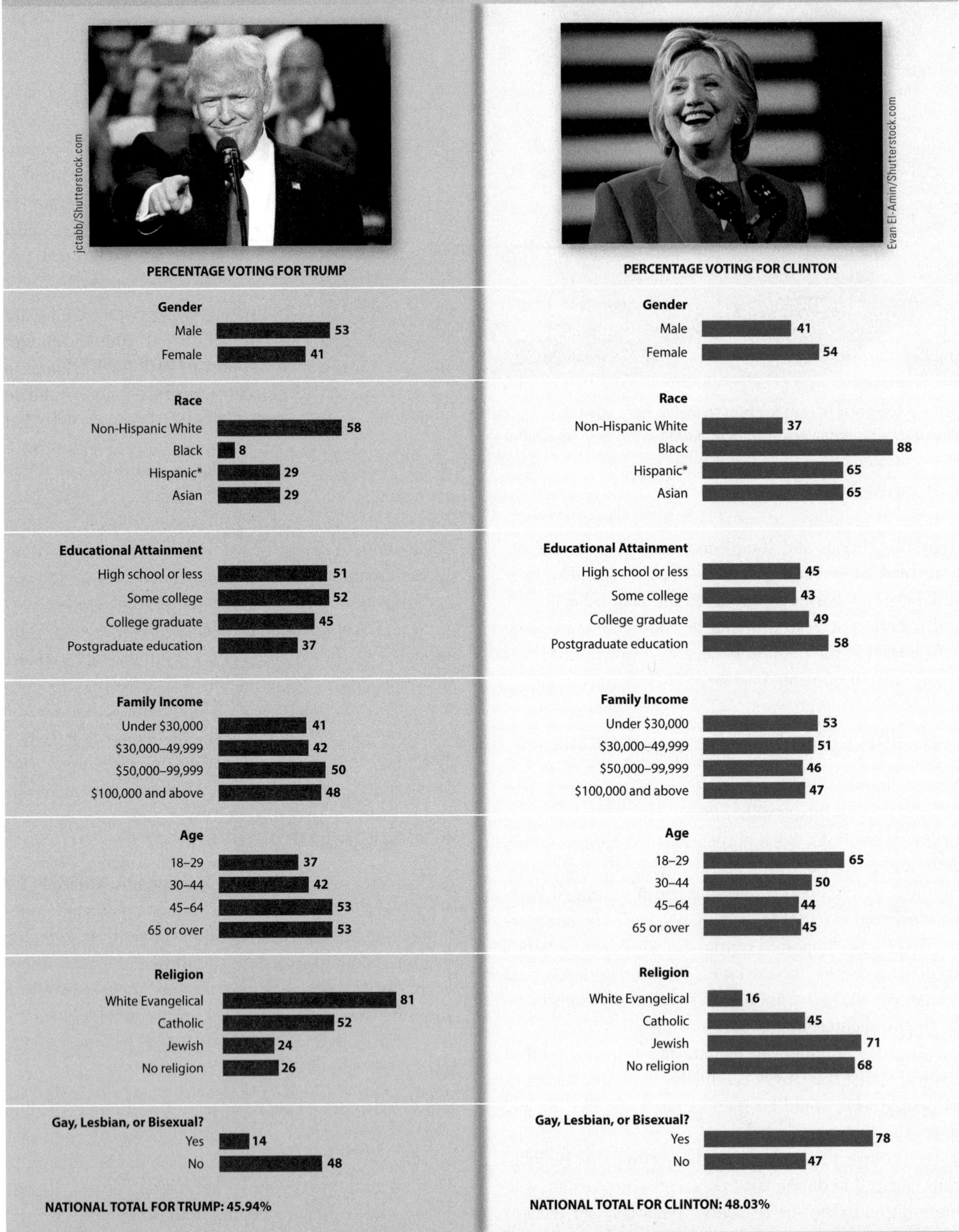

PERCENTAGE VOTING FOR TRUMP

PERCENTAGE VOTING FOR CLINTON

Gender	Trump	Clinton
Male	53	41
Female	41	54

Race	Trump	Clinton
Non-Hispanic White	58	37
Black	8	88
Hispanic*	29	65
Asian	29	65

Educational Attainment	Trump	Clinton
High school or less	51	45
Some college	52	43
College graduate	45	49
Postgraduate education	37	58

Family Income	Trump	Clinton
Under $30,000	41	53
$30,000–49,999	42	51
$50,000–99,999	50	46
$100,000 and above	48	47

Age	Trump	Clinton
18–29	37	65
30–44	42	50
45–64	53	44
65 or over	53	45

Religion	Trump	Clinton
White Evangelical	81	16
Catholic	52	45
Jewish	24	71
No religion	26	68

Gay, Lesbian, or Bisexual?	Trump	Clinton
Yes	14	78
No	48	47

NATIONAL TOTAL FOR TRUMP: 45.94%

NATIONAL TOTAL FOR CLINTON: 48.03%

* Later analyses reject these figures and estimate that Trump received 18 percent of the Latino vote and Clinton, 79 percent. See Francisco I. Pedraza and Bryan Wilcox-Archuleta, "Did Latino Voters Actually Turn Out for Trump in the Election? Not Really," *Los Angeles Times*, January 11, 2017.

Sources: The National Election Pool, as reported by the *New York Times*, CNN, and Fox News; and Dave Leip's Atlas of U.S. Presidential Elections at uselectionatlas.org.

twenty-four. In the top fifth, the figure is 73 percent. In recent years, however, well-educated persons have been moving away from the Republican Party. For the last seven presidential elections, the Democratic candidate won the largest number of votes among persons with post-graduate degrees. Republicans retained an increasingly narrow lead among persons with no more than a college degree—until 2016. In that year, Democrat Hillary Clinton carried the college-educated vote.

These results were matched by Republican gains among the less-well-educated. Since the 1992 presidential elections, the Democratic presidential candidate has usually won the largest number of votes cast by persons with no more than a high school diploma. The exceptions are 2004—the only one of the last seven presidential elections in which the Republican presidential candidate won the popular vote—and 2016. In that year, Donald Trump won decisively among voters with no college experience. Indeed, among whites at that educational level, Trump enjoyed a landslide victory. If Trump's Republican coalition holds in future years, education will again become a reliable indicator of partisan preference. Compared with how people voted in the mid-twentieth century, however, the parties have swapped positions. Well-educated individuals now tend to be Democrats, and less-well-educated persons tend to be Republicans.

Occupation and Income Businesspersons tend to vote Republican and have done so for many years. This is understandable, given the pro-business stand traditionally adopted by that party. Recently, however, professionals (such as attorneys, professors, and physicians) have been more likely to vote Democratic. It appears that institutional and social changes have made it less likely that professionals will see themselves as small businesspersons or identify with business interests. Union members are more likely to vote for the Democrats, who have a history of pro-labor positions.

Given that income and education are correlated and that less-well-educated persons now lean Republican, we might assume that today the wealthy tend to be Democrats and the poor, Republicans. In fact, however, as you can see in Figure 8–1, Clinton carried the votes of families with incomes below $50,000, while Trump carried families with higher incomes. Still, the correlation of high incomes with Republicanism is far

> "In politics, an organized minority is *a political majority*."
>
> ~ REV. JESSE JACKSON
> CIVIL RIGHTS ACTIVIST
> 1941–PRESENT

weaker today than in the past. Note also that Trump was somewhat less popular among persons in the $100,000 and above category than he was among those in the $50,000 to $99,999 range. Many of the nation's truly rich are Democrats.

It follows from these statistics that poorly educated persons who earn a good income are unusually likely to vote Republican. A successful plumber with only a high school diploma, for example, might have favored Trump. Likewise, well-educated persons with low incomes are especially drawn to the Democrats. A college graduate working at Starbucks would probably have supported Clinton.

Age The conventional wisdom is that the young are liberal and the old are conservative. Certainly, younger voters were unusually supportive of Barack Obama in the 2008 and 2012 elections, and they continued to support Hillary Clinton in 2016. Yet in earlier years, age differences in support for the parties were often quite small.

One age-related effect is that people's attitudes are shaped by the events that unfolded as they grew up. As we observed earlier, many voters who came of age during Franklin Roosevelt's New Deal held on to a preference for the Democrats. Voters who were young when Ronald Reagan was president have had a tendency to prefer the Republicans. Younger voters today are noticeably more liberal on one set of issues—those dealing with the rights of minorities, women, and LGBT individuals.

Gender In the 1960s and 1970s, there seemed to be no fixed pattern of voter preferences by gender in presidential elections. Women and men tended to vote for the various candidates in roughly equal numbers. Some political analysts believe that a gender gap became a major determinant of voter decision making in the 1980 presidential elections, however. In that year, Ronald Reagan outdrew Jimmy Carter by 16 percentage points among male voters, whereas women gave about an equal number of votes to each candidate. In the years since, the gender gap has been a continuing phenomenon. For example, in 2012 Barack Obama carried the female vote by 55 to 44 percentage points, while losing the male vote by a 45 to 52 point margin.

gender gap The difference between the percentage of votes cast for a particular candidate by women and the percentage of votes cast for the same candidate by men.

In 2016, Clinton carried the women's vote by 54 to 41 percentage points, while losing men by a 41 to 53 point margin. Of course, Clinton was female, and Trump was famous for acts of rudeness toward women.

Feminism and the recognition that women have suffered from various types of discrimination doubtless have had something to do with the gender gap. It also appears, however, that compared with men, women on average have a stronger commitment to the liberal value of community and a weaker belief in the conservative value of self-reliance.

Religion A century ago, at least in the northern states, white Catholic voters were likely to be Democrats, and white Protestant voters were probably Republicans. There are a few places around the country where this pattern continues to hold, but for the most part, non-Hispanic white Catholics are now almost as likely as their Protestant neighbors to support the Republicans.

In recent years, a different religious variable has become important in determining voting behavior. Regardless of their denomination, white Christian voters who attend church regularly have favored the Republicans by substantial margins. White Christian voters who attend church rarely or who find religion less important in their lives are more likely to vote Democratic.

Although some churches do promote liberal ways of thinking, the number of churches that promote conservative values is much larger. Note, too, that most Jewish voters are strongly Democratic, regardless of whether they attend services.

Racial and Ethnic Minorities A shared racial or ethnic identity can be one of the strongest influences on voting behavior, second only to partisan loyalty.

African Americans. Most African Americans are Protestants, but African Americans are one of the most solidly Democratic constituencies in the United States. This is a complete reversal of the circumstances that existed a century ago. For many years after the Civil War, those African Americans who could vote were overwhelmingly Republican. Not until President Franklin Roosevelt's New Deal did black voters begin to turn to the Democrats. While we would predict that today's African American voters would trend Democratic based on their low average income, black support for the Democrats far exceeds the levels that could be deduced from economics alone.

Solid South A term used to describe the tendency of the southern states to vote Democratic after the Civil War.

Hispanic and Asian Americans. Latino voters have supported the Democrats by margins of about two to one, with some exceptions: older Cuban Americans are strongly Republican. In contrast to support from African Americans, Hispanic support for the Democrats is only modestly greater than what we would predict based on low average income. This fact might encourage the minority of Republicans who have sought to win Latino votes by such measures as immigration reform.

Most Asian Americans favor the Democrats. Vietnamese Americans, however, are strongly Republican.

Muslim Americans. Muslim Americans are an interesting example of changing preferences. In 2000, a majority of Muslims of Middle Eastern background voted for Republican presidential candidate George W. Bush because of Islamic cultural conservatism. Today, Muslims are the most Democratic religious group in the nation. Anti-Muslim campaigns by certain conservative groups appear to be a major cause of this transformation.

Geographic Region In today's presidential contests, states in the South, the Great Plains, and parts of the Rocky Mountains are strongly Republican. The Northeast, the West Coast, and Illinois are firmly Democratic. Many of the swing states that decide elections are located in the Midwest, although several Rocky Mountain states swing between the parties as well.

A very different pattern existed a century ago. In those years, most white southerners were Democrats, and people spoke of the Solid South—solidly Democratic, that is. The Solid South lasted for a century after the Civil War. In large part, it resulted from southern resentment of the Republicans for their role in the "War between the States" and their support of African Americans in the postwar era. At the end of the nineteenth century, the Republicans were strong in the Northeast and much of the Midwest, while the Democrats were able to find support outside the South in the Great Plains and the Far West.

> "Whenever a fellow tells me he is bipartisan, I know he is going to vote against me."
>
> ~ HARRY TRUMAN
> THIRTY-THIRD PRESIDENT
> OF THE UNITED STATES
> 1945–1953

Muslim Americans are a growing minority group. *Whom do they tend to support politically, and why?*

The ideologies of the two parties have likewise undergone something of a reversal. One hundred years ago, the Democrats were seen as *less* likely than the Republicans to support government intervention in the economy. The Democrats were also the party that opposed civil rights. Today, the Democrats are often regarded as the party that supports "big government" and affirmative action programs.

The White Vote Even by 2050, when the United States becomes a majority-minority nation, non-Hispanic whites will still be the largest racial or ethnic group by a wide margin. The demographic dominance of whites throughout American history means that divisions among white people have been a crucial determinant of U.S. politics. By far, the most important such division was revealed in the American Civil War, which one historian has summarized as "white people slaughtering each other over what should be done about black people." (Of course, in the later years of the war, many African Americans also fought for the North.)

Southern Whites—and Blacks. It should be remembered that from a Southern point of view, the "War between the States" was a war of independence, fought to establish a new nation—the Confederate States of America. The South's loss did not erase the Southern white sense of identity. Rather, it tended to confirm it. After the war, white Southerners were a distinct people, counterposed to other national groups. This fact may help explain why so many argue that the South fought for

states' rights, not to maintain slavery. Just as the North began fighting to preserve the Union but ended up battling to abolish slavery, the South began the war to defend slavery—and finished up fighting for national survival.

For their part, the South's African Americans have always known that they were a people, but freedom from slavery allowed them to claim that status in ways that they never could before.

Northern Whites. Whites in the North never experienced the sense of collective identity felt by whites in the South. Traditionally, they were divided by religion and national origin, with old-stock Yankees, Irish Catholics, Germans, Italians, Jews, and others jostling for political advantage. By the late twentieth century, such ethnic divisions among whites had largely dissipated. Divisions among Northern whites are now based largely on cultural differences—and even ideology. In 1960, only 5 percent of Republicans and 4 percent of Democrats said they would be upset if one of their children married a supporter of the other party. Today, 49 percent of Republicans and 33 percent of Democrats express concern over interparty marriage. Psychologists have discovered that today, bias based on partisanship is substantially more powerful than bias based on race.

Consider one group: white liberals. This group has developed a strong sense of identity and a variety of cultural and political markers. A progressive might drive a Prius, not a pickup truck. Progressives often enjoy living in large cities. Conservatives largely do not. White progressives are more likely than other whites to defend—within the limits of their understanding—minority group members. White liberals today are as cohesive as any old-time, nationality-based ethnic group, and they are found in all socioeconomic classes. They form a major part of the Democratic coalition, and their existence puts a ceiling on the ability of the Republicans to recruit new whites for conservatism.

CRITICAL THINKING

▶ *For what reasons might Cuban Americans and Vietnamese Americans be more conservative than members of other minority groups?*

8-3 PUBLIC OPINION POLLS

> **LO** Explain how public opinion polls are conducted, problems with polls, and how they are used in the political process.

You may hear a news report or read a magazine article stating that "a significant number of Americans" feel a certain way about an issue. Such reports most often come from polls of public opinion.

A **public opinion poll** is a survey of the public's opinion on a particular topic at a particular moment. The results of opinion polls are most often cast in terms of percentages: 62 percent feel this way, 31 percent do not, and 7 percent have no opinion.

Of course, a poll cannot survey the entire U.S. population. Therefore, public opinion pollsters have devised scientific polling techniques for measuring public opinion through the use of **samples**—groups of people who are typical of the general population.

8-3a Early Polling Efforts

Since the 1800s, magazines and newspapers have often spiced up their articles by conducting **straw polls** of readers' opinions. Straw polls simply ask a large number of people the same question. The problem with straw polls is that the opinions expressed usually represent an atypical subgroup of the population, or a **biased sample.** A survey of those who read *People* magazine will most likely produce different results than a survey of those who read *Sports Illustrated*, for example.

The *Literary Digest* Fiasco The most famous of all straw-polling errors was committed by the *Literary Digest* in 1936 when it tried to predict the outcome of that year's presidential elections. The *Digest* forecast that Republican Alfred Landon would easily defeat Democratic incumbent Franklin D. Roosevelt. Instead, Roosevelt won by a landslide. The editors of the *Digest* had sent mail-in cards to names in telephone directories, to its own subscribers, and to automobile owners—a staggering 2,376,000 people. In the Depression year of 1936, however, people who owned a car or a telephone or who subscribed to the *Digest* were not representative of most Americans. The vast majority of Americans could not afford such luxuries. The sample turned out to be unrepresentative and consequently inaccurate.

The First Scientific Poll Takers Several newcomers to the public opinion poll industry, however, did predict Roosevelt's victory. Two of these organizations are still at the forefront of the polling industry today: the Gallup Organization, started by George Gallup, and Roper Associates, founded by Elmo Roper and now known as the Roper Center for Public Opinion Research.

8-3b How Polling Has Developed

Today, polling is used extensively by political candidates and policymakers. Politicians and the news media generally place a great deal of faith in the accuracy of poll results. Polls can be quite accurate when they are conducted properly. In the twenty presidential elections

---

public opinion poll
A survey of the public's opinion on a particular topic at a particular moment.

sample In the context of opinion polling, a group of people selected to represent the population being studied.

straw poll A nonscientific poll in which there is no way to ensure that the opinions expressed are representative of the larger population.

biased sample
A poll sample that does not accurately represent the population.

OBAMACARE IS A DISASTER. EVERYBODY KNOWS IT!

OBAMACARE IS OUT-POLLING YOU BY 9 POINTS...

in which Gallup has participated, its polls conducted in late October correctly predicted the winner in sixteen of the races.[2] Even polls taken several months in advance have been able to predict the eventual winner.

Types of Polls In the earliest days of scientific polling, interviewers typically went door to door locating respondents. Such in-person surveys were essential in the mid-twentieth century, when a surprisingly large number of homes did not have telephones.

Telephone Polls. In time, the number of homes without phones dwindled, and polling organizations determined that they could obtain satisfactory samples of voters through telephone interviews alone. In recent years, poll takers have even replaced human interviewers with prerecorded messages that solicit responses. Such methods allow companies to conduct very large numbers of polls at little cost. Questions have arisen as to whether automated polling is as accurate as polling that uses live interviewers, however.

Further complications for telephone poll takers include the increase in the use of cell phones—which not all pollsters bother to call. Today, many cell phone users no longer have a landline number. An additional problem is the public's growing use of Skype and other Internet-based telephone systems. Poll takers have not yet determined a way to integrate such users into their polls. Finally, a growing number of people simply refuse to participate in telephone surveys.

Internet Polls. Technological advances have opened up a new possibility—the Internet survey. The Harris Poll now specializes in this type of research. As when telephone interviews were introduced, serious questions exist as to whether the samples obtained by Harris and other Internet polling firms can be representative. Internet usage has become extremely widespread, but it is still not universal.

Sampling Today, the most reputable polls sample between 1,000 and 1,500 people. How can interviewing such a small group possibly indicate what millions of voters think? To be successful, a sample must consist of people who are typical of the population. If the sample is not properly chosen, then the results of the poll may not reflect the beliefs of the general population.

The most important principle in sampling is randomness. A **random sample** means that each person within the entire population being polled has an equal chance of being chosen. For example, if a poll is trying to measure how women feel about an issue, the sample should include respondents from all groups within the female population in proportion to their percentage in the entire population.

> "A popular government without popular information, or the means of acquiring it, is but a prologue to a farce or a tragedy, or perhaps both."
>
> ~ JAMES MADISON, FOURTH PRESIDENT OF THE UNITED STATES, 1809–1817

A properly drawn random sample would include appropriate numbers of women in terms of age, race and ethnicity, geography, income, and religious affiliation.

What Polls Really Tell Us As noted earlier, poll results are almost always publicized using exact numbers. A typical result would be that 80 percent of those polled are partly or completely dissatisfied with the actions of the U.S. Congress, 12 percent are partly or completely satisfied, and 8 percent have no opinion. Figures such as these, though, can provide a misleading picture of what the poll is actually saying. Public opinion polls are fundamentally *statistical*. The true result of a poll is not a single figure, but a range of probabilities. In the example just given, the figure 80 percent partly or completely dissatisfied is merely the midpoint of all the possible results.

Sampling Error. An important concept in understanding polls is **sampling error**—the difference between what the poll shows and what the results would have been if *everyone* in the relevant population had been interviewed. A professional polling firm might state of a given poll that it has "95 percent confidence that the maximum margin of sampling error is plus or minus four percentage points."

To claim "95 percent confidence" means that there is a 5 percent chance that this poll is off by four points or more. The 95 percent figure is an industry standard. That means that out of the thousands of polls released every year, 5 percent are expected to yield results that are outside their own margin of error.

random sample In the context of opinion polling, a sample in which each person within the entire population being polled has an equal chance of being chosen.

sampling error In the context of opinion polling, the difference between what the sample results show and what the true results would have been had everybody in the relevant population been interviewed.

Statistical Noise. It follows that there is not much point in paying attention to small, short-lived changes in polling results. Consider a polling firm's report that President Donald Trump's popularity rating was, in five consecutive weeks, 39 percent, 37 percent, 38 percent, 41 percent, and 39 percent. Do these figures mean that Trump was less popular in week two and more popular in week four? Almost certainly not. The fluctuation in the figures is most likely due to random error—it is statistical "noise."

8-3c Problems with Opinion Polls

Today, more than ever before, Americans are bombarded with the results of public opinion polls. As it happens, however, accurate polls can be difficult and expensive to conduct. Professional poll takers confront a variety of problems that can interfere with the validity of a poll, which we describe in this section.

In some cases, firms may not even try to prepare a valid poll. In recent years, two polling firms were accused of simply making up their results without conducting any actual surveys. Statistical evidence also exists that some firms conducting low-quality polls quietly adjust their results to be more in line with the findings of more reputable pollsters.

Statistical Modeling and House Effects   One source of error follows from the fact that it is almost impossible to obtain a body of respondents that truly reflects the population at large. Many people refuse to be interviewed. Some kinds of people—including poor people and students—are hard to reach. In addition, it happens that women answer the telephone more frequently than do men.

Weighting. Polling firms respond to these difficulties by *weighting* the responses of various groups. If the survey did not locate enough evangelical Christians, for example, the responses of the evangelicals who were contacted will be weighted more heavily. Thus, a pollster might double the numerical value of the answers provided by the evangelicals before adding the results back into the total sample. A pollster would do this if, in the initial sample, the number of evangelicals interviewed was half of what it should have been. If the statistical model that the pollster uses to weight the responses is flawed, however, the poll results will be off as well.

Weighting for purely demographic variables is a small part of the modeling problem. Errors are much more common when pollsters attempt to adjust for the number

> **house effect** In the case of a polling firm, a consistent tendency to report results more favorable to one of the political parties than the results reported by other pollsters.

Jeremy Sutton-Hibbert/Getty Images Entertainment/Getty Images

Polling expert Nate Silver appears at an event in Edinburgh, Scotland. Silver was almost alone in 2016 in stating Donald Trump had a serious chance of winning the presidential elections. *How did Trump win?*

of Republicans, Democrats, and independents in their samples. Perhaps the greatest difficulty is determining who is likely to turn out and vote. In the months leading up to the 2016 elections, each major polling firm had its own model for weighting groups of respondents and determining who was a likely voter. Most of these models were trade secrets. One result of the differing models was a substantial variation in predicted results.

House Effects. Based on their differing models, some polling firms consistently publish results more favorable to one or the other of the two major parties than the results released by other pollsters. When a pollster's results appear to consistently favor one of the parties, polling experts refer to the phenomenon as a **house effect.** Not surprisingly, firms that exhibited house effects in 2016 frequently had ties to the political party favored by their results.

The connection was not exact, however. Some partisan firms did not exhibit a house effect, and some pollsters who were well known for nonpartisanship did have one. Also, a firm with a house effect is not always wrong. It may be noticing something that most of its competitors have missed.

Bias in Framing Questions   To obtain accurate results, professional poll takers must ensure that there is no bias in their polling questions. How a question is phrased can significantly affect how people answer it.

Poorly Worded or Misleading Questions. The number of ways in which survey questions can be poorly worded is vast. Questions can contain loaded terms: "How would you rate the career of basketball legend LeBron James?"

To call James a "legend" biases the question in his favor. A question can combine two or more queries that ought to be kept separate: "Which of the following companies provides the fastest and most economical Internet service?" The most economical service is unlikely to be the fastest.

Surveys concerning the Affordable Care Act ("Obamacare") provide another example of troublesome wording. A typical survey in the years following the implementation of the act might show that 55 percent of respondents oppose the act, 40 percent support it, and 5 percent aren't sure. These results do not tell us *why* respondents oppose the reform. One poll also asked those opposing the law whether it was too liberal or not liberal enough. Among respondents, 40 percent supported the reform. In addition, 38 percent opposed it because it is too liberal, and 17 percent opposed it because it is not liberal enough. Following the inauguration of President Trump, polls reported support levels for the ACA above 50 percent for the first time ever. One reason may be that liberals no longer believed they had the luxury of opposing the law from the left.

Poll respondents are under no obligation to be consistent. A famous example is that in every poll, a majority of Americans favor cuts to federal spending. When asked whether we should cut the budget of any particular program, however, the answer is almost always "no." This raises questions as to whether politicians should—or even can—respond to survey results. For more on this topic, see this chapter's *Perception vs. Reality* feature.

Yes or No Questions. Polling questions also sometimes reduce complex issues to questions that simply call for "yes" or "no" answers. For example, a survey question might ask respondents whether they favor giving aid to foreign countries. A respondent's opinion on the issue might vary depending on the recipient country or the purpose of the aid. The poll would nonetheless force the respondent to give a "yes" or "no" answer that does not fully reflect his or her opinion.

Inadequate Information. Respondents sometimes answer "I don't know" or "I don't have enough information to answer," even when the poll does not offer such options. Interestingly, a study of how polling is conducted on the complex issue of school vouchers found that about 4 percent volunteered the answer "I don't know" when asked if they favored or opposed vouchers. When respondents were offered the option of answering "I haven't heard or read enough to answer," however, the proportion choosing that answer jumped to about 30 percent.[3]

Related Problems. In addition to potential bias in framing questions, poll takers must also be concerned with related issues that affect the reliability of their polls. For example, respondents interviewed may be influenced by the interviewer's personality or tone of voice. They may give the answer that they think will please the interviewer.

Timing of Polls Opinion polls of voter preferences cannot reflect rapid shifts in public opinion unless they are taken frequently. One example of this problem occurred during the presidential elections of 1980. The candidates in that year were incumbent Democratic president Jimmy Carter and Republican Ronald Reagan. Almost to the end of the campaign, polls showed Carter in the lead. Only the most capable analysts took note of the very large number of undecided voters. In the last week before the elections, these voters broke sharply for Reagan. Few polls were conducted late enough to detect this development.

Polling Problems in Recent Elections In the 2012 and 2014 elections, public opinion polls faced significant problems in predicting how many voters would actually cast ballots. In 2012, several major pollsters overestimated turnout among Republican voters and underestimated turnout among Democrats. Several firms actually thought that Republican presidential candidate Mitt Romney would win. In the end, President Obama was reelected with a margin of almost 4 percentage points.

In 2014, the biggest problem that pollsters faced was the very low voter turnout. Because many citizens who did not vote leaned Democratic, a majority of the polls overestimated the Democratic vote.

In 2016, Donald Trump's victory came as a surprise to almost everyone except his own supporters. As you can see in Figure 8–2, most poll takers thought that Hillary Clinton had an edge of 3 or 4 percentage points. These results were not that far off—when all the votes were counted, Clinton's popular vote margin was almost exactly 2 percentage points. This margin did not keep Donald Trump from winning a majority in the electoral college and, therefore, the presidency. It should be understood that nationwide opinion polls cannot and do not attempt to predict electoral college results. They are limited to predicting the popular vote.

That said, Trump's strong position should have shown up in state-level polls taken in Wisconsin, Michigan, and Pennsylvania—the states that gave Trump his victory. In fact, the state-level polls in question were relatively inaccurate. Among polling experts, Nate Silver of the

Do Politicians Always Follow the Polls?

During every election campaign, major candidates conduct their own polling. At the presidential level, they do so almost daily. The number of opinion polls released is enormous, not just before elections, but all year. The question is, once in office, do politicians continue to "follow the polls"? Do polls affect the kinds of legislation they support?

The Perception

Many critics of politicians argue that all they do is follow public opinion. Any personal convictions that they may have are less important than the need for political survival. These politicians rely on polls to help them vote for whatever will get them reelected.

The Reality

If politicians simply followed public opinion, our country's laws would be quite different. Take the example of religion. Polls indicate that 65 percent of Americans believe "liberals have gone too far in keeping religion out of schools and government." According

to 76 percent, public high schools should be allowed to sponsor prayer before football games. "Voluntary prayer" in the public schools (that is, prayer led by teachers from which students could "voluntarily" opt out) is favored by three-fourths of respondents. Of course, the Supreme Court has ruled that such steps would violate the First Amendment of the Constitution.

Consider also evolution versus creationism. One poll found that almost half of respondents believed that God created human beings more or less in their present form within the last ten thousand years. Not surprisingly, a majority of Americans also want creationism to be taught alongside evolution in the public schools. Both school-sponsored prayer and the teaching of creationism in public schools would require amending the Constitution. Members of Congress never seem to propose such an amendment, however.

If the public appears to be conservative on various cultural issues, it also gives stronger support than political elites do to programs such as Social Security and Medicare. Much of political Washington believes that the benefits provided by these programs need to be trimmed. In polls, however, only one American in ten agrees with this idea. A majority may prefer to see Social Security benefits increased. This group, however, is not getting its way. We might conclude from this that the "economic progressives, social conservatives" we described at the beginning of this text have little political clout.

Blog On

Pollingreport.com has a large collection of public opinion polls. Try searching for "polling report evolution." For details on the public's reluctance to cut most federal programs, search for "polling report cutting programs."

FiveThirtyEight website was almost alone in emphasizing that Trump had a serious chance of winning, though Silver, too, thought that a Clinton victory was probable.

Clearly, Trump mobilized some members of the electorate who had not voted previously. Failure to account for this mobilization is probably the reason why many pollsters had Clinton with 1 to 2 more percentage points than the actual results. A second group that seems to have turned out in record numbers is Hispanics, mobilized by a fear of Trump. They, however, had the misfortune to be concentrated in strongly partisan states such as California and Texas, where enhanced Latino turnout would not affect the results. (Note that the National Election Pool, used to generate Figure 8–1,

has had long-standing problems in accurately reporting the Latino vote.)

Misuse of Polls   Today, a frequently heard complaint is that, instead of measuring public opinion, polls can end up creating it. For example, to gain popularity, a candidate might claim that all the polls show that he or she is ahead in the race. People who want to support the winner may back this candidate despite their true feelings. This is often called the "bandwagon" effect. Presidential approval ratings lend themselves to the bandwagon effect.

The media also sometimes misuse polls. Many journalists take the easy route during campaigns and

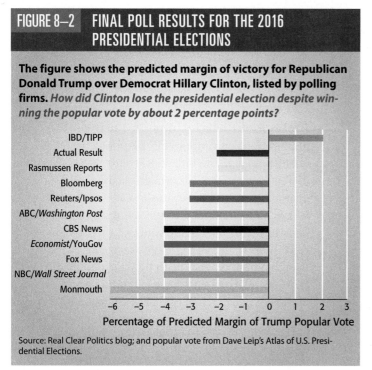

FIGURE 8–2 FINAL POLL RESULTS FOR THE 2016 PRESIDENTIAL ELECTIONS

The figure shows the predicted margin of victory for Republican Donald Trump over Democrat Hillary Clinton, listed by polling firms. *How did Clinton lose the presidential election despite winning the popular vote by about 2 percentage points?*

Percentage of Predicted Margin of Trump Popular Vote

Source: Real Clear Politics blog; and popular vote from Dave Leip's Atlas of U.S. Presidential Elections.

base their political coverage almost exclusively on poll findings. Media companies often report only the polls conducted by their affiliated pollsters, announcing the results as the absolute truth regardless of whether the results are typical or are at serious variance with polls taken by other organizations.

Indeed, given the diversity of results among different polling organizations, savvy political analysts look at as many different polls as they can. Experts often average the results of polls that ask a particular question. Some of them even weight these polls based on how reliable they believe each firm to be.

The Problem of Push Polls One tactic in political campaigns is to use **push polls,** which ask "fake" polling questions that are actually designed to "push" voters toward one candidate or another. The National Council on Public Polls describes push polls as outright political manipulation—the spreading of rumors and lies by one candidate about another. Push pollsters usually do not give their name or identify the poll's sponsor. The interviews last less than a minute, whereas legitimate pollsters typically interview a respondent for five to thirty minutes.

Some researchers argue that identifying a push poll is not always straightforward. Political analyst Charlie Cook points out that "there are legitimate polls that can ask push questions, which test potential arguments against a rival to ascertain how effective those arguments

might be in future advertising. . . . These are not only legitimate tools of survey research, but any political pollster who did not use them would be doing her or his clients a real disservice.[4]

Distinguishing between push polls and push questions, then, can be challenging—which is usually the intent of the push pollsters. A candidate does not want to be accused of conducting push polls, because the public considers them a "dirty trick" and may turn against the candidate who uses them.

CRITICAL THINKING

▸ *Suggest some poll questions that most respondents would probably answer in the same way. Think of some others that would divide those who are being interviewed into two distinct camps.*

 8-4

VOTING AND VOTER TURNOUT

LO Indicate some of the factors that affect voter turnout, and discuss what has been done to improve voter turnout and voting procedures.

Voting is arguably the most important way in which citizens participate in the political process. Because we do not live in a direct democracy, Americans use the vote to elect politicians to represent their interests, values, and opinions in government. In many states, public-policy decisions—for example, access to medical marijuana—are also decided by voters through referendums and initiatives. Our right to vote also helps keep elected officials accountable because they must face reelection.

8-4a Factors Affecting Voter Turnout

If voting is so important, then why do so many Americans fail to exercise their right to vote? Why is *voter turnout*—the percentage of those who actually turn out to vote from among those eligible to vote—relatively low? In many foreign countries, voter turnout is greater than in the United States. In a few nations, such as Australia and Brazil, citizens may be fined if they do not vote. Naturally, such policies enhance turnout.

> **push poll** A campaign tactic used to feed false or misleading information to potential voters, under the guise of taking an opinion poll, with the intent to "push" voters away from one candidate and toward another.

As you will read shortly, in the past, legal restrictions based on income, gender, race, and other factors kept many people from voting. In the last decades of the twentieth century, these restrictions were almost completely eliminated, and yet voter turnout in presidential elections still hovered around 55 percent, as shown in Figure 8–3.

According to a Pew Research Center survey, one of the reasons for low voter turnout is that many nonvoters (close to 40 percent) do not feel that they have a duty to vote. The survey also found that nearly 70 percent of nonvoters said that they did not vote because they lacked information about the candidates.[5] Finally, some people believe that their vote will not make any difference, so they do not bother to become informed about the candidates and issues or go to the polls. We compare voter turnout rates around the world in Figure 8–4.

8–4b The Legal Right to Vote

In the United States today, citizens who are at least eighteen years of age and who are not felons have the right to vote. This was not always true. Restrictions on *suffrage*, the legal right to vote, have existed since the founding of our nation. Expanding the right to vote has been an important part of the gradual democratization of the American electoral process. Table 8–1 summarizes the major amendments, Supreme Court decisions, and laws that extended the right to vote to various American groups.

Historical Restrictions on Voting   Those who drafted the Constitution left the power to set suffrage qualifications to the individual states. Most states limited suffrage to adult white males who owned a specified amount of property, but these restrictions were challenged early on in the history of the republic. By 1828, laws restricting the right to vote to Christians were abolished in all states, and property ownership and tax-payment requirements gradually began to disappear as well. By 1850, all white males were allowed to vote. Restrictions based on race and gender continued, however.

Preventing African Americans from Voting. The Fifteenth Amendment, ratified in 1870, guaranteed suffrage to African American males. Yet, for many decades, African Americans were effectively denied the ability to exercise their voting rights. Using methods ranging from mob violence to economic pressure, groups of white southerners kept black Americans from voting.

Some states required citizens to pass **literacy tests** and to answer complicated questions about government and history before they could register to vote. Registrars made sure that African Americans would almost always fail such tests. The **poll tax,** a fee of several dollars, was

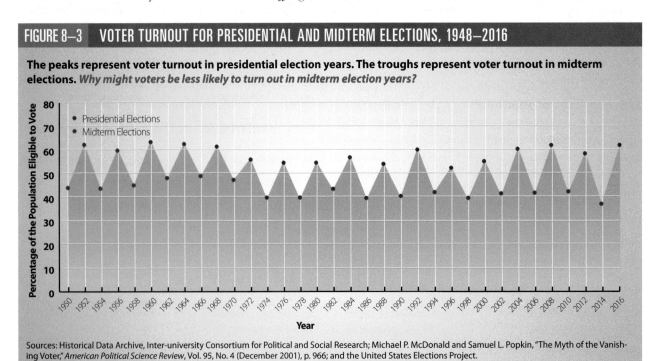

FIGURE 8–3   VOTER TURNOUT FOR PRESIDENTIAL AND MIDTERM ELECTIONS, 1948–2016

The peaks represent voter turnout in presidential election years. The troughs represent voter turnout in midterm elections. *Why might voters be less likely to turn out in midterm election years?*

Sources: Historical Data Archive, Inter-university Consortium for Political and Social Research; Michael P. McDonald and Samuel L. Popkin, "The Myth of the Vanishing Voter," *American Political Science Review*, Vol. 95, No. 4 (December 2001), p. 966; and the United States Elections Project.

FIGURE 8–4 VOTER TURNOUT AROUND THE WORLD

This list excludes nations that do not have free elections, based on ratings from Freedom House. It includes all free nations with an economy (nominal GDP) of at least $1 trillion. *What factors might cause turnout to be relatively high or low in a particular country?*

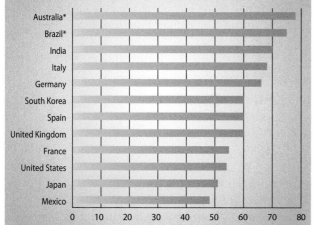

*In these countries, those who do not vote are required to pay a fine.

Source: International Institute for Democracy and Electoral Assistance. (Based on voting-age population, which depresses the U.S. percentage as explained later in this chapter.)

whose ancestors had voted before the 1860s. This technique was prohibited by the United States Supreme Court in 1915.[6]

The White Primary. Still another voting barrier was the white primary—African Americans were prohibited from voting in Democratic primary elections. (In southern states at that time, winning the Democratic primary almost always guaranteed victory in the general election.) The Supreme Court initially upheld this practice on the grounds that the political parties were private entities, not public, and thus could do as they wished. Eventually, in 1944, the Court banned the use of white primaries.[7]

Voting Rights Today Today, the four devices just discussed for restricting voting rights are explicitly outlawed by constitutional amendments and by the Voting Rights Act of 1965. Furthermore, the Nineteenth Amendment gave women the right to vote in 1920. In 1971, the Twenty-sixth Amendment reduced the minimum voting age to eighteen.

another device used to discourage African Americans from voting. At the time, this tax was a sizable burden, not only for most blacks but also for poor whites.

Another restriction was the grandfather clause, which had the effect of restricting voting rights to those

TABLE 8–1 EXTENSION OF THE RIGHT TO VOTE

Why might the grandfather clause have been one of the first voting restrictions to be abolished?

Year	Action	Impact
1870	Fifteenth Amendment	Discrimination based on race outlawed.
1915	*Guinn v. United States*	Grandfather clause ruled unconstitutional by the Supreme Court.
1920	Nineteenth Amendment	Discrimination based on gender outlawed.
1924	Congressional act	All Native Americans given citizenship.
1944	*Smith v. Allwright*	Supreme Court prohibits white primary.
1957	Civil Rights Act of 1957	Justice Department can sue to protect voting rights in various states.
1960	Civil Rights Act of 1960	Courts authorized to appoint referees to assist voter-registration procedures.
1961	Twenty-third Amendment	Residents of District of Columbia given right to vote for president and vice president.
1964	Twenty-fourth Amendment	Poll tax in national elections outlawed.
1965	Voting Rights Act of 1965	Literacy tests prohibited, federal voter registrars authorized in seven southern states, and voting rules in most southern states subject to federal oversight.
1970	Voting Rights Act Amendments of 1970	Voting age for federal elections reduced to eighteen years, maximum thirty-day residency required for presidential elections, and state literacy tests abolished.
1971	Twenty-sixth Amendment	Minimum voting age reduced to eighteen for all elections.
1975	Voting Rights Act Amendments of 1975	Federal voter registrars authorized in ten more states. Bilingual ballots to be used in certain circumstances.
1982	Voting Rights Act Amendments of 1982	Extended provisions of Voting Rights Act Amendments of 1970 and 1975. Private parties allowed to sue for violations.
2006	Voting Rights Act extension	Extended Voting Rights Act for another twenty-five years.

Registration, Residency, and Citizenship. Some restrictions on voting rights still exist. Every state except North Dakota requires voters to register with the appropriate state or local officials before voting. In eleven states and the District of Columbia, however, voters can register up to or even on voting day. California, Oregon, Vermont, and West Virginia do not require citizens to actively register. All citizens of these states who are nineteen or over and who have a driver's license or state ID card are automatically registered. In 2017, twenty-five additional states and the District of Columbia were considering similar bills.

Traditionally, residency requirements were also imposed for voting. Since 1970, however, no state can impose a residency requirement of more than thirty days. Today, twenty-six states have residency requirements, ranging from ten to thirty days. The other states do not have such requirements, but they may impose a cutoff date for registering to vote before an election.

Another voting requirement is citizenship. Noncitizens may not vote in any public election held anywhere in the United States. (Until the early twentieth century, several states allowed noncitizens to cast ballots.) Most states also do not permit prison inmates, people with mental illness, or election-law violators to vote.

The Issue of Felon Voting. A felon is someone who has been convicted of a serious crime. In some states, felons do not have the right to vote even after they have served their time in prison. Because America puts a larger share of its people behind bars than almost any other nation, the number of felons released from prison is also large. Felony disenfranchisement affects about 6 million persons in the United States. One result of this exclusion is racial discrimination. The percentage of African Americans who are felons is much greater than their share of the total population. As a result, at least 13 percent of the nation's African American male population is disenfranchised. Regardless of race, those who are convicted of felonies are disproportionately poor.

Opponents of this disenfranchisement say that by excluding many poor persons and minority group members from the voting rolls, we bias the vote. Others contend that felons are not the kind of people we want to choose our leaders. Currently, twelve states ban some or all felons from voting after their release from prison. Felons can appeal to have their rights restored. In states such as Florida, however, the appeals process is so restrictive that few felons are able to use it. About one-quarter of the nation's disenfranchised felons live in Florida.

8–4c Attempts to Improve Voter Turnout

Various attempts have been made to improve voter turnout. Typically, these attempts have a partisan dimension, because the kinds of people who find it difficult to register to vote tend to be disproportionately Democratic in their sympathies. Many, for example, are African Americans, a reliably Democratic voting bloc. As a result, Republicans are generally wary of efforts to make registration easier.

The Motor Voter Law The National Voter Registration Act (the "Motor Voter Law") of 1993 simplified the voter-registration process. The act requires states to provide all eligible citizens with the opportunity to register to vote when they apply for or renew a driver's license. The law also requires that states allow mail-in registration. Forms are available at public-assistance agencies. The law, which took effect in 1995, has facilitated millions of registrations.

A young voter casts his ballot. *What steps have some states taken to make voting easier?*

Burlingham/Shutterstock.com

JOIN THE DEBATE

Do We Need Strict Voting ID Laws?

After 2013, when the United States Supreme Court limited the effect of the Voting Rights Act of 1965, state governments in the South and elsewhere quickly implemented new voting laws. The most common change was to require voters to show photo identification at the polls, but other new laws were adopted as well. For example, Arizona and Kansas required proof of citizenship, such as a birth certificate or a passport, to vote in state elections. After the 2016 elections, many additional restrictive laws were proposed in Republican-controlled states. The goal of the new laws, according to state officials, is to reduce voter fraud. While no one is in favor of voter fraud, many argue that the new laws do more harm than good because they restrict voting rights. Do new state laws truly interfere with voting rights?

Much Ado about Nothing

Those who support the new state voting laws argue that strict laws are necessary to promote public confidence in voting systems. Photo ID requirements do not restrict anyone's rights. After all, most Americans have to show their IDs when they cash a check or board an airplane. Violations of voting laws continue to occur. Felons, for example—who are not allowed to vote in many states—may end up voting anyway. Support for ID requirements exists even within some minority communities. Polls show that Hispanic Texans support the requirement. The Supreme Court in 2008 found in an Indiana case that photo ID requirements for voting were perfectly constitutional.[8]

Also, many states have recently passed laws to make voting more convenient. Colorado now allows Election Day registration, as well as preregistration of eligible young people. Maryland has expanded its early voting system. Today, Virginia and West Virginia provide online registration, and several states automatically register everyone with a driver's license. True, some states have tightened the rules, but overall, it is as easy to vote now as it ever was.

Fewer Eligible Voters Will Vote

According to columnist Harold Meyerson of the *Los Angeles Times*, "Voter fraud is a myth—not an urban or a real myth, as such, but a Republican one." Many poorer citizens—especially minority group members—do not have the documents required by the new laws. In Texas, "free" voter IDs must be obtained from a limited number of state offices that are open only during normal business hours, a heavy burden on the working poor. Some states decided to reduce early voting, a practice that minorities have used more than others. North Carolina, for example, eliminated Sunday early voting. In that state, African American churches had adopted the practice of marching as a group to polling places at the conclusion of Sunday services.

The courts have recently begun to agree that the new laws go too far. In July 2016, a U.S. appeals court struck down a series of voting restrictions in Texas on the basis of racial discrimination.[9] In North Carolina, the courts blocked a new voting law that was aimed "with almost surgical precision" at African American voters.[10] It is time for state legislators to stop trying to disenfranchise people who might vote against them.

Critical Analysis

Some people claim that minority groups can counteract the negative effect of restrictive voting rules by increased turnout at the polls. How easy would it be to do that? Explain.

Mail-in Voting In 1998, Oregon voters approved a ballot initiative requiring that all elections in that state, including presidential elections, be conducted exclusively by mail.

Washington State required all counties to use postal ballots beginning with the 2012 elections, and Colorado began using postal ballots exclusively in 2014. Voter turnout in these states is well above the national average, especially in midterm elections, when many voters stay home. Many states have recently made such ballots an option for all voters. In the past, *absentee ballots* were often available only to those who clearly could not make it to a polling place on Election Day. Reasons for an absentee ballot might include military service, business travel, or ill health.

Other Attempts to Make Voting Easier Many states have recently passed laws to make voting more convenient. California, Hawaii, and Vermont plan to join other states in allowing Election Day registration. As of 2016, thirty-seven states and the District of Columbia permit early voting. Thirty-two states and the District of Columbia now offer online registration.

8-4d Laws That May Discourage Voting

Not all new laws have tried to make voting easier. Congress passed the Voting Rights Act in 1965 to ensure that state and local governments, particularly in the South, would not interfere with the voting rights of African Americans. One provision of the act was that state and local governments with a history of violating voters' rights must obtain "preclearance" from the federal government before making changes to voting rules and district boundaries. In 2013, however, the Supreme Court threw out the formula in the act that determined which states and localities must obtain preclearance, claiming that the rules were obsolete. Are these new state voting laws needed to reduce voter fraud—or is the true goal to make it harder for Democratic-leaning groups to vote? We look at that question in this chapter's *Join the Debate* feature. A number of state governments quickly implemented new voting laws.

8-4e Attempts to Improve Voting Procedures

Because of serious problems in achieving accurate vote counts in recent elections, steps have been taken to attempt to ensure more accuracy in the voting process. In 2002, Congress passed the Help America Vote Act, which, among other things, provided funds to the states to help them purchase new electronic voting equipment. Concerns about the possibility of fraudulent manipulation of electronic voting machines then replaced the worries over inaccurate vote counts caused by the previous equipment.

In the 2006 elections, about half of the states that were using new electronic voting systems reported problems. Because of these problems, fewer polling places used electronic systems in 2008 and 2010. Indeed, more than half of all votes cast in these years used old-fashioned paper ballots. As a result, vote counting was slow.

In 2012, the development of voter-verified paper audit trail (VVPAT) printers led to the reintroduction of electronic machines in many states. In seventeen states, however, some or all of the votes were cast through electronic devices that lacked a paper trail. A full quarter of all votes were cast using these questionable systems.[11] The trend toward the reintroduction of electronic systems continued with the 2014 and 2016 elections. Still, in 2016, five states—Delaware, Georgia, Louisiana, New Jersey, and South Carolina—did not back up any votes with a paper trail. In ten states, at least some votes had no paper trail.

8-4f Who Actually Votes

Just because an individual is eligible to vote does not necessarily mean that the person will cast a ballot. Why do some eligible voters go to the polls while others do not? Although nobody can answer this question with absolute conviction, certain factors appear to affect voter turnout.

Educational Attainment Among the factors affecting voter turnout, education appears to be the most important. The more education a person has, the more likely it is that she or he will be a regular voter. People who graduated from high school vote more regularly

Singer Christina Aguilera appears with a Rock the Vote T-shirt.
Why do young people need extra encouragement to vote?

AP Images/Lisa Rose

than those who dropped out, and college graduates vote more often than high school graduates.

Income Level and Age

Differences in income also lead to differences in voter turnout. Wealthy people tend to be overrepresented among regular voters. Generally, older voters turn out to vote more regularly than younger voters do, although participation tends to decline among the very elderly. Participation likely increases with age because older people tend to be more settled, are already registered, and have had more experience with voting.

Minority Status

Racial and ethnic minorities traditionally have been underrepresented among the ranks of voters. In several recent elections, however, participation by these groups, particularly African Americans and Hispanics, has increased. In part because the number of Latino citizens has grown rapidly, the increase in the Hispanic vote has been even larger than the increase in the black vote.

Immigration and Voter Turnout

The United States has experienced high rates of immigration in recent decades, and that has had an effect on voter-turnout figures. In the past, voter turnout was often expressed as a percentage of the **voting-age population,** the number of people residing in the United States who are at least eighteen years old. Due to legal and illegal immigration, however, many people of voting age are not eligible to vote because they are not citizens. Millions more cannot vote because they are felons. Additionally, the voting-age population excludes Americans abroad, who are eligible to cast absentee ballots.

Today, political scientists calculate the **vote-eligible population,** the number of people who are actually entitled to vote in American elections. They have found that there may be 20 million fewer eligible voters than the voting-age population suggests. Therefore, voter turnout is actually greater than the percentages sometimes cited.

Some experts have argued that the relatively low levels of voter turnout often reported for the years between 1972 and 2000 were largely due to immigration.[12] Beginning in 2004, however, presidential voter turnout improved by any calculation method.

> **voting-age population**
> The number of people residing in the United States who are at least eighteen years old.
>
> **vote-eligible population** The number of people who are actually eligible to vote in an American election.

AMERICA AT ODDS | Public Opinion and Voting

Public opinion polls reveal that Americans are in broad agreement on many issues, such as the basic political structure of our nation. Nevertheless, polls also report that Americans are at odds with one another on many other issues. After all, the questions posed by poll takers are typically divisive ones. Issues surrounding who votes and why can also be contentious. Some examples include the following:

- *Is the disenfranchisement of felons a form of racial discrimination—or a rational part of the punishment process?*

- *Given that historical events shape popular attitudes toward the parties, when all is said and done, will the impact of the Great Recession benefit one of the major parties—or will the effects of the recession prove trivial?*

- *Should legislators follow public opinion as faithfully as they can—or should lawmakers do what they think is best for the country, regardless of the polls?*

- *Should push polls be banned—or would that violate First Amendment guarantees of free speech?*

- *Should voters be more concerned with the policy positions of the presidential candidates—or are the presidential candidates' personalities and personal characteristics of equal or greater concern?*

STUDY TOOLS 8

READY TO STUDY? IN THE BOOK, YOU CAN:

☐ Review what you've read with the following chapter quiz.

☐ Check your answers in Appendix D at the back of the book.

☐ Rip out the Chapter Review Card, which includes key terms and chapter summaries.

ONLINE AT WWW.CENGAGEBRAIN.COM, YOU CAN:

☐ Watch videos to get a quick overview.

☐ Expedite your studying with Major Player readings and Focus Activities.

☐ Check your understanding with Chapter Quizzes.

FILL-IN

Learning Outcome 8–1

1. Agents of political socialization include _____.

Learning Outcome 8–2

2. For established voters, _____ is one of the most important and lasting predictors of how a person will vote.

3. When people vote for candidates who share their positions on particular issues, they are engaging in _____.

4. Socioeconomic factors that influence how people vote include _____.

5. The difference between the percentage of votes cast for a candidate by women and the percentage cast by men is called _____.

Learning Outcome 8–3

6. A random sample means that _____.

7. When a pollster's results appear to consistently favor a particular political party, polling experts refer to the phenomenon as a _____.

8. A _____ is a campaign tactic used to feed false or misleading information to potential voters, under the guise of conducting an opinion poll.

9. In the years immediately following the adoption of the Constitution, most states limited the right to vote to adult white men who _____.

Learning Outcome 8–4

10. Methods used to keep African Americans from voting even after the Fifteenth Amendment to the U.S. Constitution was ratified included _____.

MULTIPLE CHOICE

Learning Outcome 8–1

11. Most political socialization is informal, and it usually begins
    a. in college.
    b. in high school.
    c. during early childhood.

12. The family is an important agent of political socialization because
    a. most families deliberately set out to form their children's political ideas and beliefs.
    b. a child first sees the political world through the eyes of his or her family.
    c. parents are responsible for registering their children to vote.

Learning Outcome 8–2

13. Historically, _____ issues have had the strongest influence on voters' choices.
    a. foreign policy
    b. social
    c. economic

Learning Outcome 8–3

14. A *Literary Digest* poll incorrectly predicted that Alfred Landon would win the presidential election in 1936 because the
    a. pollsters used an unrepresentative sample.
    b. pollsters used a random sample.
    c. sample size was too small.

15. In 1971, the Twenty-sixth Amendment reduced the minimum voting age to

    a. sixteen.

    b. eighteen.

    c. twenty-one.

16. Among the factors affecting voter turnout, _____ appears to be the most important.

    a. educational attainment

    b. race

9 | CAMPAIGNS AND ELECTIONS

Joseph Sohm/Shutterstock.com

LEARNING OUTCOMES

After reading this chapter, you should be able to:

9-1 Explain how elections are held and how the electoral college functions in presidential elections.

9-2 Discuss how candidates are nominated.

9-3 Indicate what is involved in launching a political campaign today, and describe the structure and functions of a campaign organization.

9-4 Describe how the Internet has transformed political campaigns.

9-5 Summarize the current laws that regulate campaign financing and the role of money in modern political campaigns.

After finishing this chapter, go to **PAGE 214** for **STUDY TOOLS**

AMERICA AT ODDS | Does Money Really Buy Elections?

Money and politics. Those words go together like bacon and eggs. Of course, we are no longer in an era when politicians could be bought off with bags of hundred-dollar bills. But campaigns are expensive, and candidates can always use extra funds. In 2010, the United States Supreme Court loosened the campaign finance laws considerably. In effect, the Court blessed essentially unlimited campaign spending by corporations, unions, nonprofit groups, and individuals. The only restriction the courts have imposed is that these unlimited funds cannot go directly to a candidate's campaign but must be spent independently.

As expected, the hue and cry went out that now, more than ever, the wealthy would determine the outcome of elections. Yet not everyone is sure that the facts support this assumption.

Big Money Cannot and Does Not Buy Elections

Consider former Florida governor Jeb Bush. He raised $100 million in his quest to become the 2016 Republican presidential candidate. Yet Bush dropped out of the race after the first four state contests. Indeed, in the 2016 presidential race, there seemed to be an inverse relationship between campaign spending and winning votes. Frontrunner Donald Trump spent almost nothing in the early part of his campaign.

In the 2012 presidential contest, Mitt Romney and Barack Obama each spent more than a billion dollars. These "big bucks" do not appear to have benefited either candidate. After all, the presidential race was the biggest news story in the nation. Millions watched the candidates debate, first during the Republican primaries and then in the general elections. The audiences for these debates rivaled the audiences for NFL football games. In such circumstances, how much can a candidate really gain by spending another million dollars on TV ads?

In some state-level races, the picture was even clearer. Consider Meg Whitman, the former eBay CEO who ran as a Republican for governor of California in 2010. She spent $140 million. Democrat Jerry Brown spent less than a fifth of that, but it was enough to get his message across. Whitman lost. Californians reported that they were sick and tired of Whitman's endless ads. True, candidates rarely succeed when they have almost no money. Beyond a certain level, however, spending ceases to help.

Money Matters—But Mostly below the Presidential Level

True, the voting public pays close attention to presidential elections. Therefore, a candidate's personality, image, agenda, trustworthiness, and even physical appearance may be more important than how much money she or he has raised. As the Brown–Whitman contest illustrates, people may also give a governor's race the same level of scrutiny as a presidential contest.

In races further down the ballot, however, it's a different story. Voters are paying less attention, and money matters a lot more. In recent years, conservative groups have outspent liberal ones in state legislative races by a ratio of three to two. In 2010, such spending helped Republicans gain a net total of 675 seats in state legislatures. This outcome had major consequences. Because Republicans controlled about two-thirds of these legislative bodies, they were usually the ones to set district boundaries after the 2010 census. These boundaries were useful to the Republicans in strengthening their position in the U.S. House of Representatives.

Campaign contributions have consequences. As a member of Congress once said, "If politicians were immune to the effect of campaign contributions, they would be the only people in the history of the world who … took money from perfect strangers and made sure it had no effect on them." Big contributors expect something in return.

Where do you stand?

1. Some argue that we should eliminate campaign contributions and pay for campaigns through public funds, with equal sums given to each candidate. Would you favor such a program? Why or why not?

2. If you were a member of Congress running for reelection against a weak opponent, would you still accept large campaign contributions? Why or why not?

Explore this issue online:

- Jonathan Soros argues that money can't buy votes, but it can buy influence. Find his argument by searching for "jon soros big money."

- In the New Republic, David Dayen argues that money still matters. To learn more, search for "dayen democrats billionaires."

INTRODUCTION

During campaigns, candidates vie to become representatives of the people in both national and state offices. Campaigning for election has become an arduous task for every politician. As you will see in this chapter, American campaigns are long and expensive undertakings. Still, America's campaigns are an important part of our political process, because it is through campaigns that citizens learn about the candidates and decide how they will cast their votes.

American democracy would be impossible without campaigns and elections. For freedom to thrive, however, elections are not enough. Democracy requires the kind of shared political culture that we have described earlier. It also requires that all candidates be able to present their views to the public, regardless of whether they have wealthy backers. We looked at that issue in the chapter-opening *America at Odds* feature.

 9-1 HOW WE ELECT CANDIDATES

LO Explain how elections are held and how the electoral college functions in presidential elections.

The ultimate goal of a political campaign and the associated fund-raising efforts is, of course, winning an election. The most familiar kind of election is the **general election,** which is a regularly scheduled election held in

general election A regularly scheduled election to choose the U.S. president, vice president, and senators and representatives in Congress. General elections are held in even-numbered years on the Tuesday after the first Monday in November.

special election An election that is held at the state or local level when the voters must decide an issue before the next general election or when vacancies occur by reason of death or resignation.

Australian ballot A secret ballot that is prepared, distributed, and counted by government officials at public expense. Used by all states in the United States since 1888.

poll watcher A representative from one of the political parties who is allowed to monitor a polling place to make sure that the election is run fairly and that fraud doesn't occur.

elector In American politics, a member of the electoral college.

electoral college The group of electors who are selected by the voters in each state to officially elect the president and vice president. The number of electors in each state is equal to the number of that state's representatives in both chambers of Congress.

even-numbered years on the Tuesday after the first Monday in November. During general elections, the voters decide who will be the U.S. president, vice president, and senators and representatives in Congress. The president and vice president are elected every four years, senators every six years, and representatives every two years.

General elections are also held to choose state and local government officials, often at the same time as those for national offices. A **special election** is held at the state or local level when the voters must decide an issue before the next general election or when vacancies occur by reason of death or resignation.

9-1a Conducting Elections and Counting the Votes

Since 1888, all states in the United States have used the **Australian ballot**—a secret ballot that is prepared, distributed, and counted by government officials at public expense. As its name implies, this ballot was first developed in Australia.

Local units of government, such as cities, are divided into smaller voting districts, or precincts. Within each precinct, voters cast their ballots at a designated polling place. (An exception is the few states that conduct elections entirely by mail.)

An election board supervises the polling place and the voting process in each precinct. The board sets hours for the polls to be open according to the laws of the state and sees that ballots or voting machines are available.

In most states, the board provides the list of registered voters and makes certain that only qualified voters cast ballots in each precinct. When the polls close, staff members count the votes and report the results, usually to the county clerk or the board of elections.

Representatives from each party, called **poll watchers,** are allowed at each polling place. Their job is to make sure the election is run fairly and that fraud doesn't occur.

9-1b Presidential Elections and the Electoral College

When citizens vote for president and vice president, they are not voting directly for the candidates. Instead, they are voting for **electors** who will cast their ballots in the **electoral college.** The electors are selected during each presidential election year by the states' political parties, subject to the laws of the state. Each state has as many electoral votes as it has U.S. senators and representatives (see Figure 9–1). In addition, there are three electors from the District of Columbia, even though it is not a state.

FIGURE 9–1 STATE ELECTORAL VOTES IN 2016

The size of each state reflects the number of electoral votes that state has, following the changes required by the 2010 census. The colors show which party the state voted for in the 2016 presidential elections: red for Republican, blue for Democratic. A candidate must win 270 electoral votes to be elected president. Maine awards two of its electoral votes by congressional district, and the red square reflects that the Republicans carried one of them. *Why do some states have so many electoral votes and others so few?*

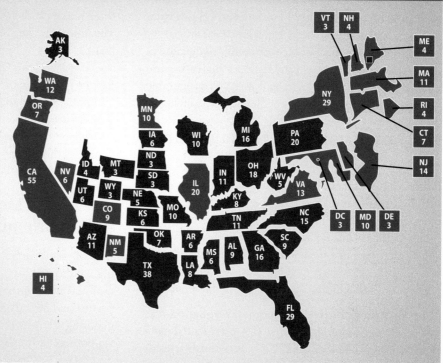

The Winner-Take-All System

The electoral college system is primarily a **winner-take-all system,** in which the candidate who receives the largest popular vote in a state is credited with all that state's electoral votes. The only exceptions are Maine and Nebraska.[1]

In December, after the general election, electors (either Republicans or Democrats, depending on which candidate has won the state's popular vote) meet in their state capitals to cast their votes for president and vice president. When the Constitution was drafted, the framers intended that the electors would use their own discretion in deciding who would make the best president. Beginning as early as 1796, however, electors have usually voted for the candidates to whom they are pledged. The electoral college ballots are then sent to the U.S. Senate, which counts and certifies them before a joint session of Congress held in early January. The candidates who receive a majority of the electoral votes are officially declared president and vice president.

What It Takes to Win

To be elected, a candidate must receive more than half of the 538 electoral votes available. Thus, a candidate needs 270 votes to win. If no presidential candidate gets an electoral college majority (which has happened twice—in 1800 and 1824), the House of Representatives chooses among the top three candidates, with each state delegation casting only a single vote. If no candidate for vice president gets a majority of electoral votes, the vice president is chosen by the Senate, with each senator casting one vote.

CRITICAL THINKING

▶ *Should the District of Columbia be admitted as a state—and therefore elect members to the U.S. House and Senate in addition to participating in the electoral college?*

9-2 HOW WE NOMINATE CANDIDATES

LO Discuss how candidates are nominated.

The first step on the long road to winning an election is the nomination process. Nominations narrow the field of possible candidates and limit each political party's choice to one person.

For many local government posts, which are often nonpartisan, self-nomination is the most common way to become a candidate. A self-proclaimed candidate usually files a petition to be listed on the ballot. Each

> **winner-take-all system** A system in which the candidate who receives the most votes wins. In contrast, proportional systems allocate votes to multiple winners.

state has laws that specify how many signatures a candidate must obtain to show that he or she has some public support. An alternative is to be a *write-in candidate*—voters write the candidate's name on the ballot on Election Day.

Candidates for major offices are rarely nominated in these ways, however. Most candidates for high office are nominated by a political party and receive considerable support from party activists throughout their campaigns.

9–2a Party Control over Nominations

The methods used by political parties to nominate candidates have changed during the course of American history. Broadly speaking, the process has grown more open over the years, with the involvement of ever-greater numbers of local leaders and ordinary citizens. Today, any voter can participate in choosing party candidates. This was not true as recently as 1968, however, and was certainly not possible during the first years of the republic.

The Caucus System   George Washington was essentially unopposed in the first U.S. presidential elections in 1789—no other candidate was seriously considered in any state. By the end of Washington's eight years in office, however, political divisions among the nation's leaders had solidified into political parties, the Federalists and Jefferson's Republicans. These early parties were organized by gatherings of important persons, who often met in secret. The meetings came to be called **caucuses**.[2]

Beginning in 1800, members of Congress who belonged to the two parties held caucuses to nominate candidates for president and vice president. The Republican caucus chose Thomas Jefferson in 1800, as expected, and the Federalist caucus nominated the incumbent president, John Adams. By 1816, the Federalist Party had ceased to exist, and the Republican congressional caucus was in complete control of selecting the president of the United States.

The Death of "King Caucus"   The congressional caucus system collapsed in 1824.[3] It was widely seen as undemocratic—opponents derided it as "King Caucus." A

much-diminished caucus nominated a presidential candidate who then came in third in the electoral vote. The other three major candidates were essentially self-nominated.[4] The four candidates split the electoral vote so completely that the House of Representatives had to decide the contest. It picked John Quincy Adams, even though Andrew Jackson had won more popular and electoral votes.

In the run-up to the 1828 elections, two new parties grew up around the major candidates. Adams's supporters called themselves the National Republicans (later known as the Whigs). Jackson's supporters organized as the Democratic Party, which won the election.

9–2b A New Method: The Nominating Convention

In 1832, both parties settled on a new method of choosing candidates for president and vice president—the national nominating convention. A number of state parties had already adopted the convention system for choosing state-level candidates. New Jersey held conventions as early as 1800.

Nominating Conventions   A **nominating convention** is an official meeting of a political party to choose its candidates. Those who attend the convention are called **delegates**, and they are chosen to represent the people of a particular geographic area. Conventions can take place at multiple levels. A county convention might choose delegates to attend a state convention. The state convention, in turn, might select delegates to the national convention. By 1840, the convention system was the most common method of nominating political party candidates at the state and national levels.

Limits of the Convention System   While the convention system drew in a much broader range of leaders than had the caucus, it was not a particularly democratic institution. Convention delegates were rarely chosen by a vote of the party's local members. Typically, they were appointed by local party officials, who were usually, with good reason, called bosses. These local leaders often gained their positions in ways that were far from democratic. Not until 1972 did ordinary voters in all states gain the right to select delegates to the national presidential nominating conventions.

9–2c Primary Elections and the Loss of Party Control

The corruption that so often accompanied the convention system led reformers to call for a new way to choose candidates—the **primary election**, in which voters go

caucus A meeting held to choose political candidates or delegates.

nominating convention An official meeting of a political party to choose its candidates. Nominating conventions at the state and local levels also select delegates to represent the citizens of their geographic areas at a higher-level party convention.

delegate A person selected to represent the people of one geographic area at a party convention.

primary election An election in which voters choose the candidates of their party, who will then run in the general election.

Vermont senator Bernie Sanders ran for the Democratic presidential nomination in 2016. *How successful was he?*

to the polls to decide among candidates who seek the nomination of their party. Candidates who win a primary election then go on to compete against the candidates from other parties in the general election.

The first primary election may have been held in 1842 by Democrats in Crawford County, Pennsylvania. The technique was not widely used, however, until the end of the nineteenth century and the beginning of the twentieth. These were years in which reform was a popular cause.

The 1972 Reforms

Despite the growing popularity of the primary system in the twentieth century, many states continued to choose delegates to the national party conventions in ways that froze out ordinary voters. Even in states that conducted presidential primaries, these elections were often *beauty contests*—that is, they chose no actual delegates. Party bosses continued to select the delegates. In 1968, however, this system led to a crisis. In that year, incumbent Democratic president Lyndon B. Johnson announced that he would not seek reelection. The Vietnam War, then at its height, had severely eroded Johnson's popularity.

Vice President Hubert Humphrey then became the establishment, pro-war candidate. Anti-war candidates prevailed in most of the presidential primaries. Humphrey did not run in any primaries but won the nomination with the votes of delegations controlled by the party establishments. Anti-war riots outside the

Chicago convention hall were forcibly suppressed by police. Humphrey went on to lose the general election to Republican Richard Nixon.

Subsequently, the Democratic National Committee appointed a special commission to reform the process of nominating presidential candidates. The heart of the reforms was a requirement that, beginning in 1972, convention delegates would be chosen through democratic processes. State conventions were allowed as an alternative to primary elections, but any nominating system would ultimately have to be based on choices by ordinary voters. Initially, party leaders and elected officials had no special privileges. In 1984, however, these individuals were allowed to participate in the convention as *superdelegates*. The Republican Party adopted reforms that were similar to those initiated by the Democrats.

Direct and Indirect Primaries

The rules for conducting primary elections are highly variable, and a number of different types of primaries exist. One major distinction is between a direct primary and an indirect primary.

In a **direct primary,** voters cast their ballots directly for candidates. The elections that nominate candidates for Congress and for state or local offices are almost always direct primaries.

In an *indirect primary*, voters choose delegates, who in turn choose the candidates. The delegates may be pledged to a particular candidate but sometimes run as *unpledged delegates*. The major parties use indirect primaries to elect delegates to the national nominating conventions, who then choose candidates for president and vice president.

The Role of the States

Primary elections are normally conducted by state governments. States set the dates and conduct the elections. They provide polling places, election officials, and registration lists, and they then count

direct primary An election held within each of the two major parties—Democratic and Republican—to choose the party's candidates for the general election. Voters choose the candidate directly, rather than through delegates.

the votes. By sponsoring the primaries, state governments have obtained considerable influence over the rules by which the primaries are conducted. The power of the states is limited, however, by the parties' First Amendment right to freedom of association, a right that has been repeatedly affirmed by the United States Supreme Court.[5]

On occasion, parties that object to the rules imposed by state governments have opted out of the state-sponsored primary system altogether.[6] Note that third parties typically do not participate in state-sponsored primaries but hold nominating conventions instead. The major parties rarely opt out of state elections, however, because the financial—and political—costs of going it alone are high. (When primary elections are used to choose candidates for local *nonpartisan* positions, state control is uncontested.)

Primary Voters

Voter turnout for primaries is lower than it is in general elections. The voters who do go to the polls are often strong supporters of their party. Indeed, as you will learn shortly, independents cannot participate in primary elections in some states, even if they lean toward one of the two major parties. As a result, the Republican primary electorate is very conservative, and Democratic primary voters are quite liberal. Candidates often find that they must run to the political right or left during the primaries. They may then move to the center during the general election campaign.

Insurgent Candidates

Primary elections were designed to take nominations out of the hands of the party bosses. Indeed, the most important result of the primary system has been to reduce dramatically the power of elected and party officials over the nominating process.

Ever since primary elections were established, the insurgent candidate who runs against the party "establishment" has been a common phenomenon. Running against the "powers that be" is often a very effective campaign strategy, and many insurgents have won victories at the local, state, and national levels.

Occasionally, an insurgent's platform is strikingly different from that of the party as a whole. Yet even when an insurgent's politics are abhorrent to the rest of the party—for example, an insurgent might make an outright appeal to racism—the party has no way of denying the insurgent the right to the party label in the general election.

Closed and Open Primaries

Primaries can be classified as closed or open.

Closed Primaries. In a closed primary, only party members can vote to choose that party's candidates, and they may vote only in the primary of their own party. Thus, only registered Democrats can vote in the Democratic primary, and only registered Republicans can vote for the Republican candidates. A person usually establishes party membership when she or he registers to vote. Some states have a *semi-closed* primary, which allows voters to register with a party or change their party affiliations on Election Day.

Regular party workers favor the closed primary because it promotes party loyalty. Independent voters usually oppose it because it forces them to select a party if they wish to participate in the nominating process.

Open Primaries. In an open primary, voters can vote for a party's candidates regardless of whether they belong to the party. In most open primaries, all voters receive both a Republican ballot and a Democratic ballot. Voters then choose either the Democratic or the Republican ballot in the privacy of the voting booth. In a *semi-open* primary, voters request the ballot for the party of their choice.

Mixed Forms. The fifty states have developed dozens of variations on the open and closed primary plans. In some states, primaries are closed only to persons registered to another party, and independents can vote in either primary. In several states, an independent who votes in a party primary is automatically enrolled in that party. In other states, the voter remains an independent. The two major parties often have different rules. For example, in five states, Democrats allow independent voters to

> **"There is no excitement anywhere in the world ... to match the excitement of an American presidential campaign."**
>
> ~ THEODORE H. WHITE
> AMERICAN JOURNALIST AND HISTORIAN
> 1915–1986

closed primary A primary in which only party members can vote to choose that party's candidates.

open primary A primary in which voters can vote for a party's candidates regardless of whether they belong to the party.

participate in primaries or caucuses, but Republicans do not. In one state, Alabama, the reverse is the case.

Blanket and "Top Two" Primaries   Until 2000, California and a few other states employed a *blanket primary*, in which voters could choose the candidates of more than one party. A voter might participate in choosing the Republican candidate for governor, for example, and at the same time vote to pick the Democratic candidate for the U.S. Senate. In that year, however, the Supreme Court ruled that the blanket primary violated the parties' right to freedom of association.[7] Similar primary systems in Washington and Alaska were struck down in later cases.

The Louisiana Model.   Beginning in 1977, Louisiana had a unique system in which all candidates participated in the same primary, regardless of party. The two candidates receiving the most votes then proceeded on to the general election. In 2008, Louisiana abandoned this "jungle primary" for the U.S. House and Senate, but kept it for state and local offices. In 2010, however, Louisiana restored the jungle system for all offices.

The "Top Two" Primary.   Even as Louisiana was questioning its system, other states began picking it up. Washington adopted the Louisiana system in 2004, and in 2008 the Supreme Court ruled that it was constitutional.[8] In June 2010, California voters adopted a system known as the *"top two" primary* that was patterned on the one in Washington. The California system went into effect in 2011, and in the 2014 general elections, seven U.S. House contests featured two members of the same party facing off against each other. The 2016 elections featured seven such races for the House and one for the Senate.

In such systems, political parties continue to have the right to designate preferred candidates, using conventions or other means, but their endorsements do not appear on the ballot. An insurgent Republican and a "regular" Republican, for example, would both be labeled simply "Republican."

9–2d Nominating Presidential Candidates

In some respects, being nominated for president is more difficult than being elected. The nominating process often narrows a very large number of hopefuls down to a single candidate from each party. Choosing a presidential candidate is unlike nominating candidates for any other office. One reason for this is that the nomination process combines several different methods.

The top three Republican presidential candidates as of early 2016: businessman Donald Trump, Texas senator Ted Cruz, and Florida senator Marco Rubio. *What are the advantages of choosing presidential candidates through primaries?*

The "Invisible Primary"   Well before the official primary season begins in the year of the election, candidates for president are busy garnering as much support as possible. In recent years, unofficial presidential campaigns have often begun as much as three years before Election Day. In this period, candidates attempt not only to enhance their public images, but also to gain the support of their party's elected officials, fund-raisers, and other leaders. This effort has been called the "invisible primary," and it can have a major impact on the primary election outcomes.[9] Historically, this was particularly true for Republicans.

The 2016 primary season, however, proved to be a dramatic counterexample. In that year, many Republican voters were in open revolt against the party's leaders. Establishment support for former Florida governor Jeb Bush, the initial front-runner, appeared to hurt, rather than help him. Donald Trump, the victorious candidate, made a point of his contempt for party leaders. The second-ranking candidate, Ted Cruz (R., Tex.), gloried in his unpopularity among his Senate colleagues.

Presidential Primaries Most of the states hold presidential primaries, beginning early in the election year. For a candidate, a good showing in the early primaries results in plenty of media attention as television networks and newspaper reporters play up the results. Subsequent primaries tend to eliminate candidates unlikely to be successful.

The presidential primaries do not necessarily follow the same rules the states use for nominating candidates for the U.S. Congress or for state and local offices. Often, the presidential primaries are not held on the same date as the other primaries. States frequently hold the presidential primaries early in hope of exercising greater influence on the outcome.

Caucuses The caucus system is an alternative to primary elections. Strictly speaking, the caucus system is a convention system. The caucuses are party conventions held at the local level that elect delegates to conventions at the county or congressional district level. These mid-level conventions then choose the delegates to the state convention, which finally elects the delegates to the national party convention.

Unlike the caucuses of two centuries ago, modern caucuses are open to all party members. It is not hard to join a party. At the famous Iowa caucuses, you become a party member simply by attending a local caucus.

While some states, such as Iowa and Minnesota, rely on the caucus/convention system to nominate candidates for state and local positions, the system is more frequently used only to choose delegates to the Democratic and Republican national conventions. Most states with presidential caucuses use primaries to nominate state and local candidates. Thirteen states choose Democratic national convention delegates through caucuses. Republicans use caucuses in fourteen states.

Primaries—The Rush to Be First Traditionally, states have held their presidential primaries at various times over the first six months of a presidential election year. In an effort to make their primaries prominent in the media and influential in the political process, however, many states moved the date of their primary to earlier in the year—a practice known as *front-loading*. In 1988, a group of southern states created a "Super Tuesday" by holding their primaries on the same day in early March. Then, other states moved their primaries to an earlier date, too.

The practice of front-loading primaries gained momentum during the first decade of the twenty-first century. The states with later primary dates found that most nominations were decided early in the season,

leaving their voters "out of the action." Many states, to compete, moved up their primaries. This rush to be first was particularly notable in the year or so preceding the 2008 presidential primaries.

The Impact of Front-Loading Many Americans worried that with a shortened primary season, long-shot candidates would no longer be able to propel themselves into serious contention by doing well in small early-voting states, such as New Hampshire and Iowa.

The practice of front-loading reached its limits in the 2008 Democratic primaries. The Democrats allocated delegates on a proportional basis, so that each candidate received delegates based on his or her share of the vote. That rule made an early decision impossible, and Barack Obama did not obtain a majority of the Democratic delegates until June 3. As a result, many of the most important Democratic primaries took place late in the season. States that had moved their primaries to Super Tuesday on February 5 discovered that they were lost in the crowd of early contests. Front-loading, in other words, had become counterproductive.

In an attempt to reduce front-loading, in 2012 the Republican National Committee ruled that only four traditionally early states—Iowa, New Hampshire, South Carolina, and Nevada—could choose delegates in February. In 2016, states other than these four could not vote until March 1. Super Tuesday, as a result, fell on March 1. Eleven largely southern states chose delegates on that date. States choosing delegates before March 15 had to allocate them proportionally. From March 15 on, delegates could be selected on a winner-take-all basis.

The Republicans had adopted similar rules in 2012, although in that year, several states violated the rules and were penalized. By 2016, the new rules were more widely accepted. The Democratic Party generally fell in line with these decisions, although the Democrats did not allow winner-take-all voting in the later primaries.

The 2016 Republican Primaries During 2015, the most striking feature of the Republican primary contest was the huge number of candidates. The field vastly exceeded the number that could reasonably participate in the Republican presidential debates. The broadcast and cable networks that sponsored the debates had to establish rules as to who could participate. Invitations were limited to the top eight to ten candidates, as shown by opinion polls. The networks also organized "junior varsity" debates among an additional half dozen candidates who were not performing as well in the polls. Scores of self-promoting candidates with no noticeable support were not invited even to the secondary debates. The main debates enjoyed enormous audiences. The first, sponsored by Fox News in August 2015, was seen by 24 million viewers. It was the most-watched live broadcast of a nonsporting event in the history of cable television.

The Rise of Trump. Early in 2015, former Florida governor John E. Bush—known as "Jeb"—led the field as the establishment favorite. Jeb is a brother of President George W. Bush and a son of President George H. W. Bush. In June 2015, however, businessman Donald J. Trump entered the race, and by July, Trump was first in the polls. Bush's support quickly eroded, while Trump's following grew from week to week.

As noted earlier in this text, Trump was such an unusual candidate that most political experts did not believe he could ultimately prevail. The experts had some reasons for this belief. In 2012, candidate after candidate challenged Mitt Romney, the front-runner and establishment favorite. All of these challengers faded, and Romney went on to secure the Republican nomination. It was widely assumed that Trump would suffer the same fate as these challengers and fade away. He did not.

The Republicans Vote. In February 2016, Trump won the New Hampshire primary, confirming his front-runner status. Most other candidates, including Bush, soon dropped out of the race. By late February, the Republicans were down to five major contenders. Only three were realistic possibilities—Texas senator Ted Cruz, Florida senator Marco Rubio, and Trump.

While in principle there were enough Republican anti-Trump votes to defeat him, that vote was split among multiple candidates. No single traditional small-government conservative had the support needed to stop Trump. Even after Super Tuesday—March 1—the anti-Trump field was split between Cruz and Rubio (and also Ohio governor John Kasich). Trump won support in large, winner-take-all states, and frantic efforts by party leaders to derail his candidacy failed. In May, Trump accumulated enough delegates for nomination at the Republican National Convention. Most, though not all, Republicans rallied behind their nominee.

The 2016 Democratic Primaries Democrat Hillary Clinton sought to win enough early support to dissuade other candidates from running against her. This effort was relatively successful, but Clinton still faced one major opponent—Vermont senator Bernie Sanders, running as a democratic socialist. Sanders won strong support from younger voters and, to an extent, from older liberals and hard-pressed white, working-class Democrats. Sanders championed liberal causes that included a universal health-care insurance program entirely run by the government, as seen in most European countries. Tuition at state colleges and universities was to be abolished. Inevitably, taxes would rise.

In contrast, Clinton emphasized her experience as First Lady, as a U.S. senator from New York, and as secretary of state during Obama's first term as president. Clinton's supporters argued that her depth of knowledge and policy expertise would translate into greater progress toward liberal goals than Sanders's ideological passion.

Clinton's Victory. Although Sanders did relatively well among white voters, he lost the African American vote by large margins. For example, Clinton beat Sanders 84 to 16 percent among black voters in South Carolina. African Americans recognized Clinton as a politician who had been their friend for decades. Clinton wrapped up enough delegates for a nomination in June.

Many of Sanders's supporters rallied around the slogan "Bernie or bust." In July, however, on the eve of the Democratic National Convention, Sanders strongly endorsed Clinton. To what extent did Sanders hurt himself by adopting the socialist label? We examine that question in this chapter's *Perception vs. Reality* feature.

Democratic presidential candidate Hillary Clinton at the first Democratic primary debate of the 2016 cycle, held in Nevada. *Would many Americans like to see a woman as president? Why or why not?*

Joseph Sohm/Shutterstock.com

Is the Word *Socialism* Still Poison in U.S. Political Campaigns?

In the early twentieth century, America had a major socialist movement. Still, the Socialist Party won very few elections. After World War II (1939–1945), the United States entered a decades-long confrontation with the Soviet Union, a Communist Party–led empire centered on what is now Russia. The Soviets described their system as *socialism* (*communism* was an ideal for the distant future). For millions of Americans, socialism became a very unpopular label. Yet Vermont senator Bernie Sanders has always called himself a "democratic socialist." In 2016, he ran for the Democratic presidential nomination. He lost, but he did carry many states in the Democratic primaries. This leads to a question: Is *socialism* still a dirty word in U.S. politics?

The Perception

For many older Americans, the word *socialism* is still political poison. Many are astonished that a major politician could embrace it.

The Reality

Informed of Sanders's considerable appeal to American youth, one resident of Cuba plaintively asked: "Don't they know that socialism is a bad thing?" Well, if you live in Cuba, where socialism can be defined as whatever the Castro brothers have done, it surely is a "bad thing." It was bad in the Soviet Union, and it has been an economic catastrophe in today's Venezuela. For many young Americans, however, the word means something else. Often, *capitalism* now appears to mean "the worst excesses of private enterprise." *Socialism*, as "anti-capitalism," thus becomes "opposition to the worst excesses of private enterprise." What's not to like?

What Sanders means by socialism is something else again. He means Denmark. Unlike Cuba or the Soviet Union, Denmark and the other Nordic countries are among the most successful societies on earth. In international comparisons, they regularly rank as among the wealthiest, freest, and happiest countries anywhere.

But as the prime minister of Denmark firmly says, Denmark is not a socialist country. It has a thriving capitalist system and adheres to free-market economic principles. What Denmark also has is a system of social benefits that is vastly more generous than what we have. (Of necessity, taxes are also much higher.) In large part, it owes these benefits to the influence of the Social Democratic Party, the largest single party in all the Nordic nations. The Social Democrats are heirs to the socialist movement, but unlike the Communists, they gave up on abolishing capitalism generations ago.

Therefore, the Nordic lands are often called social democracies. They have none of the ruthless authoritarianism and tight government control of the economy seen in a country such as Cuba. But if social democracy and socialism are not the same, is Bernie Sanders really a socialist? Many political scientists would argue that he is not.

Blog On

The worldwide organization that unites social democratic parties retains the historical name "Socialist International." Find out about these parties by visiting www.socialistinternational.org.

The Role of the Superdelegates. As of 2016, almost 15 percent of the delegates to the Democratic National Convention were **superdelegates,** that is, party leaders and elected officials who were seated automatically and who were free to support any candidate. The great majority of superdelegates supported Clinton. Sanders and many of his supporters therefore claimed that the convention was "rigged" against him. Clinton also won a majority of the regular delegates, however, so Sanders's point was somewhat irrelevant. Still, the Democratic National Committee adopted a set of reforms under which about two-thirds of all superdelegates in 2020 will be bound to vote for the winner of their state's primaries or caucuses. Top leaders, such as governors or members of Congress, will still be free to vote for any candidate.

superdelegates Party leaders and elected officials with the automatic right to attend their party's national convention and support any candidate.

The Republicans also had superdelegates, but they were far fewer in number than their Democratic counterparts. Also, as of 2016, Republican superdelegates were already bound to vote for their state's winner.

National Party Conventions At one time, national conventions were often giant free-for-alls. It wasn't always clear who the winning presidential and vice-presidential candidates would be until the delegates voted.

As more states opted to hold presidential primaries, however, the drama of national conventions diminished. Today, the conventions have been described as massive pep rallies. Nonetheless, each convention's task remains a serious one. In late summer, two thousand to three thousand delegates gather at each convention to represent the wishes of the voters and political leaders of their home states.

On the first day of the convention, delegates hear the reports of the **credentials committee,** which inspects each prospective delegate's claim to be seated as a legitimate representative of her or his state. When the eligibility of delegates is in question, the committee decides who will be seated. Then, a keynote speaker whips up enthusiasm among the delegates. Later, the convention deals with committee reports and debates on the party platform.

Balloting takes place with an alphabetical roll call in which states and territories announce their votes. The vice-presidential nomination takes place later. Acceptance speeches by the presidential and vice-presidential candidates are timed to take place during prime-time television hours.

CRITICAL THINKING

▶ *Is the caucus system undemocratic? Why or why not?*

9–3 THE MODERN POLITICAL CAMPAIGN

LO Indicate what is involved in launching a political campaign today, and describe the structure and functions of a campaign organization.

Once nominated, candidates focus on their campaigns. The term *campaign* originated in the military context. Generals mounted campaigns, using their scarce resources (soldiers and materials) to achieve military objectives. Using the term in a political context is apt. In a political campaign, candidates also use scarce resources (time and funds) in an attempt to defeat their adversaries in the battle for votes.

9–3a Responsibilities of the Campaign Staff

To run a successful campaign, a candidate's campaign staff must be able to raise funds, get media coverage, produce and pay for political ads, and schedule the candidate's time effectively with constituent groups and potential supporters. The campaign must also publicize the candidate's position on the issues, conduct research on the opposing candidate, and persuade the voters to go to the polls.

Years ago, a strong party organization on the local, state, or national level could furnish most of the services and expertise that the candidate needed. Today, party organizations are no longer as important as they once were in providing campaign services. Instead of relying so extensively on political parties, candidates now turn to professionals to manage their campaigns.

The fact that party organizations are no longer responsible for providing many campaign services, however, should not lead anyone to believe the parties are unimportant in campaigns. Because of the intense political polarization that has taken place in recent years, the parties are in some ways more important than ever. Political experts know that, today, the party label allows them to predict how a senator or representative will vote on almost all issues. Many voters are also aware of this reality.

9–3b The Professional Campaign Organization

As mentioned, the role of the political party in managing campaigns has declined, although the party continues to play an important role in recruiting volunteers and getting out the vote. Professional **political consultants** now manage nearly all aspects of a presidential candidate's campaign. Most candidates for governor, the House, and the Senate also rely on consultants. Political consultants generally specialize in a particular area of the campaign, such as researching the opposition, conducting polls, developing the candidate's advertising, or organizing "get-out-the-vote" efforts. Nonetheless, most candidates have

credentials committee
A committee of each national political party that evaluates the claims of national party convention delegates to be the legitimate representatives of their states.

political consultant
A professional political adviser who, for a fee, works on an area of a candidate's campaign. Political consultants include campaign managers, pollsters, media advisers, and "get-out-the-vote" organizers.

a campaign manager who coordinates and plans the campaign strategy. Figure 9–2 shows a typical presidential campaign organization.

A major development in contemporary American politics is the focus on reaching voters through effective use of the media, particularly television. At least half of the budget for a major political campaign is consumed by television advertising. Media consultants are therefore pivotal members of the campaign staff.

9-3c Opposition Research

Major campaigns, such as those for governor, senator, and U.S. president, typically make use of opposition research. A staff member—or even an entire team—spends time discovering as much negative information about opposing candidates as possible. Journalists often rely on opposition researchers for their stories.

Researching Hillary Clinton Beginning in 2015, Democratic candidate Hillary Clinton became the target of intense opposition research—even though she had been in the public eye since 1992, when her husband, Bill Clinton, first ran for president. Republicans recognized that any claims of improper behavior during Clinton's time as First Lady (1993–2001) or as a U.S. senator from New York (2001–2009) would be old news. The hope was to find something damaging that took place when she was secretary of state (2009–2013).

Researchers hoped to find problems in Clinton's handling of the 2012 attack on the U.S. diplomatic mission in Benghazi, Libya. Her use of a private e-mail server was criticized by the FBI. Some researchers examined contributions to the Clinton Foundation, a charity. No one ever managed to find a "smoking gun." Still, the constant drumbeat of accusations provided powerful ammunition for the Republican claim that Clinton was fundamentally dishonest. Donald Trump contributed by constantly referring to Clinton as "crooked Hillary." In the end, the campaign against Clinton may have been one of the most effective demolitions of a politician's reputation in U.S. history. Trump repeatedly stated that Clinton should not even be allowed to run for president. Such an argument opens up some interesting questions, which we discuss in this chapter's *The Rest of the World* feature.

Researching Donald Trump Donald Trump, the Republican primary winner, seemed to be

campaign strategy
The comprehensive plan developed by a candidate and his or her advisers for winning an election.

opposition research
The attempt to learn damaging information about an opponent in a political campaign.

FIGURE 9–2 A TYPICAL PRESIDENTIAL CAMPAIGN ORGANIZATION

Most aspects of a candidate's campaign are managed by professional political consultants, as this figure illustrates. *What can happen when members of the campaign organization disagree with each other about campaign strategy?*

CANDIDATE

Campaign Manager
Develops overall campaign strategy, manages finances, oversees staff

Campaign Staff
Undertake the various tasks associated with campaigning

MEDIA CONSULTANTS
Help to shape the candidate's image and manage campaign advertising

FUND-RAISERS
Raise money to pay for the campaign

LAWYERS AND ACCOUNTANTS
Monitor legal and financial aspects of the campaign

PRIVATE POLLSTER
Gathers up-to-the-minute data on public opinion

SPEECHWRITERS
Prepare speeches for the candidate's public appearances

PRESS SECRETARY
Maintains press contracts. Responsible for disseminating campaign news

RESEARCHERS
Investigate opponents' records and personal history

TRAVEL PLANNER
Arranges for the candidate's transportation and accommodations

POLICY EXPERTS
Provide input on foreign and domestic policy issues

WEB CONSULTANT
Oversees the candidate's Internet presence

State Campaign Chairpersons
Monitor state and local campaigns

Local Committees
Direct efforts of local volunteers

Volunteers
Publicize the candidate at the local level through personal visits, phone calls, direct mailings, and online activities

The Rest of the WORLD

Banning Candidates and Political Parties around the World

"It's crooked—she's—she's guilty of a very, very serious crime. She should not be allowed to run." That was how Donald Trump described Hillary Clinton. As it happens, Clinton was never charged with anything, much less convicted. Despite what Trump said, it is not possible to stop people from running for Congress or the presidency on that basis—even if they are currently serving time in prison. Eugene V. Debs, leader of the Socialist Party, ran for president in 1920 while confined to a federal penitentiary. Debs had been convicted of sedition for opposing U.S. participation in World War I. He won almost a million votes.

Constitutional rules on who can be elected to federal office are limited to age, citizenship, and residence. The Supreme Court has found that both the national and state governments may not add to these qualifications.[10] Congress has an expulsion power—it can expel a member for bad behavior but cannot prevent that person from running for reelection. (Under our federal system, however, states can ban felons from running for *state* office.)

How Do Our Allies Handle This Issue?

Are other nations as resolute in protecting the right to run for office? Rules on this topic vary. In France,

a felon cannot become president. Germany does not restrict individuals, but it can ban—and has banned—political parties on the basis that they are antidemocratic. Still, in these well-established democracies, the rules do not seem to interfere unduly with the will of the people.

The Destruction of Democracy in Thailand

There are nations, however, in which the ability to ban candidates and parties has been used as a tool to cripple democracy. Consider Thailand. Democracy has never been secure there—over the years, military dictatorships have been in power more often than not. Thailand is divided between two political factions. One, known as the yellow shirts, is based on the upper classes and is based in the capital, Bangkok. The other, the red shirts, is populist and based in the countryside. In every election since 2001, the red shirts have prevailed, sometimes by large margins. Still, the yellow shirts have sought to keep the populists from power.

In 2006, the army overthrew a populist government led by Thaksin Shinawatra. The Constitutional Court banned him from politics and dissolved his party. When elections were held in 2007, the red shirts organized

a new party, chose a new leader, and won again. In 2008, the Constitutional Court removed the new prime minister on trivial charges, banned hundreds of populists from politics, and dissolved their party. When elections were held in 2011, the red shirts won once again under Thaksin's sister. In 2014, she was thrown out by the army.

We Don't Do That in This Country

The case of Thailand shows that the American founders had good reasons to deliberately limit the requirements for office. It is simply too easy for an autocratically minded government to concoct bogus charges against a rival politician in an attempt to steal an election. Banning entire political parties can be even more dangerous. After all, throwing opposition parties out of parliament was how Adolph Hitler consolidated power in 1933.

Critical Analysis

What would happen if the majority party in the U.S. House tried to use its expulsion powers to eliminate the minority party?

vulnerable to opposition research. He had engineered four corporate bankruptcies, freezing out hundreds of creditors, many of them small businesses. Former students of Trump University sued, claiming that the defunct, nonaccredited real estate school was a scam. Still, many of Trump's followers believed that anything

said against him in the "mainstream media" was a lie. Apparently, Trump had successfully established himself as a "transgressive" politician. Making offensive remarks was part of the Trump brand, and any new instance simply confirmed what everyone already believed. Still, a few incidents during the general election seemed to cut into Trump's support, but not by enough to keep him from ultimately winning the presidency. Trump lost support when he seemed to attack ordinary citizens. An example was his remarks about the parents of U.S. Army captain Humayun Khan, a Muslim war hero killed in Iraq. Such statements were made openly—Democrats needed to publicize them, but they did not involve much research. Opposition research, however, was responsible for locating a videotape in which Trump bragged of his power to physically molest women. The effect even of that statement, however, was limited.

CRITICAL THINKING

▶ *Some people have accused political consultants of "managing the candidate" too well, making the candidate appear stilted and unnatural. How could a candidate prevent that from happening?*

 9-4

THE INTERNET CAMPAIGN

LO Describe how the Internet has transformed political campaigns.

Over the years, political leaders have benefited from understanding and using new communications technologies. In the 1930s, command of a new medium—radio—gave President Franklin D. Roosevelt an edge. In 1960, Democratic presidential candidate John F. Kennedy gained an advantage over Republican Richard Nixon because Kennedy had a better understanding of the visual impact of television.

Today, the ability to make effective use of social media and the Internet is essential to a candidate. In the 2008 presidential elections, Barack Obama gained an edge on his rivals in part because of his superior use of the new technologies. His team relied on the Internet for fund-raising, targeting potential supporters, and creating local political organizations. His 2012 campaign was even more sophisticated. By 2016, every major presidential candidate understood the need for an effective online operation.

9-4a Fund-Raising on the Internet

Internet fund-raising grew out of an earlier technique: the direct-mail campaign. In direct mailings, campaigns send solicitations to large numbers of likely prospects, typically seeking contributions. Developing good lists of prospects is central to an effective direct-mail operation, because postage, printing, and the rental of address lists make the costs of each mailing high. In many direct-mail campaigns,

most of the funds raised are used up by the costs of the campaign itself. In contrast to the costs, response rates are low—a 1 percent response rate is a tremendous success. From the 1970s on, conservative organizations became especially adept at managing direct-mail campaigns. For a time, this expertise gave conservative causes and candidates an advantage over liberals.

To understand the old system is to recognize the superiority of the new one. The cost of e-mailing is very low. Lists of prospects need not be prepared as carefully, because e-mail sent to unlikely prospects does not waste resources. E-mail fund-raising did face one problem when it was new—many people were not yet online. Today, the extent of online participation is no longer a concern.

The new technology brought with it a change in the groups that benefited the most. Conservatives were no longer the most effective fund-raisers. Instead, liberal and libertarian organizations enjoyed some of the greatest successes.

Democrats Online   As noted, Barack Obama took Internet fund-raising to a new level. One of the defining characteristics of his fund-raising was its decentralization. The Obama campaign attempted to recruit as many supporters as possible to act as fund-raisers who would solicit contributions from their friends and neighbors. As a result, Obama was spared much personal fund-raising effort during campaigns. (As president, however, he raised large sums for other Democrats). In 2015 and 2016, Hillary Clinton sought to emulate Obama's online success. Her chief opponent, Senator Bernie Sanders, was also very popular on the Internet, however. That popularity let Sanders raise more money in small donations than Clinton.

Republicans Online   Already in 2008, one Republican candidate was able to use the Internet with great success—Texas representative Ron Paul, who espoused a libertarian philosophy that was highly appealing to many high-tech enthusiasts. Paul pioneered the

> "In constant pursuit of money to finance campaigns, the political system is simply unable to function. Its deliberative powers are paralyzed."
>
> ~ JOHN RAWLS, AMERICAN EDUCATOR, 1921–2000

online *moneybomb* technique, described by the San José *Mercury News* as "a one-day fund-raising frenzy." Despite Paul's fund-raising prowess, his libertarian politics were sufficiently far from the conservative Republican mainstream that he was able to win only a handful of national convention delegates. Later Republican candidates, such as 2012 nominee Mitt Romney, had more limited Internet operations.

Donald Trump's fund-raising operation was neither large-scale nor particularly innovative. Indeed, Trump raised less money than any major-party presidential candidate in years. Trump did make great use of the Internet in rallying his supporters, however, as we will explain shortly.

9–4b Targeting Supporters

In 2004, President George W. Bush's chief political adviser, Karl Rove, pioneered a new campaign technique known as *microtargeting*. The process involves collecting as much information as possible about voters in a gigantic database and then filtering out various groups for special attention.

Through microtargeting, for example, the Bush campaign could identify Republican prospects living in heavily Democratic neighborhoods—potential supporters whom the campaign might otherwise have neglected because the neighborhood as a whole seemed so unpromising. In 2004, the Democrats had nothing to match Republican efforts. In 2012, however, Obama's microtargeting operation vastly outperformed Romney's. Both major candidates made effective use of the technique in 2016, though Clinton's operation was, of course, better funded.

9–4c Support for Organizing

Perhaps the most effective use of the Internet has been as an organizing tool. One of the earliest Internet techniques was to use the site Meetup.com to organize real-world meetings. In this way, campaigns were able to gather supporters without relying on the existing party and activist infrastructure.

The 2012 and 2016 Campaigns As with fund-raising, Barack Obama took Web-based organizing to a new level. In 2012, Obama had seven times as many Facebook supporters as Romney (28 million versus 4 million).

At the beginning of 2016, Hillary Clinton had a substantially larger social-media presence than any other candidate, including Donald Trump. By April, however, Trump passed Clinton in Twitter followers, and his social-media edge continued to grow thereafter. Trump soon became famous for his early-morning tweets, which often insulted his many foes. Trump continued his tweeting habit even after he became president. Thousands of his followers retweeted his remarks to their own followers, thus magnifying the impact of the tweets.

The Ground Game A modern campaign collects as much data as it can—in part, through use of Internet resources—to identify the people whose votes it wants. The data are used to make human contact more efficient by directing volunteers toward the voters they most need to reach. Such get-out-the-vote drives have been called the *ground game* (as opposed to advertising, which is called the *air game*.)

By 2012, Obama had had years to perfect his ground game, and it showed. The Obama campaign was able to create active local support groups in towns and counties across the country—many in areas that had traditionally supported Republicans. By comparison, Romney's ground game sometimes looked like a comedy of errors. In 2016, both Clinton and Sanders attempted to perfect their ground games. Sanders enjoyed relative success in caucus states, where turnout is lower than in primary states. That spoke well for the enthusiasm of his supporters, but it was not enough to overcome Clinton's advantages. On the Republican side, political novice Donald Trump was slow in setting up his ground game. He wound up relying largely on the Republican National Committee for local organizing. Fortunately for Trump, the RNC was able to launch a major ground-game effort on his behalf.

CRITICAL THINKING

▶ *Some candidates are more successful than others in using the Internet. Do such candidates have any traits in common? If so, what might these be?*

President Obama at a conference on climate change in Paris, France. *How important was the Internet to Obama's reelection?*

Frederic Legrand - COMEO/Shutterstock.com

WHAT IT COSTS TO WIN

LO Summarize the current laws that regulate campaign financing and the role of money in modern political campaigns.

The modern political campaign is an expensive undertaking. Candidates must spend huge sums for professional campaign managers and consultants, television and radio ads, the printing of campaign literature, travel, office rent, equipment, and other necessities.

The cost of campaigning has grown considerably. The Center for Responsive Politics has calculated that the total cost of the 2016 elections was $6.8 billion, up somewhat from 2012. This includes the primary and general elections, and races at all levels from president on down. It is true that in 2016, the Trump and Clinton candidate committees—the committees directly under candidate control—spent less than in 2012. Trump in particular spent much less. Yet spending by losing presidential candidates, congressional campaigns, the major parties, and outside groups rose substantially. Consider that the Senate race in Pennsylvania cost $175 million and the New Hampshire Senate race cost $129 million.

9–5a Presidential Spending

Presidential campaigns are even more expensive than congressional campaigns. In the 2015–2016 presidential election cycle, spending on behalf of the major-party candidates was almost $1.5 billion.

In today's campaign-finance environment, the sums spent by the candidates themselves and by the parties are only part of the story. Independent expenditures by outside groups nominally unconnected with the campaigns have become as important as spending by the candidates themselves.

The groups responsible for much of this spending, known as *super PACs*, are a new development. They became prominent only in the 2011–2012 campaign cycle. Super PACs followed from recent court decisions, especially the Supreme Court's ruling in *Citizens United v. Federal Election Commission*. We discuss that decision later in this section. First, however, we examine the development of our campaign-finance system.

9–5b The Federal Election Campaign Act

The high cost of campaigns gives rise to the fear that campaign contributors and special interest groups will try to buy favored treatment from those who are elected

Tom Steyer is a hedge fund manager, philanthropist, and environmentalist. He is also one of the largest individual contributors to Democratic candidates and has his own super PAC. *Is removing money from politics a realistic goal? Why or why not?*

to office. In an attempt to prevent these abuses, the government has tried to regulate campaign financing.

Legislation to regulate campaign finance was passed in 1925 and 1939, but these early efforts were almost completely ineffective. The first reform that actually had teeth was the Federal Election Campaign Act (FECA) of 1971.[11] The act was amended in 1974. As amended, the new law did the following:

▸ **Restricted the amount that could be spent on mass media advertising, including television.**

▸ **Limited how much individuals and groups could contribute to candidates.**

▸ **Limited the amount that candidates and their families could contribute to their own campaigns.**

▸ **Prevented corporations and labor unions from participating directly in political campaigns, but**

- allowed them to set up political action committees (discussed shortly).

▶ Required disclosure of all contributions and expenditures of more than $100.

▶ Created the Federal Election Commission (FEC) to administer and enforce the act's provisions.

In addition, the act provided public financing for presidential primaries and general elections, funded by a checkoff on federal income tax returns. From 1976 through 2000, presidential campaigns were largely funded by the public purse. Beginning in 2004, however, leading Democratic and Republican presidential candidates were refusing public funding for the primaries because they could raise much more money without it. By 2012, the public financing of presidential campaigns was effectively over.

Freeing Up Self-Financing

In 1976, the United States Supreme Court declared unconstitutional the provision in the 1971 act that limited the amount each individual could spend on his or her own campaign. The Court held that a "candidate, no less than any other person, has a First Amendment right to engage in the discussion of public issues and vigorously and tirelessly to advocate his own election."[12]

The Rise of PACs The FECA allowed corporations, labor unions, and special interest groups to set up national *political action committees (PACs)* to raise money for candidates. PACs can contribute up to $5,000 per candidate in each election, but there is no limit on the total amount of PAC contributions during an election cycle.

The number of PACs grew significantly for several decades, as did their campaign contributions. In the 2004 election cycle, about 36 percent of campaign funds spent on House races came from PACs.[13] Since 2004, however, other methods of raising campaign funds have reduced the relative importance of traditional PACs.

9–5c Skirting the Campaign-Financing Rules

The FECA was designed to regulate funds given to the campaign organizations of candidates for office. There are ways, however, to influence the political process without giving money directly to a candidate's campaign. Individuals and corporations soon developed such practices. One way to skirt the rules was to contribute to the political parties instead of the candidates. A second was to make independent expenditures not coordinated with a candidate's campaign or a political party.

Soft Money The FECA and its amendments did not prohibit individuals or corporations from contributing to political parties. Contributors could make donations to the parties to cover the costs of registering voters, printing flyers, advertising, developing campaigns to get out the vote, and holding fund-raising events. Contributions to political parties were called soft money.

By 2000, the parties were raising nearly $463 million per election season through soft money contributions. Soft dollars became the main source of campaign money in the presidential race until after the 2002 elections, when soft money was banned, as you will read shortly.

Independent Expenditures The campaign-financing laws did not prohibit corporations, labor unions, and special interest groups from making independent expenditures in an election campaign. Independent expenditures, as the term implies, are expenditures for activities that are independent of (not coordinated with) those of a candidate or a political party.

Decisions by the courts have distinguished two types of independent expenditures. In the first type, an interest group or other contributor wages an "issue campaign" without going so far as to say "Vote for Candidate X." An issue campaign might, however, go so far as to publish voter guides informing voters of candidates' positions. The courts have repeatedly upheld the right of groups to advocate their positions in this way.

Alternatively, a group might explicitly campaign for particular candidates. The Supreme Court has held that an issue-oriented group has a First Amendment right to advocate the election of its preferred candidates as long as it acts independently of the candidates' campaigns. In 1996, the Court held that these guidelines apply to expenditures by political parties as well.[14]

> **"A promising young man should go into politics so that he can go on promising for the rest of his life."**
>
> ~ ROBERT BYRNE
> AMERICAN AUTHOR
> 1930–2016

soft money Campaign contributions not regulated by federal law, such as some contributions that are made to political parties instead of to particular candidates.

independent expenditure An expenditure for activities that are independent from (not coordinated with) those of a political candidate or a political party.

Charles Koch (pronounced "coke") is the CEO of Koch Industries, the second-largest privately held company by revenue in the United States. With his brother David, he is known for massive donations to libertarian and conservative causes. *Should such donations be limited?*

9-5d The Bipartisan Campaign Reform Act of 2002

The increasing use of soft money and independent expenditures led to a demand for further campaign-finance reform. In 2002, Congress passed, and the president signed, the Bipartisan Campaign Reform Act. The measure is also known as the McCain-Feingold Act after its chief sponsors, Senators John McCain (R., Ariz.) and Russell Feingold (D., Wisc.).

The new law banned soft money at the national level. It also regulated campaign ads paid for by interest groups and prohibited any such issue-advocacy commercials within thirty days of a primary election or sixty days of a general election.

The 2002 act set the amount that an individual could contribute to a federal candidate at $2,000 and the amount that an individual could give to all federal candidates at $95,000 over a two-year election cycle. (Under the law, some individual contribution limits are indexed for inflation and thus may change slightly with every election cycle.) Individuals could still contribute to state and local parties, so long as the contributions did not exceed $10,000 per year per individual. The new law went into effect the day after the 2002 general elections.

The Supreme Court Upholds McCain-Feingold Several groups immediately filed lawsuits challenging the constitutionality of the new law. Supporters of the restrictions on campaign ads by special interest groups argued that the large amounts of funds spent on these ads create an appearance of corruption in the political process. In contrast, an attorney for the National Rifle Association (NRA) argued that because the NRA represents "millions of Americans speaking in unison ... [it] is not a *corruption* of the democratic political process; it is the democratic political process."[15] In December 2003, the Supreme Court upheld nearly all of the clauses of the act in *McConnell v. Federal Election Commission*.[16]

The Supreme Court Changes Its Mind Beginning in 2007, however, the Supreme Court began to chip away at the limits on independent expenditures contained in McCain-Feingold. In that year, in *Federal Election Commission v. Wisconsin Right to Life, Inc.*, the Court invalidated a major part of the 2002 law and overruled a portion of its own 2003 decision upholding the act. In the four years since the earlier ruling, Chief Justice John Roberts, Jr., and Associate Justice Samuel Alito, Jr., had been appointed, and both were conservatives.

In a five-to-four decision, the Court held that issue ads could not be prohibited in the time period preceding elections (thirty days before primary elections and sixty days before general elections) *unless* they were "susceptible of no reasonable interpretation other than as an appeal to vote for or against a specific candidate."[17] The Court concluded that restricting *all* television ads paid for by corporate or labor union treasuries in the weeks before an election amounted to censorship of political speech.

Citizens United v. Federal Election Commission (FEC) A January 2010 Supreme Court ruling helped establish our current wide-open campaign-finance system. This decision, *Citizens United v. FEC*, was initially seen as fostering a vast new wave of corporate spending on elections. The actual results were somewhat different, as you will read shortly.

In the *Wisconsin Right to Life* case described earlier, the Court ruled out bans on issue ads placed by corporations and other organizations in the run-up to an election. In *Citizens United v. FEC*, the Court extended this protection to ads that attack or praise specific candidates, including ads that suggest voting for particular candidates.[18] Two months later, in *Speechnow v. FEC*, a federal court of appeals held that it was not possible to limit contributions to independent-expenditure groups based on the size or source of the contribution.[19]

As a result of these two decisions, *Citizens United* and *Speechnow*, there is now no limit on the ability of corporations, unions, nonprofit groups, and individuals to fund advertising, provided that they do not contribute directly to a candidate's campaign. While Republican leaders applauded the *Citizens United* ruling as a victory for free speech, most Democrats were appalled. They feared that the ruling would result in a massive tilting of the political landscape toward corporate wealth.

McCutcheon v. FEC The Supreme Court handed down yet another ruling that freed up campaign financing in April 2014. In *McCutcheon v. FEC*, the Court struck down a decades-old cap on the total amount that any individual can contribute to federal candidates in a two-year election cycle.[20] (By 2014, the overall limit had risen to $123,000.) As a result of this ruling, to give one example, a wealthy individual could now make the maximum legal contribution to every single House candidate of a particular party.

9-5e The Current Campaign-Finance Environment

Because the *Citizens United* decision was issued less than a year before the 2010 elections, its impact in that year was modest. By 2012, however, the new rules had changed the shape of the campaign-finance environment. Individuals and PACs still faced limits on what they could contribute directly to candidates' campaigns and to the parties. Despite these limits, the campaigns and parties were still able to raise huge sums. Meanwhile, independent organizations stood out as the wild card in American politics. We list the largest independent expenditures in the 2016 election cycle in Table 9–1. (In some cases, these expenditures are made by *party committees* that are entirely under partisan control.)

Super PACs A new type of organization came into existence to take advantage of the new rules. Known officially as "independent expenditure–only committees," the new bodies were soon dubbed super PACs.

The Myth of Independence. The super PACs' supposed independence from campaigns turned out to be a convenient fiction. By 2011, every major presidential candidate had one or more affiliated super PACs, usually run by former members of the candidate's own campaign. A division of labor soon developed. Super PACs would run negative ads to damage a candidate's opponents, while the candidate committee—the committee entirely under the candidate's own control—accentuated the positive about the candidate.

The Role of the Individual Donor. When the *Citizens United* decision was handed down, a flood of corporate cash was expected to enter the political system. The ruling did result in more corporate (and union) spending, but far less than anticipated. Apparently, many companies were reluctant to take stands that might alienate a large number of customers. What caught everyone by surprise was the huge sums poured into super PACs by individuals, notably individuals of great wealth.

For example, Charles and David Koch, two brothers with a long-standing commitment to libertarian politics, soon became some of the largest political donors ever. By 2016, however, the Koch brothers faced a problem in Donald Trump, a candidate who was repugnant to the brothers' libertarian beliefs. In the end, much of the Koch money went to get-out-the-vote drives for Senate and House candidates. Such drives are potentially more effective than television advertisements.

In 2012, casino magnate Sheldon Adelson and his wife made total donations to Republican candidates that may have exceeded $100 million. In 2016, their donations to candidates in national elections were about $82 million. The Adelsons are particularly interested in supporting Israel.

While conservative donors gained much attention, some billionaires also backed Democrats. Tom Steyer, a California hedge fund billionaire and environmentalist, donated more than $65 million to national and California progressive candidates in 2012. In 2016, his federal contributions reached $91 million.

527 and 501c Committees In addition to super PACs, another type of independent committee is the *527 committee*, named after the provision of the tax code that covers it. Spending by 527s rose rapidly after 2002, and in the 2004 election cycle, the committees spent about $612 million to "advocate positions," as they were not allowed to "expressly advocate" voting for specific candidates. By 2008, the 527 committees began to decline in importance, and by 2012 they had been replaced almost completely by super PACs, which were allowed to campaign for and against candidates.

TABLE 9–1   THE TWENTY TOP GROUPS MAKING INDEPENDENT EXPENDITURES DURING THE 2015–2016 CYCLE

This table lists independent expenditures only. Some groups have designated only a part of their total fund-raising as independent expenditures. *Right to Rise later returned about $12 million to its donors. Why would it do that?*

Committee	Affiliation	Raised in 2015–2016	Type	Disclosure of Contributors
Priorities USA Action	Hillary Clinton	$133,407,972	Super PAC	full
Right to Rise USA	Jeb Bush	$86,817,138	Super PAC	full
Senate Leadership Fund	Republican	$85,994,270	Super PAC	full
Democratic Congressional Campaign Committee	Democratic	$80,321,076	Party committee	full
Senate Majority PAC	Democratic	$75,389,818	Super PAC	full
National Republican Congressional Committee	Republican	$73,601,573	Party committee	full
Conservative Solutions PAC	Marco Rubio	$55,443,483	Super PAC	full
NRA & NRA Institute for Legislative Action	gun rights	$52,532,773	501c, Super PAC	partial
Democratic Senatorial Campaign Committee	Democratic	$52,128,270	Party committee	full
Get Our Jobs Back	Donald Trump	$50,010,166	Super PAC	full
House Majority PAC	Democratic	$47,470,121	Super PAC	partial
Future 45 and the 45 Committee	Sheldon Adelson & Todd Ricketts	$45,603,026	Super PAC, 501c	partial
Congressional Leadership Fund	Republican	$40,125,691	Super PAC	partial
National Republican Senatorial Committee	Republican	$39,207,858	Party committee	full
Women Vote!	Democratic	$33,167,285	Super PAC	partial
Freedom Partners Action Fund	Koch brothers	$29,728,798	Super PAC	full
U.S. Chamber of Commerce	business	$29,106,034	501c	none
Granite State Solutions	Sen. Kelly Ayotte	$24,267,135	Super PAC	full
Great America PAC	Conservative	$23,030,467	Super PAC	full
Club for Growth Action and Club for Growth	anti-tax	$22,917,131	Super PAC, 501c	partial

Source: Center for Responsive Politics.

One reason for the decline of the 527 in 2008 was the creation of a new kind of body, the *501(c)4 organization*, known as the *501c*. Like the 527, this type of committee was named after a provision in the tax code. According to some lawyers, a 501c could make limited contributions directly to campaigns and—perhaps more importantly—could conceal the identities of its donors. So far, the FEC has refused to rule on the legality of this technique. Table 9–1 indicates which major independent committees are super PACs and which are 501c organizations. Some groups have organized both types.

The 501c's ability to hide its contributors created a new campaign-finance issue. Republicans argued that donors needed the right to remain anonymous so that they would not have to fear retribution. Democrats contended that anonymous contributions were simply a further corruption of the political process. Attempts to end donor anonymity through legislation failed. We discuss the issue of anonymous donations in this chapter's *Join the Debate* feature.

CRITICAL THINKING

▶ *Under what circumstances would you consider political contributions to be free speech—and under what circumstances would you see them as thinly veiled bribes to public officials?*

In the run-up to every November general election, television watchers can be certain that they will be bombarded with negative political ads. Such ads must identify their sponsors. But if you see an ad by the Committee for the Advancement of Everything Good, how can you tell who actually funded it?

Many such ads are put together by super PACs or 501c organizations. If you go to the websites of these organizations, you are not likely to learn who provided the funds. In some cases, you might be able to find the answer at the website of the Federal Election Commission or of a watchdog organization, such as OpenSecrets .org. Yet in 2016, all of the $29 million in donations made through the U.S. Chamber of Commerce were anonymous, and so were $33 million in contributions made through the NRA.

Full Disclosure, Please

Polls show that a strong majority of voters are concerned about the role of money in politics. No one believes that special interest money is going to disappear, but most voters from both parties say that we should know who is making the contributions.

Opponents of anonymous contributions point to a number of reasons why they should have no place in our democracy. When voters evaluate a candidate, they have the right to know who stands behind that person. Which unions, corporations, trade associations, or individual billionaires are supporting him or her? How can we battle undue influence on the part of special interests if we don't know which interests are supporting which candidates? Also, those who fund misleading advertisements or even flat-out lies should take responsibility for their messages.

Furthermore, small campaign contributors lose out when they are up against well-funded super PACs with anonymous donors. Candidates can compete fairly for public office only when we eliminate secret funding of political campaigns.

Political Privacy Should Be a Civil Right

Not everyone is in favor of forcing secret donors to political campaigns out into the open. Consider that in 1958, the United States Supreme Court ruled that Alabama could not require the NAACP to disclose its membership rolls. Why? Because if segregationists in Alabama were able to identify NAACP members, they could retaliate against the most vulnerable ones. Some members might lose their jobs or be threatened with violence. Publicizing the membership list of an organization such as the NAACP would make a mockery of the constitutional rights to free association and free speech. According to the Court, the privacy of group membership is critical to "effective advocacy of both public and private points of view, particularly controversial ones."[21]

If all political contributions were exposed, what could happen to a supporter of a liberal cause such as gay rights if he or she worked for a conservative employer? In California, supporters of same-sex marriage picketed and boycotted various groups that funded opposition to gay marriage. Banning anonymous donations harms free speech—not the other way around.

Critical Analysis

Which kind of donor might be more interested in identity protection—an individual billionaire or a corporation that sells products to the public? Why?

AMERICA AT ODDS | Campaigns and Elections

Some observers believe that if the founders could see how presidential campaigns are conducted today, they would be shocked at how candidates "pander to the masses." Whether they would be shocked at the costliness of modern campaigns is not as clear. After all, the founders themselves were an elitist, wealthy group, as are many of today's successful candidates for high political office. In any event, Americans today are certainly stunned by how much it takes to win an election. Some of the specific controversies that divide Americans concerning campaigns are the following:

- *Is the electoral college a dangerous anachronism—or a force for stability within our political system?*

- *Should all voters be free to participate in any party primary—or does such a step make it too difficult for the parties to present a coherent group of candidates and policies?*

- *Should states retain their treasured right to set the dates of their presidential primaries—or should the national parties assume responsibility for establishing a rational primary schedule?*

- *Are campaign contributions a constitutionally protected form of free speech—or are they too often a source of corruption within the political system?*

- *Should all politically active groups be required to furnish the identities of their major contributors—or should we allow contributors to remain anonymous because they might suffer reprisals due to their contributions?*

STUDY TOOLS 9

READY TO STUDY? IN THE BOOK, YOU CAN:

☐ Review what you've read with the following chapter quiz.

☐ Check your answers in Appendix D at the back of the book.

☐ Rip out the Chapter Review Card, which includes key terms and chapter summaries.

ONLINE AT WWW.CENGAGEBRAIN.COM, YOU CAN:

☐ Watch videos to get a quick overview.

☐ Expedite your studying with Major Player readings and Focus Activities.

☐ Check your understanding with Chapter Quizzes.

FILL-IN

Learning Outcome 9–1

1. The electoral college system is primarily a winner-take-all system, in which the candidate _____.

2. A candidate must win at least _____ electoral votes, cast by the electors, to become president through the electoral college system.

Learning Outcome 9–2

3. In a/an _____ primary, voters cast their ballots directly for candidates.

4. In the context of presidential primaries, the practice known as front-loading refers to _____.

5. In late summer of a presidential election year, _____ gather at their party's national convention to adopt the party platform and to nominate the party's presidential and vice-presidential candidates.

Learning Outcome 9–3

6. The attempt to learn damaging information about an opponent in a political campaign is called _____ research.

Learning Outcome 9–4

7. A campaign technique known as microtargeting involves _____.

Learning Outcome 9–5

8. The Federal Election Campaign Act of 1971 and its amendments provided public financing for presidential primaries and general elections, funded by a checkoff on _____.

9. After the Supreme Court's decision in *Citizens United v. Federal Election Commission* (2010), a new type of organization came into existence. Known officially as "independent expenditure–only committees," the new bodies were soon dubbed _____.

MULTIPLE CHOICE

Learning Outcome 9–1

10. The total number of electoral votes available is
    a. 538.　　　**b.** 535.　　　**c.** 435.

11. If no presidential candidate receives the required number of electoral votes,
    a. a runoff election is held in January.
    b. the House of Representatives votes on the top three candidates, with each state delegation casting only a single vote.
    c. the Senate votes on the candidates, with each senator casting one vote.

Learning Outcome 9–2

12. In a/an _____ primary, only party members can vote to choose that party's candidates, and they may vote only in the primary of their own party.
    a. closed　　　**b.** open　　　**c.** indirect

Learning Outcome 9–3

13. With the rise of candidate-centered campaigns in the past several decades, the role of the political party in managing campaigns has
    a. increased.
    b. stayed about the same.
    c. declined.

Learning Outcome 9–4

14. Barack Obama gained an edge on his rivals in part because of his superior use of
    a. radio.
    b. television.
    c. social media and the Internet.

Learning Outcome 9–5

15. The Federal Election Campaign Act allows corporations, labor unions, and interest groups to set up PACs to raise money for candidates. PACs can contribute up to _____ per candidate in each election, but there is no limit on the total amount of PAC contributions during an election cycle.
    a. $2,000　　　**b.** $5,000　　　**c.** $95,000

10 | POLITICS AND THE MEDIA

Chip Somodevilla/Getty Images News/Getty Images

LEARNING OUTCOMES

After reading this chapter, you should be able to:

10-1 Explain the role of the media in a democracy.

10-2 Summarize how television influences the conduct of political campaigns.

10-3 Explain why talk radio has been described as the Wild West of the media.

10-4 Describe types of media bias, and explain how such bias affects the political process.

10-5 Indicate the extent to which the Internet is reshaping news and political campaigns.

After
finishing this
chapter,
go to **PAGE 234**
for **STUDY TOOLS**

LIBEL SUIT

You can think anything that you want. When you put your thoughts into words, however, there are legal constraints. Each state (and the District of Columbia) has laws that forbid defamation, both in the form of slander and libel. *Defamation* is the communication of a false statement that harms the reputation of another. *Slander* refers to spoken statements made within the hearing of a third person. If the statement is published, it is *libel*. Someone who has suffered defamation can bring a lawsuit against the offending party—defamation is a civil wrong, not a criminal offense.

Even the most careful news organization cannot avoid making false statements from time to time. A key question is whether the falsehood injures someone's reputation. If the aggrieved party is a public official or even a public person such as an actor, she or he must adhere to stricter rules. To win a libel suit, a public official or public person must show that a media organization published false statements with "actual malice," that is, "with knowledge that they are false or in reckless disregard of their truth or falsity." The Supreme Court established this rule in 1964, in *New York Times v. Sullivan*.[1]

Both before and after he became president, Donald Trump repeatedly argued that we should "loosen up libel laws" to make it easier for aggrieved parties to win lawsuits. Is this a good idea?

No One Should Get Away with Lies

One unpleasant characteristic of current-day politics is the flood of lies peddled during every election. The old proverb says it well: "A lie will be halfway 'round the world before truth has put its boots on." Research has shown that even when a falsehood is successfully refuted, most people remember only the falsehood, not the correction. Indeed, refutation may actually strengthen belief in the falsehood, because the false statement must be repeated to refute it. It follows that we need better laws to penalize lies. If libel can be punished with large fines and public humiliation, those who employ lies as a tactic may think twice before publishing.

The irony is that hardly any public figure has made more false statements than Trump himself. Take, for example, his claim—made with no apparent evidence—that President Obama wiretapped the Trump campaign during the 2016 elections. If Obama had done this, it would have been a crime, and falsely accusing someone of a crime is the archetype of defamation. If suing for defamation were easier, President Trump might find himself buried in lawsuits.

Loose Libel Laws Threaten Our Freedom of Speech

Making it easier to sue for libel is a terrible idea. Consider why the Supreme Court established the "actual malice" doctrine for public officials. By 1964, public officials in the South had filed nearly $300 million in libel suits against news organizations that had criticized their handling of the civil rights movement. In effect, libel law was being used as a tool to defend segregation and the denial of voting rights to African Americans. No wonder the Court took action.

Anyone who wants to see what might happen if it were easier to sue for defamation can look at Great Britain, where libel is much easier to prove than in the United States. In Britain, the defendant must prove that the statement at issue is true, whereas in the United States the plaintiff (accusing party) must prove that it is false. Court cases are expensive, which makes it easy for wealthy individuals and organizations in Britain to bankrupt writers with few resources, regardless of the merits of the claim. Do we really want that in the United States? Our strict libel laws protect our freedom of speech.

Where do you stand?

1. The Constitution prohibits slander suits against members of Congress for anything they say on the floor or in committee. Were the founders wise to insert this clause, or was it a mistake?

2. Defamation on the Internet is often anonymous. How could we respond to that problem?

Explore this issue online

- The Federalist, a conservative website, argues that President Trump doesn't understand our libel laws. Find this article by searching for "federalist trump libel."

- Lawyer Richard Zorza thinks we should have a new type of legal action to establish the truth, without penalizing those who issue falsehoods. See his argument at "zorza libel."

INTRODUCTION

The debate over libel laws, described in the chapter-opening *America at Odds* feature, is just one aspect of an important topic: the role of the media in American politics. Strictly defined, the term *media* means communication channels. It is the plural form of *medium*, as in a medium, or means, of communication. In this strict sense, any method used by people to communicate—including the telephone—is a communication medium.

In this chapter, though, we look at the **mass media**—channels through which people can communicate to large audiences. These channels include the **print media** (newspapers and magazines) and the **electronic media** (radio, television, and the Internet).

10–1 THE ROLE OF THE MEDIA IN A DEMOCRACY

LO Explain the role of the media in a democracy.

What the media say and do has an impact on what Americans think about political issues. But just as clearly, the media also *reflect* what Americans think about politics. Some scholars argue that the media are the fourth "check" in our political system—checking and balancing the power of the president, the Congress, and the courts. The power of the media today is enormous, but how the media use their power is an issue about which Americans are often at odds.

10–1a Media Characteristics

mass media
Communication channels, such as newspapers and radio and television broadcasts, through which people can communicate to large audiences.

print media
Communication channels that consist of printed materials, such as newspapers and magazines.

electronic media
Communication channels that involve electronic transmissions, such as radio, television, and the Internet.

The media are a dominant presence in our lives largely because they provide entertainment. Americans today enjoy more leisure than at any time in history, and we fill it up with e-books, movies, Web surfing, texting, and television—a huge amount of television. But the media play a vital role in our political lives as well, particularly during campaigns and elections. Politicians and political candidates have learned—often the hard way—that positive media exposure and news coverage are essential to winning votes.

One of the most important civil liberties protected in the Bill of Rights is freedom of the press. Like free speech, a free press is considered a vital tool of the democratic process. If people are to cast informed votes, they must have access to a forum in which they can discuss public affairs fully and assess the conduct and competency of their officials. The media provide this forum.

In contrast, government censorship of the press is common in many nations around the globe. One example is China, where the Web is heavily censored, even though China now has more Internet users than any other country on earth.

10–1b The New Media and the Old

From the founding of the nation through the early years of the twentieth century, all media were print media—newspapers, magazines, and books. Beginning in the twentieth century, however, new media forms were introduced. Radio and motion pictures were the initial new media, and they became important in the first half of the twentieth century.

Following World War II (1939–1945), broadcast television became the dominant form of communication. Cable television networks arrived in the 1970s. The Internet, including e-mail and the World Wide Web, came into widespread use by the general public in the 1990s.

The Decline of the Old Media   Film and radio did not displace print media in the early twentieth century. Television, though, had a much greater effect. Beginning about 1950, the number of adults reading a daily paper began to decline, although circulation remained steady due to population growth.

Later, the Internet proved to be even more devastating to newspapers. Newspaper circulation fell modestly in the 1990s. In 2006, however, circulation began to collapse, declining more than 5 percent each year. We will return to these problems later in the chapter.

Youth and the New Media   Today, millions of Americans have developed unprecedented habits of media consumption. Leaders of the movement include the wealthy and "early adopters" of new technology. Above all, the new consumers include the young. As one might expect, the upcoming generation of media users rarely read newspapers. But even television is now of lesser importance.

True, young people still watch a variety of television programs. Many of them, however, primarily view such shows online, as streaming video. Often, youth and other early adopters of new technology have "cut the cord" and abandoned cable TV service altogether in favor of online streaming. Even e-mail has been abandoned by many of today's youth. Instead, messages are transmitted through Facebook, Twitter, Tumblr, WhatsApp, and texting. For such persons, old-media personalities such as television news anchors and radio talk-show hosts are completely obsolete.

New Media versus Old Voters   Yet radio, television, and print media remain important to American politics and government. Older Americans largely rely on these more traditional media outlets, and older voters outnumber the young. As of 2018, approximately 116 million Americans were age fifty or older. The number of U.S. residents age eighteen through twenty-nine was less than half that figure. Older voters are also much more likely to turn out to vote than younger ones. Finally, some of the most enthusiastic adopters of new media are not yet eighteen and cannot vote even if they want to.

To give an example, many young people may find radio host Rush Limbaugh—with his audience largely composed of middle-aged white men—to be irrelevant to their lives. Limbaugh is not irrelevant to American politics, however. His millions of listeners vote, and they can influence the outcome of Republican presidential primaries.

In short, considering the electorate as a whole, television remains a key medium in terms of political influence. Much of this chapter, therefore, deals with the impact of television.

10-1c The Media and the First Amendment

As noted earlier, freedom of the press is essential if the media are to play their role in supporting the democratic process. The concept of freedom of the press has been applied to print media since the adoption of the Bill of Rights. Such freedoms were not, however, immediately extended to other types of media as they came into existence.

Film was one of the first types of new media to be considered under the First Amendment, and in 1915 the United States Supreme Court ruled that "as a matter of common sense," freedom of the press did not apply to the movies.[2] Radio received no protection upon its

Facebook founder Mark Zuckerberg and his wife, Dr. Priscilla Chan, in Berlin. Zuckerberg was the first person to receive the Axel Springer Award, a non-monetary prize from Germany's Axel Springer media group. The award recognizes entrepreneurship and social responsibility. *How has Facebook changed the media?*

Adam Berry/Getty Images Entertainment/Getty Images

development, and neither did television. The Court did not extend First Amendment protections to the cinema until 1952.[3] Although the Court has stated that the First Amendment is relevant to broadcast media such as radio and television, to this day it has not granted these media complete protection.

In contrast, the Court extended First Amendment protections to the Internet in 1997, in its first opportunity to rule on the issue.[4] Cable TV received substantial protections in 2000.[5]

Although First Amendment protections now clearly prohibit the U.S. government from restricting speech on the Internet, other threats exist. We examine one of them in this chapter's *The Rest of the World* feature.

10-1d The Agenda-Setting Function of the Media

One of the criticisms often levied against the media is that they play too large a role in determining the issues, events, and personalities that are in the public eye. When people take in the day's top news stories, they usually assume that these stories concern the most important issues facing the nation. In actuality, the media decide the relative importance of issues by publicizing some issues and ignoring others, and by giving some stories high priority and others low priority.

By helping to determine what people will talk and think about, the media set the *political agenda*—the issues

The Internet was created by the U.S. military through the Defense Advanced Research Projects Agency—DARPA (formerly ARPA). Soon it was opened to university researchers and later to the public at large. Censoring it was almost impossible. "The Internet interprets censorship as damage," one early administrator exalted. "We will route around you!"

The Internet Goes Global

In time, the Internet became an international—not just an American—institution. Every nation with a modern economy has embraced the Internet. Poorer countries that want to develop must do so as well. A worldwide Internet, however, means participation by unfree nations. Leaders of these nations have no interest in free speech. Given this, how can the Internet remain both free and worldwide?

Threats from Abroad

No other nation can prevent a country such as China from censoring the Internet within its own borders. But could unfree nations export their controls to the rest of the world? An Obama administration plan in 2014 fueled fear of such a development. Under the plan, the U.S. Commerce Department would give up control of the Internet Corporation for Assigned Names and Numbers (ICANN). This organization is in charge of Internet names and addresses—it is the group that decided, say, that Google would own www.google.com. Many people feared that this function would pass to a United Nations body controlled by world governments.

That would bring in China, Iran, Russia, and other repressive regimes. Power over addresses could be leveraged to support censorship. New financial rules could be crippling. Russia has proposed, for example, that Facebook, Google, and other

sites pay cable companies a fee every time someone accesses them. No one has the power to impose such rules on the United States, but the Internet could become fragmented between free and unfree nations. As a result of these concerns, ICANN independence was delayed until 2016. In that year, control of ICANN was transferred to a "geek squad" of non-political technicians headquartered in Los Angeles. Governments will have almost no input into ICANN decisions. Other Internet organizations have had such a control structure for many years.

Critical Analysis

Sites such as The Pirate Bay specialize in copyright violation. Does Internet freedom mean that a nation such as Armenia or Sweden should be allowed to permit such sites? Why or why not?

---

that politicians will address. In other words, the media are engaged in **agenda setting.** To borrow from Bernard Cohen's classic statement on the media and public opinion, the press (media) may not be successful in telling people what to think, but it is "stunningly successful in telling its readers what to think about."[6]

For example, television played a significant role in shaping public opinion about the Vietnam War (1965–1975), which has been called the first "television war." Part of the

agenda setting The ability to determine which issues are considered important by the public and by politicians.

priming An agenda-setting technique in which a media outlet promotes specific facts or ideas that may affect the public's thinking on related topics.

public opposition to the war in the late 1960s came about as a result of the daily portrayal of the war's horrors on TV news programs. Film footage and narrative accounts of the destruction, death, and suffering in Vietnam brought the war into living rooms across the United States.

Priming and Framing Two additional concepts related to agenda setting are *priming* and *framing*.

Priming. In **priming,** a television show or an Internet blogger publicizes facts or ideas that may influence how the public thinks about a particular issue. As an example of priming, if the public is informed that the general rate of taxation in the United States is lower than it has been at any time since the 1950s, people are likely to be more receptive to the idea of raising tax rates on upper-income individuals.

In contrast, if the media point out that compared with other wealthy nations, the United States collects a much larger share of its tax revenue from the upper classes, then popular responses to proposals to tax our richer citizens may be quite different.

Framing. Framing an issue involves establishing the context in which it is understood. Frames are stories about how the world works. As an example, consider the different stories that can be told about someone who is experiencing poverty. A TV news show might cover a man whose condition was, to all appearances, due primarily to bad luck. Perhaps he suffered from a life-threatening disease, could not work, lost his job, and then became homeless. This description would set up a particular frame, encouraging viewers to take a positive attitude toward social spending that would provide aid to such an individual.

Another TV report might show a woman who became addicted to alcohol or drugs at an early age, dropped out of high school, and became pregnant without a partner to help support her. Such an account could lead to an entirely different frame, which could lead to a much more skeptical attitude toward spending that benefits the poor.

Limits of Agenda Setting The degree to which the media influence public opinion is not always that clear, however. Some studies show that people filter the information they receive from the media through their own preconceived ideas about issues. People bring their own frames to political stories, in other words, and these frames can be very powerful.

Scholars who try to analyze the relationship between American politics and the media inevitably confront the chicken-and-egg conundrum: Do the media cause the public to hold certain views, or do the media merely reflect the public's views?

10–1e The Medium Does Affect the Message

Of all the media, television still has the greatest impact on most Americans, especially older ones. Television reaches almost every home in the United States. Even outside their homes, Americans can watch television—in airports, shopping malls, golf clubhouses, and medical offices. People can view television shows on their computers, and they can download TV programs to their smartphones and tablet devices and view the programs whenever and wherever they want.

The Nature of Television Coverage Today, Americans watch more television than ever, and it is the primary news source for more than 65 percent of the citizenry. As you will read shortly, politicians take maximum advantage of the power and influence of television. But does the television medium alter the presentation of political information in any way? Compare the coverage given to an important political issue by the print media— including the online sites of major newspapers and magazines—with the coverage provided by broadcast and cable TV networks. You will note some striking differences.

For one thing, the print media (particularly leading newspapers such as the *Washington Post*, the *New York Times*, and the *Wall Street Journal*) deal with an important issue in much more detail than television does. In addition to news stories based on reporters' research, you will find editorials taking positions on the issue and arguments supporting those positions. Television news, in contrast, is often criticized as being too brief and too superficial.

Time Constraints. The medium of television necessarily imposes constraints on how political issues are presented. Time is limited. News stories must be reported quickly, in only a few minutes or occasionally in only a **sound bite,** a recorded comment lasting for just a few seconds that captures a thought or a perspective and has an immediate impact on the viewers.

A Visual Medium. Television reporting also relies extensively on visual elements, rather than words, to capture the viewers' attention. Inevitably, the

> "The press may not be successful much of the time in telling people what to think, *but it is stunningly successful in telling its readers what to think about.*"
>
> ~ BERNARD C. COHEN
> AMERICAN POLITICAL SCIENTIST
> BORN 1926

framing An agenda-setting technique that establishes the context of a media report. Framing can mean fitting events into a familiar story or filtering information through preconceived ideas.

sound bite A recorded comment, lasting for only a few seconds, that captures a thought or a perspective and has an immediate impact on viewers or listeners.

photos or videos selected to depict a particular political event have exaggerated importance to viewers. The visual aspect of television contributes to its power, but it also creates a potential bias. Those watching the news presentation do not know what portions of a video being shown have been deleted, what other photos may have been taken, or whether other records of the event exist.

Television Is Big Business Today's TV networks compete aggressively with one another to air "breaking news" and to produce interesting news programs. Competition in the television industry understandably has had an effect on how the news is presented. To make profits, or even to stay in business, TV stations need viewers. And to attract viewers, the news industry has turned to "infotainment"—programs that inform and entertain at the same time. Slick sets, attractive reporters, and animated graphics that dance across the television screen are commonplace on most news programs, particularly on the cable news channels.

TV networks also compete with one another for advertising income. Although the media in the United States are among the freest in the world, their programming nonetheless remains vulnerable to the influence of their advertising sponsors.

10-1f Ownership of the Media

Concentrated ownership of media is another issue. Many mainstream media outlets are owned by giant corporations, such as Time Warner, Rupert Murdoch's News Corporation, and Disney. An often-expressed concern is that these giant corporations will influence news coverage to benefit their interests.

There is little evidence, however, that these corporations significantly influence reporting. Their media outlets do show a generalized support of the capitalist economic system, but capitalism is so widely accepted in this country that the press would probably endorse it under any form of media ownership.

In some circumstances, it may benefit a media outlet to have owners with deep pockets. Consider the *Washington Post*, one of the nation's most important publications. Like many other newspapers, the *Post* has faced serious financial difficulties. Its previous owners, aware that they did not have the means to ensure the paper's quality, sold it to Jeff Bezos, founder and chief executive officer of Amazon.com. Bezos has a record of innovation and a deep understanding of the Internet. He bought the *Post* as an individual—Amazon does not own it. Still, his wealth may allow the paper the time and resources it needs to establish a new, viable business model.

Local Monopolies Concentrated ownership may be a more serious problem at the local level than at the national level. If only one or two companies own a city's newspaper and its TV stations, these outlets may not present a diversity of opinion. Further, the owners are unlikely to air information that could be damaging either to their advertisers or to themselves, or even to publicize views that they disagree with politically. For example, TV networks have refused to run antiwar commercials created by religious groups. Still, some media observers are not particularly concerned about concentrated ownership of traditional outlets, because the Internet has generated a massive diversification of media.

The Murdoch Empire A possible exception to the claim that major corporations do not influence reporting is the Murdoch media conglomerate. Murdoch's holdings in the United States, which include the Fox television networks, the *Wall Street Journal*, and the *New York Post*, are famous for promoting conservative politics. Still, Fox News is only one voice among many in America.

Jeff Bezos, CEO of Amazon. *If Amazon instead of Bezos had bought the* Washington Post, *would the public reaction have been as positive?*

10–2 THE CANDIDATES AND TELEVISION

LO Summarize how television influences the conduct of political campaigns.

Given the TV-saturated environment in which we live, it should come as no surprise that candidates spend a great deal of time—and money—cultivating a TV presence through political ads, debates, and general news coverage. Candidates and their campaign managers realize that the time and money are well spent because television has an important impact on the way people see the candidates, understand the issues, and cast their votes.

10–2a Political Advertising

Today, televised **political advertising** consumes at least half of the total budget for a major political campaign. For the 2016 election cycle, Borrell Associates has estimated that total spending on political advertisements reached $9.8 billion.

The Arrival of Negative Advertising Political advertising first appeared on television during the 1952 presidential campaign. At that time, there were only about 15 million television sets. Today, there are as many TVs as people. Initially, political TV commercials were more or less like any other type of advertising. Instead of focusing on the positive qualities of a product, thirty-second or sixty-second ads focused on the positive qualities of a political candidate. Within the decade, however, **negative political advertising** began to appear on TV.

Personal Attack Ads Despite the barrage of criticism levied against the candidates' use of negative political ads during recent election cycles, such ads are not new. Indeed, **personal attack ads**—advertising that attacks the character of a candidate—have a long tradition. In 1800, an article in the *Federalist Gazette of the United States* described Thomas Jefferson as having a "weakness of nerves, want of fortitude, and total imbecility of character."

Recent personal attacks on opponents have been so ferocious that they make old-fashioned name-calling almost quaint. Consider the 2004 campaign by Swift Boat Veterans for Truth against John Kerry, the Democratic presidential candidate. With no evidence, the group accused Kerry, a decorated Vietnam War veteran, of lying to obtain his medals. In 2016, Hillary Clinton's ads highlighted Donald Trump's habit of making contemptuous and lewd statements about women. For his part, Trump joined other Republicans in calling Clinton a criminal for maintaining a nongovernmental e-mail server while secretary of state. (This action could have made it easier for foreign hackers to obtain classified material.) The FBI criticized Clinton but refused to bring charges. The attacks were effective. Media Matters reported that in 2016, major networks gave the e-mails almost seven times as much coverage as all policy issues put together.

Issue Ads Candidates use negative **issue ads** to focus on flaws in their opponents' positions on various issues, such as immigration and terrorism. Candidates also try to undermine their opponents' credibility by pointing to discrepancies between what the opponents say in their campaign speeches, on the one hand, and their political records, such as their voting records, on the other hand. Politicians' records are available to the public and thus can be easily verified.

Issue ads can be even more devastating than personal attacks—as Barry Goldwater learned in 1964 when his opponent in the presidential race, President Lyndon Johnson, aired the "daisy girl" ad. This ad, a marked departure from the usual negative advertising, showed a little girl standing quietly in a field of daisies. She held a daisy and pulled off the petals, counting to herself. Suddenly, a deep voice was heard counting: "10, 9, 8, 7, 6, ..." When the countdown hit zero, the unmistakable mushroom cloud of an atomic explosion filled the screen. Then President Johnson's voice was heard saying, "These are the stakes: to make a world in which all of God's children can live, or to go into the dark. We must either love each other or we must die." A message on the screen then

political advertising Advertising undertaken by or on behalf of a political candidate to familiarize voters with the candidate and his or her views on campaign issues. Also, advertising for or against policy issues.

negative political advertising Political advertising undertaken for the purpose of discrediting a candidate in voters' eyes.

personal attack ad A negative political advertisement that attacks a candidate's character.

issue ad A political advertisement that focuses on a particular issue. Issue ads can be used to support or attack a candidate's position or credibility.

Presidential candidates Donald Trump and Hillary Clinton meet at the second presidential debate in St. Louis in October 2016. *What effect did the debates have on the outcome of the race?*

read: "Vote for President Johnson on November 3." The implication, of course, was that Goldwater would lead the country into a nuclear war.

Negative Advertising—Is It Good or Bad for Our Democracy? The debate over the effect of negative advertising on our political system is ongoing. Some observers argue that negative ads can backfire. Extreme ads may create sympathy for the candidate being attacked rather than support for the attacker, particularly when the charges against the candidate being attacked are not credible. Many people fear that attack ads and "dirty tricks" used by both parties during a campaign may alienate citizens from the political process itself and thus lower voter turnout in elections.

Yet candidates and their campaign managers typically assert that they use negative advertising simply because it works. Negative TV ads are more likely than positive ads to grab the viewers' attention and make an impression. Also, according to media expert Shanto Iyengar, "the more negative the ad, the more likely it is to get free media coverage. So there's a big incentive to go to extremes."[7]

Others believe that negative advertising is a force for good because it sharpens public debate, thereby enriching the democratic process. This is the position taken by Vanderbilt University political science professor John Geer. He contends that negative ads are likely to focus on substantive political issues instead of candidates' personal characteristics. Thus, negative ads do a better job of informing the voters about important campaign issues than positive ads do.[8]

10–2b Television Debates

Televised debates have been a feature of presidential campaigns since 1960, when Republican Richard M. Nixon and Democrat John F. Kennedy squared off in four famous TV debates. Television debates provide an opportunity for voters to find out how candidates differ on issues. They also allow candidates to capitalize on the power of television to improve their images or point out the failings of their opponents.

It is widely believed that Kennedy won the first of the 1960 debates in large part because of Nixon's haggard appearance and poor makeup—many people who heard the debate on the radio thought that Nixon had done well. No presidential debates were held during the general election campaigns of 1964, 1968, or 1972, but the debates have been a part of every election since 1976.

The 1992 debates, which starred Republican George H. W. Bush and Democrat Bill Clinton, also included a third-party candidate, H. Ross Perot. Since 1996, however, the Commission on Presidential Debates, which now organizes the events, has limited the participants to candidates of the two major parties.[9] The commission also organizes debates between the vice-presidential candidates.

Early TV Debates and Election Outcomes Many contend that presidential debates help shape the outcome of elections. Others doubt that the debates—or the post-debate "spin" applied by campaign operatives and political commentators—have changed many votes. Evidence on this question is mixed.

Gallup polling figures suggest that in 1960 the debates helped Kennedy to victory. In 1980, Republican Ronald Reagan did well in a final debate with Democratic incumbent Jimmy Carter. Reagan impressed many voters with his sunny temperament, which helped dispel fears that he was a right-wing radical. In Gallup's opinion, however, Reagan would have won the election even without the debate.

More Recent Debates Later presidential debates were less conclusive. In the first 2012 debate, Democrat Barack Obama turned in a surprisingly poor performance compared to Republican Mitt Romney, but Obama still won reelection easily. In 2016, Hillary Clinton was generally regarded as the debate winner, though she ultimately lost the election. Clinton was disciplined and focused, while Trump (who refused to prepare) was, at times, almost incoherent. Clinton also recognized that Trump reacted poorly to criticism. She therefore brought up an incident in which Trump had humiliated a Miss Universe winner by calling her fat. Trump took the bait, and spent days denouncing the beauty queen. The result of the three debates was that Clinton surged from a narrow lead in the polls to a seven-percentage-point advantage.

This lead soon evaporated. Several polling experts who analyzed the results came to an interesting conclusion. Despite appearances, the debates may not actually have changed many minds. Rather, they may have altered the ways in which potential respondents reacted to pollsters. In the wake of Trump's weak performance, his supporters may have felt discouraged and relatively unwilling to talk to poll-takers. Clinton's supporters, in contrast, were energized and willing to participate. If this theory is true, swings in poll results may sometimes be artificial and not reflect voters' true attitudes.

10–2c News Coverage

Whereas political ads are expensive, coverage by the news media is free. Accordingly, the candidates try to take advantage of the media's interest in campaigns to increase the quantity and quality of news coverage. This is not always easy. Often, the media devote the lion's share of their coverage to polls and other indicators of which candidate is ahead in the race.

Managed News Coverage In recent years, candidates' campaigns have shown increasing sophistication in creating newsworthy events for journalists and TV camera crews to cover. This effort is commonly referred to as **managed news coverage.** Typically, one of the jobs of the campaign manager is to create newsworthy events that demonstrate the candidate's strong points so that the media can capture this image of the candidate.[10]

In 2015, however, one candidate was such a master at winning press attention that he hardly needed the services of a campaign manager to gain coverage. That candidate was Donald Trump, who had spent many years as a TV reality show host. As a result of Trump's sometimes outrageous comments, he won more news coverage from the top three TV networks in 2015 than any other story except the weather. According to the Tyndall Report, ABC News devoted eighty-one times as much coverage to Trump as it did to Bernie Sanders.

Spinning the Story Many aspects of a campaign focus on potential news coverage. Political consultants plan political events to accommodate the press. The campaign staff attempts to make what the candidate is doing appear interesting. The staff also knows that journalists and political reporters compete for stories and that these individuals can be manipulated. Hence, they frequently are granted favors, such as exclusive personal interviews with the candidate. Each candidate also has press advisers, often called **spin doctors,** who try to convince reporters to give the story or event a **spin,** or interpretation, that is favorable to the candidate.[11]

> "For a politician to complain about the press is like *a ship's captain complaining about the sea.*"
>
> ~ ENOCH POWELL
> BRITISH POLITICIAN
> 1912–1998

10–2d "Popular" Television

Although not normally regarded as a forum for political debate, television programs such as dramas, sitcoms, and late-night comedy shows often use political themes. For example, the popular Netflix drama *House of Cards* depicts the successes of a sleazy politician played by Kevin Spacey. *Scandal* is an ABC drama focusing on a Washington, D.C. crisis management firm, with Kerry Washington as the firm's head. In the CBS show *Madam Secretary*, Téa Leoni stars as the secretary of state. For some years now, many younger viewers have obtained information and opinions from politically oriented comedy shows. Among the most famous of these is *The Daily Show* on Comedy Central. Presenting itself as a fake news program, *The Daily Show* gained a large following under host Jon Stewart. It is now hosted by Trevor Noah.

managed news coverage News coverage that is manipulated (managed) by a campaign manager or political consultant to gain positive media exposure for a political candidate.

spin doctor A political candidate's press adviser who tries to convince reporters to give a story or event concerning the candidate a particular "spin" (interpretation, or slant).

spin A reporter's slant on, or interpretation of, a particular event or action.

Bill Pugliano/Getty Images News/Getty Images

Radio talk show host Rush Limbaugh. *What is his show like?*

HBO's *Last Week Tonight with John Oliver* is another key player in political comedy. Oliver manages to combine investigative reporting with highly vulgar humor.

CRITICAL THINKING

▶ *Media experts believe that negative political advertisements often include statements that are flatly untrue. What, if anything, should the media do when that happens?*

10-3 TALK RADIO—THE WILD WEST OF THE MEDIA

LO Explain why talk radio has been described as the Wild West of the media.

Ever since Franklin D. Roosevelt held his first "fireside chats" on radio, politicians have realized the power of that medium. From the beginning, radio has been a favorite outlet for the political right.

During the 1930s, for example, the nation's most successful radio commentator was Father Charles Edward Coughlin, a Roman Catholic priest based at the National Shrine of the Little Flower church in Royal Oak, Michigan. Coughlin's audience numbered more than 40 million listeners—in a nation that had only 123 million inhabitants in 1930. Coughlin started out as a Roosevelt supporter, but he soon moved to the far right, advocating anti-Semitism and expressing sympathy for

Adolf Hitler. Coughlin's fascist connections eventually destroyed his popularity.

Modern talk radio took off in the United States during the 1990s. In 1988, there were 200 talk-show radio stations. Today, there are more than 1,200. The growth of talk radio was made possible by the Federal Communications Commission's repeal of the fairness doctrine in 1987.

Introduced in 1949, the *fairness doctrine* required the holders of broadcast licenses to present controversial issues of public importance in a manner that was (in the commission's view) honest, equitable, and balanced. That doctrine would have made it difficult for radio stations to broadcast conservative talk shows exclusively, as many now do.

Today, five of the top six talk-radio shows, as measured by Arbitron ratings, are politically conservative. No liberal commentator ranks higher than fourteenth place in the ratings. (Several of the shows ranked higher than fourteenth are not political but deal with subjects such as personal finance and paranormal activities.)

10-3a Audiences and Hosts

The Pew Research Center for the People and the Press reports that 17 percent of the public regularly listen to talk radio. This audience is predominantly male, middle aged, and conservative. Among those who regularly listen to talk radio, 45 percent consider themselves conservatives.

Talk radio is sometimes characterized as the Wild West of the media. Talk-show hosts do not attempt to hide their political biases. If anything, they exaggerate them for effect. No journalistic conventions are observed. Leading shows, such as those of Rush Limbaugh, Sean Hannity, Andrew Wilkow, and Michael Savage, espouse a brand of conservatism that is robust, even radical. Opponents are regularly characterized as Nazis, Communists, or both at the same time. Limbaugh, for example, consistently refers to feminists as "feminazis."

Talk-show hosts sometimes appear to care more about the entertainment value of their statements than whether they are, strictly speaking, true. Hosts have often publicized fringe beliefs, such as the contention that President Barack Obama was not really born in the United States. The government of Britain actually banned Michael Savage from entry into that country based on his remarks about Muslims.

226   PART THREE: The Politics of Democracy

10-3b The Impact of Talk Radio

The overwhelming dominance of strong conservative voices on talk radio is justified by supporters as a good way to counter what they perceive as the liberal bias in the mainstream print and TV media. (We discuss the question of bias in the media in the following section.) Supporters say that such shows are simply a response to consumer demand. Those who think that talk radio is good for the country argue that talk shows, taken together, provide a great populist forum. Others are uneasy because they fear that talk shows empower fringe groups, perhaps magnifying their rage.

Those who claim that talk-show hosts go too far ultimately have to deal with the constitutional issue of free speech. While the courts have always given broad support to freedom of expression, broadcast media have been something of an exception, as mentioned earlier. The Supreme Court, for example, upheld the fairness doctrine in a 1969 ruling.[12]

Presumably, the doctrine could be reinstated. In 2009, after the Democratic victories in the 2008 elections, a few liberals advocated doing just that. President Obama and the Democratic leadership in Congress, however, quickly put an end to this notion. Americans have come to accept talk radio as part of the political environment, and any attempt to curtail it would be extremely unpopular.

> "A nation that is afraid to let its people *judge truth and falsehood in an open market* is a nation that is afraid of its people."
>
> ~ JOHN FITZGERALD KENNEDY
> THIRTY-FIFTH PRESIDENT OF THE
> UNITED STATES
> 1961–1963

CRITICAL THINKING

▶ *Why, in your opinion, have liberal commentators found it so difficult to develop successful talk-radio shows?*

10-4 THE QUESTION OF MEDIA BIAS

LO Describe types of media bias, and explain how such bias affects the political process.

The question of media bias is important in any democracy. After all, for our political system to work, citizens must be well informed. And they can be well informed only if the news media, the source of much of their information, do not slant the news. Today, however, relatively few Americans believe that the news media are unbiased in their reporting. Accompanying this perception is a notable decline in the public's confidence in the news media in recent years.

In a 2017 Gallup poll measuring the public's confidence in various institutions, only 27 percent of the respondents stated that they had "a great deal" or "quite a lot" of confidence in newspapers. Among these respondents, 24 percent had the same degree of confidence in television news. Also, only 16 percent of respondents reported a similar level of confidence in Internet news sources. Because of these low percentages, some analysts believe that the media are facing a crisis of confidence.

Despite these low figures, however, the public does believe that the press is successful in fulfilling its role as a watchdog. In a recent poll by the Pew Research Center, 68 percent of respondents agreed that "press criticism of political leaders keeps them from doing things that should not be done." Republicans, Democrats, and independents were equally likely to agree with this statement.

10-4a Partisan Bias

For years, conservatives have argued that there is a liberal bias in the media, and liberals have complained that the media reflect a conservative bias. The majority of Americans think that the media reflect a bias in one direction or another. According to a 2016 Gallup poll, 40 percent of the respondents believed that the news media favored the Democrats, whereas only 14 percent thought that the news media favored the Republicans.

The Attitudes of Journalists Surveys and analyses of the attitudes and voting habits of reporters have suggested that journalists do indeed hold liberal views. The website CampaignMoney.com has calculated that from 1999 to 2016, campaign contributors who listed their occupation as journalist or reporter gave 73 percent of their donations to Democrats. Only 14 percent of the donations went to Republicans. A Pew survey shows that among journalists working for national outlets, 34 percent described themselves as liberal and only 7 percent as conservative. In contrast, 23 percent of local reporters called themselves liberals, and 12 percent adopted the conservative label.

After hosting shows on the Fox News Channel for ten years, in 2017, Megyn Kelly joined NBC News. In 2015, Kelly took part in a feud with Republican presidential candidate Donald Trump. *Was the press unfair to Trump—or did it propel his rise with vast amounts of free publicity?*

There is substantial evidence that top journalists working for the nation's most famous newspapers and networks do tend to be liberal. Many journalists themselves perceive the *New York Times* as liberal (although an even larger number view Fox News as conservative).

Still, members of the press are likely to view themselves as moderates. In a recent study, the Pew Research Center for the People and the Press found that 64 percent of reporters in both national and local media applied the term *moderate* to themselves.

The Impact on Reporting A number of media scholars, including Kathleen Hall Jamieson, suggest that even if many reporters hold liberal views, these views are not reflected in their reporting.[13] Media analysts Debra Reddin van Tuyll and Hubert P. van Tuyll have similarly concluded that left-leaning reporters do not automatically equate to left-leaning news coverage. They point out that reporters are only the starting point for news stories. Before any story goes to print or is aired on television, it has to go through a progression of editors and perhaps even the publisher. Because employees at the top of the corporate ladder in news organizations are more right leaning than left leaning, the end result of the editorial and oversight process is more balanced coverage.[14]

Perhaps the most important protection against bias in reporting is a commitment to professionalism on the part of most journalists. Professional ethics dictate a commitment to "objectivity" and truthfulness. Reporters may sometimes violate this code, but it does have an impact.

In addition, a recent, helpful development is the growing number of fact-checking operations such as PolitiFact and FactCheck. FactCheck, for example, is a project of the Annenberg Public Policy Center of the University of Pennsylvania. Services such as these enable journalists to be more objective in identifying and cracking down on political lies and misrepresentations.

10-4b The Bias against Losers

Kathleen Hall Jamieson believes that media bias does play a significant role in shaping presidential campaigns and elections, but she argues that it is not a partisan bias. Rather, it is a bias against losers. A candidate who falls behind in the race is immediately labeled a "loser," making it even more difficult for the candidate to regain favor in the voters' eyes.[15]

Jamieson says that the media use the winner–loser framework to describe events throughout the campaigns. Even a presidential debate is regarded as a "sporting match" that results in a winner and a loser. In the days leading up to the 2016 debates, reporters focused on what each candidate had to do to "win" the debate. When each debate was over, reporters immediately speculated about who had "won," as they waited for post-debate polls to answer that question. According to Jamieson, this approach "squanders the opportunity to reinforce learning." The debates are an important source of political information for the voters, and this fact is eclipsed by the media's win–lose focus.

10-4c A Changing News Culture

Today's news culture is in the midst of change. News organizations are redefining their purpose and increasingly looking for special niches in which to build their audiences. For some, the niche is *hyperlocalism*—that is, narrowing the focus of news to the local area. For

Alex Wong/Getty Images News/Getty Images

Gwen Ifill, a news anchor with the Public Broadcasting System (PBS). Ifill, who died in November 2016, was among the most respected members of the news corps. *How is PBS different from other media sources?*

others, it is personal commentary, revolving around highly politicized TV figures such as Sean Hannity (conservative) and Rachel Maddow (liberal). In a sense, news organizations have begun to base their appeal more on *how* they cover the news and less on *what* they cover. Traditional journalism—fact-based reporting instead of opinion and punditry—is becoming a smaller part of this mix.

Another development is the move toward highly specific subject matter that appeals strongly to a limited number of viewers. Magazines have always done this— consider the many magazine titles on topics such as model railroading or home decorating. With the large number of cable channels, *narrowcasting* has become important on television as well. Networks now appeal to members of particular ethnic groups (BET—Black Entertainment Television), hobbyists (Cooking Channel), or history buffs (History Channel).

Online streaming services also provide niche programming. True, users who rely only on streaming video may have trouble accessing the most up-to-the-minute network television news shows. Overall, however, there is no shortage of late-breaking news sources online.

CRITICAL THINKING

▶ *Often, media consumers prefer outlets that confirm their own personal biases. What problems might this create for American democracy?*

10–5 POLITICAL NEWS AND CAMPAIGNS ON THE WEB

LO Indicate the extent to which the Internet is reshaping news and political campaigns.

Cyberspace is getting bigger every day. About 50 percent of the world's inhabitants currently use the Internet, a total of almost 3.8 billion people. About half of all users live in Asia. Worldwide, more than 2.5 million people access the Internet using mobile phones. In the United States, 87 percent of the population are Internet users. In addition, popular social media sites have enormous numbers of personalized pages—Twitter has about 320 million active accounts, and Facebook has almost 1.9 billion.

Not surprisingly, the Internet is a major source of information. All major newspapers are online, as are transcripts of major television news programs. About two-thirds of Internet users consider the Internet to be an important source of news. In addition, having an Internet strategy has become an integral part of political campaigning.

10-5a News Organizations Online

Almost every major news organization, both print and broadcast, delivers news through the Web. Indeed, an online presence is required to compete effectively with other traditional news companies for revenues. The online share of newspaper company revenues has increased over the years. Still, only about one-quarter of U.S. newspaper revenues come from online sources.

Characteristics of Newspaper Sites Some newspaper sites simply copy articles from their printed versions. The websites for major newspapers, however, including those for the *Washington Post* and the *New York Times*, offer a different array of coverage and options than their printed editions. Websites have a notable advantage over their printed counterparts. They can add breaking news, informing readers of events that occurred just minutes before. They can also link readers to more extensive reports on particular topics. (Many papers shy away from in-text linking, though, perhaps fearing that if readers leave the news organization's site, they might not return.)

Inadequate Revenues A major problem facing news organizations is that readers or viewers of online newspapers and news programs are typically the same people who read the printed news editions and view the news programs on TV. Web-only readers of a particular newspaper make up a relatively small percentage of those going online for their news. Therefore, investing heavily in online news delivery may not be a solution for news companies seeking to increase readership and revenues.

In fact, the additional revenues that newspapers have gained from their online editions do not come close to making up for the massive losses in advertising revenue suffered by their print editions. In many instances, publications have not sold enough advertising in their online editions even to make up for the additional expense of publishing on the Web.

Google's Dominance of Online Ad Revenue
The problem is not that there is an absolute shortage of online advertising revenue. In fact, by 2012, the advertising industry was spending more on Internet advertising than it spent on all print newspapers and magazines put together.

The real problem is that *content providers*—such as newspaper sites that hire journalists and create new material—receive a very small share of the online advertising revenue. Most of the revenue goes to *aggregators*, including search engine sites that develop little new content but mostly direct users elsewhere. Google, by far the largest of these aggregators, collects one-third of all online ad revenues.

By 2016, at $25 billion, Google's U.S. ad revenues exceeded the revenues of the entire U.S. newspaper industry. Figure 10–1 shows U.S. newspaper and online ad revenues. Of course, if the business of journalism were to collapse, Google would have little to aggregate. As of now, the cybersphere is nowhere close to resolving this issue.

10-5b Blogs and the Emergence of Citizen Journalism

As mentioned earlier, the news culture is changing, and at the heart of this change—and of much innovation in news delivery today—is the blogosphere. There has been a veritable explosion of blogs in recent years. Mainstream news organizations want to make their websites more competitive and appealing, in part to counter the influence of blogs run by private citizens and those not

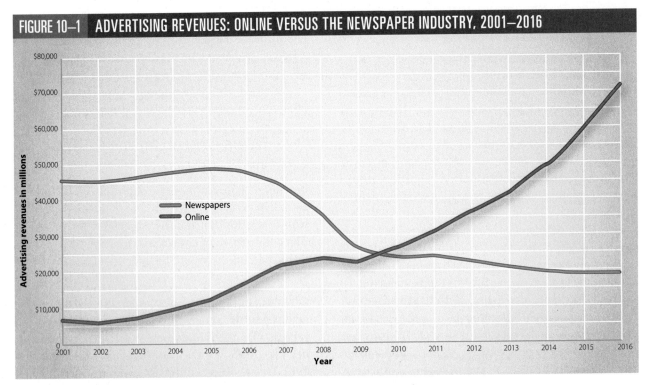

FIGURE 10–1 ADVERTISING REVENUES: ONLINE VERSUS THE NEWSPAPER INDUSTRY, 2001–2016

Sources: The Interactive Advertising Bureau and authors' calculations. Numbers are for the United States only.

in the news business. As a result, they have been adding blogs to their own websites.

Blogs are offered by independent journalists, various scholars, political activists, and the citizenry at large. Anyone can create a blog and post news or information, including videos, to share with others. Many blogs are political in nature, both reporting political developments and discussing politics. Taken as a whole, the collection, analysis, and dissemination of information online by the citizenry can be called citizen journalism. Other terms that have been used to describe the news blogosphere include *people journalism* and *participatory journalism*. When blogs focus on news and developments in a specific community, the term *community journalism* is often applied.

The increase in news blogs and do-it-yourself journalism on the Web clearly poses a threat to mainstream news sources. Compared with the operational costs faced by a major news organization, the cost of creating and maintaining blogs is trivial. Moreover, the most successful blogs are able to sell advertising. Because of their low costs, it does not take much advertising to keep such sites in business. How can major news sources adhere to their traditional standards and still compete with this new world of news generated by citizens?

10–5c Podcasting the News

Another nontraditional form of news distribution is podcasting—the distribution of audio or video files to personal computers or mobile devices, such as smartphones.[16] Though still a relatively small portion of the overall news-delivery system, podcasts are becoming increasingly popular. Almost anyone can create a podcast and make it available for downloading onto computers or mobile devices. Like blogging, podcasting is inexpensive. As you will read next, political candidates are using both blogging and podcasting as part of their Internet campaign strategies.

While podcasting, streaming video, and similar services are not expensive to offer, they do consume substantial Internet bandwidth. Is this a problem? We discuss that issue in this chapter's *Join the Debate* feature.

10–5d Cyberspace and Political Campaigns

Today's political parties and candidates realize the benefits of using the Internet to conduct online campaigns and raise funds. Voters also are increasingly using the Web to access information about parties and candidates, promote political goals, and obtain political news.

Generally, the use of the Internet is an inexpensive way for candidates to contact, recruit, and mobilize supporters, as well as to disseminate information about their positions on issues. In effect, the Internet can replace brochures, letters, and position papers. Individual voters or political party supporters can use the Internet to avoid having to go to special meetings or to a campaign site to do volunteer work or obtain information on a candidate's positions.

That the Internet is now a viable medium for communicating political information and interacting with voters was made clear in the campaigns preceding the 2016 presidential election. According to a 2016 study by the Pew Research Center, 38 percent of adults often got their news online. This statistic rose to 50 percent for the 18 to 29 age group. A full 81 percent of adults obtained news from online sources some of the time. In contrast, 20 percent of adults often got news from print newspapers, down from 27 percent in 2013. One reason for these numbers is that a majority of people who prefer to read the news now do so online. (Most of those who prefer to watch the news rather than read it continue to rely on television.) The portion of adults who obtained some of their news through a mobile device, such as a smartphone, was 72 percent, as opposed to 54 percent in 2013.

Online Fund-Raising   The Internet can be an effective—and inexpensive—way to raise campaign funds. Fund-raising on the Internet by presidential candidates became widespread after the Federal Election Commission decided, in June 1999, that the federal government could distribute matching funds for credit-card donations received by candidates through the Internet.

The Rise of the Internet Campaign   An increasingly important part of political campaigning today is the Internet campaign. Candidates typically hire Web managers to manage their Internet campaigns. The job of the Web manager, or Web strategist, is to create a well-designed, informative, and user-friendly campaign website to attract viewers, hold their attention, manage their e-mails, and track their credit-card contributions. The Web manager also hires bloggers to promote the candidate's views and arranges

citizen journalism
The collection, analysis, and dissemination of information online by independent journalists, scholars, political activists, and the general citizenry.

podcasting The distribution of audio or video files to personal computers or mobile devices, such as smartphones and tablets.

Could We Lose Our High-Speed Internet?

Most students take it for granted that they have access to high-speed Internet not only at their colleges and universities, but also in their homes. They expect to find Wi-Fi hot spots at coffee shops and other places. One of the underpinnings of Internet access is a principle known as network neutrality, or net neutrality. Under this principle, Internet service providers (ISPs), such as cable and telephone companies, are to treat all Internet traffic equally, without discrimination.

For example, if your ISP is a phone company, it can't keep you from using a competing phone-over-Internet service, such as Skype. Even more to the point, Netflix should not have to pay more for Internet access than anyone else just because it accounts for 30 percent of broadband traffic during peak hours every day. Also, no ISP should set aside a "fast lane" that allows content from favored services to load more quickly—and content from other services more slowly. Recently, the Federal Communications Commission (FCC) issued new rules to guarantee net neutrality. Not everyone, however, thinks that FCC regulations are a good idea. The Trump administration has announced plans to overturn the new rules.

Just Say No to Government Interference

Opponents of regulation point out that the Internet may have been created by the government, but it has been substantially free of regulation for decades. Now is not the time to change this system. Under the new FCC rules, ISPs would be public utilities just like companies that sell electricity or voice telephone services. ISPs such as Verizon and Comcast would not be able to charge extra for higher-speed access.

In effect, the government would tell ISPs how much they can charge for their services. Investment in Internet infrastructure would be discouraged. ISPs would lose the incentive to innovate in other ways as well. The Internet is complex. It changes all the time. No government regulator can keep up with that change. Enforced net neutrality would mean less change, less innovation, and perhaps less high-speed Internet access. In fact, major ISPs contend that broadband investment has dropped 8 percent since the FCC ruling.

Net Neutrality Means More Innovation, Not Less

Advocates of regulation contend that net neutrality is under threat by giant, monopolistic ISPs. Years ago, the number of ISPs a user could contract with was vast. No longer. A few cable and telephone companies dominate the landscape. We need regulation to keep these giants from abusing their power.

Net neutrality has lowered barriers to entry online. Entrepreneurs have been encouraged to create new services, such as Facebook, Netflix, Twitter, and YouTube. Without net neutrality rules, in the future some Internet content will get priority treatment in exchange for a fee. Other traffic will slow down. Imagine if large ISPs had been able to make videostreaming sites pay extra. YouTube would have been strangled in the crib. The Internet has always been funded by fees paid by users. These sums have paid for huge investments in infrastructure, and they will continue to do so. Major ISPs may tell the public that broadband investment is falling, but at the same time they are telling their own shareholders that investment is increasing.

Critical Analysis

Would you be willing to pay a little more for each streaming movie you watch to guarantee no interruptions? Why or why not?

---

for podcasting of campaign information and updates to supporters. The manager hires staff to monitor the Web for news about the candidates and to track the online publications of *netroots groups*. (These are online activists who support the candidate but are not controlled by the candidate's organization.)

Controlling the Netroots One of the challenges facing candidates today is delivering a consistent campaign message to voters. Netroots groups may make this task more difficult. Such a group may publish online promotional ads or other materials that do not represent a candidate's position, for instance, or attack the candidate's opponent in ways that the candidate does not approve. Yet no candidate wants to alienate these groups, because they can raise significant sums of money and garner votes for the candidate.

Candidates' 24/7 Exposure

Just as citizen journalism has altered the news culture, so have citizen videos changed the traditional campaign. For example, a candidate can never know when a comment that she or he makes may be caught on camera by someone with a cell phone or digital camera and published on the Internet for all to see.

A candidate's opponents may post a compilation of video clips showing the candidate's inconsistent comments over time on a specific topic, such as abortion or health-care reform legislation. The effect can be very damaging, because it makes the candidate's "flip-flopping" on the issue apparent.

Recent Political Gaffes

Political scientists have argued over the importance of political gaffes. Awkward comments by Mitt Romney and Barack Obama in 2012 didn't seem to have much effect on the polls. In 2016, Donald Trump constantly made statements that, based on past assumptions, should have been fatal. In reality, nothing that Trump said about politicians, journalists, Latinos and African Americans, or, for that matter, policy issues seemed to disturb loyal Republican voters. His comments about women, however, did hurt him at least somewhat. These included the tape, mentioned earlier, in which Trump boasted of his power to molest women. Thereafter, more than a dozen women stepped forward to allege that he had groped them without their consent.

Hillary Clinton was a disciplined candidate, and her list of misstatements was relatively short. A few gaffes were serious, however. One was her description of half of Trump's supporters as a "basket of deplorables." An even more damaging quote was "Because we're going to put a lot of coal miners and coal companies out of

Donald J. Trump @realDonaldTrump · Feb 2
If U.C. Berkeley does not allow free speech and practices violence on innocent people with a different point of view - NO FEDERAL FUNDS?

41K   59K   214K

Donald J. Trump @realDonaldTrump · Feb 26
Russia talk is FAKE NEWS put out by the Dems, and played up by the media, in order to mask the big election defeat and the illegal leaks!

54K   25K   115K

Donald J. Trump @realDonaldTrump · Mar 4
How low has President Obama gone to tapp my phones during the very sacred election process. This is Nixon/Watergate. Bad (or sick) guy!

105K   54K   165K

Donald Trump

Some of the more famous tweets from the Tweeter-in-Chief. *Does President Trump help or hurt himself by his use of Twitter? In either case, why?*

business, right? And we're going to make it clear that we don't want to forget those people." The problem was that Clinton seemed to be taking personal responsibility for the loss of coal jobs, when in fact almost all of them were lost to automation and competition from other energy sources, such as natural gas.

Clinton's real problem was that she disliked reporters, and they disliked her. Clinton's attitude was shaped by the decades-long effort by her opponents to find some scandal they could pin on her. Most of these scandals were bogus. Clinton's supporters were also convinced that more troublesome issues, such as her private e-mail server, had been blown out of proportion. Still, the constant barrage of bad press seriously damaged her reputation.

CRITICAL THINKING

▶ *To what extent do the media—in particular, the new media—encourage political participation? To what extent might they discourage participation by providing nonpolitical entertainment?*

 **Politics and the Media**

Americans love to hate the media, possibly because we spend so much time watching and reading them. Without a doubt, the media are undergoing a revolution today. With the loss of classified ads to the Internet, newspapers are in serious financial jeopardy. Online news sources, meanwhile, have yet to hit upon a reliable method of generating adequate income. In this changing environment, Americans are at odds over a number of media topics:

- *Do the difficulties faced by print media threaten the existence of competent journalism—or is this not an important problem?*

- *Is the media's agenda-setting function a vital contribution to the democratic process—or an improper attempt to manipulate viewers?*

- *Should protection of the First Amendment be extended to broadcast media without exception—or would such a move threaten the morals of the country and make it impossible for viewers to avoid sexual content?*

- *Are negative advertisements an inevitable and unremarkable aspect of political campaigns—or should the voters punish politicians who employ them?*

- *Does talk radio add to the vigor of our political discourse—or is it a corrupting influence that divides the nation?*

- *Do the mainstream media have a liberal bias—or do they merely publicize facts that do not square with conservative beliefs?*

STUDY TOOLS 10

READY TO STUDY? IN THE BOOK, YOU CAN:

☐ Review what you've read with the following chapter quiz.

☐ Check your answers in Appendix D at the back of the book.

☐ Rip out the Chapter Review Card, which includes key terms and chapter summaries.

ONLINE AT WWW.CENGAGEBRAIN.COM, YOU CAN:

☐ Watch videos to get a quick overview.

☐ Expedite your studying with Major Player readings and Focus Activities.

☐ Check your understanding with Chapter Quizzes.

FILL-IN

Learning Outcome 10–1

1. _____ is an agenda-setting technique in which a media outlet promotes specific facts or ideas that may affect the public's thinking on related topics.

2. Of all the media, _____ still has the greatest impact on most Americans.

3. A sound bite is _____.

4. Newspapers today are in financial difficulty because _____.

Learning Outcome 10–2

5. The first televised presidential debate, between _____, took place in 1960.

6. Spin doctors are _____.

Learning Outcome 10–3

7. The talk-radio audience is predominantly _____.

8. Talk radio is sometimes characterized as the Wild West of the media because _____.

Learning Outcome 10–4

9. It has been suggested that the media use the winner–loser framework to describe events throughout the campaigns, contributing to a bias against _____.

Learning Outcome 10–5

10. Citizen journalism refers to _____.

11. The principle that Internet service providers should treat all traffic equally is called _____.

12. When a politician uses poorly chosen words, we refer to this as a/an _____.

MULTIPLE CHOICE

Learning Outcome 10–1

13. In the news business, framing refers to
    a. fitting events into a familiar story or filtering information through preconceived ideas.
    b. news coverage that is managed by a political consultant to gain media exposure for a political candidate.
    c. narrowing the focus of news to the local area.

Learning Outcome 10–2

14. The 1964 "daisy girl" ad is an example of
    a. a personal attack ad.
    b. citizen journalism.
    c. a negative issue ad.

Learning Outcome 10–3

15. Modern talk radio took off in the United States during the
    a. 1930s, after Franklin Roosevelt's first "fireside chat."
    b. 1950s, after political advertising first appeared on television.
    c. 1990s, after the repeal of the fairness doctrine.

Learning Outcome 10–4

16. In a 2016 Gallup poll measuring the public's confidence in various institutions, _____ percent of the respondents stated that they had a "great deal" or "quite a lot" of confidence in television news.
    a. 67
    b. 42
    c. 24

Learning Outcome 10–5

17. _____ refers to the distribution of audio or video files to personal computers or mobile devices, such as smartphones.
    a. Blogging
    b. Podcasting
    c. Narrowcasting

11 | THE CONGRESS

JIM LO SCALZO/AFP/Getty Images

LEARNING OUTCOMES

After reading this chapter, you should be able to:

11-1 Explain how seats in the House of Representatives are apportioned among the states.

11-2 Describe the power of incumbency.

11-3 Identify the key leadership positions in Congress, describe the committee system, and indicate some important differences between the House of Representatives and the Senate.

11-4 Summarize the specific steps in the lawmaking process.

11-5 Identify Congress's oversight functions, and explain how Congress fulfills them.

11-6 Indicate what is involved in the congressional budgeting process.

After finishing this chapter, go to **PAGE 259** for **STUDY TOOLS**

AMERICA AT ODDS

Should It Take Sixty Senators to Pass Important Legislation?

Dtitstudio/Shutterstock.com

The number of Senate votes required to force an end to a *filibuster* is sixty. A filibuster takes place when senators use the chamber's tradition of unlimited debate to block legislation. In years past, filibustering senators would speak for hours on a proposed bill. In recent decades, however, Senate rules have permitted filibusters in which actual continuous floor speeches are not required. Senators merely announce that they are filibustering.

The threat of a filibuster has created an *ad hoc* rule that important legislation needs the support of sixty senators. (There are exceptions. Budget bills can be handled using a special *reconciliation* rule that does not permit filibusters.) If one party can elect sixty or more U.S. senators, and if they all follow the party line, they can force through any legislation they want. The Democrats, in fact, enjoyed a supermajority in the Senate for seven months, from July 7, 2009, until February 4, 2010, when they lost a seat in a special election.

Are sixty votes an appropriate requirement for passing important legislation in the Senate?

Don't Let the Majority Trample on the Minority

In the course of our history, the filibuster in the U.S. Senate has served us well. Filibusters provide the minority with an effective means of preventing the majority from ramming legislation down the throats of American voters.

A simple majority does not signify an adequate degree of consensus. It takes two-thirds of both chambers of Congress to override a veto by the president. That's another supermajority. Changing the Constitution requires three-quarters of the state legislatures. If these supermajority rules were good enough for the founders, then the principle still is good enough for the Senate.

In the past, the American public has supported the filibuster in public opinion polls—for good reason. One of the most important characteristics of our political system is that it is not easy to create new laws. The existence of two chambers of Congress—and the president's veto power—ensures this. The Senate was always meant to be a body that could delay legislation. Further, in 2013, the Senate changed the rules so that filibusters don't apply to votes on whether to approve most presidential appointees. In 2017, filibusters of Supreme Court nominees were ruled out as well. That should be more than enough reform.

Don't Let Obstructionists Determine Legislation

Supermajority rules allow a minority to block the preference of the majority. Even James Madison, who worried about the tyranny of the majority over the minority, recognized the opposite possibility. He said that "the fundamental principle of free government" might be reversed by requiring supermajorities. "It would be no longer majority that would rule: the power would be transferred to the minority."

Madison's warning has been amply justified. At one time, the filibuster was reserved for the defense of major principles. Not all of these principles were laudable—the filibuster was used to defend Jim Crow laws and to prevent African Americans from voting in much of the South. Still, the procedure was rare. Today, it is used for most legislation.

In recent years, the major parties have become politically unified and monolithic. Members of the minority are prepared to cast party-line votes to frustrate the will of the majority on most legislation. Such votes make governance almost impossible. Congress has never passed so few bills in each session as it did during President Obama's second term.

The Senate should reduce the votes required to end a filibuster to a majority of those present.

Where do you stand?

1. Why might it be appropriate to require supermajority voting for important legislation?
2. Under what circumstances do supermajority voting rules prevent democracy from being fully realized?

Explore this issue online:

- You can find out more about the filibuster by entering "filibuster" into a search engine.
- For discussions on how the filibuster has been limited recently, search on "nuclear option."

INTRODUCTION

Congress is the lawmaking branch of government. When someone says, "There ought to be a law," at the federal level it is Congress that will make that law. The framers had a strong mistrust of powerful executive authority. Consequently, they made Congress—not the executive branch (the presidency)—the central institution of American government. Still, the founders created a system of checks and balances to ensure that no branch of the federal government, including Congress, could exercise too much power.

Many Americans view Congress as a largely faceless, anonymous legislative body that is quite distant and removed from their everyday lives. Yet the people you elect to Congress represent and advocate for your interests at the very highest level of power.

Furthermore, the laws created by the men and women in the U.S. Congress affect the daily lives of every American in one way or another. Learning about your congressional representatives and how they are voting in Congress on issues that concern you is an important step toward becoming an informed voter. Even the details of how Congress makes law—such as the Senate rules described in the chapter-opening *America at Odds* feature—should be of interest to the savvy voter.

11-1 THE STRUCTURE AND MAKEUP OF CONGRESS

LO Explain how seats in the House of Representatives are apportioned among the states.

The framers agreed that the Congress should be the "first branch of the government," as James Madison said, but they did not immediately agree on its organization. Ultimately, they decided on a *bicameral legislature*—a Congress consisting of two chambers. This was part of the Great Compromise during the drafting of the Constitution.

The framers favored a bicameral legislature so that the two chambers, the House and the Senate, might serve as checks on each other's power. The House was to represent the people. The Senate was to represent the states

apportionment The distribution of House seats among the states on the basis of their respective populations.

congressional district The geographic area that is served by one member in the House of Representatives.

and would protect the interests of small states by giving them the same number of senators (two per state) as the larger states.

11-1a Apportionment of House Seats

The Constitution provides for the **apportionment** (distribution) of House seats among the states on the basis of their respective populations. States with larger populations, such as California, have many more representatives than states with smaller populations, such as Wyoming. California, for example, currently has fifty-three representatives in the House. Wyoming has only one.

Every ten years, House seats are reapportioned based on the outcome of the decennial (ten-year) census conducted by the U.S. Census Bureau. Each state is guaranteed at least one House seat, no matter what its population. Today, seven states have only one representative.[1] The District of Columbia, American Samoa, Guam, the Northern Mariana Islands, and the U.S. Virgin Islands all send nonvoting delegates to the House. Puerto Rico, a self-governing possession of the United States, is represented by a nonvoting resident commissioner.

11-1b Congressional Districts

Whereas senators are elected to represent all of the people in a state, representatives are elected by the voters of a particular area known as a **congressional district.** The Constitution makes no provisions for congressional districts. In the early 1800s, each state had the right to decide whether to have districts at all.

Most states set up single-member districts, in which voters in each district elected one of the state's representatives. In states that chose not to have districts, representatives were chosen at large, from the state as a whole. In 1842, however, Congress passed an act that required all states to send representatives to Congress from single-member districts.

The Size of the House   For many years, the number of House members increased as the population expanded. In 1929, however, a federal law fixed House membership at 435. Thus, today the 435 members of the House are chosen by the voters in 435 separate congressional districts across the country. If a state's population allows it to have only one representative, the entire state is one congressional district. In contrast, states with large populations have many districts. California's population, for example, entitles it to send fifty-three representatives to the House, so it has fifty-three congressional districts.

As a result of the rule limiting the size of the House to 435 members, U.S. congressional districts on average now have very substantial populations—about 780,000 people each.

The Requirement of Equal Representation

By default, the lines of the congressional districts are drawn by the state legislatures. Alternatively, the task may be handed off to a designated body such as an independent commission.[2] States must meet certain requirements in drawing district boundaries. To ensure equal representation in the House, districts in a given state must contain, as nearly as possible, equal numbers of people. Additionally, each district must have contiguous boundaries and must be "geographically compact," although this last requirement is not enforced very strictly.

Representative Tulsi Gabbard (D., Calif.) speaks at a concert on behalf of presidential candidate Bernie Sanders in 2016. Gabbard is the nation's first Hindu congresswoman. *Why might Asian Americans tend to back Democrats?*

Past Abuses. If congressional districts are not made up of equal populations, people's votes are not equally valuable. In the past, state legislators often used this fact to their advantage. For example, traditionally, many state legislatures were controlled by rural areas. By drawing districts that were not equal in population, rural leaders attempted to curb the number of representatives from growing urban centers. At one point in the 1960s, in many states the largest district had twice the population of the smallest district. In effect, this meant that a person's vote in the largest district had only half the value of a person's vote in the smallest district.

The Supreme Court Addresses the Issue. For some time, the United States Supreme Court refused to address this problem. In 1962, however, the Court ruled that the Tennessee state legislature's **malapportionment** was an issue that could be heard in the federal courts because it affected the constitutional requirement of equal protection under the law.[3] Two years later, the Supreme Court held that congressional districts must have equal populations.[4] This principle has come to be known as the **"one person, one vote" rule.** In other words, one person's vote has to count as much as another's vote.

Gerrymandering

Although in the 1960s the Supreme Court ruled that congressional districts must be equal in population, it continued to be silent on the issue of gerrymandered districts. **Gerrymandering**

occurs when a district's boundaries are drawn to maximize the influence of a certain group or political party.

Where a party's voters are scarce, the boundaries of a district can be drawn to include as many of the party's voters as possible. Where the party is strong, the lines are drawn so that the opponent's supporters are spread across two or more districts, thus diluting the opponent's strength. (The term *gerrymandering* was originally used to describe the district lines drawn to favor the party of Governor Elbridge Gerry of Massachusetts prior to the 1812 elections—see Figure 11–1.)

Although there have been constitutional challenges to political gerrymandering, the practice continues.[5] It was certainly evident following the 2010 census. Sophisticated computer programs were now able to analyze the partisan leanings of individual neighborhoods and city blocks. District lines were drawn to "pack" the opposing party's voters into the smallest number of districts

malapportionment
A situation in which the voting power of citizens in one district is greater than the voting power of citizens in another district.

"one person, one vote" rule A rule, or principle, requiring that congressional districts have equal populations so that one person's vote counts as much as another's vote.

gerrymandering The drawing of a legislative district's boundaries in such a way as to maximize the influence of a certain group or political party.

FIGURE 11–1   THE FIRST "GERRYMANDER"

Prior to the 1812 elections, the Massachusetts legislature divided up Essex County in a way that favored Governor Elbridge Gerry's party. The result was a district that looked something like a salamander (a mythical monster, not the amphibian). A newspaper editor of the time referred to it as a "gerrymander," and the name stuck. *Gerry was a Federalist. Why might that party have been tempted to take extreme measures to ensure election in 1812?*

Source: *Congressional Quarterly's Guide to Congress*, 3d ed. (Washington, D.C.: Congressional Quarterly Press, 1982), p. 695.

or "crack" the opposing party's voters into several different districts. Packing and cracking make congressional races less competitive.

How Gerrymandering Works.   For a better understanding of how gerrymandering works, look at the examples in Figure 11–2. In the examples, sixty-four voters must be distributed among four districts, each of which will have a population of sixteen. The two political parties are the O Party and the X Party.

In Example 1, each district contains only one kind of voter. This type of gerrymander is sometimes created when a state legislature is more interested in preserving the seats of incumbents than in benefiting a particular party. In this case, it would be almost impossible for a sitting member to lose in a general election.

minority-majority district A district in which minority groups make up a majority of the population.

In Example 2, every district is divided evenly between the parties. The slightest swing toward one of the parties could give that party all four seats. A legislature would almost never come up with these boundaries, but an independent redistricting board might do so.

Example 3 is a partisan gerrymander favoring the X Party. The district in the lower right is an example of packing—the maximum possible number of O voters is packed into the district. In the other three districts, O Party supporters are cracked apart so that they do not have a majority in any of the districts. In these districts, the X Party has majorities of eleven to five, ten to six, and eleven to five.

Gerrymandering after the 2010 Census.   The 2010 elections were a Republican triumph, and the party won control of state legislatures across the country. These victories occurred just before the states were required to redraw the boundaries of congressional districts following the 2010 census. The result was a large number of Republican gerrymanders, which had a substantial effect on the 2012 elections. In these elections, Democratic candidates for the U.S. House actually collected more votes than Republican candidates. The Democrats picked up only eight seats, however. In the end, the partisan breakdown was 200 Democrats and 235 Republicans.

Consider Pennsylvania, which went for Barack Obama by 5.4 percentage points in 2012. Pennsylvania voters cast 2.72 million votes for Democratic House candidates and 2.65 million votes for Republicans. These votes elected five Democratic representatives and thirteen Republicans—even though more votes were cast for Democrats. The Republicans look set to enjoy the fruits of their 2010 redistricting for years to come.

As you might expect, the Democrats also engaged in gerrymandering when they had a chance. Illinois is one example. The geography of that state, however, limited the effects of the Democratic gerrymander. So many Democrats are concentrated in Chicago that it was impossible to draw district boundaries that would let the city elect any more Democrats than it was already electing. The concentration of Democrats in large cities was a problem for the party in many other states as well.

Racial Gerrymandering.   Although political gerrymandering has a long history, gerrymandering to empower minority groups is a relatively new phenomenon. In the early 1990s, the U.S. Department of Justice instructed state legislatures to draw district lines to maximize the voting power of minority groups. As a result, several **minority-majority districts** were created. Many

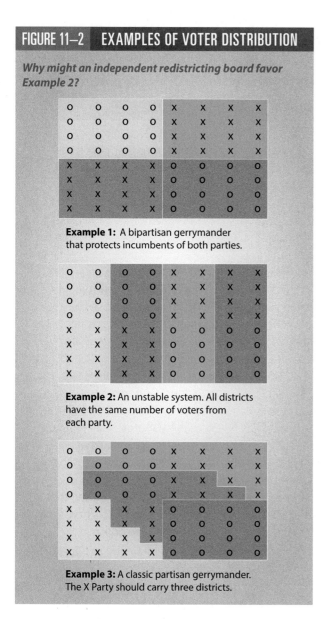

FIGURE 11-2 EXAMPLES OF VOTER DISTRIBUTION

Why might an independent redistricting board favor Example 2?

Example 1: A bipartisan gerrymander that protects incumbents of both parties.

Example 2: An unstable system. All districts have the same number of voters from each party.

Example 3: A classic partisan gerrymander. The X Party should carry three districts.

of these districts took on bizarre shapes. For example, North Carolina's newly drawn Twelfth Congressional District was 165 miles long—a narrow strip that, for the most part, followed Interstate 85.

Limits on Racial Gerrymandering. The practice of racial gerrymandering has generated heated arguments on both sides of the issue. Some groups contend that minority-majority districts are necessary to ensure equal representation of minority groups, as mandated by the Voting Rights Act of 1965. They further contend that these districts have been instrumental in increasing the number of African Americans holding political office. Before 1990, redistricting plans in the South often created only white-majority districts.[6]

Opponents of racial gerrymandering argue that such race-based districting is unconstitutional because it violates the equal protection clause. In a series of cases in the 1990s, the Supreme Court agreed and held that when race is the dominant factor in the drawing of congressional district lines, the districts are unconstitutional and must be redrawn.[7]

In 1996, for example, the Supreme Court rejected North Carolina's Twelfth District as unconstitutional. In 2001, the Court backed off somewhat and accepted a redrawn version of the district. In 2017, however, the Court toughened its position and rejected both North Carolina's Twelfth District and the First District as well.[8] The Court also clarified, however, that it does not currently object to purely partisan gerrymanders.

11-1c The Representation Function of Congress

Of the three branches of government, Congress has the closest ties to the American people. Members of Congress represent the interests and wishes of the constituents in their home states. At the same time, they must also consider larger national issues, such as the economy and the environment. Often, legislators find that the interests of their constituents are at odds with the demands of national policy.

For example, limits on emissions of carbon dioxide may help reduce climate change, to the benefit of all Americans and the people of the world generally. Yet consider members of Congress who come from states where most electricity comes from coal-burning power plants. These legislators may fear that new laws would hurt the local economy and cause companies to lay off workers.

All members of Congress face difficult votes that set representational interests against lawmaking realities. There are several views on how legislators should decide such issues.

The Trustee View of Representation Some believe that representatives should act as **trustees** of the broad interests of the entire society, rather than serving only the narrow interests of their constituents. Under the trustee view, a legislator should act according to her or his conscience and perception of national needs. For example, a senator from North Carolina might support laws regulating cigarette sales, even though the state's economy could be negatively affected.

> **trustee** A representative who tries to serve the broad interests of the entire society and not just the narrow interests of his or her constituents.

JOIN THE DEBATE

Was Banning Pork-Barrel Spending a Mistake?

Congress has voted to fund a "bridge to nowhere" in Alaska and a program to combat wild hogs in Missouri. Such special interest legislation is called pork-barrel spending—members of Congress "bring home the bacon" this way to benefit local businesses and workers.

Formally, an item of pork is called an earmark. The Congressional Research Service defines earmarks as spending provisions that apply to a very limited number of individuals or entities. The Office of Management and Budget defines earmarks as direct allocations of funds that bypass merit-based or competitive processes of the executive branch. In 2010, after winning control of the U.S. House, Republicans announced that they would ban earmarks that benefited specific individuals or corporations. (Earmarks that benefit local governments are still allowed.) This ban was widely applauded at the time. Since then, however, some people have had second thoughts.

Pork Is a Necessary Part of a Democratic System

Those who defend earmarks contend that Congress has a right to determine who benefits from government spending. After all, directing money to particular purposes is a core constitutional function of Congress. Senators and members of the House know their states and districts. Why shouldn't they play a role in funding local projects?

Another argument for pork is that it can help heal a broken Congress. Political polarization between Republicans and Democrats is not the only problem. The Republicans themselves are divided between mainstream conservatives and Freedom Caucus radicals. The Freedom Caucus is large enough that a Republican Speaker cannot pass legislation with mainstream conservatives alone. As former Speaker John Boehner said, "It's not like the old days. Without earmarks to offer, it's hard to herd the cats." Earmarks used to be the lubricant that allowed Congress to do its work. We need them back.

No Thanks—Pork Is Corruption

Opponents of earmarks reject a system in which legislators can be bribed to vote with the leadership. Laws should stand or fall on their own merits. Further, pork is a key component of excessive government spending. The cost of the earmarks themselves may not seem that large. But as Senator Tom Coburn (R., Okla.) has put it, earmarks are "the gateway drug to spending addiction in Washington."

Advocates of pork forget that the pork ban wasn't imposed on a reluctant Congress by outside reformers. Republicans in the House are responsible for the ban. These Republicans are typically elected from safe seats and don't need to bribe the voters back home. Rather, they worry about primary challenges from more conservative opponents. What better way to show that you are a conservative purist than by refusing pork? Further, the restrictions are not even that strict—many legislators have found ways around the pork ban.

Critical Analysis

If the president inserts special requests into executive funding proposals, is that also pork? Why or why not?

---

instructed delegate
A representative who deliberately mirrors the views of the majority of his or her constituents.

earmark Spending provision inserted into legislation that benefits only a small number of people.

The Instructed-Delegate View of Representation In contrast, others believe that members of Congress should behave as **instructed delegates.** The instructed-delegate view requires representatives to mirror the views of their constituents, regardless of their opinions. Under this view, a senator from Nebraska would strive to obtain subsidies for corn growers, and a representative from the Detroit area would seek to protect the automobile industry.

Legislators who are acting as instructed delegates are particularly likely to try to insert language into various bills that would benefit special interests back home. Such provisions are called **earmarks,** or pork-barrel legislation. We provide greater detail on earmarks in this chapter's *Join the Debate* feature.

The Partisan View of Representation Because the political parties often take different positions on legislative issues, there are times when members of Congress are very attentive to the wishes of the party leadership. Especially on matters that are controversial, the Democratic members of Congress will be more likely to vote in favor of policies endorsed by a Democratic president, while Republicans will be more likely to oppose them.

Typically, members of Congress combine these three approaches to representation. Legislators may take a trustee approach on some issues, adhere to the instructed-delegate view on other matters, and follow the party line on still others.

CRITICAL THINKING

▶ *Some states have tried to prevent gerrymandering by establishing independent redistricting commissions. What kinds of individuals should serve on such commissions? Why?*

 11–2 **CONGRESSIONAL ELECTIONS**

LO Describe the power of incumbency.

The U.S. Constitution requires that representatives to Congress be elected every second year by popular vote. Senators are elected every six years, also by popular vote (since the ratification of the Seventeenth Amendment). Under Article I, Section 4, of the Constitution, state legislatures control the "Times, Places and Manner of holding Elections for Senators and Representatives." Congress, however, "may at any time by Law make or alter such Regulations." You can see the results of the 2016 House elections in Figure 11–3.

11–2a Who Can Be a Member of Congress?

The Constitution sets forth only a few qualifications that those running for Congress must meet. To be a member of the House, a person must have been a citizen of the

FIGURE 11–3 MEMBERS OF THE U.S. HOUSE FOLLOWING THE 2016 ELECTIONS

Each dot represents one congressional district. Red dots show a Republican representative, and blue dots show a Democrat. In three metropolitan areas—Chicago, Los Angeles, and New York—the dots on the main map overlap so much that many of them are hidden. That is the reason for the three metro area close-ups. *Why might the Democratic vote be so concentrated in urban areas?*

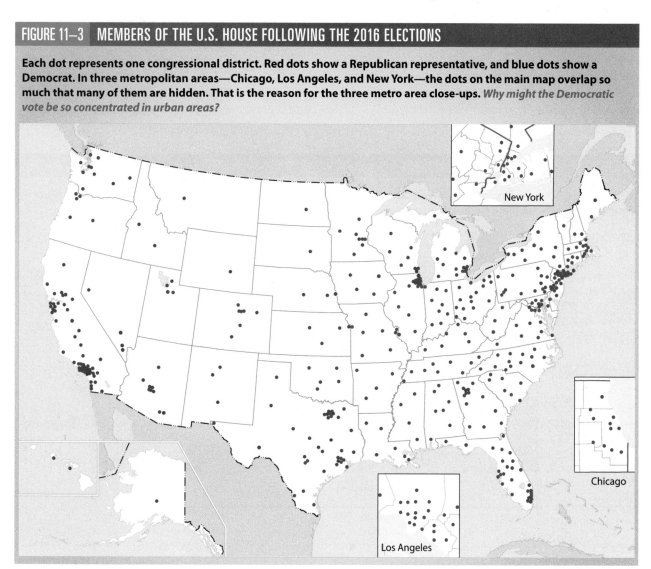

United States for at least seven years before his or her election, must be a legal resident of the state from which he or she is to be elected, and must be at least twenty-five years of age.

To be elected to the Senate, a person must have been a citizen for at least nine years, must be a legal resident of the state from which she or he is to be elected, and must be at least thirty years of age. The Supreme Court has ruled that neither the Congress nor the states can add to these three qualifications.[9]

Once elected to Congress, a senator or representative receives an annual salary from the government—$174,000 for rank-and-file members as of 2018. He or she also enjoys certain perks and privileges. Additionally, if a member of Congress wants to run for reelection in the next congressional elections, that person's chances are greatly enhanced by the power that incumbency brings to a reelection campaign.

11–2b The Power of Incumbency

An *incumbent* is someone who is already in office. The power of incumbency has long been noted in American politics. Typically, incumbents win so often and by such large margins that some observers have claimed that our electoral system involves something similar to a hereditary entitlement. As you can see in Figure 11–4, most incumbents in Congress are reelected if they run.

Incumbent politicians enjoy several advantages over their opponents. A key advantage is their fund-raising ability. Most incumbent members of Congress have a much larger network of contacts, donors, and lobbyists than their opponents have. Incumbents raise, on average, twice as much in campaign funds as their challengers. Other advantages that incumbents can put to work to aid their reelection include:

▶ *Professional staffs.* Members have large administrative staffs both in Washington, D.C., and in their home districts.

▶ *Lawmaking power.* Members can back legislation that will benefit their states or districts and then campaign on that legislative record in the next election.

▶ *Access to the media.* Because they are elected officials, members have many opportunities to stage events for the press and thereby obtain free publicity.

▶ *Name recognition.* Incumbent members are usually far better known to the voters than are challengers.

Critics argue that the advantages enjoyed by incumbents reduce the competition necessary for a healthy democracy. These incumbency advantages also serve to suppress voter turnout. Voters are less likely to turn out when an incumbent candidate is practically guaranteed reelection.

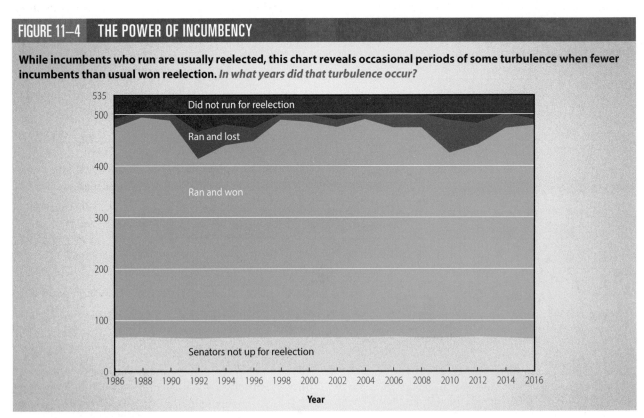

FIGURE 11–4   THE POWER OF INCUMBENCY

While incumbents who run are usually reelected, this chart reveals occasional periods of some turbulence when fewer incumbents than usual won reelection. *In what years did that turbulence occur?*

Sources: Norman Ornstein, Thomas E. Mann, and Michael J. Malbin, *Vital Statistics on Congress, 2001–2002* (Washington, D.C.: The AEI Press, 2002); and authors' updates.

11–2c Congressional Terms

As noted earlier, members of the House of Representatives serve two-year terms, and senators serve six-year terms. This means that every two years we hold congressional elections: the entire House of Representatives and a third of the Senate are up for election. In January of every odd-numbered year, a "new" Congress convenes (of course, two-thirds of the senators are not new, and most House incumbents are reelected, so they are not new to Congress either). Each Congress has been numbered consecutively, dating back to 1789. The Congress that convened in 2017 was the 115th.

Congressional Sessions Each congressional term is divided into two regular sessions, one for each year. Until about 1940, Congress remained in session for only four or five months, but the complicated rush of legislation and the public's increased demand for services in recent years have forced Congress to remain in session through most of each year.[10] Both chambers, however, schedule short recesses, or breaks, for holidays and vacations. The president may call a *special session* during a recess, but because Congress now meets on nearly a year-round basis, such sessions are rare.

Term Limits Due to the Twenty-second Amendment, the president can serve for no more than two terms in office. There is no limit on the number of terms a senator or representative can serve, however. For example, Robert Byrd (D., W.V.) served more than fifty-two years in the U.S. Senate, from 1959 until he died in June 2010, at the age of ninety-two. Some observers favor term limits for members of Congress. The Supreme Court, however, has ruled that state-level attempts to impose term limits on members of the U.S. House or Senate are unconstitutional.[11]

CRITICAL THINKING

▶ *What benefits could a state hope to gain from representation by a long-serving legislator?*

11–3 CONGRESSIONAL LEADERSHIP, THE COMMITTEE SYSTEM, AND BICAMERALISM

LO Identify the key leadership positions in Congress, describe the committee system, and indicate some important differences between the House of Representatives and the Senate.

The Constitution provides for the presiding officers of both the House and the Senate, and each chamber has added other leadership positions as it has seen fit. Leadership and organization in both chambers are based on membership in the two major political parties. The majority party in each chamber chooses the major officers of that chamber, controls debate on the floor, selects all committee chairpersons, and has a majority on all committees.

11–3a House Leadership

The Constitution states that members of the House are to choose their Speaker and other officers but says nothing more about these positions. Today, important "other officers" include the majority and minority leaders and whips.

Speaker of the House Chief among the leaders in the House of Representatives is the **Speaker of the House.** This office is filled by a vote taken at the beginning of each congressional term. The Speaker has traditionally been a member of the majority party who has risen in rank and influence through years of service in the House. The candidate for Speaker is selected by the majority-party caucus. The House as a whole then approves the selection.

Powers of the Speaker. As the presiding officer of the House and the leader of the majority party, the Speaker has a great deal of power. In the nineteenth century, the Speaker had even more authority. Speakers known by such names as "Uncle Joe Cannon" and "Czar Reed" ruled the House with a firm hand. A revolt in 1910 reduced the Speaker's powers and gave some of them to various committees. Nevertheless, the Speaker still has many important powers, including the following:

▶ The Speaker has substantial control over what bills are assigned to which committees.

▶ The Speaker may preside over the sessions of the House, recognizing or ignoring members who wish to speak.

▶ The Speaker votes in the event of a tie, interprets and applies House rules, rules on points of order (questions about procedures asked by members), puts questions to a vote, and interprets the outcome of most of the votes taken.

▶ The Speaker plays a major role in making important committee member assignments.

▶ The Speaker schedules bills for action.

When the Speaker Votes. The Speaker may choose whether to vote on any

> **Speaker of the House**
> The presiding officer in the House of Representatives. The Speaker is a member of the majority party and is the most powerful member of the House.

measure. If the Speaker chooses to vote, he or she appoints a temporary presiding officer (called a Speaker *pro tempore*), who then occupies the Speaker's chair. The Speaker does not often vote. Under the House rules, the only time the Speaker *must* vote is to break a tie. Otherwise, a tie automatically defeats a bill. On rare occasions, this rule creates an opportunity for the Speaker. If, by choosing to vote, the Speaker actually *creates* a tie, the proposal will be defeated.

From John Boehner to Paul Ryan. The powers of the Speaker are considerable, and they come with responsibilities for the effective management of the House. Such management is not always easy. For example, members of the ultraconservative Freedom Caucus tried to pass legislation that President Obama—or even the Senate—would never have accepted. To accomplish its goals, the Freedom Caucus has been willing to disrupt the normal functions of government. This tactic created major problems for Speaker John Boehner of Ohio, who resigned in frustration in October 2015. To replace Boehner, Republican leaders prevailed upon Paul Ryan of Wisconsin to become Speaker—a job he did not want. Ryan, the Republican vice-presidential candidate in 2012, had won respect as a policy leader during his time as chair of the House Budget Committee.

> **majority leader** The party leader elected by the majority party in the House or in the Senate
>
> **minority leader** The party leader elected by the minority party in the House or in the Senate.
>
> **whip** A member of Congress who assists the majority or minority leader in the House or in the Senate in managing the party's legislative program.

The Freedom Caucus gave the Speaker political heartburn even after the inauguration of President Trump. Its members refused to vote for a replacement to the Affordable Care Act (Obamacare) because they found the bill to be too generous. Republican moderates opposed it because it was too stingy. In the end, Speaker Ryan toughened the bill enough for most of the Freedom Caucus and intimidated many moderates into supporting it. The bill passed by the narrowest of margins. (The replacement effort later died in the Senate.)

Majority Leader The **majority leader** of the House is elected by the majority-party caucus to act as spokesperson for the party and to keep the party together. The majority leader's job is to help plan the party's legislative program, organize other party members to support legislation favored by the party, and make sure the chairpersons on the many committees finish work on bills that are important to the party.

Minority Leader The House **minority leader** is the leader of the minority party. Although not as powerful as the majority leader, the minority leader has similar responsibilities. The primary duty of the minority leader is to maintain solidarity within the minority party. The minority leader persuades members to follow the party's position and organizes fellow party members in criticism of the majority party's policies and programs.

Whips The leadership of each party includes assistants to the majority and minority leaders known as **whips**. Whips originated in the British House of Commons, where they were named after the " whipper in," the rider who keeps the hounds together in a fox hunt. The term is applied to assistant party leaders because of

Following the resignation of Speaker John Boehner in October 2015, Paul Ryan (R., Wisc.), left, was elected Speaker of the House. In 2014, Kevin McCarthy (R., Calif.), center, was elected House majority leader. Nancy Pelosi (D., Calif.), right, was the House minority leader. Earlier, Pelosi had been the first woman to hold the Speaker position. *How much power do these individuals have?*

the pressure that they place on party members to uphold the party's positions.

Whips try to determine how each member is going to vote on an issue and then advise the party leaders on the strength of party support. Whips also try to see that members are present when important votes are to be taken and that they vote with the party leadership. For example, if the Republican leadership strongly supports a tax-cut bill, the Republican Party whip might meet with other Republican Party members in the House to try to ensure that they will show up and vote with the party.

As a result of the 2016 elections, Mitch McConnell (R., Ky.), left, was reelected as the Senate majority leader. Charles (Chuck) Schumer (D., N.Y.), right, became the Senate minority leader in 2017 after Harry Reid (D., Nev.) retired. *What would happen if a leader disagreed with a majority of his or her caucus on an important issue?*

11–3b Senate Leadership

The Constitution makes the vice president of the United States the president of the Senate. As presiding officer, the vice president may call on members to speak and put questions to a vote. The vice president is not an elected member of the Senate, however, and may not take part in Senate debates. The vice president may cast a vote in the Senate only in the event of a tie.

President Pro Tempore   Because vice presidents are rarely available—and do not often desire—to preside over the Senate, senators elect another presiding officer, the *president pro tempore* ("pro tem"), who serves in the absence of the vice president. The president pro tem is elected by the whole Senate and is ordinarily the member of the majority party with the longest continuous term of service in the Senate. The current president pro tem is Orrin Hatch (R., Utah). In the absence of both the president pro tem and the vice president, a temporary presiding officer is selected from the ranks of the Senate, usually a junior member of the majority party.

Party Leaders   The real power in the Senate is held by the majority leader, the minority leader, and their whips. The majority leader is the most powerful individual and chief spokesperson of the majority party. The majority leader directs the legislative program and party strategy. The minority leader commands the minority party's opposition to the policies of the majority party and directs the legislative strategy of the minority party.

11–3c Congressional Committees

Thousands of bills are introduced during every session of Congress, and no single member can possibly be adequately informed on all the issues that arise. The committee system is a way to provide for specialization, or a division of the legislative labor. Members of a committee concentrate on just one area or topic—such as agriculture or transportation—and develop sufficient expertise to draft appropriate legislation when needed. The flow of legislation through both the House and the Senate is determined largely by the speed with which these committees act on bills and resolutions.

Standing Committees   The permanent and most powerful committees of Congress are called **standing committees.** Their names are listed in Table 11–1. Normally, before any bill can be considered by the entire House or Senate, it must be approved by a majority vote in the standing committee to which it was assigned.

As mentioned, standing committees are controlled by the majority party in each chamber. Committee membership is generally divided between the parties according to the number of members in each

standing committee
A permanent committee in Congress that deals with legislation concerning a particular area, such as agriculture or foreign relations.

TABLE 11–1 STANDING COMMITTEES IN THE 115TH CONGRESS, 2017–2019	
House Committees	**Senate Committees**
Agriculture	Agriculture, Nutrition, and Forestry
Appropriations	Appropriations
Armed Services	Armed Services
Budget	Banking, Housing, and Urban Affairs
Education and the Workforce	Budget
Energy and Commerce	Commerce, Science, and Transportation
Ethics	Energy and Natural Resources
Financial Services	Environment and Public Works
Foreign Affairs	Finance
Homeland Security	Foreign Relations
House Administration	Health, Education, Labor, and Pensions
Judiciary	Homeland Security and Governmental Affairs
Natural Resources	Judiciary
Oversight and Government Reform	Rules and Administration
Rules	Small Business and Entrepreneurship
Science, Space, and Technology	Veterans' Affairs
Small Business	
Transportation and Infrastructure	
Veterans' Affairs	
Ways and Means	

chamber. In both the House and the Senate, committee *seniority*—the length of continuous service on a particular committee—typically plays a role in determining the committee chairpersons.

Subcommittees and Other Committees

Most House and Senate committees also have **subcommittees** with limited areas of jurisdiction. Today, there are more than two hundred subcommittees.

Select Committees and Joint Committees.

Congress also has other types of committees. Special, or select, committees are formed to study specific problems or issues. These committees may be either permanent or temporary.

Joint committees are created by the concurrent action of both chambers of Congress and consist of members from each chamber. Joint committees have dealt with the economy, taxation, and the Library of Congress.

Conference Committees.

A **conference committee,** which also includes members from both chambers, is formed for the purpose of achieving agreement between the House and the Senate on the exact wording of a legislative act when the two chambers pass legislative proposals in different forms. No bill can be sent to the White House to be signed into law unless it first passes both chambers in identical form.

If the leadership in either chamber believes that an acceptable compromise with the other chamber is impossible, it can block legislation simply by refusing to appoint members to a conference committee. In 2013, the Republicans employed this technique on several bills.

11-3d The Differences between the House and the Senate

To understand what goes on in the chambers of Congress, we need to look at the effects of bicameralism. Each chamber has developed certain distinct features. The major differences between the House

subcommittee
A division of a larger committee that deals with a particular part of the committee's policy area. Most standing committees have several subcommittees.

conference committee
A temporary committee that is formed when the two chambers of Congress pass differing versions of the same bill. The conference committee consists of members from the House and the Senate who work out a compromise bill.

and the Senate are listed in Table 11–2.

Size Matters Obviously, with 435 voting members, the House cannot operate in the the same way as the Senate, which has only 100 members. With its larger size, the House needs both more rules and more formality—otherwise, no work would ever get done. The most obvious formal rules have to do with debate on the floor.

The Senate normally permits extended debate on all issues that arise before it. In contrast, the House uses an elaborate system: The House **Rules Committee** normally proposes time limits on debate for any bill. The rules are then accepted or modified by the House. Despite its greater size, as a consequence of its stricter time limits on debate, the House is often able to act on legislation more quickly than the Senate.

The "Hastert Rule" in the House One informal rule adopted by House Republicans can prevent consideration of legislation even if it has passed in the Senate. That is the *Hastert Rule*, named after a former Republican Speaker. Under the rule, when the Republicans have a majority in the House, the Speaker will not allow any measure to reach the floor unless it has the support of a majority of the Republican members of the House. Democratic Speakers also have the power to block legislation in this way, but they have not turned this ability into an informal rule.

The Hastert Rule came under considerable pressure in late 2012 and 2013, when Republican Speaker John Boehner felt compelled to violate it repeatedly. Legislation in December 2012 prevented large-scale tax increases at the cost of allowing taxes to rise for the wealthiest citizens. It passed without the support of most Republicans. Boehner also waived the rule to end a government shutdown that took place in October 2013. As we noted earlier, divisions in the Republican ranks led Boehner to resign from the Speaker position in 2015.

The Filibuster in the Senate At one time, both the House and the Senate allowed unlimited debate, but the House ended this practice in 1811. The use of unlimited debate in the Senate to obstruct legislation is called **filibustering** (as discussed in the chapter-opening

TABLE 11–2 MAJOR DIFFERENCES BETWEEN THE HOUSE AND THE SENATE	
House*	**Senate***
Members chosen from local districts	Members chosen from entire state
Two-year term	Six-year term
Always elected by voters	Originally (until 1913) elected by state legislatures
May impeach (accuse, indict) federal officials	May convict federal officials of impeachable offenses
Larger (435 voting members)	Smaller (100 members)
More formal rules	Fewer rules and restrictions
Debate limited	Debate extended
Floor action controlled	Unanimous consent rules
Less prestige and less individual notice	More prestige and media attention
Originates bills for raising revenues	Has power of "advice and consent" on presidential appointments and treaties
Local or narrow leadership	National leadership

*Some of these differences, such as term of office, are provided for in the Constitution, while others, such as debate rules, are not.

America at Odds feature). Until 2013, the filibuster could also be used to hold up presidential nominations for judicial or executive positions, as we explain later in this chapter.

Cloture. Today, under Senate Rule 22, filibusters may be ended by invoking **cloture**—a procedure for closing debate and bringing the matter under consideration to a vote in the Senate. Sixteen senators must sign a petition requesting cloture. Then, after two days have elapsed, three-fifths of the entire membership must vote for cloture. Normally, that means sixty senators. Once cloture is invoked, each senator may speak on a bill for no more than one hour before a vote is taken. Additionally, a final vote must take place within one hundred hours after cloture has been invoked.

Reconciliation. Another limit on the filibuster is a Senate rule known as **reconciliation.** This rule applies to revenue bills passed by the House under its constitutional obligation to initiate such laws, and which are then sent to the Senate. A reconciliation bill must meet three requirements:

▶ **It must be limited to the topics of taxing and spending,**

Rules Committee A standing committee in the House of Representatives that provides special rules governing how particular bills will be considered and debated by the House. The Rules Committee normally proposes time limits on debate for any bill.

filibustering Using the Senate tradition of unlimited debate to prevent action.

cloture A procedure for ending filibusters in the Senate and bringing the matter under consideration to a vote.

reconciliation A Senate rule under which revenue bills received from the House that meet certain requirements cannot be filibustered.

Cutting Back Our Gigantic Tax Code

A poll by the Pew Research Center shows that only a little more than a quarter of respondents consider themselves to be overtaxed. Almost half, however, believe that our tax system is too complicated.

The Perception

The House Ways and Means Committee contends that the tax code is 70,000 pages long and has tripled in length over the last thirty years. A unit within the Internal Revenue Service (IRS) itself estimates that individuals and businesses spend more than 6 billion hours each year to prepare their taxes. Clearly, this is a system that needs reform.

The Reality

Several of these perceptions are misleading. Many businesses must indeed devote major resources to their taxes, but the same IRS unit that came up with the estimate of 6 billion hours also contends that the average individual taxpayer spends only thirteen hours at the job. That's an average—people with only wage or salary income should be able to finish up much more quickly. The contention that the tax code is 70,000 pages long is also off. In fact, the current tax code is about 2,600 pages. That's still a lot, but nowhere near the headline number.

The 70,000-page collection referred to is not the tax code, but a privately produced publication called the *CCH Standard Federal Tax Reporter*, issued by CCHGroup (formerly the Commerce Clearing House). This encyclopedic reference work includes not only the tax code itself, but also all previous tax laws, plus all court decisions and regulatory rulings dealing with taxes dating back to the creation of the income tax. It is, in part, a historical record. By definition, this is not a document that anyone can shorten. Nothing is ever deleted from it, even if the tax code itself becomes simpler.

The reason that the tax code is even 2,600 pages long is that it is filled with tax breaks for special interests. Each industry with a special break knows all about its own little piece of the tax law and doesn't pay much attention to the breaks enjoyed by others. Economists have long argued that the nation as a whole would be better off if there were fewer tax breaks. We could then lower overall tax rates and still collect the same amount of money. The problem is that those who benefit from each break will fight like rabid wolves to defend it.

Still, it is at least *possible* for Congress to reform and simplify the tax system. The last major reform was undertaken in 1986—more than three decades ago. That reform required a herculean effort and bipartisan cooperation, neither of which are much in evidence today. In 2017, President Trump and Republicans in Congress announced that they were taking up the issue of tax reform once again. Given past experiences, the chances of true reform are not great.

Blog On

The news and commentary site www.vox.com explains the myth of the 70,000-page tax code— search for "vox taxes 70,000." For the Pew Research Center poll mentioned earlier, search on "pew taxes bothered."

▸ **It must not otherwise involve changes to regulations or laws, and**

▸ **It must reduce the budget deficit at the end of a ten-year period (a requirement that can be met through creative accounting).**

A reconciliation bill cannot be filibustered. Reconciliation became highly attractive to Republicans in Congress following the inauguration of President Trump, because as long as Republicans remained united, they could easily pass any law that met the reconciliation rules. As an additional attraction, it would be much easier to loosen the rules governing reconciliation than it would be to abolish the filibuster. A problem for the Republicans in 2017, however, was that they had considerable difficulty in coming to agreement even within their own party. One type of legislation that could easily meet the reconciliation requirements would be comprehensive tax reform, an issue that Congress hoped to take up in 2017. Tax reform is not particularly easy to accomplish, however, as we explain in this chapter's *Perception vs. Reality* feature.

The Senatorial Hold Senators have another tool in addition to the filibuster that they can use to delay legislation. Individual senators may place a *hold* on a particular bill. A senator simply informs the leader of his or her party of the hold. Party leaders do not announce who has placed a hold, so holds are often anonymous. Recent rule changes designed to curb anonymous holds have been ineffective. Cloture can be used to lift a hold.

Senators often place holds on nominees for executive or judicial positions in an attempt to win concessions from the executive branch. For example, in 2010, Senator Richard Shelby (R., Ala.) placed holds on at least seventy of President Obama's nominations in an attempt to force the administration to support two military spending programs in Alabama.

The Senate Wins the Prestige Race, Hands Down Because of the large number of representatives, few can garner the prestige that a senator enjoys. Senators have relatively little difficulty gaining access to the media. Members of the House, who run for reelection every two years, have to survive many reelection campaigns before they can obtain such recognition. Usually, a representative must become an important committee leader to enjoy the consistent attention of the national news media.

One consequence of the prestige difference is that it has been very difficult for a member of the House to win a presidential nomination. In contrast, the parties have often nominated senators, and a number of senators have gone on to become president.

Clearly, the Senate is the more powerful of the two chambers, given its control over presidential appointments and treaties. The right of the House to originate revenue bills does not, in practice, give that chamber an advantage. The Senate can effectively initiate a revenue bill by taking a House-passed spending measure, stripping out the language, and inserting entirely different text. (Such a step is uncommon, but it has happened from time to time.) In most other nations, however, it is the "lower house"—equivalent to our House of Representatives—that has most of the power.

CRITICAL THINKING

▶ *Vice presidents typically avoid presiding over the Senate, even though that is their chief constitutional responsibility. Why might they be so reluctant?*

 11-4 THE LEGISLATIVE PROCESS

LO Summarize the specific steps in the lawmaking process.

Look at Figure 11–5. It shows the basic process through which a bill becomes law at the national level. Not all of the complexities of the process are shown, to be sure. For example, the figure does not indicate the extensive lobbying and media politics that are often involved in the legislative process, nor does it mention the informal negotiations and "horse trading" that occur to get a bill passed.

The basic steps in the process are as follows:

1. *Introduction of legislation.* Although individual members of Congress or their staffs—as well as private citizens and lobbying groups—may come up with ideas for new legislation, most bills are proposed by the executive branch. Only a member of Congress can formally introduce legislation, however. In reality, many bills are proposed, developed, and even written by the White House or an executive agency. Then a "friendly" senator or representative introduces the bill in Congress. Such bills are rarely ignored entirely, although they are often amended or defeated.

2. *Referral to committees.* As soon as a bill is introduced and assigned a number, it is sent to the appropriate standing committee. In the House, the Speaker assigns the bill to the committee. In the Senate, the presiding officer does so. For example, a farm bill in the House would be sent to the Agriculture Committee, and a gun control bill would be sent to the Judiciary Committee.

   A committee chairperson will typically send the bill on to a subcommittee. For example, a Senate bill concerning NATO (the North Atlantic Treaty Organization), which allies the United States and Canada with most European nations, would be sent to the subcommittee dealing with European affairs. Alternatively, the chairperson may decide to put the bill aside and ignore it. Most bills that are pigeonholed in this manner receive no further action.

   If a bill is not pigeonholed, committee staff members go to work researching it. The subcommittee may hold public hearings during which people who support or oppose the bill can express their views. Subcommittees also have the power to order witnesses to testify at public hearings. Witnesses may be executive agency officials, experts on the subject, or representatives of interest groups concerned about the bill.

   The subcommittee must meet to approve the bill as it is, add new amendments, or draft a new bill. This

FIGURE 11–5 HOW A BILL BECOMES A LAW

This illustration shows the most typical way in which proposed legislation is enacted into law. It follows two hypothetical bills, House bill No. 100 (HR 100) and Senate bill No. 200 (S 200). The path of HR 100 is traced by an orange line, and that of S 200 by a green line. In practice, most bills begin as similar proposals in both chambers. Bills must be passed by both chambers in identical form before they can be sent to the president. *How does Congress ensure that the bills are identical in form?*

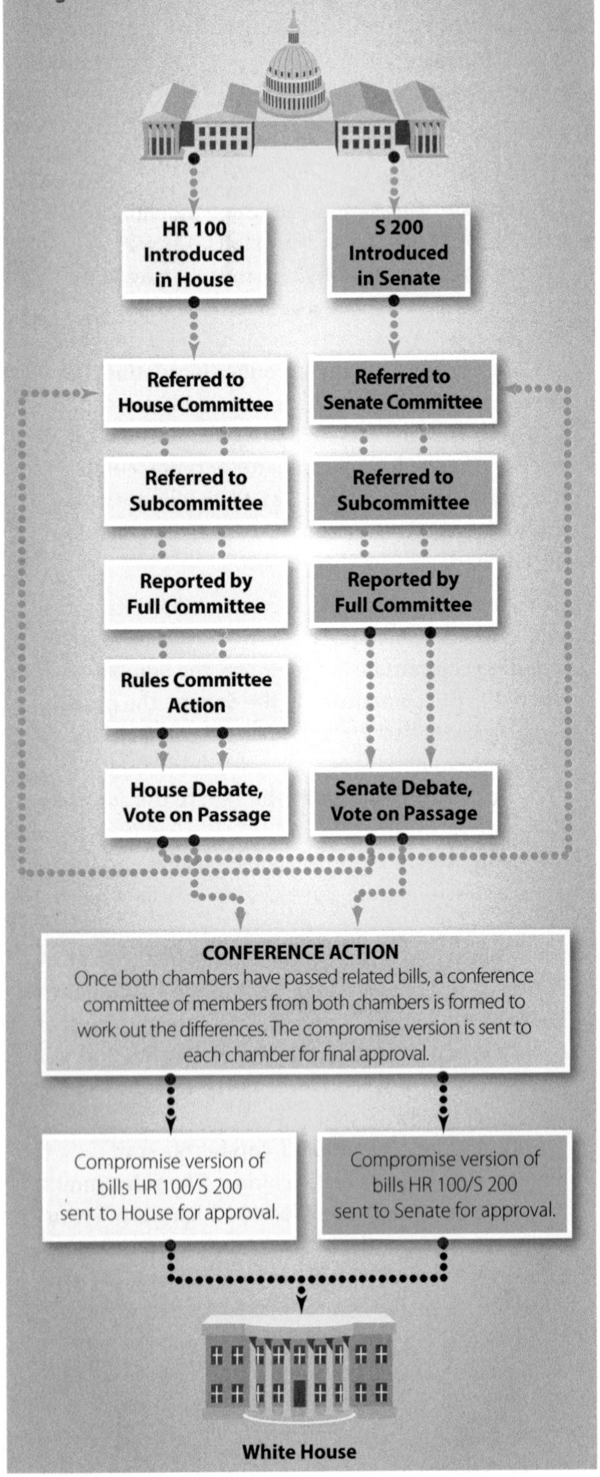

HR 100 Introduced in House

S 200 Introduced in Senate

Referred to House Committee

Referred to Senate Committee

Referred to Subcommittee

Referred to Subcommittee

Reported by Full Committee

Reported by Full Committee

Rules Committee Action

House Debate, Vote on Passage

Senate Debate, Vote on Passage

CONFERENCE ACTION
Once both chambers have passed related bills, a conference committee of members from both chambers is formed to work out the differences. The compromise version is sent to each chamber for final approval.

Compromise version of bills HR 100/S 200 sent to House for approval.

Compromise version of bills HR 100/S 200 sent to Senate for approval.

White House

meeting is known as the **markup session.** If members cannot reach a consensus on changes, a vote on the changes is taken.

When a subcommittee completes its work, the bill goes to the full standing committee, which then meets for its own markup session. The committee may hold its own hearings, amend the subcommittee's version, or simply approve the subcommittee's recommendations.

3. *Reports on a bill.* Finally, the committee will report the bill back to the full chamber. It can report the bill favorably, report the bill with amendments, or report a newly written bill. It can also report a bill unfavorably, but usually such a bill will have been pigeonholed earlier instead. Along with the bill, the committee will send to the House or Senate a written report that explains the committee's actions, describes the bill, lists the major changes made by the committee, and gives opinions on the bill.

4. *The Rules Committee and scheduling.* Scheduling is an extremely important part of getting a bill enacted into law. A bill must be put on a chamber's calendar. Typically, in the House the Rules Committee plays a major role in the scheduling process. This committee, along with the House leaders, regulates the flow of the bills through the House. The Rules Committee also specifies how much time can be spent on debate and whether amendments can be made by a floor vote.

In the Senate, a few leading members control the flow of bills. The Senate brings a bill to the floor by "unanimous consent," a motion by which all members present on the floor set aside the formal Senate rules and consider a bill. In contrast to the procedure in the House, individual senators have the power to disrupt work on legislation—refusing to agree to unanimous consent is the way in which a senatorial hold is enforced.

5. *Floor debate.* Because of its large size, the House imposes severe limits on floor debate. The Speaker recognizes those who may speak and can force any member who does not "stick to the subject" to give up the floor. Normally, the chairperson of the standing committee reporting the bill will take charge of the session during which it is debated. You can often watch such debates on C-SPAN.

Only on rare occasions does a floor debate change anybody's mind. The written record of the floor debate completes the legislative history of the proposed bill in the event that the courts have to interpret it later on. Floor debates also give the full House or Senate the opportunity to consider amendments to the original version of the bill.

6. *Vote.* In both the House and the Senate, the

markup session
A meeting held by a congressional committee or subcommittee to approve, amend, or redraft a bill.

members present generally vote for or against the bill. There are several methods of voting, including voice votes, standing votes, and recorded votes (also called roll-call votes). Since 1973, the House has had electronic voting. The Senate does not have such a system, however.

7. *Conference committee.* To become a law, a bill must be passed in identical form by both chambers. When the two chambers pass differing versions of the same bill, the measure is turned over to a conference committee—a temporary committee with members from the two chambers, as mentioned earlier.

   Most members of the committee are drawn from the standing committees that handled the bill in both chambers. In theory, the conference committee can consider only those points in a bill on which the two chambers disagree. No proposals are supposed to be added. In reality, however, the conference committee sometimes makes important changes in the bill or adds new provisions. Traditionally, these included "pork-barrel" provisions.

   Once the conference committee members agree on the final compromise bill, a **conference report** is submitted to each chamber. The bill must be accepted or rejected by both chambers as it was written by the committee, with no further amendments. If the bill is approved by both chambers, it is ready for action by the president.

8. *Presidential action.* All bills passed by Congress must be submitted to the president for approval. The president has ten days to decide whether to sign the bill or to veto it. If the president does nothing, the bill goes into effect unless Congress adjourns before the ten-day period expires. In that case, the bill dies in what is called a **pocket veto.**

9. *Overriding a veto.* If the president decides to veto a bill, Congress can still enact the bill into law. With a two-thirds majority vote in both chambers, Congress can override the president's veto.

Newly elected representative Mia Love (R., Utah) picks a lottery number that will determine where her new office will be located. Love's parents were born in Haiti, and she is the first Republican African American woman to sit in Congress. *Why would some African Americans be conservatives?*

Andrew Harrer/Bloomberg/Getty Images

11–5 INVESTIGATION AND OVERSIGHT

LO Identify Congress's oversight functions, and explain how Congress fulfills them.

Steps 8 and 9 of the legislative process just described illustrate the interlocking roles of the executive and the legislative branches in making laws. The relationship between Congress and the president is at the core of our system of government, although, to be sure, the judicial branch plays a vital role as well.

One of the most important functions of Congress is its oversight (supervision) of the executive branch and its many federal departments and agencies. The executive bureaucracy, which includes the president's cabinet departments, wields tremendous power. Congress can rein in that power by choosing not to provide the money necessary for the bureaucracy to function. (The budgeting process will be discussed later in this chapter.)

conference report
A report submitted by a conference committee after it has drafted a single version of a bill.

pocket veto A special type of veto power used by the chief executive after the legislature has adjourned. Bills that are not signed die after a specified period of time.

CRITICAL THINKING

▸ *Why do debates on the floor of the House or the Senate almost never change anyone's mind?*

Drew Angerer/Getty Images News/Getty Images

James Comey (right), then-director of the Federal Bureau of Investigation (FBI), prepares to testify before the House Select Committee on Intelligence in March 2017. The issue was Russian meddling in the 2016 elections. *How has Congress handled oversight of the Trump administration?*

11–5a The Investigative Function

Congress also has the authority to investigate the actions of the executive branch, the need for certain legislation, and even the actions of its own members. The numerous congressional committees and subcommittees regularly hold hearings to investigate the actions of the executive branch.

Going Overboard Many people believe that Congress may go overboard in its investigations when Congress and the White House are controlled by different parties. Republicans made such accusations during the Bush administration, after the Democrats gained control of Congress in the 2006 elections. When Republicans took control of both chambers in 2014, it was the Democrats' turn to complain. For example, in 2015 a House committee grilled former Secretary of State Hillary Clinton about the death of four Americans in Benghazi, Libya, in 2012. The efforts of the committee were undermined when House majority leader Kevin McCarthy admitted that one goal of the investigation was to reduce Clinton's public opinion poll numbers as a presidential candidate.

Neglecting Oversight A widely held belief is that between 2001 and 2007, when Republicans controlled both chambers of Congress and the presidency, Congress neglected its oversight function out of deference to

President Bush. Many also believe that Congress neglected its oversight function from 2009 to 2011, when the Democrats controlled both chambers of Congress and the presidency.

The issue of neglect became more important than ever after President Trump took office. Serious allegations had been raised that members of the Trump campaign may have engaged in improper communications with the Russian government during the 2016 election season. In particular, the FBI was investigating whether the Trump campaign discussed or even encouraged Russian hacking of Democratic campaign organizations. Congressional Republicans blocked Democratic demands for a special bipartisan investigation and instead planned investigations through the existing House and Senate Intelligence Committees. In the House, however, the Republican chair of the Intelligence Committee, who was leading the investigation, appeared to be so biased in favor of the Trump administration that he was forced to step down. A Republican with less seniority took over this task.

The Congressional Budget Office One way in which Congress has "kept itself honest" is by establishing oversight bodies separate from—but responsible to—Congress. One such body is the Congressional Budget Office (CBO), which evaluates the impact of proposed legislation on the federal budget and the budget deficit. The CBO has frequently been in the news in recent years due to its "scoring" of various proposals considered by the House and the Senate. Members of Congress have found themselves tailoring measures to earn a better score from the CBO.

11–5b Impeachment Power

Congress has the power to impeach and remove from office the president, vice president, and other "civil officers," such as federal judges. To *impeach* means to accuse a public official of—or charge him or her with—improper conduct in office. The House of Representatives is vested with this power. After a vote to impeach in the full House, the accused official is then tried in the

Senate. If convicted by a two-thirds vote, the official is removed from office.

Impeaching Presidents   The House has twice exercised its impeachment power against a president. It voted to impeach Andrew Johnson in 1868 and Bill Clinton in 1998. Both Johnson and Clinton were acquitted by the Senate. A vote to impeach President Richard Nixon was pending before the full House of Representatives in 1974 when Nixon chose to resign. Nixon is the only president ever to resign from office.

Impeaching Other Officers   Congress has taken action to remove officials other than the president. For example, the House of Representatives voted to impeach district court judge Thomas Porteous in March 2010 on charges of bribery and perjury. In December of that year, the Senate convicted Porteous and disqualified him from ever holding any "office of honor or profit under the United States," as the formal language puts it. Only one United States Supreme Court justice has ever been impeached. The House impeached Samuel Chase in 1804, but he was later acquitted by the Senate.

> **"Laws are like sausages. It is better if the public does not see how they are made."**
>
> ~ JOHN GODFREY SAXE
> AMERICAN POET
> 1816–1887
> (MISATTRIBUTED TO OTTO VON BISMARCK, CHANCELLOR OF GERMANY, 1871–1890)

11–5c Senate Confirmation

Article II, Section 2, of the Constitution states that the president may appoint ambassadors, justices of the Supreme Court, and other officers of the United States "with the Advice and Consent of the Senate." The Constitution leaves the precise nature of how the Senate will give this "advice and consent" up to the lawmakers.

The Traditional Confirmation Process   Traditionally, the Senate either confirms or fails to confirm the president's nominees for the Supreme Court, other federal judgeships, members of the president's cabinet, and other top executive branch officers. Nominees appear first before the appropriate Senate committee— the Judiciary Committee for federal judges or the Foreign Relations Committee for the secretary of state, for example. If the individual committee approves the nominee, the full Senate will vote on the nomination.

Senate confirmation hearings have been very politicized at times. Judicial appointments often receive the most intense scrutiny by the Senate, because federal judges serve for life. The president has a somewhat freer hand with cabinet appointments, because the heads of executive departments (unlike federal judges) are expected to be loyal to the president. Nonetheless, Senate confirmation has always been an important check on the president's power.

Appointment Delays and the "Nuclear Option"   Throughout American history, the Senate has often rejected nominees for executive and judicial positions. In recent decades, however, a new pattern has taken hold. Senators from one party have begun delaying nominations as part of an ideological struggle with a president from the other party. Given Senate traditions, such tactics have been available to both the minority and the majority party. The filibuster has often been the tool used in delaying nominations. This practice was first employed on a large scale in the 1990s by the Republicans in their battles with President Bill Clinton. Democrats then adopted it against George W. Bush. Under Obama, the Republicans resumed the practice. In 2013, however, the use of the filibuster to delay appointments was substantially curbed when the Senate exercised what has been called the *nuclear option*.

The Nuclear Option.   Senate rules that require supermajority votes for such steps as ending a filibuster have no basis in the Constitution. That document allows senators to pass legislation and approve nominees by a majority vote of those present. The filibuster—and the senatorial hold discussed earlier—exist because a Senate majority approved these rules. It follows that a majority can repeal them. In the past, such a violation of tradition would have been unthinkable. Given current political polarization, however, the unthinkable has become possible. Changing Senate rules through a simple majority vote has been called the *constitutional option*. It is also known as the **nuclear option,** an analogy to the ultimate weapon.

The Option Is Employed.

In 2005, after Senate Democrats filibustered many Bush nominees, Republicans threatened to use the nuclear option to move the nominations

> **nuclear option**
> Changing Senate rules—in particular, rules that require a supermajority—by simple majority vote. Also known as the *constitutional option*.

nominee Merrick Garland, a respected and moderate Democrat, was blocked from the Court. In November 2016, Donald Trump was elected president, and McConnell's gamble paid off. A Republican president would nominate Scalia's replacement. Trump nominated Neil Gorsuch, a respected and strictly conservative Republican. Angry over the Republican treatment of Garland, Senate Democrats planned to filibuster Gorsuch's nomination. In April 2017, however, Republican senators, on a party-line vote, abolished the filibuster as applied to Supreme Court nominations. The Senate then confirmed Gorsuch.

In April 2017, the Senate confirmed the appointment of Judge Neil Gorsuch (center) to the Supreme Court. Gorsuch fills a seat once held by Justice Antonin Scalia. Here he is flanked by Senate majority leader Mitch McConnell (left) and Vice President Mike Pence (right). *Why were Republicans so enthusiastic about Gorsuch?*

Alex Wong/Bloomberg/Getty Images

forward. At the last minute, a bipartisan group called the "gang of fourteen" engineered a compromise under which the filibuster would be reserved for "extraordinary circumstances." In 2013, with a large number of Obama nominees blocked, the Democrats claimed that the Republicans had violated this agreement. No settlement was reached, and in November the Senate voted to eliminate the use of the filibuster against all executive and judicial nominees other than those to the Supreme Court. While this step made it easier to approve candidates, the Republicans continued to use other Senate rules to delay nominations.

Extending the Nuclear Option to the Supreme Court. Of course, when the Republicans took control of the Senate after the 2014 elections, they no longer needed the filibuster to block nominations. Following the death of conservative Supreme Court justice Antonin Scalia in February 2016, Senate majority leader Mitch McConnell announced that the Republicans would refuse to hold confirmation hearings on any nominee that Obama might submit. Filling the empty seat would be delayed until after a new president took office in January 2017.

This unusual tactic met with success. Obama

authorization A part of the congressional budgeting process—the creation of the legal basis for government programs.

11-6 THE BUDGETING PROCESS

LO Indicate what is involved in the congressional budgeting process.

The Constitution makes it very clear that Congress has the power of the purse, and this power is significant. Only Congress can impose taxes, and only Congress can authorize expenditures. To be sure, the president submits a budget, but all final decisions are up to Congress.

The congressional budget is, of course, one of the most important determinants of what policies will or will not be implemented. For example, the president might order executive agencies under presidential control to undertake specific programs, but these orders are meaningless if there is no money to pay for their execution. For any program that receives an annual appropriation, Congress can nullify a president's ambitious plans simply by refusing to allocate the necessary money to executive agencies to implement the program.

11-6a Authorization and Appropriation

The budgeting process is a two-part procedure. **Authorization** is the first part. It involves the creation of the legal basis for government programs. In this phase,

Congress passes authorization bills outlining the rules governing the expenditure of funds. It may place limits on how much money can be spent and for what period of time.

Appropriation is the second part of the budgeting process. In this phase, Congress determines how many dollars will actually be spent in a given year on a particular government activity. Appropriations must never exceed the authorized amounts, but they can be less.

An exception to this process involves entitlement programs, which require the government to provide benefits, such as Social Security benefits and veterans' benefits, to persons who qualify under entitlement laws. Many such programs operate under open-ended authorizations that, in effect, place no limits on how much can be spent (although it is usually possible to estimate the cost of a particular entitlement program fairly accurately). The Affordable Care Act, also known as Obamacare, is, for the most part, an entitlement program. For this reason, repeated votes by the Republican-led House during Obama's presidency to "defund" Obamacare have had no practical effect.

The remaining federal programs fall into the category of discretionary spending, and so they can be altered at will by Congress. National defense is the most important item in the discretionary-spending part of the budget. Discretionary spending also includes earmarks, or pork, which we described earlier in this chapter in the *Join the Debate* feature.

11–6b The Actual Budgeting Process

Figure 11–6 outlines the lengthy budgeting process. The process runs from January, when the president submits a proposed federal budget for the next fiscal year, to the start of that fiscal year on October 1. In actuality, about eighteen months prior to October 1, the executive agencies submit their requests to the Office of Management and Budget (OMB), and the OMB outlines a proposed budget. If the president approves it, the budget is officially submitted to Congress.

The legislative budgeting process begins eight to nine months before the start of the fiscal year. The first budget resolution is supposed to be passed in May. It sets overall revenue goals and spending targets and, by definition, the size of the federal budget deficit or surplus.

appropriation A part of the congressional budgeting process—the determination of how many dollars will be spent in a given year on a particular government activity.

entitlement program A government program (such as Social Security) that allows, or entitles, a certain class of people (such as older persons) to receive benefits.

fiscal year A twelve-month period that is established for accounting purposes. The government's fiscal year runs from October 1 through September 30.

first budget resolution A budget resolution, which is supposed to be passed in May, that sets overall revenue goals and spending targets for the next fiscal year, beginning on October 1.

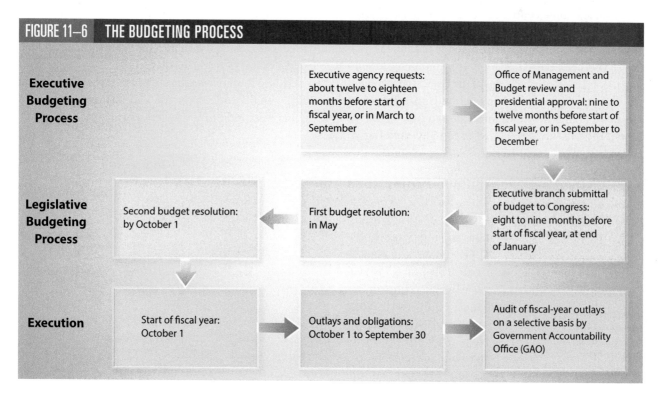

FIGURE 11–6   THE BUDGETING PROCESS

Executive Budgeting Process

Executive agency requests: about twelve to eighteen months before start of fiscal year, or in March to September → Office of Management and Budget review and presidential approval: nine to twelve months before start of fiscal year, or in September to December

Legislative Budgeting Process

Second budget resolution: by October 1 ← First budget resolution: in May ← Executive branch submittal of budget to Congress: eight to nine months before start of fiscal year, at end of January

Execution

Start of fiscal year: October 1 → Outlays and obligations: October 1 to September 30 → Audit of fiscal-year outlays on a selective basis by Government Accountability Office (GAO)

From left to right, senators Bernie Sanders (I, Vt.), Al Franken (D., Minn.), and Edward Markey (D., Mass.). The three were holding a news conference to defend net neutrality. *Why might Democrats be more sympathetic to Internet giants such as Facebook and Google that promote net neutrality than to Internet service providers such as Comcast and AT&T?*

The **second budget resolution,** which sets "binding" limits on taxes and spending, is supposed to be passed in September, before the beginning of the fiscal year on October 1. When Congress is unable to pass a complete budget by October 1—which is very common—it usually passes **continuing resolutions,** which enable the executive agencies to keep doing whatever they were doing the previous year with the same amount of funding. But even continuing resolutions have not always been passed on time. If a continuing resolution is not passed, various parts of the federal government may have to shut down temporarily. Under President Obama, Republicans twice attempted to gain legislative advantage by refusing to pass such resolutions.

Budget Projections The budget process involves making predictions about the state of the U.S. economy for years to come. This process is necessarily very imprecise. Since 1996, both Congress and the president have attempted to make ten-year projections for income (from taxes) and spending, but no one can really know what the financial picture of the United States will look like in ten years. While one- or two-year predictions are often fairly realistic, long-term projections have never come close to being accurate.

The Debt Ceiling Issue In any year in which the federal government spends more than it takes in, the resulting deficit adds to the national debt. U.S. law sets a ceiling on the size of the national debt. It is popularly believed that votes to raise the debt ceiling, which take place regularly, are ways of authorizing additional, future spending. This belief is incorrect. Congress has traditionally appropriated sums that would force the government to breach the ceiling and has then raised the ceiling at a later date.

In the past, members of Congress often took advantage of the vote to raise the ceiling to "grandstand," to show off their opposition to federal spending. They did so knowing that in the end, the ceiling would inevitably be raised. In 2011, however, Republicans in the House threatened to refuse to raise the debt ceiling unless the Obama administration made major spending concessions. If the debt ceiling was not raised, the government would not be able to pay out on already-established obligations. Bankers and economists warned that such a default would result in disaster. In the end, the Republicans were at least partially successful. A deal with the Obama administration led to a variety of restraints on spending.

House Republicans attempted to repeat the tactic in 2013, with the added pressure of refusing to pass a continuing resolution to fund the government. Democrats,

second budget resolution A budget resolution, which is supposed to be passed in September, that sets "binding" limits on taxes and spending for the next fiscal year.

continuing resolution A temporary resolution passed by Congress that enables executive agencies to continue working with the same funding that they had in the previous fiscal year.

> "You've got to work things out in the cloakroom, and when you've got them worked out, you can debate a little before you vote."
>
> ~ LYNDON B. JOHNSON,
> SENATE MAJORITY LEADER, 1955–1961
> PRESIDENT OF THE UNITED STATES,
> 1963–1969

believing they had been taken advantage of in 2011, refused to budge. The House tactics were very unpopular, and Republicans were forced to abandon them. One might think that such unpopular tactics would not be revived. Yet, in 2017, both Democrats and members of the Freedom Caucus were again considering the rejection of a continuing resolution as a way to gain leverage.

AMERICA AT ODDS | The Congress

The founders thought that Congress would be the branch of government that was closest to the people. Yet Congress is one of the least popular institutions in America. It seems that anything that Congress does annoys a substantial share of the electorate. Needless to say, Americans are at odds over Congress on a variety of issues:

- *Is the Senate's filibuster rule a legitimate safeguard of minority rights—or a disastrous handicap on Congress's ability to address the nation's problems?*

- *Is political gerrymandering just a normal part of the political game—or does it deprive voters of their rights?*

- *Does racial gerrymandering allow the voices of minority groups to be heard—or is it an unconstitutional violation of the equal protection clause?*

- *When voting on legislation, should members of Congress faithfully represent the views of their constituents—or should they stay true to their own beliefs about what is good for the nation?*

- *Should legislative earmarks, or "pork," be banned as a waste of taxpayers' resources—or is it appropriate for members of Congress to use pork to support specific projects in their own districts?*

STUDY TOOLS 11

READY TO STUDY? IN THE BOOK, YOU CAN:

- ☐ Review what you've read with the following chapter quiz.
- ☐ Check your answers in Appendix D at the back of the book.
- ☐ Rip out the Chapter Review Card, which includes key terms and chapter summaries.

ONLINE AT WWW.CENGAGEBRAIN.COM, YOU CAN:

- ☐ Watch videos to get a quick overview.
- ☐ Expedite your studying with Major Player readings and Focus Activities.
- ☐ Check your understanding with Chapter Quizzes.

FILL-IN

Learning Outcome 11–1

1. Every _____ years, seats in the House of Representatives are reapportioned based on the outcome of the census.

2. Under the trustee view of representation, a legislator should try to _____.

Learning Outcome 11–2

3. Incumbent members of Congress enjoy several advantages over their challengers in elections, including _____.

Learning Outcome 11–3

4. The Speaker of the House has the power to _____.

5. Filibusters may be ended by invoking _____.

Learning Outcome 11–4

6. A markup session is _____.

7. In the House, the _____ Committee plays a major role in the scheduling process and also specifies the amount of time to be spent on debate.

Learning Outcome 11–5

8. In practice, the Senate's power of "advice and consent" means that the Senate confirms or fails to confirm the president's nominees to _____.

Learning Outcome 11–6

9. The budgeting process is a two-part procedure that includes _____.

MULTIPLE CHOICE

Learning Outcome 11–1

10. Congressional districts in a given state must contain, as nearly as possible, equal numbers of
    a. men and women.
    b. Republicans and Democrats.
    c. people.

Learning Outcome 11–2

11. The U.S. Constitution requires that members of the House of Representatives be elected every
    a. second year by popular vote.
    b. six years by popular vote.
    c. second year by state legislatures.

Learning Outcome 11–3

12. In the Senate, the _____ is typically the most powerful individual and directs the legislative program and strategy of his or her party.
    a. vice president
    b. majority leader
    c. president pro tempore

Learning Outcome 11–4

13. As soon as a bill is introduced in either the House or the Senate, it is sent to
    a. the floor of the chamber.
    b. the appropriate standing committee.
    c. a conference committee.

Learning Outcome 11–5

14. The Senate
    a. voted to impeach Richard Nixon.
    b. convicted Bill Clinton of impeachable offenses by a two-thirds vote.
    c. tries officials who have been impeached in the House.

Learning Outcome 11–6

15. When Congress is unable to pass a budget by the beginning of the fiscal year, it usually passes _____, which lets executive agencies keep on doing whatever they were doing the previous year with the same funding.
    a. continuing resolutions
    b. entitlement programs
    c. earmarks

12 | THE PRESIDENCY

Drew Angerer/Getty Images News/Getty Images

LEARNING OUTCOMES

After reading this chapter, you should be able to:

12-1 List the constitutional requirements for becoming president.

12-2 Explain the roles that a president adopts while in office.

12-3 Indicate the scope of presidential powers.

12-4 Describe advantages enjoyed by Congress and by the president in their institutional relationship.

12-5 Discuss the organization of the executive branch and the role of cabinet members in presidential administrations.

After finishing this chapter, go to **PAGE 286** for **STUDY TOOLS**

AMERICA AT ODDS

What Should Trump Do about the Middle East?

ART production/shutterstock.com

As long as most young people can remember, Middle East headlines have involved wars and other armed conflicts. ISIS (also called the Islamic State, ISIL, or Daesh) has conquered territory in Iraq and Syria. It has released videos in which its followers behead Westerners, along with Middle Eastern Christians, Jews, and Muslims. Iran continues to sponsor terrorist groups throughout the region. Presumably, Iran has suspended work on nuclear weapons, but it is developing long-range missiles. Libya has become a "failed state" after years of bloodshed between opposing groups.

Given all this, what is the role of the United States in the Middle East? Should President Trump attempt to limit our involvement with such a troubled region?

Or should he seek to reassert American influence in the Middle East, perhaps by deploying U.S. infantry—"boots on the ground"—to stop ISIS?

Such decisions are always influenced by two great traditions in American foreign policy: idealism and realism. Currently, within the Republican establishment, a hawkish idealism prevails, often promoted by a faction known as the neoconservatives. These people strongly believe that U.S. military power can be a force for good in the world. In contrast, so-called realists seek to avoid military commitments that are not clearly and directly connected to the security of the homeland. Realism is popular among Democrats, though some of its advocates are Republicans. In the past, these Republicans have included Donald Trump.

Trump Should Be More Interventionist

Many people do not want the Middle East to be America's problem. Yet idealist hawks argue that when we do not intervene in the Middle East, it becomes an even greater problem for us. When Obama pulled out of Iraq, he left a power vacuum that was filled by Iran—and ISIS. A few years ago, Obama said that if Syrian president Bashar al-Assad used chemical weapons against his people, there would be serious consequences. But when Assad crossed the "red line," Obama backed off. He was saved from complete embarrassment by Russian president Vladimir Putin, of all people. (It was believed that Putin persuaded Assad to surrender his chemical weapons. U.S. forces then decommissioned the chemicals, but we now know Assad still has some of them.)

By now, at least a quarter of a million Syrians are dead, and almost half the nation's people have been forced to flee their homes. When our president fails to act in the Middle East, Russia and Iran step in and push us aside. Had we stepped into the Syrian civil war and really supported the rebels, ISIS would never have been allowed to establish its own state within a state. We would not see ISIS warriors beheading Americans and others.

We Don't Have a Stake in This Fight

Opponents of intervention ask: Don't the war hawks get it yet? We cannot be the world's policemen. Americans have gained nothing from sending U.S. troops to the Middle East. We went into Afghanistan to save its people from a tyranny imposed by the Taliban. True, the Taliban were driven from the capital, Kabul, but the civil war there is endless. In Iraq, what did we get for thousands of American deaths and injuries? Hawks may say Iraq fell apart because we withdrew, but the same thing probably would have happened if we left in, say, the year 2020.

As to Syria, we could easily conquer the entire country if we went in with guns blazing. And then we would own the place—"you break it, you buy it." Before long, everyone in Syria would hate us as foreign occupiers. In Libya, we helped bring down a dictator, Muammar Gaddafi. Where did that get us? The nation is a total mess, torn apart by armed factions.

Trump should not waste American lives and treasure in the Middle East. The region will not know peace until its own people are willing to fight for it.

Where do you stand?

1. Recent polls suggest that a majority of Americans want to send ground troops to fight ISIS in Iraq and Syria. Do you agree with this idea? Why or why not?

2. After Assad's chemical attacks in April 2017, President Trump ordered a one-time strike on a Syrian airbase. Did this action have any consequences? If so, what were they?

Explore this issue online:

- *Commentary* magazine is home to many of the idealist hawks known as neoconservatives. Find it at www.commentarymagazine.com.

- You can find libertarian anti-interventionists at www.antiwar.com and progressive ones at www.theglobalist.com.

INTRODUCTION

President Lyndon B. Johnson (1963–1969) stated in his autobiography that "of all the 1,886 nights I was President, there were not many when I got to sleep before 1 or 2 a.m., and there were few mornings when I didn't wake up by 6 or 6:30."[1] President Harry Truman (1945–1953) once observed that no one can really understand what it is like to be president: there is no end to "the chain of responsibility that binds him," and he is "never allowed to forget that he is president." These responsibilities are, for the most part, unremitting. Unlike Congress, the president never adjourns.

At the apex of the political ladder, the presidency is the most powerful and influential political office that any one individual can hold. Presidents can help to shape not only domestic policy but also global developments.

Since the demise of the Soviet Union and the Communist-controlled governments in eastern Europe in the early 1990s, the president of the United States has been the leader of the most powerful nation on earth. The president heads the greatest military force anywhere. Presidents have more power to reach their political objectives than any other players in the American political system. (We discussed some of the president's foreign policy options in the Middle East in this chapter's opening *America at Odds* feature.) It is not surprising, therefore, that many Americans aspire to attain this office.

Promotional poster for the feature film *Hellcats of the Navy*, starring future president Ronald Reagan (1981–1989) and his wife, Nancy Davis. *How might Reagan's career as an actor have helped him in politics?*

12–1 WHO CAN BECOME PRESIDENT?

LO List the constitutional requirements for becoming president.

The notion that anybody can become president of this country has always been a part of the American mythology. Certainly, the requirements for becoming president set forth in Article II, Section 1, of the Constitution are not difficult to meet:

> No Person except a natural born Citizen, or a Citizen of the United States, at the time of the Adoption of this Constitution, shall be eligible to the Office of President; neither shall any Person be eligible to that Office who shall not have attained to the Age of thirty-five Years, and been fourteen Years a Resident within the United States.

This language does make it impossible for a foreign-born naturalized citizen to become president, even if that person came to this country as an infant. The requirement of native birth has come up most recently because of claims by conspiracy theorists known as "birthers" that President Barack Obama (2009–2017) was not born in the United States. These individuals claim that Obama's Hawaiian birth certificate was forged, and they are undeterred by the fact that Obama's birth was also announced in two Honolulu newspapers. Among the most prominent birthers was Donald Trump, the current president.

12–1a Why Would Anyone Want to Be President?

Given the demands of the presidency, why would anyone seek the office? There are some very special perks associated with the presidency. The president enjoys, among other things, the use of the White House. At the White House, the president in residence has a staff of more than eighty persons, including chefs, gardeners, maids, butlers, and a personal tailor.

Additionally, the president has at his or her disposal a fleet of automobiles, helicopters, and jets (including *Air Force One*, which costs about $230,000 an hour to run). For relaxation, the presidential family can go to Camp David, a resort hideaway in the Catoctin Mountains of Maryland. Other perks include free dental and medical care.

12-1b Presidential Age and Occupation

President Woodrow Wilson (1913–1921) throwing out the first pitch on the opening day of the Major League Baseball season in 1916. *Why might a president wish to perform this task?*

National Photo Company Collection/Library of Congress

Modern presidents have included a haberdasher (Harry Truman), the owner of a peanut warehouse (Jimmy Carter), and an actor (Ronald Reagan), although all of these men also had significant political experience before assuming the presidency. The most common previous occupation of U.S. presidents, however, has been the legal profession. Out of forty-four presidents, twenty-six have been lawyers. Many presidents have also been wealthy.

Although the Constitution states that anyone who is thirty-five years of age or older can become president, the average age at inauguration has been fifty-five. The youngest person elected president was John F. Kennedy (1961–1963), who assumed the presidency at the age of forty-three. (The youngest person to hold the office was Theodore Roosevelt, who was forty-two when he became president in 1901 after the assassination of William McKinley.) The oldest is Donald Trump, who was seventy years old when he became president.

12-1c Race, Gender, and Religion

For most of American history, all presidential candidates, even those of minor parties, were white, male, and of the Protestant religious tradition.[2] Slowly, the pool of talent expanded. In 1928, Democrat Al Smith became the first Roman Catholic to run for president on a major-party ticket, and in 1960 Democrat John F. Kennedy was elected as the first Catholic president. Among recent unsuccessful Democratic presidential candidates, Michael Dukakis was Greek Orthodox and John Kerry was Roman Catholic.

In 2008, the doors swung wide in the presidential primaries as the Democrats chose between a white woman, Hillary Clinton, and an African American man, Barack Obama. By that time, about 90 percent of Americans told pollsters that they would be willing to support an African American for president, and the same number would support a woman.

In 2012, none of the top three finishers in the Republican primaries was Protestant. Among the 2016 finalists, however, Democrat Hillary Clinton and Republicans Ted Cruz, John Kasich, and Donald Trump are all Protestant. Republican Marco Rubio is Catholic, and Democrat Bernie Sanders is Jewish. As Cuban Americans, Cruz and Rubio are also Hispanic.

CRITICAL THINKING

▶ *Why do some people believe so strongly that Barack Obama must have been born in a foreign country?*

12–2 THE PRESIDENT'S MANY ROLES

LO Explain the roles that a president adopts while in office.

The president has the authority to exercise a variety of powers. Some of these are explicitly outlined in the Constitution, and some are simply required by the office—such as the power to persuade. In the course of exercising these powers, the president performs a variety of roles. For example, as commander in chief of the armed services, the president can exercise significant military powers.

Which roles a president executes successfully usually depends on what is happening domestically and internationally, as well as on the president's personality. Some presidents, including Bill Clinton (1993–2001) during his first term, have shown much more interest in domestic policy than in foreign policy. Others, such as George H. W. Bush (1989–1993), were more interested in foreign affairs than in domestic ones.

Table 12–1 summarizes the major roles of the president. An important role is, of course, that of chief executive. Other roles include those of commander in chief, head of state, chief diplomat, chief legislator, and political party leader.

12–2a Chief Executive

According to Article II of the Constitution,

> The executive Power shall be vested in a President of the United States of America. … [H]e may require the Opinion, in writing, of the principal Officer in each of the executive Departments, upon any Subject relating to the Duties of their respective Offices … and he shall nominate, and by and with the Advice and Consent of the Senate, shall appoint … Officers of the United States…. [H]e shall take Care that the Laws be faithfully executed.

This constitutional provision makes the president of the United States the nation's **chief executive,** or the head of the executive branch of the federal government.

When the framers created the office of the president, they created a uniquely American institution. Nowhere else in the world at that time was there a democratically chosen chief executive. The executive branch is also unique among the branches of government because it is headed by a single individual—the president.

12–2b Commander in Chief

The Constitution states that the president "shall be Commander in Chief of the Army and Navy of the United States, and of the Militia of the several States, when called into the actual Service of the United States." As **commander in chief** of the nation's armed forces, the president exercises tremendous power.

Under the Constitution, war powers are divided between Congress and the president. Congress was given the power to declare war and the

chief executive The head of the executive branch of government. In the United States, the president.

commander in chief The supreme commander of a nation's military force.

TABLE 12–1 ROLES OF THE PRESIDENT

Chief executive   Enforces laws and federal court decisions, along with treaties approved by the United States.

- Appoints, with Senate approval, and removes high-ranking officers of the federal government.
- Grants reprieves, pardons, and amnesties.
- Handles national emergencies during peacetime, such as riots or natural disasters.

Commander in chief   Leads the nation's armed forces.

- Can commit troops for up to ninety days in response to a military threat (War Powers Resolution).
- Can make secret agreements with other countries.
- Can set up military governments in occupied nations.
- Can end fighting by calling a cease-fire (armistice).

Head of state   Performs ceremonial activities as a personal symbol of the nation.

- Decorates war heroes.
- Dedicates parks and museums.
- Throws out first pitch of baseball season.
- Lights national Christmas tree and pardons the national Thanksgiving turkey.
- Receives foreign heads of state.

Chief diplomat   Directs U.S. foreign policy and is the nation's most important representative in dealing with foreign countries.

- Negotiates and signs treaties with other nations, which go into effect with Senate approval.
- Makes pacts (executive agreements) with other heads of state, without Senate approval.
- Can accept the legitimacy of another country's government (power of recognition).

Chief legislator   Informs Congress about the condition of the country and recommends legislative measures.

- Proposes legislative program to Congress in traditional State of the Union address.
- Suggests budget to Congress, and submits annual economic report.
- Can veto a bill passed by Congress.
- Can call special sessions of Congress.

Political party leader   Heads political party.

- Chooses a vice president.
- Makes several thousand top government appointments, often to party faithful (patronage).
- Tries to execute the party's platform.
- Attends party fund-raisers.
- May help reelect party members running for office as mayors, governors, or members of Congress.

power to raise and maintain the country's armed forces. The president, as commander in chief, was given the power to deploy the armed forces.

12-2c Head of State

Traditionally, a country's monarch has performed the function of head of state—the country's representative to the rest of the world. The United States, of course, has no king or queen to act as head of state. Thus, the president of the United States fulfills this role.

The president engages in many symbolic or ceremonial activities, such as throwing out the first pitch to open the baseball season (an honor Trump has declined) and turning on the lights of the national Christmas tree. The president also decorates war heroes, dedicates parks and museums, receives visiting heads of state at the White House, and goes on official state visits to other countries.

Some argue that presidents should not perform such ceremonial duties because they take time that the president should be spending on "real work." Most presidents, however, have found the role of head of state to be politically useful.

12-2d Chief Diplomat

A diplomat is a person who represents one country in dealing with representatives of another country. In the United States, the president is the nation's chief diplomat. The Constitution did not explicitly reserve this role to the president, but since the beginning of this nation, presidents have assumed the role based on their explicit constitutional powers to "receive [foreign] Ambassadors" and, with the advice and consent of the Senate, to appoint U.S. ambassadors and make treaties. As chief diplomat, the president directs the foreign policy of the United States and is our nation's most important diplomatic representative.

12-2e Chief Legislator

Nowhere in the Constitution do the words *chief legislator* appear. The Constitution, however, does require that the president "from time to time give to the Congress Information of the State of the Union, and recommend to their Consideration such Measures as he shall judge necessary and expedient." The president has, in fact, become a major player in shaping the congressional agenda—the set of measures that actually get discussed and acted on.

Presidential Activism   Presidents have not always been major players. In the nineteenth century,

some presidents preferred to let Congress lead the way in proposing and implementing policy. Since the administration of Theodore Roosevelt (1901–1909), however, presidents have taken an activist approach. Presidents are now expected to develop a legislative program and propose a budget to Congress every year.

In the past, this shared power has often put Congress and the president at odds. President Bill Clinton's administration, for example, drew up a health-care reform package in 1993 and presented it to Congress almost on a take-it-or-leave-it basis. Congress left it.

Legislation under Obama   To avoid such confrontations, President Obama frequently let Congress determine much of the content of important new legislation, such as the health-care reform bills. In the example of health-care reform, President Obama's deference to Congress had several negative consequences. These included an unusually large number of earmarks, a protracted and unpopular legislative process, and opportunities for conservatives to mobilize against the reforms. Still, in the end, Obama succeeded where Clinton had failed.

12-2f Political Party Leader

The president of the United States is also the *de facto* leader of his or her political party. The Constitution, of course, does not mention this role because, in the eyes of the founders, parties should have no place in the American political system.

As party leader, the president exercises substantial powers. For example, the president in effect chooses the chairperson of the party's national committee. The president can also exert political power within the party by using presidential appointment and removal powers.

Naturally, presidents are beholden to the party members who put them in office. Thus, usually they indulge in the practice of patronage—appointing individuals to government or public jobs to reward those who helped them win the presidential contest.

The president may also reward party members with fund-raising assistance.

> **head of state** The person who serves as the ceremonial head of a country's government and represents that country to the rest of the world.
>
> **diplomat** A person who represents one country in dealing with representatives of another country.
>
> **chief diplomat** The role of the president of the United States in recognizing and interacting with foreign governments.
>
> **patronage** The practice by which elected officials give government jobs to individuals who helped them gain office.

Paul J. Richards/Getty Images

President Obama with Japan's prime minister, Shinzo Abe. *How can the president benefit by meeting foreign leaders?*

The president is, in a sense, "fund-raiser in chief" for his or her party, and recent presidents, including Bill Clinton, George W. Bush (2001–2009), and Barack Obama, have proved themselves to be prodigious fund-raisers.

12–3 PRESIDENTIAL POWERS

LO Indicate the scope of presidential powers.

The president exercises numerous powers. Some of these powers are set forth in the Constitution. Others, known as *inherent powers*, are those that are necessary to carry out the president's constitutional duties. We look next at these powers, as well as at the expansion of presidential powers over time.

12–3a The President's Constitutional Powers

As you have read, the constitutional source for the president's authority is found in Article II of the Constitution, which states, "The executive Power shall be vested in a President of the United States of America."

treaty A formal agreement between the governments of two or more countries.

The Constitution then sets forth the president's relatively limited constitutional responsibilities.

The Specified Powers
Article II grants the president broad but vaguely described powers. From the very beginning, there were different views as to what exactly the "executive Power" clause enabled the president to do. Nonetheless, Sections 2 and 3 of Article II list the following specific presidential powers. These powers parallel the roles of the president discussed in the previous section:

▶ **To serve as commander in chief of the armed forces and the state militias.**

▶ **To appoint, with the Senate's consent, the heads of the executive departments, ambassadors, justices of the Supreme Court, and other top officials.**

▶ **To make treaties, with the advice and consent of the Senate.**

▶ **To grant reprieves and pardons, except in cases of impeachment.**

▶ **To deliver the annual State of the Union address to Congress and to send other messages to Congress from time to time.**

▶ **To call either house or both houses of Congress into special sessions.**

▶ **To receive ambassadors and other representatives from foreign countries.**

▶ **To commission all officers of the United States.**

▶ **To ensure that the laws passed by Congress "be faithfully executed."**

In addition, Article I, Section 7, gives the president the power to veto legislation. Many of the president's powers are balanced by the powers of Congress. We return to the relationship between the president and Congress later in this chapter.

Proposal and Ratification of Treaties A **treaty** is a formal agreement between two or more countries. The president has the sole power to negotiate and sign treaties with other countries. The Senate, however, must approve a treaty by a two-thirds vote of the members present before it becomes effective. If the treaty is approved by the Senate and signed by the president, it becomes law.

Nuclear Weapons Agreements.
Presidents have not always succeeded in winning the Senate's approval for treaties. In 1999, Bill Clinton was unable to persuade the Senate to approve the Comprehensive Test Ban Treaty, which would have prohibited all signers from testing nuclear weapons. Clinton argued that the United States no longer needed to test its nuclear weapons and that the treaty's restrictions on other countries would enhance our national security. The treaty was defeated largely on a party-line vote, with the Republicans opposed.

In contrast, Barack Obama convinced the Senate to approve the New Strategic Arms Reduction Treaty (New START) with Russia in December 2010. The treaty reduced by half the number of nuclear missiles in both countries and provided for inspections. New START was supported by all of the Democrats and by many Republicans.

Trade Agreements. Obama was less successful as a treaty maker in his second term, especially after the 2014 elections, which produced a Republican Senate. In 2015, he won support for the power to negotiate the Trans-Pacific Partnership (TPP), a proposed agreement between the United States and various nations that lie on the Pacific rim. The power to negotiate depended on *fast-track authority*, under which Congress agreed that it would vote the entire deal up or down without amendments. Fast-track authority for the TPP passed by a narrow margin, however, and the treaty itself was not concluded until 2016, in the middle of that year's presidential elections. When both Republican Donald Trump and Democrat Hillary Clinton came out against the deal, its failure was inevitable.

The Power to Grant Reprieves and Pardons

The president's power to grant a pardon serves as a check on judicial power. A *pardon* is a release from punishment or the legal consequences of a crime. It restores a person to the full rights and privileges of citizenship.

In 1925, the United States Supreme Court upheld an expansive interpretation of the president's pardon power in a case involving an individual convicted for contempt of court. The Court held that the power covers all offenses "either before trial, during trial, or after trial, by individuals, or by classes, conditionally or absolutely, and this without modification or regulation by Congress."[3]

President Gerald Ford appearing at a House Judiciary Committee hearing on his decision to pardon former President Richard Nixon. A presidential appearance before a congressional committee is highly unusual. *Should it happen more often? Why or why not?*

The president can grant a pardon for any federal offense, except in cases of impeachment.

One of the most controversial pardons was that granted by President Gerald Ford (1974–1977) to former president Richard Nixon (1969–1974) after the Watergate affair (to be discussed later in the chapter) before any formal charges were brought in court. The power to pardon includes the right to grant clemency, that is, the commutation (shortening) of a prison sentence. At the end of his second term, Barack Obama commuted an unusually large number of sentences. Most of those who benefited were serving long sentences for drug crimes. Obama also commuted the sentence of Chelsea Manning, an Army private who had released huge quantities of classified information to the WikiLeaks website.

Sometimes pardons are granted to a class of individuals as a general amnesty. For example, President Jimmy Carter (1977–1981) granted amnesty to tens of thousands of people who had resisted the draft during the Vietnam War by failing to register for the draft or by moving abroad. (Earlier, President Ford had established a conditional amnesty plan that required two years of public service.)

The President's Veto Power

As described earlier in this text, the president can **veto** a bill passed by Congress. Congress can override the veto with a

> **veto** A Latin word meaning "I forbid"; the refusal by an official, such as the president of the United States or a state governor, to sign a bill into law.

President Jimmy Carter (center) with Egyptian president Anwar Sadat (left) and Israeli prime minister Menachem Begin (right) at the signing of the Camp David Accords in 1978. Since then, Egypt and Israel have remained at peace with each other. *Would negotiating such agreements help a president politically? Why or why not?*

two-thirds vote by the members present in each chamber. The result of a veto override is that the bill becomes law against the wishes of the president.

If the president does not send a bill back to Congress after ten congressional working days, the bill becomes law without the president's signature. If the president refuses to sign the bill and Congress adjourns within ten working days after the bill has been submitted to the president, however, the bill is killed for that session of Congress. This step is called a *pocket veto*.

Presidents used the veto power sparingly until the administration of Andrew Johnson (1865–1869). Johnson vetoed twenty-one bills. Franklin D. Roosevelt (1933–1945) vetoed more bills by far than any of his predecessors or successors in the presidency. During his administration, there were 372 regular vetoes, 9 of which were overridden by Congress, and 263 pocket vetoes.

With a Congress led by his own party during the first two years of his presidency, President Obama exercised the veto power only twice. Surprisingly, Obama issued no vetoes during the next four years, even though the Republicans were in control of the House. Apparently, no measure that Obama would have opposed was able to make its way through the Democratic-controlled Senate. In his last two years, however, with Republicans in control of the Senate, Obama issued ten additional vetoes, one of which was overridden by Congress.

Presidents have often argued in favor of a *line-item veto* that would enable them to veto just one (or several) items in a bill. In 1996, Congress passed and President Clinton signed a line-item veto bill. In 1998, though, the Supreme Court concluded that the bill was unconstitutional.[4]

12–3b The President's Inherent Powers

In addition to the powers explicitly granted by the Constitution, the president also has *inherent powers*—powers that are necessary to carry out the specific responsibilities of the president as set forth in the Constitution.

The presidency is, of course, an institution of government, but it is also an institution that consists, at any one moment in time, of one individual. That means the lines between the presidential office and the person who holds that office often become blurred. Certain presidential powers that are generally recognized today were simply assumed by strong presidents to be inherent powers of the presidency, and their successors then continued to exercise these powers.

President Woodrow Wilson clearly indicated this interplay between presidential personality and presidential powers in the following observation:

> The President is at liberty, both in law and conscience, to be as big a man as he can. His capacity will set the limit; and if Congress be overborne by him, it will be no fault of the makers of the Constitution—it will be from no lack of constitutional powers on his part, but only because the President has the nation behind him, and Congress has not.[5]

In other words, because the Constitution is vague as to the actual carrying out of presidential powers, presidents are left to define the limits of their authority—subject, of course, to obstacles raised by the other branches of government.

12–3c The Expansion of Presidential Powers

The Constitution defines presidential powers in very general language, and even the founders were uncertain just how the president would perform the various functions.

George Washington (1789–1797) set many of the precedents that have defined presidential power. For example, he removed officials from office, interpreting the constitutional power to appoint officials as implying power to remove them as well.[6]

Washington established the practice of meeting regularly with the heads of the three departments that then existed (plus the attorney general) and of turning to them for political advice. He set a precedent for the president to act as chief legislator by submitting proposed legislation to Congress.

Outgoing President Bill Clinton addresses the troops during an awards ceremony at Fort Myer, Virginia, in January 2001. *Why do presidents enjoy visiting the troops?*

Expansion under Later Presidents

Abraham Lincoln (1861–1865), confronting the problems of the Civil War during the 1860s, took several important actions while Congress was not in session. He suspended certain constitutional liberties, spent funds that Congress had not appropriated, blockaded southern ports, and banned "treasonable correspondence" from the U.S. mail. Lincoln carried out all of these actions in the name of his power as commander in chief and his constitutional responsibility to "take Care that the Laws be faithfully executed."[7]

Other presidents, including Thomas Jefferson (1801–1809), Andrew Jackson (1829–1837), Woodrow Wilson, Franklin D. Roosevelt, and George W. Bush, also greatly expanded the powers of the president. The power of the president continues to evolve, depending on the person holding the office, the relative power of Congress, and events at home and abroad.

The President's Expanded Legislative Powers

Congress has come to expect the president to develop a legislative program. From time to time, the president submits special messages on certain subjects. These messages call on Congress to enact laws that the president thinks are necessary. The president also works closely with members of Congress to persuade them to support particular programs. The president writes, telephones, and meets with various congressional leaders to discuss pending bills. The president also sends aides to lobby on Capitol Hill.

One study of the legislative process found that "no other single actor in the political system has quite the capability of the president to set agendas in given policy areas."[8] As one lobbyist told a researcher, "Obviously, when a president sends up a bill [to Congress], it takes first place in the queue. All other bills take second place."

The Power to Persuade. The president's political skills and ability to persuade others play a large role in determining the administration's success. According to Richard Neustadt in his classic work *Presidential Power,* "Presidential power is the power to persuade."[9] For all of the resources at the president's disposal, the president still must rely on the cooperation of others if the administration's goals are to be accomplished. After three years in office, President Harry Truman made this remark about the powers of the president:

> The president may have a great many powers given to him in the Constitution and may have certain powers under certain laws which are given to him by the Congress of the United States; but the principal power that the president has is to bring people in and try to persuade them to do what they ought to do without persuasion. That's what the powers of the president amount to.[10]

Persuasive powers are particularly important when divided government exists. If a president from one political party faces a Congress dominated by the other party, the president must overcome more opposition than usual to get legislation passed.

Going Public. The president may also use a strategy known as "going public"—that is, using press conferences, public appearances, and televised events to arouse public opinion in favor of certain legislative programs.[11] The public may then pressure legislators to support the administration's programs. A president who has the support of the public can wield significant persuasive power over Congress. Presidents who are voted into office through "landslide" elections have increased bargaining power because of their widespread popularity. Those with less popular support have less bargaining leverage.

The ability of the president to "go public" effectively is dependent on popular attitudes toward the president. It is also dependent on the political climate in Washington, D.C. In periods of severe political polarization—such as the last several years—going public can actually be counterproductive. Simply by endorsing a proposal that might have had bipartisan support, the president can turn the question into a partisan issue. Without support from at least some members of both parties, the proposal then fails to pass.

The Power to Influence the Economy. Some of the greatest expansions of presidential power occurred during Franklin Roosevelt's administration. Roosevelt claimed the presidential power to regulate the economy during the Great Depression in the 1930s. Since that time, Americans have expected the president to be actively involved in economic matters and social programs. That expectation becomes especially potent during a major economic downturn, such as the Great Recession that began in December 2007.

Each year, the president sends Congress a suggested budget and the *Economic Report of the President*. The budget message proposes what amounts of money the government will need for its programs. The *Economic Report of the President* presents the state of the nation's economy and recommends ways to improve it.

Voters may rate a president based on the state of the economy. Experts have observed that the president's ability to control the level of economic activity is subject to severe limits. From the public's point of view, however, evaluating its leaders based on results makes good sense. If a president is under constant political

As chief diplomat, George Washington made foreign policy decisions without consulting Congress. This action laid the groundwork for an active presidential role in foreign policy.

By the time Abraham Lincoln gave his first Inauguration Day speech, seven southern states had already seceded from the Union. Some scholars believe that Lincoln's skillful and vigorous handling of the Civil War increased the power and prestige of the presidency.

In its attempts to counter the effects of the Great Depression, Franklin D. Roosevelt's administration not only extended the role of the national government in regulating the nation's economic life, but also further increased the power of the president.

PERCEPTION VS. REALITY

If You Like the President, You'll Love the Economy

Among political scientists, one of the most enduring beliefs is that the state of the economy is the single most important factor in determining who wins elections. In 2012, Republican presidential candidate Mitt Romney squared off against Democratic president Barack Obama. Commentators from coast to coast focused on one set of statistics—the net number of jobs created in the economy during the previous month. Polling expert Nate Silver had it down to a formula: Obama's break-even point was 150,000 new jobs per month. Much more than that and Obama was on the road to reelection. Much less and Mitt Romney would claim the Oval Office.

The Perception

James Carville, a campaign strategist for Bill Clinton in 1992, coined the classic slogan "It's the economy, stupid." This line was directed at Clinton campaign workers, but it contains an essential truth that everyone can appreciate: voters care more about the economy than anything else.

The Reality

While Carville's statement does contain a truth, as usual reality is more complicated. Sometimes the state of the economy is indeed an overwhelming determinant of the election results. In September 2008, the investment bank Lehman Brothers collapsed. This event marked the beginning of the worst economic crisis in seventy years. On Election Day 2008, no one could doubt that the state of the economy was bad. The outgoing president was a Republican—George W. Bush—and Democrat Barack Obama easily won the White House.

Popular agreement about the state of the economy did not last, however. Consider a 2014 poll by the *New York Times* and CBS. Six years after the Lehman Brothers bankruptcy, 43 percent of Democrats believed that the economy had improved in the last year. Only 20 percent of independents thought the same way, and a mere 8 percent of Republicans agreed. These people were all looking at the same economy. The only difference was how they felt about living under a Democratic president.

Immediately before the 2016 elections, 81 percent of Republicans told the Gallup Poll that the economy was getting worse. Right after the elections, only 44 percent were that pessimistic. Before the elections, 61 percent of Democrats thought the economy was getting better. Afterwards, only 46 percent agreed. Nothing about the economy changed on Election Day. It would be more than two months before president-elect Trump could do anything, for better or worse.

Clearly, if the economic news is dramatic enough, it will affect how people vote. In calmer times, however, voters' perception of the economy can be hugely influenced by whether "their team" is winning.

Blog On

To see the details of the 2016 Gallup poll just mentioned, search for "gallup confidence 2016 election." Search for "power economy president" to find Neil Irwin's explanation of the limits of a president's power over the economy.

pressure to improve the economy, he or she is likely to do whatever is possible to reach that goal. Still, popular perceptions of the state of the economy are not always accurate, as we describe in this chapter's *Perception vs. Reality* feature.

Legislative Success. Presidents' legislative success can be defined as how often they get their way on roll-call votes on which they have taken a clear position. Typically, a president's success record is very high upon first taking office and then gradually declines. This is sometimes attributed to the president's "honeymoon period," when Congress may be most likely to work with the president to achieve the president's legislative agenda.

The media often put a great deal of emphasis on how successful a president is during the "first hundred days" in office. Ironically, this is also the period when the president is least experienced in the ways of the White House, particularly if the president was a Washington outsider, such as a businessperson, before becoming president.

In 2009, President Obama had the most successful legislative year of any president in half a century. Large Democratic majorities in both chambers of Congress were surely important in explaining Obama's ability to obtain the legislation that he sought. Obama was also successful in 2010. After the Democrats lost control of the U.S. House in November 2010, however, Obama's success rate fell considerably. Trump, the archetype of an outsider, obtained no significant legislation in his first hundred days.

The Increasing Use of Executive Orders

As the nation's chief executive, the president is considered to have the inherent power to issue **executive orders,** which are presidential orders to carry out policies described in laws that have been passed by Congress. These orders have the force of law.

President George W. Bush (center) looks over a brief with Vice President Dick Cheney and National Security Adviser Condoleezza Rice (later to be secretary of state). *What are some of the tools a president can use to carry out foreign policy?*

The Purpose of Executive Orders. Presidents have issued executive orders for a variety of purposes, including to establish procedures for appointing noncareer administrators, to restructure the White House bureaucracy, and to ration consumer goods and administer wage and price controls under emergency conditions. Other goals have included classifying government information as secret, implementing affirmative action policies, and regulating the export of certain items. Presidents issue executive orders frequently, sometimes as many as one hundred a year.

Executive Orders under Obama. While Obama issued relatively few executive orders, he also issued more presidential memorandums than any president in history. In practice, memorandums and orders are indistinguishable. Other actions include presidential determinations, proclamations, letters, messages, and notices.

Some of Obama's actions were controversial. Republicans believed that several of them exceeded the president's constitutional authority. Two, in 2012 and 2014, were on the topic of immigration. The first of these, which was not challenged during Obama's time in office, suspended the deportation of several million illegal immigrants who had been brought to this country when they were small children, and who were not otherwise in trouble with the law. These "DREAMers" (named after a failed

> **executive order** A presidential order to carry out a policy or policies described in a law passed by Congress.

piece of legislation) were also allowed to obtain work permits. In 2014, Obama attempted to expand this program, largely to cover the parents of DREAMers. Federal courts blocked the expansion, however, and in 2017 President Trump revoked it altogether.

Trump's Executive Orders. Almost all of the actions undertaken by President Trump in the opening months of his administration took the form of executive orders. Many of these were not particularly consequential. Typically, Trump would order an executive department or agency to report on how it could address the policies of the Trump administration.

Trump also issued two orders that sought to block admission into the United States of persons from several Muslim-majority nations and to suspend the admission of refugees from Syria. The first of these orders was so sweeping that it covered persons who had already received visas to travel to the United States. It even included *permanent residents* ("green card" holders, who are lawful immigrants) from the affected countries who were temporarily outside of the United States. A permanent resident from Iran who was visiting Canada, for example, would be blocked from returning home. Chaos ensued at airports as visa holders and permanent residents were arrested upon deplaning—and demonstrators gathered to defend them.

This order was swiftly blocked by federal courts as a violation of the rights of lawful resident immigrants. A replacement order eliminated the ban on those holding visas or green cards. The courts suspended this order as well, on the ground that it effectively imposed discrimination on the basis of religion, contravening constitutional and legislative protections. In June 2017, however, the Supreme Court temporarily reinstated the ban for those with no "*bona fide* relationship with a person or entity in the United States." That rule stopped agencies from approving new refugees, but affected few others.

Signing Statements A signing statement is a written statement issued by a president at the time he or she signs a bill into law. James Monroe (1817–1825) was the first president to issue such a statement. For many years, signing statements were rare—before the presidency of Ronald Reagan, only seventy-five were issued. Most were " rhetorical" in character. They might praise the legislation or the Congress that passed it, or criticize the opposition. On occasion, however, the statements noted constitutional problems with one or more clauses of a bill or provided details as to how the executive branch would interpret legislative language.

Reagan and Signing Statements. Reagan issued a grand total of 249 signing statements. For the first time, each statement was published in the *U.S. Code Congressional and Administrative News*, along with the text of the bill in question. A substantial share of the statements addressed constitutional issues. Reagan staff member Samuel Alito, Jr.—who now sits on the United States Supreme Court—issued a memo in favor of using signing statements to "increase the power of the Executive to shape the law."

Signing Statements under Bush. George W. Bush took the use of signing statements to an entirely new level. Bush's 161 statements challenged more than 1,100 clauses of federal law—more legal provisions than were challenged by all previous presidents put together.[12] The powers that the statements claimed for the president alarmed some people. One statement rejected Congress's authority to ban torture. Another affirmed that

> "If one morning I walked on top of the water across the Potomac River, the headline that afternoon would read: 'President Can't Swim.'"
>
> ~ LYNDON B. JOHNSON
> THIRTY-SIXTH PRESIDENT
> OF THE UNITED STATES
> 1963–1969

the president could have anyone's mail opened without a warrant. Obama reduced the number of signing statements substantially.

Evolving Presidential Power in Foreign Affairs The precise extent of the president's power in foreign affairs is constantly evolving. The president is commander in chief and chief diplomat, but only Congress has the power to formally declare war, and the Senate must ratify any treaty that the president has negotiated with other nations. Nevertheless, from the beginning, our country has been led by the president in foreign affairs.

George Washington laid the groundwork for our long history of the president's active role in foreign policy. For example, when war broke out between Britain and France in 1793, Washington chose to disregard a treaty of alliance with France and to pursue a course of strict neutrality. Since that time, on many occasions presidents have taken military actions and made foreign policy without consulting Congress.

Executive Agreements. In foreign affairs, presidential power is enhanced by the ability to make executive agreements, which are pacts between the president and other heads of state. Executive agreements do not require Senate approval, but they have the same legal status as treaties.

Presidents form executive agreements for a wide range of purposes. Some involve routine matters, such as promises of assistance to other countries. Others concern matters of great importance. To prevent presidential abuse of the power to make executive agreements, Congress passed a law in 1972 that requires the president to inform Congress within sixty days of making any executive agreement. The law did not limit the president's power to make executive agreements, however, and

signing statement A written statement, appended to a bill at the time the president signs it into law, indicating how the president interprets that legislation.

executive agreement A binding international agreement, or pact, that is made between the president and another head of state and that does not require Senate approval.

President George H. W. Bush presents a posthumous Medal of Honor. *Why did Bush order U.S. forces into combat with Iraq in 1991?*

they continue to be used far more than treaties in making foreign policy.

For example, in 2015, the United States and five other world powers approved a deal with Iran to limit that country's ability to obtain nuclear weapons. President Obama treated the pact as an executive agreement rather than a treaty, in part because there were not enough votes in the Senate to pass it as a treaty. Needless to say, Republicans (and a few Democrats) strongly opposed this step. Because it was only an executive agreement, President Trump could have reversed Obama's decision and pulled the United States out of the deal. That would not have prevented the other nations from proceeding with it, though. In the end, Trump let the agreement stand.

Military Actions. The U.S. Constitution gives Congress the power to declare war. Consider, however, that although Congress has declared war in only five different conflicts during our nation's history, the United States has engaged in more than two hundred activities involving the armed services.[13]

Without a congressional declaration of war, President Truman sent U.S. armed forces to Korea in 1950, thus involving American troops in the conflict between North and South Korea. The United States also entered the Vietnam War (1965–1975) without a declaration of war. George H. W. Bush did, however, obtain congressional approval to use American troops to force Iraq to withdraw from Kuwait in 1991.

The War Powers Resolution. As commander in chief, the president can respond quickly to a military threat without waiting for congressional action. This power to involve the nation in a war upset many members of Congress as the undeclared war in Vietnam dragged on for years into the 1970s. Criticism of the president's role in the Vietnam conflict led to the passage of the War Powers Resolution of 1973.

The law, which was passed over President Nixon's veto, requires the president to notify Congress within forty-eight hours of deploying troops. It also prevents the president from keeping troops abroad for more than sixty days (or ninety days, if more time is needed for a successful withdrawal). If Congress does not authorize a longer period, the troops must be removed.

The War on Terrorism. President George W. Bush did not obtain a declaration of war from Congress for the war against terrorism that began on September 11, 2001. Instead, Congress passed a joint resolution authorizing the president to use "all necessary and appropriate force against those nations, organizations, or persons he determines planned, authorized, committed, or aided the terrorist attacks that occurred on September 11, 2001."

This resolution was the basis for America's subsequent involvement in Afghanistan. Also, in October 2002, Congress passed a joint resolution authorizing the use of U.S. armed forces against Iraq.

Obama at War. President Obama inherited conflicts in Afghanistan and Iraq, and he was more interested in winding these conflicts down than expanding them. No requests for congressional authority were necessary. In 2011, however, Obama used air power in Libya without congressional authorization.

In 2013, with clear reluctance, Obama asked for authority to bomb the forces of dictator Bashar al-Assad in Syria. The reason was that Assad was using poison gas against his own people. Assad later agreed to turn over his chemical weapons for destruction. This settlement was fortunate for Obama, in part because it appeared likely that Congress would refuse to give him support for military action.

Obama did not request authority to attack the terrorist group ISIS in Iraq and Syria in 2014. Some observers, contemplating Obama's request for a vote over Syria's chemical weapons and his failure to make such a request over Libya and ISIS, thought they saw a pattern. Obama was willing to seek authority for steps that he was not eager to take. For actions on which he was dead set, he preferred to ignore Congress as much as possible.

Trump, Syria—and Russia. In April 2017, Syrian dictator Bashar al-Assad employed poison gas in an attack on Syrian civilians in rebel-held territory. Hundreds died, including children. This chemical weapon was one that Assad had supposedly given up in 2013. Clearly, Assad had either hidden some of the material in 2013 or had obtained new supplies. One day later, President Trump ordered the bombing of an airfield used to undertake the chemical attack.

Russian president Vladimir Putin was a strong defender of Assad and had provided him with military support. Trump's friendly attitude toward Putin and his desire to come to an agreement with Russia were well known. The bombing of the airfield, however, put a freeze on U.S.–Russia relations, at least temporarily. It also raised the question of whether Trump's friendly attitude toward Putin could survive contact with real-world conditions.

Nuclear Weapons. Since 1945, the president, as commander in chief, has been responsible for the most difficult of all military decisions—if and when to use nuclear weapons. In 1945, President Truman made the extraordinary decision to drop atomic bombs on the Japanese cities of Hiroshima and Nagasaki. "The final decision," he said, "on where and when to use the atomic bomb was up to me. Let there be no mistake about it." Today, the president travels at all times with the "football"— the briefcase containing the codes used to launch a nuclear attack.

CRITICAL THINKING

▶ *Some observers believe that it is almost impossible for the president to change the nation's policies simply by delivering a speech, no matter how important the topic. Do you think this is true? Why or why not?*

12-4 CONGRESSIONAL AND PRESIDENTIAL RELATIONS

LO Describe advantages enjoyed by Congress and by the president in their institutional relationship.

Despite the seemingly immense powers at the president's disposal, the president is limited in what he or she can accomplish, or even attempt. In our system of checks and balances, the president must share powers with the legislative and judicial branches of government. The president's power is checked not only by these institutions, but also by the media, public opinion, and the voters. The founders hoped that this system of shared power would lessen the chance of tyranny.

Some scholars believe the relationship between Congress and the president is the most important one in the American system of government. Congress traditionally has had the upper hand in some areas, primarily in passing legislation. In some other areas, though, particularly in foreign affairs, the president can exert tremendous power that Congress has almost no ability to check.

> "As to the presidency, the two happiest days of my life were those of my entrance upon the office and my surrender of it."
>
> ~ MARTIN VAN BUREN
> EIGHTH PRESIDENT OF THE UNITED STATES
> 1837–1841

12-4a Advantage: Congress

Congress has the advantage over the president in the areas of legislative authorization, the regulation of foreign and interstate commerce, and some budgetary matters. Of course, as you have already read, the president today proposes a legislative agenda and a budget to Congress every year. Nonetheless, only Congress has the power to pass the legislation and appropriate the money. The most the president can do constitutionally is veto an entire bill if it contains something that she or he does not like. (As noted, however, recent presidents have frequently used signing statements in an attempt to nullify portions of bills that they did not approve.)

Presidential popularity is a source of power for the president in dealings with Congress. Presidents spend a great deal of time courting public opinion, eyeing their "presidential approval ratings," and meeting with the press. Much of this activity is for the purpose of gaining leverage with Congress. Yet even when the president

President-elect Trump meets with House Speaker Paul Ryan (R., Wisc.) shortly after the 2016 elections. *What are the relative powers of Congress and the president over the budget?*

puts all of his or her persuasive powers to work in achieving a legislative agenda, Congress still retains the ultimate lawmaking authority.

Divided Government When government is divided—with at least one house of Congress controlled by a different party than the White House—the president can have difficulty even getting a legislative agenda to the floor for a vote. President Barack Obama faced such a problem in 2011, when the Republicans gained a majority in the House of Representatives. During his first two years as president, Obama had worked with a very cooperative Democrat-led Congress. After the Republicans became the majority party in the House, however, divided government existed again. Indeed, few people in public life could remember a time when partisan hostilities had been so intense.

After the 2016 elections, Republicans held both chambers of Congress and the presidency. The era of divided government was over, at least for now. Still, in 2017, Republicans in the House and the Senate were unable to agree on a replacement for the Affordable Care Act (Obamacare). Apparently, congressional Republicans were capable of tying themselves in political knots without any assistance at all from the Democrats.

Different Constituencies Congress and the president have different constituencies, and this fact influences their relationship. Members of Congress represent a state or a local district, and this gives them a regional focus. Members of Congress like to have legislative successes of their own to bring home to their constituents—military bases that remain operative, public-works projects that create local jobs, or trade rules that benefit a big local employer. Ideally, the president's focus should be on the nation as a whole: national defense, homeland security, the national economy. At times, this can put the president at odds even with members of his or her own party in Congress.

Furthermore, members of Congress and the president face different election cycles (every two years in the House, every six years in the Senate, and every four years for the president), and the president is limited to two terms in office. Consequently, the president and Congress sometimes feel a different sense of urgency about implementing legislation. For example, the president often senses the need to demonstrate legislative success during the first year in office, when the excitement over the elections is still fresh in the minds of politicians and the public.

12–4b Advantage: The President

The president has the advantage over Congress in dealing with a national crisis, in setting foreign policy, and in influencing public opinion. In times of crisis, the presidency is arguably the most crucial institution in government because, when necessary, the president can act quickly, speak with one voice, and represent the nation to the world.

Some scholars have argued that recent presidents have abused the powers of the presidency by taking advantage of crises. Others have argued that there is an unwritten "doctrine of necessity" under which presidential powers can and should be expanded during a crisis. When this has happened in the past, however, Congress has always retaken some control when the crisis was over, in a natural process of institutional give-and-take.

A president is in a much stronger bargaining position if he or she has just won office in a "landslide election." Presidents elected in landslides include Reagan in 1984 (59 percent of the vote), Nixon in 1972 (61 percent), and Johnson in 1964 (also 61 percent). Given low voter turnout, however, no president has ever received the votes of a majority of all eligible adults. Johnson came closest, but even he won the votes of fewer than 40 percent of the electorate. As a result, it is questionable whether even presidents elected by a land-slide can claim to have a "mandate from the people."

The War on Terrorism A problem faced during the George W. Bush administration was that the "war on terrorism" had no obvious end or conclusion. It was not clear when the crisis would be over and the nation could return to normal government relations and procedures. Many supporters of Barack Obama believed that upon election, he would restore civil liberties lost during Bush's war on terrorism. As it turned out, the Obama administration kept most of Bush's policies in place.

Executive Privilege Congress has the authority to investigate and oversee the activities of other branches of government. Nonetheless, both Congress and the public have accepted that a certain degree of secrecy by the executive branch is necessary to protect national security. Some presidents have claimed an inherent executive power to withhold information from, or to refuse to appear before, Congress or the courts. This is called **executive privilege**, and it has been invoked by presidents from the time of George Washington to the present.

Abuses of Executive Privilege One of the problems with executive privilege is that it has been used for more purposes than simply to safeguard national security. President Nixon invoked executive privilege in an attempt to avoid handing over taped White House conversations to Congress during the **Watergate scandal.**[14] President Clinton invoked the privilege in an attempt to keep details of his sexual relationship with White House intern Monica Lewinsky a secret.

Closely related to the question of executive privilege is the issue of financial transparency on the part of the president. In contrast to every other member of the executive branch, the president is substantially free from legal limits on conflicts of interest. For many years, presidents have helped prove that their decisions were not based on personal financial interests by releasing their income tax returns. Trump, however, has refused to do so. Should he be required to release the forms? We examine that question in this chapter's *Join the Debate* feature.

CRITICAL THINKING

▶ *Would we be better off if executive privilege didn't exist, or are there some matters a president must be able to keep private? Discuss.*

President Nixon meets Chinese leader Mao Zedong. Nixon's opening to China was a foreign policy success, but his domestic abuses of power led to his resignation in 1974. *What is the mechanism by which Congress can remove a sitting president?*

12–5 THE ORGANIZATION OF THE EXECUTIVE BRANCH

LO Discuss the organization of the executive branch and the role of cabinet members in presidential administrations.

In the early days of this nation, presidents answered their own mail. Only in 1857 did Congress authorize a private secretary for the president, to be paid by the federal government. Even Woodrow Wilson typed most of his correspondence, although by that time several secretaries were assigned to the president. When Franklin Roosevelt became president in 1933, the entire executive staff consisted of thirty-seven employees. Not until Roosevelt's New Deal and World War II did the presidential staff become a sizable organization.

executive privilege An inherent executive power claimed by presidents to withhold information from, or to refuse to appear before, Congress or the courts. The president can also accord the privilege to other executive officials.

Watergate scandal A scandal involving an illegal break-in at the Democratic National Committee offices in 1972 by members of President Richard Nixon's reelection campaign staff.

12–5a The President's Cabinet

The Constitution does not specifically mention presidential assistants and advisers. The Constitution

Should We Make Trump Release His Tax Returns?

Over the last forty years, almost every major-party presidential candidate has released his or her income tax returns. Most have provided returns from multiple years, although a few have released only one or two examples. There has been one exception—Donald Trump. He has said that voters don't care about his returns, and it is a fact that he won the presidency without releasing them. Yet in polls, 74 percent of respondents say that he should make the returns public. Among Republicans alone, the share is 64 percent.

If, as seems probable, Trump continues to keep his returns secret, certain government bodies could demand them anyway as part of an investigation. Such government bodies include law enforcement agencies, such as the FBI, or congressional committees. Several Republican senators and representatives have called for Trump to release his tax forms, but no Republican-led oversight committee is likely to vote to subpoena them. That could change in the future, however—especially if the Democrats were to take control of at least one chamber of Congress in the 2018 elections. So, should we make Trump release his returns?

We Need to Know the Truth

Those who believe that Trump should release the returns note that other major presidential contenders have all understood the basic principle of transparency. The president is the most powerful official in the nation. It is important to dispel any suspicion that the president might be furthering his or her own financial interests when making important decisions. Dispelling suspicion becomes even more important with a businessman such as Trump, who has business ventures scattered across the world.

When Trump refuses to release his returns, the obvious question is: what does he have to hide? In particular, would his returns reveal any improper relations with entities tied to the Russian government? Trump's friendly attitude toward Russian president Vladimir Putin was conspicuous during the campaign and in the first months after Trump took office. Could it be that the Russians loaned Trump lots of money? The "emoluments" clause of the Constitution appears to ban U.S. officials from receiving income from foreign governments. What if Trump is in violation of this clause?

Trump's Tax Returns Are His Business, Not Ours

Others advise Trump to stand firm in keeping his taxes private. Trump's returns are several thousand pages long. If he were to release them, the world could take an unprecedented look into the detailed finances of a major entrepreneur. Trump's political opponents—and even business rivals—might locate perfectly innocent information that could still be used to harm him politically or financially. The media would devote endless hours to Trump's finances, wasting public energy that should instead be devoted to solving the nation's problems. We simply do not need to enable fishing expeditions into Trump's finances.

A more important issue may be the impact of demands for financial transparency on potential nominees for high office. Conservatives believe that businesspeople ought to take a leading role in government. How can they do that if they must open up all of their financial dealings to the public and put all of their investments in a blind trust? At least one of Trump's top nominees had to withdraw from consideration because selling some of his businesses would probably have destroyed them. We need to loosen the rules.

Critical Analysis

Is it possible for someone to serve as president and still run a private business—without running into serious ethics problems? Why or why not?

states only that the president "may require the Opinion, in writing, of the principal Officer in each of the executive Departments." Since the time of our first president, however, presidents have had an advisory group, or **cabinet,** to turn to for counsel. Originally, the cabinet consisted of only four officials—the secretaries of state, treasury, and war, plus the attorney general.

Today, the cabinet includes fourteen department secretaries, the attorney general, and a number of other officials. (See Table 12–2 for the names of the major executive departments represented in the cabinet.) Additional cabinet members vary from one presidency to the next. Typically, the vice president is a member. President George W. Bush added five officials to the cabinet, and Barack Obama added eight. Donald Trump added the following members, in addition to the vice president:

▸ **The administrator of the Environmental Protection Agency.**

▸ **The administrator of the Small Business Administration.**

▸ **The director of the Central Intelligence Agency.**

▸ **The director of National Intelligence.**

▸ **The director of the Office of Management and Budget.**

▸ **The United States ambassador to the United Nations.**

▸ **The United States trade representative.**

▸ **The White House chief of staff.**

Use of the Cabinet Because the Constitution does not require the president to consult with the cabinet, the use of this body is purely discretionary. Some presidents have relied on the counsel of their cabinets more than others. After a cabinet meeting in which a vote was seven nos against his one yes, President Lincoln supposedly said, "Seven nays and one aye, the ayes have it."[15]

Still other presidents have sought counsel from so-called **kitchen cabinets,** informal groups of unofficial advisers. The term *kitchen cabinet* originated during the presidency of Andrew Jackson, who relied on the counsel of close friends who allegedly met with him in the kitchen of the White House.

In general, presidents usually don't rely heavily on the advice of the formal cabinet. They are aware that department heads are often more responsive to the wishes of their own staffs, to their own political ambitions, or to obtaining resources for their departments than they are to the presidents they serve.

Trump's Advisers Trump scheduled only one cabinet meeting during his first hundred days in office, and he seemed unlikely to make much use of the cabinet as an advisory body. Rather, Trump received his most

TABLE 12–2 THE MAJOR EXECUTIVE DEPARTMENTS

The heads of all of these departments are members of the president's cabinet.

Department	Year of First Establishment
Department of State	1789
Department of the Treasury	1789
Department of Defense*	1789
Department of Justice (headed by the attorney general)†	1789
Department of the Interior	1849
Department of Agriculture	1889
Department of Commerce‡	1903
Department of Labor‡	1903
Department of Health and Human Services§	1953
Department of Housing and Urban Development	1965
Department of Transportation	1967
Department of Energy	1977
Department of Education	1979
Department of Veterans Affairs	1989
Department of Homeland Security	2002

*Established in 1947 by merging the Department of War, created in 1789, and the Department of the Navy, created in 1798.

†Formerly the Office of the Attorney General; renamed and reorganized in 1870.

‡Formed in 1913 by splitting the Department of Commerce and Labor, which was created in 1903.

§Formerly the Department of Health, Education, and Welfare; renamed when the Department of Education was spun off in 1979.

important advice from White House staff members, a kitchen cabinet in all but name. These advisers had a variety of backgrounds and political commitments. Some, including Vice President Mike Pence, were traditional Republicans. Another group consisted of former military generals and included not just White House staff but several members of the cabinet proper.

Two groups, however, were unusual and stood out. One consisted of members of Trump's own family and other allies from Trump's years in New York City. Above all, that meant his daughter, Ivanka Trump, and her husband, Jared Kushner. Several months

cabinet An advisory group selected by the president to assist with decision making. Traditionally, the cabinet has consisted of the heads of the executive departments and other officers whom the president may choose to appoint.

kitchen cabinet The name given to a president's unofficial advisers. The term was coined during Andrew Jackson's presidency.

into the administration, Kushner appeared to have become the most important adviser of all. A final group can be characterized as the ideologues. It was led by Steve Bannon, formerly chair of Breitbart News, a far-right news and opinion website. Bannon was linked to the *alt-right*, an online white-identity, anti-feminist movement, which easily made him Trump's most controversial adviser.

12–5b The Executive Office of the President

In 1939, President Franklin Roosevelt set up the **Executive Office of the President (EOP)** to cope with the increased responsibilities brought on by the Great Depression. Since then, the EOP has grown significantly to accommodate the increasingly expansive role played by the national government, including the executive branch, in the nation's economic and social life.

The EOP is made up of the top advisers and assistants who help the president carry out major duties. Over the years, the EOP has changed according to the needs and leadership style of each president. It has become an increasingly influential and important part of the executive branch.

Table 12–3 lists various offices within the EOP as of 2017. Note that the organization of the EOP is subject to change. Presidents have frequently added new bodies to its membership and subtracted others.

TABLE 12–3	THE EXECUTIVE OFFICE OF THE PRESIDENT AS OF 2017
Agency	
Council of Economic Advisers	
Council on Environmental Quality	
Executive Residence	
National Security Council	
Office of Administration	
Office of Management and Budget	
Office of National Drug Control Policy	
Office of Science and Technology Policy	
Office of the U.S. Trade Representative	
Office of the Vice President	
White House Office	
President's Intelligence Advisory Board	

Source: www.whitehouse.gov.

The White House Office   Of all of the executive staff agencies, the **White House Office** has the most direct contact with the president. The White House Office is headed by the **chief of staff,** who advises the president on important matters and directs the operations of the presidential staff. A number of other top officials, assistants, and special assistants to the president also provide aid in such areas as national security, the economy, and political affairs. The **press secretary**

Executive Office of the President (EOP) A group of staff agencies that assist the president in carrying out major duties.

White House Office The personal office of the president. White House Office personnel handle the president's political needs and manage the media, among other duties.

chief of staff The person who directs the operations of the White House Office and advises the president on important matters.

press secretary A member of the White House staff who holds news conferences for reporters and makes public statements for the president.

Official White House Photo by Pete Souza

President Barack Obama, Vice President Joe Biden, Secretary of State Hillary Clinton, and members of the national security team receive an update on the mission against Osama bin Laden in the Situation Room of the White House on May 1, 2011. *What happened to bin Laden?*

meets with reporters and makes public statements for the president. The counsel to the president serves as the White House lawyer and handles the president's legal matters.

The White House staff also includes speechwriters, researchers, the president's physician, and a correspondence secretary. Altogether, the White House Office has more than four hundred employees.

The White House staff has several duties. First, the staff investigates and analyzes problems that require the president's attention. Staff members who are specialists in certain areas, such as diplomatic relations or foreign trade, gather information for the president and suggest solutions. White House staff members also screen the questions, issues, and problems that people present to the president so that matters that can be handled by other officials do not reach the president's desk.

Additionally, the staff provides public relations support. For example, the press staff handles the president's relations with the White House press corps and schedules news conferences. Finally, the White House staff ensures that the president's initiatives are effectively transmitted to the relevant government personnel. Several staff members are usually assigned to work directly with members of Congress for this purpose.

The First Lady   The White House Office also includes the staff of the president's spouse. First Ladies have at times taken important roles within the White House. For example, Franklin Roosevelt's wife, Eleanor, advocated the rights of women, labor, and African Americans. As First Lady, Hillary Clinton helped develop an unsuccessful plan for a national health-care system. If she had won the 2016 elections, Bill Clinton would have become the nation's First Gentleman.

The Office of Management and Budget   The Office of Management and Budget (OMB) was originally the Bureau of the Budget. Under recent presidents, the OMB has become an important and influential unit of the Executive Office of the President. The main function of the OMB is to assist the president in preparing the proposed annual budget, which the president must submit to Congress in January of each year.

The federal budget lists the revenues and expenditures expected for the coming year. It indicates which programs the federal government will pay for and how much they will cost. Thus, the budget is an annual statement of the public policies of the United States translated into dollars and cents. Making changes in the budget is a key way for presidents to influence the direction and policies of the federal government.

Vice President Mike Pence speaks to supporters at a rally in Chesterfield, Missouri. *What powers does he have under the Constitution?*

The president appoints the director of the OMB with the consent of the Senate. The director oversees the OMB's work and argues the administration's positions before Congress. The director also lobbies members of Congress to support the president's budget or to accept key features of it. Once the budget is approved by Congress, the OMB has the responsibility of putting it into practice. The OMB oversees the execution of the budget, checking on federal agencies to ensure that they use funds efficiently.

Beyond its budget duties, the OMB also reviews new bills prepared by the executive branch. It checks all legislative matters to be certain that they agree with the president's own positions.

The National Security Council   The National Security Council (NSC) was established in 1947 to manage the domestic and foreign policies regarding the defense of the United States. Its members are the president, the vice president, and the secretaries of state and defense. It also includes several informal advisers. The NSC is the president's link to his or her key foreign and military advisers. The president's special assistant for national security affairs

Office of Management and Budget (OMB) An agency in the Executive Office of the President that has the primary duty of assisting the president in preparing and supervising the administration of the federal budget.

National Security Council (NSC) A council that advises the president on domestic and foreign matters concerning the safety and defense of the nation.

(commonly called the national security adviser) heads the NSC staff.

12–5c The Vice Presidency and Presidential Succession

As a rule, presidential nominees choose running mates who balance the ticket or whose appointment rewards or appeases party factions. For example, to balance the ticket geographically, a presidential candidate from the South may solicit a running mate from the West.

In 2008, Barack Obama picked Delaware senator Joe Biden, who had thirty-five years of experience in Congress. Obama wished to counter detractors who claimed that he was too inexperienced.

In 2012, Republican presidential candidate Mitt Romney chose Representative Paul Ryan of Wisconsin to join his ticket. Ryan helped Romney appeal to the party's conservative wing. Ryan had gained recognition as chair of the House Budget Committee when he authored a series of proposed budgets that won near-universal Republican support.

In July 2016, on the eve of the national party conventions, Donald Trump named Indiana governor Mike Pence as his running mate. Pence was as conventional as it is possible for a Republican to be, and he was clearly meant to balance the very unconventional Trump. One week later, Hillary Clinton named Virginia senator and former governor Tim Kaine to complete her ticket. Fluent in Spanish, Kaine began his legal career by representing African Americans in housing discrimination cases.

The Role of Vice Presidents For much of our history, the vice president has had almost no responsibilities. Still, the vice president is in a position to become the nation's chief executive should the president die, be impeached and convicted, or resign the presidential office. Nine vice presidents have become president because of the death or resignation of the president.

In recent years, the responsibilities of the vice president have grown substantially. The vice president has become one of the most important of the president's advisers. The first modern vice president to act as a major adviser was Walter Mondale, who served under Jimmy Carter. Later, Bill Clinton relied heavily on Vice President Al Gore, who shared many of Clinton's values and beliefs.

Without question, however, the most powerful vice president in American history was Dick Cheney, who served under George W. Bush. The unprecedented delegation of power that Cheney enjoyed would not have been possible without the president's agreement, and Bush clearly approved of it. Vice presidents Joe Biden and Mike Pence have been important advisers, but not at the level of Cheney.

Presidential Succession One of the questions left unanswered by the Constitution was what the vice president should do if the president becomes incapable of carrying out necessary duties while in office. The Twenty-fifth Amendment to the Constitution, ratified in 1967, filled this gap.

Lyndon B. Johnson is sworn in as U.S. president aboard Air Force One on November 22, 1963, shortly after the assassination of President John F. Kennedy in Dallas, Texas. Standing to the right is Kennedy's widow, Jacqueline Kennedy. To the left, behind Johnson, is his wife, Lady Bird Johnson. *How often have U.S. presidents been assassinated?*

White House Photo Office/LBJ Library photo by Cecil Stoughton

The Twenty-fifth Amendment. The amendment states that when the president believes that he or she is incapable of performing the duties of the office, he or she must inform Congress in writing of this fact. When the president is unable to communicate, a majority of the cabinet, including the vice president, can declare that fact to Congress.

In either case, the vice president then serves as acting president until the president resumes normal duties. If a dispute arises over the return of the president's ability to discharge the normal functions of the presidential office, a two-thirds vote of both chambers of Congress is required if the vice president is to remain acting president. Otherwise, the president resumes these duties.

Vice-Presidential Vacancies. The Twenty-fifth Amendment also addresses the question of how the president should fill a vacant vice presidency. Section 2 of the amendment states, "Whenever there is a vacancy in the office of the Vice President, the President shall nominate a Vice President who shall take office upon confirmation by a majority vote of both Houses of Congress."

In 1973, Gerald Ford became the first appointed vice president of the United States after Spiro Agnew was forced to resign. One year later, President Richard Nixon resigned, and Ford advanced to the office of president. President Ford named Nelson Rockefeller as his vice president. For the first time in U.S. history, neither the president nor the vice president had been elected to that position.

What if both the president and the vice president die, resign, or are disabled? According to the Succession Act of 1947, the Speaker of the House of Representatives will then act as president on her or his resignation as Speaker and as representative. If the Speaker is unavailable, next in line is the president pro tem of the Senate, followed by the permanent members of the president's cabinet in the order of the creation of their departments (see Table 12–2 earlier in this chapter).

CRITICAL THINKING

▶ *Members of the Washington political community often harbor a degree of resentment toward those who work in the White House Office. What might cause these feelings?*

AMERICA AT ODDS | The Presidency

The president is the most conspicuous figure in our political system. Everyone has opinions about what the president should do—and in a presidential election year, who the president should be. To an extent not seen in regard to other offices, the public also has a serious interest in the president's personality and character. The president, after all, represents all of us. Americans are at odds over a variety of questions relating to the presidency. These include the following:

- *Should the president try, whenever possible, to compromise with other political players, such as the Congress— or should the president generally stand on principle?*

- *Should the president seek to expand his or her authority so as to deal more effectively with the nation's problems—or should the president try to adhere to a strict constitutional understanding of the powers of the office?*

- *Is it appropriate for the president to rely primarily on staff members within the White House Office when determining*

policy—or should the president offer the cabinet a substantial policymaking role?

- *Should voters evaluate presidential candidates primarily on the positions they take on the issues— or are the president's character, personality, and decision-making style more important considerations?*

- *Should the president be the "moral leader" of the country in the sense of basing policies on religious values—or should the president avoid any intermingling of religion and policy?*

STUDY TOOLS 12

READY TO STUDY? IN THE BOOK, YOU CAN:

☐ Review what you've read with the following chapter quiz.

☐ Check your answers in Appendix D at the back of the book.

☐ Rip out the Chapter Review Card, which includes key terms and chapter summaries.

ONLINE AT WWW.CENGAGEBRAIN.COM, YOU CAN:

☐ Watch videos to get a quick overview.

☐ Expedite your studying with Major Player readings and Focus Activities.

☐ Check your understanding with Chapter Quizzes.

FILL-IN

Learning Outcome 12–1

1. The most common previous occupation of U.S. presidents has been _____

Learning Outcome 12–2

2. The president leads the nation's armed forces in his or her role as _____

3. In his or her role as _____ the president delivers the traditional State of the Union address and has the power to veto bills passed by Congress.

Learning Outcome 12–3

4. The president has the power to issue executive orders, which are _____

5. The _____ requires the president to notify Congress within forty-eight hours of deploying troops.

Learning Outcome 12–4

6. Executive privilege is _____

Learning Outcome 12–5

7. Traditionally, the cabinet has consisted of _____

8. The Executive Office of the President (EOP) is made up of a number of executive staff agencies, including the _____

MULTIPLE CHOICE

Learning Outcome 12–1

9. Which of the following is a constitutional requirement for becoming president of the United States?

   a. Must be at least thirty years old.

   b. Must be of sound moral character.

   c. Must be a natural-born citizen of the United States.

Learning Outcome 12–2

10. When the president _____, he or she is performing the role of head of state.

    a. attends party fund-raisers

    b. makes executive agreements

    c. receives foreign dignitaries

11. When the president negotiates and signs treaties with other nations, he or she is performing the role of

    a. chief diplomat.

    b. chief executive.

    c. commander in chief.

Learning Outcome 12–3

12. The presidential strategy known as "going public" refers to

    a. using press conferences, public appearances, and televised events to arouse public opinion in favor of certain legislative programs.

    b. publicly acknowledging mistakes or misconduct.

    c. appearing on talk shows.

Learning Outcome 12–4

13. The term *divided government* refers to the

    a. cultural and political differences between the red states and the blue states.

    b. case when at least one chamber of Congress is held by a different party than the White House.

    c. separation of powers.

Learning Outcome 12–5

14. If a vacancy occurs in the vice presidency,

    a. there is currently no provision for filling the office.

    b. the Speaker of the House acts as vice president.

    c. a vice president is nominated by the president and confirmed by a majority vote in both chambers of Congress.

13 | THE BUREAUCRACY

Songquan Deng/Shutterstock.com

LEARNING OUTCOMES

After reading this chapter, you should be able to:

13-1 Describe the size and functions of the U.S. bureaucracy and the major components of federal spending.

13-2 Discuss the structure and basic components of the federal bureaucracy.

13-3 Describe how the federal civil service was established and how bureaucrats get their jobs.

13-4 Explain how regulatory agencies make rules and how issue networks affect policymaking in government.

13-5 Identify some of the ways in which the government has attempted to curb waste and improve efficiency in the bureaucracy.

After
finishing this
chapter,
go to **PAGE 308**
for **STUDY TOOLS**

AMERICA AT ODDS | Does National Security Require Us to Give Up Our Privacy?

Burlingham/Shutterstock.com

The threat of terrorism in the homeland is here to stay. The nation has experienced terrorist shootings at an office Christmas party in San Bernardino, California (14 dead), at a gay nightclub in Orlando, Florida (49 dead), and elsewhere. In these two cases, the killers were inspired by ISIS—the Islamic State in Iraq and Syria, which later shortened its name to the Islamic State. Uniquely among terrorist groups, it has established a government in territory seized from Iraq and Syria. In addition to fighting in these countries, ISIS has told its followers worldwide through social media to kill residents of Western nations.

While Americans commonly think of bureaucrats as organized through such government entities as the Environmental Protection Agency (EPA) and the Department of Education, the organizations that protect our security are also bureaucracies. In particular, the nation's 1.4 million active-duty military personnel live in a thoroughly bureaucratized environment. The Federal Bureau of Investigation (FBI), the Central Intelligence Agency (CIA), and the National Security Agency (NSA) are all bureaucracies. How much of our freedom and our privacy, if any, should we yield up to these bureaucracies in our attempts to defeat ISIS and other terrorist groups?

Security First

Some point out that the oldest purpose of government is to protect its citizens from foreign and domestic violence. It follows that destroying ISIS is "job one." We should be willing to make sacrifices to defeat it. We will have to accept additional "snooping" by espionage and law enforcement agencies such as the NSA. The government must use all possible means to analyze phone, e-mail, and social media data to identify terrorists. This will cost us some of our privacy. Remember, though, the NSA is not interested in 99.9 percent of what Americans are doing, saying, or thinking. No one thinks twice today about security measures when we fly. We accept that it is better to stop terrorists from blowing up planes than to enjoy the freedom to board a flight without a security check. Polls show that a majority of Americans worry that the United States won't go far enough in monitoring potential terrorists. These citizens have got it right.

Freedom Is Fragile—Don't Crush It

Others say that Americans have spent two centuries developing and protecting our freedoms, the most important of which are found in the Bill of Rights. Now is not the time to start revoking these freedoms. The Bill of Rights requires the government to obtain a warrant from a court before conducting searches. That warrant must "particularly describe the place to be searched, and the persons or things to be seized." Given such language, how can the government indiscriminately collect information on every phone call, e-mail, and social media post?

True, our freedoms can exist only when they are protected by the government. But history shows that governments can also abuse their power and commit terrible crimes. We can recover from any particular terrorist incident, but we might not be able to recover from losses of our liberty. Defeating ISIS is a laudable goal, but we must not stifle our vibrant free society. Security at any cost is, to say the least, a bad policy choice.

Where do you stand?

1. Most Muslims abhor ISIS. Many call it *Daesh*, which is the equivalent of ISIS in Arabic. *Daesh* sounds somewhat like an Arab insult. Should Americans adopt this term?

2. Many Americans are more afraid of a terrorist attack than a heart attack. Yet death from terrorism is very rare, while heart disease kills more of us than anything else. Why might relatively rare events often be so frightening?

Explore this issue online:

- You can find detailed arguments for and against NSA surveillance online. Search for "nsa pro outline." You'll find both pro and con arguments from Debate Central, a project of the National Center for Policy Analysis.

INTRODUCTION

Did you eat breakfast this morning? If you did, **bureaucrats**—individuals who work in the offices of the government bureaucracy—had a lot to do with that breakfast.

If you had bacon, the meat was inspected by federal agents. If you drank milk, the price was affected by rules and regulations of the Department of Agriculture. If you looked at a cereal box, you saw fine print about fat and vitamins, which was the result of regulations made by several other federal agencies, including the Food and Drug Administration. If you ate leftover pizza for breakfast, state or local inspectors made sure that the kitchen of the pizza eatery was sanitary and safe. Other bureaucrats ensured that the employees who put together (and perhaps delivered) the pizza were protected against discrimination in the workplace.

Government employees deliver our mail, clean our streets, teach in our public schools, run our national parks, and attempt to ensure the safety of our food and the prescription drugs that we take, among many other things. Life as we know it would be quite different without the bureaucrats who keep our governments—federal, state, and local—in operation. Still, Americans differ about the positive and negative aspects of actions taken by federal bureaucracies, as discussed in the chapter-opening *America at Odds* feature.

 13-1 THE NATURE AND SIZE OF THE BUREAUCRACY

> **LO** Describe the size and functions of the U.S. bureaucracy and the major components of federal spending.

Today, the word *bureaucracy* often evokes a negative reaction. For some, it conjures up visions of depersonalized automatons performing chores without any sensitivity toward the needs of those they serve. For others, it is synonymous with government "red tape." A **bureaucracy,** however, is simply a large, complex administrative organization that is structured hierarchically in a pyramid-like fashion.[1] Government bureaucrats carry out the policies of elected government officials.

> **bureaucrat** An individual who works in a bureaucracy. As generally used, the term refers to a government employee.
>
> **bureaucracy** A large, complex, hierarchically structured administrative organization that carries out specific functions.

The concept of a bureaucracy is not confined to the federal government. Any large organization must have a bureaucracy. In each bureaucracy, everybody (except the head of the bureaucracy) reports to at least one other person. In the federal government, the head of the bureaucracy is the president of the United States, and the bureaucracy is part of the executive branch.[2]

13-1a The Nature of Bureaucracy

A bureaucratic form of organization allows each person to concentrate on her or his area of knowledge and expertise. In your college or university, for example, you do not expect the basketball coach to solve the problems of the finance office. The reason the federal government bureaucracy exists is that Congress, over time, has delegated certain tasks to specialists.

For example, in 1914 Congress passed the Federal Trade Commission Act, which established the Federal Trade Commission to regulate deceptive and unfair trade practices. Those appointed to the commission were specialists in that area. Similarly, Congress passed the Consumer Product Safety Act in 1972, which established the Consumer Product Safety Commission to investigate the safety of consumer products. The commission is one of many federal administrative agencies.

Another key aspect of any bureaucracy is that the power to act resides in the *position* rather than in the *person*. In your college or university, the person who is president now has more or less the same authority as any previous president. Additionally, bureaucracies usually entail *standard operating procedures*—directives on what procedures should be followed in specific circumstances. Bureaucracies normally also have a merit system, meaning that people are hired and promoted on the basis of demonstrated skills and achievements.

13-1b The Growth of Bureaucracy

The federal government that existed in 1789 was small. It had three departments, each with only a few employees: (1) the Department of State (nine employees), (2) the Department of War (two employees), and (3) the Department of the Treasury (thirty-nine employees). By 1798, nine years later, the federal bureaucracy was still quite small. The secretary of state had seven clerks. His total expenditures on stationery and printing amounted to $500, or about $10,500 in 2018 dollars. The Department of War spent, on average, a grand total of $1.4 million each year, or about $29.4 million in 2018 dollars.

Growing Government Employment   Times have changed. Figure 13–1 shows the number of government employees at the local, state, and national levels from 1959 to 2017 as a percentage of the total U.S. population. Most growth has been at the state and local levels. All in all, the three levels of government employ more than 15 percent of the civilian labor force. Today, more Americans are employed by government (at all three levels) than by the entire manufacturing sector of the U.S. economy.

As you examine Figure 13–1, you will notice a substantial increase in government employment relative to the population from 1959 up to about 1980. During those years, the absolute number of government workers nearly doubled. Government employment has been more stable since 1980, when Republican Ronald Reagan was elected president.

The Impact of President Reagan   Indeed, during Reagan's first four years in office, government employment fell. Most of this decrease was at the local level. The drop was caused in part by the recession of 1980–1982 and in part by the elimination of revenue sharing. This program had transferred large sums from the federal government to state and especially local governments. The loss of government jobs was made up in Reagan's second term, as government tended to return to business as usual. Still, the rapid rise in government employment relative to population seen before 1980 did not return.

Recently, government employment has once again dropped, in absolute as well as relative terms. President Obama's 2009 stimulus program, which transferred large sums to local governments, helped stabilize government employment through 2010. By 2017, however, almost 750,000 fewer people worked for the various levels of government. Most of those who lost their jobs had worked at the local level. It is also notable that the United States Postal Service shed more than 200,000 jobs between 2006 and 2017.

13–1c The Costs of Maintaining the Government

The costs of maintaining the government are high and growing. In 1929, government at all levels accounted for about 11 percent of the nation's gross domestic product

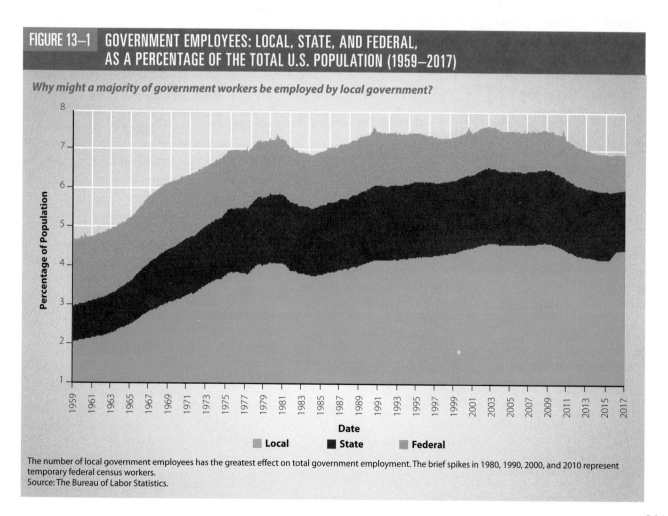

FIGURE 13–1   GOVERNMENT EMPLOYEES: LOCAL, STATE, AND FEDERAL, AS A PERCENTAGE OF THE TOTAL U.S. POPULATION (1959–2017)

Why might a majority of government workers be employed by local government?

■ Local   ■ State   ■ Federal

The number of local government employees has the greatest effect on total government employment. The brief spikes in 1980, 1990, 2000, and 2010 represent temporary federal census workers.
Source: The Bureau of Labor Statistics.

(GDP). Today, that figure is about 36 percent. Average citizens pay a significant portion of their income to federal, state, and local governments. They do this by paying income taxes, sales taxes, property taxes, and many other types of taxes and fees.

As of 2018, the individual income tax—and taxes that are collected along with it, such as the capital gains tax—make up 43 percent of the federal government's revenues. The corporate income tax adds another 11 percent. Income from the Social Security and Medicare taxes contributes about 26 percent. All other taxes and revenue sources come to 10 percent. That leaves 10 percent of the budget to be funded by borrowing. That amount is down considerably from the depths of the latest recession, but it is still high by historical standards. Figure 13–2 illustrates major sources of federal revenue.

The government is costly, to be sure, but it also provides numerous services for Americans. Cutting back on the size of government inevitably means a reduction in those services. The trade-off between government spending and popular services has been central to American politics throughout our history.

13–1d Where Does All the Money Go?

It is worth examining where federal spending actually goes. If you ask people on the street, you will get varied responses—from too much spent on welfare to too much spent on foreign aid. As it turns out, neither of those categories makes up a very large percentage of federal government spending. Consider Figure 13–3.

Social Spending As you can see in Figure 13–3, over half of the federal budget consists of various social programs. Some of these programs, such as Social Security and Medicare, are funded by payroll taxes and paid out to all qualifying persons, regardless of income. Together, these two programs make up almost 40 percent of the federal budget.

Other programs, including Medicaid and the Supplemental Nutrition Assistance Program (SNAP, formerly "food stamps"), are available only to low-income individuals. Medicaid, the Children's Health Insurance Program (CHIP), and miscellaneous low-income and disability support programs account for 22 percent of spending. Temporary Assistance for Needy Families (TANF)—traditional cash welfare—accounts for only 0.4 percent of the federal budget—$18 billion. It is completely overshadowed within the "miscellaneous low-income and disability support" pie slice by disability payments, SNAP, and the Earned Income Tax Credit (EITC) program.

Defense Defense spending is a big number—with veterans' benefits, it amounts to about a fifth of the whole. The wars in Iraq and Afghanistan were obviously expensive. One estimate of their cost under President Obama was $170 billion a year, or 4.6 percent of the total. That is serious money, but it's not really "busting the bank." Furthermore, spending on wars has fallen.

Everything Else At 11 percent of the total, "everything else" includes a vast range of programs. One example is military and economic foreign aid, at 1.4 percent of the total, or $46 billion. That's a substantial sum, but it is less than many people imagine it to be. One item that bears watching is the interest on the national

FIGURE 13–2 MAJOR SOURCES OF FEDERAL REVENUE, 2018

Why might it be hard for the federal government to avoid running a deficit?

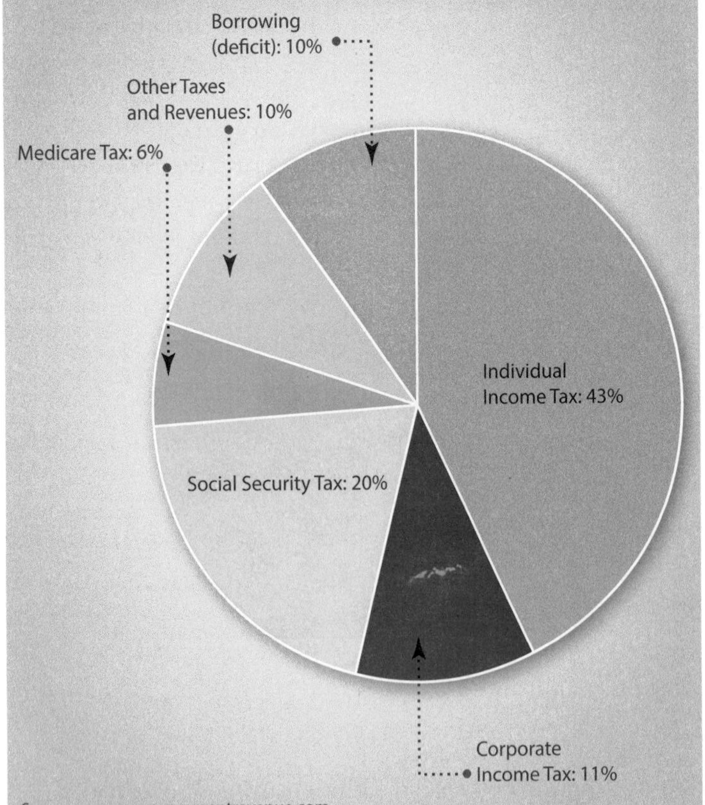

- Borrowing (deficit): 10%
- Other Taxes and Revenues: 10%
- Medicare Tax: 6%
- Individual Income Tax: 43%
- Social Security Tax: 20%
- Corporate Income Tax: 11%

Source: www.usgovernmentrevenue.com.

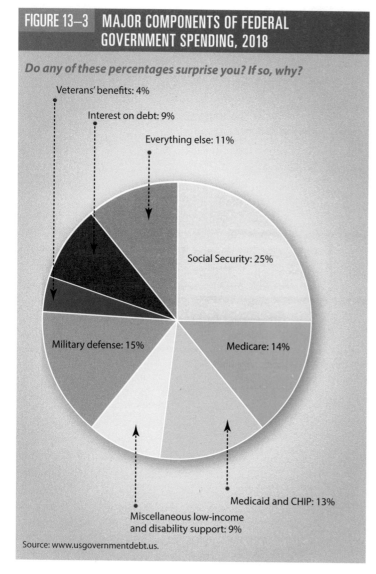

FIGURE 13–3 MAJOR COMPONENTS OF FEDERAL GOVERNMENT SPENDING, 2018

Do any of these percentages surprise you? If so, why?

Veterans' benefits: 4%

Interest on debt: 9%

Everything else: 11%

Social Security: 25%

Military defense: 15%

Medicare: 14%

Miscellaneous low-income and disability support: 9%

Medicaid and CHIP: 13%

Source: www.usgovernmentdebt.us.

debt—the interest currently is about $385 billion per year. Federal budget deficits will cause this figure to grow in future years.

CRITICAL THINKING

▶ *Does your college or university have a bureaucracy? What does it do?*

 13–2 HOW THE FEDERAL BUREAUCRACY IS ORGANIZED

LO Discuss the structure and basic components of the federal bureaucracy.

A complete organization chart of the federal government would cover an entire wall. A simplified version is provided in Figure 13–4. The executive branch consists of a number of bureaucracies that provide services to Congress, to the federal courts, and to the president directly.

The executive branch of the federal government includes four major types of structures:

▶ **Executive departments.**

▶ **Independent executive agencies.**

▶ **Independent regulatory agencies.**

▶ **Government corporations.**

Each type of structure has its own relationship to the president and its own internal workings.

13–2a The Executive Departments

The fifteen executive departments, which are directly accountable to the president, are the major service organizations of the federal government. They are responsible for performing government functions such as training troops (Department of Defense), printing currency (Department of the Treasury), and enforcing federal laws setting minimum safety and health standards for workers (Department of Labor).

Table 13–1 provides an overview of each of the departments within the executive branch. The table lists a few of the many activities undertaken by each department. Because the president appoints the department heads, they are expected to help carry out the president's policy objectives. Often, they attempt to maximize the president's political successes as well.

Each executive department was created by Congress as the perceived need for it arose, and each department manages a specific policy area. In 2002, for example, Congress created the Department of Homeland Security to deal with terrorism and other threats. The head of each department is known as the secretary, except for the Department of Justice, which is headed by the attorney general. Each department head is appointed by the president and confirmed by the Senate.

13–2b A Typical Departmental Structure

Each cabinet department consists of the department's top administrators (the secretary of the department, deputy secretary, undersecretaries, and the like), plus

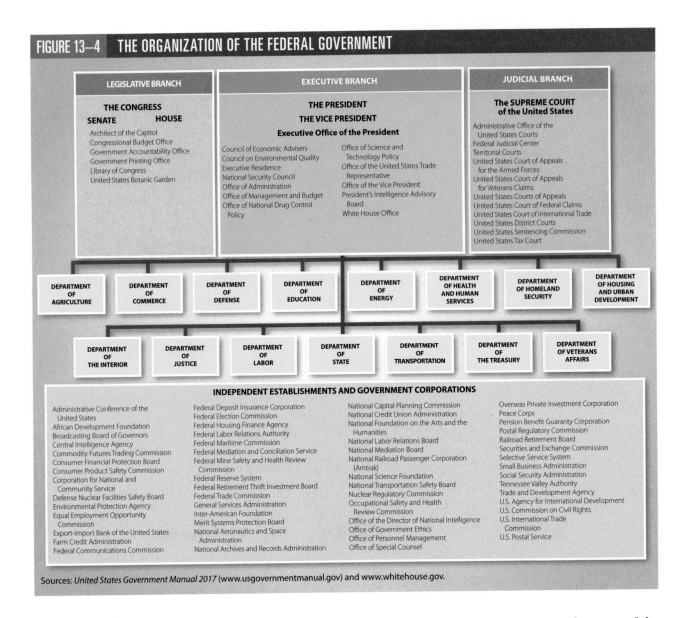

FIGURE 13–4 THE ORGANIZATION OF THE FEDERAL GOVERNMENT

LEGISLATIVE BRANCH

THE CONGRESS

SENATE   HOUSE

Architect of the Capitol
Congressional Budget Office
Government Accountability Office
Government Printing Office
Library of Congress
United States Botanic Garden

EXECUTIVE BRANCH

THE PRESIDENT

THE VICE PRESIDENT

Executive Office of the President

Council of Economic Advisers
Council on Environmental Quality
Executive Residence
National Security Council
Office of Administration
Office of Management and Budget
Office of National Drug Control
   Policy

Office of Science and
   Technology Policy
Office of the United States Trade
   Representative
Office of the Vice President
President's Intelligence Advisory
   Board
White House Office

JUDICIAL BRANCH

**The SUPREME COURT
of the United States**

Administrative Office of the
   United States Courts
Federal Judicial Center
Territorial Courts
United States Court of Appeals
   for the Armed Forces
United States Court of Appeals
   for Veterans Claims
United States Courts of Appeals
United States Court of Federal Claims
United States Court of International Trade
United States District Courts
United States Sentencing Commission
United States Tax Court

DEPARTMENT OF AGRICULTURE | DEPARTMENT OF COMMERCE | DEPARTMENT OF DEFENSE | DEPARTMENT OF EDUCATION | DEPARTMENT OF ENERGY | DEPARTMENT OF HEALTH AND HUMAN SERVICES | DEPARTMENT OF HOMELAND SECURITY | DEPARTMENT OF HOUSING AND URBAN DEVELOPMENT

DEPARTMENT OF THE INTERIOR | DEPARTMENT OF JUSTICE | DEPARTMENT OF LABOR | DEPARTMENT OF STATE | DEPARTMENT OF TRANSPORTATION | DEPARTMENT OF THE TREASURY | DEPARTMENT OF VETERANS AFFAIRS

INDEPENDENT ESTABLISHMENTS AND GOVERNMENT CORPORATIONS

Administrative Conference of the
   United States
African Development Foundation
Broadcasting Board of Governors
Central Intelligence Agency
Commodity Futures Trading Commission
Consumer Financial Protection Board
Consumer Product Safety Commission
Corporation for National and
   Community Service
Defense Nuclear Facilities Safety Board
Environmental Protection Agency
Equal Employment Opportunity
   Commission
Export-Import Bank of the United States
Farm Credit Administration
Federal Communications Commission

Federal Deposit Insurance Corporation
Federal Election Commission
Federal Housing Finance Agency
Federal Labor Relations Authority
Federal Maritime Commission
Federal Mediation and Conciliation Service
Federal Mine Safety and Health Review
   Commission
Federal Reserve System
Federal Retirement Thrift Investment Board
Federal Trade Commission
General Services Administration
Inter-American Foundation
Merit Systems Protection Board
National Aeronautics and Space
   Administration
National Archives and Records Administration

National Capital Planning Commission
National Credit Union Administration
National Foundation on the Arts and the
   Humanities
National Labor Relations Board
National Mediation Board
National Railroad Passenger Corporation
   (Amtrak)
National Science Foundation
National Transportation Safety Board
Nuclear Regulatory Commission
Occupational Safety and Health
   Review Commission
Office of the Director of National Intelligence
Office of Government Ethics
Office of Personnel Management
Office of Special Counsel

Overseas Private Investment Corporation
Peace Corps
Pension Benefit Guaranty Corporation
Postal Regulatory Commission
Railroad Retirement Board
Securities and Exchange Commission
Selective Service System
Small Business Administration
Social Security Administration
Tennessee Valley Authority
Trade and Development Agency
U.S. Agency for International Development
U.S. Commission on Civil Rights
U.S. International Trade
   Commission
U.S. Postal Service

Sources: *United States Government Manual 2017* (www.usgovernmentmanual.gov) and www.whitehouse.gov.

a number of subagencies. For example, the National Park Service is a subagency within the Department of the Interior. The Drug Enforcement Administration is a subagency within the Department of Justice.

Although there are organizational differences among the departments, each department generally follows a typical hierarchical bureaucratic structure.

One aspect of the secretary of agriculture's job is to carry out the president's agricultural policies. Another aspect is to promote and protect the department. The secretary spends time ensuring that Congress allocates enough money for the department to work effectively. The secretary also makes sure that constituents, or the people the department serves—farmers and major agricultural corporations— are happy. In general, the secretary tries to maintain or improve the status of the department with respect to all of the other departments and units of the federal bureaucracy.

The secretary of agriculture is assisted by a deputy secretary and several assistant secretaries and undersecretaries, all of whom are nominated by the president and put into office with Senate approval. The secretary and assistant secretaries have staff members who help with all sorts of jobs, such as hiring new people and generating positive public relations for the Department of Agriculture.

13–2c Independent Executive Agencies

Independent executive agencies are federal bureaucratic organizations that have a single function. They are independent in the sense that they are not located

independent executive agency
A federal agency that is not located within a cabinet department.

TABLE 13–1 EXECUTIVE DEPARTMENTS

Department (Year of Original Establishment)	Principal Duties	Selected Subagencies
State (1789)	Negotiates treaties, develops our foreign policy, protects citizens abroad.	Bureau of Consular Affairs (passports).
Treasury (1789)	Pays all federal bills, borrows money, collects federal taxes, mints coins and prints paper currency, supervises national banks.	Internal Revenue Service, U.S. Mint.
Defense (1789)*	Manages the armed forces (Army, Navy, Air Force, Marines), operates military bases.	National Security Agency, Departments of the Air Force, Navy, Army; Defense Intelligence Agency.
Justice (1789)†	Gives legal advice to the president, enforces federal criminal laws, supervises federal prisons.	Federal Bureau of Investigation, Drug Enforcement Administration, Bureau of Prisons, U.S. Marshals.
Interior (1849)	Supervises federally owned lands and parks, operates federal hydroelectric power facilities, supervises Native American affairs.	U.S. Fish and Wildlife Service, National Park Service, Bureau of Indian Affairs, Bureau of Land Management.
Agriculture (1889)	Provides assistance to farmers and ranchers, conducts research to improve agriculture, works to protect forests.	Agricultural Research Service, Food Safety and Inspection Service, Federal Crop Insurance Corporation, Forest Service.
Commerce (1903)‡	Grants patents and trademarks, conducts national census, monitors the weather, protects the interests of businesses.	Bureau of the Census, Bureau of Economic Analysis, Patent and Trademark Office, National Oceanic and Atmospheric Administration.
Labor (1903)‡	Administers federal labor laws, promotes the interests of workers.	Occupational Safety and Health Administration, Bureau of Labor Statistics, Wage and Hour Division.
Health and Human Services (1953)§	Promotes public health, enforces pure food and drug laws, sponsors health-related research.	Food and Drug Administration, Centers for Disease Control and Prevention, Centers for Medicare and Medicaid Services.
Housing and Urban Development (1965)	Deals with the nation's housing needs, develops and rehabilitates urban communities, oversees resale of mortgages.	Government National Mortgage Association, Office of Fair Housing and Equal Opportunity.
Transportation (1967)	Finances improvements in mass transit; develops and administers programs for highways, railroads, and aviation.	Federal Aviation Administration, Federal Highway Administration, National Highway Traffic Safety Administration.
Energy (1977)	Promotes the conservation of energy and resources, analyzes energy data, conducts research and development.	Office of Civilian Radioactive Waste Management, National Nuclear Security Administration.
Education (1979)	Coordinates federal programs and policies for education, administers aid to education, promotes educational research.	Office of Special Education, Office of Elementary and Secondary Education, Office of Postsecondary Education.
Veterans Affairs (1989)	Promotes the welfare of veterans of the U.S. armed forces.	Veterans Health Administration, Veterans Benefits Administration.
Homeland Security (2002)	Works to prevent terrorist attacks within the United States, control America's borders, and handle attacks and natural disasters.	U.S. Customs and Border Protection, U.S. Coast Guard, Secret Service, Federal Emergency Management Agency.

*Established in 1947 by merging the Department of War, created in 1789, and the Department of the Navy, created in 1798.
†Formerly the Office of the Attorney General, renamed and reorganized in 1870.
‡Formed in 1913 by splitting the Department of Commerce and Labor, which was created in 1903.
§Formerly the Department of Health, Education, and Welfare, renamed when the Department of Education was spun off in 1979.

within a cabinet department. Rather, independent executive agency heads report directly to the president. A new federal independent executive agency can be created only through cooperation between the president and Congress.

The Creation of Independent Agencies

Before the twentieth century, the federal government did almost all of its work through the executive departments. In the twentieth century, in contrast, presidents began to ask for certain executive agencies to be kept separate, or independent, from existing departments.

Today, there are more than two hundred independent executive agencies.

The Danger of Partisan Politics   Sometimes, agencies are kept independent because of the sensitive nature of their functions. But at other times, Congress creates independent agencies to protect them from *partisan politics*—politics in support of a particular party. The U.S. Commission on Civil Rights, which was created in 1957, is a case in point. Congress wanted to protect the work of the commission from the influences not only of Congress's own political interests, but also those of the president.

The Central Intelligence Agency (CIA), which was formed in 1947, is another good example. Both Congress and the president know that the intelligence activities of the CIA could be abused if the agency were not independent. Finally, the General Services Administration (GSA) was created as an independent executive agency in 1949 to provide services and office space for most federal agencies. To serve all parts of the government, the GSA has to be an independent agency.

Among the more than two hundred independent executive agencies, a few stand out in importance either because of the mission they were established to accomplish or because of their large size. We list selected independent executive agencies in Table 13–2.

independent regulatory agency A federal organization that is responsible for creating and implementing rules that regulate private activity and protect the public interest in a particular sector of the economy.

government corporation An agency of the government that is run as a business enterprise. Such agencies engage primarily in commercial activities, produce revenues, and require greater flexibility than most government agencies have.

13-2d Independent Regulatory Agencies

An **independent regulatory agency** is responsible for a specific type of public policy. Its function is to create and implement rules that regulate private activity and protect the public interest in a particular sector of the economy.

One of the earliest independent regulatory agencies was the Interstate Commerce Commission (ICC), established in 1887. (This agency was abolished in 1995.) After the ICC was formed, other agencies were created to regulate aviation (the Civil Aeronautics Board, or CAB, which was abolished in 1985), communications (the Federal Communications Commission, or FCC), the stock market (the Securities and Exchange Commission, or SEC), and many other areas of business. Table 13–3 lists some major independent regulatory agencies.

13-2e Government Corporations

Another form of federal bureaucratic organization is the **government corporation,** a business that is owned by the government. Government corporations are not exactly like corporations in which you buy stock and become a shareholder. The U.S. Postal Service (USPS) is a government corporation, for example, but it does not sell shares.

Government corporations are similar to private corporations in that they provide a service that could be handled by the private sector. They are also like private corporations in that they charge for their services, though sometimes they charge less than private-sector corporations do for similar services. Table 13–4 lists selected government corporations.

Facing Losses When a private business fails to make a profit, its shareholders have a problem. The value of the company may drop, in some instances to zero. If a small business loses money, its owners must either raise more capital or shut down the firm. If a government corporation runs at a loss, taxpayers may be forced to foot the bill.

TABLE 13–2	SELECTED INDEPENDENT EXECUTIVE AGENCIES	
Name	**Date Formed**	**Principal Duties**
Central Intelligence Agency (CIA)	1947	Gathers and analyzes political and military information about foreign countries, conducts covert operations outside the United States.
General Services Administration (GSA)	1949	Purchases and manages property of the federal government, oversees federal government spending projects, discovers overcharges in government programs.
Small Business Administration (SBA)	1953	Promotes the interests of small businesses, provides low-cost loans to small businesses.
National Aeronautics and Space Administration (NASA)	1958	Is responsible for the U.S. space program, including building, testing, and operating space vehicles.
Environmental Protection Agency (EPA)	1970	Undertakes programs aimed at reducing air and water pollution, works with state and local agencies to fight environmental hazards.
Social Security Administration (SSA)*	1994	Manages the government's Social Security programs, including Retirement and Survivors Insurance, Disability Insurance, and Supplemental Security Income.

*Separated from the Department of Health and Human Services in 1994, originally established in 1946.

TABLE 13–3   SELECTED INDEPENDENT REGULATORY AGENCIES

Name	Date Formed	Principal Duties
Federal Reserve System (Fed)	1913	Determines policy on interest rates, credit availability, and the money supply.
Federal Trade Commission (FTC)	1914	Works to prevent businesses from engaging in unfair trade practices and forming business monopolies.
Securities and Exchange Commission (SEC)	1934	Regulates the nation's stock exchanges, requires financial disclosure by companies that wish to sell stocks and bonds to the public.
Federal Communications Commission (FCC)	1934	Regulates interstate and international communications by radio, television, wire, satellite, and cable.
National Labor Relations Board (NLRB)	1935	Protects employees' rights to join unions and to bargain collectively with employers, attempts to prevent unfair labor practices by both employers and unions.
Equal Employment Opportunity Commission (EEOC)	1964	Works to eliminate discrimination that is based on religion, gender, race, color, national origin, age, or disability; examines claims of discrimination.

The U.S. Postal Service is an example of this problem. As Americans have increasingly relied on the Internet for communications, the volume of first-class mail has dropped considerably. As a result, the USPS has been losing money (this in spite of the fact that parcel deliveries have gone up, also because of the Internet—specifically, as a result of online shopping). The USPS has cut costs dramatically. Still, it lost $5.1 billion in 2015 and $5.6 billion in 2016. Some observers claim that the service's real problem is that Congress has forced it to prefund retiree benefits in a way that no other business or government agency must do.

To solve the problem permanently, the USPS proposed to lay off additional employees, close rural post offices, reduce pension benefits, and even end Saturday delivery. Many of these steps require congressional approval, which was not forthcoming. The alternative would be direct federal subsidies to the service, which has been self-supporting since the early 1980s.

Intermediate Forms of Organization   A number of intermediate forms of organization exist that fall between a government corporation and a private one. In some circumstances, the government can take control of a private corporation. When a company goes bankrupt, for example, it is subject to the supervision of a federal judge until it exits from bankruptcy or is liquidated. The government can also purchase stock in a private corporation. The government used this technique to funnel funds into major banks during the financial crisis that began in September 2008. In addition, the government can set up a corporation and sell stock to the public.

The Federal Home Loan Mortgage Corporation (Freddie Mac) and the Federal National Mortgage Association (Fannie Mae) are examples of stockholder-owned, government-sponsored enterprises. Fannie Mae (founded in 1938) and Freddie Mac (created in 1970) buy, resell, and guarantee home mortgages. In September 2008, the government placed the two businesses into a conservatorship—effectively, a bankruptcy overseen by the Federal Housing Finance Agency instead of a federal judge. The government also took an 80 percent

TABLE 13–4   SELECTED GOVERNMENT CORPORATIONS

Name	Date Formed	Principal Duties
Tennessee Valley Authority (TVA)	1933	Operates a Tennessee River control system and generates power for a seven-state region, controls floods and promotes the navigability of the Tennessee River.
Federal Deposit Insurance Corporation (FDIC)	1933	Insures individuals' bank deposits up to $250,000 and oversees the business activities of banks.
National Railroad Passenger Corporation (Amtrak)	1970	Provides a national and intercity rail passenger service network, controls more than 23,000 miles of track with about 505 stations.
U.S. Postal Service (formed from the old U.S. Post Office department—the Post Office itself is older than the Constitution)	1971	Delivers mail throughout the United States and its territories, is the largest government corporation.

share of the stock of each firm. Today, Fannie Mae and Freddie Mac are making money again, and their profits go into the U.S. Treasury.

CRITICAL THINKING

▸ *Some people have advocated selling off government corporations, such as the U.S. Postal Service, and turning them into truly private enterprises. Would it be a good idea to "privatize" the U.S. Postal Service? Why or why not?*

A postal worker in Boston in March 2017. Inscribed on the main post office in New York City is the motto: "Neither snow nor rain nor heat nor gloom of night stays these couriers from the swift completion of their appointed rounds." *The motto has no official, status, however. Why not?*

David L. Ryan/The Boston Globe/Getty Images

13–3 HOW BUREAUCRATS GET THEIR JOBS

LO Describe how the federal civil service was established and how bureaucrats get their jobs.

As already noted, federal bureaucrats holding top-level positions are appointed by the president and confirmed by the Senate. These bureaucrats include department and agency heads, their deputy and assistant secretaries, and the like. The list of positions that are filled by appointments is published after each presidential election in a document called *Policy and Supporting Positions*. The volume is more commonly known as the *Plum Book*, because the eight thousand jobs it summarizes are known as "political plums." Normally, these jobs go to those who supported the winning presidential candidate.

13–3a The Civil Service

The rank-and-file bureaucrats—the rest of the federal bureaucracy—are part of the **civil service** (nonmilitary employees of the government). They obtain their jobs through the Office of Personnel Management (OPM), an agency established by the Civil Service Reform Act of 1978. The OPM recruits, interviews, and tests potential government workers and determines who should be hired. The OPM makes recommendations to individual agencies as to which persons meet relevant standards (typically, the top three applicants for a position), and the agencies then generally decide which of the recommended individuals they will hire.

The 1978 act also created the Merit Systems Protection Board (MSPB) to

civil service Nonmilitary government employees.

oversee promotions, employees' rights, and other employment matters. The MSPB evaluates charges of wrongdoing, hears employee appeals from agency decisions, and can order corrective action against agencies and employees.

13–3b Origins of the Merit System

The idea that the civil service should be based on a merit system dates back more than a century. The Pendleton Civil Service Reform Act of 1883 established the principle of government employment on the basis of merit through open, competitive examinations.

Initially, only about 10 percent of federal employees were covered by the merit system. Today, more than 90 percent of the federal civil service is recruited on the basis of merit. Are public employees paid too much? For a discussion of this question, see this chapter's *Join the Debate* feature.

13–3c The OPM Hacking Scandal

In June 2015, federal cybersecurity experts discovered that hackers had downloaded personal information on millions of Americans from computers at the OPM. The database in question, EPIC, contains information from background checks that the government undertakes before issuing security clearances. EPIC includes a 127-page form that asks about past addresses and jobs, friends and relatives, and foreign contacts. It also contains data

JOIN THE DEBATE

Are Government Workers Paid Too Much?

Popular beliefs about the pay of government workers vary dramatically. Many people believe that only individuals working in private business can hope to receive large paychecks. Others, however, see government workers as an elite group whose members enjoy secure and high-paid jobs, unlike average American workers who are competing in the global economy.

Are government workers paid too much? That can be a difficult question to answer. Those arguing about this issue do not even agree on how public-sector pay compares with pay in the private sector.

Yes, They're Overpaid

Conservatives who believe that government workers are a new elite point to generous retirement benefits. Government workers typically have "defined benefit" plans that guarantee their retirement income. Private-sector employees who are lucky enough to have any kind of pension now generally have "defined contribution" plans under which benefits rise and fall with the stock market.

Government wages aren't bad, either. An article by two U.S. Bureau of Labor Statistics (BLS) economists found that, on average, workers in state government have total compensation 3 to 10 percent greater than workers in the private sector, while in local government the gap is 10 to 19 percent.[3] A 2015 study by the libertarian Cato Institute claimed that federal employees made an average of $119,934 in wages and benefits, while total compensation for private-sector workers was only $67,246. Cato based its findings on figures from the Bureau of Economic Analysis (BEA).[4] It's not fair that government workers get a better deal than the rest of us.

No, They're Not

Other studies yield different results. A paper by a Boston College team concluded that state and local workers are paid 9.5 percent less than comparable workers in the private sector, although generous benefits reduce the gap to 4 percent.[5] It's worth remembering that many government workers don't do the same kind of work as employees in the private sector. On average,

federal workers are much better educated and more likely to be employed in jobs that are also well paid in the private sector. At the local level, for example, teachers and police officers need to be well educated. At the state level, the same is true for college professors and judges, among others. Most teachers could make more money if they did something else.

At the federal level, the real point may not be that pay is high, but that pay scales are more egalitarian than in private business. The Congressional Budget Office has found that federal workers with only a high school education are paid 36 percent more than in the private sector. Employees with professional degrees, however, earn 18 percent less.[6]

Critical Analysis

Is it important for government to try to attract high-quality employees? Why or why not?

---

about problems with drugs, drinking, gambling, and mental health, criminal records, and bankruptcies. EPIC even contains 1.1 million fingerprint files. In July, experts discovered that hackers had accessed a second OPM database containing Social Security numbers and employment information on 21.5 million Americans.

Officials privately blamed a group called Deep Panda that is sponsored by the Chinese government. What the Chinese obtained may be the best database for recruiting spies in world history. EPIC also contains information on foreign contacts of those seeking security clearances. Chinese intelligence officials

have doubtless scoured the database to locate Chinese citizens who may have been in contact with Americans. Officials may be asking persons on that list some uncomfortable questions. If any of them actually provided help or information to Americans, they could be facing espionage charges.

CRITICAL ANALYSIS

▶ *When most private companies hire new employees, they don't use systems similar to those of the civil service. Why is this so?*

REGULATORY AGENCIES: ARE THEY THE FOURTH BRANCH OF GOVERNMENT?

LO Explain how regulatory agencies make rules and how issue networks affect policymaking in government.

You have learned about the system of checks and balances among the three branches of the U.S. government—executive, legislative, and judicial. Recent history, however, shows that it may be time to regard the regulatory agencies as a fourth branch of the government. Although the U.S. Constitution does not mention regulatory agencies, these agencies can and do make **legislative rules** that are as legally binding as laws passed by Congress. With such powers, regulatory agencies have an influence that rivals that of the president, Congress, and the courts. Indeed, most Americans do not realize how much of our "law" is created by regulatory agencies.

Regulatory agencies have been on the American political scene since the nineteenth century, but their golden age came during the regulatory explosion of the 1960s and 1970s. Congress itself could not have overseen the actual implementation of all of the laws that it was enacting at that time to control pollution and deal with other social problems. It therefore chose (and still chooses) to delegate to administrative agencies the tasks involved in implementing its laws. By delegating some of its authority to an administrative agency, Congress can indirectly monitor a particular area in which it has passed legislation without becoming bogged down in the details relating to the enforcement of that legislation—details that are often best left to specialists.

legislative rule An administrative agency rule that carries the same weight as a statute enacted by a legislature.

enabling legislation A law enacted by a legislature to establish an administrative agency. Enabling legislation normally specifies the name, purpose, composition, and powers of the agency being created.

adjudicate To render a judicial decision. In administrative law, it is the process in which an administrative law judge hears and decides issues that arise when an agency charges a person or firm with violating a law or regulation enforced by the agency.

rulemaking The process undertaken by an administrative agency when formally proposing, evaluating, and adopting a new regulation.

13-4a Agency Creation

To create a federal administrative agency, Congress passes **enabling legislation,** which specifies the name, purpose, composition, and powers of the agency being created.

An Example: The FTC The Federal Trade Commission (FTC), for example, was created in 1914 by the Federal Trade Commission Act, as mentioned earlier. The act prohibits unfair and deceptive trade practices. The act also describes the procedures that the agency must follow to charge persons or organizations with violations of the act, and it provides for judicial review of agency orders.

Other portions of the act grant the FTC powers to "make rules and regulations for the purpose of carrying out the Act," to conduct investigations of business practices, and to obtain reports on business practices from interstate corporations. They also allow the agency to investigate possible violations of federal antitrust statutes, to publish findings of its investigations, and to recommend new legislation.

Finally, the act empowers the FTC to hold trial-like hearings and to **adjudicate** (formally resolve) certain kinds of disputes that involve FTC regulations or federal antitrust laws. When adjudication takes place, within the FTC or any other regulatory agency, an administrative law judge (ALJ) conducts the hearing and, after weighing the evidence presented, issues an *order*. The ALJ's order may be appealed to a federal court. Unless it is overturned on appeal, the order becomes final.

The Power of Regulatory Agencies Enabling legislation makes the regulatory agency a potent organization. For example, the Securities and Exchange Commission (SEC) imposes rules regarding the disclosures a company must make to those who purchase newly issued stock. Under its enforcement authority, the SEC also investigates and prosecutes alleged violations of these regulations. Finally, SEC judges decide whether its rules have been violated and, if so, what punishment should be imposed on the offender (although, as noted, the judgment may be appealed to a federal court).

13-4b Rulemaking

A major function of a regulatory agency is **rulemaking**—the formulation of new regulations. The power that an agency has to make rules is conferred on it by Congress in the agency's enabling legislation.

For example, the Occupational Safety and Health Administration (OSHA) was authorized by the Occupational Safety and Health Act of 1970 to develop and issue rules governing safety in the workplace. Under this authority, OSHA has issued various safety standards, including rules to prevent the spread of certain diseases,

Farmers are increasingly using advanced technology to manage their crops, as shown in this California field. *What are some of the goals of the Department of Agriculture?*

such as acquired immune deficiency syndrome (AIDS). The rules specify various standards—on how contaminated needles should be handled, for instance—with which health-care workers must comply.

Requirements for Making Rules Agencies cannot just make a rule whenever they wish. Rather, they must follow certain procedural requirements, particularly those set forth in the Administrative Procedure Act of 1946. Agencies must also make sure that their rules are based on substantial evidence and are not "arbitrary and capricious." Therefore, before proposing a new rule, an agency may engage in extensive investigation to obtain data on the problem to be addressed by the rule. Based on this information, the agency may undertake a cost-benefit analysis of a new rule to determine whether its benefits outweigh its costs.

A Cost-Benefit Analysis As an example of cost-benefit analysis in rulemaking, consider the Clean Air Fine Particle Implementation Rule, issued by the Environmental Protection Agency (EPA) in 2007. The EPA estimated the costs of the regulation as $7.3 billion per year, with benefits ranging from $19 billion to $167 billion per year. The benefits largely consist of reductions in health-care costs and premature deaths—and, as these figures suggest, such calculations can be highly uncertain.

One belief that unites political conservatives is that the United States suffers from excessive regulation. Conservatives argue that regulation is inordinately expensive and also interferes with the ability of businesses to run their operations in reasonable and profitable ways. Estimates of the total costs of regulation vary dramatically. According to the Office of Management and Budget (OMB), the annual cost of federal regulations lies between $68 billion and $103 billion, with total benefits of $261 billion to $981 billion. Others argue that the OMB's sums are not comprehensive. One study quoted by conservatives puts total costs at $2.03 trillion per year. Liberals do not find this figure credible—it puts the costs at 11 percent of the entire economy.

One way in which some opponents of regulation may overestimate its costs is by treating one-time expenses as if they were ongoing. For instance, the Obama administration strengthened requirements that coal-fueled electrical power plants install expensive "scrubbers" to remove pollutants from their emissions. Such regulations were supposedly part of Obama's "war on coal." Revoking the scrubber requirements now will not make it cheaper to use coal in power plants, however, because most of the scrubbers are already installed, they would be expensive to remove, and they cost relatively little to run.

13–4c Policymaking

Bureaucrats in federal agencies are expected to exhibit **neutral competency,** which means that they are supposed to apply their technical skills to their jobs without regard to political issues. In principle, they should not be swayed by the thought of personal or political gain. In reality, each independent agency and each executive department is interested in its own survival and expansion. All agencies and departments wish to retain or expand their functions and staffs. To do this, they must gain the goodwill of both the White House and Congress.

Support from Congress While the administrative agencies of the federal government are prohibited from directly lobbying Congress, departments and agencies have developed techniques to help them gain congressional support. Each organization maintains a congressional information office, which specializes in helping members of Congress by supplying any requested information and solving casework problems.

For example, if a member of the House of Representatives receives a complaint from a constituent that his Social Security

neutral competency
The application of technical skills to jobs without regard to political issues.

payments are not arriving on time, that member of Congress may contact the Social Security Administration and ask that something be done. Typically, requests from members of Congress receive immediate attention.

Iron Triangles Analysts have determined that one way to understand the bureaucracy's role in policymaking is to examine the **iron triangle,** which is a three-way alliance among legislators (members of Congress), bureaucrats, and interest groups. Presumably, the laws that are passed and the policies that are established benefit the interests of all three corners of the iron triangle, as shown in Figure 13–5. Iron triangles are well established in almost every part of the bureaucracy.

Who Belongs to an Iron Triangle? As an example, consider agricultural policy. The Department of Agriculture consists of almost 90,000 individuals working directly for the federal government and thousands of other individuals who work indirectly for the department as contractors, subcontractors, and consultants. Now think about the various interest groups and client groups that are concerned with what the bureaus and agencies in the Agriculture Department can do for them. These groups include the American Farm Bureau Federation, the National Milk Producers Federation, various regional citrus growers associations, and many others. Finally, in Congress two major committees are concerned with agriculture: the House Committee on Agriculture and the Senate Committee on Agriculture, Nutrition, and Forestry.

The bureaucrats, interest groups, and legislators who make up this iron triangle cooperate to create mutually beneficial regulations and legislation. Because of the connections between agricultural interest groups and policymakers within the government, the agricultural industry has benefited greatly over the years from significant farm subsidies.

Congress's Role. The Department of Agriculture is headed by the secretary of agriculture, who is nominated by the president (and confirmed by the Senate). But that secretary cannot even buy a desk lamp if Congress does not approve the appropriations for the department's budget.

Within Congress, the responsibility for considering the Department of Agriculture's request for funding belongs first to the House and Senate appropriations committees and then to the agriculture subcommittees of the appropriations committees. The members of those committees, most of whom represent agricultural states, have been around a long time and have their own ideas about what is appropriate for the Agriculture Department's budget. They carefully scrutinize the ideas of the president and the secretary of agriculture.

The Influence of Interest Groups. The various interest groups—including producers of farm chemicals and farm machinery, agricultural cooperatives, grain dealers, and exporters—have vested interests in what the Department of Agriculture does and in what Congress lets the department do. Those interests are well represented by the lobbyists who crowd the halls of Congress. Many lobbyists have been working for agricultural interest groups for decades. They know the congressional committee members and Agriculture Department staff very well and meet with them routinely.

Issue Networks The iron triangle relationship does not apply to all policy domains. When making policy decisions on environmental and welfare issues, for example, many members of Congress and agency officials rely heavily on "experts." Legislators and agency heads also tend to depend on their staff members for specialized knowledge of rules, regulations, and legislation.

iron triangle A three-way alliance among legislators, bureaucrats, and interest groups to make or preserve policies that benefit their respective interests.

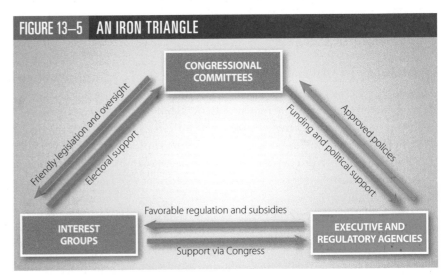

FIGURE 13–5 AN IRON TRIANGLE

CONGRESSIONAL COMMITTEES

Friendly legislation and oversight

Electoral support

Funding and political support

Approved policies

Favorable regulation and subsidies

INTEREST GROUPS

Support via Congress

EXECUTIVE AND REGULATORY AGENCIES

These experts have frequently served variously as interest group lobbyists and as public-sector staff members during their careers, creating a revolving-door effect. They often have strong opinions and interests regarding the direction of policy and are thus able to exert a great deal of influence on legislators and bureaucratic agencies.

The relationships among these experts, which are less structured than iron triangles, are often referred to as **issue networks.** Like iron triangles, issue networks are made up of people with similar policy concerns. Issue networks are less interdependent and unified than iron triangles, however, and often include more players, such as media outlets.[7] (See Figure 13–6.)

A key characteristic of issue networks is that there can be more than one network in a given policy area. To take the example of the environment, one issue network tends to advocate greater environmental regulation, while another network opposes such regulations as undue burdens on businesses and landowners. In other words, competing interests often form rival issue networks that tend to limit each other's power.

CRITICAL ANALYSIS

▶ *Who—or what—can stop an iron triangle from absorbing ever-greater amounts of government resources?*

13–5 CURBING WASTE AND IMPROVING EFFICIENCY

> **LO** Identify some of the ways in which the government has attempted to curb waste and improve efficiency in the bureaucracy.

There is no doubt that our bureaucracy is costly. There is also little doubt that at times it can be wasteful and inefficient. The government has made many attempts to reduce waste, inefficiency, and wrongdoing. For example, federal and state governments have passed laws requiring more openness in government. Other laws encourage employees to report any waste and wrongdoing that they observe.

13–5a Whistleblowers

The term **whistleblower** as applied to the federal bureaucracy, has a special meaning: it is someone who blows the whistle, or reports, on gross governmental inefficiency, illegal activities, or other wrongdoing. Whistleblowers often take their complaints to the press.

Laws Protecting Whistleblowers Federal employees may be reluctant to blow the whistle on their superiors for fear of reprisals. To encourage federal employees to report government wrongdoing, Congress has passed laws to protect whistleblowers.

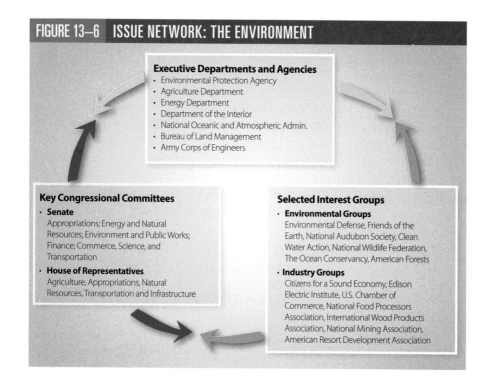

FIGURE 13–6 ISSUE NETWORK: THE ENVIRONMENT

Executive Departments and Agencies
- Environmental Protection Agency
- Agriculture Department
- Energy Department
- Department of the Interior
- National Oceanic and Atmospheric Admin.
- Bureau of Land Management
- Army Corps of Engineers

Key Congressional Committees
- **Senate**
  Appropriations; Energy and Natural Resources; Environment and Public Works; Finance; Commerce, Science, and Transportation
- **House of Representatives**
  Agriculture, Appropriations, Natural Resources, Transportation and Infrastructure

Selected Interest Groups
- **Environmental Groups**
  Environmental Defense, Friends of the Earth, National Audubon Society, Clean Water Action, National Wildlife Federation, The Ocean Conservancy, American Forests
- **Industry Groups**
  Citizens for a Sound Economy, Edison Electric Institute, U.S. Chamber of Commerce, National Food Processors Association, International Wood Products Association, National Mining Association, American Resort Development Association

issue networks
Groups of individuals or organizations—which consist of legislators and legislative staff members, interest group leaders, bureaucrats, the media, scholars, and other experts—that support particular policy positions on a given issue.

whistleblower In the context of government employment, someone who "blows the whistle" (reports to authorities or the press) on gross governmental inefficiency, illegal action, or other wrongdoing.

Marchers in a gay pride parade demand freedom for Chelsea Manning, a convicted national security leaker. Manning, who is transsexual, was freed in May 2017 following a commutation order by President Obama as he left office. *Are long prison sentences for such leakers appropriate?*

The Whistleblower Protection Act of 1989 authorized the Office of Special Counsel (OSC), an independent agency, to investigate complaints of reprisals against whistleblowers. Many federal agencies also have toll-free hotlines that employees can use to anonymously report bureaucratic waste and inappropriate behavior.

One set of laws encourages reports by making cash rewards to whistleblowers. Under four different programs, if the government saves or retrieves a significant sum as a result of a tip-off, a percentage of the government's gain can be paid to the whistleblower. Under the False Claims Act, a private individual can even pursue a claim in court if the Justice Department fails to proceed.

Many such cases involve tax fraud by corporations and individuals, not government malfeasance. In September 2012, the government paid out the largest such reward ever—$104 million. The money went to a banker who blew the whistle on a Swiss bank that was helping U.S. citizens defraud the Internal Revenue Service. The whistleblower, however, also had to serve forty months in prison for his part in the fraud.

Whistleblowers Continue to Face Problems

In spite of these laws, there is little evidence that whistleblowers are adequately protected against retaliation. According to a study conducted by the Government Accountability Office, 41 percent of the whistleblowers who turned to the OSC for protection during a recent three-year period reported that they were no longer employed by the agencies on which they blew the whistle. Indeed, given how difficult it is to fire a federal employee under normal circumstances, it is amazing how quickly most whistleblowers are "shown the door."

Many federal employees who have blown the whistle say that they would not do so again because it was so difficult to get help. Even when they did get help, they faced a stressful ordeal.

Whistleblowers under Obama.

Barack Obama's supporters expected that, as president, he would protect whistleblowers. Many of them were disappointed, however, when the Obama administration took an unusually harsh line regarding information disclosures. Indeed, some believe that Obama's record on whistleblowers was the worst of any president's.

The Obama administration charged seven individuals who leaked information to the press with violations of the Espionage Act of 1917. Before Obama took office, only three persons had ever been charged under that act for talking to the press. Some of those charged may have endangered national security. In other cases, though, the true crime may simply have been embarrassing the government.

Whistleblowers and National Security.

It is, of course, possible that leaking information can simultaneously endanger national security and also expose government actions that are unethical and possibly illegal or unconstitutional. Some of the revelations provided by Edward Snowden concerning activities of the National Security Agency may have fallen into such a category. The news that the government had spied on various foreign leaders created substantial problems for the U.S. government. Reports of spying on American citizens, however, generated outrage in many quarters. The Trump administration has also been outraged at national security leaks. We provide some background to that issue in this chapter's *The Rest of the World* feature.

13–5b Improving Efficiency and Getting Results

The Government Performance and Results Act, which went into effect in 1993, has forced the federal government to change the way it does business. Since 1997, almost every agency (except the intelligence agencies) has had to describe its goals and identify methods for evaluating how well those goals are met. A goal can be as

In the months following President Trump's inauguration, we have heard a new term—the *deep state*. Supposedly, a shadowy conspiracy of national security operatives and civilian bureaucrats is plotting to block the Trump agenda through bureaucratic resistance and leaks to the press. Trump's own advisers have advocated this concept.

As one example, leaks from security agency sources in February 2017 revealed that Michael Flynn, Trump's White House national security adviser at the time, had questionable contacts with the Russian ambassador. Flynn was forced to resign. Trump supporters blamed the leaks on the deep state. What, then, is a deep state?

The Deep State in Turkey

The term *deep state* originated in Turkey. This conspiracy dates back to a secret Turkish military unit set up after World War II (1939–1945) with the help of the CIA. If Turkey were conquered by the Soviet Union—a real concern at the time—this unit would organize guerrilla resistance against the Soviets. That threat passed, but a clandestine, ultra-nationalist organization survived, based in the military and security forces. Later known as *Ergenekon*, the group sought to infiltrate the police, judiciary, and media.

It may even have established relations with organized crime.

For decades, the Turkish military sought to defend Turkey's secular establishment against Islamist political parties. This defense included at least one *coup d'etat* (seizure of power) to keep an elected Islamist regime from taking office. In 2002, however, the Justice and Development Party, moderate Islamists led by Recep Erdoğan, was elected by margins large enough to forestall military action. Step by step, Prime Minister Erdoğan proceeded to neutralize the military. Ergenekon remained, however. Its members appear to have used assassinations, phony evidence, and threats of violence to bring down its enemies.

One of Erdoğan's allies against the military was a religious movement led by Fethullah Gülen, a cleric who lives in exile in Pennsylvania. Apparently, the Gülenists also set up a clandestine operation that infiltrated Turkish institutions. Gülenists were prominent in the arrest and trial of scores of military officers with alleged ties to Ergenekon. The Gülenists eventually broke with Erdoğan, however, and allied with elements of the military. In 2016, the government blamed an attempted coup on the Gülenists, and tens of thousands of Turks were arrested or fired for Gülenist associations. Erdoğan

is now well on his way to becoming an absolute dictator.

Leaky Government— an American Tradition

Ergenekon—and later the Gülenists— established deep states. Clearly, nothing of the sort exists in our country. Michael Flynn was brought down by information that was leaked to the press and which sparked an FBI investigation. When President Trump fired FBI director James Comey in an attempt to halt the inquiry, the Justice Department appointed a special counsel to investigate not only Flynn, but Comey's firing. The Trump administration was now in serious trouble.

In short, the due process of law has taken its course. Indeed, government officials have passed sensitive information to reporters for as long as our system has existed. Trump's own White House is an absolute font of leaks. National security leakers may be called criminals, but there is no broad conspiracy and no deep state.

Critical Thinking

Why might security officials be more likely to leak sensitive information today than in the past?

broad as lowering the number of highway traffic deaths or as narrow as reducing the number of times an agency's phone rings before it is answered.

As one example, consider the National Oceanic and Atmospheric Administration (NOAA). It has improved the effectiveness of its short-term forecasting services, particularly in issuing warnings of

tornadoes. The warning time has increased from seven to fifteen minutes. This may not seem significant, but it provides additional critical time for those in the path of a tornado.

President Obama's contribution to the attempt to improve government effectiveness was to create a chief performance officer. This individual reported directly to the president and worked with other economic officials in an attempt to increase efficiency and eliminate waste in government.

13-5c Another Approach—Pay-for-Performance Plans

For some time, the private sector has used pay-for-performance plans as a means to increase employee productivity and efficiency. About one-third of the major firms in this country use some kind of alternative pay system, such as team-based pay, skill-based pay, profit-sharing plans, or individual bonuses. In contrast, workers for the federal government traditionally have received fixed salaries. Promotions and salary increases are given on the basis of seniority, not output.

The federal government has been experimenting with pay-for-performance systems. For example, the U.S. Postal Service has implemented the Economic Value Added Variable Pay Program, which ties bonuses to performance. As part of a five-year test of a new pay system, three thousand scientists working in Air Force laboratories received salaries based on results.

13-5d Privatization

Another idea for reforming government bureaucracies is **privatization,** which means turning over certain types of government work to the private sector. Privatization can take place by contracting out (outsourcing) work to the private sector or by *managed competition*, in which the task of providing public services is opened up to competition. In managed competition, both the relevant government agency and private firms can compete for the work.

State and local governments have been experimenting with privatization for some time. Almost all of the states have privatized at least a few of their services, and some states, including California, Colorado, and Florida, have privatized more than one hundred activities formerly undertaken by government. In Scottsdale, Arizona, the city contracts for fire protection. In Baltimore, Maryland, nine of the city's schools are outsourced to private entities.

privatization The transfer of the task of providing services traditionally provided by government to the private sector.

> "*The only thing that saves us from the bureaucracy is its inefficiency.*"
>
> ~ EUGENE J. MCCARTHY
> U.S. SENATOR FROM MINNESOTA
> 1959–1971

13-5e Government in the Sunshine

The last four decades of the twentieth century saw a trend toward more openness in government. The theory was that because Americans pay for the government, they own it—and they have a right to know what the government is doing with the taxpayers' dollars.

The Freedom of Information Act In response to pressure for more government openness and disclosure, Congress passed the Freedom of Information Act in 1966. This act requires federal agencies to disclose any information in agency files, with some exceptions, to any persons requesting it. Since the 1970s, *sunshine laws*, which require government meetings to be open to the public, have been enacted at all levels of American government.

Government Openness after 9/11 The trend toward greater openness in government came to an abrupt halt on September 11, 2001. In the wake of the terrorist attacks on the World Trade Center and the Pentagon, the government began tightening its grip on information. In the months following the attacks, hundreds of thousands of documents were removed from government websites. No longer can the public access layouts of nuclear power plants, descriptions of airline security violations, or maps of pipeline routes. Agencies were instructed to be more cautious about releasing information in their files and were given new guidelines on what should be considered public information.

13-5f Government Online

Increasingly, government agencies have attempted to improve their effectiveness and efficiency by making use of the Internet. One method has been to make information available to the public online. This may appear to run counter to the information restrictions imposed following 9/11, but much government information is not relevant to national security issues.

It is now possible to get annual data on immigration, on airline flight delays, and on job-related deaths that name the employer of the deceased. The *Federal Register*, a record of government notices, can now be read online.

Local governments have posted such information as real estate records, restaurant health inspection scores, and the geographic locations of crimes. Some parts of

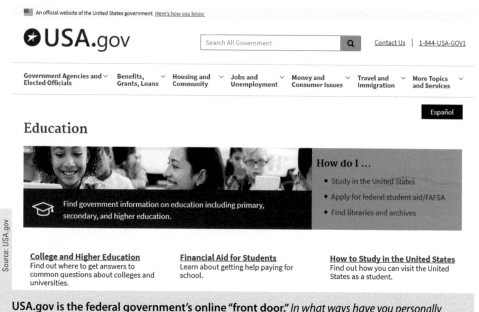

An official website of the United States government Here's how you know

⊙ USA.gov

Search All Government 🔍   Contact Us | 1-844-USA-GOV1

Government Agencies and ⌄   Benefits, ⌄   Housing and ⌄   Jobs and ⌄   Money and ⌄   Travel and ⌄   More Topics ⌄
Elected Officials   Grants, Loans   Community   Unemployment   Consumer Issues   Immigration   and Services

Español

Education

How do I ...

- Study in the United States
- Apply for federal student aid/FAFSA
- Find libraries and archives

Find government information on education including primary, secondary, and higher education.

College and Higher Education
Find out where to get answers to common questions about colleges and universities.

Financial Aid for Students
Learn about getting help paying for school.

How to Study in the United States
Find out how you can visit the United States as a student.

Source: USA.gov

USA.gov is the federal government's online "front door." *In what ways have you personally interacted with the federal government?*

the government have resisted the trend toward openness, however. Lawyers and other interested parties must often pay to obtain information held by the courts.

Filing Forms Online   Another way that government agencies are using the Internet to improve services is to let citizens file forms and apply for services online. For example, if you change your address, you may be able to request an update sticker for your driver's license by visiting a state website. Also, you may be able to apply for unemployment benefits without visiting an unemployment office and receive payments through a government-issued debit card. The federal government distributes payments for Medicare, tax refunds, and a variety of other programs automatically and electronically.

E-Fraud   One danger of automatic payments is the possibility of fraud. This problem is not new. Criminals have long attempted to defraud the government—and the taxpayer—by filing false income tax forms or by making improper claims following natural disasters. The Internet, however, has made it possible for crooks to "game the system" more easily. Claims can be processed without examination by an actual person. Such faulty payment systems demonstrate that bureaucrats still have a role to play, even in the high-tech era.

Law Enforcement versus Online Privacy

A major recent issue concerning the government's online presence has been the extent to which the government can require cooperation from Internet service providers and technology companies. Law enforcement agencies such as the Federal Bureau of Investigation (FBI) naturally want the widest possible powers to demand cooperation. Such demands, however, run the danger of infringing on the privacy rights of Americans (and foreigners as well). In 2014, the United States Supreme Court ruled unanimously that law enforcement personnel cannot search cell phones without a search warrant. It remains an open question, however, as to what kinds of demands law enforcement agencies can make if they have a search warrant.

In one major incident, following a terrorist attack in San Bernardino, California, in 2015, the FBI recovered an Apple iPhone that had been used by one of the perpetrators. The FBI was not immediately able to access the information stored on the phone because the data were encrypted. The FBI therefore demanded that Apple write a new operating system that would bypass the phone's security features. Apple refused, citing security risks that such a "backdoor" would pose for its customers. The FBI then obtained a court order requiring Apple to cooperate. Shortly thereafter, however, the FBI announced that it had found a way to "crack" the iPhone without Apple's help. The court order was lifted, but the underlying issue remains.

CRITICAL ANALYSIS

▶ *In the name of security, some states have gone so far as to bar access to emergency evacuation plans. Why might these states have done this? What problems could result if citizens lack access to this information?*

AMERICA AT ODDS | The Bureaucracy

Although the story is often told about red tape and wasteful spending generated by our bureaucracy, all in all, the U.S. bureaucracy compares favorably with bureaucracies in other countries. Citizens typically overestimate the amount of "government waste" by very large margins. Still, the U.S. government faces the same problems with its bureaucracy—sluggishness, inefficiency, and even incompetence—that large businesses and organizations throughout the country face. Americans are at odds over a number of issues relating to the bureaucracy, including the following:

- *Can new financial regulations eliminate the danger of a catastrophe such as the one we experienced in September 2008—or will clever financiers find ways around any regulations?*

- *Does the Affordable Care Act (Obamacare) provide vital protections to the citizenry—or is it an example of excessive government meddling in the private sector?*

- *Are government employees overpaid—or is their pay appropriate, given their responsibilities?*

- *Is the outsourcing of government services a way to improve efficiency—or does it mostly serve to hide the true cost and scope of government?*

- *Should our leaders focus on openness and transparency in government—or are such measures dangerous during the war on terrorism?*

STUDY TOOLS 13

READY TO STUDY? IN THE BOOK, YOU CAN:

☐ Review what you've read with the following chapter quiz.

☐ Check your answers in Appendix D at the back of the book.

☐ Rip out the Chapter Review Card, which includes key terms and chapter summaries.

ONLINE AT WWW.CENGAGEBRAIN.COM, YOU CAN:

☐ Watch videos to get a quick overview.

☐ Expedite your studying with Major Player readings and Focus Activities.

☐ Check your understanding with Chapter Quizzes.

FILL-IN

Learning Outcome 13–1

1. All in all, the three levels of government employ more than _____ percent of the civilian labor force.

Learning Outcome 13–2

2. The head of each executive department is known as the _____, except for the Department of Justice, which is headed by the attorney general.

3. The _____ Department grants patents and trademarks, conducts the national census, and monitors the weather.

Learning Outcome 13–3

4. Federal bureaucrats holding top-level positions are appointed by the _____ and confirmed by the _____.

5. The Civil Service Reform Act of 1883 established the principle of government employment on the basis of _____.

Learning Outcome 13–4

6. To create a federal administrative agency, Congress passes _____, which specifies the name, purpose, composition, and powers of the agency being created.

7. An iron triangle is _____.

Learning Outcome 13–5

8. A whistleblower is someone who _____.

MULTIPLE-CHOICE

Learning Outcome 13–1

9. The amount spent on defense, together with veterans' benefits, accounts for about _____ percent of federal spending.
   a. 5   **b.** 19   **c.** 49

Learning Outcome 13–2

10. The principal duties of the _____ Department include negotiating treaties, developing foreign policy, and protecting citizens abroad.
    a. State
    b. Homeland Security
    c. Defense

11. The independent executive agencies
    a. are businesses owned by the government.
    b. create and implement rules that regulate private activity and protect the public interest in a particular sector of the economy.
    c. are federal bureaucratic organizations that have a single function.

12. The _____ is a government corporation.
    a. General Services Administration
    b. U.S. Postal Service
    c. Securities and Exchange Commission

Learning Outcome 13–3

13. The document called *Policy and Supporting Positions* (the *Plum Book*) summarizes about _____ jobs that are filled by appointments after each presidential election.
    a. six hundred
    b. one thousand
    c. eight thousand

Learning Outcome 13–4

14. The process undertaken by an administrative agency when formally proposing, evaluating, and adopting a new regulation is called
    a. adjudication.
    b. rulemaking.
    c. neutral competency.

Learning Outcome 13–5

15. "Sunshine laws" require government
    a. meetings to be open to the public.
    b. agencies to outsource work to the private sector.
    c. agencies to let citizens file forms and apply for services online.

14 | THE JUDICIARY

Samuel Corum/Anadolu Agency/Getty Images

LEARNING OUTCOMES

After reading this chapter, you should be able to:

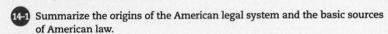

14-1 Summarize the origins of the American legal system and the basic sources of American law.

14-2 Delineate the structure of the federal court system.

14-3 Say how federal judges are appointed.

14-4 Explain how the federal courts make policy, and describe the role of ideology and judicial philosophies in judicial decision making.

14-5 Identify some of the criticisms of the federal courts and some of the checks on the power of the courts.

After finishing this chapter, go to **PAGE 332** for **STUDY TOOLS**

AMERICA AT ODDS

Should the People Elect Judges?

Lukasz Siekierski/Shutterstock.com

The founders of the American republic were concerned that too great a degree of popular control over the government could lead to "mob rule," and so they sought to insulate various institutions from direct popular elections. Federal judges, in particular, were to be appointed and serve for life. In contrast, in many states, all judges are popularly elected.

From time to time, judges are defeated at the polls. The most common way to defeat a judge is to accuse that official of being "soft on crime." Some people believe that despite the long prison sentences common in recent years, the judicial system is still too friendly to criminals. Others believe that elections tempt judges to cut corners on civil liberties. (In general, voters are not sympathetic to the civil liberties of alleged criminals.) So, should state judges be named through appointment? Or should the states rely on popular election?

The People Should Rule

Those who favor electing judges do not believe that judges can be insulated from politics. Governors, who often do the appointing when judges aren't elected, are highly political creatures. They tend to appoint supporters of their own party. If politics is going to play a role in judicial selection, then the people ought to have their say directly. Let the voters decide whether a judge is tough enough on crime or too tough on business. We admit ordinary people into the judicial process through juries, and judges should respond to public opinion as well. Officials who do not have to win a popular election may become remote from the people. Living in upscale neighborhoods, they will never experience what it is like to walk home at night fearing for their safety. Instead, they can end up living in a legal never-never land, where abstractions matter more than the real world. It takes elections to give us the kinds of judges that we really want.

The Courts Must Be Insulated from Popular Pressure

Many opponents of judicial elections believe that they allow too much opportunity for panics and prejudices to influence the process. Popular "lock 'em up" attitudes toward criminals do not lead to an optimum strategy for crime reduction. Rather, we need to study what works and what doesn't. In some states, "get tough" policies have led to absurd cases of individuals serving life sentences for trivial offenses. Indeed, in states such as Texas, even conservative Republicans have recently concluded that we are imprisoning too many people at too great an expense. The last thing we need is to place additional pressure on judges by threatening them with removal.

Any move toward greater use of elections would bring with it a further problem—the corrupting influence of campaign contributions. Several states that use judicial elections are famous for their harsh sentences and enthusiasm for the death penalty. Judges in these states are also conspicuously friendly toward the moneyed interests that helped get them elected.

Where do you stand?

1. How much information do voters typically have about judicial candidates?
2. If judges had to raise campaign contributions, what kinds of people would be most likely to contribute? Why?

Explore this issue online:

- *The Atlantic* magazine interviews Don Willett, a Texas judge opposed to judicial elections. Find it by searching on "Atlantic Don Willet."
- Randolph Hammock, a Los Angeles County Superior Court judge, has written an article defending the election of judges. Search on "hammock judicial elections."

INTRODUCTION

As you read in this chapter's opening *America at Odds* feature, the question of whether judges should be elected has elicited controversy. Also controversial is the policy-making function of the United States Supreme Court. After all, when the Court renders an opinion on how the Constitution is to be interpreted, it is, necessarily, making policy on a national level.

To examine the nature of this controversy, we first need to explain how the **judiciary** (the court system) functions in this country. We begin by looking at the origins and sources of American law. We then describe the federal court system, at the apex of which is the United States Supreme Court, and consider various issues relating to the courts.

> "It is confidence *in the men and women who administer the judicial system* that is the true backbone of the rule of law."
>
> ~ JOHN PAUL STEVENS
> ASSOCIATE JUSTICE OF THE
> UNITED STATES SUPREME COURT
> 1975–2010

his successors began the process of unifying the country under their rule. One of the methods they used was the establishment of the "king's courts," or *curiae regis*. Before the Norman Conquest, disputes had been settled according to the local legal customs in various regions of the country. The law developed in the king's courts, however, applied to the country as a whole. What evolved in these courts was the beginning of the **common law**— the body of general rules that was applied throughout the entire English realm.

The Rule of Precedent

The early English courts developed the common law rules from the principles underlying judges' decisions in actual legal controversies. Judges tried to be consistent, and whenever possible, they based their decisions on the principles applied in earlier cases. They also considered new kinds of cases with the awareness that their decisions would make new law. Each interpretation became part of the law on the subject and served as a legal **precedent**—that is, a decision that furnished an example or authority for deciding subsequent cases involving similar legal issues and facts.

14–1 THE ORIGINS AND SOURCES OF AMERICAN LAW

LO Summarize the origins of the American legal system and the basic sources of American law.

judiciary The court system. One of the three branches of government in the United States.

common law The body of law developed from judicial decisions in English and U.S. courts, not attributable to a legislature.

precedent A court decision that furnishes an example or authority for deciding subsequent cases involving identical or similar facts and legal issues.

stare decisis A common law doctrine under which judges normally are obligated to follow the precedents established by prior court decisions. Pronounced *ster*-ay *dih-si-sis*.

The American colonists brought with them the legal system that had developed in England over hundreds of years. Thus, to understand how the American legal system operates, we need to go back in time to the early English courts and the traditions they established.

14–1a The Common Law Tradition

After the Normans conquered England in 1066, William the Conqueror and

Stare Decisis The practice of deciding new cases with reference to former decisions, or precedents, eventually became a cornerstone of the English and American judicial systems. The practice formed a doctrine called ***stare decisis*** ("to stand on decided cases").

Under this doctrine, judges are obligated to follow the precedents established in their jurisdictions. For example, if the Supreme Court of Georgia holds that a state law requiring candidates for state office to pass drug tests is unconstitutional, that decision will control the outcome of future cases on that issue brought before the state courts in Georgia.

Similarly, a decision made on a given issue by the United States Supreme Court (the nation's highest court) is binding on all inferior (lower) courts. For example, the Georgia case on drug testing might be appealed to the United States Supreme Court. If the Court agrees that the Georgia law is unconstitutional, the high court's ruling will be binding on *all* courts in the United States. In other words, similar drug-testing laws in other states will be invalid and unenforceable.

Departures from Precedent Sometimes a court will depart from the rule of precedent if it decides that a precedent is simply incorrect or that technological or social changes have rendered the precedent inapplicable. Cases that overturn precedent often receive a great deal of publicity.

An Example: *Brown v. Board of Education.* For example, in 1954, in *Brown v. Board of Education of Topeka,*[1] the United States Supreme Court expressly overturned precedent. Separate educational facilities for African Americans had been upheld as constitutional in many earlier cases under the "separate-but-equal" doctrine.[2] The Court now concluded, however, that such separation was inherently unequal and violated the equal protection clause. The Supreme Court's departure from precedent in *Brown* received a tremendous amount of publicity as people began to realize the political and social ramifications of this change in the law.

Another Example: *Citizens United v. FEC.* More recently, the Supreme Court departed from precedent in its 2010 ruling *Citizens United v. Federal Election Commission.*[3] In this decision, the Court determined that the government may not ban political spending by corporations in elections when the spending is undertaken independently of the campaigns of individual candidates. (The ruling implicitly covers unions and nonprofit groups as well.) The Court's decision overturned two precedents that had upheld restrictions on corporate spending.[4]

14–1b Primary Sources of American Law

In any governmental system, the main function of the courts is to interpret and apply the law. In the United States, the courts interpret and apply several sources of law when deciding cases. We look here only at the **primary sources of law**—that is, sources that *establish* the law—and the relative priority of these sources when particular laws come into conflict.

Constitutional Law The U.S. government and each of the fifty states have separate written constitutions that set forth the general organization, powers, and limits of their respective governments. **Constitutional law** consists of the rights and duties set forth in these constitutions.

The U.S. Constitution is the supreme law of the land. As such, it is the basis of all law in the United States. Any law that violates the Constitution is invalid and unenforceable. Because of the paramount importance of the U.S. Constitution in the American legal system, the complete text of the Constitution is found in Appendix B.

Chief Justice John Roberts. *What does it mean when the Supreme Court stands on precedent?*

Each state in the union also has its own constitution. Unless they conflict with the U.S. Constitution or a federal law, state constitutions are supreme within the borders of their respective states.

Statutory Law Statutes enacted by legislative bodies at any level of government make up another source of law, which is generally referred to as **statutory law**. Federal statutes—laws enacted by the U.S. Congress—apply to all of the states. State statutes—laws enacted by state legislatures—apply only within the state that enacted the laws. Any state statute that conflicts with the U.S. Constitution, with federal laws enacted by Congress, or with the state's constitution will be deemed invalid if challenged in court and will not be enforced.

Statutory law also includes the ordinances (such as local zoning or

primary source of law A source of law that establishes the law. Primary sources of law include constitutions, statutes, administrative agency rules and regulations, and decisions rendered by the courts.

constitutional law Law based on the U.S. Constitution and the constitutions of the various states.

statutory law The body of law enacted by legislatures (as opposed to constitutional law, administrative law, or case law).

housing-construction laws) passed by cities and counties. None of these may violate the U.S. Constitution, the relevant state constitution, or any existing federal or state laws.

Administrative Law   Another important source of American law consists of administrative law—the rules, regulations, orders, and decisions of administrative agencies. At the federal level, Congress creates executive agencies, such as the Food and Drug Administration and the Environmental Protection Agency, to perform specific functions. Typically, when Congress establishes an agency, it authorizes the agency to create rules that have the force of law and to enforce those rules by bringing legal actions against violators.

Rules issued by various government agencies now affect nearly every aspect of our lives. For example, almost all of a business's operations are subject to government regulation. These include the firm's capital structure and financing, its hiring and firing practices, its relations with employees and unions, and the way it manufactures and markets its products.

Government agencies exist at the state and local levels as well. States commonly create agencies that parallel federal agencies. Just as federal statutes take precedence over conflicting state statutes, federal agency regulations take precedence over conflicting state regulations.

Case Law   As is evident from the earlier discussion of the common law tradition, another basic source of American law consists of the rules of law announced in court decisions, or case law. These rules of law include interpretations of constitutional provisions, of statutes enacted by legislatures, and of regulations issued by administrative agencies.

Thus, even though a legislature passes a law to govern a certain area, how that law is interpreted and applied depends on the courts. The importance of case law, or *judge-made law*, is one of the distinguishing characteristics of the common law tradition.

14-1c Civil Law and Criminal Law

All of the sources of law just discussed can be classified in other ways as well. One of the most significant classification systems divides all law into two categories: civil law and criminal law.

Civil law spells out the duties that individuals in society owe to other persons or to their governments, excluding the duty not to commit crimes. Typically, in a civil case, a private party sues another private party (although the government can also sue a party for a civil law violation). The object of a civil lawsuit is to make the defendant—the person being sued—comply with a legal duty (such as a contractual promise) or pay money damages for failing to comply with that duty.

Criminal law, in contrast, has to do with wrongs committed against the public as a whole. Criminal acts are prohibited by local, state, and federal government statutes. Thus, criminal defendants are prosecuted by public officials, such as a district attorney (D.A.), on behalf of the government, not by their victims or other private parties.

In a criminal case, the government seeks to impose a penalty (usually a fine and/or imprisonment) on a person who has violated a criminal law. For example, when someone robs a convenience store, that person has committed a crime and, if caught and proved guilty, will usually spend time in prison.

14-1d Basic Judicial Requirements

A court cannot decide just any issue at any time. Before a court can hear and decide a case, specific requirements must be met. To a certain extent, these requirements act as restraints on the judiciary because they limit the types of cases that courts can hear and decide. Courts also have procedural requirements that judges must follow.

Jurisdiction   In Latin, *juris* means "law," and *diction* means "to speak." Therefore, jurisdiction literally refers

> "Our Constitution is color-blind, *and neither knows nor tolerates classes among citizens.*"
>
> ~ JOHN MARSHALL HARLAN
> ASSOCIATE JUSTICE OF THE
> UNITED STATES SUPREME COURT
> 1877–1911

administrative law The body of law created by administrative agencies (in the form of rules, regulations, orders, and decisions) in order to carry out their duties and responsibilities.

case law The rules of law announced in court decisions. Case law is the aggregate of reported cases that interpret judicial precedents, statutes, regulations, and constitutional provisions.

civil law The branch of law that spells out the duties that individuals in society owe to other persons or to their governments, excluding the duty not to commit crimes.

criminal law The branch of law that defines and governs actions that constitute crimes. Generally, criminal law has to do with wrongful actions committed against society for which society demands redress.

jurisdiction The authority of a court to hear and decide a particular case.

An attorney addressing a jury. If a criminal case goes to trial, a jury of ordinary citizens typically determines guilt or innocence. *How might trials by jury help protect our rights?*

and Treaties made, or which shall be made, under their Authority." Whenever a case involves a claim based, at least in part, on the U.S. Constitution, a treaty, or a federal law, a **federal question** arises. Any lawsuit involving a federal question can originate in a federal court.

Federal courts can also exercise jurisdiction over cases involving **diversity of citizenship.** Such cases may arise when the parties in a lawsuit live in different states or when one of the parties is a foreign government or a foreign citizen. Before a federal court can take jurisdiction in a diversity case, the amount in controversy must be more than $75,000. (Congress raised the limit to $75,000 in 1996. In 1789, the sum was $500, which is about $14,750 in 2018 dollars.)

to the power "to speak the law." Jurisdiction applies either to the geographic area in which a court has the right and power to decide cases, or to the right and power of a court to decide matters concerning certain persons, types of property, or subjects. Before any court can hear a case, it must have jurisdiction over the person against whom the suit is brought, the property involved in the suit, and the subject matter.

State Court Jurisdiction. A state trial court usually has jurisdictional authority over the residents of a particular area of the state, such as a county or district. (A **trial court** is, as the term implies, a court in which trials are held and testimony is taken.) A state's highest court (often called the *state supreme court*)[5] has jurisdictional authority over all residents within the state. In some cases, if an individual has committed an offense such as injuring someone in an automobile accident or selling defective goods within the state, the court can exercise jurisdiction even if the individual is a resident of another state.

State courts can also exercise jurisdiction over those who do business within the state. A New York company that distributes its products in California, for example, can be sued by a California resident in a California state court.

Federal Court Jurisdiction. Because the federal government is a government of limited powers, the jurisdiction of the federal courts is limited. Article III, Section 2, of the Constitution states that the federal courts can exercise jurisdiction over all cases "arising under this Constitution, the Laws of the United States,

Standing to Sue To bring a lawsuit before a court, a person must have **standing to sue,** or a sufficient "stake" in the matter to justify bringing a suit. Thus, the party bringing the suit must have suffered a harm or been threatened with a harm by the action at issue, and the issue must be justiciable. A **justiciable controversy** is one that is real and substantial, as opposed to hypothetical or academic.

The requirement of standing to sue clearly limits the issues that can be decided by the courts. Furthermore, both state and federal governments can specify by law when an individual or group has standing to sue. For example, the federal government will not allow a taxpayer to sue the Department of Defense for spending tax dollars wastefully.

trial court A court in which trials are held and testimony is taken.

federal question A question that pertains to the U.S. Constitution, acts of Congress, or treaties. A federal question provides a basis for federal court jurisdiction.

diversity of citizenship A basis for federal court jurisdiction over a lawsuit that arises when (1) the parties in the lawsuit live in different states or when one of the parties is a foreign government or a foreign citizen, and (2) the amount in controversy is more than $75,000.

standing to sue The requirement that an individual must have a sufficient stake in a controversy before he or she can bring a lawsuit. The party bringing the suit must demonstrate that he or she has either been harmed or been threatened with a harm.

justiciable controversy A controversy that is not hypothetical or academic but real and substantial. This requirement must be satisfied before a court will hear a case. *Justiciable* is pronounced jus-*tish*-a-bul.

Court Procedures Both the federal and the state courts have established procedural rules that apply in all cases. These procedures are designed to protect the rights and interests of the parties, ensure that the litigation proceeds in a fair and orderly manner, and identify the issues that must be decided by the court—thus saving court time and costs. Different procedural rules apply in criminal and civil cases. Generally, criminal procedural rules attempt to ensure that defendants are not deprived of their constitutional rights.

Parties involved in civil or criminal cases must comply with court procedural rules or risk being held in contempt of court. A party who is held in **contempt of court** can be fined, taken into custody, or both. A court must take care to ensure that the parties—and the court itself—comply with procedural requirements. Procedural errors often serve as grounds for a mistrial or for appealing the court's decision to a higher tribunal.

CRITICAL THINKING

▶ *Why does national law—even administrative law established by a federal agency—overrule conflicting state law, even when a state law is based on the state constitution?*

14–2 **THE FEDERAL COURT SYSTEM**

LO Delineate the structure of the federal court system.

The federal court system is a three-tiered model consisting of U.S. district courts and specialized courts (trial courts), U.S. courts of appeals, and the United States Supreme Court. Figure 14–1 shows the organization of the federal court system.

Bear in mind that the federal courts constitute only one of the fifty-two court systems in the United States. Each of the fifty states has its own court system, as does the District of Columbia. No two state court systems are exactly the same. In general, though, the states have different levels, or tiers, of courts, just as the federal system does.

Normally, state courts deal with questions of state law, and the decisions of a state's highest court on matters of state law are normally final. If a federal question is involved, however, a decision of a state supreme court may be appealed to the federal court system.

contempt of court
A ruling that a person has disobeyed a court order or has shown disrespect to the court or to a judicial proceeding.

FIGURE 14–1 THE ORGANIZATION OF THE FEDERAL COURT SYSTEM

Why might the government have created specialized courts?

Supreme Court of the United States

Courts of Appeals

Court of Appeals for the Federal Circuit

District Courts

Specialized Courts (Including the Court of Federal Claims, Court of International Trade, and Court of Appeals for Veterans Claims)

Note: Some specialized courts, such as the Tax Court, are not included in this figure.

We will discuss the federal court system in the pages that follow.

14–2a **U.S. District and Specialized Courts**

On the lowest tier of the federal court system are the U.S. district courts, or federal trial courts—the courts in which cases involving federal laws begin. The cases in these courts are decided by a judge or a jury. There is at least one federal district court in every state, and there is one in the District of Columbia. The number of judicial districts has varied historically, but no new district has been created since 1966. Figure 14–2 shows their geographic boundaries. Currently, there are 94 judicial districts and 678 district court judgeships. The number of judges per district varies from two in North Dakota to twenty-eight in the Southern District of New York.

The federal system also includes other trial courts, such as the Court of International Trade and others listed in Figure 14–1. These courts have limited, or specialized, subject-matter jurisdiction—that is, they can exercise authority over only certain kinds of cases.

One specialized court has recently received exceptional scrutiny—the Foreign Intelligence Surveillance Court (FISC). This court was initially created to issue search warrants against suspected foreign spies inside the United States. The USA Patriot Act of 2001 greatly

FIGURE 14–2 U.S. COURTS OF APPEALS AND U.S. DISTRICT COURTS

Why, under our system of government, is it almost inevitable that each state will have at least one U.S. district court?

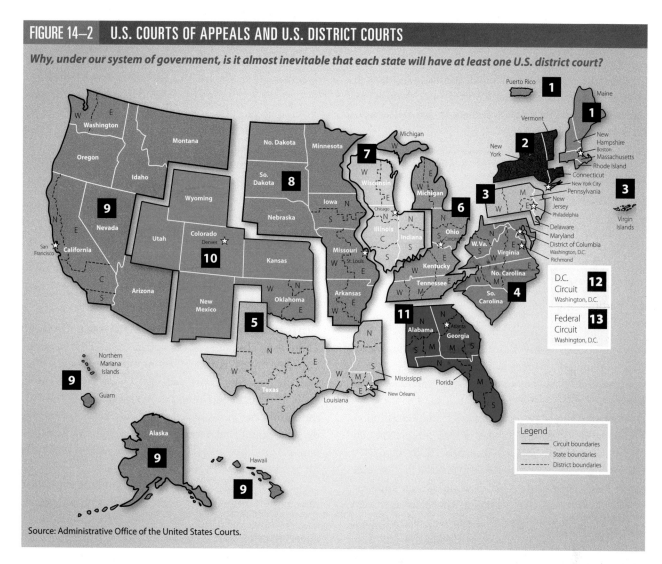

Source: Administrative Office of the United States Courts.

expanded its powers. The FISC almost never rejects a warrant request. It meets in secret and releases no information on individual cases.

More controversially, the court does not report the legal interpretations under which it issues its rulings. In 2013, revelations of large-scale surveillance by the National Security Agency (NSA) raised questions about the FISC's practices. (NSA actions must be approved by the FISC.) Some legal experts doubted that the FISC's decisions could be squared with the Fourth Amendment to the U.S. Constitution, which bars unreasonable searches. The USA Freedom Act of 2015 sought to submit the FISC to greater scrutiny.

14–2b U.S. Courts of Appeals

On the middle tier of the federal court system are the U.S. courts of appeals. Courts of appeals, or **appellate courts,** do not hear evidence or testimony. Rather, an appellate court reviews the transcript of the trial court's

proceedings, other records relating to the case, and attorneys' arguments as to why the trial court's decision should or should not stand.

In contrast to a trial court, where normally a single judge presides, an appellate court consists of a panel of three or more judges. The task of the appellate court is to determine whether the trial court erred in applying the law to the facts and issues involved in a particular case.

There are thirteen federal courts of appeals in the United States. The courts of appeals for twelve of the circuits, including the Court of Appeals for the D.C. Circuit, hear appeals from the U.S. district courts located within their respective judicial circuits (see Figure 14–2).

Decisions made by federal administrative agencies may be reviewed by either a district court or a court of appeals, depending on the agency. The Court of

appellate court A court of appeals, consisting of a panel of three or more judges. It does not hear evidence or testimony. Its task is to determine whether the trial court erred in applying the law in a particular case.

Appeals for the Federal Circuit has national jurisdiction over certain types of cases, such as those concerning patent law and some claims against the national government.

The decisions of the federal appellate courts may be appealed to the Supreme Court. If a decision is not appealed, or if the high court declines to review the case, the appellate court's decision is final.

14–2c The United States Supreme Court

The highest level of the three-tiered model of the federal court system is the United States Supreme Court. According to Article III of the U.S. Constitution, there is only one national Supreme Court, but Congress is empowered to create additional ("inferior") courts as it deems necessary. The inferior courts that Congress has created include the second tier in our model—the U.S. courts of appeals—as well as the district courts and other courts of limited, or specialized, jurisdiction.

The United States Supreme Court consists of nine justices—a chief justice and eight associate justices—although that number is not mandated by the Constitution. The Supreme Court has original, or trial, jurisdiction only in unusual instances (set forth in Article III, Section 2). In other words, only rarely does a case originate at the Supreme Court level. Most of the Court's work is as an appellate court. The Supreme Court has appellate authority over cases decided by the U.S. courts of appeals, as well as over some cases decided in the state courts when federal questions are at issue.

writ of *certiorari*
An order from a higher court asking a lower court for the record of a case. *Certiorari* is pronounced sur-shee-uh-*rah*-ree.

The Writ of *Certiorari*   To bring a case before the Supreme Court, a party may request that the Court issue a writ of *certiorari,* often called "cert." The writ of *certiorari* is an order that the Supreme Court issues to a lower court requesting the latter to send it the record of the case in question.

Parties can petition the Supreme Court to issue a writ of *certiorari*, but whether the Court will do so is entirely within its discretion. The Court will not issue a writ unless at least four of the nine justices approve. In no instance is the Court required to issue a writ of *certiorari*.[6]

Most petitions for writs of *certiorari* are denied. A denial is not a decision on the merits of a case, nor does it indicate that the Court agrees with a lower court's opinion. The denial of a writ has no value as a precedent. A denial simply means that the decision of the lower court remains the law within that court's jurisdiction.

Which Cases Reach the Supreme Court?

There is no absolute right to appeal to the United States Supreme Court. Although thousands of cases are filed with the Supreme Court each year, on average the Court hears fewer than one hundred. As shown in Figure 14–3, the number of cases heard by the Court each year has declined significantly since the 1980s. In large part, this has occurred because the Court has raised its standards for accepting cases in recent years.

Typically, the Court grants petitions for cases that raise important policy issues that need to be addressed. In its 2016–2017 term, for example, the Court heard cases involving such issues as the following:

▶ **Can a state, based on its own constitution, refuse to issue a grant to upgrade a playground solely because the playground belonged to a church? The Court ruled that this refusal amounted to religious discrimination.[7]**

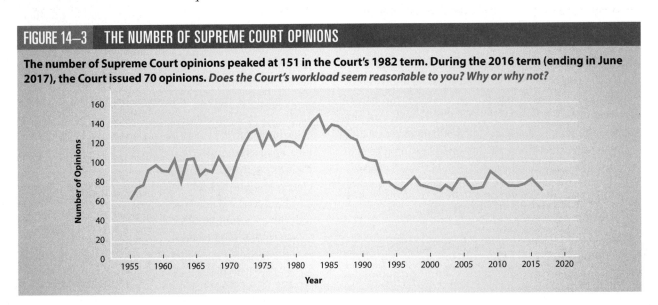

FIGURE 14–3   THE NUMBER OF SUPREME COURT OPINIONS

The number of Supreme Court opinions peaked at 151 in the Court's 1982 term. During the 2016 term (ending in June 2017), the Court issued 70 opinions. *Does the Court's workload seem reasonable to you? Why or why not?*

- Can Muslims subject to illegal treatment by federal officials in the months following the 9/11 attack sue those officials for monetary damages? The Court found that no law existed that would allow such a penalty.[8]

- Can a public school prevent a girl with severe cerebral palsy from bringing her service dog to school? The Court determined that the school's refusal violated federal law and could result in a denial of federal funds.[9]

- Did the North Carolina legislature engage in unlawful racial gerrymandering when it drew the boundaries of two U.S. House districts? The Court ruled that it did.[10]

If the lower courts have rendered conflicting opinions on an important issue, the Supreme Court often reviews one or more cases involving that issue to define the law on the matter. For example, in 2014 four appellate courts ruled that same-sex couples had a constitutional right to marry. The Sixth Circuit Court, however, issued an opinion denying that right. These conflicting judgments forced a somewhat reluctant Supreme Court to take up the issue. The result was *Obergefell v. Hodges* (2015), which established a nationwide right to same-sex marriage.[11]

Supreme Court Opinions   Like other appellate courts, the United States Supreme Court normally does not hear any evidence. The Court's decision in a particular case is based on the written record of the case and the written arguments (legal briefs) that the attorneys submit. The attorneys also present **oral arguments**—spoken arguments presented in person rather than on paper—to the Court. Some observers of the Court have advocated that the oral arguments be video-recorded and provided to the public through C-SPAN. The Court does not agree, however, and cameras are banned.

Reaching an Opinion.   After considering all this information, the justices discuss the case in **conference.** The conference is strictly private—only the justices are allowed in the room.

When the Court has reached a decision, the chief justice, if in the majority, assigns the task of writing the Court's **opinion** to one of the justices. When the chief justice is not in the majority, the most senior justice voting with the majority assigns the writing of the Court's opinion. The opinion outlines the reasons for the Court's decision, the rules of law that apply, and the judgment. An opinion that commands the support of more than half of the justices is called a *majority opinion.*

Concurring and Dissenting Opinions.   Often, one or more justices who agree with the Court's decision do so for reasons different from those outlined in the

majority opinion. These justices may write **concurring opinions,** setting forth their own legal reasoning on the issue. Frequently, one or more justices disagree with the Court's conclusion. These justices may write **dissenting opinions,** outlining the reasons they feel the majority erred in arriving at its decision.

Although a dissenting opinion does not affect the outcome of the case before the Court, it may be important later. In a subsequent case concerning the same issue, a jurist or attorney may use the legal reasoning in the dissenting opinion as the basis for an argument to reverse the previous decision and establish a new precedent.

Sometimes, the opinion with the support of the largest number of justices does not command a majority of the Court. Such an opinion is called a *plurality opinion*. It becomes the Court's opinion only if it is supported by enough concurring opinions to form a majority. It is possible, though rare, for a plurality opinion to be a dissent if a large enough number of alternative opinions are in agreement.

oral argument A spoken argument presented to a judge (or justices) in person by an attorney on behalf of her or his client.

conference In regard to the Supreme Court, a private meeting of the justices in which they present their arguments concerning a case under consideration.

opinion A written statement by a court expressing the reasons for its decision in a case.

concurring opinion A statement written by a judge or justice who agrees (concurs) with the court's decision, but for reasons different from those in the majority opinion.

dissenting opinion A statement written by a judge or justice who disagrees with the majority opinion.

CRITICAL THINKING

- *Some people believe that the Supreme Court should accept more cases and thereby resolve more issues. Others contend that such a move would result in fewer well-thought-out opinions. Who do you think has the better argument, and why?*

FEDERAL JUDICIAL APPOINTMENTS

LO Say how federal judges are appointed.

Unlike state court judges, who are often elected, all federal judges are appointed. Article II, Section 2, of the Constitution authorizes the president to appoint the justices of the Supreme Court with the advice and consent of the Senate. Laws enacted by Congress provide that the same procedure is to be used for appointing judges to the lower federal courts as well.

Federal judges receive lifetime appointments (because under Article III of the Constitution they "hold their Offices during good Behaviour"). Federal judges may be removed from office through the impeachment process, but such proceedings are extremely rare and are usually undertaken only if a judge engages in blatantly illegal conduct, such as bribery. In the history of this nation, only fifteen federal judges have been impeached, and only eleven left office due to a conviction or resignation. Normally, federal judges serve until they resign, retire, or die.

Although the Constitution sets no specific qualifications for those who serve on the Supreme Court, those who have done so share one characteristic: all have been attorneys. The backgrounds of the Supreme Court justices have been far from typical of the characteristics of the American public as a whole. Table 14–1 summarizes the backgrounds of all of the 113 United States Supreme Court justices to 2018.

14–3a The Nomination Process

The president receives suggestions and recommendations of potential nominees for judicial positions from various sources. These include the Justice Department, senators, other judges, the candidates themselves, state political leaders, bar associations, and other interest groups. After selecting a nominee, the president submits her or his name to the Senate for approval. The Senate Judiciary Committee then holds hearings and makes its recommendation to the Senate, where it takes a majority vote to confirm the nomination.

Senatorial Courtesy When judges are nominated to the district courts (and, to a lesser extent, the U.S. courts of appeals), a senator of the president's political party from the state where there is a vacancy traditionally has been allowed to veto the president's choice. This

TABLE 14–1 BACKGROUNDS OF UNITED STATES SUPREME COURT JUSTICES TO 2018	Number of Justices (113 = Total)
Occupational Position before Appointment	
Private legal practice	25
State judgeship	21
Federal judgeship	32
U.S. attorney general	7
Deputy or assistant U.S. attorney general	2
U.S. solicitor general	3
U.S. senator	6
U.S. representative	2
State governor	3
Federal executive post	9
Other	3
Religious Affiliation	
Protestant	84
Roman Catholic	14
Jewish	7
Unitarian	7
No religious affiliation	1
Age on Appointment	
Under 40	5
41–50	34
51–60	60
61–70	14
Political Party Affiliation	
Federalist (to 1835)	13
Jeffersonian Republican (to 1828)	7
Whig (to 1861)	1
Democrat	46
Republican	45
Independent	1
Education	
College graduate	97
Not a college graduate	16
Gender	
Male	109
Female	4
Race	
White (non-Hispanic)	110
African American	2
Hispanic	1

Sources: *Congressional Quarterly's Guide to the U.S. Supreme Court* (Washington, D.C.: Congressional Quarterly Press, 1997); and authors' updates.

Sonia Sotomayor became the first Latina on the Supreme Court when she was confirmed by the Senate in 2009. *Why might President Obama have chosen her?*

practice is known as **senatorial courtesy.** At times, senatorial courtesy even permits senators from the opposing party to veto presidential choices. Because of senatorial courtesy, home-state senators of the president's party may be able to influence the choice of the nominee.

Partisanship   It should come as no surprise that partisanship plays a significant role in the president's selection of nominees to the federal bench, particularly to the Supreme Court, the crown jewel of the federal judiciary. Traditionally, presidents have attempted to strengthen their legacies by appointing federal judges with political and philosophical views similar to their own. In the history of the Supreme Court, fewer than 13 percent of the justices nominated by a president have been from an opposing political party.

That said, presidents have often discovered that the justices they appointed took very different positions than expected. President Dwight D. Eisenhower (1953–1961), for example, had no idea when he appointed Chief Justice Earl Warren that Warren would seek to overturn the system of racial segregation. The Court accomplished this goal through rulings such as *Brown v. Board of Education*.[12]

Courts of Appeals   Appointments to the U.S. courts of appeals can also have a lasting impact. Recall that these courts occupy the level just below the

Supreme Court in the federal court system. Also recall that the decisions rendered by these courts—about sixty thousand per year—are final unless overturned by the Supreme Court. Given that the Supreme Court renders opinions in fewer than one hundred cases a year, the decisions of the federal appellate courts have a wide-reaching effect on American society.

For example, consider a decision interpreting the federal Constitution by the U.S. Court of Appeals for the Ninth Circuit. If not overruled by the Supreme Court, it establishes a precedent that will be followed in the states of Alaska, Arizona, California, Hawaii, Idaho, Montana, Nevada, Oregon, and Washington.

14–3b Confirmation or Rejection by the Senate

The president's nominations are not always confirmed. In fact, almost 20 percent of presidential nominations for the Supreme Court have been either rejected or not acted on by the Senate. The process of nominating and confirming federal judges, especially Supreme Court justices, often involves political debate and controversy. Many bitter battles over Supreme Court appointments have ensued when the Senate and the president have disagreed on political issues.

From 1893 until 1968, the Senate rejected only three Court nominees. From 1968 through 1986, however, two presidential nominees to the highest court were rejected, and two more nominations, both by President Ronald Reagan, failed in 1987. The most significant of these nominees was Robert Bork, who faced hostile questioning about his strongly conservative views during the confirmation hearings. The Bork hearings are often considered to be a turning point, after which confirmation hearings became much more contentious.

One of President George H. W. Bush's nominees to the Supreme Court—Clarence Thomas—was also the subject of considerable controversy. The nation watched on television as Anita Hill, a former aide, leveled charges of sexual harassment at Thomas, who nevertheless was confirmed.

George W. Bush's Appointments   During George W. Bush's second term, Chief Justice William Rehnquist died, and Sandra Day O'Connor, the Court's first woman justice, retired. These events allowed Bush to nominate John G. Roberts, Jr., to replace Rehnquist and

senatorial courtesy A practice that allows a senator of the president's party to veto the president's nominee to a federal court judgeship within the senator's state.

Samuel A. Alito, Jr., to replace O'Connor. Both nominations were confirmed by the Senate with relatively little difficulty. The appointment of Alito, in particular, changed the character of the Court, because he was distinctly more conservative than O'Connor.

Obama's Nominees In May 2009, as a result of a judicial retirement, President Barack Obama named Sonia Sotomayor to the Court. Sotomayor had served for more than a decade as a judge of the U.S. Court of Appeals for the Second Circuit and was the first Hispanic American ever nominated to the Supreme Court.

A second retirement gave Obama an additional chance to pick a nominee, in May 2010. He chose Elena Kagan, his solicitor general. It was a sign of the increased political polarization in the Senate that neither Sotomayor nor Kagan received more than a handful of votes from Republican senators.

The Death of Justice Scalia In February 2016, Justice Antonin Scalia died unexpectedly. Scalia and Justice Clarence Thomas were the two most conservative members of the Court. The chances of Barack Obama—or any Democratic president—nominating a replacement as conservative as Scalia were zero. It appeared possible that the Court was about to take an abrupt lurch to the left. Senate majority leader Mitch McConnell therefore announced that the Republicans would refuse to consider any nominee that Obama might submit. Filling Scalia's seat might have to wait until after January 2017, when a new president would assume office. Republican senators clearly hoped that the new president would be a Republican.

The first result of McConnell's decision was to block Obama's appointment of Merrick Garland, chief judge of the D.C. Circuit Court and a well-regarded moderate Democrat. The second result was a 14-month period in which the Court had only eight members, raising the possibility of four-to-four tie votes. When that happens, the decision of the lower court is sustained. The Court's action does not, however, serve as a precedent. While

> **"As nightfall doesn't come at once, neither does oppression.** *In both instances, . . . We must be aware of change in the air, however slight, lest we become unwitting victims of the darkness."*
>
> ~ WILLIAM O. DOUGLAS
> ASSOCIATE JUSTICE OF THE
> UNITED STATES SUPREME COURT
> 1939–1975

Chief Justice Roberts sought consensus on the Court, a few four-to-four deadlocks did occur. In one case, a four-to-four split sustained a lower court ruling that allowed teachers' unions to collect service fees from nonmembers.[13]

McConnell's bet on delay paid off in November 2016 as Republican Donald Trump became president-elect. Shortly after his inauguration, Trump nominated Neil Gorsuch to the Court. Gorsuch, an appeals court judge, was a well-regarded staunch conservative. Senate Democrats sought to block the Gorsuch appointment through a filibuster. Although filibusters had been banned when considering lower court judges and executive branch personnel, such a step was still available to block Supreme Court nominations. Republicans promptly deployed the "nuclear option," described earlier in this text, and extended the filibuster ban to votes on Supreme Court nominees. In April, Gorsuch took his seat on the Court. Are appointments to the Supreme Court too politicized? We examine that question in this chapter's *Join the Debate* feature.

CRITICAL THINKING

▸ *In what kinds of cases does it matter whether the Supreme Court tilts liberal or conservative?*

 14–4 THE COURTS AS POLICYMAKERS

LO Explain how the federal courts make policy, and describe the role of ideology and judicial philosophies in judicial decision making.

In the United States, judges and justices play a major role in government. Unlike judges in some other countries, U.S. judges have the power to decide on the constitutionality of laws or actions undertaken by the other branches of government.

JOIN THE DEBATE

Are Supreme Court Confirmations Too Political?

The U.S. Constitution gives the president the power to nominate Supreme Court justices, who are then confirmed with the "Advice and Consent" of the Senate. How should the Senate carry out its duties? Should it limit itself to examining the qualifications of the nominee? For most of the twentieth century, the Senate did limit itself in this way. As recently as the 1990s, justices have been approved with only a handful of votes cast in opposition.

Alternatively, the Senate could approve only justices whose political opinions are likely to please the majority party. Today, a president from one party can assume that members of the Senate from the other party will vote against any nominee. In 2016, Republicans in the Senate refused even to hold hearings on President Obama's choice for the Supreme Court. They hoped that a Republican would win the 2016 elections and name a more conservative candidate. So, have we gone too far in politicizing the Court?

Politics is Too Important to Ignore

In 2016, millions of people who had grave reservations about Donald Trump still voted for him—because they believed he would appoint a conservative to the open seat on the Supreme Court. Trump did just that. These voters demonstrated the obvious: we cannot take politics out of Supreme Court nominations. Every year, the Court rules on cases that are fundamentally political. What should the rules be on abortion? Voting rights? Affirmative action?

There is no requirement in the Constitution that the Senate hold hearings on any presidential nomination. If elections are underway, it is only right to wait and let the people's choice for president name the new nominee. Democrats who objected to the delay in 2016 should have heeded the voice of one of their own. In 1992, an election year, Senator Joe Biden (later Obama's vice president) argued that Republican president George H.W. Bush should avoid naming a Supreme Court replacement. "Once the political season is underway, action on a Supreme Court nomination must be put off until after the election campaign is over."

Too Much Politics Threatens the Court

Others say that playing politics with nominations is not right. Supreme Court nominees deserve a fair hearing, even during an election year. It is true that political polarization has become intense. That does not mean that we need to make the problem worse by politicizing Court appointments. Despite appearances, in most cases it is possible to apply the law without partisanship.

Consider the 2012 ruling on the constitutionality of Obamacare. The Court stated that Congress could encourage people to buy health-care insurance by imposing a tax if they did not. Republicans condemned this ruling. The Court also found that Congress could not force states to expand Medicaid by threatening to take away all of their Medicaid funds. Democrats denounced this decision. Yet both opinions were fully in line with precedent. That is why liberal justices Stephen Breyer and Elena Kagan joined Chief Justice John Roberts in the Medicaid ruling. Despite intense pressure, the Court rose above politics. The Senate should encourage such behavior by approving qualified nominees, no matter which president nominates them.

Critical Analysis

If the Democrats were to retake the Senate in 2018, what do you think would happen if a Republican president tried to fill a Supreme Court vacancy?

Clearly, the function of the courts is to interpret and apply the law, not to make law—that is the function of the legislative branch of government. Yet judges can and do "make law." Indeed, they cannot avoid making law in some cases, because the law does not always provide clear answers to questions that come before the courts.

14–4a The Issue of Broad Language

The text of the U.S. Constitution is set forth in broad terms. When a court interprets a constitutional provision and applies that interpretation to a specific set of circumstances, the court is essentially "making the law"

In 2017, Neil Gorsuch was nominated to the Supreme Court by President Trump and confirmed by the Senate. *Why was his appointment controversial?*

communications technologies, including the Internet. Until legislative bodies enact laws governing these issues, it is up to the courts to fashion the law that will apply—and thus make policy.

14-4b The Power of Judicial Review

The U.S. Constitution divides government powers among the executive, legislative, and judicial branches. This division of powers is part of our system of checks and balances. Essentially, the founders gave each branch of government the constitutional authority to check the other two branches. The federal judiciary can exercise a check on the actions of either of the other branches through its power of **judicial review.**

on that issue. Examples of how the courts, and especially the United States Supreme Court, do this abound.

The Right to Privacy Consider privacy rights. Nothing in the Constitution or its amendments specifically states that we have a right to privacy. Yet the Supreme Court, through various decisions, has established such a right by deciding that it is implied by several constitutional amendments. The Court has also held that this right to privacy includes a number of specific rights, such as the right to have an abortion.

Vague Language and New Technologies Statutory provisions and other legal rules also tend to be expressed in general terms, and the courts must decide how those general provisions and rules apply to specific cases. The Americans with Disabilities Act of 1990 is an example. The act requires employers to reasonably accommodate the needs of employees with disabilities. But the act does not say exactly what employers must do to "reasonably accommodate" such persons. Thus, the courts must decide, on a case-by-case basis, what this phrase means.

Additionally, in some cases there is no relevant law or precedent to follow. In recent years, for example, courts have been struggling with new kinds of legal issues stemming from new

judicial review The power of the courts to decide on the constitutionality of legislative enactments and of actions taken by the executive branch.

Marbury v. Madison The Constitution does not actually mention judicial review. Rather, the Supreme Court claimed the power for itself in *Marbury v. Madison*.[14] In that case, which was decided by the Court in 1803, Chief Justice John Marshall held that a provision of a 1789 law affecting the Supreme Court's jurisdiction violated the Constitution and was thus void. Marshall declared, "It is emphatically the province and duty of the judicial department [the courts] to say what the law is. . . . If two laws conflict with each other, the courts must decide on the operation of each. . . . [I]f a law be in opposition to the constitution . . . the court must determine which of these conflicting rules governs the case. This is the very essence of judicial duty."

The Views of the Founders Most constitutional scholars believe that the framers intended that the federal courts should have the power of judicial review. In *Federalist Paper* No. 78, Alexander Hamilton clearly espoused the doctrine. Hamilton stressed the importance of the "complete independence" of federal judges and their special duty to "invalidate all acts contrary to the manifest tenor of the Constitution." Without judicial review by impartial courts, there would be nothing to ensure that the other branches of government stayed within constitutional limits when exercising their powers, and "all the reservations of particular rights or privileges would amount to nothing." Chief Justice Marshall shared Hamilton's views and adopted Hamilton's reasoning in *Marbury v. Madison.*

Justice Samuel Alito, Jr., and Justice Stephen Breyer. *How did the appointment of these two justices change the Court?*

of legislative acts unless those acts are clearly unconstitutional.

Political Ideology and Judicial Activism/ Restraint One of the Supreme Court's most activist eras occurred during the period from 1953 to 1969 under the leadership of Chief Justice Earl Warren. The Warren Court propelled the civil rights movement forward by holding, among other things, that laws permitting racial segregation violated the equal protection clause.

Because of the activism of the Warren Court, the term *judicial activism* has often been linked with liberalism. Neither judicial activism nor judicial restraint is necessarily linked to a particular political ideology, however. In fact, many observers claim that today's Supreme Court is often activist on behalf of a conservative agenda.

14-4c Judicial Activism versus Judicial Restraint

As already noted, making policy is not the primary function of the federal courts. Yet it is unavoidable that courts do, in fact, influence or even establish policy when they interpret and apply the law. Further, the power of judicial review gives the courts, and particularly the Supreme Court, an important policymaking tool. When the Supreme Court upholds or invalidates a state or federal statute, the consequences for the nation can be profound.

One issue that is often debated is how the federal courts should wield their policymaking power, particularly the power of judicial review. Often, this debate is couched in terms of judicial activism versus judicial restraint.

Activist versus Restraintist Justices The terms *judicial activism* and *judicial restraint* do not have precise meanings. Generally, however, an activist judge or justice believes that the courts should actively use their powers to check the legislative and executive branches to ensure that they do not exceed their authority. A restraintist judge or justice, in contrast, generally assumes that the courts should defer to the decisions of the legislative and executive branches. After all, members of Congress and the president are elected by the people, whereas federal court judges are not. In other words, the courts should not thwart the implementation

14-4d Ideology and the Courts

The policymaking role of the courts gives rise to an important question: To what extent do ideology and personal policy preferences affect judicial decision making? Numerous scholars have attempted to answer this question, especially as it applies to Supreme Court justices.

Few doubt that ideology affects judicial decision making, although, of course, other factors play a role as well. Certainly, there are numerous examples of ideology affecting Supreme Court decisions. As new justices replace old ones and new ideological alignments are formed, the Court's decisions are affected. The real question is whether personal preferences influence Supreme Court decisions to an *unacceptable* extent.

Keep in mind that judicial decision making, particularly at the Supreme Court level, can be very complex. When deciding cases, the Supreme Court often must consider any number of sources of law, including constitutions, statutes, and administrative agency regulations—as well as cases interpreting relevant portions of those sources. At times, the Court may also take demographic data, public opinion, foreign laws, and other factors into account. How much weight is given to each of these sources or factors will vary from justice to justice. After all, reasoning of any kind, including judicial reasoning, does not take place in a vacuum.

It is only natural that a justice's life experiences, personal biases, and intellectual abilities and predispositions will influence the reasoning process. Nevertheless, it is expected that when reviewing a case, a Supreme Court justice will not start out with a conclusion (such as "I don't like this particular law that Congress passed") and then look for legal sources to support that conclusion. Still, recent research suggests that justices sometimes behave in exactly this fashion. Consciously or unconsciously, they may begin with a conclusion and then engage in "motivated reasoning" to justify their beliefs.

14-4e Ideology and Today's Supreme Court

In contrast to the liberal Supreme Court under Earl Warren, today's Court has been generally conservative. The Court began its rightward shift after President Ronald Reagan (1981–1989) appointed conservative William Rehnquist as chief justice in 1986, and the Court moved further to the right as other conservative appointments to the bench were made by Reagan and George H. W. Bush (1989–1993).

The Roberts Court Many Supreme Court scholars believe that the appointments of John Roberts (as chief justice) and especially Samuel Alito (as associate justice) caused the Court to drift even further to the right. Certainly, the five conservative justices on the bench during the Roberts Court's first several terms voted together and cast the deciding votes in numerous cases. The remaining justices held liberal to moderate views and often formed an opposing bloc.

A notable change in the Court occurred when Alito replaced retiring justice Sandra Day O'Connor. O'Connor had often been the "swing" vote on the Court, sometimes voting with the liberal bloc and at other times siding with the conservatives.

On the Roberts Court, the swing voter is usually Justice Anthony Kennedy, who is generally more conservative in his views than O'Connor was. Although Justice Kennedy dislikes being described as a swing voter, he often decides the outcome of a case. From October 2010 through June 2016, Kennedy was in the majority in 84 percent of the cases decided by a narrow five-to-four vote. No other justice came close to this percentage.

President Obama's naming of Justices Elena Kagan and Sonia Sotomayor to the Court did not change its

Justice Ruth Bader Ginsburg. Earlier in her career, Ginsburg argued a series of key cases on women's rights. *How might such advocacy affect a justice's view of the issues before the Court?*

ideological balance. Both women joined the liberal bloc, but the men they replaced had been fairly liberal as well. Likewise, President Trump's appointment of Neil Gorsuch involved no long-term change in the Court's ideological balance, because Trump replaced one conservative justice—Scalia—with another. (The eight-person Court that served from February 2016 to April 2017 was somewhat more liberal, of course, because it was short one conservative justice.)

The Court's Conservatism In recent years, the nature of the Court's conservatism has come into sharper focus. It is a mistake to equate the ideology of the Court's majority with the conservatism, say, of the Republicans in Congress or with the ideology of the conservative movement. To be sure, there are members of the Court who are unmistakably *movement conservatives*—that is, members in good standing of the conservative movement. Justice Clarence Thomas is in this camp, and so was the late Justice Antonin Scalia. Yet Justice Kennedy and Chief Justice Roberts—and even Justice Alito—often "march to their own drummer."

Obamacare. A leading example was Chief Justice Roberts's 2015 ruling on Obamacare. In *King v. Burwell*, the question was how to interpret the text of the Affordable Care Act. The case focused on one clause in a long bill (the act is about the length of *Harry Potter and the Order of the Phoenix*). The clause referred to subsidies granted to low-income individuals who used state exchanges to buy health-care insurance. The federal exchange was not mentioned. Opponents of Obamacare argued that subsidies for the federal exchange were contrary to the plain text of the legislation. In a six-to-three majority opinion, Chief Justice Roberts found that it was clear from the language of the bill taken as a whole that Congress meant to grant federal exchange subsidies.[15] The ruling angered many conservatives.

Gay Rights. Another area in which Court conservatives have parted from the conservative movement is that of gay rights. Justice Kennedy, in particular, has favored gay rights ever since *Lawrence v. Texas*, a 2003 ruling that abolished laws against homosexual acts.[16] Kennedy joined with the Court's majority in that case, providing an important vote to decide the issue. Kennedy's vote was also decisive in later gay rights cases, such as *Obergefell v. Hodges*, the 2015 ruling that established a right to same-sex marriage in all fifty states.[17]

Toward a More Conservative Court? Progressives celebrated a number of victories in the Court's 2014–2015 term. The *Obergefell v. Hodges* same-sex marriage ruling was a major example of a liberal decision. Some Court watchers explained the liberal trend by noting that in 2014–2015, conservatives sponsored a large number of cases in an attempt to push the law to the right. Often, the Court resisted. In June 2015, however, the Court announced that it would take up several questions on which it had a conservative record.

The return to conservatism was clear in February 2016, when the Court, by a five-to-four vote, stayed (blocked) implementation of an EPA attempt to regulate carbon dioxide emissions from power plants.[18] Four days after this ruling, Justice Antonin Scalia died. The Court's conservative majority was now replaced by a four-to-four split. Conservatives regained their majority in April 2017, however, with the confirmation of Justice Neil Gorsuch. Furthermore, the distinct possibility existed that a Republican president would have the power to nominate new justices through 2020. Supreme Court justices are generally healthy and long-lived, but as of 2017, three of them were age 75 or more. These three were liberal justices Ruth Bader Ginsburg and Stephen Breyer, plus Anthony Kennedy. Given Kennedy's history as a swing voter, replacing him with a firm conservative would push the Court to the right. Replacing a liberal with a conservative would have an even more dramatic effect.

> "The Constitution itself should be our guide, not our own concept of what is fair, decent, and right."
>
> ~ HUGO L. BLACK
> ASSOCIATE JUSTICE OF THE
> UNITED STATES SUPREME COURT
> 1937–1971

Justice Anthony Kennedy tours the aircraft carrier USS John C. Stennis. Kennedy has typically held the "swing" vote on the closely divided Roberts Court. *On what kinds of cases has Kennedy broken with the conservative movement?*

Andre T. Richard/Mass Communication Specialist/U.S. Navy

14–4f Approaches to Legal Interpretation

It would be a mistake to look at the judicial philosophy of today's Supreme Court solely in terms of the political ideologies of liberalism and conservatism. In fact, some Supreme Court scholars have suggested that other factors are as important as, or more important than, the justices' political philosophies in determining why they decide as they do. These factors include the justices' attitudes toward legal interpretation and their perceptions of the Supreme Court's role in the federal judiciary. Two important judicial philosophies, both of which are often associated with conservative principles, are *strict construction* and *originalism*.

Strict Construction The term *strict construction* is widely used in the press and by politicians. Republican presidential candidates routinely promise to appoint justices who will interpret the Constitution strictly and not "legislate from the bench." The opposite of strict construction is *broad construction*. Advocates of strict construction often contend that the government should do nothing that is not specifically mentioned in the Constitution. In 1803, for example, some strict constructionists argued that the national government had no power to double the size of the country by purchasing the Louisiana Territory. Such radical strict constructionism had little support in 1803 and is accepted by few people today.

Despite the wide popularity of strict construction as a concept, members of the Supreme Court generally reject the description. The late Justice Scalia, for example, who is usually considered to have been one of the purest examples of a strict constructionist on the Court, preferred to call himself a *textualist* instead. Scalia wrote, "I am not a strict constructionist, and no one ought to be. . . . A text should not be construed strictly, and it should not be construed leniently; it should be construed reasonably, to contain all that it fairly means."[19]

What Scalia meant by textualism is that when determining the meaning of legislation, he refused to consider the legislative debates that took place when the measure was passed, the nature of the problem the legislation was meant to address, or anything other than the actual text of the law.

Original Intent A second conservative philosophy is called *originalism*. Justice Thomas is a well-known advocate of this approach. Originalists believe that to determine the meaning of a particular constitutional

Justice Clarence Thomas is widely seen as a conservative. *How might he approach the text of legislation?*

phrase, the Court should look to the intentions of the founders. What did the framers of the Constitution themselves intend when they included the phrase in the document? To discern the intent of the founders, justices might look to sources that shed light on the founders' views. These sources could include writings by the founders, newspaper articles from that period, the *Federalist Papers*, and notes taken during the Constitutional Convention.

Originalism, Textualism, and Modernism Such analysis of source materials is precisely what textualists wish to avoid when it comes to assessing modern day statutory law. Nevertheless, Justice Scalia considered himself an originalist as well as a textualist. In the 2014–2015 term, (his last) Scalia was in agreement with Justice Thomas more often than any other justice.

Originalism can be contrasted with what has been called *modernism*. Modernists seek to examine the Constitution in the context of today's society and to consider how modern life affects the words in the document. For an example of how originalism and modernism contrast, consider *Lawrence v Texas*, a case mentioned earlier.

Justice Kennedy's majority opinion in the case held that laws that criminalize same-sex intimate relations are unconstitutional under the Fourteenth Amendment. An originalist could object to this judgment because the legislators who adopted the amendment never considered that it might apply to gay men and lesbians. In fact, both Scalia and Thomas opposed the ruling on this basis. In contrast, modernists might argue that discrimination against gays and lesbians is exactly the type of evil that the amendment sought to prevent, even though such an application never occurred to those who wrote it.

CRITICAL THINKING

▶ *If, in the future, a more conservative Supreme Court were to rule that women have no constitutional right to an abortion, what do you think would happen?*

Chip Somodevilla/Getty Images News/Getty Images

Justice Elena Kagan. Along with five other justices, she attended Harvard Law School. The remaining three graduated from Yale Law School. *Is it a problem that the entire Supreme Court attended one of these two law schools? Why or why not?*

14–5 ASSESSING THE ROLE OF THE FEDERAL COURTS

LO Identify some of the criticisms of the federal courts and some of the checks on the power of the courts.

The federal courts have often come under attack, particularly in the last decade or so, for many reasons. This should come as no surprise in view of the policymaking power of the courts. After all, a Supreme Court decision can establish national policy on such issues as abortion, racial segregation, and gay rights. Critics, especially on the political right, frequently accuse the judiciary of "legislating from the bench." We discuss these criticisms in this chapter's *Perception vs. Reality* feature.

14–5a Criticisms of the Federal Courts

Certainly, policymaking by unelected judges and justices in the federal courts has serious implications in a democracy. Some Americans, including many conservatives, contend that making policy from the bench has upset the balance of powers envisioned by the framers of the Constitution. They cite Thomas Jefferson, who once said, "To consider the judges as the ultimate arbiters of all constitutional questions [is] a very dangerous doctrine indeed, and one which would place us under the despotism of an oligarchy."[20] This group believes that we should rein in the power of the federal courts and, particularly, judicial activism.

14–5b The Case for the Courts

On the other side of the debate over the courts are those who argue in favor of leaving the courts alone. Several federal court judges have sharply criticized congressional efforts to interfere with their authority. They claim that such efforts violate the Constitution's separation of powers. James M. Jeffords, a former independent senator from Vermont, likened the federal court system to a referee: "The first lesson we teach children when they enter competitive sports is to respect the referee, even if we think he [or she] might have made the wrong call. If our children can understand this, why can't our political leaders?"[21]

Others argue that there are already sufficient checks on the courts. We look at some of those next.

Judicial Traditions and Doctrines   One check on the courts is judicial restraint. Supreme Court justices

The Supreme Court Legislates from the Bench

Our Constitution gives legislative powers to the Congress exclusively. All executive powers are granted to the president. And all judicial powers are given to the judiciary. The United States Supreme Court is the final arbiter and interpreter of what is and is not constitutional. Because of its power of judicial review, it has the ability to "make law," or so it seems.

The Perception

Using the power of judicial review, the Supreme Court creates new laws. In 1954, the Court determined that racial segregation was illegal, a position that is universally accepted today but was hugely controversial back in the 1950s. The Court has also legalized same-sex marriage and, of course, abortion. These decisions, especially the legalization of abortion, remain very divisive today.

Such decisions have had a major impact on the nature of American society. Because citizens elect members of Congress and the president only—and not members of the Supreme Court—it is undemocratic to allow these nine justices to determine laws for our nation.

The Reality

The Supreme Court cannot actually write new laws. It can only eliminate old ones. When the Court threw out laws that criminalized adult sexual activity by gay men and lesbians, it was abolishing laws, not creating them. The Court does not have the power to legislate—to create new laws.

Consider what would happen if the Court decided that some basic level of health care is a constitutional right—a highly unlikely event. Could the Court establish mechanisms by which such a right could be enforced? It normally could not. It takes members of Congress months of hard work to craft bills that affect our health-care system. Such legislation fills thousands of pages and can be developed only with the assistance of large numbers of experts and lobbyists. The federal courts could not undertake such projects even if they wanted to.

The courts must decide how they will handle the cases that are brought before them. To do so establishes judicial policy. It does not constitute lawmaking. In any event, we have no alternative to judicial review when it comes to determining what is or is not constitutional. Without the Supreme Court, Congress and the president could make all sorts of laws that violate our Constitution and infringe on our rights, and there would be nothing to stop them. As Chief Justice John Roberts said during his confirmation hearings, "Judges are like umpires. Umpires don't make the rules; they apply them."

Blog On

Plenty of bloggers follow the activities of the Supreme Court. One of the best is SCOTUSblog, at www.scotusblog.com.

---

traditionally have exercised a great deal of self-restraint. Justices sometimes admit to making decisions that fly in the face of their personal values and policy preferences, simply because they feel obligated to do so in view of existing law.

Self-restraint is also mandated by various established judicial traditions and doctrines, including the doctrine of *stare decisis*, which theoretically obligates the Supreme Court to follow its own precedents. Furthermore, the Supreme Court will not hear a meritless appeal just so it can rule on the issue.

Finally, the justices often narrow their rulings to focus on just one aspect of an issue, even though there may be nothing to stop them from broadening their focus and thus widening the impact of their decisions.

Other Checks   The judiciary is subject to other checks as well. Courts may make rulings, but they cannot force federal and state legislatures to appropriate the funds necessary to carry out those rulings. For example, if a state supreme court decides that prison conditions must be improved, the state legislature has to find the funds to carry out the ruling or the improvements will not take place.

Additionally, legislatures can revise old laws or pass new ones in an attempt to negate a court's ruling. This may happen when a court interprets a statute in a way that Congress did not intend. Congress may also propose amendments to the Constitution to reverse Supreme Court rulings, and Congress has the authority to limit or otherwise alter the jurisdiction of the lower federal courts. Finally, although it is most unlikely, Congress could even change the number of justices on the Supreme Court, in an attempt to change the ideological balance on the Court. (President Franklin D. Roosevelt proposed such a plan in 1937—without success.)

The Public's Regard for the Supreme Court

Some have proposed that Congress, not the Supreme Court, be the final arbiter of the Constitution. In debates on this topic, one factor is often overlooked: the American public's high regard for the Supreme Court and the federal courts generally. The Court continues to be respected as a fair arbiter of conflicting interests and the protector of constitutional rights and liberties.

Even when the Court issued its decision to halt the manual recount of votes in Florida following the 2000 elections, which effectively handed the presidency to George W. Bush, Americans respected the Court's decision-making authority—although many disagreed with the Court's decision. Polls continue to show that Americans have much more trust and confidence in the Supreme Court than they do in Congress.

CRITICAL THINKING

▶ *Why do you think that Americans trust the Supreme Court much more than they do Congress?*

AMERICA AT ODDS | The Judiciary

A Supreme Court decision can affect the lives of millions of Americans. For example, in 1973 the Supreme Court, in *Roe v. Wade*, held that the constitutional right to privacy included the right to have an abortion. The influence wielded by the Court today is a far cry from the Court's relative obscurity at the founding of this nation. Initially, the Supreme Court was not even included in the plans for government buildings in the national capital. It did not have its own building until 1935. Over time, however, the Court has established a reputation with the public for dispensing justice in a fair and reasonable manner. Still, Americans are at odds over a number of judicial issues:

- *Should state judges be elected—or does selection by appointment lead to a better court system?*

- *Should the United States Supreme Court accept more cases to provide a greater number of definitive rulings—or should it take on relatively few cases so that it can treat each one thoroughly?*

- *Should senators accept a Supreme Court nomination by a president of the opposing party whenever the nominee appears to have sound judicial temperament—or should senators vote only for those nominees who share their political philosophies?*

- *Should judges defer to the decisions of legislatures and administrative agencies whenever possible—or should they strictly police the constitutionality of legislative and executive decisions?*

- *Is it crucial that the Constitution be interpreted in terms of the beliefs of the founders—or should justices take account of modern circumstances that the founders could not have envisioned?*

STUDY TOOLS 14

READY TO STUDY? IN THE BOOK, YOU CAN:

☐ Review what you've read with the following chapter quiz.

☐ Check your answers in Appendix D at the back of the book.

☐ Rip out the Chapter Review Card, which includes key terms and chapter summaries.

ONLINE AT WWW.CENGAGEBRAIN.COM, YOU CAN:

☐ Watch videos to get a quick overview.

☐ Expedite your studying with Major Player readings and Focus Activities.

☐ Check your understanding with Chapter Quizzes.

FILL-IN

Learning Outcome 14–1

1. Primary sources of American law include _____.

2. In the context of the courts, *jurisdiction* means

   _____.

Learning Outcome 14–2

3. To bring a case before the Supreme Court, a party may request a _____, which is an order the Court issues to a lower court asking that court to send it the record of the case in question.

4. The attorneys involved with a case will present _____, to the Supreme Court, after which the justices discuss the case in conference.

5. A/An _____ opinion is a statement written by a justice who agrees with the Court's decision, but for reasons different from those outlined by the majority.

Learning Outcome 14–3

6. Because of a practice known as _____, home-state senators of the president's political party may be able to influence the choice of a nominee for the U.S. district court in that state.

Learning Outcome 14–4

7. Two important judicial philosophies that describe justices' attitudes toward legal interpretation, both of which are often associated with conservative principles, are

   _____.

8. In recent years, the "swing vote" on the Supreme Court has been Justice _____.

Learning Outcome 14–5

9. Congress can check the power of the courts in several ways, including _____.

MULTIPLE CHOICE

Learning Outcome 14–1

10. A precedent is best defined as a
    a. controversy that is real and substantial.
    b. court decision that furnishes an example or authority for deciding subsequent cases.
    c. ruling that a person has disobeyed a court order.

Learning Outcome 14–2

11. The U.S. courts of appeals
    a. are the courts in which cases involving federal law begin.
    b. hear appeals from the U.S. district courts located within their respective judicial circuits.
    c. hear testimony and evidence before they make decisions in cases.

Learning Outcome 14–3

12. A nominee for the Supreme Court must be confirmed by a
    a. majority vote in the Senate.
    b. two-thirds vote in the Senate.
    c. majority vote in the House Judiciary Committee.

Learning Outcome 14–4

13. The power of the courts to decide on the constitutionality of legislative enactments and of actions taken by the executive branch is called
    a. judicial review.
    b. *stare decisis.*
    c. jurisdiction.

Learning Outcome 14–5

14. Judicial self-restraint is mandated by various judicial traditions and doctrines, such as _____, which theoretically obligates the Supreme Court to follow its own precedents.
    a. *curiae regis*
    b. *stare decisis*
    c. justiciable controversy

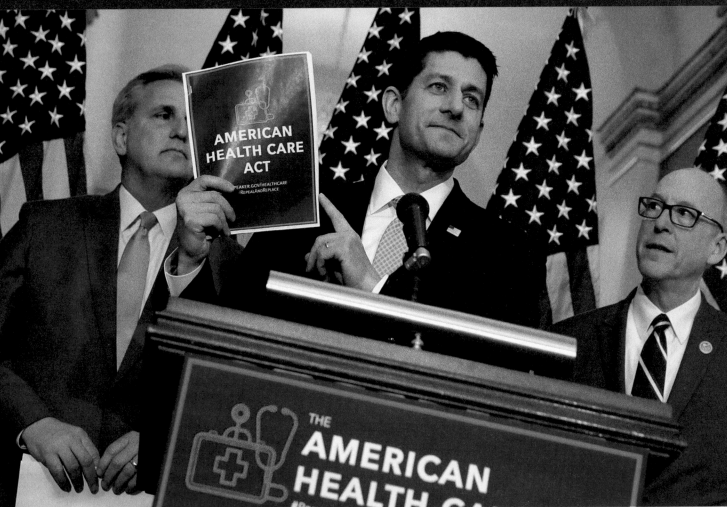

Chip Somodevilla/Getty Images News/Getty Images

LEARNING OUTCOMES

After reading this chapter, you should be able to:

15-1 Define domestic policy, and summarize the steps in the policymaking process.

15-2 Discuss the issue of health-care funding and recent legislation on universal health insurance.

15-3 Summarize the issues of energy independence, climate change, and alternative energy sources.

15-4 Describe the two major areas of economic policymaking, and discuss the issue of the public debt.

After finishing this chapter, go to **PAGE 353** for **STUDY TOOLS**

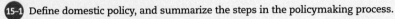

Currently, there are about 2.3 million people in U.S. prisons and jails. That's roughly one in every one hundred adults. We are setting records—the share of our population in prison is thirteen times more than in Japan, nine times more than in Germany, and five times more than in Britain.

In 1970, the proportion of Americans behind bars—the *incarceration rate*—was only one-fourth of what it is today. Not surprisingly, the number of drug offenders in prison is responsible for much of this increase. Such lockups have multiplied thirteenfold since 1980.

Defense attorney Jim Felman of Tampa, Florida, said that America is conducting "an experiment in imprisoning first-time nonviolent offenders for periods of time previously reserved only for those who had killed someone." Holding that many prisoners is not cheap. It costs between $20,000 and $60,000 a year to house a convicted criminal in a state prison, depending on the state. Because of these costs, a number of conservative governors have begun to rethink their commitment to high rates of incarceration. Indeed, the massive growth in prison populations that marked the last few decades appears to have come to an end, and the incarceration rate is no longer growing. Given all this, do we still send too many Americans to prison?

Keep Criminals behind Bars—It Works

Supporters of aggressive incarceration policies argue that still more criminals should be behind bars. Putting more people in prison reduces crime rates. After all, incentives matter. If potential criminals know that they will be thrown in jail more readily and stay there longer, they will have less incentive to engage in illegal activities.

Also, the crime rate is strongly determined by the number of criminals at large. When we remove a criminal from the streets and put that person in prison, the prisoner can no longer commit crimes that harm the public. This effect of removal from society is called *incapacitation*. Evidence shows that during the 1960s, when incarceration rates fell, the crime rate more than doubled. As incarceration rates rose sharply in the 1990s, the crime rate went steadily down. As a comparison, the risk of criminal punishment in England has been falling. In consequence, crime rates have risen in England, while they have fallen in the United States.

Tough sentencing is effective. We should not turn career criminals loose on the streets.

Too Many Laws and Too Many Prisoners

Those who argue against our high rates of incarceration point out that many individuals are convicted of nonviolent crimes. The government should not be spending tens of thousands of dollars to keep such people in prison. In fact, among those in jail, 63 percent have not been convicted of the crime for which they are held. Since 2000, almost all of the growth in the jail population has consisted of unconvicted persons.

Too many acts have been criminalized, particularly at the federal level. Many crimes are so vaguely defined that most Americans would not know if they were breaking the law. Granted, hard-core criminals should be behind bars. But what about the casual pot smoker? Lying to a federal official is a felony. Who can say how many people might be imprisoned based on such an act?

In California, until recently, about 7,600 persons were serving life sentences because they were convicted of a third offense—and in almost half of these cases, the third crime was nonserious or nonviolent. In 2012, voters changed the law to allow the release of nonviolent offenders. California voters recognized the truth: the cost to society of putting drug users and other minor offenders behind bars is much greater than the benefits.

Where do you stand?

1. Could factors other than high incarceration rates be causing our current low crime rates? What might those factors be?

2. Why do you think federal, state, and local governments arrest so many drug-law violators?

Explore this issue online:

- You can find several articles in *The Economist*, a British magazine, arguing that the United States imprisons too many people. Search on "economist us incarceration."

- The Criminal Justice Legal Foundation is among the few groups that advocate increased rates of incarceration. See its arguments at www.cjlf.org.

INTRODUCTION

Whether we send too many people to prison is just one of the issues that confront our nation's policymakers today. How are questions of national importance, such as this one, decided? Who are the major participants in the decision-making process?

To learn the answers to these questions, we need to delve into the politics of policymaking. *Policy*, or *public policy*, can be defined as a plan or course of action taken by the government to respond to a political issue or to enhance the social or political well-being of society. Public policy is the end result of the policymaking process, which will be described shortly.

In this chapter, after discussing how policy is made, we look at several aspects of **domestic policy**, which consists of public policy concerning issues *within* a national unit. Specifically, we examine health-care policy, energy policy, and economic policy. We focus on these policy areas because they have been among the federal government's top priorities. Another major

domestic policy Public policy concerning issues within a national unit, such as national policy on health care or the economy.

issue has been unauthorized immigration. We examine that problem in this chapter's *Join the Debate* feature.

Bear in mind that although the focus here is on policy and policymaking at the national level, state and local governments also engage in policymaking. These governments establish policies to achieve goals relating to activities within their boundaries. This process is evident in the criminal justice issues discussed in this chapter's opening *America at Odds* feature.

15–1 THE POLICYMAKING PROCESS

LO Define domestic policy, and summarize the steps in the policymaking process.

A new law does not appear out of the blue. First, the problem addressed by the new law has to become part of the political agenda—that is, the problem must be defined as a political issue to be resolved by government action. Furthermore, once the issue gets on the political agenda, proposed solutions to the problem have to be formulated and then adopted. Issue identification and agenda setting, policy formulation, and policy adoption are all parts of how policy is made, illustrated in Figure 15–1.

FIGURE 15–1 THE POLICYMAKING PROCESS

Why would the policymaking process be so complicated?

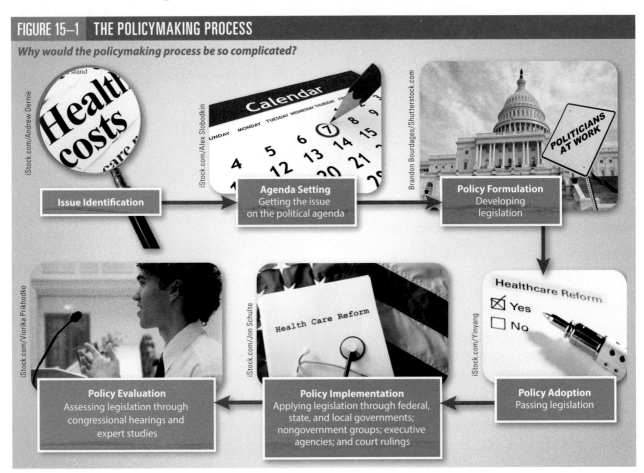

Issue Identification

Agenda Setting
Getting the issue on the political agenda

Policy Formulation
Developing legislation

Policy Adoption
Passing legislation

Policy Implementation
Applying legislation through federal, state, and local governments; nongovernment groups; executive agencies; and court rulings

Policy Evaluation
Assessing legislation through congressional hearings and expert studies

JOIN THE DEBATE

What Should We Do about Unauthorized Immigrants?

Illegal immigration is a major issue in part because of the dramatic statements made by Donald Trump when he was the Republican presidential candidate. During the 2016 campaign, candidate Trump favored total deportation of all illegal immigrants (known as *unauthorized immigrants* by the Department of Homeland Security). In contrast, Democrat Hillary Clinton favored a path to citizenship.

Currently, about 11 million unauthorized immigrants live in the United States. Some crossed the border illegally, and others arrived legally but overstayed their visas. A majority of these persons are from Latin America, particularly Mexico. Because Congress has failed to reform our immigration laws, little has been done about this problem for years. So the debate continues. Should we deport them, or should we offer them a path to citizenship or at least legal status?

Ship Them Home

The greatest applause line in any of Trump's campaign speeches represented one extreme position: deport them all, build a "great wall" on the southern border, and make Mexico pay for it. There's a reason these people are called *illegal*—they are breaking the law. Lawbreakers should not stay. After we deport them, then they

can apply legally to become U.S. residents.

Illegal immigrants are mainly low-skilled, low-wage workers. They compete against our poorest citizens and drive down their wages. They cause overcrowding in schools and hospital emergency rooms. If we do not actually deport them all, we must at least prevent those who stay from becoming U.S. citizens. Democrats would like them to become citizens, of course. That would amount to a scheme to add 11 million new Democratic voters. Such a result is not fair to our existing citizens, who were never asked whether they wanted this influx. How would the liberal citizens of Berkeley, California, react to a plan to import thousands of new right-wing voters into town, with the result that the City Council flips from Democrat to Republican?

Do What Is Right— Give Them a Path to Citizenship

Others point out that the costs of total deportation would be staggering. We would need hundreds of thousands of new federal enforcement officers. Such a project would turn us into a police state. What would it be like to be a U.S. citizen of Mexican ancestry living in the middle of such an operation? Your civil rights would fly out

the window. Already, under President Trump, millions of immigrants are living in fear.

In fact, deporting unauthorized immigrants would not improve the wages or job prospects of lower-income citizens. Immigrants not only work, but they consume. This additional spending leads to more employment, not less. A UCLA study predicted that mass deportation would reduce California's tax revenues by 8.5 percent and would shrink the state economy by tens of billions of dollars.

We have unauthorized immigrants because it is almost impossible for a low-skilled person to legally enter the United States. Now that they are here, we cannot allow them to remain as second-class residents. America tried that with African Americans, and it was a disaster. A path to citizenship is the only solution.

Critical Analysis

If immigrants who become citizens vote overwhelmingly for Democrats, is that the fault of the Democrats—or the Republicans? In either case, why?

The **policymaking process** does not end there, however. Once the law is passed, it has to be implemented and then evaluated.

Each phase of the policymaking process involves interactions among various individuals and groups. The president and members of Congress are obviously important participants in the process. Interest groups also play a key role. Groups that may be affected adversely by a new

policy will try to convince Congress not to adopt the policy. Groups that will benefit from the policy will exert whatever influence they can on Congress to do the opposite. Congressional committees and subcommittees

policymaking process
The procedures involved in identifying an issue and then getting it on the political agenda; formulating, adopting, and implementing a policy with regard to the issue; and then evaluating the results of the policy.

may investigate the problem to be addressed by the policy and, in so doing, solicit input from members of various groups or industries.

The participants in policymaking and the nature of the debates involved depend on the particular policy being proposed, formed, or implemented. Whatever the policy, however, debate over its pros and cons occurs during each stage of the policymaking process. Additionally, making policy decisions typically involves *trade-offs*, in which policymakers must sacrifice one goal to achieve another because of budget constraints and other factors.

15–1a Issue Identification and Agenda Setting

If no one recognizes a problem, then no matter how important the problem may be, politically it does not yet really exist. Thus, *issue identification* is part of the first stage of the policymaking process. Some group—whether it be the media, the public, politicians, or even foreign commentators—must identify a problem that can be solved politically. The second part of this stage of the policymaking process involves getting the issue on the political agenda to be addressed by Congress. This is called agenda setting, or *agenda building*.

A problem in society may be identified as an issue and included on the political agenda when an event or series of events leads to a call for action. For example, the failure of a major bank may lead to the conclusion that the financial industry is in trouble and that the government should take action to rectify the problem. More recently, dramatic increases in opioid abuse have caused the media and other groups to consider the opioid epidemic a priority that should be on the national political agenda. Sometimes, the social or economic effects of a national calamity, such as the Great Depression of the 1930s or the terrorist attacks of September 11, 2001, create a pressing need for government action.

15–1b Policy Formulation and Adoption

The second stage in the policymaking process involves the formulation and adoption of specific plans for achieving a particular goal. The president, members of Congress, administrative agencies, and interest group leaders typically are the key participants in developing proposed legislation. Iron triangles and issue networks try to develop mutually beneficial policies.

agenda setting In policymaking, getting an issue on the political agenda to be addressed by Congress. Part of the first stage of the policymaking process.

To a certain extent, the courts also establish policies when they interpret statutes passed by legislative bodies or make decisions concerning disputes not yet addressed by any law, such as disputes involving new technology.

Note that some issues may become a part of the political agenda but never proceed beyond that stage of the policymaking process. Usually, this happens when it is impossible to achieve a consensus on what policy should be adopted.

15–1c Policy Implementation

Because of our federal system, the implementation of national policies works most smoothly when there is cooperation among the federal government and the state and local governments. For example, the Affordable Care Act, nicknamed Obamacare, assumed that the states would set up marketplaces where individuals could buy health-care insurance. This example also shows that the federal government can act without the states if it must—in thirty-six states, the federal government set up a marketplace because the state government refused to participate.

Successful implementation usually requires the support of groups outside the government. For example, the state health-care insurance marketplaces established under Obamacare were effective only because of the participation of commercial insurance companies.

Policy implementation also involves agencies in the executive branch. Once Congress establishes a policy by enacting legislation, the executive branch, through its agencies, enforces the new policy. Furthermore, the courts are involved in policy implementation, because the legislation and administrative regulations enunciating the new policy must be interpreted and applied to specific situations by the courts.

15–1d Policy Evaluation

The final stage of policymaking involves evaluating the success of a policy during and following its implementation. Groups both inside and outside the government participate in the evaluation process.

Congress may hold hearings to obtain feedback from different groups on how a statute or regulation has affected them. Scholars and scientists may conduct studies to determine whether a particular law, such as an environmental law designed to reduce air pollution, has achieved the desired result—less air pollution. Sometimes, feedback obtained in these or other ways indicates that a policy has failed in whole or in part, and a new policymaking process may be undertaken to modify the policy or create a more effective one.

15-1e Policymaking and Special Interests

The policymaking steps just discussed may seem straightforward, but they are not. Every bill that passes through Congress is a compromise. Every bill that passes through Congress is also an opportunity for individual members of Congress to help constituents, particularly those who were kind enough to contribute financially to the members' reelection campaigns.

The Farm Bill Consider the Agricultural Act of 2014, commonly known as the 2014 farm bill. The act authorizes about $95 billion per year over the next decade. About $75 billion is actually for the Special Nutrition Assistance Program (SNAP), or food stamps. Combining food stamp authorization with agricultural subsidies has been a way to get urban liberals to vote for the legislation.

The centerpiece of the farm bill was the abolition of *direct payments* for certain crops—payments made regardless of whether the recipient actually planted the crops in question. Most of the funds saved were transferred to a much-enlarged crop insurance program. Supporters claimed that the new bill would reduce federal expenditures. Critics, pointing to falling prices for corn, soybeans, and wheat, argued that it would in fact be more expensive.

Special Provisions to Help the Bill Along
A polarized Congress meant that the bill would be hard to pass—indeed, it was two years late. Special provisions, not requested by the Department of Agriculture, helped the bill along. A pilot program for industrial hemp production helped secure the support of members from Kentucky. Profit-margin insurance for catfish farmers helped sew up the Mississippi delegation. Newly insured products include biofuels, lamb, peanuts, poultry, sesame, sushi rice, and swine. Various GMO (genetically modified organism) crops now receive special insurance treatment. The bill included livestock disaster relief and funds to combat a disease called citrus greening in Florida.

Some provisions had little to do with agriculture or nutrition. The EPA was prohibited from proceeding with a program against overfishing. Central State University in Ohio, a historically black college, received additional federal aid. Clearly, policymaking is a complicated process.

CRITICAL THINKING

▶ *What role do the media have in the agenda-setting process?*

15-2 HEALTH-CARE POLICY

LO Discuss the issue of health-care funding and recent legislation on universal health insurance.

In March 2010, Congress passed the Patient Protection and Affordable Care Act (the ACA) and a companion bill. The two bills, which President Barack Obama immediately signed, contained health-care reforms that were among the most consequential government initiatives in many years.

Even before the new legislation was adopted, the federal government was paying the health-care costs of more than 100 million Americans. When President Obama took office, the government was picking up the tab for about 50 percent of the nation's health-care costs. Private insurance was responsible for about a third of all health-care payments, and the rest was met either by patients themselves or by charity. Paying for health-care expenses, in other words, was already a major federal responsibility, and questions about how the government should carry out that function in the future were unavoidable.

15-2a Two Problems with U.S. Health Care

Critics of our system for funding health care have identified two major problems. One is that health care is expensive. As of 2017, almost 18 percent of national spending in the United States went to health care, compared with 11 percent in France, 10 percent in Canada, and 8.5 percent in Britain. U.S. health-care costs have been rising for years, as you can see in Figure 15–2.

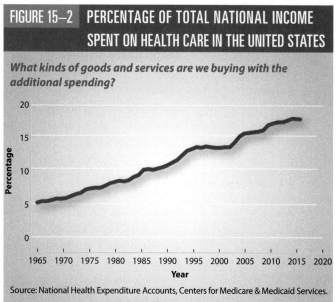

FIGURE 15–2 PERCENTAGE OF TOTAL NATIONAL INCOME SPENT ON HEALTH CARE IN THE UNITED STATES

What kinds of goods and services are we buying with the additional spending?

Source: National Health Expenditure Accounts, Centers for Medicare & Medicaid Services.

A second problem has been lack of health-care insurance. About 18 percent of the population had no health-care insurance as of 2013, before the ACA was fully implemented. Lack of coverage means that people may put off seeing a physician until it is too late for effective treatment or may be forced into bankruptcy due to large medical bills. One study has estimated that before 2013, twenty thousand people per year died prematurely because they lacked health insurance.[1] (Others dispute these findings.) Still, a substantial body of conservatives believed then and now that the government has no business providing health-care insurance, even if the result is that some people go without coverage.

Before discussing the ACA, let's first look at the programs that were in place before it was passed. The most important of these are Medicare, which provides health-care insurance to Americans aged sixty-five and over, and Medicaid, which funds health-care coverage for low-income persons.

15–2b Medicaid and Medicare

Like many major employers, the federal government buys health-care insurance for its employees. Members of the armed forces, veterans, and Native Americans receive medical services provided directly by the government. Most federal spending on health care, however, is accounted for by Medicare and Medicaid.

Medicaid A joint federal–state program, Medicaid provides health-care subsidies to low-income persons. The federal government provides more than 80 percent of the Medicaid budget, and the states provide the rest. About 70 million people are in the program. Many Medicaid recipients are elderly residents of nursing homes—the Medicare program does not pay for nursing home expenses.

> "It helps to think of the government as *an insurance company with an army*."
>
> ~ MIKE HOLLAND
> OFFICE OF SCIENCE
> AND TECHNOLOGY POLICY
> UNDER PRESIDENT GEORGE W. BUSH

Although recent cost-containment measures have slowed the growth of Medicaid spending, the cost of Medicaid has doubled in the last decade. Fortunately for state budgets, the ACA has increased the share of Medicaid spending assumed by the federal government. It now amounts to 6.5 percent of state budgets, down from about 17 percent. Another program, the Children's Health Insurance Program (CHIP), covers children in families with incomes that are modest but too high to qualify for Medicaid. By fiscal year 2018, the total cost of Medicaid and CHIP for all levels of government was $646 billion.

Medicare Medicare is the federal government's health-care program for persons sixty-five years of age and older. Medicare is now the government's second-largest domestic spending program, after Social Security. Medicare currently accounts for more than 3 percent of GDP, and costs are expected to rise as millions of "baby boomers" retire over the next two decades.

By 2030, the sixty-five-and-older population is expected to double. Further, advancements in medical science are driving medical costs up every year. There are simply more actions that medical science can take to keep people alive—and Americans naturally want to take advantage of these services.

Entitlement Programs Medicare and Medicaid are examples of government entitlement programs. Social Security and unemployment compensation are two other examples. Entitlement programs pay out benefits to persons who meet specified requirements. In the case of Social Security, for example, the government issues payments based on a recipient's age at retirement and past wage or salary income.

A special characteristic of entitlement programs is that they continue from year to year, regardless of whether Congress passes an annual funding measure. An entitlement continues until the government explicitly adopts a new law to change the benefits or otherwise alter the program. Further, Congress has no direct control over how much an entitlement program will cost in any particular year. It is usually possible to estimate the costs, but the actual amount of spending depends on how many eligible persons sign up for the benefits. In understanding the Affordable Care Act, it

---

Medicare A federal government program that pays for health-care insurance for Americans aged sixty-five years and over.

Medicaid A joint federal–state program that pays for health-care services for low-income persons.

Children's Health Insurance Program (CHIP) A joint federal–state program that provides health-care insurance for low-income children.

entitlement program A government program that provides benefits to all persons who meet specified requirements.

is important to realize that the program was primarily designed as an entitlement.

Because entitlements do not need to be explicitly renewed, they are different from *discretionary spending*. In a discretionary program, Congress establishes a binding annual budget for a government agency that the agency cannot exceed. Note that "discretionary" does not mean "unimportant." As an example, the nation's armed forces are funded through discretionary spending.

15-2c The Democrats Propose Universal Coverage

For a long time, the United States was the only economically advanced nation that did not provide universal health-insurance coverage to its citizens. Democratic president Bill Clinton (1993–2001) and first lady Hillary Clinton made a serious push for a universal plan during President Clinton's first term, but the project failed to pass Congress.

Congress Addresses the Issue The program developed by Congress in 2009 assumed that employer-provided health insurance would continue to be a major part of the system. Medicaid would be available to individuals with incomes up to about 1.5 times the federal poverty level. (In 2017, the poverty level for a family of four was $24,600.) A new health-insurance marketplace, the Health Insurance Exchange, would allow individuals and small employers to shop for plans. Insurance companies would not be allowed to deny anyone coverage.

Most individuals would be required to obtain coverage or pay an income tax penalty. This requirement is known as the **individual mandate.** Those with low-to-middle incomes would receive help in paying their premiums. Subsidies would be phased out for those earning more than four times the federal poverty level.

To fund the program, Congress adopted various new taxes and fees, such as a new tax on investments for high-income persons and an increased Medicare tax rate.

Expected Results The ACA was to become effective over a period of several years. One immediate change was that young people could remain covered by their parents' insurance until they turned twenty-six. Another immediate result was subsidies to small employers that obtained insurance plans for their employees. The most

> *"Nature provides a free lunch, but only if we control our appetites."*
> ~ WILLIAM DOYLE RUCKELSHAUS
> FIRST HEAD OF THE ENVIRONMENTAL PROTECTION AGENCY
> 1970–1973

important provisions, however, did not take effect until January 1, 2014. From that day on, subsidies were available to help citizens purchase health-care insurance if they were not covered by Medicare, Medicaid, or an employer's plan.

The Conservative Reaction In 2009, the Democrats were able to win the support—or at least the acquiescence—of groups that had opposed universal health-care plans in the past. That included the American Medical Association, hospitals, insurance companies, and pharmaceutical firms. Nevertheless, opposition to the reforms was widespread and strong. Conservatives saw the Affordable Care Act as a "big government takeover" of health care and a threat to popular freedoms. The individual mandate was at the heart of much of the opposition. After all, it was a way of pressuring people to do something that they might not otherwise do. Supporters of reform could point out that the system would face financial collapse unless everyone, healthy or unhealthy, bought insurance. This fact did nothing to make the reforms more palatable.

Attempts to challenge the constitutionality of the reforms failed, although the Supreme Court did allow state governments to opt out of expanding the Medicaid program.[2] Repeated attempts by Republicans in the House to repeal or delay Obamacare were ineffectual. The Republicans would need control of both chambers of Congress and the presidency to abolish it. In 2012, however, Obama was reelected and the Democrats retained control of the Senate. In 2015, the Supreme Court rejected a claim that major parts of the Affordable Care Act should be thrown out due to poorly worded language.[3]

Implementation On October 1, 2013, Americans who were eligible to buy health-care insurance through a state or federal exchange had their first chance to do so. It was expected, though not required, that most of the signups would take place online. Many of the state online exchanges functioned effectively. A few never worked properly, forcing signups to take place offline. The federal site turned out to be almost completely nonfunctional. The site was not fully operational until the end of the

> **individual mandate**
> In the context of health-care reform, a requirement that all persons obtain health-care insurance from one source or another. Those failing to do so must pay a penalty.

This patient is being discharged from a hospital. Under federal law, emergency rooms cannot turn away patients who cannot pay. *How might this affect the positions that hospitals take on health insurance legislation?*

year. Obamacare's troubled rollout was a political blow to the Democrats.

By the end of the signup period in April 2014, however, 8 million Americans had obtained insurance policies through the state and federal exchanges. This was 2 million more than predicted by the Congressional Budget Office. By 2017, the number enrolled was more than 11 million.

Evaluation and Potential Replacements

The ACA sought to restructure one of the nation's largest industries—medical care. It was an enormous piece of legislation, with many moving parts. Inevitably, some did not work as well as intended. Normally, Congress would revisit such a program and make various fixes to it. That proved impossible with the ACA, because Republicans in Congress were interested only in repealing the legislation. By 2017, when President Trump took office at the head of a unified Republican government, a widespread consensus had emerged about the key problems with Obamacare.

Criticisms of the ACA. Other than the individual mandate—always unpopular—the main criticism was that policies bought through the exchanges did not cover enough of the costs incurred by those who needed health care. *Co-pays*, the consumer's share of the cost of an office visit or medication, were too great. *Deductibles*, the sums a consumer would have to pay before insurance kicked in, were too high. Also, while subsidies kept the cost of policies reasonable for low-income persons, those

with an income just high enough to receive no subsidies found their premiums to be uncomfortably large. These criticisms were leveled not just by Democrats, but by Republicans, including Senate majority leader Mitch McConnell and President Trump.

The Republicans Propose Replacements. If the problem with Obamacare was that it was insufficiently generous, however, repealing it altogether posed a problem for Republicans. "Repeal and replace" became the Republican slogan. In 2017, the party advanced several successive replacement programs. No attempt was made to win Democratic support for any of them. Both chambers bypassed the normal committee process—bills were drafted in private by Republican leaders.

The House was the first to report a bill. This legislation was substantially less generous than the ACA. True, some younger persons would see their premiums drop. Low-income persons, however, especially older ones, might see premiums that exceeded half of their total income. Effectively, they would be uninsurable. The bill would also phase out the expansion of Medicaid in those states that had adopted it and, in time, cut Medicaid benefits below what they were before Obamacare was even adopted. According to the Congressional Budget Office (CBO), 24 million people would eventually lose their insurance. The program would also cut taxes for upper-income persons by almost $90 billion per year.

The initial version of the legislation was opposed both by the Freedom Caucus (which thought it too expensive) and by Republican moderates (who saw it as too stingy). A second version was even less generous—enough so to earn Freedom Caucus support. The bill passed the House by a single vote. On receiving this bill, Senate Republicans resolved to start over. Republicans in the Senate ran into some of the same political problems as in the House, however, and they could afford to lose fewer votes. In the end, the legislation failed to pass the Senate.

Can Obamacare Survive? In short, Republicans found Obamacare remarkably hard to kill. From the beginning, Democrats had hoped that once it was actually in effect, the ACA would become popular. For years, that did not happen. By 2017, however, for the first time ever, polls showed majority support for the ACA. In contrast, only 17 percent of the public supported the initial House bill. Even if Obamacare survived, however, it faced a problem—the personnel that Trump appointed to administer the program were opposed to its very existence. Faced with uncertainty, several insurance companies withdrew from the exchanges.

CRITICAL THINKING

▸ *Is it reasonable for health care to continue to absorb increasingly larger shares of the nation's budget—or will that interfere too much with our country's ability to purchase other goods and services? Explain your reasoning.*

15-3 ENERGY AND THE ENVIRONMENT

LO Summarize the issues of energy independence, climate change, and alternative energy sources.

Energy policy has also been a major issue at the national level. Energy policy is important because of two problems: (1) our reliance on imported oil, and (2) the possibility of global climate change.

15-3a The Problem of Imported Oil

It is estimated that in 2017, our nation's net imports of petroleum amounted to about one-quarter of our total consumption. This figure has fallen substantially in recent years. In 2005, imports were more than 60 percent of consumption. Still, oil imports are a potential

A technician installs solar panels on a roof. *How might traditional electric utility companies react to the growing use of solar power?*

problem largely because many of the nations that export oil are not particularly friendly to the United States. Some, such as Iran, are outright adversaries. Other oil exporters that could pose difficulties include Iraq, Libya, Nigeria, Russia, and Venezuela.

Fortunately for the United States, the sources of our imported oil are diversified, and we are not excessively dependent on unfriendly nations. Canada, a friendly neighbor, supplies 60 percent of our net imports. Many of our European and Asian allies, however, are dependent on imports from questionable regimes.

The Price of Oil Rises . . .   Until 2003, the price of oil was low, and the U.S. government was under little pressure to address our dependence on imports. In 1998, the price per barrel fell below $12. In July 2008, however, the price of oil spiked to more than $140 a barrel, forcing U.S. gasoline prices above $4 per gallon.

. . . and Falls   The most recent change in oil prices has been more encouraging. In July 2014, the price of oil, then at about $110 per barrel, began to fall. By January 2015, the price was below $50 per barrel. After bottoming out close to $30, it appears likely to stay in the $50 range for some time to come. What happened? The answer is that the high prices of the preceding years persuaded the oil industry to make substantial—and successful—efforts to increase the oil supply. We discuss that development later in the chapter.

15-3b Climate Change

Observations collected by agencies such as the National Aeronautics and Space Administration (NASA) suggest that during the last half century, average global temperatures increased by about 0.85 degree Celsius (1.53 degrees Fahrenheit). Most climatologists believe that this **climate change** is the result of human activities, especially the release of **greenhouse gases** such as carbon dioxide (CO_2) into the atmosphere.

A United Nations (UN) body, the Intergovernmental Panel on Climate Change, has estimated that by the end of the twenty-first century global temperatures could rise to 2.25 to 5.65 degrees Celsius (4 to 10 degrees Fahrenheit) above preindustrial levels. These estimates assume that little more will be done to curb greenhouse gas

climate change The increase in the average temperature of the earth's surface over the last half century and its projected continuation. Also referred to as *global warming*.

greenhouse gas A gas that, when released into the atmosphere, traps the sun's heat and slows its release into outer space. Carbon dioxide (CO_2) is a major example.

emissions. In fact, major efforts to counteract global warming are already underway. At a conference sponsored by the UN in Paris in 2015, representatives of 195 countries endorsed an agreement aimed at keeping average global temperatures to 2.0 degrees Celsius (3.6 degrees Fahrenheit) above preindustrial levels by 2050. This goal established by the Paris Convention may be hard to meet.

Effects of Climate Change   The predicted outcomes of climate change vary, depending on the climate models on which they are based. If the oceans grow warmer, seawater will expand, and polar ice will melt. (This last event is already underway.) These two developments will cause sea levels to rise, negatively affecting coastal areas. Rainfall patterns are expected to change, turning some areas into deserts but allowing agriculture to expand elsewhere. Other likely effects could include increases in extreme weather.

The Climate Change Debate   Some dispute the consensus view of climate change. They argue that any observed warming is due largely to natural causes and may not continue into the future. Although this position is rare among scientists, it has been common in the broader community of Americans. A 2017 Gallup poll, for example, revealed that 31 percent of Americans believe either that global warming is due to natural causes or that it does not exist. This number was as high as 46 percent as recently as 2010.

Attitudes toward climate change have become highly politicized. Some commentators on the political right contend that global warming is a giant liberal hoax designed to clear the way for increased government control of the economy and society. At the same time, many on the political left believe that the right-wing refusal to accept the existence of climate change threatens the very future of the human race.

Obama and Trump on Climate Change   Political deadlock meant that Congress would take no action on CO_2 emissions. The Obama administration therefore sought to act on its own. In 2015, the Environmental Protection Agency (EPA) issued the Clean Power Plan (CPP), a program to reduce CO_2 emissions from existing power plants. Twenty-nine states sued to stop the CPP. In 2016, the Supreme Court blocked the plan pending a Court ruling. Then, in November of that year, Donald Trump was elected president. Trump immediately halted support for the CPP. In addition, in June 2017 he withdrew the United States from the Paris Convention on climate change.

15–3c New Energy Sources

The issues of U.S. energy security and climate change raise the question of whether we can develop new energy sources. Energy security means finding energy sources that are produced either in this country or by friendly neighbors such as Canada. A reduction in global warming means deploying energy sources that do not release CO_2 and other greenhouse gases into the atmosphere. As explained next, however, new energy sources may be accompanied by problems.

Expanded Supplies of Oil and Natural Gas
By 2012, many Americans had begun to realize that they were entering a new era of energy production. U.S. oil production, which declined rapidly after 1985, began to grow again in 2009. This development was based in part on technological improvements and in part on higher prices. For example, production from oil sands in Alberta, Canada, was not profitable when prices for petroleum were low. With gasoline prices approaching $4 per gallon, however, extraction was economical.

The Natural Gas Boom.   An even more dramatic development was the increase in supplies of natural gas. Only

A fracking derrick in a Colorado field. New fracking sites can be developed relatively quickly compared to traditional drilling sites. That means that the rate of development can easily respond to the price of oil or natural gas. *Why do some people oppose fracking?*

a few years ago, experts believed that the United States would soon need to import natural gas. Because gas cannot be transported by ship efficiently unless it is converted to *liquefied natural gas (LNG)*, imports would be costly.

By 2012, however, gas producers were planning to export LNG. The nation was running out of facilities to store all the new gas, some of which was simply flamed off into the atmosphere. Low natural gas prices plus new EPA air-pollution regulations made coal uncompetitive as a source of electricity. As a result, about 130 coal-based power plants were closed or scheduled for retirement, and construction of new coal-based plants was at a standstill. Coal-producing regions such as eastern Kentucky and West Virginia faced serious economic difficulties.

An unexpected consequence of the boom in natural gas production was its environmental impact. Burning natural gas does release some CO_2 into the atmosphere, but less than half as much as coal. By 2009, U.S. emissions of CO_2 were falling. (They leveled off from 2010 on.) More fuel-efficient vehicles on the road added to the reduction.

The Fracking Revolution.   Why has it been possible for the United States to ramp up oil and natural gas production so greatly during the last several years? The answer is an extraction technique known as hydraulic fracturing, or **fracking.** This method involves pumping a high-pressure mixture of water, sand, and chemicals into oil- or gas-bearing underground rock, usually shale, to release the oil or gas. Fracking is not actually a new technique. High prices of oil and gas combined with improvements in the process, however, have made fracking cost-effective.

New oilfields in Texas and North Dakota are based on fracking. A growing concern, though, is that the technology could lead to the contamination of underground water sources. Accordingly, various state governments are developing regulations aimed at preventing such contamination.[4]

By 2014, fracking had turned the United States into the number-one oil producer in the world. As we observed earlier, by then increased supplies of petroleum had caused the price of oil to fall dramatically. In the past, Saudi Arabia would have cut its production in an attempt to keep prices up. In 2014, however, the Saudis maintained production in the hopes of driving high-cost U.S. fracking companies out of business. The Saudi move did reduce the number of new wells developed by U.S. oil firms. Vigorous cost-cutting measures by the

U.S. industry, however, meant that the United States was able to maintain oil production despite lower prices.

Nuclear Energy   One energy source that cannot contribute to global warming is nuclear power—nuclear reactors do not release greenhouse gases. Still, due to concern over possible dangers and the difficulty of storing spent nuclear fuel, no new nuclear power plants have been built in the United States in more than thirty years. The key obstacle to the construction of new nuclear plants is cost. Nuclear power plants must compete on price with natural gas plants. Currently, nuclear energy simply cannot compete.

Nuclear power also suffered a severe blow in 2011 as a result of a series of disasters. A giant tsunami devastated the northeast coast of Japan, and more than 25,000 people died. Four reactors located on the coast were flooded, and radioactive material was released. Following the disasters, support for new nuclear plants in the United States fell.

Renewable Energy   Not all methods of supplying energy come with potentially hazardous by-products, such as greenhouse gases or nuclear waste. For example, hydroelectric energy, generated by water flowing through dams, is a widely used technology that employs no coal, natural gas, oil, or other fossil fuels. Energy from such technologies is referred to as **renewable energy,** because it does not rely on extracting resources that can run out, such as oil, coal, and uranium ore.

Until recently, the problem was that most existing renewable technologies, such as solar power cells, were expensive. However, the cost of solar power and wind energy has been falling fast. In some locations, wind power now competes with natural gas in price. As a result, the number of solar- and wind-power installations has grown rapidly. Of course, the wind does not always blow, and the sun does not always shine, so absent large improvements in battery technology, there are practical limits to how much of our electricity can be provided by these technologies.

CRITICAL THINKING

▶ *One possible way to reduce greenhouse gas emissions would be to tax them by imposing a "carbon tax" on fuels that contain carbon. Why hasn't Congress taken such a solution seriously?*

fracking A technique for extracting oil or natural gas from underground rock by the high-power injection of a mixture of water, sand, and chemicals.

renewable energy Energy from technologies that do not rely on extracted resources, such as oil and coal, that can run out.

15-4 ECONOMIC POLICY AND TAXES

LO Describe the two major areas of economic policymaking, and discuss the issue of the public debt.

When economic conditions are troubled, policies that affect the economy are more important than any other set of activities the government undertakes. **Economic policy** consists of all actions taken by the government to address the ups and downs in the nation's level of business activity. National economic policy is solely the responsibility of the national government.

15-4a The Goals of Economic Policy

Everyone understands that the nation's economy passes through periods of "boom and bust" and that in 2008 and following years, we experienced a major bust known as the *Great Recession*. Even in times when the economy has been less turbulent, however, the nation has alternated between periods of strong economic growth and periods of weak or no growth. This rhythm seems to be inherent in the capitalist system, and it is called the *business cycle*.

A period in which the economy stops growing altogether and undergoes a contraction is called a **recession.** The most recent recession began in December 2007 and officially ended in June 2009. We say "officially," because even though economic growth resumed in 2009, the nation's economy was still operating below its potential.

Unemployment The most important sign of an economic downturn is a high rate of **unemployment.** The rate of unemployment is measured by a government survey. People are defined as unemployed if they are without a job and are actively looking for one. An unemployment rate of 7 percent means that there are seven people looking for work for every ninety-three people who have a job. If "discouraged workers," who have given up looking for work, are also counted, the unemployment rate is substantially higher. Figure 15–3 shows an alternative method of examining the problem. Rather than counting the unemployed, this chart counts those who are actually working.

Even in the best of times, there is always a degree of unemployment, because some people are between jobs. Unemployment rates of 8 or 9 percent, however, are clear signs of economic and social distress. Few experiences are more psychologically damaging than extended unemployment. Reducing unemployment is a major policy objective.

Inflation Unemployment and recession go hand in hand. A second economic problem that the government must occasionally address is associated with economic booms. That problem is **inflation,** a sustained rise in average prices. A rise in prices is equivalent to a decline in the value of the dollar. High rates of inflation were a serious problem in the 1970s, but rates have fallen since. Even though the rate of inflation is now low, many people are fearful that high rates could return at some point in the future.

The national government has two main tools to smooth the business cycle and to reduce unemployment and inflation. These tools are monetary policy and fiscal policy, and we describe them in the following sections.

15-4b Monetary Policy

One of the tools used in managing the economy is **monetary policy,** which involves changing the amount of money in circulation to affect interest rates, credit markets, the rate of inflation, the rate of economic growth, and the rate of unemployment. Monetary policy is under the control of the Federal Reserve System, an independent regulatory agency.

The Federal Reserve System (the Fed) was established by Congress as the nation's central banking system in 1913. The Fed is overseen by a board of seven governors, including the very influential chairperson. The president appoints the members of the board of governors, and the Senate must approve the nominations. Members of the board serve for fourteen-year terms. In addition to controlling the money supply, the Fed has a number of responsibilities in supervising and regulating the nation's banking system.

Easy Money, Tight Money The Fed and its **Federal Open Market Committee (FOMC)** make decisions about monetary policy several times each year. In theory, monetary policy is relatively straightforward.

---

economic policy All actions taken by the national government to address ups and downs in the nation's level of business activity.

recession A period in which the level of economic activity falls. It is usually defined as two or more quarters of economic decline.

unemployment The state of not having a job when actively seeking one.

inflation A sustained rise in average prices. It is equivalent to a decline in the value of the dollar.

monetary policy Actions taken by the Federal Reserve to change the amount of money in circulation to affect interest rates, credit markets, the rate of inflation, the rate of economic growth, and the rate of unemployment.

Federal Open Market Committee (FOMC) The most important body within the Federal Reserve System. It decides how monetary policy should be carried out.

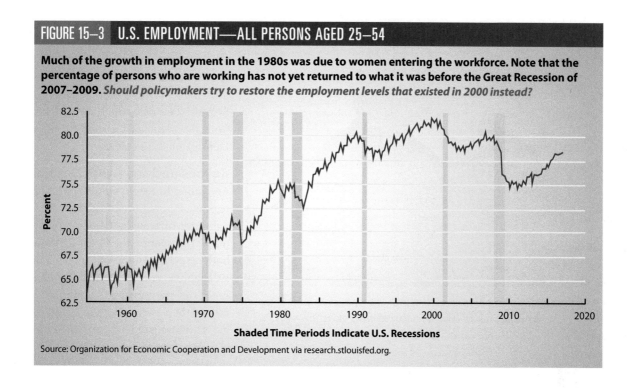

FIGURE 15–3 U.S. EMPLOYMENT—ALL PERSONS AGED 25–54

Much of the growth in employment in the 1980s was due to women entering the workforce. Note that the percentage of persons who are working has not yet returned to what it was before the Great Recession of 2007–2009. *Should policymakers try to restore the employment levels that existed in 2000 instead?*

Shaded Time Periods Indicate U.S. Recessions

Source: Organization for Economic Cooperation and Development via research.stlouisfed.org.

In periods of recession and high unemployment, the Fed pursues an **easy-money policy** to stimulate the economy by expanding the rate of growth of the money supply. An easy-money policy supposedly will lead to lower interest rates and induce consumers to spend more and producers to invest more.

In periods of rising inflation, the Fed does the reverse: it reduces the rate of growth in the amount of money in circulation. This is called a *tight-money policy*. This policy should cause interest rates to rise, thus inducing consumers to spend less and businesses to invest less.

"Pushing on a String" Although an easy-money policy may sound simple, the reality is not simple at all. To give one example, if times are hard enough, people and businesses may not want to borrow even if interest rates go down to zero. The government cannot force anyone to borrow, after all.

This state of affairs is not hypothetical—it characterized the economy for many years after 2008. The Fed managed to keep the interest rate for short-term federal debt almost at zero, but rates of borrowing were still depressed. Instead of percolating into the actual economy, much of the extra money created by the Fed piled up in excess bank reserves. With some reason, the failure of easy-money policy to spur the economy has been described as "pushing on a string."

The Fed responded to the failure of its easy-money policy by adopting some unorthodox tactics. Ordinarily, the Fed expands the money supply by using the newly created money to purchase short-term federal government debt. After 2010, however, it undertook programs of buying long-term federal debt in the hope that long-term purchases would be more effective than short-term ones. In addition, it began purchasing private-sector debt obligations, such as securities based on residential mortgages.

Beginning in 2013, the Fed began winding down its unusual policies. In 2014, it stopped its unorthodox bond purchases. In December 2015, for the first time since the Great Recession, the Fed raised its key interest rate by 0.25 percent. It raised the rate by another 0.25 percent in December 2016 and again in March 2017. Some economists, however, argued that the Fed was moving too fast. These economists recommended hiking interest rates only after the economy was clearly overheating.

Conservative Criticisms A number of conservatives have expressed alarm at the Fed's recent policies. Some fear that the extra money created by the Fed—which is currently just sitting there—could pass into the real economy with explosive speed. The result would be increased inflation.

A second response has been the growth in the philosophy of "hard money" among radical conservatives. Hard-money advocates believe that the government should tie the value of the dollar to commodities such as gold. Mainstream economists believe

> **easy-money policy**
> A monetary policy that involves stimulating the economy by expanding the rate of growth of the money supply.

Federal Reserve chair Janet Yellen speaks on monetary policy to a convention of business journalists. *How does the Fed make monetary policy?*

that such a policy would lead to a dramatic contraction in the money supply and a recession of unprecedented severity.

15–4c Fiscal Policy

Prior to the onset of the Great Recession, mainstream economists agreed on one point: under ordinary circumstances, monetary policy would be sufficient to steer the economy. If monetary policy proved to be inadequate, however, many economists also recommended use of a second tool—fiscal policy.

The principle underlying **fiscal policy,** like the one that underlies monetary policy, is relatively simple: when unemployment is rising and the economy is entering a recession, fiscal policy should stimulate economic activity by decreasing taxes, increasing government spending, or both. When unemployment is decreasing and prices are rising (that is, when we have inflation), fiscal policy should curb economic activity by reducing government spending, increasing taxes, or both.

In the past, fiscal policy meant raising or lowering rates of taxation. Such changes could be accomplished quickly and would not trigger disputes about government spending. The severity of the Great Recession, however, led some economists

fiscal policy The use of changes in government expenditures and taxes to alter national economic variables.

Keynesian economics An economic theory proposed by British economist John Maynard Keynes that is typically associated with the use of fiscal policy to alter national economic variables.

to recommend increases in government spending as well.

U.S. fiscal policy is associated with the economic theories of the British economist John Maynard Keynes (1883–1946). Keynes's theories, which we address next, were the result of his study of the Great Depression of the 1930s.

Keynes and the Great Depression

According to **Keynesian economics,** the nation cannot automatically recover from a disaster such as the Great Depression—or, for that matter, the Great Recession. In both cases, the shock that initiates the crisis frightens consumers and businesses so much that they, in great numbers, begin to reduce their borrowing and spending.

Unfortunately, if everyone in the economy tries to cut spending at the same time, demand for goods and services drops sharply. That, in turn, reduces the income of everyone selling these goods and services. People become even more reluctant to borrow and spend. The cycle feeds on itself.

The Keynesian solution to this type of impasse is for the government to provide the demand through a huge, if temporary, spending program. The spending must not be paid for through taxes but typically will be financed by borrowing. The government, in other words, begins borrowing when the private sector stops. Some economists believe that just such a spending program broke the back of the Great Depression—that is, the "spending program" known as World War II (1939–1945).

Keynes and the Great Recession   Until

recently, support for Keynesianism was relatively bipartisan. Republican president Richard Nixon once said, "I am now a Keynesian." Even President George W. Bush justified his tax cuts with Keynesian rhetoric. From the years after World War II until the first years of the twenty-first century, it was relatively easy to be a Keynesian. After all, Keynesian solutions could be implemented through relatively small changes to rates of taxation. The Bush administration sponsored just such a tax-based stimulus in early 2008, when the Great Recession had already begun but was not yet a major disaster.

Obama versus the Republicans.   In February 2009, with the full scope of the recession evident, Obama proposed and Congress passed a stimulus package of roughly $800 billion, made up mostly of spending, not tax cuts. This was a classical Keynesian response to the recession, but it turned out to be a one-time measure. From

2009 on, Republicans in Congress strongly rejected Keynesianism. An important group of economists had long opposed Keynesian theories. They argued that it is not possible to stimulate the economy through federal borrowing. The borrowing just drains funds from some other part of the economy. A few members of Congress turned to these thinkers. Most of the Republicans, however, simply objected to the use of budget deficits as a recession-fighting tool.

The Eclipse of Keynesianism. If it took World War II to eliminate unemployment in the 1940s, Keynesian economics faced a problem in 2009. The increase in the federal budget deficit necessary to end the economic crisis could be very large. Some Keynesians outside the Obama administration calculated that, to have a real impact, stimulus spending would have to be three times the $800 billion already committed.[5] That type of program was politically impossible. Few Americans would accept new government spending programs amounting to trillions of dollars. By the time of his State of the Union address in 2010, Obama himself was employing rhetoric that was substantially anti-Keynesian.

State and local government spending dropped sharply after the expiration of the 2009 stimulus, and more than half a million state and local workers lost their jobs. At the federal level, even though explicitly Keynesian fiscal policies were off the table, the government continued to run trillion-dollar budget deficits through 2012. The size of these deficits became a major political issue. By 2013, however, the deficit had begun to decline noticeably.

15-4d The Federal Tax System

The government raises money to pay its expenses in two ways: through taxes levied on business and personal income and through borrowing. The American income

British economist John Maynard Keynes developed theories of how to pull the world out of the Great Depression in the 1930s. *What policies did Keynes advocate to end a depression?*

tax system is progressive—meaning that as you earn more income, you pay a higher tax rate on the additional income earned.

The 2017 tax rates are shown in Table 15–1. The rates shown are marginal ones. That means that they are the rates imposed on the last dollar you earn. An individual may be a multimillionaire, but he or she will still pay only 10 percent on taxable income up to $9,325. The 39.6 percent rate is charged only on income in excess of $418,401. (Note that the second-highest income bracket is absurdly narrow—a side effect of a surcharge to pay for the Affordable Care Act.)

TABLE 15–1	TAX RATES FOR SINGLE PERSONS AND MARRIED COUPLES: TAX YEAR 2017, FILED IN APRIL 2018		
Individual		**Married filling Jointly**	
Marginal Tax Bracket	**Marginal Tax Rate**	**Marginal Tax Bracket**	**Marginal Tax Rate**
0 – $9,325	10%	0 – $18,650	10%
$9,326 – $37,950	15%	$18,651 – $75,900	15%
$37,951 – $91,900	25%	$75,901 – $153,100	25%
$91,901 – $191,650	28%	$153,101 – $233,350	28%
$191,651 – $416,700	33%	$233,351 – $416,700	33%
$416,701 – $418,400	35%	$416,701 – $470,700	35%
$418,401 +	39.6%	$470,701 +	39.6%

Universal History Archive/Universal Images Group/Getty Images

PERCEPTION VS. REALITY

Tax-Rate Cuts for the Rich

Republicans experienced difficulties in 2017 as they attempted to pass legislation. Almost everyone, however, was certain that the Republicans would eventually win one victory—reducing tax rates on upper-income Americans. Such tax-rate cuts were a top political goal for traditional Republicans, and President Trump was quite willing to go along with this plan.

The Perception

Many believe that it is only fair if those who have the most also contribute the most. That means higher tax rates for the rich. If the existing higher rates are cut, we could see an increase in the federal budget deficit.

The Reality

As is so often the case, reality is more complicated. First, we must distinguish between tax rates and taxes paid. In 2003, under President George W. Bush, tax rates on the wealthy were cut substantially. The percentage of income that the top 1 percent of earners paid in taxes fell from 27.3 percent in 2002 to 22.5 percent in 2007. Yet the percentage of all income taxes paid by the rich went up, not down. The top 1 percent paid 34 percent of all income taxes in 2002. By 2007, it was 40 percent. (We stop at 2007 because, after that year, the Great Recession temporarily scrambled all the tax numbers, and in 2010 tax rates on the rich went up again.)

One cause of this apparent discrepancy is that incomes of the top 1 percent of earners rose even faster than their taxes. While the total taxes in dollars paid by the 1 percent rose 68 percent from 2002 to 2007, the dollar income of this group rose 104 percent—it more than doubled. Another consideration is that reductions in tax rates could lead the rich to work harder and earn more. Such incentives may be at least one reason that the income of the 1 percent doubled.

It is a fact that when it comes to income taxes, the rich pay a lot. According to the Congressional Budget Office, the top 10 percent of income earners pay more than 70 percent of all income taxes. At the bottom end of the scale, more than 40 percent of households pay no income taxes at all (though they do pay substantial Social Security and Medicare taxes).

Some conservatives argue that the kinds of tax rate cuts advocated by President Trump would pay for themselves through economic growth. A panel of top economists organized by the University of Chicago, however, disagreed with this proposition unanimously. Still, there are those who argue that at least for now, increases to the federal budget deficit are not really a problem. Figure 15–3 shows that many people have still not returned to work since the Great Recession. If the Keynesian theories described earlier in this chapter are correct, we may yet have at least some room to increase the deficit.

Blog On

For an up-to-date analysis by the Tax Foundation of taxes paid by the rich, search for "tax foundation summary income."

More than 40 percent of American families earn so little that they have no income tax liability at all, and this figure temporarily hit 47 percent at the height of the recession. (For a discussion of the taxes paid by the rich see this chapter's *Perception vs. Reality* feature.)

Tax Loopholes Generally, the higher the tax rate, the greater the public's reaction to that tax rate. Individuals and corporations facing high tax rates will react by making concerted attempts to get Congress to add various loopholes to the tax law that will allow them to reduce their taxable incomes.

Years ago, when Congress imposed very high tax rates on high incomes, it also provided for more loopholes. These loopholes enabled many wealthy individuals to decrease their tax bills significantly. For example, special tax provisions allowed investors in oil and gas wells to reduce their taxable income.

Will We Ever Have a Truly Simple Tax System? The Tax Reform Act of 1986 was intended to lower taxes and simplify the tax code—and it did just that for most taxpayers. A few years later, however, large federal deficits forced Congress to choose between cutting spending and raising taxes, and Congress opted to do the latter. Tax increases occurred under the administrations of both George H. W. Bush (1989–1993) and Bill Clinton (1993–2001). In fact, the tax rate for the highest income bracket rose from 28 percent in 1986 to 39.6 percent in 1993. Thus, the effective highest marginal tax rate increased significantly.

In response to this sharp increase in taxes, those who were affected lobbied Congress to legislate special exceptions and loopholes so that the full impact of the rate increase would not be felt by the wealthiest Americans. As a result, the tax code is more complicated than it was before the 1986 Tax Reform Act.

While in principle everyone is for a simpler tax code, in practice Congress rarely is able to pass tax-reform legislation. Why? The reason is that those who now benefit from our complicated tax code will not give up their tax breaks without a fight.

15–4e The Public Debt

When the government spends more than it receives, it has to finance this shortfall. Typically, it borrows. The U.S. Treasury sells IOUs on behalf of the U.S. government. They are called U.S. Treasury bills, notes, or bonds, depending on how long the funds are borrowed. All are commonly called *treasuries*.

The sale of these obligations to corporations, private individuals, pension plans, foreign governments, foreign companies, and foreign individuals is big business. After all, except for a few years in the late 1990s and early 2000s, federal government expenditures have always exceeded federal government revenues.

Every time there is a federal government deficit, there is an increase in the total accumulated **public debt** (also called the *national debt*), which is defined as the total value of all outstanding federal government borrowing. If the existing public debt is $5 trillion and the government runs a deficit of $100 billion, then at the end of the year the public debt is $5.1 trillion. Figure 15–4 shows what has happened to the *net* public debt over time, in comparison with the overall size of the economy. (The net public debt doesn't count sums that the government owes to itself, although it does include funds held by the Fed.)

The Burden of the Public Debt We often hear about the burden of the public debt. Some even maintain that the government will eventually go bankrupt. As long as the government can collect taxes to pay interest on its public debt, however, that will never happen. What happens instead is that when treasuries come due, they are simply "rolled over," or refinanced. That is, if a $1 million Treasury bond comes due today and

> **public debt** The total amount of money that the national government owes as a result of borrowing. Also called the *national debt*.

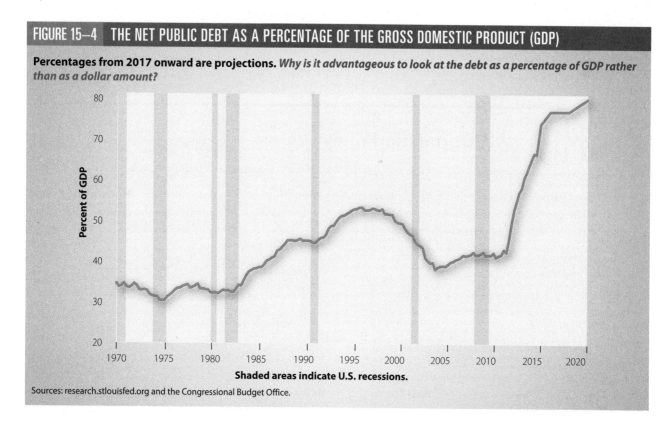

FIGURE 15–4   THE NET PUBLIC DEBT AS A PERCENTAGE OF THE GROSS DOMESTIC PRODUCT (GDP)

Percentages from 2017 onward are projections. *Why is it advantageous to look at the debt as a percentage of GDP rather than as a dollar amount?*

Shaded areas indicate U.S. recessions.

Sources: research.stlouisfed.org and the Congressional Budget Office.

No one likes paying taxes, but they have been called "the dues we pay to live in a civilized society." *What would it be like to live in a society with little or no government?*

The Deficit after the Great Recession and the Deficit Today

As discussed earlier, the initial response of the federal government to the Great Recession was to increase spending. At the same time, the economy was shrinking, so tax revenues were shrinking, too. Between increased spending and lower revenues, the federal budget deficit shot up. The deficit for 2011 was $1.3 trillion. That was about 8.6 percent of the entire economy. If we look at all levels of government together, for every five dollars of spending, three were backed up by tax receipts. The other two were borrowed.

By 2016, however, the federal budget deficit was down to $587 billion. (This number is up somewhat from 2015 because Congress relaxed certain constraints on federal spending.) Given current policies, the deficit should not exceed $750 billion until the 2020s. Thereafter, if no policy changes are made, the deficit is predicted to grow rapidly. Some economists contend that so long as the deficit does not cause the public debt to grow faster than the economy as a whole, we have no problem. To meet that standard, however, the deficit would need to fall below $430 billion and stay low thereafter.

is cashed in, the U.S. Treasury pays it off with the money it gets from selling another $1 million bond.

The interest on treasuries is paid by federal taxes. Even though much of the interest is being paid to American citizens, the more the federal government borrows to meet these payments, the greater the percentage of its budget is committed to making interest payments. This reduces the government's ability to supply funds for anything else, including transportation, education, housing programs, and the military.

CRITICAL THINKING

▶ *Does your family benefit from any tax breaks that you know of? If so, what are they?*

AMERICA AT ODDS | Domestic Policy

The Preamble to the U.S. Constitution states that one of the goals of the new government was to "promote the general Welfare." Domestic policy is certainly the main way in which our government seeks to promote the general welfare. But how should this be done? Americans are at odds over many domestic issues. A few of them are listed here:

- *Do we send too many people to prison—or do our current incarceration policies protect the public?*

- *Should health-care insurance be a right of all citizens—or does such a program sap individual initiative and lead to an over-mighty government?*

- *Is climate change a serious problem that must be addressed now—or are the risks overblown and the proposed solutions a danger to our economy?*

- *When dealing with the issue of unauthorized immigrants, should we seek to normalize the status of these persons—or is deportation the answer?*

- *Should the wealthiest Americans pay more in taxes—or would such a policy be unfair or counterproductive?*

STUDY TOOLS 15

READY TO STUDY? IN THE BOOK, YOU CAN:

☐ Review what you've read with the following chapter quiz.

☐ Check your answers in Appendix D at the back of the book.

☐ Rip out the Chapter Review Card, which includes key terms and chapter summaries.

ONLINE AT WWW.CENGAGEBRAIN.COM, YOU CAN:

☐ Watch videos to get a quick overview.

☐ Expedite your studying with Major Player readings and Focus Activities.

☐ Check your understanding with Chapter Quizzes.

FILL-IN

Learning Outcome 15–1

1. The stages of the policymaking process are _____.

Learning Outcome 15–2

2. _____ is now the federal government's second-largest domestic spending program, after Social Security.

3. The individual mandate in the 2010 health-care reform legislation is a requirement that _____.

Learning Outcome 15–3

4. The foreign nation that today supplies more than half of our imported oil is _____.

5. The predicted outcomes of climate change include _____.

6. Renewable energy technologies include _____.

Learning Outcome 15–4

7. A period in which the economy stops growing altogether and undergoes a contraction is called a _____.

8. Monetary policy is under the control of the _____, an independent regulatory agency.

MULTIPLE CHOICE

Learning Outcome 15–1

9. A discussion in the media about a problem that might have a political solution is an example of
   a. policy adoption.
   b. policy implementation.
   c. issue identification.

Learning Outcome 15–2

10. About _____ percent of national spending in the United States goes to health care.
    a. 4
    b. 18
    c. 29.5

11. One immediate change brought about by the health-care reform bills that passed in 2010 was that young people can remain covered by their parents' insurance until they turn
    a. 26.
    b. 21.
    c. 18.

Learning Outcome 15–3

12. By 2017, the price of a barrel of crude oil, which in 2014 was about $110, was
    a. closer to $175.
    b. averaging between $90 and $100.
    c. about $50.

Learning Outcome 15–4

13. _____ policy uses changes in government expenditures and taxes to alter national economic variables.
    a. Monetary
    b. Fiscal
    c. Domestic

14. According to the nonpartisan Congressional Budget Office, about _____ percent of this nation's households pay no income taxes at all.
    a. 10
    b. 23
    c. 40

16 FOREIGN POLICY

United Nation Relief and Works Agency/Getty Images News/ Getty Images

LEARNING OUTCOMES

After reading this chapter, you should be able to:

16–1 Discuss how foreign policy is made, and identify the key players in this process.

16–2 Summarize the history of American foreign policy.

16–3 Identify the foreign policy challenges that our government has sought to meet by using military force.

16–4 Describe issues that the government has handled primarily through diplomacy, including the Israeli-Palestinian conflict, curbing weapons of mass destruction, and the rise of China as a world power.

After finishing this chapter, go to **PAGE 374** for **STUDY TOOLS**

AMERICA AT ODDS | How Much of a Threat Is Putin's Russia?

Semen Lixodeev/Shutterstock.com

Most students today are too young to remember the Union of Soviet Socialist Republics—the Soviet Union, or USSR. That country broke up into fifteen independent republics in 1991. From the end of World War II until the late 1980s, America and its allies were pitted against the Soviet Union in what was called the "Cold War." (You'll read more about the Cold War in this chapter.)

Millions of Soviet soldiers were under arms during the Cold War. The USSR had a world-class navy and a vast arsenal of nuclear weapons. The heart of the old Soviet Union was the Russian Republic, which contained about half the USSR's population. Today's Russia is much weaker than the Soviet Union. Yet in recent years, Russia's president, Vladimir Putin, has begun to demonstrate an alarming degree of aggressiveness. How much of a threat does Putin's Russia present?

Russia Is a Very Serious Threat

Consider what Putin has done. He has threatened Europe by cutting off natural gas supplies. He has waged war on the small nation of Georgia, detaching portions of Georgian territory. Because Putin opposed Ukraine's new Europe-friendly government, he invaded and annexed Ukraine's Crimean peninsula. He then sponsored an insurrection in Russian-speaking areas of eastern Ukraine. When it seemed that the Ukrainian government would put down the rebellion, Russia moved its own troops into Ukraine to prevent such a result. Putin has initiated a series of provocations aimed at the small Baltic nations. Unlike Ukraine, however, the Baltic states are members of the North Atlantic Treaty Organization (NATO). That means that America and most of Europe are sworn to defend their territory as if it were our own.

Putin has said that the biggest geopolitical disaster of the twentieth century was the fall of the Soviet Union. He wants to restore its former glory. An example is Russia's recent intervention into the Syrian civil war, which involved bombings and even the use of troops. In the long run, economic troubles may limit Russia's capabilities. In the short run, however, they may provoke Putin into distracting his citizens through military adventures.

In the Long Run, Russia Is Weak

There is no question that Putin has begun making trouble for the world. Yet consider the balance of forces. Add the European Union to the United States and you have an economy sixteen times the size of Russia's. The U.S. defense budget is seven times that of Russia. The old Soviet Union drew strength from the ideology of communism, which had supporters around the world. Today's Russia has no ideology that can match the attractions of the West. Indeed, the crisis in Ukraine began because that nation wanted to draw closer to the European Union—an organization that is truly attractive to the peoples of Eastern Europe.

Russia's state-controlled economy is fragile and inefficient. Russia's population is even declining. The United States and our European allies have imposed sanctions (punishments) on Russia due to its Ukraine policy. Sanctions, together with the fall in the price of oil—Russia's chief export—have pushed the Russian economy into recession. As a regional power, Russia can make trouble. It does not, however, threaten the world.

Where do you stand?

1. Does it matter that most of the nations Putin has threatened militarily are former members of the Soviet Union? Why or why not?

2. Does President Trump's attempt to warm up to Putin have a chance of success? Why or why not?

Explore this issue online:

- The *New Yorker* magazine discusses Russia's attempt to interfere with the 2016 elections and other topics. Search for "trump putin cold war."

- The Vox website has a card stack titled "Everything You Need to Know about Ukraine." Find it by searching on "vox cards ukraine."

INTRODUCTION

What we call **foreign policy** is a systematic and general plan that guides a country's attitudes and actions toward the rest of the world. Foreign policy includes all of the economic, military, commercial, and diplomatic positions and actions that a nation takes in its relationships with other countries. Although foreign policy may seem quite removed from the concerns of everyday life, it can and does have a significant impact on the day-to-day lives of Americans.

American foreign policy has been shaped by two principles that are often seen as contradicting each other. One is **moral idealism,** the belief that the most important goal in foreign policy is to do what is right. Moral idealists think that it is possible for nations to relate to each other as part of a rule-based community. Moral idealism appeals to the often-held American belief that our nation is special and should provide an example to the rest of the world.

A contrasting view is **political realism,** the belief that nations are inevitably selfish. In this view, foreign countries are by definition dangerous. The chapter-opening *America at Odds* feature, for example, discusses the dangers posed by Russia. Foreign policy must therefore be based on protecting our national security, regardless of moral arguments. Although there have been times when one or the other of these two principles has dominated, U.S. foreign policy has usually been a mixture of both.

An Iranian woman in her hotel room in California after her release from custody in January 2017. She was one of dozens of people from seven Muslim-majority nations with valid visas or green cards who were detained at Los Angeles International Airport. The arrests followed an executive order by President Trump. *Why would federal judges have suspended Trump's order?*

Francine Orr/Los Angeles Times/Getty Images

---

foreign policy A systematic and general plan that guides a country's attitudes and actions toward the rest of the world. Foreign policy includes all of the economic, military, commercial, and diplomatic positions and actions that a nation takes in its relationships with other countries.

moral idealism In foreign policy, the belief that the most important goal is to do what is right. Moral idealists think that it is possible for nations to cooperate as part of a rule-based community.

political realism In foreign policy, the belief that nations are inevitably selfish and that we should seek to protect our national security, regardless of moral arguments.

16–1 WHO MAKES U.S. FOREIGN POLICY?

LO Discuss how foreign policy is made, and identify the key players in this process.

The framers of the Constitution envisioned that the president and Congress would cooperate in developing American foreign policy. The Constitution did not spell out exactly how this was to be done, though. As commander in chief, the president has assumed much of the decision-making power in the area of foreign policy. Nonetheless, members of Congress, a number of officials, and a vast national security bureaucracy help to shape the president's decisions and to limit the president's powers.

16–1a The President's Role

Article II, Section 2, of the Constitution names the president commander in chief of the armed forces. As commander in chief, the president oversees the military and guides defense policies. Presidents have interpreted this role broadly, sending American troops, ships, and weapons to trouble spots at home and around the world.

The Constitution authorizes the president to make treaties, which must be approved by two-thirds of the

Senate. In addition, the president is empowered to form executive agreements—pacts between the president and the heads of other nations. These executive agreements do not require Senate approval.

The president's foreign policy responsibilities have special significance in that the president has ultimate control over the use of nuclear weapons. The president also influences foreign policymaking in the role of head of state. As the symbolic head of our government, the president represents the United States to the rest of the world. When a serious foreign policy issue or international question arises, the nation expects the president to provide leadership.

> "*To be prepared for war* is one of the most effectual means of preserving peace."
>
> ~ GEORGE WASHINGTON, COMMANDER OF THE CONTINENTAL ARMY AND FIRST PRESIDENT OF THE UNITED STATES 1789–1797

16-1b The Cabinet

Many members of the president's cabinet concern themselves with international problems and recommend policies to deal with them. As U.S. power in the world has grown and as economic factors have become increasingly important, the departments of Agriculture, Commerce, Energy, and Treasury have become more involved in foreign policy decisions. The secretary of state and the secretary of defense, however, are the only cabinet members who concern themselves with foreign policy matters on a full-time basis.

The Department of State The Department of State is, in principle, the government agency most directly involved in foreign policy. The department is responsible for diplomatic relations with nearly two hundred independent nations around the globe, as well as with the United Nations and other multilateral organizations, such as the Organization of American States. Most U.S. relations with other countries are maintained through embassies, consulates, and other U.S. offices around the world.

As the head of the State Department, the secretary of state has traditionally played a key role in foreign policymaking, and many presidents have relied heavily on the advice of their secretaries of state. Under many presidents since the end of World War II, however, the State Department

has taken a back seat in foreign policy to the president's National Security Council, described later. The Obama administration was an exception to this trend—secretaries of state Hillary Clinton and John Kerry played leading roles in foreign policy issues. Under President Trump, however, the State Department has again receded into the background. Indeed, Trump has proposed major cuts to the State Department budget.

The Department of Defense

The Department of Defense is the principal executive department that establishes and carries out defense policy and protects our national security. The secretary of defense advises the president on all aspects of U.S. military and defense policy, supervises all of the military activities of the U.S. government, and works to see that the decisions of the president as commander in chief are carried out. The secretary advises and informs the president on the nation's military forces, weapons, and bases and works closely with U.S. military leaders, especially the Joint Chiefs of Staff, in gathering and studying defense information.

The Joint Chiefs of Staff (JCS) include the chair and vice chair of the JCS; the military service chiefs of the Army, Navy, Air Force, and Marines; and the chief of the National Guard. All are appointed by the president and confirmed by the Senate.

German Chancellor Angela Merkel meets with President Trump at the White House in March 2017. Germany runs a large trade surplus with the United States. *Why would that concern Trump?*

SAUL LOEB/AFP/Getty Images

The joint chiefs regularly serve as the key military advisers to the president, the secretary of defense, and the National Security Council. They are responsible for handing down the president's orders to the nation's military units, preparing strategic plans, and recommending military actions. They also propose military budgets, new weapons systems, and military regulations.

16-1c Other Agencies

Several other government agencies are also involved in the foreign relations of the United States. Two key agencies in the area of foreign policy are the National Security Council and the Central Intelligence Agency.

The National Security Council   The National Security Council (NSC) was established by the National Security Act of 1947. The formal members of the NSC include the president, the vice president, the secretary of state, and the secretary of defense. Meetings are often attended by the chairperson of the Joint Chiefs of Staff, the director of the Central Intelligence Agency, and representatives from other departments.

The national security adviser, who is a member of the president's White House staff, is the director of the NSC. The adviser informs the president, coordinates advice and information on foreign policy, and serves as a liaison with other officials.

The NSC and its members can be as important and powerful as the president wants them to be. Some presidents have made frequent use of the NSC, whereas others have convened it infrequently. Similarly, the importance of the role played by the national security adviser in shaping foreign policy can vary significantly, depending on the administration and the adviser's identity.

The Central Intelligence Agency   The Central Intelligence Agency (CIA) was created after World War II to coordinate American intelligence activities abroad. The CIA provides the president and his or her advisers with up-to-date information about the political, military, and economic activities of foreign governments.

The CIA gathers much of its intelligence from overt sources, such as foreign radio broadcasts and newspapers, people who travel abroad, the Internet, and satellite photographs. Other information is gathered from covert activities, such as the CIA's own secret investigations into the economic or political affairs of other nations. Covert operations may involve secretly supplying weapons to a force rebelling against an unfriendly government or seizing suspected terrorists in a clandestine operation and holding them for questioning.

The CIA has tended to operate autonomously, and the details of its work, methods, and operating funds have been kept secret. Intelligence reform passed by Congress in 2004, however, makes the CIA accountable to a new national intelligence director. The CIA is now required to cooperate more with other U.S. intelligence agencies and has lost a degree of the autonomy it once enjoyed.

16-1d Powers of Congress

Although the executive branch takes the lead in foreign policy matters, Congress also has some power over foreign policy. Remember that Congress alone has the power to declare war. It also has the power to appropriate funds to build new weapons systems, equip the U.S. armed forces, and provide foreign aid. The Senate has the power to approve or reject treaties and the appointment of ambassadors.

In 1973, Congress passed the War Powers Resolution, which limits the president's use of troops in military action without congressional approval. Presidents since then, however, have not interpreted the resolution to mean that Congress must be consulted before military action is taken. On several occasions, presidents have ordered military action and then informed Congress after the fact.

A few congressional committees are directly concerned with foreign affairs. The most important are the Armed Services Committee and the Foreign Affairs Committee in the House, and the Committee on Armed Services and the Committee on Foreign Relations in the Senate. Other congressional committees deal with matters that indirectly influence foreign policy, such as oil, agriculture, and imports.

CRITICAL THINKING

▶ *Should American citizens know more about what the CIA does, or would such knowledge merely benefit our opponents? In either case, why?*

16-2   A SHORT HISTORY OF AMERICAN FOREIGN POLICY

LO   Summarize the history of American foreign policy.

A primary consideration in U.S. foreign policy has always been *national security*—the protection of the independence and political integrity of the nation.

Over the years, the United States has attempted to preserve its national security in many ways. These ways have changed over time and are not always internally consistent. This inconsistency results from the fact that foreign policymaking, like domestic policymaking, reflects the influence of various political groups in the United States. These groups—including the voting public, interest groups, Congress, and the president and relevant agencies of the executive branch—are often at odds over what the U.S. position should be on particular foreign policy issues.

16–2a Isolationism

The nation's founders and the early presidents believed that isolationism—avoiding political involvement with other nations—was the best way to protect American interests. The United States was certainly not yet strong enough to directly influence European developments. During the 1700s and 1800s, the United States generally attempted to avoid conflicts and political engagements elsewhere.

In accordance with this isolationist philosophy, President James Monroe in 1823 proclaimed what became known as the **Monroe Doctrine.** Monroe stated that the United States would not tolerate foreign intervention in the Western Hemisphere. In return, Monroe promised that the United States would stay out of European affairs.

16–2b The Beginning of Interventionism

Isolationism gradually gave way to interventionism (direct involvement in foreign affairs). The first true step toward interventionism occurred with the Spanish-American War of 1898. The United States fought this war to free Cuba from Spanish rule. Spain lost and subsequently ceded control of several of its possessions, including Guam, Puerto Rico, and the Philippines, to the United States. The United States thus acquired a colonial empire and was acknowledged as a world power.

The growth of the United States as an industrial economy also confirmed the nation's position as a

world power. For example, in the early 1900s, President Theodore Roosevelt proposed that the United States could invade Latin American countries when it was necessary to guarantee political or economic stability.

16–2c The World Wars

When World War I broke out in 1914, President Woodrow Wilson initially proclaimed a policy of neutrality—the United States would not take sides in the conflict. The United States did not enter the war until 1917, after U.S. ships in international waters were attacked by German submarines that were blockading Britain.

Wilson called the war a way to "make the world safe for democracy." In his eyes, Germany was not merely dangerous but evil. Wilson, in short, was our most famous presidential advocate of moral idealism.

After World War I ended in 1918, the United States returned to a policy of isolationism. Consequently, we refused to join the League of Nations, an international body intended to resolve peacefully any future conflicts between nations.

The U.S. policy of isolationism ended when the Japanese attacked Pearl Harbor in 1941. We joined the Allies—Australia, Britain, Canada, China, France, and the Soviet Union—to fight the Axis nations of Germany, Italy, and Japan. One of the

President James Monroe (1817–1825) said that the United States would not allow foreign intervention in the Western Hemisphere. *What position did Monroe take on U.S. intervention in Europe?*

Everett - Art/Shutterstock.com

isolationism A political policy of noninvolvement in world affairs.

Monroe Doctrine A U.S. policy, announced in 1823 by President James Monroe, that the United States would not tolerate foreign intervention in the Western Hemisphere and, in return, would stay out of European affairs.

interventionism Direct involvement by one country in another country's affairs.

colonial empire A group of dependent nations that are under the rule of an imperial power.

neutrality The position of not being aligned with either side in a dispute or conflict, such as a war.

most significant foreign policy actions during World War II was the dropping of atomic bombs on the Japanese cities of Hiroshima and Nagasaki in August 1945, which forced Japan to surrender.

16-2d The Cold War

After World War II ended in 1945, the wartime alliance between the United States and the Soviet Union began to deteriorate quickly. The Soviet Union opposed America's political and economic systems. Many Americans considered Soviet attempts to spread communist systems to other countries a major threat to democracy. After the war ended, countries in Eastern Europe—Bulgaria, Czechoslovakia, East Germany, Hungary, Poland, and Romania—fell under Soviet domination, forming what became known as the **Soviet bloc.**

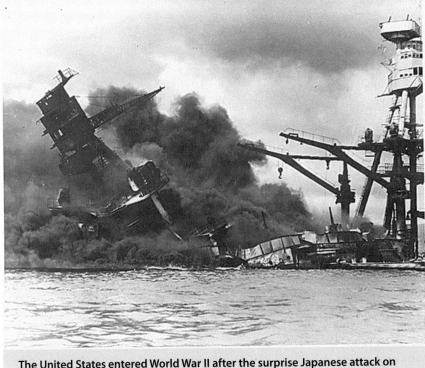

The United States entered World War II after the surprise Japanese attack on Pearl Harbor, Hawaii, on December 7, 1941. *Which nations were our allies in this conflict?*

National Archives

The Marshall Plan and the Policy of Containment   In 1947, when it appeared that local Communist parties, backed by the Soviets, would take over Greece and Turkey, President Harry Truman took action. He convinced Congress to appropriate $400 million ($4.2 billion in 2018 dollars) in aid for those countries to prevent the spread of communism.

The Truman Doctrine and the Marshall Plan.   The president also proclaimed what became known as the *Truman Doctrine*. It would be "the policy of the United States to support free peoples who are resisting attempted subjugation by armed minorities or by outside pressures."[1]

The Truman administration also instituted a policy of economic assistance to war-torn Europe, called the **Marshall Plan** after George Marshall, who was then the U.S. secretary of state. During the next five years, Congress appropriated $17 billion (about $176 billion in 2018 dollars) for aid to sixteen European countries. By 1952, the nations of Western Europe, with U.S. help, had recovered and were again prospering.

The Containment Policy and NATO.   These actions marked the beginning of a policy of **containment,** designed to contain (prevent) the spread of communism by offering U.S. military and economic aid to threatened nations.[2] To make the policy of containment effective, the United States initiated a program of collective security involving the formation of mutual defense alliances with other nations.

In 1949, through the North Atlantic Treaty, the United States, Canada, and ten European nations formed a military alliance—the North Atlantic Treaty Organization (NATO). The treaty declared that an attack on any member of the alliance would be considered an attack against all members.

The Cold War Begins   By 1949, almost all illusions of friendship between the Soviet Union and the Western allies had disappeared. The United States became the leader of a bloc of democratic nations in Western Europe, the Pacific, and elsewhere.

Soviet bloc The group of Eastern European nations that fell under the control of the Soviet Union following World War II.

Marshall Plan A plan providing for U.S. economic assistance to European nations following World War II to help those nations recover from the war. The plan was named after George C. Marshall, secretary of state from 1947 to 1949.

containment A U.S. policy designed to contain the spread of communism by offering military and economic aid to threatened nations.

Britain's Winston Churchill was a valuable friend of the United States during World War II. *What did Britain promise when it joined NATO after the war?*

The tensions between the Soviet Union and the United States became known as the Cold War—a war of words, warnings, and ideologies that lasted from the late 1940s through the late 1980s. Although the Cold War was mainly a war of words and belief systems, "hot" wars in Korea (1950–1953) and Vietnam (1965–1975) grew out of the efforts to contain communism.

The Arms Race and Deterrence   The tensions induced by the Cold War led both the Soviet Union and the United States to try to surpass each other militarily. They began competing for more and better weapons, particularly nuclear weapons, with greater destructive power.

This phenomenon, known as the *arms race*, was supported by a policy of deterrence—of rendering ourselves and our allies so strong militarily that our very strength would deter (stop or discourage) any attack on us. Out of deterrence came the theory of mutually assured destruction (MAD), which held that if the forces of two nations were capable of destroying each other, neither nation would take a chance on war.

The Cuban Missile Crisis   In 1962, the United States and the Soviet Union came close to a nuclear confrontation in what became known as the Cuban missile crisis. The United States learned that the Soviet Union had placed nuclear weapons on the island of Cuba, ninety miles from the coast of Florida.

The crisis was defused without military conflict. A U.S. naval blockade of Cuba convinced the Soviet Union to agree to remove the missiles. The United States also agreed to remove some of its missiles near the Soviet border in Turkey. Both sides recognized that a nuclear war between the two superpowers was unthinkable.

Although the United States agreed not to invade Cuba or attempt to overthrow its government, it did institute an embargo against the island. (An *embargo* is a ban on trade.) The United States also refused to recognize the Cuban government. That policy lasted until December 2014, when President Obama and Cuban president Raúl Castro announced plans to normalize relations between the two countries. Diplomatic relations were officially restored in July 2015, and Obama visited the island in March 2016. Only Congress can lift the embargo, however, and Congress has not yet shown an interest in taking such a step.

Détente and Arms Control   In 1969, the United States and the Soviet Union began negotiations on a treaty to limit the number of antiballistic missiles (ABMs) and offensive missiles that each country could develop and deploy. In 1972, both sides signed the Strategic Arms Limitation Treaty (SALT I). This event marked the beginning of a period of détente, a French word that means a "relaxation of tensions."

In 1983, President Ronald Reagan (1981–1989) nearly reignited the arms race by proposing a missile defense system known as the strategic defense initiative (SDI, or "Star Wars"). Nonetheless,

Cold War The war of words, warnings, and ideologies between the Soviet Union and the United States that lasted from the late 1940s through the late 1980s.

deterrence A policy of building up military strength for the purpose of discouraging (deterring) military attacks by other nations. This policy supported the arms race between the United States and the Soviet Union during the Cold War.

mutually assured destruction (MAD) A phrase referring to the assumption that if the forces of two nations are capable of destroying each other, neither nation will take a chance on war.

Cuban missile crisis A nuclear standoff that occurred in 1962 when the United States learned that the Soviet Union had placed nuclear warheads in Cuba.

détente A French word meaning a "relaxation of tensions." Détente characterized the relationship between the United States and the Soviet Union in the 1970s as they attempted to pursue cooperative dealings and arms control.

Reagan pursued arms control agreements with Soviet leaders, as did Reagan's successor, President George H. W. Bush (1989–1993).

The Dissolution of the Soviet Union In the late 1980s, the political situation inside the Soviet Union began to change rapidly. Mikhail Gorbachev, the new leader, had initiated an effort to democratize the Soviet political system and decentralize the economy. The reforms quickly spread to other countries in the Soviet bloc. In 1989, the Berlin Wall, constructed nearly thirty years earlier to separate Soviet-dominated East Berlin from West Berlin, was torn down. East Germany and West Germany were reunited in 1990.

In August 1991, a number of disgruntled Communist Party leaders who wanted to reverse the reforms briefly seized control of the Soviet central government. Russian citizens rose up in revolt and defied those leaders. The democratically elected president of the Russian republic (the largest republic in the Soviet Union), Boris Yeltsin, confronted troops in Moscow that were under the control of the conspirators. The attempted coup collapsed after three days. The Communist Party in the Soviet Union lost almost all of its power.

The fifteen republics constituting the Soviet Union—including the Russian republic—declared their independence. By the end of the year, the Union of Soviet Socialist Republics (USSR) no longer existed. For years following the collapse of the Soviet Union, Russia—the main successor state—posed little or no threat to world peace. Under President Vladimir Putin, however, Russian policy has been much more aggressive. We discussed these developments in the chapter-opening *America at Odds* feature.

16–2e Post–Cold War Foreign Policy

The demise of the Soviet Union altered the framework and goals of U.S. foreign policy. During the Cold War, the moral underpinnings of American foreign policy were clear to all—the United States was the defender of the "free world" against the Soviet aggressor.

U.S. foreign policymakers have struggled since the end of the Cold War to determine the degree of intervention that is appropriate and prudent for the U.S. military. Should we intervene in a humanitarian crisis, such as a famine? Should the U.S. military participate

> "Soviet Union foreign policy is a puzzle, inside a riddle wrapped in an enigma."
>
> ~ WINSTON CHURCHILL
> BRITISH PRIME MINISTER
> DURING WORLD WAR II
> 1874–1965

in peacekeeping missions, such as those instituted after civil or ethnic strife in other countries? Americans have faced these questions in Bosnia, Kosovo, Rwanda, Somalia, and Sudan.

Yet no overriding framework emerged in U.S. foreign policy until September 11, 2001. Since that date, our primary goal has been to capture and punish the terrorists who planned and perpetrated the events of that day and to prevent future terrorist attacks against Americans. Sometimes, that goal has involved "regime change," one of the objectives of the war against Iraq in 2003.

CRITICAL THINKING

▶ *The Cold War between the United States and the Soviet Union never turned into a shooting war. Why not?*

16–3 PROBLEMS REQUIRING THE USE OF FORCE

LO Identify the foreign policy challenges that our government has sought to meet by using military force.

We can divide the main foreign policy problems that confront the United States into two types. One set of issues is dealt with primarily through diplomacy. We discuss these issues later in this chapter. In contrast, some problems must be handled through the use of force. When in foreign lands, the use of force means deployment of the U.S. armed forces. When the problem is terrorism, which can involve attacks on the American homeland, the primary response may be provided instead by U.S. police agencies such as the FBI. We consider terrorism next.

16–3a The Problem of Terrorism

One of the most difficult challenges faced by governments around the world is how to control terrorism. *Terrorism* is defined as the use of staged violence, often against civilians, to achieve political goals. Terrorism has occurred in almost every region of the world.

The most devastating terrorist attack in U.S. history occurred on September 11, 2001, when radical

Islamist terrorists used hijacked airliners as missiles to bring down the World Trade Center towers in New York City and to destroy part of the Pentagon building in Washington, D.C. A fourth airplane crashed in a Pennsylvania field after passengers fought back against the hijackers. In all, almost three thousand innocent civilians were killed as a result of these terrorist acts.

Terrorists are willing to destroy others' lives and property, and often sacrifice their own lives, for a variety of reasons. Terrorist acts generally fall into one of three broad categories, discussed next.

Mourners in Orlando, Florida, in June 2016 remember the shooting victims at the Pulse nightclub in that city. Most victims were Latino and gay. The American gunman was radicalized by ISIS propaganda. *Why would the killer have targeted gay men and lesbians?*

Nationalist Terrorism

Some terrorist acts have been committed by extremists motivated by the desire to obtain freedom from a nation or government that they regard as an oppressor. Another motivation for terrorism is to disrupt peace talks. In Israel, for example, numerous suicide bombings by Palestinians against Israeli civilians have served to stall efforts to negotiate a peace between Israel and the Palestinians.

The Irish Republican Army, which sought to unite British-governed Northern Ireland with the independent Republic of Ireland, conducted bombings and other terrorist acts in Northern Ireland and England over a period of many years. The attacks came to an end in 1997 as part of a peace process that lasted from 1995 until 2005.

Basque separatists in Spain have engaged in terrorism for decades. The separatists were initially—and incorrectly—blamed for bombing a commuter train in Madrid, Spain, on March 11, 2004. That terrorist attack, actually perpetrated by Islamic radicals, killed 191 people and injured hundreds of others.

Domestic Terrorism

In parts of the South, whites used terrorist methods to prevent African Americans from voting all the way from the late nineteenth century until the 1960s. In other words, domestic terrorism in America has a long history. Indeed, attacks on minority group members continue to be a problem to this day.

In the Vietnam War era, antiwar radicals engaged in a series of bombings.[3] In the 1990s, right-wing extremism was an issue. The bombing of the Oklahoma City federal building in 1995, which killed 168 people, was the act of vengeful extremists who claimed to fear an oppressive federal government. Although Timothy McVeigh and Terry Nichols, who were convicted of the crime, were not directly connected to a particular political group, they expressed views characteristic of the extreme right-wing militia movement in the United States.

A more recent problem in the United States has been attacks by domestic Islamists who have been "self-radicalized" through the Internet. While these individuals may communicate with foreign terrorist organizations, they are not under foreign control. An example is the two self-radicalized Muslim brothers who set off bombs at the Boston Marathon in 2013. Three people died in this incident, and many more lost the use of one or both of their legs. The terrorist attack in San Bernardino, California, in 2015 that killed fourteen was another example, as was the attack on a gay nightclub in Orlando, Florida, on its "Latin night" in 2016. The death toll in Orlando was forty-nine.

Foreign Terrorist Networks

A relatively new phenomenon in the late 1990s and early 2000s was the emergence of terrorist networks, such as al Qaeda. Al Qaeda is the nongovernmental organization that planned and carried out the terrorist attacks of September 11, 2001. Its leader until his death in 2011 was the Saudi dissident Osama bin Laden.

Throughout the 1990s, al Qaeda conducted training camps in the mountains of Afghanistan, which was ruled by an ultraconservative Islamic faction known as the Taliban. The U.S. government determined that al Qaeda was responsible for terrorist attacks on two U.S. embassies in Africa in 1998 and the bombing of the USS *Cole* in 2000. In 1998, President Bill Clinton (1993–2001) ordered the bombing of terrorist camps in Afghanistan in retaliation for the embassy bombings, but with little effect. Al Qaeda cells continued to operate largely unimpeded until the terrorist attacks of September 11.

> *"Fighting terrorism is like being a goalkeeper. You can make a hundred brilliant saves but the only shot that people remember is the one that gets past you."*
>
> ~ PAUL WILKINSON
> BRITISH TERRORISM EXPERT

conflict with that country. In 1990, Hussein had attacked and occupied Kuwait, a small neighboring country. This unprovoked aggression was, at the time, perhaps the most flagrant violation of international law since World War II. U.S. President George H. W. Bush (George W. Bush's father) organized an international coalition to free Kuwait. The coalition forces did not advance into Iraq to unseat Hussein, however.

Reasons for the Second Gulf War The cease-fire that ended the first Gulf War required Iraq to submit to inspections for chemical, biological, and nuclear weapons—**weapons of mass destruction**. In 1998, however, Hussein ceased to cooperate with the inspections. The George W. Bush administration believed that Hussein was developing an atomic bomb and that the Iraqi regime was in some way responsible for the 9/11 terrorist attacks. (Both beliefs later proved to be incorrect.) Bush sought United Nations support for the use of military force, but China, France, and Russia blocked the move. In March 2003, Bush told Hussein to leave Iraq or face war. Hussein was defiant, and war followed.

16-3b The U.S. Response to 9/11—The War in Afghanistan

Immediately after the 9/11 terrorist attacks, Congress passed a joint resolution authorizing President George W. Bush (2001–2009) to use "all necessary and appropriate force" against nations, organizations, and individuals that the president determined had "planned, authorized, committed, or aided the terrorist attacks."

In late 2001, supported by a **coalition** of allies, the U.S. military attacked al Qaeda camps in Afghanistan and the ruling Taliban regime that harbored those terrorists. Once the Taliban had been ousted, the United States helped to establish a government in Afghanistan that did not support terrorism. Instead of continuing the hunt for al Qaeda members in Afghanistan, however, the Bush administration increasingly viewed Iraq as a threat to U.S. security.

16-3c The Focus on Iraq

coalition An alliance of nations formed to undertake a foreign policy action, particularly a military action. A coalition is often a temporary alliance that dissolves after the action is concluded.

weapons of mass destruction Chemical, biological, and nuclear weapons that can inflict massive casualties.

On March 20, 2003, U.S. and British forces attacked the nation of Iraq. Iraqi military units crumbled quickly. Saddam Hussein, Iraq's dictator, was captured in December 2003 and executed in 2006.

The First Gulf War The 2003 attack on Iraq was in fact the second U.S.

The Rise and Fall of the Insurgency Iraq is divided into three main ethnic or religious groups: Kurds, Arabs of the Sunni branch of Islam, and Arabs of the Shiite branch of Islam. The Kurdish-speaking people live in the north. The Sunni Muslims live mostly in west-central Iraq and had been the group in power under Hussein's rule. The Shiite Muslims, who live mostly in the south, make up the majority of the population, but they had been persecuted by the Sunnis under Hussein.

After the overthrow of Hussein's government, Sunni rebels soon launched an insurrection against the occupation forces. The insurgents, including the newly organized al Qaeda in Iraq, attacked not only U.S. and Iraqi government forces but also Shiite civilians. Shiite radicals responded with attacks on Sunnis, and Iraq appeared to be drifting toward interethnic civil war. American voters began to turn against the war, and in the 2006 elections they handed Congress to the Democrats.

Instead of withdrawing U.S. troops, however, the Bush administration increased troop levels in 2007. The "surge," as it was called, was surprisingly successful. Many Sunnis, who also had been terrorized by al Qaeda, turned against the insurgency and allied with the Americans.

With the insurgency fatally undermined, the United States planned its withdrawal. President Barack Obama announced that U.S. combat forces would leave Iraq by the end of August 2010, and the rest of the troops would be out by the end of 2011. In fact, U.S. forces departed slightly ahead of schedule.

16-3d Again, Afghanistan

The war in Iraq tended to draw the Bush administration's attention away from Afghanistan, which was never completely at peace even after the Taliban had been ousted from Kabul, the capital. By 2006, the Taliban had regrouped and were waging a war of insurgency against the new government. The United States and its NATO allies were now the new government's principal military defenders.

Kurdish fighters at the outskirts of the Syrian town of Kobane. The town was almost completely destroyed during attacks by ISIS. Kurdish forces were eventually able to drive off the attackers. *What vital interests does the United States have in the Middle East, if any?*

The Afghan-Pakistani Border A problem for the coalition forces was that the Taliban were able to take shelter on the far side of the Afghan-Pakistani border, in Pakistan's Federally Administered Tribal Areas. These districts are largely free from central government control.

Under the George W. Bush administration, the CIA began operating remote-controlled aircraft (drones) known as Predators over Pakistan. Predators are equipped with small missiles, which were used to kill a number of Taliban and al Qaeda leaders. President Obama ramped up the Predator program significantly.

One result was increasing tensions with Pakistan, which could not openly support the Predator campaign. Pakistan's role in Afghanistan, in fact, has been quite complicated. The nation has been nominally allied with the United States. At the same time, Pakistan's intelligence agency, Inter-Services Intelligence, has funded a variety of Islamist militant groups, including units that have engaged in terrorist attacks on the government of Afghanistan and U.S. forces in that country.

The Death of Bin Laden During the winter of 2010–2011, U.S. intelligence agencies learned that al Qaeda leader Osama bin Laden might be hiding in the Pakistani city of Abbottabad. On May 1, 2011, U.S. Navy

Seals entered bin Laden's residential compound and killed him. The reaction in America was one of relief and satisfaction. The reaction in Pakistan was quite different. Many Pakistanis considered the incident a violation of their country's sovereignty.

Afghanistan, Obama, and Trump In 2009, President Obama increased the number of U.S. troops in Afghanistan by 47,000. At the same time, he indicated that he hoped to withdraw some U.S. forces as early as 2011. In fact, only ten thousand U.S. soldiers left Afghanistan that year. Withdrawals picked up speed in 2012. By 2016, the American presence was down to about ten thousand troops. The remaining U.S. forces have executed air strikes and provided close air support to Afghan forces. In May 2017, however, President Trump approved a request by U.S. military leaders for an additional five thousand soldiers, many of them infantry who would train members of the Afghan Army.

16-3e The Civil War in Syria and the Growth of ISIS

In September 2014, the air forces of the United States and five Arab states began a campaign of bombing in Iraq and Syria. The campaign was directed at an organization known as ISIS. President Obama had spent much of his administration attempting to reduce and eventually end

Iraqi soldiers display a captured ISIS flag in November 2016. The soldiers have just recaptured a town outside of Mosul in preparation for retaking the city itself. *Why is the United States reluctant to deploy U.S. infantry in the struggle against ISIS?*

United States interventions in Middle Eastern nations, but now we were back at war. What happened?

The Legacy of the "Arab Spring" Beginning in December 2010, the Arab world was swept by a wave of protests against autocratic rulers. With the sole exception of Tunisia, the protesters failed to win their democratic objectives. In Egypt, the dictator Hosni Mubarak was ousted, but a democratic regime was overthrown by the nation's military. A civil war in Libya dislodged the dictator Muammar Gaddafi, but Libyans thereafter were unable to establish an effective national government. (The rebels were greatly aided by international air support organized by President Obama.)

The Civil War in Syria Protests in Syria developed into a civil war, as rebels attempted to forcibly overthrow the regime of Bashar al-Assad. By 2017, the fighting had killed more than 400,000 Syrians. More than 11 million out of a total population of 23 million had been driven from their homes. Of these, more than 6 million were displaced within Syria and about 5 million had been driven out of the country altogether. Almost 3 million were in Turkey alone. Many people around the world called for Western intervention to assist the rebels, but aid was limited. A problem for the United States and its allies was

ISIS The Islamic State in Iraq and Greater Syria—a terrorist organization that by 2014 had taken over substantial portions of Iraq and Syria. Also known as *ISIL* (the Islamic State in Iraq and the Levant) or the Islamic State.

that only a minority of the rebels could be called pro-democratic. Others were Islamists of varying levels of radicalism.

The Rise of ISIS The most radical faction fighting in Syria was called ISIS, short for the "Islamic State in Iraq and Greater Syria." An alternative transliteration of the Arabic is ISIL, the "Islamic State in Iraq and the Levant." (Both "Greater Syria" and "the Levant" refer to the lands on the eastern shore of the Mediterranean from the Gaza Strip north to Syria proper.) As the name indicates, ISIS was active in both Syria and Iraq. In fact, ISIS is a reorganized version of the group once known as al Qaeda in Iraq. In February 2014, however, al Qaeda expelled ISIS, citing the group's brutality.

ISIS Attacks Iraq. In June 2014, ISIS swept through northern Iraq, almost to Baghdad. The Iraqi army fled, despite outnumbering ISIS forces greatly. ISIS changed its name to simply "the Islamic State" and set up a government in the Iraqi city of Mosul. When its forces threatened to overrun the autonomous Kurdish region in Northern Iraq, President Obama provided air support to the Kurds.

Obama and the Iraqi Government. The advance of ISIS through Iraq was aided by the hostility felt by Sunnis toward the government of Iraq, which had mistreated them. Initially, Obama held off on direct support for the Iraqi government because he did not want America to provide a "Shiite air force" that protected sectarian interests within Iraq. After the Iraqi government was reorganized in an attempt to conciliate the Sunnis, however, the United States agreed to provide it air support. Obama promised the American people that the United States would not provide "boots on the ground"—infantry forces would need to be organized by the Iraqis themselves. By 2016, ISIS was losing territory in Iraq and Syria. Possibly in response, the group had also initiated a new strategy—terrorist attacks on Western nations such as France and Belgium.

By 2017, Iraqi forces had retaken Mosul and were fighting to seize the rest. Iraqis were uncertain, however, about what policies President Trump might adopt in the future. Trump had said that the United States should not have entered Iraq in the first place. Yet he also promised massive bombings of ISIS. As president, Trump initially said little about Iraq, and he did not appear to be making major policy changes.

▶ *Sometimes, it is possible to negotiate with certain terrorist groups, such as the Irish Republican Army, and "bring them in from the cold." Why might such a strategy be impossible with ISIS?*

16–4 DIPLOMACY IN AN UNSTABLE WORLD

LO Describe issues that the government has handled primarily through diplomacy, including the Israeli-Palestinian conflict, curbing weapons of mass destruction, and the rise of China as a world power.

> "The purpose of foreign policy is not to provide an outlet for our own sentiments of hope or indignation; it is to shape real events in a real world."
>
> ~ JOHN F. KENNEDY, THIRTY-FIFTH PRESIDENT OF THE UNITED STATES, 1961–1963

Given the death and destruction that result from the use of military force, there is much to be said for resolving problems through diplomacy whenever possible. Diplomacy, however, can involve the use of nonviolent coercive measures, such as sanctions that limit a target nation's ability to participate in the world economy. In the past, sanctions have been used to pressure nations ranging from South Africa under the apartheid system through Hussein's Iraq to Cuba.

Diplomacy can also be important in addressing problems with nations that are friendly to or even allied with us. Economic and social problems experienced by our European allies, for example, have been a source of concern. We look at Europe's problems in this chapter's *The Rest of the World* feature. We discuss other diplomatic issues in the following sections.

16–4a The Israeli-Palestinian Conflict

The long-running conflict between Israel and its Arab neighbors has poisoned the atmosphere in the Middle East for more than half a century. American presidents dating back at least to Richard Nixon (1969–1974) have attempted to persuade the parties to reach a settlement. Obama and Trump are only the latest American leaders to address the problem.

The Arab-Israeli Wars For many years after Israel was founded in 1948, the neighboring Arab states did not accept its legitimacy as a nation. The result was a series of wars between Israel and those states, including Egypt, Jordan, and Syria, waged in 1948, 1956, 1967, and 1973. Following the 1948 Arab-Israeli War, a large number of Palestinians—Arab residents of the area known as Palestine until 1948—were forced into exile, adding to Arab grievances.

The failure of the Arab states in the 1967 war led to additional Palestinian refugees and the rise of the

Palestine Liberation Organization (PLO), a nonstate body committed to armed struggle against Israel. In the late 1960s and early 1970s, Palestinian groups launched a wave of terrorist attacks against Israeli targets around the world.

Following the 1973 Yom Kippur War, Egyptian president Anwar el-Sadat launched a major peace initiative. U.S. president Jimmy Carter (1977–1981) then sponsored intensive negotiations. Egypt and Israel signed a peace treaty in 1979 that marked the end of an era of major wars between Israel and other states. Lower-level conflicts continued, however. Israel and Jordan eventually signed a peace treaty in 1994, but no peace treaty between Israel and Syria has yet been negotiated, and the conflict between Israel and the Palestinians continues.

Israel and the Palestinians Resolving the Israeli-Palestinian dispute has always presented more difficulties than achieving peace between Israel and neighbors such as Egypt. One problem is that the hostilities between the two parties run deeper.

Israeli and Palestinian Grievances. On the Palestinian side, many families lost their homes after the 1948 war. Then, after the 1967 war, the West Bank of the Jordan River and the Gaza Strip fell under Israeli control, and the Palestinians living in these areas became an occupied people.

On the Israeli side, the sheer viciousness of the Palestinian terrorist attacks—which frequently resulted in the deaths of civilians, including children—made negotiations with those responsible hard to imagine.

> **Palestine Liberation Organization (PLO)** An organization formed in 1964 to represent the Palestinian people. The PLO has a long history of terrorism but for some years has functioned primarily as a political party.

THE REST OF THE WORLD

Europe in Crisis

During presidential election years, you'll hear plenty about our nation's problems. But how are other nations doing? Consider the twenty-eight nations of the European Union (EU). They have a level of development comparable to that of the United States. And they have some large problems.

The Refugee Crisis

Immigration has become a huge issue in Europe. Of course, immigration is also an issue in the United States. Still, the number of people who are in the United States illegally has at least stopped growing. In 2015, more than a million refugees entered Europe, the largest number headed for Germany. (Beginning in 2016, however, the flow of asylum-seekers slowed, in part because of a deal with Turkey, through which many of the refugees had come.)

These refugees had fled their home countries because of war, death threats, and religious persecution. Many are from Syria, but others are from Afghanistan, Iraq, and the nations of Africa. The refugees are often Muslim, and assimilation is not easy. For example, the newcomers often have beliefs about the role of women that are far from the European norm.

Terrorist Attacks

Terrorist attacks are a concern in America, but the problem is worse in Europe. U.S. Muslims are relatively well assimilated. In contrast, the EU has a large population of impoverished and poorly integrated Muslims, including many alienated young men. This provides a natural recruiting ground for the jihadi terrorists who recently struck in Paris and Nice in France.

The Wages of Austerity

Nineteen members of the EU share a common currency, the euro. They are members of the *Eurozone*. Following the world economic crisis of 2008, however, evidence began to accumulate that the design of the Eurozone was catastrophically flawed. Members of the zone had never adopted the common institutions that would have been necessary to make it work.

Further, a program of *austerity*—enforced by leading nations such as Germany—made it impossible for individual nations to use monetary or fiscal policy to stimulate their economies. This was a serious problem for the zone's weakest members, such as Ireland, Portugal, Spain, and above all Greece. The United States, in contrast, was much more effective at shaking off the effects of the Great Recession.

Notably, the Fed adopted an aggressive monetary policy.

Britain Leaves the Union

Despite severe pressures, Greece held on and stayed in the Eurozone. The British, at the opposite end of the EU, had other ideas. Britain always considered itself distinct from the rest of Europe—in particular, it never adopted the euro. Immigration, terrorism, and financial crises surely made the EU even less attractive. In 2016, Britain held a referendum on whether to leave the EU altogether—a step known as *Brexit*. The vote was close, but Brexit won. EU leaders vowed to make Britain's departure as painful as possible, as a warning to others. In effect, European unity would depend in part on fear of punishment, not just the attraction of shared values. Unity on such a basis, however, can never be fully secure.

Critical Analysis

The twenty-eight EU countries (soon to be twenty-seven) have a variety of cultures and languages. How hard would it be for the United States to remain a union if it had more than twenty official languages?

A further complication was the Israeli settlements on the West Bank, which the Palestinians considered their own. Israeli settlers on the West Bank had an obvious interest in opposing any peace deal that required them to move.

International Principles. Despite the difficulties, the international community, including the United States, was in agreement on several principles for settling the conflict. Lands seized by Israel in the 1967 war should be restored to the Palestinians, who could organize their own independent nation-state there. In turn, the Palestinians would have to recognize Israel's right to exist and take concrete steps to guarantee Israel's security.

The international consensus, however, did not address some important issues. These include what compensation, if any, should go to Palestinians who lost homes in what is now Israel. In fact, the Palestinian leadership has never abandoned its demand that the descendants of Palestinians forced out of Israel be allowed to return. Still, it is generally recognized that this demand must be given up as part of a final deal. A second issue is whether Israel could adjust its borders to incorporate some of the Israeli settlement areas, plus part or all of eastern Jerusalem, which had been under Arab control before 1967.

Negotiations   In 1993 in Oslo, Norway, Israel and the PLO met officially for the first time. The resulting Oslo Accords were signed in Washington under the watchful eye of President Bill Clinton. A major result was the establishment of a Palestinian Authority, under Israeli control, on the West Bank and the Gaza Strip.

Negotiations Collapse.   In 2000, talks between Israel and the Palestinian Authority collapsed in acrimony. After the failure of these talks, an uprising by Palestinian militants led to Israeli military incursions into the West Bank and the temporary collapse of the Palestinian Authority. In 2005, Israeli prime minister Ariel Sharon carried out a plan to unilaterally withdraw from the Gaza Strip and to build an enormous security fence between Israel and the West Bank. The fence came under strong international criticism because it incorporated parts of the West Bank into Israel.

A Divided Palestine.   Gaza was taken over in 2007 by Hamas, a radical Islamist party that refuses to recognize Israel. The West Bank remained under the control of the PLO-led Palestinian Authority, and so the Palestinians, now politically divided, were in an even worse bargaining position than before. Attempts by the United States to restart talks between the Israelis and Palestinians collapsed in 2014. By 2015, the United States had given up, at least temporarily, on attempts to restart the peace process. In 2017, President Trump announced his desire to reopen peace talks. Trump, however, was likely to face the same problems in achieving peace that have troubled previous presidents.

16-4b Weapons of Mass Destruction

The Cold War may be over, but the threat of nuclear warfare—which formed the backdrop of foreign policy during the Cold War—has by no means disappeared. The existence of nuclear weapons in Russia and in other countries around the world continues to challenge U.S. foreign policymakers.

Concerns about nuclear proliferation mounted in 1998 when India and Pakistan detonated nuclear devices

Palestinian and Jewish antiwar activists hug during a peace rally. The gathering was organized following the death of a Palestinian child in an arson attack. *What issues stand in the way of peace between the Israelis and the Palestinians?*

Hasem Bader/AFP/Getty Images

within a few weeks of each other. Increasingly, American officials have focused on the threat of an attack by a rogue nation or a terrorist group that possesses weapons of mass destruction. Of most concern recently have been attempts by North Korea and Iran to develop nuclear capabilities and the use of chemical weapons by the Assad regime in Syria.

North Korea's Nuclear Program   North Korea signed the Treaty on the Non-Proliferation of Nuclear Weapons in 1985 and submitted to weapons inspections by the International Atomic Energy Agency (IAEA) in 1992. Throughout the 1990s, however, there were discrepancies between North Korean declarations and IAEA inspection findings. In 2002, North Korea expelled the IAEA inspectors.

Opening Negotiations. The administration of George W. Bush insisted that any talks with North Korea must also include all of North Korea's

> **Oslo Accords** The first agreement signed between Israel and the PLO. The accords led to the establishment of the Palestinian Authority in the occupied territories.

The launch of a North Korean intermediate-range ballistic missile in May 2017. It can reach South Korea, Japan, the U.S. island of Guam, Russia's Far East, and most of China. North Korea is developing nuclear devices compact enough to fit on such a missile. *Why would North Korea want nuclear weapons?*

new series of tests involving nuclear weapons and long-range missiles. One of the missiles, if ever perfected, would be able to reach the U.S. mainland. In response, Trump described North Korea as our number-one military threat. In talks with Chinese leaders, Trump offered to abandon some trade grievances with China in exchange for Chinese help in dealing with North Korea. In fact, China responded to North Korea's tests by halting coal imports from that country. (This was not a difficult step, because China was suffering from a coal glut.) Chinese leaders also explained to Trump that their leverage over North Korea was limited.

Indeed, China was greatly concerned with the belligerence of Kim Jong-un, North Korea's latest leader. Yet China also had a major interest in ensuring that the North Korea regime did not collapse altogether. Such an event would drive thousands of refugees across the border into China. It could also result in a unified Korea, allied to the United States, immediately on China's border.

neighbors—China, Japan, Russia, and South Korea. In 2003, North Korea finally agreed to such talks.

Since that time, it has proved quite difficult to keep North Korea at the bargaining table—its representatives have stormed out of the talks repeatedly, for the most trivial reasons. China is the one power with substantial economic leverage over North Korea, and typically, Chinese leaders have been the ones to lead the North Koreans back to the table.

Tensions heightened in 2006, when North Korea conducted its first nuclear test. In the spring of 2007, North Korea agreed that it would begin to dismantle its nuclear facilities and would allow inspectors from the United Nations (UN) into the country. In return, the other nations agreed to provide various kinds of aid.

The Collapse of Negotiations. In 2009, North Korea tested a long-range missile under the guise of attempting to launch a satellite. The UN Security Council voted unanimously to condemn the test. North Korea then pulled out of the six-party talks and expelled all nuclear inspectors from the country.

After a third missile test in 2013, China for the first time imposed significant economic sanctions on North Korea. The UN Security Council imposed its own sanctions, which led to an explosion of violent rhetoric from the northern regime.

North Korea, China, and Trump. Following the inauguration of President Trump, North Korea engaged in a

Iran: An Emerging Nuclear Threat? In recent years, the world has learned Iran was engaged in a covert nuclear program. Investigators for the International Atomic Energy Agency reported that Iran was enriching uranium that could be used in the fabrication of a nuclear bomb.

Iran as a Security Threat. Like North Korea, Iran has been openly hostile to the United States. In addition, Mahmoud Ahmadinejad, president of Iran from 2005 to 2013, repeatedly called for the complete destruction of Israel. It is no surprise, therefore, that Israel considers Iranian nuclear weapons to be a threat to its existence. Perhaps more surprising is that Iran's Arab neighbors consider these weapons a threat as well. Leaked U.S. diplomatic cables reveal that Arab leaders have urged the United States to take out the Iranian nuclear program by force.

War or Peace? When negotiations with Iran appeared to be going nowhere, the United States and its allies increasingly turned to coercive measures. These included sanctions, imposed by the United States, the European Union, and the United Nations. The United States was able to persuade or pressure a majority of the world's nations not to buy Iran's oil. The United States was also able to cut Iran off from the international banking system. This step made it extremely difficult for Iran to finance imports and exports. By 2013, the Iranian economy was in serious trouble.

Another coercive measure would be to bomb Iran's nuclear sites. In 2008, Israel began preparations that would allow it to launch such a strike if necessary. After Benjamin Netanyahu became prime minister of Israel in 2009, he called for air strikes with increasing urgency. One type of attack, in fact, was launched immediately. In 2010, a sophisticated U.S. computer "worm" took down about a thousand of the five thousand centrifuges used in Iran's uranium enrichment program. Many were completely destroyed.

Again, Negotiations. In 2013, Iran elected a new president, Hassan Rouhani. In short order, Rouhani initiated a charm offensive aimed at reestablishing diplomatic negotiations. The new leader repudiated the anti-Israel rhetoric of previous Iranian president Ahmadinejad.

Serious negotiations soon began between Iran and six other nations: Britain, China, France, Germany, Russia, and the United States. In November 2013, Iran and the multinational team announced a six-month interim deal. Iran would freeze parts of its nuclear program in return for the lifting of some sanctions.

Finally, in July 2015, Iran and the six world powers came to an agreement. Under the terms of the deal, Iran would be able to hold only about half the uranium needed to make one bomb. Its number of centrifuges would be reduced dramatically. International representatives would have the right to demand inspections of Iranian nuclear facilities. In return for these measures, all sanctions tied to Iran's nuclear program would be lifted. Certain U.S. sanctions not tied to the nuclear program remain in effect, however.

Opposition to the Deal. Given that the agreement was signed by six world powers and the European Union, it clearly had international support. The agreement had its opponents, however, including Israeli prime minister Benjamin Netanyahu.

The opponents of the deal had two problems. One was that rejecting the deal would effectively remove all limits on Iran's nuclear program. The second was that

The Ayatollah Ali Khamenei, supreme leader of Iran. *Why is he, and not Iran's president, the supreme leader?*

"no deal" would lead to the collapse of the sanctions, because nations other than the United States would no longer agree to impose them. The only realistic options for blocking an Iranian bomb would then be military. As a presidential candidate, Donald Trump had promised to pull the United States out of the deal. As president, he abandoned such a move.

Use of Chemical Weapons by Syria Most nations have signed treaties banning the use of chemical weapons—they were, in fact, one of the few instruments of horror that were never used on the battlefield in World War II.[4] Only a handful of nations have refused to sign, including North Korea, Iraq (under Saddam Hussein), and Syria. In August 2013, the government of Syria used the nerve gas sarin against residents of Damascus suburbs that were under the control of antiregime rebels. The attack killed more than a thousand civilians. Syrian dictator Bashar al-Assad may have used chemical weapons earlier, but this incident was so conspicuous that it could not be ignored.

President Obama equivocated over punishing the Assad regime for its use of poison gas by launching air strikes. In September, however, the government of Russia announced that Syria was willing to sign the Chemical Weapons Convention, a treaty governing chemical weapons, and place its weapons under international control. This initiative was a diplomatic triumph for Russian president Vladimir Putin.

Chinese President Xi Jinping. Xi has launched a major crackdown on official corruption in China. *Why might the absence of democracy foster corruption among Chinese officials?*

By October 2013, to the surprise of many, the Assad regime appeared to be cooperating with international inspectors. The chemical weapons were removed from Syria to a U.S. ship equipped with special decontamination systems. In August 2014, President Obama announced that the destruction of the weapons was complete.

In 2015, however, Assad's forces apparently used chlorine gas to attack rebels. Chlorine has many industrial uses and is not a controlled substance. Employing it as a weapon, though, violates the Chemical Weapons Convention.

In April 2017, the Assad regime dropped the nerve gas sarin on a rebel-held town in northern Syria. The attack killed at least seventy-four people, many of them children. Clearly, either Assad had failed to yield up all of his chemical weapons or he had managed to secure new supplies. In response, President Trump employed cruise missiles to bomb the airbase from which the attack took place. Trump's action appeared to be a one-time effort, however. Russia's Putin condemned the American response.

16-4c China—The Next Superpower?

A major challenge to the United States may be the growing importance of China. Following President Richard Nixon's historic visit to China in 1972, American diplomatic and economic relations with the Chinese gradually improved. Diplomacy with China focused on cultivating a more pro-Western disposition in the formerly isolationist nation. Relations with China are important in part because until recently, that nation has enjoyed economic growth averaging almost 10 percent a year for more than thirty years in a row. Such growth has turned China into a great power.

Chinese-American Trade Relations China has one of the fastest-growing economies in the world, along with a population of 1.3 billion. Measured in terms of purchasing power, its gross domestic product (GDP) surpassed that of the United States in 2014. In terms of its own currency, China's GDP is *two hundred times* what it was in 1978, when China implemented reforms to make the economy more market oriented. Never in the history of the world have so many people been lifted out of poverty so quickly.

China's rapid growth has been fueled in part by an enormous manufacturing export sector. One result is that Americans can buy Chinese products for much less than U.S.-manufactured goods would cost. Toys, electronics, hardware, clothing, and many other items are cheaper than they otherwise would be. The flip side is that the American workers who used to make such products lost their jobs. Studies have shown that workers who lose employment due to foreign competition have a hard time recovering. It is no surprise, therefore, that in the 2016 presidential race, many candidates criticized imports. Donald Trump in particular demanded huge cuts in foreign trade.

The Issue of Taiwan Although China has not demonstrated any ambition to acquire non-Chinese territory, it has a rather expansive definition of what Chinese territory is. China considers Taiwan, a former Chinese province, to be a legal part of China. In practice, however, since 1949 the island has functioned as an independent nation. The United States has historically supported a free and separate Taiwan and has stated that any reunion of China and Taiwan must come about by peaceful means.

Recent Chinese Nationalism In recent years, China has exhibited nationalist tendencies that have alarmed some of its neighbors. China is engaged in a territorial dispute with Japan over uninhabited islands in the East China Sea. China has also claimed almost all of the uninhabited islands located in the South China Sea, even ones that are a considerable distance from the Chinese mainland. These claims have resulted in military confrontations with the Philippines and Vietnam.

In 2012, President Obama announced a "pivot" to East Asia. The pivot involves shifting naval resources into the region and negotiating enhanced security relationships with area nations. China's response was to accuse the United States of attempting to "contain" China.

Within China itself, nationalism has often taken the form of discrimination against minority nationalities. These include the people of Tibet and also the Uighurs, a Muslim people in the western region of Xinjiang. Both Tibet and Xinjiang have experienced very large inflows of the majority Chinese group, known as *Han Chinese*. Many Tibetans and Uighurs believe that they are becoming oppressed minorities within their own countries. As a result, disturbances have been common.

CRITICAL THINKING

▶ *If we have strong trade relations with a country, does that make it less likely that we would ever go to war with that country? Why or why not?*

AMERICA AT ODDS | Foreign Policy

In 1947, Republican senator Arthur Vandenberg of Michigan announced, "Politics stops at the water's edge." By this, Vandenberg, formerly a fierce isolationist, meant that Republicans and Democrats should cooperate in dealing with such foreign policy issues as the Cold War with the Soviet Union.

Bipartisanship is less common now than it was in Vandenberg's day. True, the two major parties are more likely to cooperate over a foreign policy issue than over domestic policy. Nevertheless, Americans are at odds over many foreign policy issues, as reflected in Congress. The following are a few of these issues:

- *In foreign policy, is it best to ally with other nations whenever possible—or should America carefully guard its ability to act alone?*

- *Should the president take complete charge of the foreign policy process, including the use of armed force—or should the president collaborate closely with Congress?*

- *Should the war on terrorism be the central focus of U.S. foreign policy—or should we devote equal energy to managing our relations with rising powers such as China?*

- *Should the United States take a firm line with Russia over Ukraine, or is it more important to head off a new Cold War?*

- *In attempting to promote peace between Israelis and Palestinians, should the United States put most of its pressure on the Palestinians—or should it also pressure the Israelis to, for example, suspend the construction of new Jewish settlements in the West Bank?*

- *Is the recent nuclear arms agreement between Iran and six world powers a blessing—or a catastrophe?*

STUDY TOOLS 16

READY TO STUDY? IN THE BOOK, YOU CAN:

☐ Review what you've read with the following chapter quiz.

☐ Check your answers in Appendix D at the back of the book.

☐ Rip out the Chapter Review Card, which includes key terms and chapter summaries.

ONLINE AT WWW.CENGAGEBRAIN.COM, YOU CAN:

☐ Watch videos to get a quick overview.

☐ Expedite your studying with Major Player readings and Focus Activities.

☐ Check your understanding with Chapter Quizzes.

FILL-IN

Learning Outcome 16–1

1. The executive departments and other government agencies that are most directly involved in foreign policy include the _____.

Learning Outcome 16–2

2. The nation's founders and the early presidents believed that a policy of _____ was the best way to protect American interests.

3. The _____ was a war of words, warnings, and ideologies between the Soviet Union and the United States that lasted from the late 1940s through the late 1980s.

Learning Outcome 16–3

4. In 2001, supported by a coalition of allies, the U.S. military attacked al Qaeda camps in _____ and the ruling Taliban regime that harbored those terrorists.

5. In 2011, U.S. Navy Seals killed Osama bin Laden in Abbottabad, a city in _____.

Learning Outcome 16–4

6. The 1993 Oslo Accords led to the establishment of the _____ in the occupied territories.

7. American officials are most concerned about nuclear proliferation in the countries of _____.

8. The danger exists of a possible future crisis in U.S.-Chinese relations over the status of _____.

MULTIPLE CHOICE

9. The power to declare war belongs to
   a. the president.
   b. Congress.
   c. the Joint Chiefs of Staff.

Learning Outcome 16–2

10. Direct involvement by one country in another country's affairs best describes
    a. political realism.
    b. collective security.
    c. interventionism.

11. Actions taken under the Truman Doctrine and the Marshall Plan marked the beginning of a policy of
    a. containment.
    b. deterrence.
    c. mutually assured destruction.

Learning Outcome 16–3

12. The phrase *weapons of mass destruction* refers to
    a. landmines and cluster munitions.
    b. improvised explosive devices (IEDs).
    c. chemical, biological, and nuclear weapons.

Learning Outcome 16–4

13. For many years after Israel was founded in 1948,
    a. the neighboring Arab states did not accept its legitimacy as a nation.
    b. the only peace treaty that it was able to negotiate was one with Syria.
    c. it lived in peace with its neighbors in the Middle East.

14. During 2010, a sophisticated computer "worm" attacked centrifuges used in _____ uranium enrichment program.
    a. North Korea's
    b. Iran's
    c. Israel's

THE DECLARATION OF INDEPENDENCE

IN CONGRESS, JULY 4, 1776

A Declaration by the Representatives of the United States of America, in General Congress assembled. When in the Course of human Events, it becomes necessary for one People to dissolve the Political Bands which have connected them with another, and to assume among the Powers of the Earth, the separate and equal Station to which the Laws of Nature and of Nature's God entitle them, a decent Respect to the Opinions of Mankind requires that they should declare the causes which impel them to the Separation.

We hold these Truths to be self-evident, that all Men are created equal, that they are endowed by their Creator with certain unalienable Rights, that among these are Life, Liberty, and the Pursuit of Happiness—That to secure these Rights, Governments are instituted among Men, deriving their just Powers from the Consent of the Governed, that whenever any Form of Government becomes destructive of these Ends, it is the Right of the People to alter or to abolish it, and to institute new Government, laying its Foundation on such Principles, and organizing its Powers in such Forms, as to them shall seem most likely to effect their Safety and Happiness. Prudence, indeed, will dictate that Governments long established should not be changed for light and transient Causes; and accordingly all Experience hath shewn, that Mankind are more disposed to suffer, while Evils are sufferable, than to right themselves by abolishing the Forms to which they are accustomed. But when a long Train of Abuses and Usurpations, pursuing invariably the same Object, evinces a Design to reduce them under absolute Despotism, it is their Right, it is their Duty, to throw off such Government, and to provide new Guards for their future Security. Such has been the patient Sufferance of these Colonies; and such is now the Necessity which constrains them to alter their former Systems of Government. The History of the present King of Great-Britain is a History of repeated Injuries and Usurpations, all having in direct Object the Establishment of an absolute Tyranny over these States. To prove this, let Facts be submitted to a candid World.

He has refused his Assent to Laws, the most wholesome and necessary for the public Good.

He has forbidden his Governors to pass Laws of immediate and pressing Importance, unless suspended in their Operation till his Assent should be obtained; and when so suspended, he has utterly neglected to attend to them.

He has refused to pass other Laws for the Accommodation of large Districts of People, unless those People would relinquish the Right of Representation in the Legislature, a Right inestimable to them, and formidable to Tyrants only.

He has called together Legislative Bodies at Places unusual, uncomfortable, and distant from the Depository of their Public Records, for the sole Purpose of fatiguing them into Compliance with his Measures.

He has dissolved Representative Houses repeatedly, for opposing with manly Firmness his Invasions on the Rights of the People.

He has refused for a long Time, after such Dissolutions, to cause others to be elected; whereby the Legislative Powers, incapable of Annihilation, have returned to the People at large for their exercise; the State remaining in the mean time exposed to all the Dangers of Invasion from without, and Convulsions within.

He has endeavoured to prevent the Population of these States; for that Purpose obstructing the Laws for Naturalization of Foreigners; refusing to pass others to encourage their Migrations hither, and raising the Conditions of new Appropriations of Lands.

He has obstructed the Administration of Justice, by refusing his Assent to Laws for establishing Judiciary Powers.

He has made Judges dependent on his Will alone, for the Tenure of their offices, and the Amount and payment of their Salaries.

He has erected a Multitude of new Offices, and sent hither Swarms of Officers to harrass our People, and eat out their Substance.

He has kept among us, in Times of Peace, Standing Armies, without the consent of our Legislatures.

He has affected to render the Military independent of, and superior to the Civil Power.

He has combined with others to subject us to a Jurisdiction foreign to our Constitution, and unacknowledged by our Laws; giving his Assent to their Acts of pretended Legislation:

For quartering large Bodies of Armed Troops among us:

For protecting them, by a mock Trial, from Punishment for any Murders which they should commit on the Inhabitants of these States:

For cutting off our Trade with all Parts of the World:

For imposing Taxes on us without our Consent:

For depriving us, in many cases, of the Benefits of Trial by Jury:

For transporting us beyond Seas to be tried for pretended Offences:

For abolishing the free System of English Laws in a neighbouring Province, establishing therein an arbitrary Government, and enlarging its Boundaries, so as to render it at once an Example and fit Instrument for introducing the same absolute Rule into these Colonies:

For taking away our Charters, abolishing our most valuable Laws, and altering fundamentally the Forms of our Governments:

For suspending our own Legislatures, and declaring themselves invested with Power to legislate for us in all Cases whatsoever.

He has abdicated Government here, by declaring us out of his Protection and waging War against us.

He has plundered our Seas, ravaged our Coasts, burnt our towns, and destroyed the Lives of our People.

He is, at this Time, transporting large Armies of foreign Mercenaries to compleat the works of Death, Desolation, and Tyranny, already begun with circumstances of Cruelty and Perfidy, scarcely parallelled in the most barbarous Ages, and totally unworthy the Head of a civilized Nation.

He has constrained our fellow Citizens taken Captive on the high Seas to bear Arms against their Country, to become the Executioners of their Friends and Brethren, or to fall themselves by their Hands.

He has excited domestic Insurrections amongst us, and has endeavoured to bring on the Inhabitants of our Frontiers, the merciless Indian Savages, whose known Rule of Warfare, is an undistinguished Destruction, of all Ages, Sexes and Conditions.

In every state of these Oppressions we have Petitioned for Redress in the most humble Terms: Our repeated Petitions have been answered only by repeated Injury. A Prince, whose Character is thus marked by every act which may define a Tyrant, is unfit to be the Ruler of a free People.

Nor have we been wanting in Attentions to our British Brethren. We have warned them from Time to Time of Attempts by their Legislature to extend an unwarrantable Jurisdiction over us. We have reminded them of the Circumstances of our Emigration and Settlement here. We have appealed to their native Justice and Magnanimity, and we have conjured them by the Ties of our common Kindred to disavow these Usurpations, which, would inevitably interrupt our Connections and Correspondence. They too have been deaf to the Voice of Justice and of Consanguinity. We must, therefore, acquiesce in the Necessity, which denounces our Separation, and hold them, as we hold the rest of Mankind, Enemies in War, in Peace, Friends.

We, therefore, the Representatives of the UNITED STATES OF AMERICA, in General Congress Assembled, appealing to the Supreme Judge of the World for the Rectitude of our Intentions, do, in the Name, and by the Authority of the good People of these Colonies, solemnly Publish and Declare, That these United Colonies are, and of Right ought to be, Free and Independent States; that they are absolved from all Allegiance to the British Crown, and that all political Connection between them and the State of Great-Britain, is and ought to be totally dissolved; and that as Free and Independent States, they have full Power to levy War, conclude Peace, contract Alliances, establish Commerce, and to do all other Acts and Things which Independent States may of right do. And for the support of this declaration, with a firm Reliance on the Protection of divine Providence, we mutually pledge to each other our lives, our Fortunes, and our sacred Honor.

THE CONSTITUTION OF THE UNITED STATES

PREAMBLE

We the People of the United States, in Order to form a more perfect Union, establish Justice, insure domestic Tranquility, provide for the common defence, promote the general Welfare, and secure the Blessings of Liberty to ourselves and our Posterity, do ordain and establish this Constitution for the United States of America.

ARTICLE I

Section 1. All legislative Powers herein granted shall be vested in a Congress of the United States, which shall consist of a Senate and House of Representatives.

Section 2. The House of Representatives shall be composed of Members chosen every second Year by the People of the several States, and the Electors in each State shall have the Qualifications requisite for Electors of the most numerous Branch of the State Legislature.

No Person shall be a Representative who shall not have attained to the Age of twenty five Years, and been seven Years a Citizen of the United States, and who shall not, when elected, be an Inhabitant of that State in which he shall be chosen.

Representatives and direct Taxes shall be apportioned among the several States which may be included within this Union, according to their respective Numbers, which shall be determined by adding to the whole Number of free Persons, including those bound to Service for a Term of Years, and excluding Indians not taxed, three fifths of all other Persons. The actual Enumeration shall be made within three Years after the first Meeting of the Congress of the United States, and within every subsequent Term of ten Years, in such Manner as they shall by Law direct. The Number of Representatives shall not exceed one for every thirty Thousand, but each State shall have at Least one Representative; and until such enumeration shall be made, the State of New Hampshire shall be entitled to chuse three, Massachusetts eight, Rhode Island and Providence Plantations one, Connecticut five, New York six, New Jersey four, Pennsylvania eight, Delaware one, Maryland six, Virginia ten, North Carolina five, South Carolina five, and Georgia three.

When vacancies happen in the Representation from any State, the Executive Authority thereof shall issue Writs of Election to fill such Vacancies.

The House of Representatives shall chuse their Speaker and other Officers; and shall have the sole Power of Impeachment.

Section 3. The Senate of the United States shall be composed of two Senators from each State, chosen by the Legislature thereof, for six Years; and each Senator shall have one Vote.

Immediately after they shall be assembled in Consequence of the first Election, they shall be divided as equally as may be into three Classes. The Seats of the Senators of the first Class shall be vacated at the Expiration of the second Year, of the second Class at the Expiration of the fourth Year, and of the third Class at the Expiration of the sixth Year, so that one third may be chosen every second Year; and if Vacancies happen by Resignation, or otherwise, during the Recess of the Legislature of any State, the Executive thereof may make temporary Appointments until the next Meeting of the Legislature, which shall then fill such Vacancies.

No Person shall be a Senator who shall not have attained to the Age of thirty Years, and been nine Years a Citizen of the United States, and who shall not, when elected, be an Inhabitant of that State for which he shall be chosen.

The Vice President of the United States shall be President of the Senate, but shall have no Vote, unless they be equally divided.

The Senate shall chuse their other Officers, and also a President pro tempore, in the Absence of the Vice President, or when he shall exercise the Office of President of the United States.

The Senate shall have the sole Power to try all Impeachments. When sitting for that Purpose, they shall be on Oath or Affirmation. When the President of the United States is tried, the Chief Justice shall preside: And no Person shall be convicted without the Concurrence of two thirds of the Members present.

Judgment in Cases of Impeachment shall not extend further than to removal from Office, and disqualification to hold and enjoy any Office of honor, Trust, or Profit under the United States: but the Party convicted shall nevertheless be liable and subject to Indictment, Trial, Judgment, and Punishment, according to Law.

Section 4. The Times, Places and Manner of holding Elections for Senators and Representatives, shall be prescribed in each State by the Legislature thereof; but the Congress may at any time by Law make or alter such Regulations, except as to the Places of chusing Senators.

The Congress shall assemble at least once in every Year, and such Meeting shall be on the first Monday in December, unless they shall by Law appoint a different Day.

Section 5. Each House shall be the Judge of the Elections, Returns, and Qualifications of its own Members, and a Majority of each shall constitute a Quorum to do Business; but a smaller Number may adjourn from day to day, and may be authorized to compel the Attendance of absent Members, in such Manner, and under such Penalties as each House may provide.

Each House may determine the Rules of its Proceedings, punish its Members for disorderly Behavior, and, with the Concurrence of two thirds, expel a Member.

Each House shall keep a Journal of its Proceedings, and from time to time publish the same, excepting such Parts as may in their Judgment require Secrecy; and the Yeas and Nays of the Members of either House on any question shall, at the Desire of one fifth of those Present, be entered on the Journal.

Neither House, during the Session of Congress, shall, without the Consent of the other, adjourn for more than three days, nor to any other Place than that in which the two Houses shall be sitting.

Section 6. The Senators and Representatives shall receive a Compensation for their Services, to be ascertained by Law, and paid out of the Treasury of the United States. They shall in all Cases, except Treason, Felony and Breach of the Peace, be privileged from Arrest during their Attendance at the Session of their respective Houses, and in going to and returning from the same; and for any Speech or Debate in either House, they shall not be questioned in any other Place.

No Senator or Representative shall, during the Time for which he was elected, be appointed to any civil Office under the Authority of the United States, which shall have been created, or the Emoluments whereof shall have been increased during such time; and no Person holding any Office under the United States, shall be a Member of either House during his Continuance in Office.

Section 7. All Bills for raising Revenue shall originate in the House of Representatives; but the Senate may propose or concur with Amendments as on other Bills.

Every Bill which shall have passed the House of Representatives and the Senate, shall, before it become a Law, be presented to the President of the United States; If he approve he shall sign it, but if not he shall return it, with his Objections to the House in which it shall have originated, who shall enter the Objections at large on their Journal, and proceed to reconsider it. If after such Reconsideration two thirds of that House shall agree to pass the Bill, it shall be sent together with the Objections, to the other House, by which it shall likewise be reconsidered, and if approved by two thirds of that House, it shall become a Law. But in all such Cases the Votes of both Houses shall be determined by Yeas and Nays, and the Names of the Persons voting for and against the Bill shall be entered on the Journal of each House respectively. If any Bill shall not be returned by the President within ten Days (Sundays excepted) after it shall have been presented to him, the Same shall be a Law, in like Manner as if he had signed it,

unless the Congress by their Adjournment prevent its Return in which Case it shall not be a Law.

Every Order, Resolution, or Vote, to which the Concurrence of the Senate and House of Representatives may be necessary (except on a question of Adjournment) shall be presented to the President of the United States; and before the Same shall take Effect, shall be approved by him, or being disapproved by him, shall be repassed by two thirds of the Senate and House of Representatives, according to the Rules and Limitations prescribed in the Case of a Bill.

Section 8. The Congress shall have Power To lay and collect Taxes, Duties, Imposts and Excises, to pay the Debts and provide for the common Defence and general Welfare of the United States; but all Duties, Imposts and Excises shall be uniform throughout the United States;

To borrow Money on the credit of the United States;

To regulate Commerce with foreign Nations, and among the several States, and with the Indian Tribes;

To establish an uniform Rule of Naturalization, and uniform Laws on the subject of Bankruptcies throughout the United States;

To coin Money, regulate the Value thereof, and of foreign Coin, and fix the Standard of Weights and Measures;

To provide for the Punishment of counterfeiting the Securities and current Coin of the United States;

To establish Post Offices and post Roads;

To promote the Progress of Science and useful Arts, by securing for limited Times to Authors and Inventors the exclusive Right to their respective Writings and Discoveries;

To constitute Tribunals inferior to the supreme Court;

To define and punish Piracies and Felonies committed on the high Seas, and Offenses against the Law of Nations;

To declare War, grant Letters of Marque and Reprisal, and make Rules concerning Captures on Land and Water;

To raise and support Armies, but no Appropriation of Money to that Use shall be for a longer Term than two Years;

To provide and maintain a Navy;

To make Rules for the Government and Regulation of the land and naval Forces;

To provide for calling forth the Militia to execute the Laws of the Union, suppress Insurrections and repel Invasions;

To provide for organizing, arming, and disciplining, the Militia, and for governing such Part of them as may be employed in the Service of the United States, reserving to the States respectively, the Appointment of the Officers, and the Authority of training the Militia according to the discipline prescribed by Congress;

To exercise exclusive Legislation in all Cases whatsoever, over such District (not exceeding ten Miles square) as may, by Cession of particular States, and the Acceptance of Congress, become the Seat of the Government of the United States, and to exercise like Authority over all Places purchased by the Consent of the Legislature of the State in which the Same shall be, for the Erection of Forts, Magazines, Arsenals, dock-Yards, and other needful Buildings;—And

To make all Laws which shall be necessary and proper for carrying into Execution the foregoing Powers, and all other Powers vested by this Constitution in the Government of the United States, or in any Department or Officer thereof.

Section 9. The Migration or Importation of such Persons as any of the States now existing shall think proper to admit, shall not be prohibited by the Congress prior to the Year one thousand eight hundred and eight, but a Tax or duty may be imposed on such Importation, not exceeding ten dollars for each Person.

The privilege of the Writ of Habeas Corpus shall not be suspended, unless when in Cases of Rebellion or Invasion the public Safety may require it.

No Bill of Attainder or ex post facto Law shall be passed.

No Capitation, or other direct, Tax shall be laid, unless in Proportion to the Census or Enumeration herein before directed to be taken.

No Tax or Duty shall be laid on Articles exported from any State.

No Preference shall be given by any Regulation of Commerce or Revenue to the Ports of one State over those of another: nor shall Vessels bound to, or from, one State be obliged to enter, clear, or pay Duties in another.

No Money shall be drawn from the Treasury, but in Consequence of Appropriations made by Law; and a regular Statement and Account of the Receipts and Expenditures of all public Money shall be published from time to time.

No Title of Nobility shall be granted by the United States: And no Person holding any Office of Profit or Trust under them, shall, without the Consent of the Congress, accept of any present, Emolument, Office, or Title, of any kind whatever, from any King, Prince, or foreign State.

Section 10. No State shall enter into any Treaty, Alliance, or Confederation; grant Letters of Marque and Reprisal; coin Money; emit Bills of Credit; make any Thing but gold and silver Coin a Tender in Payment of Debts; pass any Bill of Attainder, ex post facto Law, or Law impairing the Obligation of Contracts, or grant any Title of Nobility.

No State shall, without the Consent of the Congress, lay any Imposts or Duties on Imports or Exports, except what may be absolutely necessary for executing its inspection Laws: and the net Produce of all Duties and Imposts, laid by any State on Imports or Exports, shall be for the Use of the Treasury of the United States; and all such Laws shall be subject to the Revision and Controul of the Congress.

No State shall, without the Consent of Congress, lay any Duty of Tonnage, keep Troops, or Ships of War in time of Peace, enter into any Agreement or Compact with another State, or with a foreign Power, or engage in War, unless actually invaded, or in such imminent Danger as will not admit of delay.

ARTICLE II

Section 1. The executive Power shall be vested in a President of the United States of America. He shall hold his Office during the Term of four Years, and, together with the Vice President, chosen for the same Term, be elected, as follows:

Each State shall appoint, in such Manner as the Legislature thereof may direct, a Number of Electors, equal to the whole Number of Senators and Representatives to which the State may be entitled in the Congress; but no Senator or Representative, or Person holding an Office of Trust or Profit under the United States, shall be appointed an Elector.

The Electors shall meet in their respective States, and vote by Ballot for two Persons, of whom one at least shall not be an Inhabitant of the same State with themselves. And they shall make a List of all the Persons voted for, and of the Number of Votes for each; which List they shall sign and certify, and transmit sealed to the Seat of the Government of the United States, directed to the President of the Senate. The President of the Senate shall, in the Presence of the Senate and House of Representatives, open all the Certificates, and the Votes shall then be counted. The Person having the greatest Number of Votes shall be the President, if such Number be a Majority of the whole Number of Electors appointed; and if there be more than one who have such Majority, and have an equal Number of Votes, then the House of Representatives shall immediately chuse by Ballot one of them for President; and if no Person have a Majority, then from the five highest on the List the said House shall in like Manner chuse the President. But in chusing the President, the Votes shall be taken by States, the Representation from each State having one Vote; A quorum for this Purpose shall consist of a Member or Members from two thirds of the States, and a Majority of all the States shall be necessary to a Choice. In every Case, after the Choice of the President, the Person having the greater Number of Votes of the Electors shall be the Vice President. But if there should remain two or more who have equal Votes, the Senate shall chuse from them by Ballot the Vice President.

The Congress may determine the Time of chusing the Electors, and the Day on which they shall give their Votes; which Day shall be the same throughout the United States.

No person except a natural born Citizen, or a Citizen of the United States, at the time of the Adoption of this Constitution, shall be eligible to the Office of President; neither shall any Person be eligible to that Office who shall not have attained to the Age of thirty five Years, and been fourteen Years a Resident within the United States.

In Case of the Removal of the President from Office, or of his Death, Resignation or Inability to discharge the Powers and Duties of the said Office, the same shall devolve on the Vice President, and the Congress may by Law provide for the Case of Removal, Death, Resignation or Inability, both of the President and Vice President, declaring what Officer shall then act as President, and such Officer shall act accordingly, until the Disability be removed, or a President shall be elected.

The President shall, at stated Times, receive for his Services, a Compensation, which shall neither be increased nor diminished during the Period for which he shall have been elected, and he shall not receive within that Period any other Emolument from the United States, or any of them.

Before he enter on the Execution of his Office, he shall take the following Oath or Affirmation: "I do solemnly swear (or affirm) that I will faithfully execute the Office of President of the United States, and will to the best of my Ability, preserve, protect and defend the Constitution of the United States."

Section 2. The President shall be Commander in Chief of the Army and Navy of the United States, and of the Militia of the several States, when called into the actual Service of the United States; he may require the Opinion, in writing, of the principal Officer in each of the executive Departments, upon any Subject relating to the Duties of their respective Offices, and he shall have Power to grant Reprieves and Pardons for Offenses against the United States, except in Cases of Impeachment.

He shall have Power, by and with the Advice and Consent of the Senate to make Treaties, provided two thirds of the Senators present concur; and he shall nominate, and by and with the Advice and Consent of the Senate, shall appoint Ambassadors, other public Ministers and Consuls, Judges of the supreme Court, and all other Officers of the United States, whose Appointments are not herein otherwise provided for, and which shall be established by Law; but the Congress may by Law vest the Appointment of such inferior Officers, as they think proper, in the President alone, in the Courts of Law, or in the Heads of Departments.

The President shall have Power to fill up all Vacancies that may happen during the Recess of the Senate, by granting Commissions which shall expire at the End of their next Session.

Section 3. He shall from time to time give to the Congress Information of the State of the Union, and recommend to their Consideration such Measures as he shall judge necessary and expedient; he may, on extraordinary Occasions, convene both Houses, or either of them, and in Case of Disagreement between them, with Respect to the Time of Adjournment, he may adjourn them to such Time as he shall think proper; he shall receive Ambassadors and other public Ministers; he shall take Care that the Laws be faithfully executed, and shall Commission all the Officers of the United States.

Section 4. The President, Vice President and all civil Officers of the United States, shall be removed from Office on Impeachment for, and Conviction of, Treason, Bribery, or other high Crimes and Misdemeanors.

ARTICLE III

Section 1. The judicial Power of the United States, shall be vested in one supreme Court, and in such inferior Courts as the Congress may from time to time ordain and establish. The Judges, both of the supreme and inferior Courts, shall hold their Offices during good Behaviour, and shall, at stated Times, receive for their Services a Compensation, which shall not be diminished during their Continuance in Office.

Section 2. The judicial Power shall extend to all Cases, in Law and Equity, arising under this Constitution, the Laws of the United States, and Treaties made, or which shall be made, under their Authority;—to all Cases affecting Ambassadors, other public Ministers and Consuls;—to all Cases of admiralty and maritime Jurisdiction;—to Controversies to which the United States shall be a Party;—to Controversies between two or more States;—between a State and Citizens of another State;—between Citizens of different States;—between Citizens of the same State claiming Lands under Grants of different States, and between a State, or the Citizens thereof, and foreign States, Citizens or Subjects.

In all Cases affecting Ambassadors, other public Ministers and Consuls, and those in which a State shall be a Party, the supreme Court shall have original Jurisdiction. In all the other Cases before mentioned, the supreme Court shall have appellate Jurisdiction, both as to Law and Fact, with such Exceptions, and under such Regulations as the Congress shall make.

The Trial of all Crimes, except in Cases of Impeachment, shall be by Jury; and such Trial shall be held in the State where the said Crimes shall have been committed; but when not committed within any State, the Trial shall be at such Place or Places as the Congress may by Law have directed.

Section 3. Treason against the United States, shall consist only in levying War against them, or, in adhering to their Enemies, giving them Aid and Comfort. No Person shall be convicted of Treason unless on the Testimony of two Witnesses to the same overt Act, or on Confession in open Court.

The Congress shall have Power to declare the Punishment of Treason, but no Attainder of Treason shall work Corruption of Blood, or Forfeiture except during the Life of the Person attainted.

ARTICLE IV

Section 1. Full Faith and Credit shall be given in each State to the public Acts, Records, and judicial Proceedings of every other State. And the Congress may by general Laws prescribe the Manner in which such Acts, Records and Proceedings shall be proved, and the Effect thereof.

Section 2. The Citizens of each State shall be entitled to all Privileges and Immunities of Citizens in the several States.

A Person charged in any State with Treason, Felony, or other Crime, who shall flee from Justice, and be found in another State, shall on Demand of the executive Authority of the State from which he fled, be delivered up, to be removed to the State having Jurisdiction of the Crime.

No Person held to Service or Labour in one State, under the Laws thereof, escaping into another, shall, in Consequence of any Law or Regulation therein, be discharged from such Service or Labour, but shall be delivered up on Claim of the Party to whom such Service or Labour may be due.

Section 3. New States may be admitted by the Congress into this Union; but no new State shall be formed or erected within the Jurisdiction of any other State; nor any State be formed by the Junction of two or more States, or Parts of

States, without the Consent of the Legislatures of the States concerned as well as of the Congress.

The Congress shall have Power to dispose of and make all needful Rules and Regulations respecting the Territory or other Property belonging to the United States; and nothing in this Constitution shall be so construed as to Prejudice any Claims of the United States, or of any particular State.

Section 4. The United States shall guarantee to every State in this Union a Republican Form of Government, and shall protect each of them against Invasion; and on Application of the Legislature, or of the Executive (when the Legislature cannot be convened) against domestic Violence.

ARTICLE V

The Congress, whenever two thirds of both Houses shall deem it necessary, shall propose Amendments to this Constitution, or, on the Application of the Legislatures of two thirds of the several States, shall call a Convention for proposing Amendments, which, in either Case, shall be valid to all Intents and Purposes, as part of this Constitution, when ratified by the Legislatures of three fourths of the several States, or by Conventions in three fourths thereof, as the one or the other Mode of Ratification may be proposed by the Congress; Provided that no Amendment which may be made prior to the Year One thousand eight hundred and eight shall in any Manner affect the first and fourth Clauses in the Ninth Section of the first Article; and that no State, without its Consent, shall be deprived of its equal Suffrage in the Senate.

ARTICLE VI

All Debts contracted and Engagements entered into, before the Adoption of this Constitution shall be as valid against the United States under this Constitution, as under the Confederation.

This Constitution, and the Laws of the United States which shall be made in Pursuance thereof; and all Treaties made, or which shall be made, under the Authority of the United States, shall be the supreme Law of the Land; and the Judges in every State shall be bound thereby, any Thing in the Constitution or Laws of any State to the Contrary notwithstanding.

The Senators and Representatives before mentioned, and the Members of the several State Legislatures, and all executive and judicial Officers, both of the United States and of the several States, shall be bound by Oath or Affirmation, to support this Constitution; but no religious Test shall ever be required as a Qualification to any Office or public Trust under the United States.

ARTICLE VII

The Ratification of the Conventions of nine States shall be sufficient for the Establishment of this Constitution between the States so ratifying the Same.

AMENDMENT I [1791]

Congress shall make no law respecting an establishment of religion, or prohibiting the free exercise thereof; or abridging the freedom of speech, or of the press; or the right of the people peaceably to assemble, and to petition the Government for a redress of grievances.

AMENDMENT II [1791]

A well regulated Militia, being necessary to the security of a free State, the right of the people to keep and bear Arms, shall not be infringed.

AMENDMENT III [1791]

No Soldier shall, in time of peace be quartered in any house, without the consent of the Owner, nor in time of war, but in a manner to be prescribed by law.

AMENDMENT IV [1791]

The right of the people to be secure in their persons, houses, papers, and effects, against unreasonable searches and seizures, shall not be violated, and no Warrants shall issue, but upon probable cause, supported by Oath or affirmation, and particularly describing the place to be searched, and the persons or things to be seized.

AMENDMENT V [1791]

No person shall be held to answer for a capital, or otherwise infamous crime, unless on a presentment or indictment of a Grand Jury, except in cases arising in the land or naval forces, or in the Militia, when in actual service in time of War or public danger; nor shall any person be subject for the same offense to be twice put in jeopardy of life or limb; nor shall be compelled in any criminal case to be a witness against himself, nor be deprived of life, liberty, or property, without due process of law; nor shall private property be taken for public use, without just compensation.

AMENDMENT VI [1791]

In all criminal prosecutions, the accused shall enjoy the right to a speedy and public trial, by an impartial jury of the State and district wherein the crime shall have been committed, which district shall have been previously ascertained by law, and to be informed of the nature and cause of the accusation; to be confronted with the witnesses against him; to have compulsory process for obtaining witnesses in his favor, and to have the Assistance of Counsel for his defence.

AMENDMENT VII [1791]

In Suits at common law, where the value in controversy shall exceed twenty dollars, the right of trial by jury shall be preserved, and no fact tried by a jury, shall be otherwise re-examined in any Court of the United States, than according to the rules of the common law.

AMENDMENT VIII [1791]

Excessive bail shall not be required, nor excessive fines imposed, nor cruel and unusual punishments inflicted.

AMENDMENT IX [1791]

The enumeration in the Constitution, of certain rights, shall not be construed to deny or disparage others retained by the people.

AMENDMENT X [1791]

The powers not delegated to the United States by the Constitution, nor prohibited by it to the States, are reserved to the States respectively, or to the people.

AMENDMENT XI [1795]

The Judicial power of the United States shall not be construed to extend to any suit in law or equity, commenced or prosecuted against one of the United States by Citizens of another State, or by Citizens or Subjects of any Foreign State.

AMENDMENT XII [1804]

The Electors shall meet in their respective states, and vote by ballot for President and Vice-President, one of whom, at least, shall not be an inhabitant of the same state with themselves; they shall name in their ballots the person voted for as President, and in distinct ballots the person voted for as Vice-President, and they shall make distinct lists of all persons voted for as President, and of all persons voted for as Vice-President, and of the number of votes for each, which lists they shall sign and certify, and transmit sealed to the seat of the government of the United States, directed to the President of the Senate;—The President of the Senate shall, in the presence of the Senate and House of Representatives, open all the certificates and the votes shall then be counted;—The person having the greatest number of votes for President, shall be the President, if such number be a majority of the whole number of Electors appointed; and if no person have such majority, then from the persons having the highest numbers not exceeding three on the list of those voted for as President, the House of Representatives shall choose immediately, by ballot, the President. But in choosing the President, the votes shall be taken by states, the representation from each state having one vote; a quorum for this purpose shall consist of a member or members from two-thirds of the states, and a majority of all states shall be necessary to a choice. And if the House of Representatives shall not choose a President whenever the right of choice shall devolve upon them, before the fourth day of March next following, then the Vice-President shall act as President, as in the case of the death or other constitutional disability of the President.—The person having the greatest number of votes as Vice-President, shall be the Vice-President, if such number be a majority of the whole number of Electors appointed, and if no person have a majority, then from the two highest numbers on the list, the Senate shall choose the Vice-President; a quorum for the purpose shall consist of two-thirds of the whole number of Senators, and a majority of the whole number shall be necessary to a choice. But no person constitutionally ineligible to the office of President shall be eligible to that of Vice-President of the United States.

AMENDMENT XIII [1865]

Section 1. Neither slavery nor involuntary servitude, except as a punishment for crime whereof the party shall have been duly convicted, shall exist within the United States, or any place subject to their jurisdiction.

Section 2. Congress shall have power to enforce this article by appropriate legislation.

AMENDMENT XIV [1868]

Section 1. All persons born or naturalized in the United States, and subject to the jurisdiction thereof, are citizens of the United States and of the State wherein they reside. No State shall make or enforce any law which shall abridge the privileges or immunities of citizens of the United States; nor shall any State deprive any person of life, liberty, or property, without due process of law; nor deny to any person within its jurisdiction the equal protection of the laws.

Section 2. Representatives shall be apportioned among the several States according to their respective numbers, counting the whole number of persons in each State, excluding Indians not taxed. But when the right to vote at any election for the choice of electors for President and Vice President of the United States, Representatives in Congress, the Executive and Judicial officers of a State, or the members of the Legislature thereof, is denied to any of the male inhabitants of such State, being twenty-one years of age, and citizens of the United States, or in any way abridged, except for participation in rebellion, or other crime, the basis of representation therein shall be reduced in the proportion which the number of such male citizens shall bear to the whole number of male citizens twenty-one years of age in such State.

Section 3. No person shall be a Senator or Representative in Congress, or elector of President and Vice President, or hold any office, civil or military, under the United States, or under any State, who having previously taken an oath, as a member of Congress, or as an officer of the United States, or as a member of any State legislature, or as an executive or judicial officer of any State, to support the Constitution of the United States, shall have engaged in insurrection or rebellion against the same, or given aid or comfort to the enemies thereof. But Congress may by a vote of two-thirds of each House, remove such disability.

Section 4. The validity of the public debt of the United States, authorized by law, including debts incurred for payment of pensions and bounties for services in suppressing insurrection or rebellion, shall not be questioned. But neither the United States nor any State shall assume or pay any debt or obligation incurred in aid of insurrection or rebellion against the United States, or any claim for the loss or emancipation of any slave; but all such debts, obligations and claims shall be held illegal and void.

Section 5. The Congress shall have power to enforce, by appropriate legislation, the provisions of this article.

AMENDMENT XV [1870]

Section 1. The right of citizens of the United States to vote shall not be denied or abridged by the United States or by any State on account of race, color, or previous condition of servitude.

Section 2. The Congress shall have power to enforce this article by appropriate legislation.

AMENDMENT XVI [1913]

The Congress shall have power to lay and collect taxes on incomes, from whatever source derived, without apportionment among the several States, and without regard to any census or enumeration.

AMENDMENT XVII [1913]

Section 1. The Senate of the United States shall be composed of two Senators from each State, elected by the people thereof, for six years; and each Senator shall have one vote. The electors in each State shall have the qualifications requisite for electors of the most numerous branch of the State legislatures.

Section 2. When vacancies happen in the representation of any State in the Senate, the executive authority of such State shall issue writs of election to fill such vacancies: Provided, That the legislature of any State may empower the executive thereof to make temporary appointments until the people fill the vacancies by election as the legislature may direct.

Section 3. This amendment shall not be so construed as to affect the election or term of any Senator chosen before it becomes valid as part of the Constitution.

AMENDMENT XVIII [1919]

Section 1. After one year from the ratification of this article the manufacture, sale, or transportation of intoxicating liquors within, the importation thereof into, or the exportation thereof from the United States and all territory subject to the jurisdiction thereof for beverage purposes is hereby prohibited.

Section 2. The Congress and the several States shall have concurrent power to enforce this article by appropriate legislation.

Section 3. This article shall be inoperative unless it shall have been ratified as an amendment to the Constitution by the legislatures of the several States, as provided in the Constitution, within seven years from the date of the submission hereof to the States by the Congress.

AMENDMENT XIX [1920]

Section 1. The right of citizens of the United States to vote shall not be denied or abridged by the United States or by any State on account of sex.

Section 2. Congress shall have power to enforce this article by appropriate legislation.

AMENDMENT XX [1933]

Section 1. The terms of the President and Vice President shall end at noon on the 20th day of January, and the terms of Senators and Representatives at noon on the 3d day of January, of the years in which such terms would have ended if this article had not been ratified; and the terms of their successors shall then begin.

Section 2. The Congress shall assemble at least once in every year, and such meeting shall begin at noon on the 3d day of January, unless they shall by law appoint a different day.

Section 3. If, at the time fixed for the beginning of the term of the President, the President elect shall have died, the Vice President elect shall become President. If the President shall not have been chosen before the time fixed for the beginning of his term, or if the President elect shall have failed to qualify, then the Vice President elect shall act as President until a President shall have qualified; and the Congress may by law provide for the case wherein neither a President elect nor a Vice President elect shall have qualified, declaring who shall then act as President, or the manner in which one who is to act shall be selected, and such person shall act accordingly until a President or Vice President shall have qualified.

Section 4. The Congress may by law provide for the case of the death of any of the persons from whom the House of Representatives may choose a President whenever the right of choice shall have devolved upon them, and for the case of the death of any of the persons from whom the Senate may choose a Vice President whenever the right of choice shall have devolved upon them.

Section 5. Sections 1 and 2 shall take effect on the 15th day of October following the ratification of this article.

Section 6. This article shall be inoperative unless it shall have been ratified as an amendment to the Constitution by the legislatures of three-fourths of the several States within seven years from the date of its submission.

AMENDMENT XXI [1933]

Section 1. The eighteenth article of amendment to the Constitution of the United States is hereby repealed.

Section 2. The transportation or importation into any State, Territory, or possession of the United States for delivery or use therein of intoxicating liquors, in violation of the laws thereof, is hereby prohibited.

Section 3. This article shall be inoperative unless it shall have been ratified as an amendment to the Constitution by conventions in the several States, as provided in the Constitution, within seven years from the date of the submission hereof to the States by the Congress.

AMENDMENT XXII [1951]

Section 1. No person shall be elected to the office of the President more than twice, and no person who has held the office of President, or acted as President, for more than two years of a term to which some other person was elected President shall be elected to the office of President more than once. But this Article shall not apply to any person holding the office of President when this Article was proposed by the Congress, and shall not prevent any person who may be holding the office of President, or acting as President, during the term within which this Article becomes operative from holding the office of President or acting as President during the remainder of such term.

Section 2. This article shall be inoperative unless it shall have been ratified as an amendment to the Constitution by the legislatures of three-fourths of the several States within seven years from the date of its submission to the States by the Congress.

AMENDMENT XXIII [1961]

Section 1. The District constituting the seat of Government of the United States shall appoint in such manner as the Congress may direct:

A number of electors of President and Vice President equal to the whole number of Senators and Representatives in Congress to which the District would be entitled if it were a State, but in no event more than the least populous state; they shall be in addition to those appointed by the states, but they shall be considered, for the purposes of the election of President and Vice President, to be electors appointed by a state; and they shall meet in the District and perform such duties as provided by the twelfth article of amendment.

Section 2. The Congress shall have power to enforce this article by appropriate legislation.

AMENDMENT XXIV [1964]

Section 1. The right of citizens of the United States to vote in any primary or other election for President or Vice President, for electors for President or Vice President, or for Senator or Representative in Congress, shall not be denied or abridged by the United States, or any State by reason of failure to pay any poll tax or other tax.

Section 2. The Congress shall have power to enforce this article by appropriate legislation.

AMENDMENT XXV [1967]

Section 1. In case of the removal of the President from office or of his death or resignation, the Vice President shall become President.

Section 2. Whenever there is a vacancy in the office of the Vice President, the President shall nominate a Vice President who shall take office upon confirmation by a majority vote of both Houses of Congress.

Section 3. Whenever the President transmits to the President pro tempore of the Senate and the Speaker of the House of Representatives his written declaration that he is unable to discharge the powers and duties of his office, and until he transmits to them a written declaration to the contrary, such powers and duties shall be discharged by the Vice President as Acting President.

Section 4. Whenever the Vice President and a majority of either the principal officers of the executive departments or of such other body as Congress may by law provide, transmit to the President pro tempore of the Senate and the Speaker of the House of Representatives their written declaration that the President is unable to discharge the powers and duties of his office, the Vice President shall immediately assume the powers and duties of the office as Acting President.

Thereafter, when the President transmits to the President pro tempore of the Senate and the Speaker of the House of Representatives his written declaration that no inability exists, he shall resume the powers and duties of his office unless the Vice President and a majority of either the principal officers of the executive department or of such other body as

Congress may by law provide, transmit within four days to the President pro tempore of the Senate and the Speaker of the House of Representatives their written declaration that the President is unable to discharge the powers and duties of his office. Thereupon Congress shall decide the issue, assembling within forty-eight hours for that purpose if not in session. If the Congress, within twenty-one days after receipt of the latter written declaration, or, if Congress is not in session, within twenty-one days after Congress is required to assemble, determines by two-thirds vote of both Houses that the President is unable to discharge the powers and duties of his office, the Vice President shall continue to discharge the same as Acting President; otherwise, the President shall resume the powers and duties of his office.

AMENDMENT XXVI [1971]

Section 1.   The right of citizens of the United States, who are eighteen years of age or older, to vote shall not be denied or abridged by the United States or by any State on account of age.

Section 2.   The Congress shall have power to enforce this article by appropriate legislation.

AMENDMENT XXVII [1992]

No law, varying the compensation for the services of the Senators and Representatives, shall take effect, until an election of Representatives shall have intervened.

APPENDIX C

FEDERALIST PAPERS NO. 10 AND NO. 51

The founders completed drafting the U.S. Constitution in 1787. It was then submitted to the thirteen states for ratification, and a major debate ensued. As you read in Chapter 2, on the one side of this debate were the Federalists, who urged that the new Constitution be adopted. On the other side of the debate were the Anti-Federalists, who argued against ratification.

During the course of this debate, three men well known for their Federalist views—Alexander Hamilton, James Madison, and John Jay—wrote a series of essays in which they argued for immediate ratifcation of the Constitution. The essays appeared in the New York City Independent Journal *in October 1787, just a little over a month after the Constitutional Convention adjourned. Later, Hamilton arranged to have the essays collected and published in book form. The articles filled two volumes, both of which were published by May 1788. The essays are often referred to collectively as the* Federalist Papers.

Scholars disagree as to whether the Federalist Papers *had a significant impact on the decision of the states to ratify the Constitution. Nonetheless, many of the essays are masterpieces of political reasoning and have left a lasting imprint on American politics and government. Above all, the* Federalist Papers *shed an important light on what the founders intended when they drafted various constitutional provisions.*

Here we present just two of these essays, Federalist Paper No. 10 *and* Federalist Paper No. 51. *Each essay was written by James Madison, who referred to himself as "Publius." We have annotated each document to clarify the meaning of particular passages. The annotations are set in italics to distinguish them from the original text of the documents.*

#10

Federalist Paper No. 10 is a classic document that is often referred to by teachers of American government. Authored by James Madison, it sets forth Madison's views on factions in politics. The essay was written, in large part, to counter the arguments put forth by the Anti-Federalists that small factions might take control of the government, thus destroying the representative nature of the republican form of government established by the Constitution. The essay opens with a discussion of the "dangerous vice" of factions and the importance of devising a form of government in which this vice will be controlled.

Among the numerous advantages promised by a well-constructed Union, none deserves to be more accurately developed than its tendency to break and control the violence of faction. The friend of popular governments never finds himself so much alarmed for their character and fate as when he contemplates their propensity to this dangerous vice. He will not fail, therefore, to set a due value on any plan which, without violating the principles to which he is attached, provides a proper cure for it. The instability, injustice, and confusion introduced into the public councils have, in truth, been the mortal diseases under which popular governments have everywhere perished, as they continue to be the favorite and fruitful topics from which the adversaries to liberty derive their most specious declamations. The valuable improvements made by the American constitutions on the popular models, both ancient and modern, cannot certainly be too much admired; but it would be an unwarrantable partiality to contend that they have as effectually obviated the danger on this side, as was wished and expected. Complaints are everywhere heard from our most considerate and virtuous citizens, equally the friends of public and private faith and of public and personal liberty, that our governments are too unstable, that the public good is disregarded in the conflicts of rival parties, and that measures are too often decided, not according to the rules of justice and the rights of the minor party, but by the superior force of an interested and overbearing majority. However anxiously we may wish that these complaints had no foundation, the evidence of known facts will not permit us to deny that they are in some degree true. It will be found, indeed, on a candid review of our situation, that some of the distresses under which we labor have been erroneously charged on the operation of our governments; but it will be found, at the same time, that other causes will not alone account for many of our heaviest misfortunes; and, particularly, for that prevailing and increasing distrust of public engagements and alarm for private rights which are echoed from one end of the continent to the other. These must be chiefly, if not wholly, effects of the unsteadiness and injustice with which a factious spirit has tainted our public administration.

In the following paragraph, Madison clarifies for his readers his understanding of what the term faction means.

By a faction I understand a number of citizens, whether amounting to a majority or minority of the whole, who are united and actuated by some common impulse of passion, or of interest, adverse to the rights of other citizens, or the permanent and aggregate interests of the community.

In the following passages, Madison looks at the two methods of curing the "mischiefs of factions." One of these methods is removing the causes of faction. The other is to control the effects of factions.

There are two methods of curing the mischiefs of faction: the one, by removing its causes; the other, by controlling its effects.

There are again two methods of removing the causes of faction: the one, by destroying the liberty which is essential to its existence; the other, by giving to every citizen the same opinions, the same passions, and the same interests.

It could never be more truly said than of the first remedy that it was worse than the disease. Liberty is to faction what air is to fire, an aliment without which it instantly expires. But it could not be a less folly to abolish liberty, which is essential to political life, because it nourishes faction than it would be to wish the annihilation of air, which is essential to animal life, because it imparts to fire its destructive agency.

The second expedient is as impracticable as the first would be unwise. As long as the reason of man continues fallible, and his is at liberty to exercise it, different opinions will be formed. As long as the connection subsists between his reason and his self-love, his opinions and his passions will have a reciprocal influence on each other; and the former will be objects to which the latter will attach themselves. The diversity in the faculties of men, from which the rights of property originate, is not less an insuperable obstacle to a uniformity of interests. The protection of these faculties is the first object of government. From the protection of different and unequal faculties of acquiring property, the possession of different degrees and kinds of property immediately results; and from the influence of these on the sentiments and views of the respective proprietors ensues a division of the society into different interests and parties.

The latent causes of faction are thus sown in the nature of man; and we see them everywhere brought into different degrees of activity, according to the different circumstances of civil society. A zeal for different opinions concerning religion, concerning government, and many other points, as well of speculation as of practice; an attachment to different leaders ambitiously contending for pre-eminence and power; or to persons of other descriptions whose fortunes have been interesting to the human passions, have, in turn, divided mankind into parties, inflamed them with mutual animosity, and rendered them much more disposed to vex and oppress each other than to co-operate for their common good. So strong is this propensity of mankind to fall into mutual animosities that where no substantial occasion presents itself the most frivolous and fanciful distinctions have been sufficient to kindle their unfriendly passions and excite their most violent conflicts. But the most common and durable source of factions has been the various and unequal distribution of property. Those who hold and those who are without property have ever formed distinct interests in society. Those who are creditors, and those who are debtors, fall under a like discrimination. A landed interest, a manufacturing interest, a mercantile interest, a moneyed interest, with many lesser interests, grow up of necessity in civilized nations, and divide them into different classes, actuated by different sentiments and views. The regulation of these various and interfering interests forms the principal task of modern legislation and involves the spirit of party and faction in the necessary and ordinary operations of government.

No man is allowed to be a judge in his own cause, because his interest would certainly bias his judgment, and, not improbably, corrupt his integrity. With equal, nay with greater reason, a body of men are unfit to be both judges and parties at the same time; yet what are many of the most important acts of legislation but so many judicial determinations, not indeed concerning the rights of single persons, but concerning the rights of large bodies of citizens? And what are the different classes of legislators but advocates and parties to the causes which they determine? Is a law proposed concerning private debts? It is a question to which the creditors are parties on one side and the debtors on the other. Justice ought to hold the balance between them. Yet the parties are, and must be, themselves the judges; and the most numerous party, or in other words, the most powerful faction must be expected to prevail. Shall domestic manufacturers be encouraged, and in what degree, by restrictions on foreign manufacturers? Are questions which would be differently decided by the landed and the manufacturing classes, and probably by neither with a sole regard to justice and the public good. The apportionment of taxes on the various descriptions of property is an act which seems to require the most exact impartiality; yet there is, perhaps, no legislative act in which greater opportunity and temptation are given to a predominant party to trample on the rules of justice. Every shilling with which they overburden the inferior number is a shilling saved to their own pockets.

It is in vain to say that enlightened statesmen will be able to adjust these clashing interests and render them all subservient to the public good. Enlightened statesmen will not always be at the helm. Nor, in many cases, can such an adjustment be made at all without taking into view indirect and remote considerations, which will rarely prevail over the immediate interest which one party may find in disregarding the rights of another or the good of the whole.

The inference to which we are brought is that the causes of faction cannot be removed and that relief is only to be sought in the means of controlling its effects.

In the preceding passages, Madison has explored the causes of factions and has concluded that they cannot "be removed" without removing liberty itself, which is one of the causes, or altering human nature. He now turns to a discussion of how the effects of factions might be controlled.

If a faction consists of less than a majority, relief is supplied by the republican principle, which enables the majority to defeat its sinister views by regular vote. It may clog the administration, it may convulse the society; but it will be unable to execute and mask its violence under the forms of the Constitution. When a majority is included in a faction, the form of popular government, on the other hand, enables it to sacrifice to its ruling passion or interest both the public good and the rights of other citizens. To secure the public good and private rights against the danger of such a faction, and at the same time to preserve the spirit and the form of popular government, is then the great object to which our inquiries are directed. Let me add that it is the great desideratum by which alone this form of government can be rescued from the opprobrium under which it has so long labored and be recommended to the esteem and adoption of mankind.

According to Madison, one way of controlling the effects of factions is to make sure that the majority is not able to act in "concert," or jointly, to "carry into effect schemes of oppression."

By what means is this object attainable? Evidently by one of two only. Either the existence of the same passion or interest in a majority at the same time must be prevented, or the majority, having such coexistent passion or interest, must be rendered, by their number and local situation, unable to concert and carry into effect schemes of oppression. If the impulse and the opportunity be suffered to coincide, we well know that neither moral nor religious motives can be relied on as an adequate control. They are not found to be such on the injustice and violence of individuals, and lose their efficacy in proportion to the number combined together, that is, in proportion as their efficacy becomes needful.

From this view of the subject it may be concluded that a pure democracy, by which I mean a society consisting of a small number of citizens, who assemble and administer the government in person, can admit of no cure for the mischiefs of faction. A common passion or interest will, in almost every case, be felt by a majority of the whole; a communication and concert results from the form of government itself; and there is nothing to check the inducements to sacrifice the weaker party or an obnoxious individual. Hence it is that such democracies have ever been spectacles of turbulence and contention; have ever been found incompatible with personal security or the rights of property; and have in general been as short in their lives as they have been violent in their deaths. Theoretic politicians, who have patronized this species of government, have erroneously supposed that by reducing mankind to a perfect equality in their political rights, they would at the same time be perfectly equalized and assimilated in their possessions, their opinions, and their passions.

In the following six paragraphs, Madison sets forth some of the reasons why a republican form of government promises a "cure" for the mischiefs of factions. He begins by clarifying the difference between a republic and a democracy. He then describes how in a large republic, the elected representatives of the people will be large enough in number to guard against factions—the "cabals," or concerted actions, of "a few." On the one hand, representatives will not be so removed from their local districts as to be unacquainted with their constituents' needs. On the other hand, they will not be "unduly attached" to local interests and unfit to understand "great and national objects." Madison concludes that the Constitution "forms a happy combination in this respect."

A republic, by which I mean a government in which the scheme of representation takes place, opens a different prospect and promises the cure for which we are seeking. Let us examine the points in which it varies from pure democracy, and we shall comprehend both the nature of the cure and the efficacy which it must derive from the Union.

The two great points of difference between a democracy and a republic are: first, the delegation of the government, in the latter, to a small number of citizens elected by the rest; secondly, the greater number of citizens and greater sphere of country over which the latter may be extended.

The effect of the first difference is, on the one hand, to refine and enlarge the public views by passing them through the medium of a chosen body of citizens, whose wisdom may best discern the true interest of their country and whose patriotism and love of justice will be least likely to sacrifice it to temporary or partial considerations. Under such a regulation it may well happen that the public voice, pronounced by the representatives of the people, will be more consonant to the public good than if pronounced by the people themselves, convened for the purpose. On the other hand, the effect may be inverted. Men of factious tempers, of local prejudices, or of sinister designs, may, by intrigue, by corruption, or by other means, first obtain the suffrages, and then betray the interests of the people. The question resulting is, whether small or extensive republics are most favorable to the election of proper guardians of the public weal; and it is clearly decided in favor of the latter by two obvious considerations.

In the first place it is to be remarked that however small the republic may be the representatives must be raised to a certain number in order to guard against the cabals of a few; and that however large it may be they must be limited to a certain number in order to guard against the confusion of a multitude. Hence, the number of representatives in the two cases not being in proportion to that of the constituents, and being proportionally greatest in the small republic, it follows that if the proportion of fit characters be not less in the large than in the small republic, the former will present a greater option, and consequently a greater probability of a fit choice.

In the next place, as each representative will be chosen by a greater number of citizens in the large than in the small republic, it will be more difficult for unworthy candidates to practice with success the vicious arts by which elections are too often carried; and the suffrages of the people being more free, will be more likely to center on men who possess the most attractive merit and the most diffusive and established characters.

It must be confessed that in this, as in most other cases, there is a mean, on both sides of which inconveniencies will be found to lie. By enlarging too much the number of electors, you render the representative too little acquainted with all their local circumstances and lesser interests; as by reducing it too much, you render him unduly attached to these, and too little fit to comprehend and pursue great and national objects. The federal Constitution forms a happy combination in this respect; the great and aggregate interests being referred to the national, the local and particular to the State legislatures.

In the remaining passages of this essay, Madison looks at another "point of difference" between a republic and a democracy. Specifically, a republic can encompass a larger territory and a greater number of citizens than a democracy can. This fact, too, argues Madison, will help to control the influence of factions because the interests that draw people together to act in concert are typically at the local level and would be unlikely to affect or dominate the national government. As Madison states, "The influence of factious leaders may kindle a flame within their particular States but will be unable to spread a general conflagration through the other States." Generally, in a large republic, there will be numerous factions, and no particular faction will be able to "pervade the whole body of the Union."

The other point of difference is the greater number of citizens and extent of territory which may be brought within the compass of republican than of democratic government; and it is this circumstance principally which renders factious combinations less to be dreaded in the former than in the latter. The smaller the society, the fewer probably will be the distinct parties and interests composing it; the fewer the distinct parties and interests, the more frequently will a majority be found of the same party; and the smaller the number of individuals composing a majority, and the smaller the compass within which they are placed, the more easily will they concert and execute their plans of oppression. Extend the sphere and you take in a greater variety of parties and interests; you make it less probable that a majority of the whole will have a common motive to invade the rights of other citizens; or if such a common motive exists, it will be more difficult for all who feel it to discover their own strength and to act in unison with each other. Besides other impediments, it may be remarked that, where there is a consciousness of unjust or dishonorable purposes, communication is always checked by distrust in proportion to the number whose concurrence is necessary.

Hence, it clearly appears that the same advantage which a republic has over a democracy in controlling the effects of faction is enjoyed by a large over a small republic—is enjoyed by the Union over the States composing it. Does this advantage consist in the substitution of representatives whose enlightened views and virtuous sentiments render them superior to local prejudices and to schemes of injustice? It will not be denied that the representation of the Union will be most likely to possess these requisite endowments. Does it consist in the greater security afforded by a greater variety of parties, against the event of any one party being able to outnumber and oppress the rest? In an equal degree does the increased variety of parties comprised within the Union increase this security. Does it, in fine, consist in the greater obstacles opposed to the concert and accomplishment of the secret wishes of an unjust and interested majority? Here again the extent of the Union gives it the most palpable advantage.

The influence of factious leaders may kindle a flame within their particular States but will be unable to spread a general conflagration through the other States. A religious sect may

degenerate into a political faction in a part of the Confederacy; but the variety of sects dispersed over the entire face of it must secure the national councils against any danger from that source. A rage for paper money, for an abolition of debts, for an equal division of property, or for any other improper or wicked project, will be less apt to pervade the whole body of the Union than a particular member of it, in the same proportion as such a malady is more likely to taint a particular county or district than an entire State.

In the extent and proper structure of the Union, therefore, we behold a republican remedy for the diseases most incident to republican government. And according to the degree of pleasure and pride we feel in being republicans ought to be our zeal in cherishing the spirit and supporting the character of federalists.

Publius
(James Madison)

#51

Federalist Paper No. 51, which was also authored by James Madison, is one of the classics in American political theory. Recall from Chapter 2 that a major concern of the founders was to create a relatively strong national government but one that would not be capable of tyrannizing over the populace. In the following essay, Madison sets forth the theory of "checks and balances." He explains that the new Constitution, by dividing the national government into three branches (executive, legislative, and judicial), offers protection against tyranny.

To what expedient, then, shall we finally resort, for maintaining in practice the necessary partition of power among the several departments as laid down in the Constitution? The only answer that can be given is that as all these exterior provisions are found to be inadequate the defect must be supplied, by so contriving the interior structure of the government as that its several constituent parts may, by their mutual relations, be the means of keeping each other in their proper places. Without presuming to undertake a full development of this important idea I will hazard a few general observations which may perhaps place it in a clearer light, and enable us to form a more correct judgment of the principles and structure of the government planned by the convention.

In the following two paragraphs, Madison explains that to ensure that the powers of government are genuinely separated, it is important that each of the three branches of government (executive, legislative, and judicial) should have a "will of its own." Among other things, this means that persons in one branch should not depend on persons in another branch for the "emoluments annexed to their offices" (pay, perks, and privileges). If they did, then the branches would not be truly independent of one another.

In order to lay a due foundation for that separate and distinct exercise of the different powers of government, which to a certain extent is admitted on all hands to be essential to the preservation of liberty, it is evident that each department should have a will of its own; and consequently should be so constituted that the members of each should have as little agency as possible in the appointment of the members of the others. Were this principle rigorously adhered to, it would require that all the appointments for the supreme executive, legislative, and judiciary magistracies should be drawn from the same fountain of authority, the people, through channels having no communication whatever with one another. Perhaps such a plan of constructing the several departments would be less difficult in practice than it may in contemplation appear. Some difficulties, however, and some additional expense would attend the execution of it. Some deviations, therefore, from the principle must be admitted. In the constitution of the judiciary department in particular, it might be inexpedient to insist rigorously on the principle: first, because peculiar qualifications being essential in the members, the primary consideration ought to be to select that mode of choice which best secures these qualifications; second, because the permanent tenure by which the appointments are held in that department must soon destroy all sense of dependence on the authority conferring them.

It is equally evident that the members of each department should be as little dependent as possible on those of the others for the emoluments annexed to their offices. Were the executive magistrate, or the judges, not independent of the legislature in this particular, their independence in every other would be merely nominal.

One of the striking qualities of the theory of checks and balances as posited by Madison is that it assumes that persons are not angels but driven by personal interests and motives. In the following two paragraphs, which are among the most widely quoted of Madison's writings, he stresses that the division of the government into three branches helps to check personal ambitions. Personal ambitions will naturally arise, but they will be linked to the constitutional powers of each branch. In effect, they will help to keep the three branches separate and thus serve the public interest.

But the great security against a gradual concentration of the several powers in the same department consists in giving to those who administer each department the necessary constitutional means and personal motives to resist encroachments of the others. The provision for defense must in this, as in all other cases, be made commensurate to the danger of attack. Ambition must be made to counteract ambition. The interest of the man must be connected with the constitutional rights of the place. It may be a reflection on human nature that such devices should be necessary to control the abuses of government. But what is government itself but the greatest of all reflections on human nature? If men were angels, no government would be necessary. If angels were to govern men, neither external nor internal controls on government would be necessary. In framing a government which is to be administered by men over men, the great difficulty lies in this: you must first enable the government to control the governed; and

in the next place oblige it to control itself. A dependence on the people is, no doubt, the primary control on the government; but experience has taught mankind the necessity of auxiliary precautions.

This policy of supplying, by opposite and rival interests, the defect of better motives, might be traced through the whole system of human affairs, private as well as public. We see it particularly displayed in all the subordinate distributions of power, where the constant aim is to divide and arrange the several offices in such a manner as that each may be a check on the other—that the private interest of every individual may be a sentinel over the public rights. These inventions of prudence cannot be less requisite in the distribution of the supreme powers of the State.

In the next two paragraphs, Madison first points out that the "legislative authority necessarily predominates" in a republican form of government. The "remedy" for this lack of balance with the other branches of government is to divide the legislative branch into two chambers with "different modes of election and different principles of action."

But it is not possible to give to each department an equal power of self-defense. In republican government, the legislative authority necessarily predominates. The remedy for this inconveniency is to divide the legislature into different branches; and to render them, by different modes of election and different principles of action, as little connected with each other as the nature of their common functions and their common dependence on the society will admit. It may even be necessary to guard against dangerous encroachments by still further precautions. As the weight of the legislative authority requires that it should be thus divided, the weakness of the executive may require, on the other hand, that it should be fortified. An absolute negative on the legislature appears, at first view, to be the natural defense with which the executive magistrate should be armed. But perhaps it would be neither altogether safe nor alone sufficient. On ordinary occasions it might not be exerted with the requisite firmness, and on extraordinary occasions it might be perfidiously abused. May not this defect of an absolute negative be supplied by some qualified connection between this weaker department and the weaker branch of the stronger department, by which the latter may be led to support the constitutional rights of the former, without being too much detached from the rights of its own department?

If the principles on which these observations are founded be just, as I persuade myself they are, and they be applied as a criterion to the several State constitutions, and to the federal Constitution, it will be found that if the latter does not perfectly correspond with them, the former are infinitely less able to bear such a test.

In the remaining passages of this essay, Madison discusses the importance of the division of government powers between the states and the national government. This division of powers, by providing additional checks and balances, offers a "double security" against tyranny.

There are, moreover, two considerations particularly applicable to the federal system of America, which place that system in a very interesting point of view.

First. In a single republic, all the power surrendered by the people is submitted to the administration of a single government; and the usurpations are guarded against by a division of the government into distinct and separate departments. In the compound republic of America, the power surrendered by the people is first divided between two distinct governments, and then the portion allotted to each subdivided among distinct and separate departments. Hence a double security arises to the rights of the people. The different governments will control each other, at the same time that each will be controlled by itself.

Second. It is of great importance in a republic not only to guard the society against the oppression of its rulers, but to guard one part of the society against the injustice of the other part. Different interests necessarily exist in different classes of citizens. If a majority be united by a common interest, the rights of the minority will be insecure. There are but two methods of providing against this evil: the one by creating a will in the community independent of the majority—that is, of the society itself; the other, by comprehending in the society so many separate descriptions of citizens as will render an unjust combination of a majority of the whole very improbable, if not impracticable. The first method prevails in all governments possessing an hereditary or self-appointed authority. This, at best, is but a precarious security; because a power independent of the society may as well espouse the unjust views of the major as the rightful interests of the minor party, and may possibly be turned against both parties. The second method will be exemplified in the federal republic of the United States. Whilst all authority in it will be derived from and dependent on the society, the society itself will be broken into so many parts, interests and classes of citizens, that the rights of individuals, or of the minority, will be in little danger from interested combinations of the majority. In a free government the security for civil rights must be the same as that for religious rights. It consists in the one case in the multiplicity of interests, and in the other in the multiplicity of sects. The degree of security in both cases will depend on the number of interests and sects; and this may be presumed to depend on the extent of country and number of people comprehended under the same government. This view of the subject must particularly recommend a proper federal system to all the sincere and considerate friends of republican government, since it shows that in exact proportion as the territory of the Union may be formed into more circumscribed Confederacies, or States, oppressive combinations of a majority will be facilitated; the best security, under the republican forms, for the rights of every class of citizen, will be diminished; and consequently the stability and independence of some member of the government, the only other security, must be proportionally increased. Justice is the end of government. It is the end of civil society. It ever has been and ever will be pursued until it be obtained, or until liberty be lost in the pursuit. In a society under the forms of which the stronger faction can readily unite and oppress the weaker, anarchy may as truly be said to reign as in a state of nature, where the weaker individual is not secured against the violence of the stronger; and as, in the latter state, even the stronger individuals are prompted, by the uncertainty of their condition, to submit to a government which may protect the weak as well as themselves; so, in the former state, will the more powerful factions or parties be gradually induced, by a like motive, to wish for a government which will protect all parties, the weaker as well as the more powerful. It can be little doubted that if the State of Rhode Island was separated from the Confederacy and left to itself, the insecurity of rights under the popular form of government within such narrow limits would be displayed by such reiterated oppressions of factious majorities that some power altogether independent of the people would soon be called for by the voice of the very factions whose misrule had proved the necessity of it. In the extended republic of the United States, and among the great variety of interests, parties, and sects which it embraces, a coalition of a majority of the whole society could seldom take place on any other principles than those of justice and the general good; whilst there being thus less danger to a minor from the will of a major party, there must be less pretext, also, to provide for the security of the former, by introducing into the government a will not dependent on the latter, or, in other words, a will independent of the society itself. It is no less certain than it is important, notwithstanding the contrary opinions which have been entertained, that the larger the society, provided it lie within a practicable sphere, the more duly capable it will be of self-government. And happily for the *republican cause*, the practicable sphere may be carried to a very great extent by a judicious modification and mixture of the *federal principle*.

Publius
(James Madison)

APPENDIX D

ANSWERS TO CHAPTER QUIZ QUESTIONS

Chapter 1

Fill-In

1. Government (Learning Outcome 1–1)
2. it resolves conflicts, provides public services, and defends the nation and its culture against attacks by other nations (Learning Outcome 1–1)
3. autocracy (Learning Outcome 1–2)
4. representative democracy (Learning Outcome 1–2)
5. life, liberty, and property (Learning Outcome 1–3)
6. equality in voting, individual freedom, equal protection of the law, majority rule and minority rights, and voluntary consent to be governed (Learning Outcome 1–3)
7. conservatives and liberals (Learning Outcome 1–4)
8. conservatives (Learning Outcome 1–4)
9. moderates (Learning Outcome 1–4)
10. Libertarians (Learning Outcome 1–4)

Multiple Choice

11. c. (Learning Outcome 1–1)
12. a. (Learning Outcome 1–1)
13. b. (Learning Outcome 1–2)
14. c. (Learning Outcome 1–2)
15. b. (Learning Outcome 1–3)
16. a. (Learning Outcome 1–3)
17. c. (Learning Outcome 1–4)
18. a. (Learning Outcome 1–4)

Chapter 2

Fill-In

1. Mayflower Compact (Learning Outcome 2–1)
2. imposing taxes on the American colonists and exercising more direct control over colonial trade (Learning Outcome 2–2)
3. Sugar Act, the Stamp Act, and taxes on glass, paint, and lead (Learning Outcome 2–2)
4. Congress of the Confederation (Learning Outcome 2–3)
5. Shays' Rebellion (Learning Outcome 2–3)
6. House of Representatives and the Senate (Learning Outcome 2–4)
7. "Treason, Bribery, or other high Crimes and Misdemeanors" (Learning Outcome 2–4)
8. bill of rights (Learning Outcome 2–4)
9. separation of powers (Learning Outcome 2–5)
10. judicial review (Learning Outcome 2–5)

Multiple Choice

11. c. (Learning Outcome 2–1)
12. b. (Learning Outcome 2–2)
13. b. (Learning Outcome 2–3)
14. a. (Learning Outcome 2–4)
15. a. (Learning Outcome 2–5)

Chapter 3

Fill-In

1. the ability to experiment with innovative policies at the state or local level, and the opportunity for the political and cultural interests of regional groups to be reflected in the laws governing those groups (Learning Outcome 3–1)
2. necessary and proper (Learning Outcome 3–2)
3. full faith and credit (Learning Outcome 3–2)
4. implied powers and national supremacy (Learning Outcome 3–3)
5. the Great Depression (Learning Outcome 3–3)
6. picket-fence (Learning Outcome 3–3)
7. federal mandate (Learning Outcome 3–4)
8. fiscal federalism (Learning Outcome 3–4)
9. threatening to withhold federal highway funds from states that did not comply (Learning Outcome 3–5)
10. No Child Left Behind (Learning Outcome 3–5)

Multiple Choice

11. a. (Learning Outcome 3–1)
12. c. (Learning Outcome 3–1)
13. b. (Learning Outcome 3–2)

14. c. (Learning Outcome 3–2)

15. a. (Learning Outcome 3–3)

16. c. (Learning Outcome 3–4)

17. b. (Learning Outcome 3–5)

Chapter 4

Fill-In

1. due process (Learning Outcome 4–1)

2. (1) be for a clearly secular purpose; (2) neither advance nor inhibit religion in its primary effect; and (3) avoid an "excessive government entanglement with religion" (Learning Outcome 4–2)

3. subversive speech (Learning Outcome 4–2)

4. Libel (Learning Outcome 4–2)

5. "National Security Letters" (Learning Outcome 4–3)

6. Roe v. Wade (1973) (Learning Outcome 4–3)

7. Fourth (Learning Outcome 4–4)

8. the Miranda warnings (Learning Outcome 4–4)

Multiple Choice

9. b. (Learning Outcome 4–1)

10. b. (Learning Outcome 4–1)

11. a. (Learning Outcome 4–2)

12. c. (Learning Outcome 4–2)

13. b. (Learning Outcome 4–3)

14. a. (Learning Outcome 4–4)

Chapter 5

Fill-In

1. suspect classification (Learning Outcome 5–1)

2. separate-but-equal (Learning Outcome 5–2)

3. race, color, religion, gender, and national origin (Learning Outcome 5–2)

4. full political, economic, and social equality (Learning Outcome 5–3)

5. 83 cents (Learning Outcome 5–3)

6. Latinos (Learning Outcome 5–4)

7. Japanese (Learning Outcome 5–4)

8. Americans with Disabilities Act (Learning Outcome 5–4)

9. that gives special consideration, in jobs and college admissions, to members of groups that have been discriminated against in the past (Learning Outcome 5–5)

10. strict (Learning Outcome 5–5)

Multiple Choice

11. b. (Learning Outcome 5–1)

12. a. (Learning Outcome 5–2)

13. a. (Learning Outcome 5–3)

14. c. (Learning Outcome 5–4)

15. b. (Learning Outcome 5–4)

16. a. (Learning Outcome 5–5)

Chapter 6

Fill-In

1. First (Learning Outcome 6–1)

2. Disturbance (Learning Outcome 6–1)

3. 10.7 (Learning Outcome 6–2)

4. Right-to-work (Learning Outcome 6–2)

5. identity interest group (Learning Outcome 6–2)

6. all of the attempts by organizations or by individuals to influence the passage, defeat, or contents of legislation or to influence the administrative decisions of government (Learning Outcome 6–3)

7. amicus curiae briefs (Learning Outcome 6–3)

8. are not coordinated with a candidate's campaign.

9. revolving door (Learning Outcome 6–4)

Multiple Choice

10. b. (Learning Outcome 6–1)

11. c. (Learning Outcome 6–1)

12. a. (Learning Outcome 6–2)

13. c. (Learning Outcome 6–2)

14. b. (Learning Outcome 6–3)

15. c. (Learning Outcome 6–3)

16. c. (Learning Outcome 6–4)

Chapter 7

Fill-In

1. Federalists and the Jeffersonian Republicans (Learning Outcome 7–1)

2. Whig (Learning Outcome 7–1)

3. Republican (Learning Outcomes 7–1)

4. Democrats (Learning Outcomes 7–2)

5. a growing detachment from both major political parties (Learning Outcome 7–2)

6. primary (Learning Outcome 7–3)

7. national convention (Learning Outcome 7–4)

8. Theodore Roosevelt

Multiple Choice

9. a. (Learning Outcome 7–1)

10. c. (Learning Outcome 7–2)

11. b. (Learning Outcome 7–3)

12. c. (Learning Outcome 7–4)

13. b. (Learning Outcome 7–5)

Chapter 8

Fill-In

1. family, schools, churches, the media, opinion leaders, and peer groups (Learning Outcome 8–1)

2. party identification (Learning Outcome 8–2)

3. policy voting (Learning Outcome 8–2)

4. educational attainment; occupation and income; age, gender, religion and ethnic background; and geographic region (Learning Outcome 8–2)

5. the gender gap (Learning Outcome 8–2)

6. each person within the entire population being polled has an equal chance of being chosen (Learning Outcome 8–3)

7. house effect (Learning Outcome 8–3)

8. push poll (Learning Outcome 8–3)

9. owned property (Learning Outcome 8–4)

10. literacy tests, poll taxes, the grandfather clause, and white primaries (Learning Outcome 8–4)

Multiple Choice

11. c. (Learning Outcome 8–1)

12. b. (Learning Outcome 8–1)

13. c. (Learning Outcome 8–2)

14. a. (Learning Outcome 8–3)

15. b. (Learning Outcome 8–4)

16. a. (Learning Outcome 8–4)

Chapter 9

Fill-In

1. who receives the largest popular vote in a state is credited with all that state's electoral votes (Learning Outcome 9–1)

2. 270 (Learning Outcome 9–1)

3. direct (Learning Outcome 9–2)

4. the states moving their primaries to earlier in the year in an effort to make their primaries more prominent in the media and influential in the political process (Learning Outcome 9–2)

5. delegates (Learning Outcome 9–2)

6. opposition (Learning Outcome 9–3)

7. collecting as much information as possible about voters in a database and then filtering out various groups for special attention (Learning Outcome 9–4)

8. federal income tax returns (Learning Outcome 9–5)

9. super PACs (Learning Outcome 9–5)

Multiple Choice

10. a. (Learning Outcome 9–1)

11. b. (Learning Outcome 9–1)

12. a. (Learning Outcome 9–2)

13. c. (Learning Outcome 9–3)

14. c. (Learning Outcome 9–4)

15. b. (Learning Outcome 9–5)

Chapter 10

Fill-In

1. Priming (Learning Outcome 10–1)

2. television (Learning Outcome 10–1)

3. televised comment, lasting for only a few seconds, that captures a thought or a perspective and has an immediate impact on the viewers (Learning Outcome 10–1)

4. they have lost a major share of their advertising revenue to online sites. (Learning Outcome 10–1)

5. John F. Kennedy and Richard Nixon (Learning Outcome 10–2)

6. political candidates' press advisers, who try to convince reporters to give a story or event concerning a candidate a particular interpretation or slant (Learning Outcome 10–2)

7. male, middle-aged, and conservative (Learning Outcome 10–3)

8. talk-show hosts often exaggerate their political biases for effect. Hosts sometimes appear to care more about the entertainment value of their statements than whether they are, strictly speaking, true. No journalistic conventions are observed (Learning Outcome 10–3)

9. losers (Learning Outcome 10–4)

10. the collection, analysis, and dissemination of information online by independent journalists, scholars, political activists, and the general citizenry (Learning Outcome 10–5)

11. net neutrality (Learning Outcome 10–5)

12. gaffe (Learning Outcome 10–5)

Multiple Choice

13. a. (Learning Outcome 10–1)

14. c. (Learning Outcome 10–2)

15. c. (Learning Outcome 10–3)

16. c. (Learning Outcome 10–4)

17. b. (Learning Outcome 10–5)

Chapter 11

Fill-In

1. ten (Learning Outcome 11–1)

2. serve the broad interests of the entire society and act according to his or her perception of national needs (Learning Outcome 11–1)

3. fund-raising ability, franking privileges, professional staffs, lawmaking power, access to the media, and name recognition (Learning Outcome 11–2)

4. preside over sessions of the House, vote in the event of a tie, put questions to a vote, participate in making important committee assignments, and schedule bills for action (Learning Outcome 11–3)

5. cloture (Learning Outcome 11–3)

6. a meeting held by a congressional committee or subcommittee to approve, amend, or redraft a bill (Learning Outcome 11–4)

7. Rules (Learning Outcome 11–4)

8. the federal judiciary and to the cabinet (Learning Outcome 11–5)

9. authorization and appropriation (Learning Outcome 11–6)

Multiple Choice

10. c. (Learning Outcome 11–1)

11. a. (Learning Outcome 11–2)

12. b. (Learning Outcome 11–3)

13. b. (Learning Outcome 11–4)

14. c. (Learning Outcome 11–5)

15. a. (Learning Outcome 11–6)

Chapter 12

Fill-In

1. the legal profession (Learning Outcome 12–1)

2. commander in chief (Learning Outcome 12–2)

3. chief legislator (Learning Outcome 12–2)

4. presidential orders to carry out policies described in laws passed by Congress (Learning Outcome 12–3)

5. War Powers Resolution (Learning Outcome 12–3)

6. an inherent executive power claimed by presidents to withhold information from, or to refuse to appear before, Congress or the courts (Learning Outcome 12–4)

7. the heads of the executive departments and other officials whom the president may choose to appoint (Learning Outcome 12–5)

8. White House Office, the Office of Management and Budget, and the National Security Council (Learning Outcome 12–5)

Multiple Choice

9. c. (Learning Outcome 12–1)

10. c. (Learning Outcome 12–2)

11. a. (Learning Outcome 12–2)

12. a. (Learning Outcome 12–3)

13. b. (Learning Outcome 12–4)

14. c. (Learning Outcome 12–5)

Chapter 13

Fill-In

1. 15 (Learning Outcome 13–1)

2. secretary (Learning Outcome 13–2)

3. Commerce (Learning Outcome 13–2)

4. president; Senate (Learning Outcome 13–3)

5. merit through open, competitive examinations (Learning Outcome 13–3)

6. enabling legislation (Learning Outcome 13–4)

7. a three-way alliance among legislators, bureaucrats, and interest groups to make or preserve policies that benefit their respective interests (Learning Outcome 13–4)

8. reports on gross governmental inefficiency, illegal action, or other wrongdoing (Learning Outcome 13–5)

Multiple Choice

9. b. (Learning Outcome 13–1)

10. a. (Learning Outcome 13–2)

11. c. (Learning Outcome 13–2)

12. b. (Learning Outcome 13–2)

13. c. (Learning Outcome 13–3)

14. b. (Learning Outcome 13–4)

15. a. (Learning Outcome 13–5)

Chapter 14

Fill-In

1. constitutions, statutes, administrative agency rules and regulations, and decisions by courts (Learning Outcome 14–1)
2. the authority of a court to hear and decide a particular case (Learning Outcome 14–2)
3. writ of certiorari (Learning Outcome 14–2)
4. oral arguments (Learning Outcome 14–2)
5. concurring (Learning Outcome 14–2)
6. senatorial courtesy (Learning Outcome 14–3)
7. strict construction and originalism (Learning Outcome 14–4)
8. Anthony Kennedy (Learning Outcome 14–4)
9. rewriting a statute to negate a court's ruling, proposing constitutional amendments to reverse Supreme Court decisions, or limiting the jurisdiction of the federal courts (Learning Outcome 14–5)

Multiple Choice

10. b. (Learning Outcome 14–1)
11. b. (Learning Outcome 14–2)
12. a. (Learning Outcome 14–3)
13. a. (Learning Outcome 14–4)
14. b. (Learning Outcome 14–5)

Chapter 15

Fill-In

1. issue identification and agenda setting, policy formulation and adoption, and policy implementation and evaluation (Learning Outcome 15–1)
2. Medicare (Learning Outcome 15–2)
3. all persons obtain health-care insurance from one source or another, or pay a penalty (Learning Outcome 15–2)
4. Canada (Learning Outcome 15–3)
5. a rise in sea levels, changes in rainfall patterns, and increases in extreme weather (Learning Outcome 15–3)
6. solar power, hydropower, and wind power (Learning Outcome 15–3)
7. recession (Learning Outcome 15–4)
8. Federal Reserve System (Learning Outcome 15–4)

Multiple Choice

9. c. (Learning Outcome 15–1)
10. b. (Learning Outcome 15–2)
11. a. (Learning Outcome 15–2)
12. c. (Learning Outcome 15–3)
13. b. (Learning Outcome 15–4)
14. c. (Learning Outcome 15–4)

Chapter 16

Fill-In

1. departments of state and defense, and the National Security Council and the Central Intelligence Agency (Learning Outcome 16–1)
2. isolationism (Learning Outcome 16–2)
3. Cold War (Learning Outcome 16–2)
4. Afghanistan (Learning Outcome 16–3)
5. Pakistan (Learning Outcome 16–3)
6. Palestinian Authority (Learning Outcome 16–4)
7. North Korea and Iran (Learning Outcome 16–4)
8. Taiwan (Learning Outcome 16–4)

Multiple Choice

9. b. (Learning Outcome 16–1)
10. c. (Learning Outcome 16–2)
11. a. (Learning Outcome 16–2)
12. c. (Learning Outcome 16–3)
13. a. (Learning Outcome 16–4)
14. b. (Learning Outcome 16–4)

NOTES

Chapter 1

1. Harold Laswell, *Politics: Who Gets What, When, and How* (1936; repr., Whitefish, Mont.: Literary Licensing LLC, 2011).

2. As quoted in Mario M. Cuomo and Harold Holzer, *Lincoln on Democracy* (New York: Fordham University Press, 2004), p. 64.

3. It is worth noting that all citizens of Athens were expected to serve in the city-state's army or navy. The assembly that decided on issues of war and peace was made up of the same people who would have to do the fighting.

4. From Lincoln's first inaugural address. See Abraham Lincoln, *Axioms and Aphorisms from Abraham Lincoln* (Seattle: CreateSpace, an Amazon company, 2012), p. 26.

5. Mike Males, "The Stunning Facts on Crime and Imprisonment Everyone Is Ignoring," *Washington Monthly*, March 10, 2016.

Chapter 2

1. The first *European* settlement in today's United States was St. Augustine, Florida, which was founded on September 8, 1565, by the Spaniard Pedro Menéndez de Avilés.

2. Archaeologists recently discovered the remains of a colony at Popham Beach, on the southern coast of what is now Maine, that was established at the same time as the colony at Jamestown. The Popham colony disbanded after thirteen months, however, when the leader, after learning that he had inherited property back home, returned—with the other colonists—to England.

3. John Camp, *Out of the Wilderness: The Emergence of an American Identity in Colonial New England* (Middletown, Conn.: Wesleyan University Press, 1990).

4. Ironically, the colonists were, in fact, protesting a tax reduction. The British government believed that if tea were cheaper, Americans would be more willing to drink it, even though it was still taxed. The Americans viewed the tax reduction as an attempt to trick them into accepting the principle of taxation. If the tea had been expensive, it would have been easy to organize a boycott. Because the tea was cheap, the protesters destroyed it so that no one would be tempted to buy it. (Also, many of the protesters were in the business of smuggling tea, and they would have been put out of business by the cheap competition.)

5. Much of the colonists' fury over British policies was directed personally at King George III, who had ascended the British throne in 1760 at the age of twenty-two, rather than at Britain or British rule *per se.* If you look at the Declaration of Independence in Appendix A, you will note that much of that document focuses on what "He" (George III) has or has not done. George III's lack of political experience, his personality, and his temperament all combined to lend instability to the British government at this crucial point in history.

6. *Thomas Paine: Collected Writings* (New York: Library of America, 1995), p. 36.

7. As quoted in Joseph J. Ellis, *Passionate Sage: The Character and Legacy of John Adams* (1993; repr., New York: W. W. Norton, 2001), p. 104.

8. Locke had coined the phrase "pursuit of happiness" in *An Essay Concerning Human Understanding*. Still, some scholars feel that Locke's influence on the colonists, including Thomas Jefferson, has been exaggerated. For example, Jay Fliegelman states that Jefferson's fascination with the ideas of Homer, Ossian, and Patrick Henry "is of greater significance than his indebtedness to Locke." See Jay Fliegelman, *Declaring Independence: Jefferson, Natural Language, and the Culture of Performance* (Stanford, Calif.: Stanford University Press, 1993).

9. Well before the Articles were ratified, many of them had, in fact, already been implemented. The Second Continental Congress and the thirteen states conducted American military, economic, and political affairs according to the standards and form specified later in the Articles of Confederation. See Robert W. Hoffert, *A Politics of Tensions: The Articles of Confederation and American Political Ideas* (Niwot, Colo.: University Press of Colorado, 1992).

10. Shays' Rebellion was not merely made up of a small group of poor farmers. The participants and their supporters represented whole communities, including some of the wealthiest and most influential families of Massachusetts. See Leonard L. Richards, *Shays' Rebellion: The American Revolution's Final Battle* (Philadelphia: University of Pennsylvania Press, 2003).

11. Madison, however, was much more "republican" in his views—that is, less of a centralist—than Hamilton. See Lance Banning, *The Sacred Fire of Liberty: James Madison and the Founding of the Federal Republic* (Ithaca, N.Y.: Cornell University Press, 1998).

12. The State House was later named Independence Hall. The East Room was the same room in which the Declaration of Independence had been signed eleven years earlier.

13. Charles A. Beard, *An Economic Interpretation of the Constitution of the United States* (1913; repr., Mineola, N.Y.: Dover, 2004.)

14. In 1961, the Twenty-third Amendment added three additional members to the electoral college to represent the District of Columbia.

15. Morris was partly of French descent, which is why his first name may seem unusual. Note, however, that naming one's child "Governor" was not common at the time in any language, including French.

16. Scott J. Hammond, Kevin R. Hardwick, and Howard Leslie Lubert, *Classics of American Political and Constitutional Thought: Origins through the Civil War, Volume 1* (Cambridge, Mass.: Hackett Publishing, 2007), p. 441.

17. For further detail on Wood's depiction of the founders' views, see Gordon S. Wood, *Revolutionary Characters: What Made the Founders Different* (New York: Penguin Press, 2006).

18. Some scholarship suggests that the *Federalist Papers* did not play a significant role in bringing about the ratification of the Constitution. Nonetheless, the papers have lasting value as an authoritative explanation of the Constitution.

19. The papers written by the Anti-Federalists can be found at www.constitution.org/afp/afp.htm.

For essays on the positions, arranged in topical order, of both the Federalists and the Anti-Federalists in the ratification debate, see John P. Kaminski and Richard Leffler, *Federalists and Antifederalists: The Debate over the Ratification of the Constitution*, 2d ed. (Madison, Wis.: Madison House, 1998).

20. The concept of the separation of powers generally is credited to the French political philosopher Montesquieu (1689–1755), who included it in his monumental two-volume work entitled *The Spirit of Laws*, published in 1750. See Charles de Montesquieu, *The Spirit of Laws*, trans. Thomas Nugent (New York: Cosimo Classics, 2011).

21. The Constitution does not explicitly mention the power of judicial review, but the delegates at the Constitutional Convention probably assumed that the courts would have this power. Indeed, Alexander Hamilton, in *Federalist Paper* No. 78, explicitly outlined the concept of judicial review. In any event, whether the founders intended for the courts to exercise this power is a moot point, because in an 1803 decision, *Marbury v. Madison*, the Supreme Court successfully claimed this power for the courts.

22. An amendment concerning compensation of members of Congress, included with the Bill of Rights but not adopted, became the Twenty-seventh Amendment to the Constitution when it was ratified 203 years later, in 1992.

23. The Twenty-first Amendment repealed the Eighteenth Amendment, which had prohibited the manufacture or sale of alcoholic beverages nationwide (Prohibition). Special conventions were necessary because prohibitionist forces controlled legislatures in many states where a majority of the voters supported repeal.

Chapter 3

1. The federal models used by the German and Canadian governments provide interesting comparisons with the U.S. system. See Arthur B. Gunlicks, *The Länder and German Federalism* (Manchester, England: Manchester University Press, 2003); and Jennifer Smith, *Federalism* (Vancouver: University of British Columbia Press, 2004).

2. Text of an address by President Reagan to the National Conference of State Legislatures, Atlanta, Georgia (Washington, D.C.: The White House, Office of the Press Secretary, July 30, 1981).

3. Until the 1960s, U.S. paper currency—known informally as greenbacks—could be redeemed (in peacetime) for an equivalent value in silver. In 1964, the Treasury stopped issuing new silver-backed notes, and in 1968 it halted silver redemption for older notes as well. Today, you can "redeem" an old dollar bill—for a freshly printed one.

4. 133 S.Ct. 2675 (2013).

5. 135 S.Ct. 2584 (2015).

6. An excellent illustration of this principle was President Dwight Eisenhower's disciplining of Arkansas governor Orval Faubus when Faubus refused to allow a Little Rock high school to be desegregated in 1957. Eisenhower federalized

the National Guard to enforce the court-ordered desegregation of the school.

7. 5 U.S. 137 (1803).

8. 17 U.S. 316 (1819).

9. 22 U.S. 1 (1824).

10. *Hammer v. Dagenhart*, 247 U.S. 251 (1918). This decision was overturned in *United States v. Darby*, 312 U.S. 100 (1941).

11. *Wickard v. Filburn*, 317 U.S. 111 (1942).

12. *McLain v. Real Estate Board of New Orleans, Inc.*, 444 U.S. 232 (1980).

13. 514 U.S. 549 (1995).

14. *Printz v. United States*, 521 U.S. 898 (1997).

15. *United States v. Morrison*, 529 U.S. 598 (2000).

16. 549 U.S. 497 (2007).

17. 132 S.Ct. 2492 (2012).

18. 132 S.Ct. 2566 (2012).

19. *South Dakota v. Dole*, 483 U.S. 203 (1987).

20. 133 S.Ct. 2612 (2013).

21. Thomas R. Dye, *American Federalism: Competition Among Governments* (Lanham, Md.: Lexington Books, 1990).

Chapter 4

1. 32 U.S. 243 (1833).

2. *Yamataya v. Fischer*, 189 U.S. 86 (1903).

3. *Reno v. American-Arab Anti-Discrimination Committee*, 325 U.S. 471 (1999).

4. 134 S.Ct. 1811.

5. *Everson v. Board of Education*, 330 U.S. 1 (1947).

6. 370 U.S. 421 (1962).

7. *Stone v. Graham*, 449 U.S. 39 (1980).

8. *Wallace v. Jaffree*, 472 U.S. 38 (1985).

9. See, for example, *Brown v. Gwinnett County School District*, 112 F.3d 1464 (1997).

10. *Santa Fe Independent School District v. Doe*, 530 U.S. 290 (2000).

11. *Epperson v. Arkansas*, 393 U.S. 97 (1968).

12. *Edwards v. Aguillard*, 482 U.S. 578 (1987).

13. *Kitzmiller v. Dover Area School District*, 400 F. Supp.2d 707 (M.D.Pa. 2005).

14. 403 U.S. 602 (1971).

15. In addition, Maine and Vermont have long-standing voucher programs for students in school districts that are too small to support a high school. These vouchers can only be used to attend schools in neighboring public school districts.

16. *Zelman v. Simmons-Harris*, 536 U.S. 639 (2002).

17. *Holmes v. Bush* (Fla.Cir.Ct. 2002). For details about this case, see David Royse, "Judge Rules School Voucher Law Violates Florida Constitution," *USA Today*, August 6, 2002, p. 7D.

18. 98 U.S. 145 (1878).

19. *Police v. City of Newark*, 170 F.3d 359 (3d Cir. 1999).

20. *Equal Employment Opportunity Commission v. Abercrombie & Fitch Stores*, 135 S.Ct. 2038 (2015).

21. 134 S.Ct. 2751 (2014).

22. *Schenck v. United States*, 249 U.S. 47 (1919).

23. The bad tendency test was used later in a famous 1925 case, *Gitlow v. New York* (268 U.S. 652).

24. *Schenck v. United States*, op. cit.

25. *Brandenburg v. Ohio*, 395 U.S. 444 (1969).

26. *Liquormart v. Rhode Island*, 517 U.S. 484 (1996).

27. 413 U.S. 15 (1973).

28. *Reno v. American Civil Liberties Union*, 521 U.S. 844 (1997); and *Ashcroft v. American Civil Liberties Union*, 542 U.S. 656 (2004). In *United States v. American Library Association*, 539 U.S. 194 (2003), the Court finally found that the government could require libraries that received certain federal subsidies to install filtering software to prevent minors from viewing pornographic material. The filters could be turned off at adult request. The subsidies were small, however, and about one-third of libraries nationwide rejected them and did not install the software.

29. *Morse v. Frederick*, 551 U.S. 393 (2007).

30. See, for example, *Doe v. University of Michigan*, 721 F.Supp. 852 (1989).

31. *Hazelwood School District v. Kuhlmeier*, 484 U.S. 260 (1988).

32. Brandeis made this statement in a dissenting opinion in *Olmstead v. United States*, 277 U.S. 438 (1928).

33. 381 U.S. 479 (1965). In this case, the Supreme Court found that Connecticut could not ban birth control methods.

34. 410 U.S. 113 (1973). Jane Roe was not the real name of the woman in this case. It is a common legal pseudonym used to protect a party's privacy.

35. See, for example, the Supreme Court's decision in *Lambert v. Wicklund*, 520 U.S. 1169 (1997). The Court held that a Montana law requiring a minor to notify one of her parents before getting an abortion was constitutional.

36. *Schenck v. ProChoice Network*, 519 U.S. 357 (1997); and *Hill v. Colorado*, 530 U.S. 703 (2000).

37. *McCullen v. Coakley*, 134 S.Ct. 2518 (2014).

38. *Stenberg v. Carhart*, 530 U.S. 914 (2000).

39. *Gonzales v. Carhart*, 550 U.S. 124 (2007).

40. *Washington v. Glucksberg*, 521 U.S. 702 (1997).

41. *Gonzales v. Oregon*, 546 U.S. 243 (2006).

42. The state of South Carolina challenged the constitutionality of this act, claiming that the law violated states' rights under the Tenth Amendment. The Supreme Court, however, held that Congress had the authority, under its commerce power, to pass the act because drivers' personal information had become an article of interstate commerce. See *Reno v. Condon*, 528 U.S. 141 (2000).

43. *Sorrell v. IMS Health*, 564 U.S. 552 (2011).

44. Yiannopoulos finally stumbled badly in February 2017, when a videotape surfaced in which he seemed to endorse *pederasty*—sexual relations between adult men and teenage boys. (Yiannopoulos is gay.) The tape cost him a book contract, speaking engagements, and his position as an editor with the ultra-right Breitbart website. Ironically, from a liberal point of view, Yiannopoulos's remarks in this case were not nearly as offensive as his statements about feminists and transgender persons. They were unacceptable to his conservative allies, however.

45. 372 U.S. 335 (1963).

46. *Mapp v. Ohio*, 367 U.S. 643 (1961).

47. *Riley v. California*, 134 S.Ct. 2473 (2014).

48. 384 U.S. 436 (1966). In 1968, Congress passed legislation including a provision that reinstated the previous rule that statements made by defendants can be used against them as long as the statements were made voluntarily. This provision was never enforced, however, and only in 1999 did a court try to enforce it. The case ultimately came before the Supreme Court, which held that the *Miranda* rights were based on the Constitution and thus could not be overruled by legislative act. See *Dickerson v. United States*, 530 U.S. 428 (2000).

49. *Arizona v. Fulminante*, 499 U.S. 279 (1991).

50. *J.D.B. v. North Carolina*, 564 U.S. 261 (2011).

51. Thomas P. Sullivan, *Police Experiences with Recording Custodial Interrogations* (Chicago: Northwestern University School of Law Center on Wrongful Convictions, Summer 2004), p. 4.

Chapter 5

1. *Michael M. v. Superior Court*, 450 U.S. 464 (1981).

2. See, for example, *Craig v. Boren*, 429 U.S. 190 (1976).

3. *Orr v. Orr*, 440 U.S. 268 (1979).

4. *Mississippi University for Women v. Hogan*, 458 U.S. 718 (1982).

5. 163 U.S. 537 (1896).

6. 347 U.S. 483 (1954).

7. 349 U.S. 294 (1955).

8. *Swann v. Charlotte-Mecklenburg Board of Education*, 402 U.S. 1 (1971).

9. 133 S.Ct. 2612 (2013).

10. *Ledbetter v. Goodyear Tire & Rubber Co.*, 550 U.S. 618 (2007).

11. Claudia Goldin, "A Grand Gender Convergence: Its Last Chapter," *American Economic Review 104*, no. 4 (2014): 1091–1119.

12. *Oncale v. Sundowner Offshore Services*, 523 U.S. 75 (1998).

13. *Faragher v. City of Boca Raton*, 524 U.S. 775 (1998).

14. The Supreme Court upheld these actions in *Hirabayashi v. United States*, 320 U.S. 81 (1943); and *Korematsu v. United States*, 323 U.S. 214 (1944).

15. Historians in the early and mid-twentieth century gave much lower figures for the pre-Columbian population—as low as 14 million people for the entire New World. Today, 40 million is considered a conservative estimate, and an estimate of 100 million has some support among demographers. If 100 million is correct, the epidemics that followed the arrival of the Europeans killed one out of every five people alive in the world at that time. See Charles C. Mann, *1491* (New York: Vintage, 2006).

16. *County of Oneida, New York v. Oneida Indian Nation*, 470 U.S. 226 (1985).

17. *Sutton v. United Airlines*, 527 U.S. 471 (1999); and *Toyota v. Williams*, 534 U.S. 184 (2002).

18. *Board of Trustees of the University of Alabama v. Garrett*, 531 U.S. 356 (2001).

19. 539 U.S. 558 (2003).

20. 135 S.Ct. 2584 (2015).

21. *Goodridge v. Department of Public Health*, 798 N.E.2d 941 (Mass. 2003).

22. 438 U.S. 265 (1978).

23. 515 U.S. 200 (1995).

24. 539 U.S. 244 (2003).

25. 539 U.S. 306 (2003).

26. *Parents Involved in Community Schools v. Seattle School District No. 1*, 551 U.S. 701 (2007).

27. 133 S.Ct. 2411 (2013) and 136 S.Ct. 2198 (2016).

28. *Schuette v. Coalition to Defend Affirmative Action*, 134 S.Ct. 1623 (2014).

Chapter 6

1. David Bicknell Truman, *The Governmental Process: Political Interests and Public Opinion* (Santa Barbara, Calif.: Praeger, 1981). This work is a political science classic.

2. Robert H. Salisbury, *Interests and Institutions: Substance and Structure in American Politics* (Pittsburgh: University of Pittsburgh Press, 1992).

3. Phillips Bradley, ed., *Democracy in America*, Vol. 1 (New York: Knopf, 1980), p. 191.

4. Mancur Olson, *The Logic of Collective Action: Public Goods and the Theory of Groups*, rev. ed. (Cambridge, Mass.: Harvard University Press, 1971).

5. Martin Gilens and Benjamin I. Page, "Testing Theories of American Politics: Elites, Interest Groups, and Average Citizens," *Perspectives on Politics* 12, no. 3 (Fall 2014).

6. 558 U.S. 50 (2010).

7. 132 S.Ct. 2492 (2012).

8. *Caperton v. A. T. Massey Coal Co.*, 556 U.S. 868 (2009).

9. *United States v. Harriss*, 347 U.S. 612 (1954).

Chapter 7

1. Letter to Francis Hopkinson written from Paris while Jefferson was ambassador to France, as cited in John P. Foley, ed., *The Jeffersonian Cyclopedia* (New York: Russell & Russell, 1967), p. 677.

2. The U.S. Senate presents the text of the address at www.access.gpo.gov/congress/senate/farewell/sd106-21.pdf.

3. The association of red with the Republicans and blue with the Democrats is little more than a decade old. The terms *red* and *blue* are derived from the colors used by the major television networks to show the states carried by the Republican and Democratic presidential candidates. This use of colors deliberately reverses a traditional pattern. In most European countries, the right-of-center party uses blue, while the left-of-center party employs red. The use of red originated in the socialist movement, from which most European left-of-center parties descend. From time to time, Republicans have accused Democrats of socialism. U.S. television networks thus assigned red to the Republicans precisely so that the networks would not appear to be endorsing that accusation.

4. Theda Skocpol and Vanessa Williamson, *The Tea Party and the Remaking of Republican Conservatism* (New York: Oxford University Press, 2013).

5. John B. Judis and Ruy Teixeira, *The Emerging Democratic Majority* (New York: Scribner, 2002).

6. Matt Grossmann and David A. Hopkins, "Ideological Republicans and Group Interest Democrats: The Asymmetry of American Party Politics," *Perspectives on Politics* 13, no. 1 (March 2015): 119-139.

7. For an interesting discussion of the pros and cons of patronage from a constitutional perspective, see the majority opinion versus the dissent in the Supreme Court case *Board of County Commissioners v. Umbehr*, 518 U.S. 668 (1996).

8. The term *third party*, although not literally accurate (because sometimes there has been a fourth party, a fifth party, and even more), is commonly used to refer to a minor party.

9. Today, ten states have multimember districts for their state houses, and two also have have multimember districts for their state senates.

Chapter 8

1. Doris A. Graber, *Mass Media and American Politics*, 9th ed. (Washington, D.C.: CQ Press, 2014).

2. The elections that Gallup predicted incorrectly were usually close ones. In 2004, Gallup reported a statistical tie—49 percent each—between Republican George W. Bush and Democrat John Kerry. In 1976, Gallup falsely predicted that Republican incumbent Gerald Ford would prevail over Democrat Jimmy Carter. In 1948, Gallup wrongly predicted that Republican Thomas Dewey would defeat Democratic incumbent Harry Truman. The 2012 elections, however, may have been Gallup's biggest embarrassment to date. Assuming very low Democratic voter turnout, Gallup had Romney well in the lead throughout October. It corrected its last poll to reflect greater turnout, but it still predicted a Romney victory.

3. John M. Benson, "When Is an Opinion Really an Opinion?" *Public Perspective*, September/October 2001, pp. 40–41.

4. As quoted in Karl G. Feld, "When Push Comes to Shove: A Polling Industry Call to Arms," *Public Perspective*, September/October 2001, p. 38.

5. Pew Research Center for the People and the Press, survey conducted September 21–October 4, 2006, and reported in "Who Votes, Who Doesn't, and Why," released October 28, 2006.

6. *Guinn v. United States*, 238 U.S. 347 (1915).

7. *Smith v. Allwright*, 321 U.S. 649 (1944).

8. *Crawford v. Marion County Election Board*, 553 U.S. 181 (2008).

9. *Veasey v. Abbott*, 815 F.3d 958 (2016).

10. *North Carolina NAACP v. McCrory*, 831 F.3d 204, 241 (4th Cir. 2016).

11. For more information on voting systems, see the website of verifiedvoting.org.

12. The argument about the vote-eligible population was first made by Michael P. McDonald and Samuel L. Popkin, "The Myth of the Vanishing Voter," *American Political Science Review*, 95, no. 4 (December 2001), p. 963.

Chapter 9

1. These states award one electoral vote to the candidate who wins the popular vote in a congressional district and an additional two electoral votes to the winner of the statewide popular vote. Other states have considered similar plans.

2. The word *caucus* apparently was first used in the name of a men's club, the Caucus Club of colonial Boston, sometime between 1755 and 1765. (Many early political and government meetings took place in pubs.) We have no certain knowledge of the origin of the word, but it may be from an Algonquin term meaning "elder" or from the Latin name of a drinking vessel.

3. Today, the Democratic and Republican caucuses in the House and Senate (the Republicans now use the term *conference* instead of *caucus*) choose each party's congressional leadership and sometimes discuss legislation and legislative strategy.

4. Due to the customs of the time, none of the candidates could admit that he had made a personal decision to run. All claimed to have entered the race in response to popular demand.

5. Parties cannot use their freedom-of-association rights to practice racial discrimination in state-sponsored elections: *Smith v. Allwright*, 321 U.S. 649 (1944). When racial discrimination is not involved, the parties have regularly won freedom-of-association suits against state governments. Examples are *Tashjian v. Republican Party of Connecticut*, 479 U.S. 208 (1986), and *California Democratic Party v. Jones*, 530 U.S. 567 (2000).

6. In Washington, the state government holds presidential primaries for both parties. The Democratic Party, however, ignores the Democratic primary and chooses its national convention delegates through a caucus/convention system. In 1984, following a dispute with the state of Michigan over primary rules, the state Democratic Party organized a presidential primary election that was run completely by party volunteers. In 2008, after a similar dispute with its state, the Virginia Republican Party chose its candidate for the U.S. Senate at its state party convention instead of through the Virginia primary elections.

7. The case was *California Democratic Party v. Jones*, cited in endnote 5.

8. *Washington State Grange v. Washington State Republican Party et al.*, 552 U.S. 442 (2008).

9. See Marty Cohen, David Karol, Hans Noel, and John Zaller, *The Party Decides: Presidential Nominations Before and After Reform* (Chicago: University of Chicago Press, 2008). This enormously influential work argues that party leaders usually determine primary outcomes. Donald Trump's political career placed this theory into question.

10. *U.S. Term Limits, Inc. v. Thornton*, 514 U.S. 779 (1995).

11. This act is sometimes referred to as the Federal Election Campaign Act of 1972 because it became effective in that year. The official date of the act, however, is 1971.

12. *Buckley v. Valeo*, 424 U.S. 1 (1976).

13. This figure is from the Center for Responsive Politics.

14. *Colorado Republican Federal Campaign Committee v. Federal Election Commission*, 518 U.S. 604 (1996).

15. Quoted in George Will, "The First Amendment on Trial," *The Washington Post*, December 1, 2002, p. B7.

16. 540 U.S. 93 (2003).

17. 551 U.S. 449 (2007).

18. 558 U.S. 50 (2010).

19. 599 F.3d 686 (D.C.Cir. 2010).

20. 134 S.Ct. 1434.

21. *NAACP v. Alabama*, 357 U.S. 449 (1958).

Chapter 10

1. 376 U.S. 254 (1964).

2. *Mutual Film Corporation v. Industrial Commission of Ohio*, 236 U.S. 230 (1915).

3. *Joseph Burstyn, Inc. v. Wilson*, 343 U.S. 495 (1952).

4. *Reno v. American Civil Liberties Union*, 521 U.S. 844 (1997).

5. *United States v. Playboy Entertainment Group*, 529 U.S. 803 (2000).

6. Bernard Cohen, *The Press and Foreign Policy* (Princeton, N.J.: Princeton University Press, 1963), p. 81.

7. As quoted in Michael Grunwald, "The Year of Playing Dirtier," *Washington Post*, October 27, 2006, p. A1.

8. John G. Geer, *In Defense of Negativity: Attack Ads in Presidential Campaigns* (Chicago: University of Chicago Press, 2006).

9. The commission's action was upheld by a federal court. See *Perot v. Federal Election Commission*, 97 F.3d 553 (D.C.Cir. 1996).

10. For more details on how political candidates manage news coverage, see Doris A. Graber, *Mass Media and American Politics*, 9th ed. (Washington, D.C.: CQ Press, 2014).

11. For suggestions on how to dissect spin and detect when language is steering people toward a conclusion, see Brooks Jackson and Kathleen Hall Jamieson, *unSpun: Finding Facts in a World of Disinformation* (New York: Random House, 2007).

12. *Red Lion Broadcasting Co. v. FCC*, 395 U.S. 367 (1969).

13. Kathleen Hall Jamieson, *Everything You Think You Know about Politics . . . and Why You're Wrong* (New York: Basic Books, 2000), pp. 187–195.

14. Debra Reddin van Tuyll and Hubert P. van Tuyll, "Political Partisanship," in William David Sloan and Jenn Burleson Mackay, eds., *Media Bias: Finding It, Fixing It* (Jefferson, N.C.: McFarland, 2007), pp. 35-49.

15. Jamieson, *op. cit.*, pp. xiii–xiv.

16. The term *podcasting* is used for this type of information delivery because initially podcasts were downloaded onto Apple's iPods.

Chapter 11

1. These states are Alaska, Delaware, Montana, North Dakota, South Dakota, Vermont, and Wyoming.

2. In June 2015, the United States Supreme Court upheld the right of state voters to transfer redistricting to independent commissions. Voters can do this even if the state legislature objects. See *Arizona State Legislature v. Arizona Independent Redistricting Commission*, 576 U.S. ____ (2015).

3. *Baker v. Carr*, 369 U.S. 186 (1962).

4. *Wesberry v. Sanders*, 376 U.S. 1 (1964).

5. See, for example, *Davis v. Bandemer*, 478 U.S. 109 (1986).

6. *Amicus curiae* brief filed by the American Civil Liberties Union (ACLU) in support of the appellants in *Easley v. Cromartie*, 532 U.S. 234 (2001).

7. See, for example, *Miller v. Johnson*, 515 U.S. 900 (1995); *Shaw v. Reno*, 509 U.S. 630 (1993); *Shaw v. Hunt*, 517 U.S. 899 (1996); and *Bush v. Vera*, 517 U.S. 952 (1996).

8. *Cooper v. Harris*, ____ U.S.____ (2017).

9. *Powell v. McCormack*, 395 U.S. 486 (1969).

10. Some observers maintain that another reason Congress stays in session longer is the invention of air-conditioning. Until the advent of air-conditioning, no member of Congress wanted to stay in session during the hot and sticky late spring, summer, and early fall months in Washington, D.C.

11. *U.S. Term Limits, Inc. v. Thornton*, 514 U.S. 779 (1995).

Chapter 12

1. Lyndon B. Johnson, *The Vantage Point: Perspectives of the Presidency, 1963–1969* (New York: Henry Holt & Co., 1971).

2. Four presidents have been Unitarians, members of a church directly descended from the (Protestant) Massachusetts Puritans. Because Unitarianism is not strictly Christian, however, it cannot be called Protestant either. Mitt Romney, if elected in 2012, would have been the first Mormon president. Some may consider the Mormons, or Latter-Day Saints, to be in the Protestant tradition, but their theology differs radically from that of both Protestant and Catholic Christianity.

3. *Ex parte Grossman*, 267 U.S. 87 (1925). *Ex parte Grossman*, 267 U.S. 87 (1925).

4. *Clinton v. City of New York*, 524 U.S. 417 (1998). *Clinton v. City of New York*, 524 U.S. 417 (1998).

5. Woodrow Wilson, *Constitutional Government in the United States* (1908; repr., Washington, D.C.: Woodrow Wilson Press, 2008), p. 70.

6. The Constitution does not grant the president explicit power to remove from office officials who are not performing satisfactorily or who do not agree with the president. In 1926, however, the Supreme Court prevented Congress from interfering with the president's ability to fire those executive-branch officials whom he had appointed with Senate approval. See *Myers v. United States*, 272 U.S. 52 (1926).

7. Ironically, Lincoln believed that the actions of the president ought to be strictly limited when war powers were not concerned. He therefore left most domestic issues that did not involve the war entirely to Congress. In doing so, Lincoln was true to the ideas of his former party, the Whigs. That party advocated a limited role for the presidency in reaction to the sweeping assumption of authority by President Andrew Jackson, their great opponent. See David Donald's classic essay "Abraham Lincoln: Whig in the White House," in *Lincoln Reconsidered: Essays on the Civil War Era*, 3d ed. (New York: Vintage, 2001), pp. 133–147.

8. John W. Kingdon, *Agendas, Alternatives, and Public Policies* (Boston: Little, Brown, 1984), p. 25.

9. Richard E. Neustadt, *Presidential Power: The Politics of Leadership* (New York: John Wiley, 1960), p. 10.

10. As quoted in Richard M. Pious, *The American Presidency* (New York: Basic Books, 1979), pp. 51–52.

11. A phrase coined by Samuel Kernell in *Going Public: New Strategies of Presidential Leadership*, 4th ed. (Washington, D.C.: Congressional Quarterly Press, 2006).

12. Christopher S. Kelley and Bryan W. Marshall, "Assessing Presidential Power: Signing Statements and Veto Threats as Coordinated Strategies," *American Politics Research* 37, no. 3 (May 2009): 508.

13. Congress used its power to declare war in the War of 1812, the Mexican War (1846–1848), the Spanish-American War (1898), and World War I (U.S. involvement lasted from 1917 until 1918), and on six different occasions during World War II (U.S. involvement lasted from 1941 until 1945).

14. The scandal involved an illegal break-in at the Democratic National Committee offices in 1972 by members of President Richard Nixon's reelection campaign staff. The offices were located in the Watergate hotel/office complex in Washington, hence the name.

15. As quoted in Thomas E. Cronin, *The State of the Presidency*, 2d ed. (Boston: Little, Brown, 1980), p. 11.

Chapter 13

1. This definition follows the classic model of bureaucracy put forth by German sociologist Max Weber. See Max Weber, *The Theory of Social and Economic Organization*, ed. Talcott Parsons (New York: Oxford University Press, 1947; repr. Eastford, Conn.: Martino Fine Books, 2012).

2. It should be noted that although the president is technically the head of the bureaucracy, the president cannot always control the bureaucracy—as you will read later in this chapter.

3. Maury Gittleman and Brooks Pierce, "Compensation for State and Local Government Workers,"

Journal of Economic Perspectives 26, no. 1 (Winter 2012), pp. 217–242 (www.aeaweb.org/articles.php?doi=10.1257/jep.26.1.217).

4. Chris Edwards, "Reducing the Costs of Federal Worker Pay and Benefits," October 1, 2015 (www.downsizinggovernment.org/federal-worker-pay).

5. Alicia Munnell, Jean-Pierre Aubry, Josh Hurwitz, and Laura Quinby, *Comparing Compensation: State-Local versus Private Sector Workers*, Center for Retirement Research at Boston College, September 2011 (slge.org/publications/comparing-compensation-state-local-versus-private-sectorworkers).

6. Congressional Budget Office, "Comparing the Compensation of Federal and Private-Sector Employees," January 30, 2012 (www.cbo.gov/publication/42921).

7. For an insightful analysis of the policymaking process in Washington, D.C., and the role played by various groups in the process, see Morton H. Halperin and Priscilla A. Clapp, with Arnold Kanter, *Bureaucratic Politics and Foreign Policy*, 2d ed. (Washington, D.C.: The Brookings Institution, 2006). Although the focus of the book is on foreign policy, the analysis applies in many ways to the general policymaking process.

Chapter 14

1. 347 U.S. 483 (1954).

2. See *Plessy v. Ferguson*, 163 U.S. 537(1896).

3. 558 U.S. 310(2010).

4. *Austin v. Michigan Chamber of Commerce*, 494 U.S. 652 (1990) and *McConnell v. Federal Election Commission*,540 U.S. 93 (2003).

5. Although a state's highest court is often referred to as the state supreme court, there are exceptions. In the New York court system, for example, the supreme court is a trial court, and the highest court is called the New York Court of Appeals.

6. Between 1790 and 1891, Congress allowed the Supreme Court almost no discretion over which cases to decide. After 1925, in almost 95 percent of appealed cases the Court could choose whether to hear arguments and issue an opinion. Beginning in October 1988, mandatory review was nearly eliminated.

7. *Trinity Lutheran Church v. Comer*, ___ U.S. ___ (2017).

8. *Ziglar v. Abbasi*, ___ U.S. ___ (2017).

9. *Fry v. Napoleon Community Schools*, ___ U.S. ___ (2017).

10. *Cooper v. Harris*, ___ U.S. ___ (2017).

11. 135 S.Ct. 2584 (2015).

12. 347 U.S. 483 (1954).

13. *Friedrichs v. California Teachers Association*, 136 S.Ct. 1083 (2016).

14. 5 U.S. 137 (1803). The Supreme Court had considered the constitutionality of an act of Congress in *Hylton v. United States*, 3 U.S. 171 (1796), in which Congress's power to levy certain taxes was challenged. That particular act was ruled constitutional, rather than unconstitutional, however, so this first federal exercise of judicial review was not clearly recognized as such. Also, during the decade before the adoption of the federal Constitution, courts in at least eight states had exercised the power of judicial review.

15. *King v. Burwell*, 135 S.Ct. 2480 (2015).

16. 539 U.S. 558 (2003).

17. 135 S.Ct. 2584 (2015).

18. *West Virginia v. EPA* (pending).

19. Antonin Scalia, *A Matter of Interpretation: Federal Courts and the Law* (Princeton, N.J.: Princeton University Press, 1997; new edition 2017).

20. Letter by Thomas Jefferson to William C. Jarvis, 1820, in Andrew A. Lipscomb and Albert Ellery Bergh, *The Writings of Thomas Jefferson*, Memorial Edition (Washington, D.C.: Thomas Jefferson Memorial Association of the United States, 1904).

21. As quoted in Carl Hulse and David D. Kirkpatrick, "DeLay Says Federal Judiciary Has 'Run Amok,' Adding Congress Is Partly to Blame," *New York Times*, April 8, 2005, p. 5.

Chapter 15

1. Stan Dorn, *Uninsured and Dying Because of It: Updating the Institute of Medicine Analysis on the Impact of Uninsurance on Mortality* (Washington, D.C.: Urban Institute, 2008).

2. *National Federation of Independent Business v. Sebelius*, 132 S.Ct. 2566 (2012).

3. *King v. Burwell*, 135 S.Ct. 2480 (2015).

4. A recent investigation has shown that hydraulic fracturing that takes place deep underground has no effect on underground water sources used for human consumption. The distance between the fracking zone and the water table is too great. However, contamination *is* possible if the pipes leading down to the fracking are not properly sealed. A second study has linked the underground disposal of wastewater generated by fracking to an increase in the number of small earthquakes. Fracking itself rarely induces quakes.

5. Paul Krugman, "Romer and Bernstein on Stimulus," Conscience of a Liberal (blog), January 10, 2009.

Chapter 16

1. *Public Papers of the Presidents of the United States: Harry S. Truman, 1947* (Washington, D.C.: U.S. Government Printing Office, 1963), pp. 176–180.

2. The containment policy was outlined by George F. Kennan, the chief of the policy-planning staff for the Department of State at that time, in an article that appeared in *Foreign Affairs*, July 1947, p. 575. The author's name was given as "X."

3. Antiwar bombings differed from more recent ones: Antiwar bombers made a general practice of phoning in warnings with the goal of preventing casualties. In most cases, the warnings were successful. The right-wing bombers of the 1990s and today's jihadi terrorists, in contrast, clearly have sought to kill as many people as possible.

4. The Nazis did, however, use poison gas against civilians as part of the *holocaust*, the attempt to murder the entire Jewish population of Europe.

GLOSSARY

A

adjudicate To render a judicial decision. In administrative law, it is the process in which an administrative law judge hears and decides issues that arise when an agency charges a person or firm with violating a law or regulation enforced by the agency.

administrative law The body of law created by administrative agencies (in the form of rules, regulations, orders, and decisions) in order to carry out their duties and responsibilities.

affirmative action A policy that gives special consideration, in jobs and college admissions, to members of groups that have been discriminated against in the past.

agenda setting The ability to determine which issues are considered important by the public and by politicians.

agents of political socialization People and institutions that influence the political views of others.

Anti-Federalists A political group that opposed the adoption of the Constitution.

appellate court A court of appeals, consisting of a panel of three or more judges. It does not hear evidence or testimony. Its task is to determine whether the trial court erred in applying the law in a particular case.

apportionment The distribution of House seats among the states on the basis of their respective populations.

appropriation A part of the congressional budgeting process—the determination of how many dollars will be spent in a given year on a particular government activity.

Articles of Confederation The nation's first constitution, which established a national form of government following the American Revolution. The Articles provided for a confederal form of government in which the central government had few powers.

Australian ballot A secret ballot that is prepared, distributed, and counted by government officials at public expense. Used by all states in the United States since 1888.

authority The ability to legitimately exercise power, such as the power to make and enforce laws.

authorization A part of the congressional budgeting process—the creation of the legal basis for government programs.

autocracy A form of government in which the power and authority of the government are in the hands of a single person.

B

biased sample A poll sample that does not accurately represent the population.

bicameral legislature A legislature made up of two chambers, or parts.

bill of attainder A legislative act that inflicts punishment on particular persons or groups without granting them the right to a trial.

Bill of Rights The first ten amendments to the U.S. Constitution. They list the freedoms—such as the freedoms of speech, press, and religion—that a citizen enjoys and that cannot be infringed on by the government.

block grant A federal grant given to a state for a broad area, such as criminal justice or mental-health programs.

bureaucracy A large, complex, hierarchically structured administrative organization that carries out specific functions.

bureaucrat An individual who works in a bureaucracy. As generally used, the term refers to a government employee.

C

cabinet An advisory group selected by the president to assist with decision making. Traditionally, the cabinet has consisted of the heads of the executive departments and other officers whom the president may choose to appoint.

campaign strategy The comprehensive plan developed by a candidate and his or her advisers for winning an election.

capitalism An economic system based on the private ownership of wealth-producing property, free markets, and freedom of contract. The privately owned corporation is the preeminent capitalist institution.

case law The rules of law announced in court decisions. Case law is the aggregate of reported cases that interpret judicial precedents, statutes, regulations, and constitutional provisions.

categorical grant A federal grant targeted for a specific purpose as defined by federal law.

caucus A meeting held to choose political candidates or delegates.

checks and balances A major principle of American government in which each of the three branches is given the means to check (to restrain or balance) the actions of the others.

chief diplomat The role of the president of the United States in recognizing and interacting with foreign governments.

chief executive The head of the executive branch of government. In the United States, the president.

chief of staff The person who directs the operations of the White House Office and advises the president on important matters.

Children's Health Insurance Program (CHIP) A joint federal–state program that provides health-care insurance for children from low-income families.

citizen journalism The collection, analysis, and dissemination of information online by independent journalists, scholars, political activists, and the general citizenry.

civil disobedience The deliberate and public act of refusing to obey laws thought to be unjust.

civil law The branch of law that spells out the duties that individuals in society owe to other persons or to their governments, excluding the duty not to commit crimes.

civil liberties Individual rights protected by the Constitution against the powers of the government.

civil rights The rights of all Americans to equal treatment under the law, as provided by the Fourteenth Amendment to the Constitution.

civil rights movement The movement in the 1950s and 1960s, by minorities and concerned whites, to end racial discrimination.

civil service Nonmilitary government employees.

climate change The increase in the average temperature of the earth's surface over the last half century and its projected continuation. Also referred to as *global warming*.

closed primary A primary in which only party members can vote to choose that party's candidates.

cloture A procedure for ending filibusters in the Senate and bringing the matter under consideration to a vote.

coalition An alliance of individuals or groups with a variety of interests and opinions who join together to support all or part of a political party's platform. Also, an alliance of nations formed to undertake a foreign policy action, particularly a military action. A coalition is often a temporary alliance that dissolves after the action is concluded.

Cold War The war of words, warnings, and ideologies between the Soviet Union and the United States that lasted from the late 1940s through the late 1980s.

colonial empire A group of dependent nations that are under the rule of an imperial power.

commander in chief The supreme commander of a nation's military force.

commerce clause The clause in Article I, Section 8, of the Constitution that gives Congress the power to regulate interstate commerce (commerce involving more than one state).

commercial speech Advertising statements that describe products. Commercial speech receives less protection under the First Amendment than ordinary speech.

common law The body of law developed from judicial decisions in English and U.S. courts, not attributable to a legislature.

competitive federalism A model of federalism in which state and local governments compete for businesses and citizens, who in effect "vote with their feet" by moving to jurisdictions that offer a competitive advantage.

concurrent powers Powers held by both the federal and the state governments in a federal system.

concurring opinion A statement written by a judge or justice who agrees (concurs) with the court's decision, but for reasons different from those in the majority opinion.

confederal system A league of independent sovereign states, joined together by a central government that has only limited powers over them.

confederation A league of independent states that are united only for the purpose of achieving common goals.

conference In regard to the Supreme Court, a private meeting of the justices in which they present their arguments concerning a case under consideration.

conference committee A temporary committee that is formed when the two chambers of Congress pass differing versions of the same bill. The conference committee consists of members from the House and the Senate who work out a compromise bill.

conference report A report submitted by a conference committee after it has drafted a single version of a bill.

congressional district The geographic area that is served by one member in the House of Representatives.

conservatism A set of political beliefs that include a limited role for the national government in helping individuals and in the economic affairs of the nation, as well as support for traditional values and lifestyles.

conservative movement An ideological movement that arose in the 1950s and 1960s and continues to shape conservative beliefs.

Constitutional Convention The convention of delegates from the states that was held in Philadelphia in 1787 for the purpose of amending the Articles of Confederation. In fact, the delegates wrote a new constitution (the U.S. Constitution) that established a federal form of government.

constitutional law Law based on the U.S. Constitution and the constitutions of the various states.

containment A U.S. policy designed to contain the spread of communism by offering military and economic aid to threatened nations.

contempt of court A ruling that a person has disobeyed a court order or has shown disrespect to the court or to a judicial proceeding.

continuing resolution A temporary resolution passed by Congress that enables executive agencies to continue working with the same funding that they had in the previous fiscal year.

cooperative federalism A model of federalism in which the states and the federal government cooperate in solving problems.

credentials committee A committee of each national political party that evaluates the claims of national party convention delegates to be the legitimate representatives of their states.

criminal law The branch of law that defines and governs actions that constitute crimes. Generally, criminal law has to do with wrongful actions committed against society for which society demands redress.

cross-cutting requirements Requirements that apply to all federal grants.

Cuban missile crisis A nuclear standoff that occurred in 1962 when the United States learned that the Soviet Union had placed nuclear warheads in Cuba.

D

dealignment Among voters, a growing detachment from both major political parties.

de facto segregation Racial segregation that occurs not as a result of government actions but because of social and economic conditions and residential patterns.

de jure segregation Racial segregation that occurs because of laws or decisions by government agencies.

delegate A person selected to represent the people of one geographic area at a party convention.

democracy A system of government in which the people have ultimate political authority. The word is derived from the Greek demos ("the people") and kratia ("rule").

détente A French word meaning a "relaxation of tensions." Détente characterized the relationship between the United States and the Soviet Union in the 1970s as they attempted to pursue cooperative dealings and arms control.

deterrence A policy of building up military strength for the purpose of discouraging (deterring) military attacks by other nations. This policy supported the arms race between the United States and the Soviet Union during the Cold War.

devolution The surrender or transfer of powers to local authorities by a central government.

dictatorship A form of government in which absolute power is exercised by an individual or group whose power is not supported by tradition.

diplomat A person who represents one country in dealing with representatives of another country.

direct democracy A system of government in which political decisions are made by the people themselves rather than by elected representatives. This form of government was practiced in some parts of ancient Greece.

direct primary An election held within each of the two major parties—Democratic and Republican—to choose the party's candidates for the general election. Voters choose the candidate directly, rather than through delegates.

direct technique Any method used by an interest group to interact with government officials directly to further the group's goals.

dissenting opinion A statement written by a judge or justice who disagrees with the majority opinion.

diversity of citizenship A basis for federal court jurisdiction over a lawsuit that arises when (1) the parties in the lawsuit live in different states or when one of the parties is a foreign government or a foreign citizen, and (2) the amount in controversy is more than $75,000.

divine right theory The theory that a monarch's right to rule was derived directly from God rather than from the consent of the people.

division of powers A basic principle of federalism established by the U.S. Constitution, by which powers are divided between the national and state governments.

domestic policy Public policy concerning issues within a national unit, such as national policy on health care or the economy.

double jeopardy The prosecution of a person twice for the same criminal offense. Prohibited by the Fifth Amendment in all but a few circumstances.

dual federalism A system of government in which the federal and the state governments maintain diverse but sovereign powers.

due process clause The constitutional guarantee, set out in the Fifth and Fourteenth Amendments, that the government will not illegally or arbitrarily deprive a person of life, liberty, or property.

due process of law The requirement that the government use fair, reasonable, and standard procedures whenever it takes any legal action against an individual.

E

earmark Spending provision inserted into legislation that benefits only a small number of people.

easy-money policy A monetary policy that involves stimulating the economy by expanding the rate of growth of the money supply.

economic policy All actions taken by the national government to address ups and downs in the nation's level of business activity.

elector In American politics, a member of the electoral college.

electoral college The group of electors who are selected by the voters in each state to officially elect the president and vice president. The number of electors in each state is equal to the number of that state's representatives in both chambers of Congress.

electorate All of the citizens eligible to vote in a given election.

electronic media Communication channels that involve electronic transmissions, such as radio, television, and the Internet.

elite theory The belief that the government is controlled by one or more elite groups.

enabling legislation A law enacted by a legislature to establish an administrative agency. Enabling legislation normally specifies the name, purpose, composition, and powers of the agency being created.

entitlement program A government program that provides benefits to all persons who meet specified requirements.

equality A concept that holds, at a minimum, that all people are entitled to equal protection under the law.

equal protection clause Section 1 of the Fourteenth Amendment, which says that no state shall "deny to any person within its jurisdiction the equal protection of the laws."

establishment clause The section of the First Amendment that prohibits Congress from passing laws "respecting an establishment of religion."

exclusionary rule A criminal procedural rule stating that illegally obtained evidence is not admissible in court.

executive agreement A binding international agreement, or pact, that is made between the president and another head of state and that does not require Senate approval.

Executive Office of the President (EOP) A group of staff agencies that assist the president in carrying out major duties.

executive order A presidential order to carry out a policy or policies described in a law passed by Congress.

executive privilege An inherent executive power claimed by presidents to withhold information from, or to refuse to appear before, Congress or the courts. The president can also accord the privilege to other executive officials.

***ex post facto* law** A criminal law that punishes individuals for committing an act that was legal when the act was committed.

expressed powers Constitutional or statutory powers that are expressly provided for by the U.S. Constitution; also called *enumerated powers*.

F

faction A group of individuals forming a cohesive minority.

federalism A system of shared sovereignty between two levels of government— one national and one subnational—occupying the same geographic region.

Federalists A political group, led by Alexander Hamilton and John Adams, that supported the adoption of the Constitution and the creation of a federal form of government.

federal mandate A requirement in federal legislation that pressures states and municipalities to comply with certain rules.

Federal Open Market Committee (FOMC) The most important body within the Federal Reserve System. It decides how monetary policy should be carried out.

federal question A question that pertains to the U.S. Constitution, acts of Congress, or treaties. A federal question provides a basis for federal court jurisdiction.

federal system A form of government that provides for a division of powers between a central government and several regional governments.

feminism A doctrine advocating full political, economic, and social equality for women.

filibustering Using the Senate tradition of unlimited debate to prevent action.

first budget resolution A budget resolution, which is supposed to be passed in May, that sets overall revenue goals and spending targets for the next fiscal year, beginning on October 1.

First Continental Congress A gathering of delegates from twelve of the thirteen colonies, held in 1774 to protest the Coercive Acts.

fiscal federalism The allocation of taxes collected by one level of government (typically the national government) to another level (typically state or local governments).

fiscal policy The use of changes in government expenditures and taxes to alter national economic variables.

fiscal year A twelve-month period that is established for accounting purposes. The government's fiscal year runs from October 1 through September 30.

foreign policy A systematic and general plan that guides a country's attitudes and actions toward the rest of the world. Foreign policy includes all of the economic, military, commercial, and diplomatic positions and actions that a nation takes in its relationships with other countries.

fracking A technique for extracting oil or natural gas from underground rock by the high-power injection of a mixture of water, sand, and chemicals.

framing An agenda-setting technique that establishes the context of a media report. Framing can mean fitting events into a familiar story or filtering information through preconceived ideas.

free exercise clause The provision of the First Amendment stating that the government cannot pass laws "prohibiting the free exercise" of religion.

free rider problem The existence of persons who benefit from the actions of a group but do not contribute to the group.

fundamental right A basic right of all Americans, such as First Amendment rights. Any law or action that prevents some group of persons from exercising a fundamental right is subject to the *strict scrutiny standard*.

G

gender gap The difference between the percentage of votes cast for a particular candidate by women and the percentage of votes cast for the same candidate by men.

general election A regularly scheduled election to choose the U.S. president, vice president, and senators and representatives in Congress. General elections are held in even-numbered years on the Tuesday after the first Monday in November.

gerrymandering The drawing of a legislative district's boundaries in such a way as to maximize the influence of a certain group or political party.

glass ceiling An invisible but real discriminatory barrier that prevents women and minorities from rising to top positions of power or responsibility.

GOP A nickname for the Republican Party—"grand old party."

government The individuals and institutions that make society's rules and possess the power and authority to enforce those rules.

government corporation An agency of the government that is run as a business enterprise. Such agencies engage primarily in commercial activities, produce revenues, and require greater flexibility than most government agencies have.

grandfather clause A clause in a state law that had the effect of restricting voting rights to those whose ancestors had voted before the 1860s. It was one of the techniques used in the South to prevent African Americans from exercising their right to vote.

Great Compromise A plan for a bicameral legislature in which one chamber would be based on population and the other chamber would represent each state equally. Also known as the Connecticut Compromise.

greenhouse gas A gas that, when released into the atmosphere, traps the sun's heat and slows its release into outer space. Carbon dioxide (CO_2) is a major example.

H

head of state The person who serves as the ceremonial head of a country's government and represents that country to the rest of the world.

house effect In the case of a polling firm, a consistent tendency to report results more favorable to one of the political parties than the results reported by other pollsters.

I

ideology Generally, a system of political ideas that are rooted in religious or philosophical beliefs concerning human nature, society, and government.

imminent lawless action test The current Supreme Court doctrine for assessing the constitutionality of subversive speech. To be illegal, speech must be "directed to inciting . . . imminent lawless action."

implied powers The powers of the federal government that are implied by the expressed powers in the Constitution, particularly in Article I, Section 8.

independent executive agency A federal agency that is not located within a cabinet department.

independent expenditure An expenditure for activities that are independent from (not coordinated with) those of a political candidate or a political party.

independent regulatory agency A federal organization that is responsible for creating and implementing rules that regulate private activity and protect the public interest in a particular sector of the economy.

indirect technique Any method used by interest groups to influence government officials through third parties, such as voters.

individual mandate In the context of health-care reform, a requirement that all persons obtain health-care insurance from one source or another. Those failing to do so must pay a penalty.

inflation A sustained rise in average prices. It is equivalent to a decline in the value of the dollar.

inherent powers The powers of the national government that, although not always expressly granted by the Constitution, are necessary to ensure the nation's integrity and survival as a political unit.

institution An ongoing organization that performs certain functions for society.

instructed delegate A representative who deliberately mirrors the views of the majority of his or her constituents.

interest group An organized group of individuals sharing common objectives who actively attempt to influence policymakers.

interstate commerce Trade that involves more than one state.

interventionism Direct involvement by one country in another country's affairs.

iron triangle A three-way alliance among legislators, bureaucrats, and interest groups to make or preserve policies that benefit their respective interests.

ISIS The Islamic State in Iraq and Greater Syria—a terrorist organization that by 2014 had taken over substantial portions of Iraq and Syria. Also known as *ISIL* (the Islamic State in Iraq and the Levant) or the Islamic State.

isolationism A political policy of noninvolvement in world affairs.

issue ad A political advertisement that focuses on a particular issue. Issue ads can be used to support or attack a candidate's position or credibility.

issue networks Groups of individuals or organizations—which consist of legislators and legislative staff members, interest group leaders, bureaucrats, the media, scholars, and other experts— that support particular policy positions on a given issue.

J

judicial review The power of the courts to decide on the constitutionality of legislative enactments and of actions taken by the executive branch.

judiciary The court system. One of the three branches of government in the United States.

jurisdiction The authority of a court to hear and decide a particular case.

justiciable controversy A controversy that is not hypothetical or academic but real and substantial. This requirement must be satisfied before a court will hear a case. *Justiciable* is pronounced jus-*tish*-a-bul.

K

Keynesian economics An economic theory proposed by British economist John Maynard Keynes that is typically associated with the use of fiscal policy to alter national economic variables.

kitchen cabinet The name given to a president's unofficial advisers. The term was coined during Andrew Jackson's presidency.

L

legislative rule An administrative agency rule that carries the same weight as a statute enacted by a legislature.

Lemon **test** A three-part test enunciated by the Supreme Court in the 1971 case of *Lemon v. Kurtzman* to determine whether government aid to parochial schools is constitutional.

LGBT persons Individuals who are lesbian, gay men, bisexual, or transgender.

libel A published report of a falsehood that tends to injure a person's reputation or character.

liberalism A set of political beliefs that include the advocacy of active government, including government intervention to improve the common welfare and to protect civil rights.

libertarianism The belief that government should do as little as possible, not only in the economic sphere, but also in regulating morality and personal behavior.

liberty The freedom of individuals to believe, act, and express themselves as they choose so long as doing so does not infringe on the rights of other individuals in the society.

limited government A form of government based on the principle that the powers of government should be clearly limited either through a written document or through wide public understanding.

literacy test A test given to voters to ensure that they could read and write and thus evaluate political information. This technique was used in many southern states to restrict African American participation in elections.

lobbying All of the attempts by organizations or by individuals to influence the passage, defeat, or contents of legislation or to influence the administrative decisions of government.

lobbyist An individual who handles a particular interest group's lobbying efforts.

M

Madisonian Model The model of government devised by James Madison, in which the powers of the government are separated into three branches: legislative, executive, and judicial.

majoritarianism The belief that public policy is or should be set in accordance with the opinions of a majority of the people.

majority leader The party leader elected by the majority party in the House or in the Senate.

majority party The political party that has more members in the legislature than the opposing party.

malapportionment A situation in which the voting power of citizens in one district is greater than the voting power of citizens in another district.

managed news coverage News coverage that is manipulated (managed) by a campaign manager or political consultant to gain positive media exposure for a political candidate.

markup session A meeting held by a congressional committee or subcommittee to approve, amend, or redraft a bill.

Marshall Plan A plan providing for U.S. economic assistance to European nations following World War II to help those nations recover from the war. The plan was named after George C. Marshall, secretary of state from 1947 to 1949.

mass media Communication channels, such as newspapers and radio and television broadcasts, through which people can communicate to large audiences.

material incentive A reason to join an interest group—practical benefits such as discounts, subscriptions, or group insurance.

Mayflower Compact A document drawn up by Pilgrim leaders in 1620 on the ship *Mayflower*. The document set up a provisional government.

media Newspapers, magazines, television, radio, the Internet, and any other printed or electronic means of communication.

Medicaid A joint federal–state program that pays for health-care services for low-income persons.

Medicare A federal government program that pays for health-care insurance for Americans aged sixty-five years and over.

minority leader The party leader elected by the minority party in the House or in the Senate.

minority-majority district A district in which minority groups make up a majority of the population.

minority party The political party that has fewer members in the legislature than the opposing party.

Miranda **warnings** A series of statements informing criminal suspects, on their arrest, of their constitutional rights, such as the right to remain silent and the right to counsel. Required by the Supreme Court's 1966 decision in *Miranda v. Arizona*.

moderates Persons whose views fall in the middle of the political spectrum.

monarchy A form of autocracy in which a king, queen, or other aristocrat is the highest authority in the government. Monarchs usually obtain their power through inheritance.

monetary policy Actions taken by the Federal Reserve to change the amount of money in circulation to affect interest rates, credit markets, the rate of inflation, the rate of economic growth, and the rate of unemployment.

Monroe Doctrine A U.S. policy, announced in 1823 by President James Monroe, that the United States would not tolerate foreign intervention in the Western Hemisphere and, in return, would stay out of European affairs.

moral idealism In foreign policy, the belief that the most important goal is to do what is right. Moral idealists think that it is possible for nations to cooperate as part of a rule-based community.

mutually assured destruction (MAD) A phrase referring to the assumption that if the forces of two nations are capable of destroying each other, neither nation will take a chance on war.

N

national convention The meeting held by each major party every four years to nominate presidential and vice-presidential candidates, write a party platform, and conduct other party business.

national party chairperson An individual who serves as a political party's administrative head at the national level and directs the work of the party's national committee.

national party committee The political party leaders who direct party business during the four years between the national party conventions, organize the next national convention, and plan how to support the party's candidate in the next presidential election.

National Security Council (NSC) A council that advises the president on domestic and foreign matters concerning the safety and defense of the nation.

natural rights Rights that are not bestowed by governments but are inherent within every man, woman, and child by virtue of the fact that he or she is a human being.

necessary and proper clause Article I, Section 8, Clause 18, of the Constitution, which gives Congress the power to make all laws "necessary and proper" for the federal government to carry out its responsibilities; also called the *elastic clause*.

negative political advertising Political advertising undertaken for the purpose of discrediting a candidate in voters' eyes.

neutral competency The application of technical skills to jobs without regard to political issues.

neutrality The position of not being aligned with either side in a dispute or conflict, such as a war.

New Deal The policies ushered in by the Roosevelt administration in 1933 in an attempt to bring the United States out of the Great Depression.

new federalism A plan to limit the federal government's role in regulating state governments and to give the states increased power in deciding how they should spend government revenues.

nominating convention An official meeting of a political party to choose its candidates. Nominating conventions at the state and local levels also select delegates to represent the citizens of their geographic areas at a higher-level party convention.

nuclear option Changing Senate rules—in particular, rules that require a supermajority—by simple majority vote. Also known as the constitutional option.

O

obscenity Indecency or offensiveness in speech, expression, behavior, or appearance.

Office of Management and Budget (OMB) An agency in the Executive Office of the President that has the primary duty of assisting the president in preparing and supervising the administration of the federal budget.

"one person, one vote" rule A rule, or principle, requiring that congressional districts have equal populations so that one person's vote counts as much as another's vote.

open primary A primary in which voters can vote for a party's candidates regardless of whether they belong to the party.

opinion A written statement by a court expressing the reasons for its decision in a case.

opposition research The attempt to learn damaging information about an opponent in a political campaign.

oral argument A spoken argument presented to a judge (or justices) in person by an attorney on behalf of her or his client.

Oslo Accords The first agreement signed between Israel and the PLO. The accords led to the establishment of the Palestinian Authority in the occupied territories.

P

Palestine Liberation Organization (PLO) An organization formed in 1964 to represent the Palestinian people. The PLO has a long history of terrorism but for some years has functioned primarily as a political party.

parliament The national legislative body in countries governed by a parliamentary system, such as Britain and Canada.

party activists A party member who helps to organize and oversee party functions and planning during and between campaigns, and may even become a candidate for office.

party identifiers A person who identifies himself or herself as being a supporter of a particular political party.

party platform The document drawn up by each party at its national convention that outlines the policies and positions of the party.

party ticket A list of a political party's candidates for various offices. In national elections, the party ticket consists of the presidential and vice-presidential candidates.

patronage A system of rewarding the party faithful with government jobs or contracts.

peer group Associates, often close in age to one another. May include friends, classmates, co-workers, club members, or religious group members.

personal attack ad A negative political advertisement that attacks a candidate's character.

picket-fence federalism A model of federalism in which specific policies and programs are administered by all levels of government—national, state, and local.

pluralist theory A theory that views politics as a contest among various interest groups—at all levels of government—to gain benefits for their members.

pocket veto A special type of veto power used by the chief executive after the legislature has adjourned. Bills that are not signed die after a specified period of time.

podcasting The distribution of audio or video files to personal computers or mobile devices, such as smartphones and tablets.

police powers The powers of a government body that enable it to create laws for the protection of the health, safety, welfare, and morals of the people. In the United States, most police powers are reserved to the states.

policymaking process The procedures involved in identifying an issue and then getting it on the political agenda; formulating, adopting, and implementing a policy with regard to the issue; and then evaluating the results of the policy.

political action committee (PAC) A committee that is established by a corporation, labor union, or special interest group to raise funds and make campaign contributions on the establishing organization's behalf.

political advertising Advertising undertaken by or on behalf of a political candidate to familiarize voters with the candidate and his or her views on campaign issues. Also, advertising for or against policy issues.

political consultant A professional political adviser who, for a fee, works on an area of a candidate's campaign. Political consultants include campaign managers, pollsters, media advisers, and "get-out-the-vote" organizers.

political correctness Criticism or other actions taken against others for speech that is offensive to minority group members, women, or LGBT persons. (*LGBT* stands for lesbian, gay male, bisexual, or transgender.)

political culture The set of ideas, values, and attitudes about government and the political process held by a community or a nation.

political party A group of individuals who organize to win elections, operate the government, and determine policy.

political realism In foreign policy, the belief that nations are inevitably selfish and that we should seek to protect our national security, regardless of moral arguments.

political socialization The learning process through which most people acquire their political attitudes, opinions, beliefs, and knowledge.

politics The process of resolving conflicts over how society should use its scarce resources and who should receive various benefits, such as public health care and public higher education.

poll tax A fee of several dollars that had to be paid before a person could vote. This device was used in some southern states to discourage African Americans and low-income whites from voting.

poll watcher A representative from one of the political parties who is allowed to monitor a polling place to make sure that the election is run fairly and that fraud doesn't occur.

power The ability to influence the behavior of others, usually through the use of force, persuasion, or rewards.

precedent A court decision that furnishes an example or authority for deciding subsequent cases involving identical or similar facts and legal issues.

precinct A political district within a city, such as a block or a neighborhood, or a rural portion of a county. The smallest voting district at the local level.

preemption A doctrine rooted in the supremacy clause of the Constitution that provides that national laws or regulations governing a certain area take precedence over conflicting state laws or regulations governing that same area.

press secretary A member of the White House staff who holds news conferences for reporters and makes public statements for the president.

primary A preliminary election held for the purpose of choosing a party's final candidate.

primary election An election in which voters choose the candidates of their party, who will then run in the general election.

primary source of law A source of law that establishes the law. Primary sources of law include constitutions, statutes, administrative agency rules and regulations, and decisions rendered by the courts.

priming An agenda-setting technique in which a media outlet promotes specific facts or ideas that may affect the public's thinking on related topics.

print media Communication channels that consist of printed materials, such as newspapers and magazines.

privatization The transfer of the task of providing services traditionally provided by government to the private sector.

probable cause Cause for believing that there is a substantial likelihood that a person has committed or is about to commit a crime.

progressivism Today, an alternative, more popular term for the set of political beliefs also known as liberalism.

public debt The total amount of money that the national government owes as a result of borrowing. Also called the *national debt*.

public-interest group An interest group formed for the purpose of working for the "public good." Examples are the American Civil Liberties Union and Common Cause.

public opinion The views of the citizenry about politics, public issues, and public policies. A complex collection of opinions held by many people on issues in the public arena.

public opinion poll A survey of the public's opinion on a particular topic at a particular moment.

public services Essential services that individuals cannot provide for themselves, such as building and maintaining roads, establishing welfare programs, operating public schools, and preserving national parks.

purposive incentive A reason to join an interest group— satisfaction resulting from working for a cause in which one believes.

push poll A campaign tactic used to feed false or misleading information to potential voters, under the guise of taking an opinion poll, with the intent to "push" voters away from one candidate and toward another.

Q

quota system A policy under which a specific number of jobs, promotions, or other types of placements, such as university admissions, are given to members of selected groups.

R

random sample In the context of opinion polling, a sample in which each person within the entire population being polled has an equal chance of being chosen.

rating system A system by which a particular interest group evaluates (rates) the performance of legislators based on how often the legislators have voted with the group's position on particular issues.

rational basis test A test (also known as the *ordinary scrutiny standard*) used by the Supreme Court to decide whether a discriminatory law violates the equal protection clause of the Constitution. It is used only when there is no classification—such as race or gender—that would require a higher level of scrutiny.

realignment A process in which the popular support for and relative strength of the parties shift, and the parties are reestablished with different coalitions of supporters.

recession A period in which the level of economic activity falls. It is usually defined as two or more quarters of economic decline.

reconciliation A Senate rule under which revenue bills received from the House that meet certain requirements cannot be filibustered.

renewable energy Energy from technologies that do not rely on extracted resources, such as oil and coal, that can run out.

representative democracy A form of democracy in which the will of the majority is expressed through groups of individuals elected by the people to act as their representatives.

republic Essentially, a representative system in which there is no king or queen and the people are sovereign.

reverse discrimination Discrimination against those who have no minority status.

right-to-work laws Laws that ban unions from collecting dues or other fees from workers whom they represent but who have not actually joined the union.

rulemaking The process undertaken by an administrative agency when formally proposing, evaluating, and adopting a new regulation.

rule of law A basic principle of government that requires those who govern to act in accordance with established law.

Rules Committee A standing committee in the House of Representatives that provides special rules governing how particular bills will be considered and debated by the House. The Rules Committee normally proposes time limits on debate for any bill.

S

sample In the context of opinion polling, a group of people selected to represent the population being studied.

sampling error In the context of opinion polling, the difference between what the sample results show and what the true results would have been had everybody in the relevant population been interviewed.

school voucher An educational certificate, provided by a government, that allows a student to use public funds to pay for a private or a public school chosen by the student or his or her parents.

secession The act of formally withdrawing from membership in an alliance; the withdrawal of a state from the federal Union.

second budget resolution A budget resolution, which is supposed to be passed in September, that sets "binding" limits on taxes and spending for the next fiscal year.

Second Continental Congress The congress of the colonies that met in 1775 to assume the powers of a central government and to establish an army.

seditious speech Speech that urges resistance to lawful authority or that advocates the overthrow of a government.

self-incrimination Providing damaging information or testimony against oneself in court.

senatorial courtesy A practice that allows a senator of the president's party to veto the president's nominee to a federal court judgeship within the senator's state.

separate-but-equal doctrine A Supreme Court doctrine holding that the equal protection clause of the Fourteenth Amendment did not forbid racial segregation as long as the facilities for blacks were equal to those for whites.

separation of powers The principle of dividing governmental powers among the legislative, executive, and judicial branches of government.

sexual harassment Unwanted physical contact, verbal conduct, or abuse of a sexual nature that interferes with a recipient's job performance, creates a hostile environment, or carries with it an implicit or explicit threat of adverse employment consequences.

Shays' Rebellion A rebellion of angry farmers in western Massachusetts in 1786, led by former Revolutionary War captain Daniel Shays.

signing statement A written statement, appended to a bill at the time the president signs it into law, indicating how the president interprets that legislation.

sit-ins A tactic of nonviolent civil disobedience. Demonstrators enter a business, college building, or other public place and remain seated until they are forcibly removed or until their demands are met.

slander The public utterance (speaking) of a statement that holds a person up for contempt, ridicule, or hatred.

social conflict Disagreements among people in a society over what the society's priorities should be.

social contract A voluntary agreement among individuals to create a government and to give that government adequate power to secure the mutual protection and welfare of all individuals.

socialism A political ideology, often critical of capitalism, that lies to the left of liberalism on the traditional political spectrum. Socialists are scarce in the United States but common in many other countries.

soft money Campaign contributions not regulated by federal law, such as some contributions that are made to political parties instead of to particular candidates.

solidarity Mutual agreement among the members of a particular group.

solidary incentive A reason to join an interest group—pleasure in associating with like-minded individuals.

Solid South A term used to describe the tendency of the southern states to vote Democratic after the Civil War.

sound bite A recorded comment, lasting for only a few seconds, that captures a thought or a perspective and has an immediate impact on viewers or listeners.

Soviet bloc The group of Eastern European nations that fell under the control of the Soviet Union following World War II.

Speaker of the House The presiding officer in the House of Representatives. The Speaker is a member of the majority party and is the most powerful member of the House.

special election An election that is held at the state or local level when the voters must decide an issue before the next general election or when vacancies occur by reason of death or resignation.

spin A reporter's slant on, or interpretation of, a particular event or action.

spin doctor A political candidate's press adviser who tries to convince reporters to give a story or event concerning the candidate a particular "spin" (interpretation, or slant).

standing committee A permanent committee in Congress that deals with legislation concerning a particular area, such as agriculture or foreign relations.

standing to sue The requirement that an individual must have a sufficient stake in a controversy before he or she can bring a lawsuit. The party bringing the suit must demonstrate that he or she has either been harmed or been threatened with a harm.

stare decisis A common law doctrine under which judges normally are obligated to follow the precedents established by prior court decisions. Pronounced *ster*-ay dih-*si*-sis.

statutory law The body of law enacted by legislatures (as opposed to constitutional law, administrative law, or case law).

straw poll A nonscientific poll in which there is no way to ensure that the opinions expressed are representative of the larger population.

strict scrutiny standard A standard under which a law or action must be necessary to promote a compelling state interest and must be narrowly tailored to meet that interest.

subcommittee A division of a larger committee that deals with a particular part of the committee's policy area. Most standing committees have several subcommittees.

suffrage The right to vote; the franchise.

superdelegates Party leaders and elected officials with the automatic right to attend their party's national convention and support any candidate.

supremacy clause Article VI, Clause 2, of the Constitution, which makes the Constitution and federal laws superior to all conflicting state and local laws.

suspect classification A classification, such as race, that provides the basis for a discriminatory law. Any law based on a suspect classification is subject to strict scrutiny by the courts, meaning that the law must be justified by a compelling state interest.

symbolic speech The expression of beliefs, opinions, or ideas through forms other than verbal speech or print. Also speech involving actions and other nonverbal expressions.

T

Tea Party movement A grassroots conservative movement that arose in 2009 after Barack Obama became president. The movement opposes big government and current levels of taxation, and also rejects political compromise.

third party In the United States, any party other than the two major parties (Republican and Democratic).

three-fifths compromise A compromise reached during the Constitutional Convention by which three-fifths of all slaves were to be counted for purposes of representation in the House of Representatives.

trade organization An association formed by members of a particular industry, such as the oil or trucking industries, to develop common standards and goals for the industry. Trade organizations, as interest groups, lobby government for legislation or regulations that specifically benefit their members.

transgender person Someone born with the physical characteristics of one sex, but whose sense of gender and identity corresponds with that of the other sex.

treaty A formal agreement between the governments of two or more countries.

trial court A court in which trials are held and testimony is taken.

trustee A representative who tries to serve the broad interests of the entire society and not just the narrow interests of his or her constituents.

two-party system A political system in which two strong and established parties compete for political offices.

tyranny The arbitrary or unrestrained exercise of power by an oppressive individual or government.

U

unemployment The state of not having a job when actively seeking one.

unicameral legislature A legislature with only one chamber.

unitary system A centralized governmental system in which local or subdivisional governments exercise only those powers given to them by the central government.

V

veto A Latin word meaning "I forbid"; the refusal by an official, such as the president of the United States or a state governor, to sign a bill into law.

veto power A constitutional power that enables the chief executive (president or governor) to reject legislation and return it to the legislature with reasons for the rejection. This either prevents or delays the bill from becoming law.

vote-eligible population The number of people who are actually eligible to vote in an American election.

voting-age population The number of people residing in the United States who are at least eighteen years old.

W

ward A local unit of a political party's organization, consisting of a division or district within a city.

Watergate scandal A scandal involving an illegal break-in at the Democratic National Committee offices in 1972 by members of President Richard Nixon's reelection campaign staff.

weapons of mass destruction Chemical, biological, and nuclear weapons that can inflict massive casualties.

whip A member of Congress who assists the majority or minority leader in the House or in the Senate in managing the party's legislative program.

whistleblower In the context of government employment, someone who "blows the whistle" (reports to authorities or the press) on gross governmental inefficiency, illegal action, or other wrongdoing.

White House Office The personal office of the president. White House Office personnel handle the president's political needs and manage the media, among other duties.

white primary A primary election in which African Americans were prohibited from voting. The practice was banned by the Supreme Court in 1944.

winner-take-all system A system in which the candidate who receives the most votes wins. In contrast, proportional systems allocate votes to multiple winners.

working class Today, persons with no more than a high school diploma. Formerly, families in which the head of household was employed in manual or unskilled labor.

writ of *certiorari* An order from a higher court asking a lower court for the record of a case. *Certiorari* is pronounced sur-shee-uh-*rah*-ree.

writ of *habeas corpus* An order that requires an official to bring a specified prisoner into court and explain to the judge why the person is being held in jail.

INDEX

weapons of mass destruction thought to be in, 364

WMD inspections, 364

Iraq War
authorization of armed forces in, 276
federal budget spent on, 292
First Gulf War
background, 364
invasion of, 364
Obama and, 365
President Bush and, 276
public opinion of, 14
rise and fall of insurgency, 364–365
withdrawal, 365

Ireland, Irish Republic Army and peace process England, 363

Irish Republican Army, 363

Iron triangle, policymaking and, 338

ISIS (Islamic State)
air strikes against, 366
attacks in Iraq and Syria, 276–277, 366
defending against and privacy issues, 289
rise of, 365–366
self-radicalized terrorists, 363
United States involvement and, 263

Islam, Yusuf, 78

Isolationism, 359

Israel, 363
conflict with Palestinians, 367–369
Gaza Strip War, 369
negotiations with, 369
as unitary system, 51

Issue ads, 136–137
defined, 223
effectiveness of, 224

Issue campaigns, 209

Issue identification, 338

Issue networks, 302–303

Issue-oriented parties, 163–164

Italy, 359

Iyengar, Shanto, 224

J

Jackson, Andrew, 27, 60, 271
Democrats and, 148
election of 1824, 196
election of 1828, 147
kitchen cabinet, 281

Jamestown colony, 26

Jamieson, Kathleen Hall, 228

Japan
aging population in, 16
nuclear crisis in, 345
Pearl Harbor attacked by, 359–360
as unitary system, 51
World War II, 359–360

Japanese Americans, 113

Jay, John, 40

Jefferson, Thomas, 27, 32, 58, 84, 223, 271, 329
Constitutional Convention and, 36
Declaration of Independence, 31–32
election of 1796, 147
election of 1800, 147, 196
election of 1804, 147
establishment clause, 78, 79
on political parties, 146
on slavery, 40
wall of separation, 78, 79

Jeffersonian Republicans, 147–148, 196

Jeffords, James M., 329

Jews, voting behavior, 176

Jim Crow laws, 102

Job Corps, 62

John, King (England), 10

Johnson, Andrew
impeachment, 255
vetoes by, 270

Johnson, Lyndon B., 18, 62, 264, 284
affirmative action, 118
block grants, 67
daisy girl ad, 223–224
decision to not seek reelection, 197
election of 1964, 150
percentage of votes for, 278–279
Great Society, 66
Medicare and Medicaid, 18–19

Joint Chiefs of Staff, 357

Jolie, Angelina, 171

Jones, Leslie, 91

Jordan, 367

Judge-made law, 314

Judicial activism, 325

Judicial branch
authority of, and Constitution, 39
checks and balances and, 43–44
judicial review, 44
separation of powers, 43

Judicial restraint, 325

Judicial review, 44, 58
defined, 324
power of, 324

Judiciary, 311–331
broad language and, 323–324
checks and balances, 324, 329–3331
defined, 312
electing judges, 311
federal court system, 316–319
federal judicial appointments, 320–322
ideology and, 325–329
jurisdiction, 314–315

origins and sources of American law, 312–316
power of judicial review, 324
standing to sue, 315

Judis, John, 155

Jurisdiction, 314–315

Jury trials, 93
common law tradition, 312–313
impartial jury, 77
right to, 75

Justice, Department of, 281, 294, 295

Justiciable controversy, 315

K

Kagan, Elena, 108, 322, 323, 326, 329

Kaine, Tim, 284

Kasich, John, 201, 265

Kelly, Megyn, 111, 228

Kennedy, Anthony, 326, 327, 329

Kennedy, Jacqueline, 284

Kennedy, John F., 265
election of 1960, television debates, 206, 224

Kerry, John, 223, 265
as secretary of state, 357

Keynes, John Maynard, 348–349

Keynesian economics, 348–349

Khan, Humayun, 206

Kim Jong-un, 8, 370

King, Martin Luther, Jr., 104, 105

King Caucus, 196

King's court, 312

King v. Burwell, 327

Kitchen cabinet, 281

Klopfer v. North Carolina, 77

Koch, Charles, 157, 210, 211

Koch, David, 157, 210, 211

Korean War, 276, 361

Kosovo, 362

Ku Klux Klan, 102, 103

Kurds, 364

Kushner, Jared, 281–282

Kuwait, invaded by Iraq, 364

L

Labor, Department of, 281, 295

Labor interest groups, 130–132

Labor unions. *See* Unions

Lady Gaga, 171

Land-grant colleges, 66

Landon, Alfred, 178

Landslide election, 278–2790

Lasswell, Harold, 5

Last Week Tonight with John Oliver, 226

Latinos, 110
civil rights of, 110–113
as economic progressive and social conservatives, 21
income, 111

Latino/Latina term, 110
party identification, 111–113, 145, 155
percent of population, 110
place of origin, 110–111
political participation, 113
poverty, 110
project racial and ethnic distribution of U.S., 15–16
Republican party and immigration policy, 145
voter turnout, 189
voting behavior, 176

Latter-Day Saints, 82

Law enforcement
bias debate, 99, 106
online privacy versus, 307

Lawrence v. Texas, 117, 327, 329

Law(s)
administrative, 314
case, 314
civil, 314
common law tradition, 312–313
constitutional, 313
criminal, 314
due process of, 76
election laws favoring two-party system, 161
equal protection of, 11
ex post facto law, 74
Jim Crow, 102
legislative process, 251–253
primary sources of, 313–314
rule of law, 42
rule of precedent, 312
sodomy, 116–117
sources of, 313–314
statutory, 313–314
steps in bill becoming a law, 251–253
sunshine, 306

League of Nations, 359

Ledbetter, Lilly, 109

Lee, Richard Henry, 31

Legislation
enabling, 300
supermajority to pass important legislation, 237
by Supreme Court, 330

Legislative branch
checks and balances and, 43–44
separation of powers, 43

Legislative process, 251–253

Legislative rules, 300

Legislature
bicameral, 37
unicameral, 32

Lehman Brothers, 273

Lemon test, 81

Lemon v. Kurtzman, 81

Leoni, Téa, 225

Le Pen, Marine, 154

1-1 **Explain what is meant by the terms *politics* and *government*.** Resolving conflicts over how society should use its scarce resources and who should receive various benefits is the essence of **politics. Government**—the individuals and **institutions** that make society's rules and possess the **power** and **authority** to enforce those rules—resolves **social conflicts,** provides **public services,** and defends the nation and its culture against attacks by other nations.

authority The ability to legitimately exercise power, such as the power to make and enforce laws.

government The individuals and institutions that make society's rules and possess the power and authority to enforce those rules.

institution An ongoing organization that performs certain functions for society.

politics The process of resolving conflicts over how society should use its scarce resources and who should receive various benefits, such as public health care and public higher education.

power The ability to influence the behavior of others, usually through the use of force, persuasion, or rewards.

public services Essential services that individuals cannot provide for themselves, such as building and maintaining roads, establishing welfare programs, operating public schools, and preserving national parks.

social conflict Disagreements among people in a society over what the society's priorities should be.

1-2 **Identify the various types of government systems.** Authoritarian rule by an individual is called **autocracy.** In a **monarchy,** a king, queen, or other aristocrat usually obtains power through inheritance. A **dictatorship** is authoritarian rule by an individual or group whose power is not supported by tradition. **Democracy** is a system of government in which supreme political authority rests with the people. One modern institution with some of the characteristics of **direct democracy** is the ballot proposal. In a **representative democracy,** the will of the people is expressed through groups of individuals elected by the people to act as their representatives. Other forms of government include aristocracy, plutocracy, and theocracy.

autocracy A form of government in which the power and authority of the government are in the hands of a single person.

democracy A system of government in which the people have ultimate political authority. The word is derived from the Greek *demos* ("the people") and *kratia* ("rule").

dictatorship A form of government in which absolute power is exercised by an individual or group whose power is not supported by tradition.

direct democracy A system of government in which political decisions are made by the people themselves rather than by elected representatives. This form of government was practiced in some parts of ancient Greece.

divine right theory The theory that a monarch's right to rule was derived directly from God rather than from the consent of the people.

monarchy A form of autocracy in which a king, queen, or other aristocrat is the highest authority in the government. Monarchs usually obtain their power through inheritance.

parliament The national legislative body in countries governed by a parliamentary system, such as Britain and Canada.

representative democracy A form of democracy in which the will of the majority is expressed through groups of individuals elected by the people to act as their representatives.

republic Essentially, a representative democracy in which there is no king or queen and the people are sovereign.

1-3 **Summarize some of the basic principles of American democracy and basic American political values.** In writing the U.S. Constitution, the framers incorporated two basic principles of government that had evolved in England: **limited government** and representative government. Our democracy resulted from a type of **social contract** among early Americans to create and abide by a set of governing rules. American democracy is based on several principles, including equality in voting, individual freedom, equal protection of the law, majority rule and minority rights, and collective voluntary consent to be governed. The rights to **liberty, equality,** and property are fundamental political values shared by most Americans. Differences among Americans in interpreting these values underlie the division between the Democratic and Republican parties, as demonstrated during the 2016 elections.

capitalism An economic system based on the private ownership of wealth-producing property, free markets, and freedom of contract. The privately owned corporation is the preeminent capitalist institution.

equality A concept that holds, at a minimum, that all people are entitled to equal protection under the law.

liberty The freedom of individuals to believe, act, and express themselves as they choose so long as doing so does not infringe on the rights of other individuals in the society.

limited government A form of government based on the principle that the powers of government should be clearly limited either through a written document or through wide public understanding.

natural rights Rights that are not bestowed by governments but are inherent within every man, woman, and child by virtue of the fact that he or she is a human being.

political culture The set of ideas, values, and attitudes about government and the political process held by a community or a nation.

social contract A voluntary agreement among individuals to create a government and to give that government adequate power to secure the mutual protection and welfare of all individuals.

working class Today, persons with no more than a high school diploma. Formerly, families in which the head of household was employed in manual or unskilled labor.

1-4 **Define common American ideological positions, such as "conservatism" and "liberalism."** The emergence of the **conservative movement** in the 1950s and 1960s was essential to the development of modern American **conservatism.** Conservatives believe that individuals and families should take responsibility for their own economic circumstances, and they place a high value on the principle of order, on family values, and on patriotism. Conservatism includes those who want society and the government to reflect traditional religious values. While tracing its roots to the New Deal programs of Franklin D. Roosevelt, American **liberalism** took its modern form in the 1960s. Support for minority rights of all kinds became an important part of liberal ideology. Liberals, or **progressives,** argue that big government is a necessary tool for promoting the common welfare, and strongly favor the separation of church and state. Liberals identify with the Democratic Party, and conservatives typically identify themselves politically as Republicans. People whose views fall in the middle of the traditional political spectrum are generally called **moderates.** Many Americans have opinions that do not fit neatly under the liberal or conservative label. Some Americans, for example, are both economic progressives and social conservatives. The **ideology** of **socialism** has few adherents in the United States. **Libertarianism,** on the other hand, has unusually strong support.

FIGURE 1–3   THE TRADITIONAL POLITICAL SPECTRUM

This spectrum is based primarily on economic policies. *What issues do not fit under "economic policy"?*

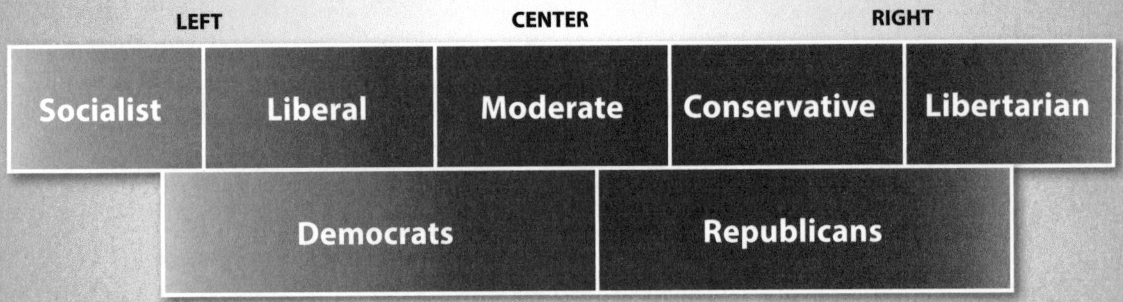

	LEFT		CENTER		RIGHT	

Socialist	Liberal	Moderate	Conservative	Libertarian

Democrats	Republicans

---

conservatism A set of political beliefs that include a limited role for the national government in helping individuals and in the economic affairs of the nation, as well as support for traditional values and lifestyles.

conservative movement An ideological movement that arose in the 1950s and 1960s and continues to shape conservative beliefs.

ideology Generally, a system of political ideas that are rooted in religious or philosophical beliefs concerning human nature, society, and government.

liberalism A set of political beliefs that include the advocacy of active government, including government intervention to improve the common welfare and to protect civil rights.

libertarianism The belief that government should do as little as possible, not only in the economic sphere, but also in regulating morality and personal behavior.

moderates Persons whose views fall in the middle of the political spectrum.

progressivism Today, an alternative, more popular term for the set of political beliefs also known as liberalism.

socialism A political ideology, often critical of capitalism, that lies to the left of liberalism on the traditional political spectrum. Socialists are scarce in the United States but common in many other countries.

2-1 **Point out some of the influences on the American political tradition in the colonial years.** American politics owes much to the English political tradition, but the colonists derived most of their understanding of limited government and representative government from their own experiences. In 1620, the Pilgrims drew up the **Mayflower Compact,** in which they set up a government and promised to obey its laws.

Other colonies, in turn, established fundamental governing rules and principles that were later expressed in the U.S. Constitution and **Bill of Rights.** Colonial leaders became familiar with the practical problems of governing. They learned how to build coalitions among groups with diverse interests and how to make compromises.

Bill of Rights The first ten amendments to the U.S. Constitution. They list the freedoms—such as the freedoms of speech, press, and religion— that a citizen enjoys and that cannot be infringed on by the government.

Mayflower Compact A document drawn up by Pilgrim leaders in 1620 on the ship *Mayflower*. The document set up a provisional government.

2-2 **Explain why the American colonies rebelled against Britain.** After the French and Indian War, the British government decided to pay its war debts and to finance the defense of its North American empire by imposing taxes on the colonists. The colonists protested, and Britain responded with a series of repressive measures. The colonists established the **First Continental Congress** and sent a petition to King George III to explain their

grievances. The congress also called for a continued boycott of British goods and required each colony to establish an army. Soon after British soldiers fought colonial citizen soldiers in the first battles of the American Revolution in 1775, delegates gathered for the **Second Continental Congress,** which assumed the powers of a central government. The congress adopted the Declaration of Independence on July 4, 1776.

First Continental Congress A gathering of delegates from twelve of the thirteen colonies, held in 1774 to protest the Coercive Acts.

Second Continental Congress The congress of the colonies that met in 1775 to assume the powers of a central government and to establish an army.

unicameral legislature A legislature with only one chamber.

2-3 **Describe the structure of government established by the Articles of Confederation and some of the strengths and weaknesses of the Articles.** The **Articles of Confederation** established the Congress of the Confederation as the central governing body. It was a **unicameral legislature** in which each state had one vote. Congress had several powers, including the power to declare war, to enter into treaties, and to settle disputes among the states under certain circumstances. Nevertheless, the central government created

by the Articles was weak. Congress could not force the states to meet military quotas. It could not regulate trade or agreements between the states or with other nations. Disruptions such as **Shays' Rebellion** frightened political and business leaders and persuaded more and more Americans that a true national government had to be created. Congress called on the states to send delegates to a meeting in Philadelphia in 1787 that became the **Constitutional Convention.**

Articles of Confederation The nation's first national constitution, which established a national form of government following the American Revolution. The Articles provided for a confederal form of government in which the central government had few powers.

confederation A league of independent states that are united only for the purpose of achieving common goals.

Constitutional Convention The convention of delegates from the states that was held in Philadelphia in 1787 for the purpose of amending the Articles of Confederation. In fact, the delegates wrote a new constitution (the U.S. Constitution) that established a federal form of government.

Shays' Rebellion A rebellion of angry farmers in western Massachusetts in 1786, led by former Revolutionary War captain Daniel Shays.

2-4 **List the major compromises made by the delegates at the Constitutional Convention, and discuss the Federalist and Anti-Federalist positions on ratifying the Constitution.** Delegates resolved the small-state/large-state controversy over representation in Congress with the **Great Compromise,** which established a **bicameral legislature.** The **three-fifths compromise** settled a deadlock on how slaves would be counted to determine representation in the House of Representatives. The delegates also agreed that Congress could prohibit the importation of slaves beginning in 1808. The South agreed to let Congress have the power to regulate both interstate commerce and commerce with other nations in exchange for a ban on export taxes. Other actions taken at the convention included the creation of an independent executive and the establishment of the United States Supreme Court. The battle over ratification was fought between the **Federalists,** who favored a strong central government and the new Constitution, and the **Anti-Federalists,** who argued that the Constitution would lead to aristocratic **tyranny** or an overly powerful central government that would limit personal freedom. To gain support for ratification, the Federalists promised to add a bill of rights to the Constitution.

Anti-Federalists A political group that opposed the adoption of the Constitution.

bicameral legislature A legislature made up of two chambers, or parts.

faction A group of persons forming a cohesive minority.

Federalists A political group, led by Alexander Hamilton and John Adams, that supported the adoption of the Constitution and the creation of a federal form of government.

Great Compromise A plan for a bicameral legislature in which one chamber would be based on population and the other chamber would represent each state equally. Also known as the Connecticut Compromise.

interstate commerce Trade that involves more than one state.

three-fifths compromise A compromise reached during the Constitutional Convention by which three-fifths of all slaves were to be counted for purposes of representation in the House of Representatives.

tyranny The arbitrary or unrestrained exercise of power by an oppressive individual or government.

2-5 **Summarize the Constitution's major principles of government, and describe how the Constitution can be amended.** The Constitution incorporated the principles of limited government, popular sovereignty, and the **rule of law.** A **federal system,** in which the national government shares sovereign powers with the state governments, was established. **Separation of powers** and a system of **checks and balances** ensure that no one branch—legislative, executive, or judicial—can exercise exclusive control. An amendment to the Constitution can be proposed either by a two-thirds vote in each chamber of Congress or by a national convention called at the request of two-thirds of the state legislatures. Ratification of an amendment requires approval either by three-fourths of the state legislatures or by three-fourths of the states in special conventions.

FIGURE 2–6   THE PROCESS OF AMENDING THE CONSTITUTION

How is it that the president has no role in amending the Constitution?

AN AMENDMENT CAN BE PROPOSED BY . . .

A two-thirds vote in both houses of Congress

A vote at a national constitutional convention called by Congress at the request of two-thirds of state legislatures

AN AMENDMENT CAN BE RATIFIED BY . . .

Three-fourths of state legislatures

Three-fourths of states at special conventions

Traditional   Used once (21st Amendment)   Never used

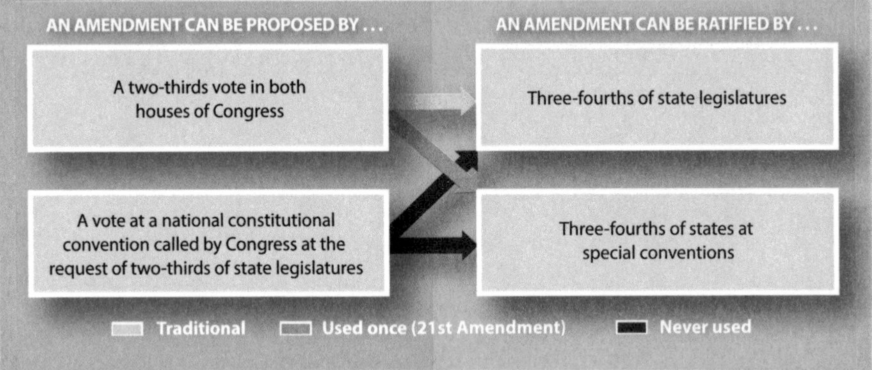

checks and balances A major principle of American government in which each of the three branches is given the means to check (to restrain or balance) the actions of the others.

commerce clause The clause in Article I, Section 8 of the Constitution that gives Congress the power to regulate interstate commerce (commerce involving more than one state).

federal system A form of government that provides for a division of powers between a central government and several regional governments.

Madisonian Model The model of government devised by James Madison, in which the powers of the government are separated into three branches: legislative, executive, and judicial.

rule of law A basic principle of government that requires those who govern to act in accordance with established law.

separation of powers The principle of dividing governmental powers among the legislative, the executive, and the judicial branches of government.

veto power A constitutional power that enables the chief executive (president or governor) to reject legislation and return it to the legislature with reasons for the rejection. This either prevents or delays the bill from becoming law.

3-1 Explain what federalism means, how federalism differs from other systems of government, and why it exists in the United States. Government powers in a federal system are divided between a national government and subnational governments. The powers of both levels of government are specified and limited. Alternatives to **federalism** include a **unitary system,** in which subnational governments exercise only those powers given to them by the national government, and a **confederal system,** in which the national government exists and operates only at the direction of the subnational governments. The Articles of Confederation failed because they did not allow for a sufficiently strong central government, but the framers of the Constitution were fearful of a too-powerful central government. The appeal of federalism was that it retained state powers and local traditions while establishing a strong national government capable of handling common problems.

confederal system A league of independent sovereign states, joined together by a central government that has only limited powers over them.

federalism A system of shared sovereignty between two levels of government—one national and one subnational—occupying the same geographic region.

unitary system A centralized governmental system in which local or subdivisional governments exercise only those powers given to them by the central government.

3-2 Indicate how the Constitution divides governing powers in our federal system. The national government possesses three types of powers: **expressed, implied,** and **inherent.** The Constitution expressly enumerates twenty-seven powers that Congress may exercise, while the **necessary and proper clause** is the basis for implied powers. The national government also enjoys certain inherent powers—powers that governments must have simply to ensure the nation's integrity and survival. In addition, the Constitution expressly prohibits the national government from undertaking certain actions. The Tenth Amendment states that powers that are not delegated to the national government by the Constitution nor prohibited to the states are "reserved" to the states or to the people. In principle, each state has **police powers**—the ability to regulate its internal affairs and to enact whatever laws are necessary to protect the health, safety, welfare, and morals of its people. The Constitution also contains provisions, such as the full faith and credit clause, relating to interstate relations. **Concurrent powers** can be exercised by both the state governments and the federal government. The **supremacy clause** asserts that national government power takes precedence over any conflicting state action.

concurrent powers Powers held by both the federal and the state governments in a federal system.

division of powers A basic principle of federalism established by the U.S. Constitution, by which powers are divided between the national and state governments.

expressed powers Constitutional or statutory powers that are expressly provided for by the U.S. Constitution; also called *enumerated powers.*

implied powers The powers of the federal government that are implied by the expressed powers in the Constitution, particularly in Article I, Section 8.

inherent powers The powers of the national government that, although not always expressly granted by the Constitution, are necessary to ensure the nation's integrity and survival as a political unit.

necessary and proper clause Article I, Section 8, Clause 18 of the Constitution, which gives Congress the power to make all laws "necessary and proper" for the federal government to carry out its responsibilities; also called the *elastic clause.*

police powers The powers of a government body that enable it to create laws for the protection of the health, safety, welfare, and morals of the people. In the United States, most police powers are reserved to the states.

supremacy clause Article VI, Clause 2 of the Constitution, which makes the Constitution and federal laws superior to all conflicting state and local laws.

3-3 Summarize the evolution of federal-state relationships in the United States over time. The United States Supreme Court, in *McCulloch v. Maryland* (1819) and *Gibbons v. Ogden* (1824), played a key role in establishing the constitutional foundations for the supremacy of the national government. An increase in the political power of the national government was also a result of the South's defeat in the Civil War. The relationship between the states and the national government has evolved through several stages. The model of **dual federalism,** which prevailed after the Civil War until the 1930s, assumes that the states and the national government are more or less equals, with each level of government having separate and distinct functions and responsibilities. The model of **cooperative federalism,** which views the national and state governments as complementary parts of a single governmental mechanism, grew out of the need to solve the pressing national problems caused by the Great Depression. The 1960s and 1970s saw an even greater expansion of the national government's role in domestic policy, but the massive social programs undertaken during this period also resulted in greater involvement by state and local governments. The model in which every level of government is involved in implementing a policy is sometimes referred to as **picket-fence federalism.**

cooperative federalism A model of federalism in which the states and the federal government cooperate in solving problems.

dual federalism A system of government in which the federal and the state governments maintain diverse but sovereign powers.

New Deal The policies ushered in by the Roosevelt administration in 1933 in an attempt to bring the United States out of the Great Depression.

picket-fence federalism A model of federalism in which specific policies and programs are administered by all levels of government—national, state, and local.

preemption A doctrine rooted in the supremacy clause of the Constitution that provides that national laws or regulations governing a certain area take precedence over conflicting state laws or regulations governing that same area.

secession The act of formally withdrawing from membership in an alliance; the withdrawal of a state from the federal Union.

3-4 **Describe developments in federalism in recent years.** Starting in the 1970s, several administrations favored a shift from nation-centered federalism to state-centered federalism. One of the goals of the "**new federalism**" was to return to the states certain powers that had been exercised by the national government since the 1930s—a process called **devolution.** The federal government and the states seem to be in a constant tug-of-war over federal regulations, federal programs, and federal demands on the states. In the last several years, Supreme Court decisions regarding state immigration laws, health-care reform, and voting rights have affected the shape of our federal system. The politics of federalism include controversies surrounding **federal mandates.**

---

devolution The surrender or transfer of powers to local authorities by a central government.

federal mandate A requirement in federal legislation that forces states and municipalities to comply with certain rules.

new federalism A plan to limit the federal government's role in regulating state governments and to give the states increased power in deciding how they should spend government revenues.

3-5 **Explain what is meant by the term *fiscal federalism.*** To help the states pay for some of the costs associated with implementing national policies, the national government gives back some of the tax dollars it collects to the states—in the form of **categorical** and **block grants.** States have come to depend on this process of **fiscal federalism** as an important source of revenue. By giving or withholding federal grant dollars, the federal government has been able to exercise control over matters that traditionally have been under the control of state governments. Sometimes state and local governments engage in **competitive federalism** by offering lower taxes or more services to attract businesses and citizens.

FIGURE 3–4 STATE AND LOCAL GOVERNMENT REVENUE SOURCES

Do the sizes of any of these pie slices surprise you? If so, which ones?

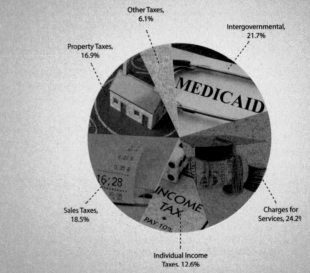

- Other Taxes, 6.1%
- Intergovernmental, 21.7%
- Property Taxes, 16.9%
- Sales Taxes, 18.5%
- Individual Income Taxes, 12.6%
- Charges for Services, 24.2%

Source: U.S. Census Bureau, *Annual Survey of State and Local Government Finances,* 2015.

CW from top right: Designer491/Shutterstock.com, Zimmytws/Shutterstock.com, CaseyMartin/Shutterstock.com, Qvist/Shutterstock.com, ChameleonsEye/Shutterstock.com

---

block grant A federal grant given to a state for a broad area, such as criminal justice or mental-health programs.

categorical grant A federal grant targeted for a specific purpose as defined by federal law.

competitive federalism A model of federalism in which state and local governments compete for businesses and citizens, who in effect "vote with their feet" by moving to jurisdictions that offer a competitive advantage.

cross-cutting requirements Requirements that apply to all federal grants.

fiscal federalism The allocation of taxes collected by one level of government (typically the national government) to another level (typically state or local governments).

4-1 Define the term *civil liberties,* explain how civil liberties differ from civil rights, and state the constitutional basis for our civil liberties. **Civil liberties** are legal and constitutional rights that protect citizens from government actions. Civil rights specify what the government *must* do. Civil liberties set forth what the government *cannot* do. Many of our liberties were added by the Bill of Rights, ratified in 1791. The United States Supreme Court has used the **due process clause** to incorporate most of the protections guaranteed by the Bill of Rights into the liberties protected from state government actions under the Fourteenth Amendment.

TABLE 4–2 INCORPORATING THE BILL OF RIGHTS INTO THE FOURTEENTH AMENDMENT

Year	Issue	Amendment Involved	Court Case
1925	Freedom of speech	I	*Gitlow v. New York,* 268 U.S. 652
1931	Freedom of the press	I	*Near v. Minnesota,* 283 U.S. 697
1932	Right to a lawyer in capital punishment cases	VI	*Powell v. Alabama,* 287 U.S. 45
1937	Freedom of assembly and right to petition	I	*De Jonge v. Oregon,* 299 U.S. 353
1940	Freedom of religion	I	*Cantwell v. Connecticut,* 310 U.S. 296
1947	Separation of church and state	I	*Everson v. Board of Education,* 330 U.S. 1
1948	Right to a public trial	VI	*In re Oliver,* 333 U.S. 257
1949	No unreasonable searches and seizures	IV	*Wolf v. Colorado,* 338 U.S. 25
1961	Exclusionary rule (See "The Rights of the Accused" section in Chapter 4.)	IV	*Mapp v. Ohio,* 367 U.S. 643
1962	No cruel and unusual punishments	VIII	*Robinson v. California,* 370 U.S. 660
1963	Right to a lawyer in all criminal felony cases	VI	*Gideon v. Wainwright,* 372 U.S. 335
1964	No compulsory self-incrimination	V	*Malloy v. Hogan,* 378 U.S. 1
1965	Right to privacy	Various	*Griswold v. Connecticut,* 381 U.S. 479
1966	Right to an impartial jury	VI	*Parker v. Gladden,* 385 U.S. 363
1967	Right to a speedy trial	VI	*Klopfer v. North Carolina,* 386 U.S. 213
1969	No double jeopardy	V	*Benton v. Maryland,* 395 U.S. 784
1982	Right to refuse to quarter soldiers	III	*Englblom v. Carey,* 677 F.2d 957 (2d Cir.)
2010	Right to bear arms	II	*McDonald v. Chicago,* 561 U.S. 3025

bill of attainder A legislative act that inflicts punishment on particular persons or groups without granting them the right to a trial.

civil liberties Individual rights protected by the Constitution against the powers of the government.

due process clause The constitutional guarantee, set out in the Fifth and Fourteenth Amendments, that the government will not illegally or arbitrarily deprive a person of life, liberty, or property.

due process of law The requirement that the government use fair, reasonable, and standard procedures whenever it takes any legal action against an individual.

ex post facto law A criminal law that punishes individuals for committing an act that was legal when the act was committed.

writ of habeas corpus An order that requires an official to bring a specified prisoner into court and explain to the judge why the person is being held in jail.

4-2 List the religious freedoms guaranteed by the First Amendment, and explain how the courts have interpreted and applied these freedoms. The First Amendment prohibits Congress from passing laws "respecting an establishment of religion, or prohibiting the free exercise thereof." Issues involving the **establishment clause** include prayer in the public schools, the teaching of evolution versus creationism or intelligent design, and government aid to parochial schools. The Supreme Court has ruled that public schools cannot sponsor religious activities and has held unconstitutional state laws forbidding the teaching of evolution in the schools. Some aid to parochial schools has been held to violate the establishment clause, while other forms of aid have been held permissible. In its interpretation of the **free exercise clause,** the Court has ruled consistently that the right to hold any religious belief is absolute. The right to practice one's beliefs may have some limits. Title VII of the 1964 Civil Rights Act, however, bolstered free exercise of religion in the workplace.

establishment clause The section of the First Amendment that prohibits Congress from passing laws "respecting an establishment of religion."

free exercise clause The provision of the First Amendment stating that the government cannot pass laws "prohibiting the free exercise" of religion.

***Lemon* test** A three-part test enunciated by the Supreme Court in the 1971 case of *Lemon v. Kurtzman* to determine whether government aid to parochial schools is constitutional.

school voucher An educational certificate, provided by a government, that allows a student to use public funds to pay for a private or a public school chosen by the student or his or her parents.

4-3 **Describe how freedom of speech is protected by the First Amendment, and show how the courts have implemented this freedom.** Although the Supreme Court has zealously safeguarded the right to free speech, including **symbolic speech,** under the First Amendment, at times it has imposed limits on speech in the interests of protecting other rights. These rights include security against harm to one's person or reputation, the need for public order, and the need to preserve the government. The current standard for evaluating the legality of speech opposing the government is the **imminent lawless action test.** The First Amendment freedom of the press generally protects the right to publish a wide range of opinions and information. Over the years, the Court has developed various guidelines and doctrines to use in deciding whether freedom of expression can be restrained.

commercial speech Advertising statements that describe products. Commercial speech receives less protection under the First Amendment than ordinary speech.

imminent lawless action test The current Supreme Court doctrine for assessing the constitutionality of subversive speech. To be illegal, speech must be "directed to inciting . . . imminent lawless action."

libel A published report of a falsehood that tends to injure a person's reputation or character.

obscenity Indecency or offensiveness in speech, expression, behavior, or appearance.

political correctness Criticism or other actions taken against others for speech that is offensive to minority group members, women, or LGBT persons. (LGBT stands for lesbian, gay, bisexual, or transgender.)

seditious speech Speech that urges resistance to lawful authority or that advocates the overthrow of a government.

slander The public utterance (speaking) of a statement that holds a person up for contempt, ridicule, or hatred.

symbolic speech The expression of beliefs, opinions, or ideas through forms other than verbal speech or print. Also, speech involving actions and other nonverbal expressions.

4-4 **Discuss why Americans are increasingly concerned about privacy rights.** The Supreme Court has held that a right to privacy is implied by other constitutional rights guaranteed in the Bill of Rights. The nature and scope of this right, however, are not always clear. In 1973, the Court held that the right to privacy is broad enough to encompass a woman's decision to terminate a pregnancy, though the right is not absolute throughout pregnancy. Since that decision, the Court has upheld some restrictive state laws requiring certain actions prior to abortions. Privacy issues have also been raised in the context of physician-assisted suicide; several states now allow the practice. A concern among Americans in recent years is that their personal information could be collected by organizations that use the data improperly, and some laws have been passed to protect the privacy rights of individuals. Since the terrorist attacks of September 11, 2001, the news media and Congress have debated how the United States can strengthen national security while still protecting civil liberties, particularly the right to privacy. The USA Patriot Act, the revelations regarding the NSA's collection of metadata, programs such as PRISM, and the tapping of foreign leaders' phones have all been part of the ongoing discussion. The 2015 USA Freedom Act sought to limit some aspects of data collection by the government.

4-5 **Summarize how the Constitution and the Bill of Rights protect the rights of accused persons.** Constitutional safeguards include the Fourth Amendment protection from unreasonable searches and seizures and the requirement that no warrant for a search or an arrest be issued without **probable cause;** the Fifth Amendment prohibition against **double jeopardy** and the protection against **self-incrimination;** the Sixth Amendment guarantees of a speedy trial, a trial by jury, a public trial, the right to confront witnesses, and the right to counsel at various stages in criminal proceedings; and the Eighth Amendment prohibitions against excessive bail and fines and against cruel and unusual punishments. The Constitution also provides for the **writ of habeas corpus**—an order requiring that an official bring a specified prisoner into court and explain to the judge why the person is being held in jail.

double jeopardy The prosecution of a person twice for the same criminal offense. Prohibited by the Fifth Amendment in all but a few circumstances.

exclusionary rule A criminal procedural rule stating that illegally obtained evidence is not admissible in court.

***Miranda* warnings** A series of statements informing criminal suspects, on their arrest, of their constitutional rights, such as the right to remain silent and the right to counsel. Required by the Supreme Court's 1966 decision in *Miranda v. Arizona.*

probable cause Cause for believing that there is a substantial likelihood that a person has committed or is about to commit a crime.

self-incrimination Providing damaging information or testimony against oneself in court.

CHAPTER 5 LEARNING OUTCOMES / KEY TERMS

5-1 **Explain the constitutional basis for our civil rights and for laws prohibiting discrimination. Civil rights** are the rights of all Americans to equal treatment under the law. The **equal protection clause** of the Fourteenth Amendment has been interpreted by the courts to mean that states may not discriminate unreasonably against a particular group or class of individuals. The amendment also provides a legal basis for federal civil rights legislation. The U.S. Supreme Court has developed various standards for determining whether the equal protection clause has been violated. A law based on a **suspect classification,** for example, is subject to the **strict scrutiny standard.**

civil rights The rights of all Americans to equal treatment under the law, as provided by the Fourteenth Amendment to the Constitution.

equal protection clause Section 1 of the Fourteenth Amendment, which states that no state shall "deny to any person within its jurisdiction the equal protection of the laws."

fundamental right A basic right of all Americans, such as First Amendment rights. Any law or action that prevents some group of persons from exercising a fundamental right is subject to the *strict scrutiny standard.*

rational basis test A test (also known as the *ordinary scrutiny standard*) used by the Supreme Court to decide whether a discriminatory law violates the equal protection clause of the Constitution. It is used only when there is no classification—such as race or gender—that would require a higher level of scrutiny.

strict scrutiny standard A standard under which a law or action must be necessary to promote a compelling state interest and must be narrowly tailored to meet that interest.

suspect classification A classification, such as race, that provides the basis for a discriminatory law. Any law based on a suspect classification is subject to strict scrutiny by the courts, meaning that the law must be justified by a compelling state interest.

5-2 **Discuss the reasons for the civil rights movement and the changes it caused in American politics and government.** The equal protection clause was originally intended to protect the newly freed slaves from discrimination after the Civil War. By the late 1880s, however, southern states had begun to pass a series of segregation laws. In 1896, the Supreme Court established the **separate-but-equal doctrine,** which was used to justify segregation for nearly sixty years. In 1954, the Court held that segregation by race in public education was unconstitutional. One year later, the arrest of Rosa Parks for violating local segregation laws spurred a boycott of the bus system in Montgomery, Alabama. The protest was led by the Reverend Dr. Martin Luther King, Jr. In 1956, a federal court prohibited the segregation of buses in Montgomery, marking the beginning of the **civil rights movement.** Civil rights protesters in the 1960s applied the tactic of nonviolent **civil disobedience** in actions throughout the South. As the civil rights movement demonstrated its strength, Congress passed a series of civil rights laws, including the Civil Rights Act of 1964, the Voting Rights Act of 1965, and the Civil Rights Act of 1968. Today, the percentages of voting-age blacks and whites registered to vote are nearly equal. Political participation by African Americans has increased, as has the number of African American elected officials. African Americans continue to struggle for income and educational parity with whites.

civil disobedience The deliberate and public act of refusing to obey laws thought to be unjust.

civil rights movement The movement in the 1950s and 1960s, by minorities and concerned whites, to end racial discrimination.

de facto segregation Racial segregation that occurs not as a result of government actions but because of social and economic conditions and residential patterns.

de jure segregation Racial segregation that occurs because of laws or decisions by government agencies.

separate-but-equal doctrine A Supreme Court doctrine holding that the equal protection clause of the Fourteenth Amendment did not forbid racial segregation as long as the facilities for blacks were equal to those for whites.

sit-in A tactic of nonviolent civil disobedience. Demonstrators enter a business, college building, or other public place and remain seated until they are forcibly removed or until their demands are met.

5-3 **Describe the political and economic achievements of women in this country over time, and identify some obstacles to equality that women continue to face.** The struggle of women for equal treatment initially focused on **suffrage.** In 1920, the Nineteenth Amendment was ratified, granting voting rights to women. **Feminism** shaped a new movement that began in the 1960s. Congress and state legislatures enacted measures to provide equal rights for women, and the courts accepted the argument that gender discrimination violates the equal protection clause. Although women remain underrepresented in politics, increasingly women have gained power as public officials. In spite of federal legislation to promote equal treatment of women in the workplace, women continue to face various forms of discrimination, including the **glass ceiling.** The prohibition of gender discrimination has been extended to prohibit **sexual harassment.**

feminism A doctrine advocating full political, economic, and social equality for women.

glass ceiling An invisible but real discriminatory barrier that prevents women and minorities from rising to top positions of power or responsibility.

sexual harassment Unwanted physical contact, verbal conduct, or abuse of a sexual nature that interferes with a recipient's job performance, creates a hostile environment, or carries with it an implicit or explicit threat of adverse employment consequences.

suffrage The right to vote; the franchise.

5-4 **Summarize the struggles for equality that other groups in America have experienced.** Latinos constitute the largest ethnic minority in the United States. Economically, Latino households are often members of this country's working poor. Immigration reform has been an important issue for many Latinos. After the 2016 elections, Latino representation in Congress reached thirty-eight members. Asian Americans suffered from discriminatory treatment in the late 1800s and early 1900s, and again during World War II. Today, Asian Americans lead other minority groups in median income and median education. Native Americans were not considered U.S. citizens until 1924. Beginning in the 1960s, some American Indians formed organizations to strike back at the U.S. government and to reclaim their heritage, including their lands. Persons with disabilities first became a political force in the 1970s. The Americans with Disabilities Act (ADA) of 1990 is the most significant legislation protecting the rights of this group of Americans. In the decades following the 1969 Stonewall Inn incident, laws and court decisions protecting the rights of gay men and lesbians have reflected changing social attitudes. In 2015, the Supreme Court ruled that the Constitution guarantees a right to same-sex marriage in every state. In the wake of the gay rights movement, transgender individuals have also come forward and demanded equal rights.

LGBT persons Individuals who are lesbian, gay, bisexual, or transgender.

transgender person Someone born with the physical characteristics of one sex, but whose sense of gender and identity corresponds with that of the other sex.

5-5 **Explain what affirmative action is and why it has been so controversial. Affirmative action** programs have been tested in court cases involving claims of **reverse discrimination.** Some states have banned affirmative action or replaced it with alternative policies.

affirmative action A policy that gives special consideration, in jobs and college admissions, to members of groups that have been discriminated against in the past.

quota system A policy under which a specific number of jobs, promotions, or other types of placements, such as university admissions, are given to members of selected groups.

reverse discrimination Discrimination against those who have no minority status.

FIGURE 5–1 PERSONS IN POVERTY IN THE UNITED STATES BY RACE AND HISPANIC ORIGIN

Blacks, Hispanics, and American Indians are more likely than whites or Asians to have incomes below the poverty line. *Why are children more likely than adults to live in families with incomes below the poverty line?*

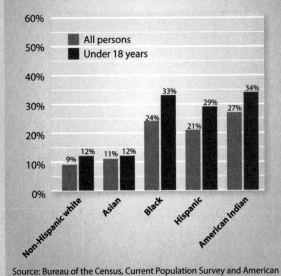

Source: Bureau of the Census, Current Population Survey and American Population Survey, 2015.

CHAPTER 6 LEARNING OUTCOMES / KEY TERMS

6-1 **Explain what an interest group is, why interest groups form, and how interest groups function in American politics.** An **interest group** is an organized group of people sharing common objectives who actively attempt to influence government policymakers through direct and indirect methods. The right to form interest groups and to lobby the government is protected by the First Amendment. Interest groups may form—and existing groups may become more politically active—when the government expands its scope of activities. Interest groups also come into existence in response to a perceived threat to a group's interests, or they can form in reaction to the creation of other groups. **Purposive incentives, solidary incentives,** and

material incentives are among the reasons people join interest groups. Interest groups (a) help bridge the gap between citizens and government; (b) help raise public awareness and inspire action on various issues; (c) provide public officials with specialized information that may be useful in making policy choices; and (d) serve as another check on public officials. The **pluralist theory** of American democracy views politics as a contest among various interest groups to gain benefits for their members. Two other theories to describe American democracy are **majoritarianism** and **elite theory.** Although both interest groups and political parties are groups of people joined together for political purposes, they differ in several ways.

elite theory The belief that the government is controlled by one or more elite groups.

free rider problem The difficulty that exists when individuals can enjoy the outcome of an interest group's efforts without having to contribute, such as by becoming members of the group.

interest group An organized group of individuals sharing common objectives who actively attempt to influence policymakers.

majoritarianism The belief that public policy is or should be set in accordance with the opinions of a majority of the people.

material incentive A reason to join an interest group—practical benefits such as discounts, subscriptions, or group insurance.

pluralist theory A theory that views politics as a contest among various interest groups—at all levels of government—to gain benefits for their members.

purposive incentive A reason to join an interest group—satisfaction resulting from working for a cause in which one believes.

solidary incentive A reason to join an interest group—pleasure in associating with like-minded individuals.

6-2 **Identify the various types of interest groups.** The most common interest groups are those that promote private interests. Business has long been well organized for effective action. Hundreds of business groups operate at all levels of government, and there are also umbrella organizations, including the U.S. Chamber of Commerce, that represent business interests. **Trade organizations** support policies that benefit specific industries. Producers of various specific farm commodities have formed organizations to promote their own interests, and many groups work for general agricultural interests. Interest groups representing labor have been some of the most influential groups in the nation's history. While the strength and political power of labor unions have waned in the past several decades, more than one-third of all public-sector workers are union members. Most professions

that require advanced education or specialized training have organizations to protect and promote their interests. Other types of groups include **public-interest groups,** which are formed with the broader goal of working for the "public good." In reality, however, all lobbying groups represent special interests. Groups organized for the protection of consumer rights were very active in the 1960s and 1970s, and some are still active today. Americans who share the same race, ethnicity, gender, or other characteristic often have important common interests and form identity interest groups. Some interest groups, including environmental and religious groups, promote a shared political perspective or ideology. Numerous interest groups focus on a single issue. Efforts by state and local governments to lobby the federal government have escalated in recent years.

public-interest group An interest group formed for the purpose of working for the "public good." Examples are the American Civil Liberties Union and Common Cause.

right-to-work laws Laws that ban unions from collecting dues or other fees from workers whom they represent but who have not actually joined the union.

trade organization An association formed by members of a particular industry, such as the oil or trucking industries, to develop common standards and goals for the industry. Trade organizations, as interest groups, lobby government for legislation or regulations that specifically benefit their members.

6-3 **Discuss how the activities of interest groups help to shape government policymaking.** Interest groups use a variety of strategies to steer policies in ways beneficial to their interests. Sometimes, they attempt to influence policymakers directly, but at other times they try to exert indirect influence on policymakers by shaping public opinion. **Lobbying** and providing election support are two important **direct techniques** used by interest groups. Groups also try to influence public policy through the general public. **Indirect techniques** include advertising, **rating systems,** issue advocacy through **independent expenditures,** mobilizing constituents, going to court, and organizing demonstrations.

TABLE 6–5 DIRECT LOBBYING TECHNIQUES	
Technique	**Description**
Making Personal Contacts with Key Legislators	A lobbyist's personal contacts with key legislators or other government officials—in their offices, in the halls of Congress, or on social occasions such as dinners, boating expeditions, and the like—are one of the most effective direct lobbying techniques.
Providing Expertise and Research Results for Legislators	Lobbyists often have knowledge and expertise that are useful in drafting legislation, and these can be major strengths for an interest group. Harried members of Congress cannot possibly be experts on everything they vote on and therefore eagerly seek information to help them make up their minds.
Offering "Expert" Testimony before Congressional Committees	Lobbyists often provide "expert" testimony before congressional committees for or against proposed legislation. Each expert offers as much evidence as possible to support her or his position.
Providing Legal Advice to Legislators	Many lobbyists assist legislators in drafting legislation or prospective regulations. Lobbyists are a source of ideas and sometimes offer legal advice on specific details.
Following Up on Legislation	Because executive agencies responsible for carrying out legislation can often change the scope of the new law, lobbyists may also try to influence the bureaucrats who implement the policy.

© 2018 Cengage Learning

direct technique Any method used by an interest group to interact with government officials directly to further the group's goals.

independent expenditure An expenditure for activities that are independent from (not coordinated with) those of a political candidate or a political party.

indirect technique Any method used by interest groups to influence government officials through third parties, such as voters.

lobbying All of the attempts by organizations or by individuals to influence the passage, defeat, or contents of legislation or to influence the administrative decisions of government.

lobbyist An individual who handles a particular interest group's lobbying efforts.

political action committee (PAC) A committee that is established by a corporation, labor union, or special interest group to raise funds and make campaign contributions on the establishing organization's behalf.

rating system A system by which a particular interest group evaluates (rates) the performance of legislators based on how often the legislators have voted with the group's position on particular issues.

6-4 **Describe how interest groups are regulated by government.** In spite of legislation designed to reduce the "revolving door" syndrome, it remains common for those who leave positions with the federal government to become **lobbyists** or consultants for the interest groups they helped to regulate. The Lobbying Disclosure Act of 1995 reformed a 1946 law in several ways, particularly by creating stricter definitions of who is a lobbyist.

In the wake of lobbying scandals in the early 2000s, additional lobbying reform efforts were undertaken. The Honest Leadership and Open Government Act of 2007 increased lobbying disclosure requirements and placed further restrictions on the receipt of gifts and travel by members of Congress paid for by lobbyists and the organizations they represent.

CHAPTER 7 LEARNING OUTCOMES / KEY TERMS

7-1 **Summarize the origins and development of the two-party system in the United States.** After the Constitution was ratified, the Federalist Party supported a strong central government that would encourage the development of commerce and manufacturing. The party's opponents, Jefferson's Republicans, favored a more limited role for government. After suffering electoral defeats in the early 1800s, the Federalists went out of existence, resulting in a **realignment** of the party system. In the mid-1820s, Jefferson's Republicans split into two groups—the Democrats and the National Republicans (later the Whig Party). As the Democrats and Whigs competed for the presidency from 1835 to 1854, the **two-party system** as we know it today emerged. By the mid-1850s, most northern Whigs were absorbed into the new Republican Party, which opposed the extension of slavery.

After the Civil War, the Republicans and Democrats were roughly even in strength, although the Republicans were more successful in presidential contests. After the realigning election of 1896, many Americans viewed the **GOP** as the party that knew how to manage the nation's economy, and it remained dominant in national politics until the Great Depression. The election of 1932 brought Franklin D. Roosevelt to the presidency and the Democrats back to power at the national level. In the 1960s, however, conservative Democrats did not like the direction in which their party seemed to be taking them, and over time most of them became Republican voters. The result of this "rolling realignment" was that by 2000, the two major parties were fairly evenly matched.

GOP A nickname for the Republican Party—"grand old party."

political party A group of individuals who organize to win elections, operate the government, and determine policy.

realignment A process in which the popular support for and relative strength of the parties shift, and the parties are reestablished with different coalitions of supporters.

7-2 **Describe the current status of the two major parties.** A key characteristic of recent politics has been the extreme partisanship of party activists and members of Congress. The rolling realignment after the elections of 1968 resulted in parties that were much more homogeneous. By 2009, the most conservative Democrat in the House was to the left of the most moderate Republican. This ideological uniformity made it easier for the parties to maintain discipline in Congress. Political polarization

grew even more severe after the 2010 elections. Many of the new Republican members of Congress were pledged to the Tea Party philosophy of no-compromise conservatism. The ascension of Donald Trump in 2016, however, signaled that new rifts might be emerging in the Republican Party. Also significant is the growing number of independent voters, contributing to a potential **dealignment** in the party system.

dealignment Among voters, a growing detachment from both major political parties.

Tea Party movement A grassroots conservative movement that arose in 2009 after Barack Obama became president. The movement opposes big government and current levels of taxation, and also rejects political compromise.

7-3 **Explain how political parties function in our democratic system. Political parties** link the people's policy preferences to actual government policies. They recruit and nominate candidates for political office, coordinate campaigns, and take care of a number of tasks that are essential to the smooth functioning of the electoral process. Parties also help educate the public about

important political issues. Parties coordinate policy among the various branches and levels of government, and balance the competing interests of those who support the party. In government, the **minority party** checks the actions of the party in power.

coalition An alliance of individuals or groups with a variety of interests and opinions who join together to support all or part of a political party's platform.

majority party The political party that has more members in the legislature than the opposing party.

minority party The political party that has fewer members in the legislature than the opposing party.

primary A preliminary election held for the purpose of choosing a party's final candidate.

7-4 **Discuss the structure of American political parties.** The party in the **electorate** consists of **party identifiers** and **party activists** plus supportive celebrities and interest groups. Each party is decentralized, with national, state, and local organizations. Delegates to the **national convention** nominate the party's presidential and vice-presidential candidates, and they adopt the **party platform.** The national party organization

includes a **national party committee,** a **national party chairperson,** and congressional campaign committees. The party in government consists of all of the party's candidates who have won elections and now hold public office. The party in government helps to organize the government's agenda by convincing its own party members in office to vote for its policies.

electorate All of the citizens eligible to vote in a given election.

national convention The meeting held by each major party every four years to nominate presidential and vice-presidential candidates, write a party platform, and conduct other party business.

national party chairperson An individual who serves as a political party's administrative head at the national level and directs the work of the party's national committee.

national party committee The political party leaders who direct party business during the four years between the national party conventions, organize the next national convention, and plan how to support the party's candidate in the next presidential election.

party activist A party member who helps to organize and oversee party functions and planning during and between campaigns, and may even become a candidate for office.

party identifier A person who identifies himself or herself as being a supporter of a particular political party.

party platform The document drawn up by each party at its national convention that outlines the policies and positions of the party.

party ticket A list of a political party's candidates for various offices. In national elections, the party ticket consists of the presidential and vice-presidential candidates.

patronage A system of rewarding the party faithful with government jobs or contracts.

precinct A political district within a city, such as a block or a neighborhood, or a rural portion of a county. The smallest voting district at the local level.

solidarity Mutual agreement among the members of a particular group.

ward A local unit of a political party's organization, consisting of a division or district within a city.

7-5 **Describe the different types of third parties and how they function in the American political system.** The United States has a two-party system in which the Democrats and the Republicans dominate national politics. American election laws and the rules governing campaign financing tend to favor the major parties. There are also institutional barriers, such as single-member legislative districts and the electoral college system, that prevent **third parties** from enjoying electoral success. There are different kinds of third parties. An issue-oriented party is formed to promote a particular cause or timely issue. An ideological party supports a particular political doctrine or a set of beliefs. A splinter party develops out of a split within a major party, which may be part of an attempt to elect a specific person. Third parties have brought many issues to the public's attention and can influence election outcomes. Third parties also provide a voice for voters who are frustrated with the Republican and Democratic parties.

TABLE 7–1 THE MOST SUCCESSFUL THIRD-PARTY PRESIDENTIAL CAMPAIGNS SINCE 1865

This table includes all third-party candidates winning more than 5 percent of the popular vote or any electoral votes since 1865. It does not count "unfaithful electors" in the electoral college who did not vote for the candidate to whom they were pledged. *What kinds of issue positions might make a third party especially popular?*

Year	Third Party	Third-Party Presidential Candidate	Percent of the Popular Vote	Electoral Votes	Winning Presidential Candidate and Party
1892	Populist	James Weaver	8.5%	22	Grover Cleveland (D)
1912	Progressive	Theodore Roosevelt	27.4	88	Woodrow Wilson (D)
	Socialist	Eugene Debs	6.0	—	
1924	Progressive	Robert La Follette	16.6	13	Calvin Coolidge (R)
1948	States' Rights	Strom Thurmond	2.4	39	Harry Truman (D)
1960	Independent Democrat	Harry Byrd	0.4	15*	John F. Kennedy (D)
1968	American Independent	George Wallace	13.5	46	Richard Nixon (R)
1980	National Union	John Anderson	6.6	—	Ronald Reagan (R)
1992	Independent	Ross Perot	18.9	—	Bill Clinton (D)
1996	Reform	Ross Perot	8.4	—	Bill Clinton (D)

*Byrd received fifteen electoral votes from unpledged electors in Alabama and Mississippi.
Source: Dave Leip's Atlas of U.S. Presidential Elections at www.uselectionatlas.org.

---

third party In the United States, any party other than the two major parties (Republican and Democratic).

two-party system A political system in which two strong and established parties compete for political offices.

8-1   Describe the political socialization process. Most people acquire their political attitudes, opinions, beliefs, and knowledge through a complex learning process called **political socialization.** Most political socialization is informal. The strong early influence of the family later gives way to the multiple influences of schools, churches, the **media,** opinion leaders, major life events, **peer groups,** and economic status and occupation. People and institutions that influence the political views of others are called **agents of political socialization.**

agents of political socialization People and institutions that influence the political views of others.

media Newspapers, magazines, television, radio, the Internet, and any other printed or electronic means of communication.

peer group Associates, often close in age to one another; may include friends, classmates, co-workers, club members, or religious group members.

political socialization The learning process through which most people acquire their political attitudes, opinions, beliefs, and knowledge.

public opinion The views of the citizenry about politics, public issues, and public policies; a complex collection of opinions held by many people on issues in the public arena.

8-2   Discuss the different factors that affect voter choices. For established voters, party identification is one of the most important and lasting predictors of how a person will vote. Voters' choices often depend on the perceived character of the candidates rather than on their qualifications or policy positions. When people vote for candidates who share their positions on particular issues, they are engaging in policy voting. Historically, economic issues have had the strongest influence on voters' choices. Socioeconomic factors, including educational attainment, occupation and income, age, gender, religion, race and ethnic background, and geographic region, also influence how people vote. Ideology is another indicator of voting behavior.

gender gap The difference between the percentage of votes cast for a particular candidate by women and the percentage of votes cast for the same candidate by men.

Solid South A term used to describe the tendency of the southern states to vote Democratic after the Civil War.

8-3   Explain how public opinion polls are conducted, problems with polls, and how they are used in the political process. A **public opinion poll** is a survey of the **public's opinion** on a particular topic at a particular moment, as measured through the use of **samples.** Early polling efforts often relied on **straw polls.** The opinions expressed in straw polls, however, usually represent an atypical subgroup of the population, or a **biased sample.** Over time, more scientific polling techniques were developed. Today, polling is used extensively by political candidates and policymakers. Polls can be quite accurate when conducted properly. In-person surveys have been replaced by telephone interviews, often with prerecorded messages that solicit responses. Some pollsters specialize in Internet surveys. To achieve the most accurate results possible, pollsters use **random samples,** in which each person within the entire population being polled has an equal chance of being chosen. A properly drawn random sample will be representative of the population as a whole, though responses of various groups are sometimes weighted in an effort to achieve representativeness. Public opinion polls are fundamentally statistical. The true result of a poll is not a single figure, but a range of probabilities. All polls contain a **sampling error. effect.** Polling firms often use differing models that contribute to a **house effect.** Problems with polls can stem from the way questions are worded, and polls often reduce complex issues to questions that simply call for "yes" or "no" answers. Moreover, polls of voter preferences cannot reflect rapid shifts in public opinion unless they are taken frequently. Many journalists base their political coverage during campaigns almost exclusively on poll findings, and media companies often report only the polls conducted by their affiliated pollsters. A tactic used in some political campaigns is a **push poll,** which asks "fake" polling questions that are designed to "push" voters toward one candidate or another.

biased sample A poll sample that does not accurately represent the population.

house effect In the case of a polling firm, a consistent tendency to report results more favorable to one of the political parties than the results reported by other pollsters.

public opinion poll A survey of the public's opinion on a particular topic at a particular moment.

push poll A campaign tactic used to feed false or misleading information to potential voters, under the guise of taking an opinion poll, with the intent to "push" voters away from one candidate and toward another.

random sample In the context of opinion polling, a sample in which each person within the entire population being polled has an equal chance of being chosen.

sample In the context of opinion polling, a group of people selected to represent the population being studied.

sampling error In the context of opinion polling, the difference between what the sample results show and what the true results would have been had everybody in the relevant population been interviewed.

straw poll A nonscientific poll in which there is no way to ensure that the opinions expressed are representative of the larger population.

CHAPTER REVIEW — LEARNING OUTCOMES / KEY TERMS

CHAPTER 8 LEARNING OUTCOMES / KEY TERMS

8-4

Indicate some of the factors that affect voter turnout, and discuss what has been done to improve voter turnout and voting procedures. The Fifteenth Amendment to the Constitution (1870) guaranteed suffrage to African American males. Yet, for many decades, African Americans were effectively denied the ability to exercise their voting rights. Today, devices used to restrict voting rights, such as the **poll tax, literacy tests,** the **grandfather clause,** and **white primaries,** are explicitly prohibited by constitutional amendments, by the Voting Rights Act of 1965, or by court decisions. The Nineteenth Amendment (1920) gave women the right to vote, and the Twenty-sixth Amendment (1971) reduced the minimum voting age to eighteen. Some restrictions on voting rights, such as registration, residency, and citizenship requirements, still exist. Most states also do not permit prison inmates or felons to vote. Attempts to improve voter turnout and voting procedures include simplifying the voter-registration process, conducting voting by mail, updating voting equipment, and allowing early voting. In recent years, a number of states have passed laws that may have the effect of making it harder to vote, not easier. Voter turnout is affected by several factors, including educational attainment, income level, age, and minority status.

FIGURE 8–4 VOTER TURNOUT AROUND THE WORLD

This list excludes nations that do not have free elections, based on ratings from Freedom House. It includes all free nations with an economy (nominal GDP) of at least $1 trillion. *What factors might cause turnout to be relatively high or low in a particular country?*

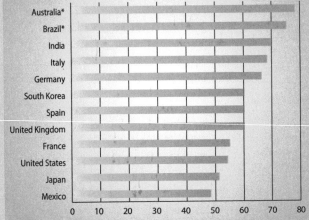

*In these countries, those who do not vote are required to pay a fine.

Source: International Institute for Democracy and Electoral Assistance. (Based on voting-age population, which depresses the U.S. percentage as explained later in this chapter.)

grandfather clause A clause in a state law that had the effect of restricting voting rights to those whose ancestors had voted before the 1860s. It was one of the techniques used in the South to prevent African Americans from exercising their right to vote.

literacy test A test given to voters to ensure that they could read and write and thus evaluate political information. This technique was used in many southern states to restrict African American participation in elections.

poll tax A fee of several dollars that had to be paid before a person could vote. This device was used in some southern states to discourage African Americans and low-income whites from voting.

vote-eligible population The number of people who are actually eligible to vote in an American election.

voting-age population The number of people residing in the United States who are at least eighteen years old.

white primary A primary election in which African Americans were prohibited from voting. The practice was banned by the Supreme Court in 1944.

9-1 **Explain how elections are held and how the electoral college functions in presidential elections.** During **general elections,** voters decide who will be the U.S. president, vice president, and members of Congress. An election board supervises the voting process in each precinct. **Poll watchers** from each of the two major parties typically monitor the polling place as well. Citizens do not vote directly for the president and vice president. Instead, they vote for **electors** who will cast their ballots in the **electoral college.** Each state has as many electoral votes as it has U.S. senators and representatives. There are also three electors from the District of Columbia. The electoral college system is primarily a **winner-take-all system** because, in nearly all states, the candidate who receives the most popular votes in the state is credited with all of that state's electoral votes. To be elected through this system, a candidate must receive at least 270 electoral votes, a majority of the 538 electoral votes available.

FIGURE 9–1   STATE ELECTORAL VOTES IN 2016

The size of each state reflects the number of electoral votes that state has, following the changes required by the 2010 census. The colors show which party the state voted for in the 2016 presidential elections: red for Republican, blue for Democratic. A candidate must win 270 electoral votes to be elected president. Maine awards two of its electoral votes by congressional district, and the red square reflects that the Republicans carried one of them. *Why do some states have so many electoral votes and others so few?*

Australian ballot A secret ballot that is prepared, distributed, and counted by government officials at public expense. Used by all states in the United States since 1888.

elector A member of the electoral college.

electoral college The group of electors who are selected by the voters in each state to officially elect the president and vice president. The number of electors in each state is equal to the number of that state's representatives in both chambers of Congress.

general election A regularly scheduled election to choose the U.S. president, vice president, and senators and representatives in Congress. General elections are held in even-numbered years on the Tuesday after the first Monday in November.

poll watcher A representative from one of the political parties who is allowed to monitor a polling place to make sure that the election is run fairly and that fraud doesn't occur.

special election An election that is held at the state or local level when the voters must decide an issue before the next general election or when vacancies occur by reason of death or resignation.

winner-take-all system A system in which the candidate who receives the most votes wins. In contrast, proportional systems allocate votes to multiple winners.

9-2 **Discuss how candidates are nominated.** The methods used by political parties to nominate candidates have changed over time and have included **caucuses** and **nominating conventions.** Today, candidates who win **primary elections** go on to compete against the candidates from other parties in the general election. In variations of **closed** or **open direct primaries,** voters cast their ballots directly for candidates. The elections that nominate candidates for Congress and for state or local offices are almost always direct primaries. Most of the states hold presidential primaries, which are indirect primaries used to choose **delegates** to the national nominating conventions. In some states, delegates are chosen through a caucus/convention system. Each political party holds a national convention at which delegates adopt the party platform and nominate the party's presidential and vice-presidential candidates.

caucus A meeting held to choose political candidates or delegates.

closed primary A primary in which only party members can vote to choose that party's candidates.

Credentials Committee A committee of each national political party that evaluates the claims of national party convention delegates to be the legitimate representatives of their states.

delegate A person selected to represent the people of one geographic area at a party convention.

direct primary An election held within each of the two major parties—Democratic and Republican—to choose the party's candidates for the general election. Voters choose the candidate directly, rather than through delegates.

nominating convention An official meeting of a political party to choose its candidates. Nominating conventions at the state and local levels also select delegates to represent the citizens of their geographic areas at a higher-level party convention.

open primary A primary in which voters can vote for a party's candidates regardless of whether they belong to the party.

primary election An election in which voters choose the candidates of their party, who will then run in the general election.

superdelegates Party leaders and elected officials with the automatic right to attend their party's national convention and support any candidate.

9-3 **Indicate what is involved in launching a political campaign today, and describe the structure and functions of a campaign organization.** To run a successful campaign, a candidate's campaign staff must be able to raise funds, get media coverage, produce and pay for political ads, schedule the candidate's time effectively with constituent groups and potential supporters, convey the candidate's position on the issues, conduct **opposition research,** and persuade the voters to go to the polls. Political party organizations are no longer as important as they once were in providing campaign services. Candidates now turn to **political consultants** who specialize in a particular area of the campaign such as conducting polls or developing the candidate's advertising. Most candidates have a campaign manager who coordinates and plans the **campaign strategy.**

campaign strategy The comprehensive plan developed by a candidate and his or her advisers for winning an election.

opposition research The attempt to learn damaging information about an opponent in a political campaign.

political consultant A professional political adviser who, for a fee, works on an area of a candidate's campaign. Political consultants include campaign managers, pollsters, media advisers, and "get-out-the-vote" organizers.

9-4 **Describe how the Internet has transformed political campaigns.** Today, the ability to make effective use of social media and the Internet is essential to a candidate. In 2008, Barack Obama gained an edge on his rivals in part because of his superior use of new technologies, and his 2012 campaign was even more sophisticated, taking Internet fund-raising to a new level. Donald Trump's fund-raising operation was neither large-scale nor particularly innovative. Indeed, Trump raised less money than any major-party presidential candidate in years. Trump did make great use of the Internet in rallying his supporters, however. At the beginning of 2016, Hillary Clinton had a substantially larger social-media presence than any other candidate, including Trump. By April, however, Trump passed Clinton in Twitter followers, and his social-media edge continued to grow thereafter.

9-5 **Summarize the current laws that regulate campaign financing and the role of money in modern political campaigns.** The modern campaign is an expensive undertaking. Campaign-financing laws enacted in the 1970s provided public funding for presidential primaries and general elections, limited individual and group contributions to candidates, and created the Federal Election Commission. Beginning in 2004, leading Democratic and Republican presidential candidates were refusing public funding for the primaries because they could raise much more money without it. By 2012, the public financing of presidential campaigns was effectively over. The Bipartisan Campaign Reform Act of 2002 addressed the increasing use of **soft money** and **independent expenditures** to a certain extent. Several court decisions, however, have altered the rules of campaign financing. Notable consequences of these rulings include the rise of super PACs and fewer restrictions on wealthy individuals who wish to spend significant amounts of money during political campaigns. Another campaign-finance issue arose after the creation of a new kind of organization, known as the 501c, which has the ability to spend money during campaigns and to conceal the identity of its donors.

independent expenditure An expenditure for activities that are independent from (not coordinated with) those of a political candidate or a political party.

soft money Campaign contributions not regulated by federal law, such as some contributions that are made to political parties instead of to particular candidates.

CHAPTER 10 LEARNING OUTCOMES / KEY TERMS

10-1 **Explain the role of the media in a democracy.** What the media say and do has an impact on what Americans think about political issues, but the media also reflect what Americans think about politics. While the new media based on the Internet are becoming increasingly important, the traditional media—radio, television, and print—remain important to American politics and government. By helping to determine what people will talk and think about, the media play a role in setting the political agenda. Two techniques of **agenda setting** are **priming** and **framing.** Of all the media, television still has the greatest impact on most Americans, but the medium of television imposes constraints on how political issues are presented. Television reporting relies extensively on visual elements, and stories may be communicated in only a **sound bite.**

agenda setting The ability to determine which issues are considered important by the public and by politicians.

electronic media Communication channels that involve electronic transmissions, such as radio, television, and the Internet.

framing An agenda-setting technique that establishes the context of a media report. Framing can mean fitting events into a familiar story or filtering information through preconceived ideas.

mass media Communication channels, such as newspapers and radio and television broadcasts, through which people can communicate to large audiences.

priming An agenda-setting technique in which a media outlet promotes specific facts or ideas that may affect the public's thinking on related topics.

print media Communication channels that consist of printed materials, such as newspapers and magazines.

sound bite A recorded comment, lasting for only a few seconds, that captures a thought or a perspective and has an immediate impact on viewers or listeners.

10-2 **Summarize how television influences the conduct of political campaigns.** Candidates for political office spend a great deal of time and money cultivating a TV presence through political ads, debates, and general news coverage. Televised **political advertising** consumes at least half of the total budget for a major political campaign. **Negative political advertising,** including **personal attack ads** and **issue ads,** is frequently used. Televised debates are a feature of presidential campaigns. They provide an opportunity for voters to find out how candidates differ on issues and allow candidates to capitalize on the power of television to improve their images or point out the failings of their opponents. Candidates' campaigns have become increasingly sophisticated in **managing news coverage.** Press advisers often try to convince reporters to give a story or event a **spin** that is favorable to the candidate.

issue ad A political advertisement that focuses on a particular issue. Issue ads can be used to support or attack a candidate's position or credibility.

managed news coverage News coverage that is manipulated (managed) by a campaign manager or political consultant to gain media exposure for a political candidate.

negative political advertising Political advertising undertaken for the purpose of discrediting a candidate in voters' eyes.

personal attack ad A negative political advertisement that attacks a candidate's character.

political advertising Advertising undertaken by or on behalf of a political candidate to familiarize voters with the candidate and his or her views on campaign issues. Also, advertising for or against policy issues.

spin A reporter's slant on, or interpretation of, a particular event or action.

spin doctor A political candidate's press adviser who tries to convince reporters to give a story or event concerning the candidate a particular "spin" (interpretation, or slant).

10-3 **Explain why talk radio has been described as the Wild West of the media.** Talk radio is dominated by conservatives. Talk-show hosts do not attempt to hide their political biases; if anything, they exaggerate them for effect. Sometimes, hosts appear to care more about the entertainment value of their statements than whether they are, strictly speaking, true. No journalistic conventions are observed. Those who think that talk radio is good for the country argue that talk shows, taken together, provide a great populist forum. Others fear that talk shows empower fringe groups, perhaps magnifying their rage.

10-4 **Describe types of media bias, and explain how such bias affects the political process.** Relatively few Americans believe that the news media are unbiased in their reporting, and there has been a notable decline in the public's confidence in news media in recent years. Nevertheless, the public does believe that the media are successful in fulfilling their role as a watchdog. While the majority of Americans think that the media reflect a bias in a liberal—or sometimes a conservative direction, it is a media bias against losers that may play a significant role in shaping presidential campaigns and elections. The media use the winner–loser framework to describe events throughout the campaigns. Today's news culture is in the midst of change. News organizations are redefining their purpose and looking for special niches in which to build their audiences. For some, the niche is hyperlocalism; for others, it is personal commentary. In many ways, news organizations have begun to base their appeal more on how they cover the news and less on what they cover. Narrowcasting has also become important on television.

10-5

Indicate the extent to which the Internet is reshaping news and political campaigns. The Internet is a major source of information. Almost every major news organization, both print and broadcast, delivers news online. In addition, there has been a veritable explosion of **citizen journalism** in recent years. Blogs are offered by independent journalists, scholars, political activists, and the citizenry at large. **Podcasting** is another form of news distribution. The Internet is an inexpensive way for candidates to contact, recruit, and mobilize supporters, as well as to disseminate information about their positions on issues. Candidates hire Web managers to create well-designed campaign websites to attract viewers, manage their e-mail, and track their credit-card contributions. The Web manager also hires bloggers to promote the candidate's views, arranges for podcasting of campaign information, and hires staff to monitor the Web for news about the candidates and to track the online publications of netroots groups. Citizen videos have also changed the traditional campaign. Comments a candidate makes may be caught on camera by someone with a cell phone or digital camera and published on the Internet for all to see. Many politicians have experienced the dangers of 24/7 exposure.

FIGURE 10–1   ADVERTISING REVENUES: ONLINE VERSUS THE NEWSPAPER INDUSTRY, 2001–2016

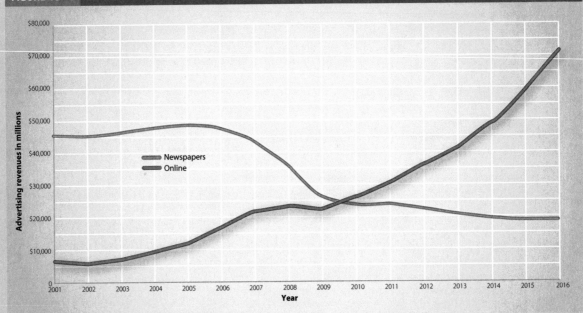

Sources: The Interactive Advertising Bureau and authors' calculations. Numbers are for the United States only.

citizen journalism The collection, analysis, and dissemination of information online by independent journalists, scholars, political activists, and the general citizenry.

podcasting The distribution of audio or video files to personal computers or mobile devices, such as smartphones and tablets.

CHAPTER 11 LEARNING OUTCOMES / KEY TERMS

11-1 **Explain how seats in the House of Representatives are apportioned among the states.** The Constitution provides for the **apportionment** of House seats among the states on the basis of their respective populations, though each state is guaranteed at least one seat. Every ten years, the 435 House seats are reapportioned based on the outcome of the census. Each representative to the House is elected by voters in a **congressional district.** Within each state, districts must contain, as nearly as possible, equal numbers of people. This principle is known as the **"one person, one vote" rule.** Gerrymandering occurs when a district's boundaries are drawn to maximize the influence of a certain group or political party.

apportionment The distribution of House seats among the states on the basis of their respective populations.

congressional district The geographic area that is served by one member in the House of Representatives.

earmark Spending provision inserted into legislation that benefits only a small number of people.

gerrymandering The drawing of a legislative district's boundaries in such a way as to maximize the influence of a certain group or political party.

instructed delegate A representative who deliberately mirrors the views of the majority of his or her constituents.

malapportionment A situation in which the voting power of citizens in one district is greater than the voting power of citizens in another district.

minority-majority district A district in which minority groups make up a majority of the population.

"one person, one vote" rule A rule, or principle, requiring that congressional districts have equal populations so that one person's vote counts as much as another's vote.

trustee A representative who tries to serve the broad interests of the entire society and not just the narrow interests of his or her constituents.

11-2 **Describe the power of incumbency.** If legislators choose to run for reelection, they enjoy several advantages over their opponents, including name recognition, access to the media, and lawmaking power. Members of Congress also have administrative staffs in Washington, D.C., and in their home districts. A key advantage is their fund-raising ability. Most incumbent members of Congress have a much larger network of contacts, donors, and lobbyists than their challengers have. Although incumbents who run are usually reelected, there have been occasional periods of some turbulence when fewer incumbents than usual won reelection.

11-3 **Identify the key leadership positions in Congress, describe the committee system, and indicate some important differences between the House of Representatives and the Senate.** The Constitution provides for the presiding officers of both the House and the Senate, and each chamber has added other leadership positions. The majority party in each chamber chooses the major officers of that chamber, selects committee chairpersons, and has a majority on all committees. Chief among the leaders in the House of Representatives is the **Speaker of the House,** who has a great deal of power. Other leaders include the **majority and minority leaders** and the **whips.** The vice president of the United States is the president of the Senate, and senators elect the president pro tempore ("pro tem"). The real power in the Senate is held by the majority and minority leaders, and their whips. The committee system is a way to provide for specialization, or a division of legislative labor. Much of the work of legislating is performed by the **standing committees** and their **subcommittees** in the House and the Senate. A **conference committee** is formed for the purpose of achieving agreement between the House and the Senate on the wording of a legislative act. With its larger size, the House needs more rules and more formality than the Senate. The House **Rules Committee** proposes time limits on debate for most bills. The Senate normally permits extended debate. The use of unlimited debate to obstruct legislation is called **filibustering,** which may be ended by invoking **cloture.** There are other important differences between the House and the Senate as well. The Senate, for example, has the power of "advice and consent" on presidential appointments and treaties.

TABLE 11–2	MAJOR DIFFERENCES BETWEEN THE HOUSE AND THE SENATE	
House*	**Senate***
Members chosen from local districts	Members chosen from entire state
Two-year term	Six-year term
Always elected by voters	Originally (until 1913) elected by state legislatures
May impeach (accuse, indict) federal officials	May convict federal officials of impeachable offenses
Larger (435 voting members)	Smaller (100 members)
More formal rules	Fewer rules and restrictions
Debate limited	Debate extended
Floor action controlled	Unanimous consent rules
Less prestige and less individual notice	More prestige and media attention
Originates bills for raising revenues	Has power of "advice and consent" on presidential appointments and treaties
Local or narrow leadership	National leadership

*Some of these differences, such as term of office, are provided for in the Constitution, while others, such as debate rules, are not.

cloture A procedure for ending filibusters in the Senate and bringing the matter under consideration to a vote.

conference committee A temporary committee that consists of members from the House and the Senate who work out a compromise bill.

filibustering Using the Senate tradition of unlimited debate to prevent action.

majority leader The party leader elected by the majority party in the House or in the Senate.

minority leader The party leader elected by the minority party in the House or in the Senate.

reconciliation A Senate rule under which revenue bills received from the House that meet certain requirements cannot be filibustered.

Rules Committee A standing committee in the House that provides special rules governing how particular bills will be considered and debated.

Speaker of the House The presiding officer in the House of Representatives. A member of the majority party who is the most powerful member of the House.

standing committee A permanent committee in Congress that deals with legislation concerning a particular area, such as agriculture or foreign relations.

subcommittee A division of a larger committee that deals with a particular part of the committee's policy area.

whip A member of Congress who assists the majority or minority leader in managing the party's legislative program.

11-4 **Summarize the specific steps in the lawmaking process.** After a bill is introduced, it is sent to the appropriate standing committee. A committee chairperson will typically send the bill on to a subcommittee, where public hearings may be held. After a **markup session,** the bill goes to the full committee for further action. After a bill is reported to the chamber, it is scheduled for floor debate. If, after votes are taken on the legislation, the House and the Senate have passed differing versions of the same bill, a conference committee is formed to produce a compromise bill. A **conference report** is submitted to each chamber. If the bill is approved by both chambers, it is ready for action by the president.

conference report A report submitted by a conference committee after it has drafted a single version of a bill.

markup session A meeting held by a congressional committee or subcommittee to approve, amend, or redraft a bill.

pocket veto A special type of veto power used by the president after the legislature has adjourned.

11-5 **Identify Congress's oversight functions, and explain how Congress fulfills them.** Congress oversees the departments and agencies of the executive branch, and can rein in the power of the bureaucracy by choosing not to provide the money necessary for the bureaucracy to function. Congress also has the authority to investigate the actions of the executive branch, the need for certain legislation, and even the actions of its own members. Congress has the power to impeach federal officials and remove them from office. The Senate either confirms or fails to confirm the president's nominees for federal judgeships and top executive branch officers.

nuclear option Changing Senate rules—in particular, rules that require a supermajority—by simple majority vote. Also known as the *constitutional option.*

11-6 **Indicate what is involved in the congressional budgeting process.** The budgeting process, which involves **authorization** and **appropriation,** begins when the president submits a proposed federal budget for the next **fiscal year.** In the **first budget resolution,** Congress sets overall revenue goals and spending targets. The **second budget resolution** sets "binding" limits on taxes and spending. When Congress is unable to pass a complete budget by October 1, it usually passes **continuing resolutions,** which enable executive agencies to keep on doing whatever they were doing the previous year with the same amount of funding. **Entitlement programs** operate under open-ended budget authorizations.

appropriation The determination of how many dollars will be spent in a given year on a particular government activity.

authorization The creation of the legal basis for government programs.

continuing resolution A temporary resolution that enables executive agencies to continue working with the same funding that they had in the previous fiscal year.

entitlement program A government program (such as Social Security) that allows, or entitles, a certain class of people (such as older persons) to receive benefits.

first budget resolution A budget resolution, which is supposed to be passed in May, that sets overall revenue goals and spending targets for the next fiscal year, beginning on October 1.

fiscal year A twelve-month period that is established for accounting purposes. The government's fiscal year runs from October 1 through September 30.

second budget resolution A budget resolution, which is supposed to be passed in September, that sets "binding" limits on taxes and spending for the next fiscal year.

12-1 **List the constitutional requirements for becoming president.** Article II of the Constitution sets forth relatively few requirements for becoming president. A person must be a natural-born citizen, at least thirty-five years of age, and a resident within the United States for at least fourteen years.

12-2 **Explain the roles that a president adopts while in office.** In the course of exercising his or her powers, the president performs a variety of roles. The president is the nation's **chief executive**—the head of the executive branch— and enforces laws and federal court decisions. The president leads the nation's armed forces as **commander in chief.** As **head of state,** the president performs ceremonial activities as a personal symbol of the nation. As **chief diplomat,** the president directs U.S. foreign policy and is the nation's most important representative in dealing with foreign governments. The president has become the chief legislator, informing Congress about the condition of the country and recommending legislative measures. As political party leader, the president chooses the chairperson of his or her party's national committee, attends party fund-raisers, and exerts influence within the party by using presidential appointment powers and engaging in the practice of **patronage.**

chief diplomat The role of the president of the United States in recognizing and interacting with foreign governments.

chief executive The head of the executive branch of government. In the United States, the president.

commander in chief The supreme commander of a nation's military force.

diplomat A person who represents one country in dealing with representatives of another country.

head of state The person who serves as the ceremonial head of a country's government and represents that country to the rest of the world.

patronage The practice by which elected officials give government jobs to individuals who helped them gain office.

12-3 **Indicate the scope of presidential powers.** The Constitution gives the president specific powers, such as the power to make **treaties,** to grant reprieves and pardons, and to **veto** bills passed by Congress. The president also has inherent powers—powers that are necessary to carry out the specific constitutional duties of the presidency. Several presidents have greatly expanded the powers of the office. The president, for example, is now expected to develop a legislative program. The president's political skills, the ability to persuade others, and the strategy of "going public" all play a role in determining legislative success. The president's executive authority has been expanded by the use of **executive orders** and **signing statements,** and the ability to make **executive agreements** has enhanced presidential power in foreign affairs. As commander in chief, the president can respond quickly to a military threat without waiting for congressional action, and since 1945, the president has been responsible for deciding if and when to use nuclear weapons.

executive agreement A binding international agreement, or pact, that is made between the president and another head of state and that does not require Senate approval.

executive order A presidential order to carry out a policy or policies described in a law passed by Congress.

signing statement A written statement, appended to a bill at the time the president signs it into law, indicating how the president interprets that legislation.

treaty A formal agreement between the governments of two or more countries.

veto A Latin word meaning "I forbid"; the refusal by an official, such as the president of the United States or a state governor, to sign a bill into law.

12-4 **Describe advantages enjoyed by Congress and by the president in their institutional relationship.** Congress has the advantage over the president in the areas of legislative authorization, the regulation of foreign and interstate commerce, and some budgetary matters. The president has the advantage over Congress in dealing with a national crisis, in setting foreign policy, and in influencing public opinion. The relationship between Congress and the president is affected by their different constituencies and election cycles, and the fact that the president is limited to two terms in office. Their relationship is also affected when government is divided, with at least one house of Congress controlled by a party different from the White House.

executive privilege An inherent executive power claimed by presidents to withhold information from, or to refuse to appear before, Congress or the courts. The president can also accord the privilege to other executive officials.

Watergate scandal A scandal involving an illegal break-in at the Democratic National Committee offices in 1972 by members of President Richard Nixon's reelection campaign staff.

12-5 **Discuss the organization of the executive branch and the role of cabinet members in presidential administrations.** The heads of the executive departments are members of the president's **cabinet.** The president may add other officials to the cabinet as well. In general, presidents don't rely heavily on the advice of the formal cabinet. Department heads are often more responsive to the wishes of their own staffs, to their own political ambitions, or to obtaining resources for their departments than they are to the presidents they serve. Since 1939, top advisers and assistants in the **Executive Office of the President (EOP)** have helped the president carry out major duties. Some of the most important staff agencies in the EOP are the **White House Office,** which is headed by the **chief of staff** and includes the **press secretary;** the **Office of Management and Budget;** and the **National Security Council.** In recent years, the responsibilities of the vice president have grown immensely, and the vice president has become one of the most important of the president's advisers.

TABLE 12–3 THE EXECUTIVE OFFICE OF THE PRESIDENT AS OF 2017

Agency
Council of Economic Advisers
Council on Environmental Quality
Executive Residence
National Security Council
Office of Administration
Office of Management and Budget
Office of National Drug Control Policy
Office of Science and Technology Policy
Office of the U.S. Trade Representative
Office of the Vice President
White House Office
President's Intelligence Advisory Board

Source: www.whitehouse.gov.

cabinet An advisory group selected by the president to assist with decision making. Traditionally, the cabinet has consisted of the heads of the executive departments and other officers whom the president may choose to appoint.

chief of staff The person who directs the operations of the White House Office and advises the president on important matters.

Executive Office of the President (EOP) A group of staff agencies that assist the president in carrying out major duties.

kitchen cabinet The name given to a president's unofficial advisers. The term was coined during Andrew Jackson's presidency.

National Security Council (NSC) A council that advises the president on domestic and foreign matters concerning the safety and defense of the nation.

Office of Management and Budget (OMB) An agency in the Executive Office of the President that has the primary duty of assisting the president in preparing and supervising the administration of the federal budget.

press secretary A member of the White House staff who holds news conferences for reporters and makes public statements for the president.

White House Office The personal office of the president. White House Office personnel handle the president's political needs and manage the media, among other duties.

13-1 **Describe the size and functions of the U.S. bureaucracy and the major components of federal spending.** A **bureaucracy** is a large, complex administrative organization that is structured hierarchically. In the federal government, the bureaucracy is part of the executive branch, and its head is the president of the United States. The federal bureaucracy exists because Congress, over time, has delegated certain tasks to specialists. The three levels of government employ more than 15 percent of the civilian labor force. Over half of the federal budget consists of various social programs. Defense spending, including veterans' benefits, also accounts for a significant amount of total federal spending. Other categories of spending include military and economic foreign aid, as well as interest on the national debt.

bureaucracy A large, complex, hierarchically structured administrative organization that carries out specific functions.

bureaucrat An individual who works in a bureaucracy. As generally used, the term refers to a government employee.

13-2 **Discuss the structure and basic components of the federal bureaucracy.** The fifteen executive departments are the major service organizations of the federal government. Each department was created by Congress as the perceived need for it arose, and each manages a specific policy area. Department heads are appointed by the president and confirmed by the Senate. Each department includes several subagencies. **Independent executive agencies** have a single function. Sometimes agencies are kept independent because of the sensitive nature of their functions, but at other times, Congress creates independent agencies to protect them from partisan politics. There are more than two hundred independent executive agencies. An **independent regulatory agency** is responsible for a specific type of policy. Its function is to create and implement rules that regulate private activity and protect the public interest in a particular sector of the economy. **Government corporations** are businesses owned by the government. They provide a service that could be handled by the private sector, and they charge for their services. A number of intermediate forms of organization exist that fall between a government corporation and a private one.

TABLE 13–3 SELECTED INDEPENDENT REGULATORY AGENCIES

Name	Date Formed	Principal Duties
Federal Reserve System (Fed)	1913	Determines policy on interest rates, credit availability, and the money supply.
Federal Trade Commission (FTC)	1914	Works to prevent businesses from engaging in unfair trade practices and forming business monopolies.
Securities and Exchange Commission (SEC)	1934	Regulates the nation's stock exchanges, requires financial disclosure by companies that wish to sell stocks and bonds to the public.
Federal Communications Commission (FCC)	1934	Regulates interstate and international communications by radio, television, wire, satellite, and cable.
National Labor Relations Board (NLRB)	1935	Protects employees' rights to join unions and to bargain collectively with employers, attempts to prevent unfair labor practices by both employers and unions.
Equal Employment Opportunity Commission (EEOC)	1964	Works to eliminate discrimination that is based on religion, gender, race, color, national origin, age, or disability; examines claims of discrimination.

government corporation An agency of the government that is run as a business enterprise. Such agencies engage primarily in commercial activities, produce revenues, and require greater flexibility than most government agencies have.

independent executive agency A federal agency that is not located within a cabinet department.

independent regulatory agency A federal organization that is responsible for creating and implementing rules that regulate private activity and protect the public interest in a particular sector of the economy.

13-3 **Describe how the federal civil service was established and how bureaucrats get their jobs.** Federal **bureaucrats** holding top-level positions are appointed by the president and confirmed by the Senate. The list of positions that are filled by appointments is published after each presidential election in a book that summarizes about eight thousand jobs. The rank-and-file bureaucrats—the rest of the federal bureaucracy—are part of the **civil service.** They obtain their jobs through the Office of Personnel Management (OPM). The OPM recruits, interviews, and tests potential government workers and makes recommendations to individual agencies as to which persons meet relevant standards. The Civil Service Reform Act of 1883 established the principle of government employment on the basis of merit through open, competitive examinations.

civil service Nonmilitary government employees.

13-4 **Explain how regulatory agencies make rules and how issue networks affect policymaking in government.** Regulatory agencies are sometimes regarded as the fourth branch of government. **Enabling legislation** makes the regulatory agency a potent organization. Agencies make **legislative rules** that are as legally binding as laws passed by Congress. When they are engaging in **rulemaking,** agencies must follow certain procedural requirements and must also make sure that their rules are based on substantial evidence. Bureaucrats in federal agencies are expected to exhibit **neutral competency,** which means that they are supposed to apply their technical skills to their jobs without regard to political issues. In reality, however, each independent agency and each executive department is interested in its own survival and expansion. **Iron triangles** are well established in almost every part of the bureaucracy. In some policy areas, there are less structured relationships among experts who have strong opinions and interests regarding the direction of policy. These **issue networks** are able to exert a great deal of influence on legislators and bureaucratic agencies.

FIGURE 13–6   ISSUE NETWORK: THE ENVIRONMENT

Executive Departments and Agencies
- Environmental Protection Agency
- Agriculture Department
- Energy Department
- Department of the Interior
- National Oceanic and Atmospheric Admin.
- Bureau of Land Management
- Army Corps of Engineers

Key Congressional Committees
- **Senate**
  Appropriations; Energy and Natural Resources; Environment and Public Works; Finance; Commerce, Science, and Transportation
- **House of Representatives**
  Agriculture, Appropriations, Natural Resources, Transportation and Infrastructure

Selected Interest Groups
- **Environmental Groups**
  Environmental Defense, Friends of the Earth, National Audubon Society, Clean Water Action, National Wildlife Federation, The Ocean Conservancy, American Forests
- **Industry Groups**
  Citizens for a Sound Economy, Edison Electric Institute, U.S. Chamber of Commerce, National Food Processors Association, International Wood Products Association, National Mining Association, American Resort Development Association

adjudicate To render a judicial decision. In administrative law, it is the process in which an administrative law judge hears and decides issues that arise when an agency charges a person or firm with violating a law or regulation enforced by the agency.

enabling legislation A law enacted by a legislature to establish an administrative agency. Enabling legislation normally specifies the name, purpose, composition, and powers of the agency being created.

iron triangle A three-way alliance among legislators, bureaucrats, and interest groups to make or preserve policies that benefit their respective interests.

issue networks Groups of individuals or organizations—which consist of legislators and legislative staff members, interest group leaders, bureaucrats, the media, scholars, and other experts—that support particular policy positions on a given issue.

legislative rule An administrative agency rule that carries the same weight as a statute enacted by a legislature.

neutral competency The application of technical skills to jobs without regard to political issues.

rulemaking The process undertaken by an administrative agency when formally proposing, evaluating, and adopting a new regulation.

13-5 **Identify some of the ways in which the government has attempted to curb waste and improve efficiency in the bureaucracy.** To encourage federal employees to report gross governmental inefficiency or wrongdoing, Congress has passed laws to protect **whistleblowers** and to make cash rewards to them. To improve efficiency, almost every federal agency has had to describe its goals and identify methods for evaluating how well those goals are met. President Obama created the position of a chief performance officer who works with other economic officials in an attempt to increase efficiency and eliminate waste in government. Other ideas for reforming government bureaucracies include pay-for-performance plans, **privatization,** and using the Internet to let citizens file forms and apply for services online.

privatization The transfer of the task of providing services traditionally provided by government to the private sector.

whistleblower In the context of government employment, someone who "blows the whistle" (reports to authorities or the press) on gross governmental inefficiency, illegal action, or other wrongdoing.

CHAPTER 14 LEARNING OUTCOMES / KEY TERMS

14-1 **Summarize the origins of the American legal system and the basic sources of American law.** The American legal system evolved from the **common law** tradition that developed in England. The practice of deciding new cases with reference to **precedents** *(stare decisis)* became a cornerstone of the American judicial system. Various **primary sources of law** provide the basis for **constitutional law, statutory law, administrative law,** and **case law. Civil law** spells out the duties that individuals in society owe to other persons or to their governments. **Criminal law** has to do with wrongs committed against the public as a whole. A court must have **jurisdiction** to hear and decide a particular case. A **federal question** provides a basis for federal court jurisdiction. Federal courts can also hear **diversity-of-citizenship** cases. To bring a lawsuit before a court, a person must have **standing to sue,** and the issue must be a **justiciable controversy.** The courts have also established procedural rules that apply in all cases.

administrative law The body of law created by administrative agencies (in the form of rules, regulations, orders, and decisions) in order to carry out their duties and responsibilities.

case law The rules of law announced in court decisions. Case law is the aggregate of reported cases that interpret judicial precedents, statutes, regulations, and constitutional provisions.

civil law The branch of law that spells out the duties that individuals in society owe to other persons or to their governments, excluding the duty not to commit crimes.

common law The body of law developed from judicial decisions in English and U.S. courts, not attributable to a legislature.

constitutional law Law based on the U.S. Constitution and the constitutions of the various states.

contempt of court A ruling that a person has disobeyed a court order or has shown disrespect to the court or to a judicial proceeding.

criminal law The branch of law that defines and governs actions that constitute crimes. Generally, criminal law has to do with wrongful actions committed against society for which society demands redress.

diversity of citizenship A basis for federal court jurisdiction over a lawsuit that arises when (1) the parties in the lawsuit live in different states or when one of the parties is a foreign government or a foreign citizen, and (2) the amount in controversy is more than $75,000.

federal question A question that pertains to the U.S. Constitution, acts of Congress, or treaties. A federal question provides a basis for federal court jurisdiction.

judiciary The court system. One of the three branches of government in the United States.

jurisdiction The authority of a court to hear and decide a particular case.

justiciable controversy A controversy that is not hypothetical or academic but real and substantial. This requirement must be satisfied before a court will hear a case. *Justiciable* is pronounced jus-*tish*-a-bul.

precedent A court decision that furnishes an example or authority for deciding subsequent cases involving identical or similar facts and legal issues.

primary source of law A source of law that establishes the law. Primary sources of law include constitutions, statutes, administrative agency rules and regulations, and decisions rendered by the courts.

standing to sue The requirement that an individual must have a sufficient stake in a controversy before he or she can bring a lawsuit. The party bringing the suit must demonstrate that he or she has either been harmed or been threatened with a harm.

stare decisis A common law doctrine under which judges normally are obligated to follow the precedents established by prior court decisions. Pronounced *ster*-ay dih-*si*-sis.

statutory law The body of law enacted by legislatures (as opposed to constitutional law, administrative law, or case law).

trial court A court in which trials are held and testimony is taken.

14-2 **Delineate the structure of the federal court system.** The U.S. district courts are **trial courts**—the courts in which cases involving federal laws begin. There is at least one federal district court in every state, and there is one in the District of Columbia. The U.S. courts of appeals are **appellate courts** that hear cases on review from the U.S. district courts located within their respective judicial circuits. Some federal administrative agency decisions may also be appealed to these courts. The Court of Appeals for the Federal Circuit has national jurisdiction over certain types of cases. The United States Supreme Court has some original jurisdiction, but most of its work is as an appellate court. The Supreme Court may take appeals of decisions made by the U.S. courts of appeals as well as appeals of cases decided in the state courts when federal questions are at issue. To bring a case before the Supreme Court, a party may request that the Court issue a **writ of *certiorari.*** If the Court grants "cert," it will typically hear **oral arguments.** The justices will then discuss the case in **conference.** When the Court has reached a decision, the justices explain their reasoning in written **opinions.**

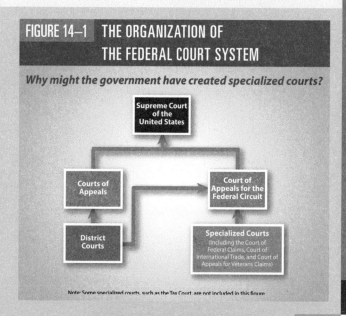

FIGURE 14–1 **THE ORGANIZATION OF THE FEDERAL COURT SYSTEM**

Why might the government have created specialized courts?

Supreme Court of the United States

Courts of Appeals

Court of Appeals for the Federal Circuit

District Courts

Specialized Courts
(Including the Court of Federal Claims, Court of International Trade, and Court of Appeals for Veterans Claims)

Note: Some specialized courts, such as the Tax Court, are not included in this figure.

CHAPTER REVIEW

CHAPTER 14 LEARNING OUTCOMES / KEY TERMS

appellate court A court of appeals, consisting of a panel of three or more judges. It does not hear evidence or testimony. Its task is to determine whether the trial court erred in applying the law in a particular case.

concurring opinion A statement written by a judge or justice who agrees (concurs) with the court's decision, but for reasons different from those in the majority opinion.

conference In regard to the Supreme Court, a private meeting of the justices in which they present their arguments concerning a case under consideration.

dissenting opinion A statement written by a judge or justice who disagrees with the majority opinion.

opinion A written statement by a court expressing the reasons for its decision in a case.

oral argument A spoken argument presented to a judge (or justices) in person by an attorney on behalf of her or his client.

writ of *certiorari* An order from a higher court asking a lower court for the record of a case. *Certiorari* is pronounced sur-shee-uh-*rah*-ree.

14-3 **Say how federal judges are appointed.** Federal judges are appointed by the president with the advice and consent of the Senate. They receive lifetime appointments. The Senate Judiciary Committee holds hearings on judicial nominees and makes its recommendations to the Senate, where it takes a majority vote to confirm nominations. **Senatorial courtesy** gives home-state senators of the president's party influence over the president's choice of nominees for district courts (and, to a lesser extent, the U.S. courts of appeals). The process of nominating and confirming federal judges often involves political debate and controversy.

senatorial courtesy A practice that allows a senator of the president's party to veto the president's nominee to a federal court judgeship within the senator's state.

14-4 **Explain how the federal courts make policy, and describe the role of ideology and judicial philosophies in judicial decision making.** It is unavoidable that judges influence or even establish policy when they interpret and apply the law, because the law does not always provide clear answers to questions that come before the courts. Federal judges can also decide on the constitutionality of laws or actions undertaken by the other branches of government through the power of **judicial review.** Generally, activist judges believe that the courts should actively use their powers to check the other two branches of government to ensure that they do not exceed their authority.

Restraintist judges generally assume that the courts should defer to the decisions of the other branches. Neither judicial activism nor judicial restraint is necessarily linked to a particular political ideology. There are numerous examples of ideology affecting Supreme Court decisions. Judicial decision making, however, can be complex. How much weight is given to the factors that may be taken into account when deciding cases depends, in part, on the approaches justices take toward the interpretation of laws and the Constitution. Important judicial philosophies include originalism, textualism, and modernism.

judicial review The power of the courts to decide on the constitutionality of legislative enactments and of actions taken by the executive branch.

14-5 **Identify some of the criticisms of the federal courts and some of the checks on the power of the courts.** Policymaking by unelected judges has important implications in a democracy. Critics, especially on the political right, frequently accuse the **judiciary** of "legislating from the bench." There are several checks on the courts, however, including judicial traditions and doctrines, the judiciary's lack of enforcement powers, and potential congressional actions in response to court decisions. The American public continues to have a fairly high regard for the federal judiciary.

15-1 **Define domestic policy, and summarize the steps in the policymaking process.** Domestic policy consists of public policy concerning issues within a national unit. The **policymaking process** involves several phases. Identifying a problem that can be solved politically (issue identification) and getting the issue on the political agenda **(agenda setting)** begin the process.

The second stage involves the formulation and adoption of specific plans for achieving a particular goal. The final stages of the process focus on the implementation of the policy and evaluating its success. Each phase of the policymaking process involves interactions among various individuals and groups.

agenda setting In policymaking, getting an issue on the political agenda to be addressed by Congress. Part of the first stage of the policymaking process.

domestic policy Public policy concerning issues within a national unit, such as national policy concerning health care or the economy.

policymaking process The procedures involved in getting an issue on the political agenda; formulating, adopting, and implementing a policy with regard to the issue; and then evaluating the results of the policy.

15-2 **Discuss the issue of health-care funding and recent legislation on universal health insurance.** Most federal spending on health care is accounted for by two **entitlement programs, Medicaid** and **Medicare.** Medicare is the government's second-largest domestic spending program. Under the Patient Protection and Affordable Care Act, signed into law in 2010 by President Obama, employer-provided health insurance continues, and a new health-insurance marketplace allows small businesses and individuals to shop for plans. The legislation also includes an **individual mandate**—most individuals are required to obtain coverage or pay an income tax penalty. One immediate change was that young people could remain covered by their parents' insurance until they turn twenty-six, but the most important provisions of the new law were not to take effect until

2014, when subsidies were available to help citizens purchase health-care insurance if they were not covered by Medicare, Medicaid, or an employer's plan. Conservatives were opposed to the Affordable Care Act (Obamacare), but repeated attempts by Republicans in the House to repeal Obamacare were ineffectual. The roll-out of the federal health insurance exchange in 2013 did not go smoothly but by April 2014, the end of the sign-up period, 8 million Americans had obtained insurance policies through the state and federal exchanges. When the Republicans took control of the presidency in 2016, attempted to replace the ACA with a less expensive and generous program, but divisions within their ranks on what the legislation should do made the replacement process difficult.

Children's Health Insurance Program (CHIP) A joint federal–state program that provides health-care insurance for low-income children.

entitlement program A government program that provides benefits to all persons who meet specified requirements.

individual mandate In the context of health-care reform, a requirement that all persons obtain health-care insurance from one source or another. Those failing to do so must pay a penalty.

Medicaid A joint federal–state program that pays for health-care services for low-income persons.

Medicare A federal government program that pays for health-care insurance for Americans aged sixty-five years and over.

15-3 **Summarize the issues of energy independence, climate change, and alternative energy sources.** In 2017, our nation imported a quarter of its petroleum supply, much less than in the past. Fortunately, friendly neighbor Canada supplies 60 percent of those imports. Most climatologists believe that **climate change** is the result of human activities, especially the release of **greenhouse gases** into the atmosphere. The predicted outcomes of climate change vary, and attitudes toward it have become highly politicized. The issues of U.S. energy

security and climate change raise the question of whether we can develop new energy sources. In part because of newly affordable techniques, such as **fracking,** the United States has increased its domestic supplies of natural gas and oil. Nuclear power does not contribute to global warming; a key obstacle to the construction of new nuclear power plants, however, is cost. There are also concerns about the possible dangers of storing spent nuclear fuel. **Renewable energy** technologies, such as solar power and wind energy, continue to be developed.

climate change The increase in the average temperature of the Earth's surface over the last half century and its projected continuation. Also referred to as *global warming.*

fracking A technique for extracting oil or natural gas from underground rock by the high-power injection of a mixture of water, sand, and chemicals.

greenhouse gas A gas that, when released into the atmosphere, traps the sun's heat and slows its release into outer space. Carbon dioxide (CO_2) is a major example.

renewable energy Energy from technologies that do not rely on extracted resources, such as oil and coal, that can run out.

15-4 **Describe the two major areas of economic policymaking, and discuss the issue of the public debt. Economic policy** consists of all actions taken by the government to address the ups and downs in the nation's level of business activity. The national government has two main tools to smooth the business cycle and to reduce **unemployment** and **inflation.** **Monetary policy** is under the control of the Federal Reserve System (the Fed), an independent regulatory agency. The Fed and its **Federal Open Market Committee (FOMC)** make decisions about monetary policy several times each year. In periods of recession and high unemployment, the Fed pursues an **easy-money policy.** In periods of rising inflation, the Fed adopts a tight-money policy. **Fiscal policy,** associated with **Keynesian economics,** involves the use of changes in government spending or taxes to stimulate or curb economic activity. The government raises money to pay its expenses through taxes levied on business and personal income and through borrowing. When the government spends more than it receives, it borrows to finance the shortfall. Every time there is a federal government deficit, there is an increase in the total accumulated **public debt.** The federal budget deficit has gone down in recent years.

FIGURE 15–4 THE NET PUBLIC DEBT AS A PERCENTAGE OF THE GROSS DOMESTIC PRODUCT (GDP)

Percentages from 2017 onward are projections. *Why is it advantageous to look at the debt as a percentage of GDP rather than as a dollar amount?*

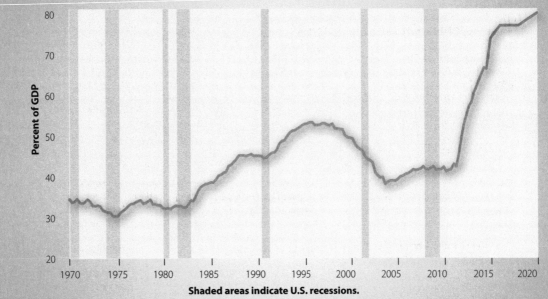

Shaded areas indicate U.S. recessions.

Sources: research.stlouisfed.org and the Congressional Budget Office.

---

easy-money policy A monetary policy that involves stimulating the economy by expanding the rate of growth of the money supply.

economic policy All actions taken by the national government to address ups and downs in the nation's level of business activity.

Federal Open Market Committee (FOMC) The most important body within the Federal Reserve System. It decides how monetary policy should be carried out.

fiscal policy The use of changes in government expenditures and taxes to alter national economic variables.

inflation A sustained rise in average prices. It is equivalent to a decline in the value of the dollar.

Keynesian economics An economic theory proposed by British economist John Maynard Keynes that is typically associated with the use of fiscal policy to alter national economic variables.

monetary policy Actions taken by the Federal Reserve to change the amount of money in circulation to affect interest rates, credit markets, the rate of inflation, the rate of economic growth, and the rate of unemployment.

public debt The total amount of money that the national government owes as a result of borrowing. Also called the *national debt.*

recession A period in which the level of economic activity falls. It is usually defined as two or more quarters of economic decline.

unemployment The state of not having a job when actively seeking one.

16-1 **Discuss how foreign policy is made, and identify the key players in this process.** As commander in chief, the president oversees the military and guides defense policies. The president also represents the United States to the rest of the world. The Department of State is directly involved in **foreign policy** and is responsible for diplomatic relations with other nations and multilateral organizations. The Department of Defense establishes and carries out defense policy and protects our national security.

The secretary of defense works closely with the U.S. military, especially the Joint Chiefs of Staff, in gathering and analyzing defense information. Two key agencies in the area of foreign policy are the National Security Council and the Central Intelligence Agency. Congress has the power to declare war and the power to appropriate funds to equip the armed forces and provide for foreign aid. The Senate has the power to ratify treaties. A few congressional committees are directly concerned with foreign affairs.

foreign policy A systematic and general plan that guides a country's attitudes and actions toward the rest of the world. Foreign policy includes all of the economic, military, commercial, and diplomatic positions and actions that a nation takes in its relationships with other countries.

moral idealism In foreign policy, the belief that the most important goal is to do what is right. Moral idealists think that it is possible for nations to cooperate as part of a rule-based community.

political realism In foreign policy, the belief that nations are inevitably selfish and that we should seek to protect our national security, regardless of moral arguments.

16-2 **Summarize the history of American foreign policy.** Early political leaders sought to protect American interests through policies of **isolationism** such as the **Monroe Doctrine.** The Spanish-American War of 1898 marked the first step toward **interventionism.** In World War I, the United States initially adopted a policy of **neutrality,** and after the war, returned to a policy of isolationism. That policy ended when Pearl Harbor was attacked in 1941. After World War II, the wartime alliance between the United States and the Soviet Union deteriorated. Countries in Eastern Europe became part of the **Soviet bloc.** The Truman Doctrine

and the **Marshall Plan** marked the beginning of a policy of **containment** designed to prevent the spread of communism. During the **Cold War,** the United States and the Soviet Union engaged in an arms race supported by a policy of **deterrence,** in keeping with the theory of **mutually assured destruction (MAD).** In 1962, the two countries came close to a nuclear confrontation during the **Cuban missile crisis.** The fall of the Berlin Wall in 1989 and the collapse of the Soviet Union in 1991 altered the framework and goals of U.S. foreign policy.

Cold War The war of words, warnings, and ideologies between the Soviet Union and the United States that lasted from the late 1940s through the late 1980s.

colonial empire A group of dependent nations that are under the rule of an imperial power.

containment A U.S. policy designed to contain the spread of communism by offering military and economic aid to threatened nations.

Cuban missile crisis A nuclear standoff that occurred in 1962 when the United States learned that the Soviet Union had placed nuclear warheads in Cuba.

détente A French word meaning a "relaxation of tensions." Détente characterized the relationship between the United States and the Soviet Union in the 1970s as they attempted to pursue cooperative dealings and arms control.

deterrence A policy of building up military strength for the purpose of discouraging (deterring) military attacks by other nations. This policy supported the arms race between the United States and the Soviet Union during the Cold War.

interventionism Direct involvement by one country in another country's affairs.

isolationism A political policy of noninvolvement in world affairs.

Marshall Plan A plan providing for U.S. economic assistance to European nations following World War II to help those nations recover from the war. The plan was named after George C. Marshall, secretary of state from 1947 to 1949.

Monroe Doctrine A U.S. policy, announced in 1823 by President James Monroe, that the United States would not tolerate foreign intervention in the Western Hemisphere and, in return, would stay out of European affairs.

mutually assured destruction (MAD) A phrase referring to the assumption that if the forces of two nations are capable of destroying each other, neither nation will take a chance on war.

neutrality The position of not being aligned with either side in a dispute or conflict, such as a war.

Soviet bloc The group of Eastern European nations that fell under the control of the Soviet Union following World War II.

16-3

Identify the foreign policy challenges that our government has sought to meet by using military force. Terrorism is defined as the use of staged violence, often against civilians, to achieve political goals. Governments around the world face the challenges of dealing with nationalist terrorism, domestic terrorism, and foreign terrorist networks. After the 9/11 terrorist attacks, the U.S. military, supported by a **coalition** of allies, attacked al Qaeda camps in Afghanistan and the ruling Taliban regime that harbored those terrorists. In 2003, U.S. and British forces attacked the nation of Iraq, believing (though incorrectly) that Iraq's dictator, Saddam Hussein, was developing **weapons of mass destruction** and that the Iraqi regime was in some way responsible for the 9/11 terrorist attacks. After overthrowing

Hussein's government and undermining an insurgency that included the newly organized al Qaeda in Iraq, U.S. combat forces left Iraq in 2011. By 2006, the Taliban had regrouped and were waging a war of insurgency against the new government in Afghanistan. President Obama increased the number of U.S. troops in that country in 2009, and in 2011, U.S. Navy Seals killed al Qaeda leader Osama bin Laden in his Pakistani compound. Most U.S. troops were out of Afghanistan by the end of 2014. In the aftermath of the "Arab Spring," however, new terrorist groups emerged. The most radical faction fighting in Syria was **ISIS,** which also became active in Iraq. How the United States should deal with the threat posed by ISIS is a subject of continuing debate and controversy.

coalition An alliance of nations formed to undertake a foreign policy action, particularly a military action. A coalition is often a temporary alliance that dissolves after the action is concluded.

ISIS The Islamic State in Iraq and Greater Syria—a terrorist organization that by 2014 had taken over substantial portions of Iraq and Syria. Also known as ISIL (the Islamic State in Iraq and the Levant) or the Islamic State.

weapons of mass destruction Chemical, biological, or nuclear weapons that can inflict massive casualties.

16-4

Describe issues that the government has handled primarily through diplomacy, including the Israeli-Palestinian conflict, curbing weapons of mass destruction, and the rise of China as a world power. For years after Israel was founded in 1948, the neighboring Arab states did not accept its legitimacy as a nation, resulting in a series of wars. After the 1967 war, Palestinians living in the West Bank and Gaza Strip became an occupied people. Attempts to negotiate a permanent peace settlement have been unsuccessful. North Korea conducted nuclear tests in 2006, 2009, and 2013. Following the inauguration of President Trump, North Korea engaged in a new series of tests involving nuclear weapons and long-range missiles. One of the missiles, if ever perfected, would be able to reach the U.S. mainland. In response, Trump described North Korea as our number-one military threat. Like North Korea, Iran has been openly hostile to the United States and has engaged in a nuclear program.

From 2009 on, the diplomatic team confronting Iran about its nuclear ambitions consisted of Britain, China, France, Germany, Russia, and the United States. When negotiations appeared to be going nowhere, sanctions were imposed by the United States, the European Union, and the United Nations. In 2015, an agreement was reached: There would be a reduction in the amount of uranium and the number of centrifuges Iran could have in exchange for lifting the sanctions. As a presidential candidate, Donald Trump had promised to pull the United States out of the deal. As president, he abandoned such a move. China has one of the fastest-growing economies in the world, along with a population of 1.3 billion. In recent years, China has exhibited nationalist tendencies that have alarmed some of its neighbors. In 2012, President Obama announced a "pivot" to East Asia involving shifting naval resources into the region and negotiating enhanced security relationships with area nations.

Oslo Accords The first agreement signed between Israel and the Palestinian Liberation Organization (PLO). The accords to the establishment of the Palestinian Authority in the occupied territories.

Palestine Liberation Organization (PLO) An organization formed in 1964 to represent the Palestinian people. The PLO has a long history of terrorism but more recently has functioned primarily as a political party.